THE OXFORD EDITION OF THE
WORKS OF JOHN WESLEY

Editor in chief FRANK BAKER

THE WORKS OF
JOHN WESLEY

VOLUME 11

———

The Appeals to Men of
Reason and Religion

and Certain Related
Open Letters

EDITED BY

GERALD R. CRAGG

Brown Professor of Ecclesiastical History
Andover Newton Theological School
Newton Centre, Massachusetts

OXFORD
AT THE CLARENDON PRESS
1975

Oxford University Press, Ely House, London W.1

GLASGOW NEW YORK TORONTO MELBOURNE WELLINGTON
CAPE TOWN IBADAN NAIROBI DAR ES SALAAM LUSAKA ADDIS ABABA
DELHI BOMBAY CALCUTTA MADRAS KARACHI LAHORE DACCA
KUALA LUMPUR SINGAPORE HONG KONG TOKYO

ISBN 0 19 812498 8

The Directors of the Oxford Edition of Wesley's Works gratefully acknowledge the financial support of Dennis Myers, of Charlotte, North Carolina, and of Noah O. Pitts, Jr., of Morganton, North Carolina, in the preparation of this volume

The monogram used on the case and half-title is adapted by Richard P. Heitzenrater from one of John Wesley's personal seals

*Printed in Great Britain
at the University Press, Oxford
by Vivian Ridler
Printer to the University*

THE OXFORD EDITION OF
WESLEY'S WORKS

THIS edition of the works of John Wesley reflects the quickened interest in the heritage of Christian thought that has characterized both ecumenical churchmanship and dominant theological perspectives during the last half-century. A fully critical presentation of his writings had long been a desideratum in order to furnish documentary sources illustrating his contributions to both catholic and evangelical Christianity.

Several scholars, notably Professor Albert C. Outler, Professor Franz Hildebrandt, Dean Merrimon Cuninggim, and Dean Robert E. Cushman, discussed the possibility of such an edition. Under the leadership of Dean Cushman, a Board of Directors was formed in 1960 composed of the deans of four sponsoring theological schools of Methodist-related universities in the United States (Drew, Duke, Emory, and Southern Methodist). They appointed an Editorial Committee to formulate plans, and enlisted an international and interdenominational team of scholars for the 'Wesley's Works Editorial Project'. The Delegates of the Oxford University Press agreed to undertake publication.

The works were divided into units of cognate material, with a separate editor (or joint editors) responsible for each unit. Dr. Frank Baker was appointed textual editor for the whole project, with responsibility for supplying each unit editor with a collated critical text for his consideration and use. The text seeks to represent Wesley's thought in its fullest and most deliberate expression, in so far as this can be determined from the available evidence. Substantive variant readings in any British edition published during Wesley's lifetime are shown in the appendixes of the units, preceded by a summary of the problems faced and the solutions reached in the complex task of securing and presenting Wesley's text. The aim throughout is to enable Wesley to be read with maximum ease and understanding, and with minimal intrusion by the editors.

It was decided that the edition should include all Wesley's original or mainly original prose works, together with one volume devoted to his *Collection of Hymns for the Use of the People called Methodists,* and another to his extensive work as editor and publisher of extracts from the writings of others. An essential feature of the project is a bibliography outlining the historical settings of over 450 items published by Wesley and his brother Charles, sometimes jointly, sometimes separately. The bibliography also offers full analytical data for identifying each of the 2,000 editions published during the lifetime of John Wesley, and notes the location of copies. An index is supplied for each unit, and a general index for the whole edition.

During the decade 1961–70, planning was carried forward by the Editorial Committee under the chairmanship of Dean Joseph D. Quillian, Jr. International conferences were convened in 1966 and 1970, bringing together all available unit editors with the committee, who thus completed their task of achieving a common mind upon editorial principles and procedure. Throughout this decade Dr. Eric W. Baker of London, England, serving as a General Editor, assisted the Directors in British negotiations, as well as at the conferences. In 1969 the Directors appointed Dr. Frank Baker, early attached to the project as bibliographer, and later as textual editor, their Editor-in-Chief. In 1971 they appointed a new Editorial Board to assist him in co-ordinating the preparation of the different units for publication.

Other sponsoring bodies were successively added to the original four: The Department of the Ministry of the Methodist Church, The Commission on Archives and History of The United Methodist Church, and Boston University School of Theology. For the continuing support of the sponsoring institutions the Directors express their profound thanks. They gratefully acknowledge also the encouragement and financial support that have come from the Historical Societies and Commissions on Archives and History of many Annual Conferences, as well as the patronage of the World Methodist Council, The British Methodist Church, private individuals, and foundations.   THE BOARD OF DIRECTORS

Editor-in-Chief

FRANK BAKER, The Divinity School, Duke University, Durham, North Carolina

General Editors

WILLIAM R. CANNON, Bishop, The United Methodist Church, Atlanta, Georgia

PREFACE

The works published in this volume are indispensable for an understanding of John Wesley and his movement. They provide his own interpretation both of his task and of the way he discharged it. From one point of view these writings were defensive and apologetic in character: their purpose was to correct current misconceptions. They were also constructive in effect: they enabled Wesley to present a positive statement of his position. While refuting attacks upon himself, he expounded his views on many of the doctrines which he regarded as central to the Christian faith. Prevalent misinterpretations of his mission were often concerned with theological issues, but critics also objected to the methods he employed. Here, too, Wesley offered a careful justification even of the features which struck his contemporaries as bizarre or reprehensible. The unity possessed by the material in this volume is consequently due to its concentration on these two areas of doctrine and method. Wesley published other open letters: they have not been included because they do not deal chiefly with the subjects central to this volume.

These writings also illuminate a significant aspect of the intellectual life of the eighteenth century. Religious controversy occupied an important place in the disputes that were so characteristic of the age. Clergymen engaged in these debates with zest. Laymen followed them with interest and concern—which guaranteed a market for the large number of works that were published. This volume illustrates in some detail the methods commonly employed. The results may not always be attractive to the modern reader, but they are an accurate reflection of certain characteristic aspects of the mentality of the eighteenth century.

The editor of a volume of this kind incurs heavy obligations. My first and greatest debt is to Professor Frank Baker. His wide familiarity with everything connected with Wesley's life and his minute knowledge of the text of Wesley's works have made his help invaluable at every point. It is obvious that he knows a great deal more about the text than anyone since Wesley: indeed, he probably knows more about many aspects of it than did Wesley himself. I am also indebted, of course, to the Board of Directors and the

Editorial Board of this edition: to the contributors who have provided financial support for their work, and to Mr. John Vickers, the indexer for the edition. I would also like to thank those who have helped to identify some of Wesley's more elusive quotations. Professor Robert Renehan and Father Thomas O'Malley, S. J., of Boston College, and Professor W. K. C. Guthrie, of Downing College, Cambridge, traced some of the classical allusions. The Revd. J. Leonard Waddy provided details about the Wednesbury riots. A large number of scholars, especially in the Boston area and in the University of Cambridge, patiently submitted to my intrusions when I was trying to locate the source of three or four quotations which have stubbornly defied all attempts to find them. My wife has helped me in more ways than it is possible to specify.

G. R. C.

CONTENTS

SIGNS, SPECIAL USAGES, ABBREVIATIONS

[ ] entries within square brackets indicate editorial insertions within Wesley's text or notes.

a, b, c small superscript letters indicate footnotes supplied by Wesley.

1, 2, 3 small superscript figures indicate footnotes supplied by the editor.

Cf. is used for a scriptural or other citation when Wesley indicated that he was quoting—usually by italicization, but sometimes by quotation marks —but his quotation is more than minimally inexact.

See is used to cite an undoubted allusion or quotation which was not indicated as such by Wesley, and is more than minimally inexact.

In general the footnotes attempt to cite all quotations in Wesley's text except those within other quotations, whether from Wesley himself or from other writers; one source only has been given for quotations from the Synoptic Gospels.

Where a work by Wesley was first published separately its title is italicized; where it first appeared in a collected volume the title is given within quotation marks.

A.V. Authorized Version of the Bible, 1611 ('King James Version').

B.C.P. The Book of Common Prayer, London, 1662.

D.N.B. *The Dictionary of National Biography*, ed. Sir Leslie Stephen and Sir Sidney Lee, Oxford University Press, 1921–2.

Loeb The Loeb Classical Library, London, Heinemann; Cambridge, Massachusetts, Harvard University Press.

Migne J. P. Migne, ed., *Patrologiae Cursus Completus: Series Graeca* (Paris, 1857–66), and *Series Latina* (Paris, 1878–90).

Notes John Wesley, *Explanatory Notes upon the New Testament*, London, 1755.

O.E.D. *The Oxford English Dictionary upon Historical Principles*, Oxford, Clarendon Press, 1933.

Poet. Wks. John and Charles Wesley, *The Poetical Works*, 13 vols., ed. G. Osborn, Wesleyan-Methodist Conference Office, 1868–72.

W.H.S. *The Proceedings of the Wesley Historical Society*, Burnley and London, 1898– .

Works John Wesley, *Works*, 32 vols., Bristol, Pine, 1771–4.

INTRODUCTION

I

WHEN John Wesley died on March 2, 1791 he was in his eighty-eighth year. More than half a century had passed since he had thrown himself into his crusade to revitalize religion in England. Time had brought remarkable changes. He had won a recognized, even a respected, place in public life. 'It seems', he wrote in 1777, 'after being scandalous near fifty years, I am at length growing into an honourable man.'[1] Admittedly many of his contemporaries still disagreed with certain of his views; others were distressed by some of his methods, but even his critics conceded that he had profoundly affected the lives of multitudes of Englishmen. In due course, with the spectre of the French Revolution before their eyes, even the sceptics applauded his constructive influence and made allowances for what they considered his eccentricities. Wherever he went he was treated with respect.

Such recognition had been slow in coming. It had been won both by decades of unceasing labour and by an unremitting effort to remove misunderstanding. Initially Wesley had faced much hostility. Usually it had sprung from ignorance. Often it had erupted in violence. Riots could normally be subdued by a courageous refusal to be intimidated, 'it being my rule', he said, 'confirmed by long experience, always to look a mob in the face'.[2] Some misconceptions could be ignored: time and the witness of truth would provide sufficient refutation. But certain errors had to be corrected. When critics misinterpreted his gospel or misconstrued his purposes, silence on his part might have implied that the accusations were founded on fact. By giving free course to falsehood, he might have diminished the impact of truth. Certainly disruptive criticism added immeasurably to his burden. At one stage he was compelled to ride repeatedly from London to Bristol, then from Bristol back to London to try to heal the dissensions which were tearing apart his societies in Fetter Lane, at the Foundery, or at Kingswood.[3] These

[1] *Journal*, Jan. 26, 1777.   [2] Ibid., Aug. 6, 1746.
[3] Cf. *Journal*, *III* and *IV*, *passim*. (Wesley issued his *Journal* in instalments. In the footnotes of the present volume references are usually identified by the date of the

troubles were fomented from without: 'an enemy hath done this.'
Some of the opposition that Wesley encountered seemed to be
wilful interference by people who were not essentially interested in
his message, and who had suffered no inconvenience from his
mission. 'What have we done to *you*, that you should join in the
common cry against us?'[1] Some of the resistance he branded as
malicious and unprincipled. But whatever the character of these
attacks, their possible effects could not be ignored. They might
prejudice the reading public against Wesley, so that people who
might normally have given him a serious hearing would now be
tempted to dismiss his message as the vapourings of a mere 'enthusiast'. Slanderous accusations might stir up antagonisms against
his members and thus aggravate the persecution to which they were
so often exposed. Persistent criticism might even shake the confidence of his converts.

At all events Wesley felt compelled to intervene in the public
discussion which his movement inspired. Certain topics demanded
his attention: 'These partly relate to the *doctrines* I teach, partly to
my *manner* of teaching them, and partly to the *effects* which are
supposed to follow from teaching these doctrines in this manner.'[2]
Gradually he built up a distinctive type of apologetic literature;
with this material the present volume is concerned. Wesley was
a prolific though a reluctant author. He harboured no literary
ambitions. Other activities had a far stronger claim on his time and
attention. All his works were written in intervals snatched from his
primary task of evangelism. In every case they were designed to
meet a specific need. If Wesley begrudged the time devoted to
authorship, he particularly resented the demands of controversy.
He quoted with approval the ancient saying, 'God made practical
divinity necessary, the devil controversial.'[3] 'I have neither time
nor inclination for controversy with any', he wrote.[4] 'O that I might

entry quoted; when that is not sufficient, a roman numeral identifies the instalment.
In most of Wesley's other works he himself provided a system of numbering by roman
and arabic numerals. References to such works are thus governed by his own method of
identifying material.) The Foundery (always so spelled by Wesley) was a disused cannon
factory which Wesley bought, remodelled, and used as his London headquarters. For its
beginnings as a centre of religious work, see *An Earnest Appeal to Men of Reason and
Religion*, § 90. Kingswood, a coal-mining village near Bristol, was the scene of some of
his most striking successes, and the site of the school he founded.

[1] *An Earnest Appeal*, § 12.
[2] *A Farther Appeal to Men of Reason and Religion*, Wesley's opening paragraph.
[3] *Journal*, Nov. 19, 1751.   [4] Ibid., Aug. 27, 1739. Cf. ibid., Jan. 2, 1749.

dispute with no man!' he exclaimed on another occasion, 'but, if I must dispute, let it be with men of sense!'[1]

Wesley disliked controversy, but when he felt obliged to engage in it, he took it seriously. In fact, he consistently showed himself a formidable debater. His training at Oxford, both as undergraduate and as don, had equipped him with considerable dialectical skill. He had an unerring eye for the weak point in an opponent's argument, and he mercilessly exposed and demolished it. When a fact was wrong, he did not mince matters. 'My lord', he wrote to Bishop Gibson, 'this is not so.'[2] His clear and lucid style never befogged his argument or left his meaning in doubt. He refused to be deflected by specious arguments or by verbal sleight-of-hand. He consistently appealed to 'the plain natural meaning of the passage'.[3] He maintained certain standards of intellectual integrity; he expected others to do likewise. 'Surely a writer should reverence himself, how much soever he despises his opponent.'[4] A 'candid man' ought not blithely to assume that after a debate he would think precisely as he did before. 'You have heard one side already. Hear the other. Weigh both. Allow for human weakness. And then judge as you desire to be judged.'[5]

Integrity, he believed, presupposed accuracy. He expected that a quotation would correspond in some reasonable degree to the original. He shrank from controversy with Roman Catholics for two reasons: because he was convinced that they had often tampered with the sources to which they appealed, and 'because I cannot trust any of their quotations without consulting every sentence they quote in the originals'.[6] He vigorously attacked Bishop Warburton and Bishop Lavington for what he considered the slipshod and unprincipled way in which both these prelates treated material taken from his *Journal*. Warburton was not merely inexact; he conflated passages relating to different persons so that they appeared to refer to a single individual. He wrenched phrases from their context so as to leave an impression exactly the opposite of what the passage as a whole was clearly intended to convey. He confused dates, not by days or even months, but by years. He based major accusations on

---

[1] Ibid., Mar. 8, 1762.
[2] *A Letter to the Right Reverend the Lord Bishop of London*, § 16.
[3] *A Letter to the Right Reverend the Lord Bishop of Gloucester*, II. 8.
[4] Ibid. I. 39.
[5] *Journal III*, Preface § 2.   [6] Ibid., Aug. 27, 1739.

incidents which he treated with neither 'seriousness nor truth'.[1] This, of course, raises an interesting question about Wesley's own controversial methods. In many of his writings he quoted widely but often inexactly. He admitted as much. 'You can easily see', he wrote, 'that I quoted the Council of Trent by memory, not having the book then by me.'[2] The important issue is the type of mistakes that he made. He frequently inserted in his writings the kind of passages from ancient or modern literature which linger in the memory of a widely read man, and he did so with the approximate accuracy which often marks the references of those unable to verify what they wish to quote. Wesley lived on horseback, not in libraries. But he was also verbally inexact in controversy. He attacked Warburton's treatment of quotations, and then quoted Warburton incorrectly. The eighteenth century was less insistent than the twentieth on the need to reproduce the *ipsissima verba* in references.[3] Wesley was concerned about essential accuracy in reflecting an author's meaning, not in verbal exactitude in reproducing his words. He claimed that he satisfied this fundamental requirement; Lavington and Warburton, he contended, did not.

Quotations of any kind presupposed that the controversialist had taken the pains to read with care what his antagonist had written. Nothing exasperated Wesley so profoundly as the consistent refusal of his critics to take account of what he actually had said. They ignored not only his narratives, but his refutations, his explanations, his corrections, and kept on repeating the same exploded myths.[4] He was quite content that any critic should brand the Methodists as heretics or schismatics—provided that 'he will not condemn us unheard, but first read what we have written, and pray earnestly that God may direct him in the right way'.[5] Twenty-five years later

---

[1] *A Letter to the Bishop of Gloucester*, I. 38. Cf. the similar charges against Bishop Lavington of grossly distorted quotations: e.g. '. . . you cite (and murder) four or five lines from one of my *Journals*'; 'At present I need only return the compliment by charging you with wilful prevarication from the beginning of your book to the end.' *A Second Letter to the Author of the Enthusiasm of Methodists and Papists Compared*, §§ 2, 6; see also §§ 3, 4, 7, 9, etc.

[2] *A Farther Appeal*, Pt. I, IV. 3.

[3] Cf. *The Spectator*, No. 33, where Steele quotes Ben Jonson with a freedom comparable with that which Wesley frequently employs. Note also Wesley's candid account of how he treated Young's *Night Thoughts* when making it 'more intelligible to ordinary readers', *Journal*, Dec. 20, 1768.

[4] Cf. *A Second Letter to the Author of the Enthusiasm of Methodists and Papists Compared*, § 8. Cf. *A Letter to the Bishop of London*, §§ 10, 16.

[4] *Journal*, Mar. 11, 1745. Cf. *Journal III*, Preface § 7.

he was still making the same complaint. Lord Lyttelton[1] seemed to him a perfect example of the intelligent man who disparaged the Methodists without first bothering to ascertain the facts.

> What does he know of them but from the caricatures drawn by Bishop Lavington and Bishop Warburton? And did he ever give himself the trouble of reading the answers to those warm lively men? Why should a good natured and a thinking man thus condemn whole bodies of men by the lump? In this I can neither read the gentleman, the scholar, nor the Christian.[2]

For Wesley controversy was a serious matter. He did not engage in it for diversion, and he expected results from his efforts. He appealed for a decision. 'Either profess you are an infidel, or be a Christian. Halt no longer thus between two opinions. Either cast off the Bible or your sins.'[3]

II

Wesley was ridiculed and abused because the eighteenth century was not prepared to tolerate, still less to welcome, an ardent evangelical revival. But it was an anomaly that Wesley should have been the leader of such a movement. There was little in his upbringing or in his early ministry to promise such a development. All indications pointed to a sedate and decorous career in the Church of England. His home training had been rigorous but not extreme. From his parents he had imbibed High Church principles and Tory loyalties.[4] Charterhouse School and Christ Church, Oxford, had made him a sound scholar; in due course he was elected a fellow of Lincoln. His earliest Diaries reveal a demure but not an austere young man. He shared in the life of the Senior Common Room of his college; he cultivated friendships with other senior members of the university; he participated in the social life of rectories in the Cotswold

---

[1] Author of *Dialogues of the Dead* (1760), which Wesley had been reading. Lord Lyttelton (1709–73) was a friend of Pope, a generous patron of literature, and himself a minor literary figure. He was a statesman of some importance, and in 1755 became Chancellor of the Exchequer.

[2] *Journal*, Aug. 31, 1770.   [3] *An Earnest Appeal*, § 40.

[4] In later years, reflecting on a particular incident in Georgia, he was amazed at his former rigidity. 'Can one carry High Church zeal higher than this?' *Journal*, Sept. 29, 1749. Cf. also ibid., Apr. 20, 1753, Apr. 3, 1754; *A Farther Appeal*, Pt. III, III. 19. But note also his subsequent description of himself as 'a High Churchman, the son of a High Churchman', letter to Lord North and Lord Dartmouth, June 14, 1775.

country. When in residence he conscientiously discharged his duties. 'I should have thought myself little better than a highwayman', he wrote, 'if I had not lectured them [his pupils] every day in the year but Sundays.'[1] He had no patience with the kind of 'college-drone' whom Gibbon pilloried so mercilessly in his famous description of the fellows of Magdalen. Wesley knew the type. He spoke with contempt of the 'wretch who has received ten talents, and employs none; that is not only promised a reward hereafter, but is also paid beforehand for his work, and yet works not at all'. He had no intention of subsiding into 'the drowsy ingratitude, the lazy perjury, of those who are commonly called harmless men, a fair proportion of whom I must, to our shame, confess are to be found in colleges'.[2] The dominant tradition in the University of Oxford still bore the stamp of Laud; it was Catholic, it appealed to the Fathers, it maintained the emphases of the Caroline divines. It had little sympathy with Latitudinarianism or with Hanoverian Erastianism. Wesley found it congenial. It would have been plausible to predict that he would remain a fellow of Lincoln until a college living fell vacant and that thereafter he would be a conscientious parish priest for the remainder of his life. He probably lacked the patronage to have become one of 'the dignified clergy', but he would have been highly respected, and he would not have become the centre of acrimonious controversy.

The predictable did not prove to be the actual. For a man of Wesley's temperament it was not enough to be competent and conscientious. He could not reconcile himself to the view that Christianity existed to foster propriety. He was increasingly conscious of a demand which he was unable to satisfy. He was convinced that faith ought to be a vital experience; yet he knew that for him it was merely a formal orthodoxy.[3] His problem was clear: how

---

[1] *Journal*, May 27, 1776. He was shocked at the holidays allowed the undergraduates at St. Andrew's University.

[2] Letter of Dec. 10, 1734 to the Revd. Samuel Wesley, sen., inserted in *Journal III*. Wesley was defending his moral and religious responsibility in remaining a college tutor. Cf. also his sharp attacks on Oxford fellows in his sermon, *Scriptural Christianity*, IV. 3–10; also his sermon 'Oxford in Apostasy' (on Isa. 1: 21), II. The former was preached before the University of Oxford; the latter was written for that purpose, but friends (whose advice he heeded) thought it too provocative—when published in Joseph Benson's edition of Wesley's *Works* (1809–13) it was entitled 'True Christianity Defended'. (N.B. The titles of works which Wesley first published separately are here italicized; titles of those which originally appeared in collections are given in quotation marks.)   [3] Cf. *Journal*, Aug. 15, 1750

could he convert it from the one to the other? He multiplied good works; he increased his austerities; he even volunteered to go as a missionary to the American Indians. His expedition to Georgia laid bare, in humiliating detail, his utter insufficiency, but it also brought him into contact with the Moravians. In the crises in which he proved to be fearful and ineffective, they showed themselves serene, courageous, and filled with undaunted faith. He asked himself the reason for the contrast; in pursuing that question he found the answer to a more fundamental need. He discovered the reality of forgiveness; faith became a transforming power.

Experience naturally issued in testimony. After describing the religious quickening that came to him at Aldersgate on May 24, 1738 he added these words: 'I then testified openly to all there what I now first felt in my heart.'[1] He did not immediately discover the appropriate pattern for his new endeavours. He preached in churches till, one by one, he found them closed against him. Then, at George Whitefield's persuasion, he began to preach in the open air. He also began to publish instalments of his *Journal*. His motives for doing so were varied. He wished to inform the world of what was happening. So he described with remarkable candour his strivings and his spiritual frustrations before his conversion, and, after it, provided a day-by-day account of the way in which his mission was progressing. He stressed the central convictions which had clarified in his mind and which formed the heart of his message, but he did not amplify them—he left that to his Sermons and his other published works. Inevitably, therefore, the *Journal* gave a one-sided account of his theology and invited misrepresentation. Wesley also intended that the *Journal* should provide a link between himself and the scattered members of his Societies. Many of them would see him only briefly and at lengthy intervals; this detailed account of where he went and what he did would enable them to follow the progress of his work and to share vicariously in its trials and triumphs. But the details which might encourage a recent convert— remarkable providences, striking cures, dramatic conversions, the emotional excitements which attended the early stages of the revival —were certain to offend the upholders of ecclesiastical propriety in the eighteenth century. Here could be found in abundance ammunition with which to attack the new movement. It will be noticed in this volume how often the criticisms which Wesley could

[1] Ibid., May 24, 1738.

not ignore were based on evidence which he himself had supplied in his *Journal*.

At all events the issues with which controversy would be concerned began to emerge soon after the launching of the revival. Some were theological: What does it mean to be saved? Is the 'New Birth' merely a phrase or is it a fact? How is the Christian justified in the sight of God? What are the work and witness of the Holy Spirit? To what extent can the doctrines proclaimed by the Methodists be reconciled with the norms of Anglican theology? More striking to many people were the outward phenomena associated with the revival. By eighteenth-century standards much that happened was bizarre, if not offensive. It was universally assumed that the proclamation of the Gospel would never be accompanied by violent seizures, nor by the ravings of those who (it was asserted) were wrestling with Satan. Open-air preaching was in itself an impropriety, and Wesley's calm assumption that he was entitled to invade anybody's parish offended all the canons of eighteenth-century professional ethics. At every point the Methodist movement seemed to be marked in the deepest degree by that most offensive of all aberrations, 'enthusiasm'. From this there naturally followed a further question: What kind of man was the leader of this movement? Was he a fanatic, a charlatan, an impostor, a lunatic, perhaps even a Papist? And what of Methodism itself and the kind of life which it fostered in its converts?

Such were the staple elements in anti-Methodist controversy. To these Wesley addressed himself in the works contained in this volume. With the background of these issues and with Wesley's approach to them, this introduction is chiefly concerned.

III

Wesley was a serious though not a systematic theologian. Implicit in his preaching as well as in everything he wrote was a body of doctrine carefully elaborated and entirely faithful (as he believed) to the most authentic sources of Christian truth. Wesley had studied the Fathers attentively. He particularly emphasized 'those who wrote before the Council of Nicea', but he readily conceded the equal importance of Chrysostom, Basil, Jerome, and Augustine, 'and above all, the man of a broken heart, Ephraim Syrus'.[1] He

---

[1] *An Address to the Clergy*, I. 2.

regularly appealed to the cardinal documents of the English Reformation—the Thirty-nine Articles, the Book of Common Prayer, and the *Homilies*. One immediate effect of his conversion was to drive him to a more exact study of these normative documents. What he found in them, he felt, must be made readily available to others. 'I began', he wrote, 'more narrowly to inquire what the doctrine of the Church of England is, concerning the much controverted point of justification by faith; and the sum of what I found in the *Homilies* I extracted and printed for the use of others.'[1] Thus in his search for authentic Anglicanism he turned first to the Tudor documents, but it must be remembered that he interpreted them in the light of the works of the great seventeenth-century divines. He was satisfied that he was at all times scrupulously loyal to his heritage; he was equally convinced that many of his detractors had lost vital contact with the true sources of his Church's theology.[2] It was particularly galling to him when men whom he regarded as little better than Latitudinarians or even Deists loftily rebuked him for his aberrations from authentic Anglicanism.

The substance of Wesley's theology came from unexceptionable sources, but the emphasis and balance of his thought were profoundly modified by other influences. Some of these were unavowed, perhaps unconscious. Both of Wesley's grandfathers were Puritan ministers ejected in 1662, and Samuel Wesley and Susanna Annesley must have transmitted to their son more of that heritage than they acknowledged or he admitted. When he encountered Puritanism in in its authentic purity—as in the works of 'that loving serious Christian', Richard Baxter, or in 'the life of that truly great and good man, Mr. Philip Henry'—he joyfully responded to its quality.[3] But more is here involved than a vague affinity. To read concurrently the works of John Wesley and those of certain of the later Puritans—John Flavel is a good example—is to encounter a startling similarity in content and emphasis. His contemporaries were not consciously aware of this affinity; they seldom made it a pretext for

[1] *Journal*, Nov. 12, 1738. The printed work is *The Doctrine of Salvation, Faith, and Good Works, Extracted from the Homilies of the Church of England* (1738). (See Vol. 1 of this edition, *Sermons*.)

[2] Cf. *Journal*, May 25, 1737; sermon, *The Lord our Righteousness* (1766), II. 14; sermon, 'Oxford in Apostasy', I. 3.

[3] *Journal*, May 1, 1755; ibid., Nov. 7-15, 1741. Cf. also ibid., Apr. 3, 1754, Aug. 11, 1755; *A Farther Appeal*, Pt. III, IV. 8. In *A Christian Library* (vols. 8-12), he included material drawn from Robert Bolton, John Preston, Richard Sibbes, Thomas Goodwin, William Dell, and Thomas Manton—redoubtable names in the history of Puritanism.

attack, but its presence certainly did not ingratiate him to a generation nurtured on John Locke, John Tillotson, and Samuel Clarke.[1]

Some of his other debts were easily identified and just as easily
distorted to suit controversial needs. William Law was a prominent
figure in recent English religious life, and Wesley acknowledged
a deep indebtedness to him. He gladly admitted that *A Practical
Treatise upon Christian Perfection* and *A Serious Call to a Devout
and Holy Life* had powerfully influenced him for good. Both the
Wesley brothers had treated Law with the deference that young
disciples owe to their master. Up to a point it was legitimate for
Bishop Warburton to claim that 'Mr. William Law begot Methodism . . .',[2] but in his treatment of this relation he deliberately
ignored all the evidence of a change in attitude on John Wesley's
part. In 1738 he had broken with Law. The older man had veered off
into a world of mystical ecstasy, and Wesley was increasingly
suspicious of its implications. In many respects Wesley was a typical
eighteenth-century Englishman. Temperamentally he was too cool,
intellectually he was too reasonable, to tolerate willingly the
irrationalities of mysticism. When in the course of his own mission
he encountered spiritual phenomena which he could not understand, he adjusted to them with a common-sense pragmatism which
accepted what he could not explain. But the advocacy of such things
in print seemed to him a very different matter. Basically Wesley was
a fair man; he distrusted mystics, but he did not denounce them
unread. 'In riding to Bradford', he notes, 'I read over Mr. Law's
book on the New Birth: philosophical, speculative, precarious;
Behmenish, void and vain!

O what a fall is here.'[3]

When Wesley pressed behind Law's writings to Jacob Boehme, one
of the sources of Law's inspiration, his reaction was the same:
'it is the most sublime nonsense; inimitable bombast; fustian not to
be paralleled!'[4] Nor was Wesley content to form a judgement and

[1] Cf. *Journal*, Aug. 16, 1740. When Warburton attacked Wesley as a 'precisian' (i.e.
a Puritan), it was because of standards of behaviour rather than because of theological
emphasis.

[2] Warburton, *Works* (ed. Richard Hurd, 11 vols., London, 1811), VIII. 343.

[3] *Journal*, Oct. 23, 1739. Wesley was quoting (with adaptation) from Mark Anthony's
speech in Shakespeare, *Julius Caesar*, III. ii. 195.

[4] Ibid., June 4, 1742. In the eighteenth century Boehme's name was often spelt
Behmen. Wesley published two short pieces on Boehme: 'Thoughts upon Jacob
Behmen' and 'A Specimen of the Divinity and Philosophy of the Highly-Illuminated
Jacob Behmen'.

then dismiss the subject. Seven years later he was still examining the evidence. 'I read Mr. Law on *The Spirit of Prayer*. There are many masterly strokes therein, and the whole is lively and entertaining; but it is another gospel; for if God is never angry (as this tract asserts) he could never be reconciled; and consequently the whole Christian doctrine of reconciliation by Christ falls to the ground at once. An excellent way of converting deists! by giving up the very essence of Christianity.'[1] From the *Journal* Warburton identified Law as one of Wesley's spiritual progenitors, and attacked him because of it; if he had treated his source with any integrity he would have found ample evidence that Wesley had repudiated in the strongest terms the tendencies in Law with which Warburton proposed to besmear the Methodists. Wesley, of course, was by no means the first victim of Warburton's high-handed controversial methods.

The relations of the Methodists with the Moravians were close, confused, and increasingly embittered. The extent of Wesley's debt to these German pietists is beyond question. When first he met them on shipboard during the voyage to America he was a frustrated middle-aged cleric who knew that his kind of religion bore little relation to what the New Testament commended. The crucial question concerned the nature of faith. Much earnest discussion, combined with much eager search, brought Wesley the release and power for which he longed. If it had not been for the wise and patient guidance of the Moravians, Wesley might never have experienced this new birth. In that case his own history—and indeed that of his age—would have been very different. He never forgot this fact, and he never ceased to be thankful. But his gratitude did not blind his judgement. He went to Herrnhut, the headquarters of the Moravians, and though deeply impressed by some of the things he saw, he was equally disturbed by others. On his return to England matters rapidly moved toward a clash. The Moravians had shown Wesley the true nature of saving faith; he was astonished that they seemed so blind to its necessary implications. Their Lutheran background made them recoil from anything suggestive of good works. Wesley believed that they were making the religious life a flight from responsibility. 'German stillness' increasingly became a threat to Christian witness. On visiting Birstall, he found that all

---

[1] Ibid., July 27, 1749. The first part of the final sentence refers to Law's *The Case of Reason* (1731), a powerful attack on the deists.

who had experienced the grace of God 'had been vehemently
pressed, "Not to run about to church and sacrament", and "to keep
their religion to themselves; to be still; not to talk about what they
had experienced."'[1]

For a time personal affection was strong enough to offset the
theological antagonism. 'I had a long conversation with Peter
Böhler', wrote Wesley in 1741 (after nearly three years of rising
tension). 'I marvel how I refrain from joining these men; I scarce
ever see any of them but my heart burns within me; I long to be
with them, and yet I am kept from them.'[2] A few days later he wrote
to his brother Charles explaining why 'as yet I dare in no wise join
with the Moravians', and he briefly enumerated five points on
which he believed that their differences constituted an insuperable
barrier.[3] Their disagreements were not about purely speculative
matters. When Wesley identified the errors of the Moravians as
'universal salvation, antinomianism, and a kind of new-reformed
quietism',[4] he made the issues appear theological, but he admitted
that they were largely practical: for years the stability, even the
survival of Wesley's societies was endangered. The seriousness of
the threat is reflected in the amount of attention it received in the
fourth, fifth, and sixth instalments of the *Journal*. He was also
concerned that 'every serious person [should] see the true picture
of antinomianism full grown'.[5] Therefore he maintained an unremitting campaign of education. He published a letter to the
Moravian Church, pointing out the reasons which compelled him
to differ from them.[6] To 'an old friend, whose spirit and life once
adorned the Gospel', he wrote at even greater length, and once more
covered in detail the areas of controversy.[7] By publishing these
letters in the *Journal* he made them part of his ceaseless struggle to
keep his converts uncorrupted by destructive error. 'I found it
absolutely necessary', he wrote, 'openly and explicitly to warn all
that feared God to beware of the German wolves (falsely called
Moravians).'[8]

[1] *Journal*, May 26, 1742.
[2] Ibid., Apr. 6, 1741. Peter Böhler was a Moravian who had played an important role
in Wesley's conversion in 1738. Cf. below, p. 337, n. 1.   [3] Ibid., Apr. 21, 1741.
[4] *Journal IV, ad fin.* Wesley quotes from a letter of Sept. 1738, which he did not
send, but which three years later he found very apposite.   [5] Ibid., Mar. 23, 1746.
[6] June 24, 1744, printed as the preface to *Journal IV*.
[7] Ibid., Nov. 27, 1750.
[8] Ibid., Oct. 20, 1750. Cf. *A Short View of the Difference between the Moravian
Brethren Lately in England and the Rev. John and Charles Wesley* (1745).

This was a complex story, difficult for contemporaries to follow or to understand. From that great quarry for anti-Methodist diatribe, the *Journal*, they learned that Wesley had had intimate relations with these people, and was indebted to them for the powerful impetus that launched this Oxford don on the seemingly incongruous career of a travelling evangelist. On this basis critics felt entitled to attribute to the Methodists many of the views admittedly held by the Moravians. On a given doctrine (e.g. faith) Wesley and his former friends agreed on some points but differed radically on others. In spite of the amount of space given in his writings to anti-Moravian polemic, Wesley's antagonists seemed incapable of recognizing certain of the distinctions which were repeatedly and emphatically drawn. If the discussion of Wesley's views on faith, justification, salvation, and good works sometimes becomes tortuous, it is because his critics insisted that his doctrines must have been determined by what they regarded as his primary theological source.

IV

Many of the attacks on Wesley were prompted by the belief that his distinctive doctrines were dangerous. Even those who did not trouble to investigate the source of his errors felt that they must be corrected at once. Actually Wesley's characteristic themes were always set within a certain context. He believed that, when seen in proper perspective, they would be recognized as orthodox and thoroughly Anglican. He developed this body of teaching in his sermons; till these were available to the reading public, his critics depended on isolated comments in the *Journal* or in the tracts.[1] This may have been unfair to Wesley's total position, but it was encouraged by his own practices. He was an evangelist; he strove to awaken in his hearers a sense of need, and then to bring them, beyond a conviction of sin, to the experience of justification. A complete doctrine of salvation is a relatively complex delineation of the graduated and ascending steps that lead men to newness of life. Wesley knew this; his critics were sure that he did not.

The pattern of Wesley's theology and the nature of some of his

---

[1] The *Sermons* were first published in 1746. The *Appeals* antedate their appearance; most of the open letters do not. It is clear, however, that even after the *Sermons* appeared, critics still drew most of what they knew about Wesley and his message from the *Journal*.

controverted views are highly relevant to the material in this volume, but as a preliminary it is necessary to consider a charge often levelled against him. He appealed to the emotions, it was said; he did, because they formed a part of the whole man, and were therefore vital to a full appropriation of religious experience. The eighteenth century was suspicious of any such argument. Bishop Gibson insisted that the Methodists endangered the acceptance of religious truth by 'making inward, secret, and sudden impulses the guides of their actions, resolutions, and designs'.[1] It was often claimed that Wesley depreciated reason and denied it its legitimate role in man's religious quest.[2] He repudiated the charge. He was eager to safeguard its proper place. 'When you despise or depreciate reason, you must not imagine that you are doing God service; least of all are you promoting the cause of God when you are endeavouring to exclude reason out of religion.'[3] He was horrified to discover that Luther had been willing to 'decry reason, right or wrong, as an irreconcilable enemy to the Gospel of Christ'.[4] Wesley refused to sanction any separation of faith from reason. 'I am for both', he said; 'for faith to perfect my reason, that by the Spirit of God not putting out the eyes of my understanding, but enlightening them more and more, I may "be ready to give a clear", scriptural "answer to every man that asketh me a reason of the hope that is in me"!'[5] The religion he preached was 'a religion evidently founded on, and every way agreeable to, eternal reason, to the essential nature of things'.[6] It presupposed revelation on the part of God as well as appropriation by the mind of man; it maintained the due subordination of the second to the first, but it presupposed the exercise of the faculties God had given men. 'We therefore not only allow, but earnestly exhort all who seek after true religion to use all the reason which God hath given them in seeking out the things of God.'[7]

As we have seen, the shape of Wesley's theology was affected by certain historical influences—patristic, Reformed, and Caroline—

---

[1] [Edmund Gibson], *Observations upon the Conduct and Behaviour of a Certain Sect, usually distinguished by the Name of Methodists*, p. 14. Cf. Wesley, *A Letter to the Bishop of London*, § 5.

[2] Cf. Warburton, *The Doctrine of Grace*, in *Works*, vol. VIII, Ch. vii.

[3] Sermon, 'The Case of Reason Impartially Considered', II. 10.

[4] *Journal*, June 15, 1741. He had been reading Luther's Commentary on Galatians.

[5] Ibid., Nov. 27, 1750.

[6] *An Earnest Appeal*, § 28. Cf. ibid., §§ 20–7. [7] Ibid., § 31.

but its substance was determined by its Biblical sources. 'My ground is the Bible', he wrote; '. . . I follow it in all things both great and small.'[1] The particular emphasis of his theology derived from his preoccupation with evangelism. He included all the traditional elements of the Christian system of belief, but he so arranged them as to bring into the sharpest relief the doctrine of salvation.[2] He began with the fact of man's need; he found its explanation in original sin. 'Our old man', he wrote, is 'coeval with our being and as old as the fall; our evil nature; a strong and beautiful expression for that entire depravity and corruption which by nature spreads itself over the whole man, leaving no part uninfected.'[3] In preaching to a congregation at Bath which included many wealthy and prominent people, Wesley 'declared with all plainness of speech: (1) that by nature they were all children of wrath; (2) that all their natural tempers were corrupt and abominable, and (3) all their words and works, which could never be any better but by faith; and that, (4) a natural man has no more faith than a devil, if so much'.[4] It might seem that man is condemned to choose evil, but the sequence from guilt to condemnation is broken because God's grace is at work. 'By nature ye are wholly corrupted: but by grace ye shall be wholly renewed.'[5] 'Preventing grace' arrests the sinner's attention; the saving word makes him aware of his sin and of Christ's redeeming power; he repudiates his past, acknowledges his sin, commits himself in humble trust to God's mercy, and finds that he achieves a new standing and enters into a new relationship with God.

This then is the salvation which is through faith, even in the present world: a salvation from sin, and the consequences of sin, both often expressed in the word *justification*; which, taken in the largest sense, implies a deliverance from guilt and punishment, by the atonement of Christ actually applied to the soul of the sinner now believing on him, and a deliverance from the whole body of sin, through Christ formed in his heart. So that he who is thus justified, or saved by faith, is indeed *born again*.[6]

Here are concentrated many of the key words and crucial concepts in Wesley's theology. Justification opens the way to a new life. He

[1] *Journal*, June 5, 1766.
[2] Cf. *The Doctrine of Original Sin; According to Scripture, Reason, and Experience* (1757).   [3] *Explanatory Notes upon the New Testament*, on Rom. 6: 6.
[4] *Journal*, Jan. 24, 1743.   [5] *A Sermon on Original Sin*, III. 5.
[6] *A Sermon on Salvation by Faith*, II. 7.

was much too concerned with practical issues to be content merely to expound a theory of salvation. His theology was never divorced from ethics. 'Scriptural Christianity' means that the new convert is 'athirst to do good'.[1] Faith, as he once said, is the door, but holiness is 'religion itself'.[2] The ethical transformation of the believer is inevitably the consequence of the new life. 'He thinks, speaks and lives according to the method laid down in the revelation of Jesus Christ. His soul is renewed after the image of God, in righteousness and in all true holiness. And having that mind that was in Christ, he walks as Christ also walked.'[3]

So justification by faith led to sanctification. The one could not be divorced from the other. The particular form under which he expounded his understanding of the new life was the doctrine of Christian perfection. It proved to be no simple matter to reduce to consistent and intelligible form exactly what he meant by this term. The conviction, however, was so central and so characteristic that it was responsible for much of the controversy in which he was involved. Its stress on spiritual vitality alienated the formalist who was content with a life of religious propriety. Its active, strenuous implications set it in conflict with all types of antinomianism or acquiescent pietism. What did not always emerge in the controversies in which Wesley found himself involved was the basic fact that he always presupposed certain doctrines which did not necessarily emerge above the surface of debate. The sovereignty of God, the incarnation of the Son, the atonement of Christ—these were not as immediately controversial as the witness of the Spirit or the character of faith; but they always underlay the doctrines which attracted more immediate attention. The latter now require more detailed consideration.

V

Justification by faith had an impressive lineage. It was Pauline and Augustinian. It had been taught by the great continental reformers and so had found its way into the formularies of the Church of England, but it was not popular with eighteenth-century Anglicans, and when Wesley began to preach it, he invited attack. Warburton

[1] Sermon, *Scriptural Christianity*, I. 9.
[2] *The Principles of a Methodist Farther Explained*, VI. 4.
[3] *The Character of a Methodist*, § 17. Cf. ibid., § 4: 'By salvation he means holiness of heart and life.'

conceded that it was a great Reformation principle, but 'enthusiasm', he said, had carried it 'into dangerous and impure antinomianism'.[1] The Revd. George Horne, later bishop of Norwich, adopted the same attitude; in justification by faith he detected a threat to good works, and consequently a repudiation of Christian responsibility.[2] He, too, believed that it was an open invitation to antinomianism.[3] Wesley had been fully occupied in resisting antinomianism himself. He did not believe that he was vulnerable to that particular charge. As we have already seen, he believed that he was more faithful to Anglican standards than most of his critics. When 'a serious clergyman' asked 'in what points we differed from the Church of England', Wesley answered, 'To the best of my knowledge, in none; the doctrines we preach are the doctrines of the Church of England; indeed, the fundamental doctrines of the Church, clearly laid down, both in her prayers, articles and homilies.' When pressed to specify points of difference 'from that part of the clergy who dissent from the Church (though they own it not)' he mentioned first justification, and then added good works, sanctification, and the new birth.[4] He regarded with dismay the way many clergymen—even 'many wise and learned men'—explained away the clear meaning of St. Paul's teaching on this subject.[5] It was an unhappy but undeniable fact that what often passed muster as Anglican doctrine was really only 'popery refined or veiled'.[6]

From the outset justification by faith had been a favourite Methodist emphasis. 'Meanwhile,' Wesley wrote, when reviewing the beginnings of his movement, 'they began to be convinced that "by grace we are saved through faith"; that justification by faith was the doctrine of the Church, as well as of the Bible. As soon as they believed, they spake; salvation by faith being now their standing topic.'[7] As it began, so it continued. 'Now, all I teach respects either the nature and condition of justification, the nature and condition of salvation, the nature of justifying and saving faith, or the Author of faith and salvation.'[8] A doctrine so crucial to his

---

[1] Warburton, *Works*, VIII. 442.
[2] For Wesley's letter to Horne, see below, pp. 438 ff.
[3] Horne, *Works Wrought through Faith a Condition of our Justification*, pp. 5–6.
[4] *Journal*, Sept. 13, 1739. Cf. ibid., Oct. 15, 1739.
[5] Ibid., Dec. 13, 1740.
[6] Ibid., June 27, 1742. In the sermon, 'Oxford in Apostasy', Wesley claimed that Tillotson and Bull sapped 'the very foundation of our Church' by their teaching on justification and holiness. I. 5.
[7] *A Short History of Methodism*, § 10.   [8] *A Farther Appeal*, Pt. I, I. 1.

message but so often misinterpreted by his critics obviously needed careful definition. 'It is the present remission of our sins, or our first acceptance with God.'[1] The heart of the matter, he insisted, is pardon. 'It is that act of God the Father whereby, for the sake of the propitiation made by the blood of his Son, he "showeth forth his righteousness" (or mercy) "by the remission of the sins that are past".'[2] Those who tried to distinguish two types of justification, or who made the conditions that govern it complex and complicated, distorted 'the easy natural account of it given by St. Paul'.[3]

Wesley scandalized his contemporaries by associating justification so exclusively with faith. Faith, he declared, 'is the necessary condition of justification; yea, and the only necessary condition thereof'.[4] Pelagianism, always so congenial to the Anglo-Saxon mind, and so prevalent in the eighteenth century, reacted strongly against the Augustinianism of such teaching. Wesley knew that many Anglicans appealed to Archbishop Tillotson, who preached 'the necessity of regeneration in order to justification'; in quoting the archbishop's words Wesley inserted, as his own interpretation of their meaning, the clause, 'which he at large proves to imply holiness of heart and life'.[5] The same Anglicans quoted Bishop Bull: 'Good works are the condition, according to the divine appointment, established in the gospel covenant, requisite and necessary to a man's justification.'[6] For the generally accepted position, Dr. Horne was a faithful spokesman. He admitted that faith was 'a necessary condition' of justification: 'on that all Christians are agreed'. But it was not the sole requirement—as Wesley claimed. 'That works are so likewise I shall prove—from Scripture testimonies; from Scripture examples; from the nature of faith; after which I shall show from St. Paul's own words that he preaches the very same doctrine with St. James; and close the whole with the state of that doctrine given by Bishop Bull in the noble confession of his faith in this particular made by him when on his death-bed.'[7] It is scarcely surprising that Wesley felt obliged to answer so explicit a challenge to his views.

---

[1] *Journal*, Dec. 13, 1739.

[2] Sermon, 'Justification by Faith', II. 5.   [3] Ibid.

[4] Ibid. IV. 5. Sermon, *The Scripture Way of Salvation*, III. 1: 'Faith is the condition, the only condition, of justification.'

[5] Sermon, 'Oxford in Apostasy', I. 5. Tillotson preached a series of five sermons entitled 'Of the Nature of Regeneration, and its Necessity, in order to Justification and Salvation'.   [6] George Bull, *Harmonia Apostolica*, p. 4.

[7] Horne, op. cit., pp. 8–9. The above quotation provides the outline of the discourse to which Wesley replies in *A Letter to the Rev. Mr. Horne*.

One reason Wesley drew so sharp a line between faith and works (as the condition of justification) was his conviction that both our new standing and the grounds on which we claim it must be the gift of God. This is certainly true of faith: 'all faith is the gift of God.'[1] We cannot earn it or deserve it. 'No merit, no goodness in man, precedes the forgiving love of God. His pardoning mercy supposes nothing in us but a sense of mere sin and misery; and to all who see and feel and own their wants and their utter inability to remove them, God freely gives faith, for the sake of him "in whom he is always well pleased".'[2] Wesley was aware of a problem of definition. Faith might mean intellectual assent ('a bare believing that Jesus is the Christ') or it might mean 'a living, growing, purifying principle'.[3] He described this vital faith as a man's 'sure trust and confidence in God, that by the merits of Christ his sins are forgiven, and he reconciled to the favour of God'.[4]

The clash about faith was partly due to fear about its implications. Bishop Gibson spoke apprehensively about the 'doctrines big with pernicious influences upon practice'.[5] It is easy to understand this concern. There were plenty of historical precedents to show that those who exalt faith sometimes depress morals. Wesley was aware of this danger; it was a constant menace to his movement, and he was not likely to fall into that particular pitfall. But this was a matter of fundamental conviction, not of incidental tactics. One of his complaints about the Moravians was that they 'undervalue good works (especially works of outward mercy)'.[6] A perceptive listener who came to hear Wesley preach (though with little predisposition in his favour) realized at once how wide of the mark were the charges often levelled against him. Wesley's exhortation to his listeners to add to faith all the Christian virtues, 'and to show forth their faith by every kind of good work, convinced me', he wrote, 'of the great wrong done you by a public report, common in people's mouths, that you preach faith without good works'.[7] Right belief issues in proper conduct; faith is the foundation of true morality. Wesley inculcated this theme with tireless insistence. He saw 'faith, holiness and good works as the root, the tree, and the fruit, which

---

[1] *Journal*, Dec. 24, 1740.
[2] *An Earnest Appeal*, § 11. Cf. also § 9.   [3] *Journal*, Nov. 1, 1739.
[4] Ibid., July 31, 1739. Cf. the very similar definitions in *Scriptural Christianity*, I. 2, and the sermon on 'Justification by Faith', IV. 2.
[5] *A Letter to the Bishop of London*, § 4.
[6] *Journal*, Sept. 3, 1741. Cf. ibid., June 15, 1741.   [7] Ibid., Nov. 1, 1739.

God had joined and man ought not to put asunder'.[1] He was explicit about the kind of conduct that should characterize his converts. 'I endeavoured', he recorded, 'to explain and enforce the Apostle's direction, that those "who believed be careful to maintain good works". The works I particularly mentioned were praying, communicating, searching the Scriptures; feeding the hungry, clothing the naked, assisting the stranger, and visiting or relieving those that are sick or in prison.'[2] Faith and works belonged together; he intended to keep them so, but he insisted that they must remain in the right sequence. Good works could not justify a man. Only faith could do that; but the justified man began to live the sanctified life, and good works were the inevitable fruit.[3] This is one of the themes to which Wesley constantly returned. It was a triumph of obtuseness for Warburton to ignore it as he leafed through the *Journal*.

The doctrine of the new birth was not popular in most eighteenth-century circles. It was so central to Wesley's thought that inevitably it invited attacks from his critics. Warburton indulged in a particularly disagreeable sneer: in Wesley's movement, he suggested, the devil evidently acted 'in the office of *man-midwife* to the *new birth*'.[4] The New Testament, reinforced by his own experience, compelled Wesley to come to terms with the concept. Within a few months of his conversion we find him advancing, as the surest test of the reality of faith, St. Paul's criterion: 'if any man be in Christ, he is a new creature. Old things are passed away; behold all things are become new.'[5] A radical transformation takes place. The new birth is 'that grand change which God works in the soul when he brings it to life: when he raises it from the death of sin to the life of righteousness'.[6] The man who is born anew manifests the primary evangelical graces—faith, hope, and love.[7] In replying to the author of *A Caution against Religious Delusion*, Wesley emphasized the difference between the old man and the new. 'The "old man" implies infinitely more than outward evil conversation; even "an evil heart of unbelief" corrupted by pride and a thousand deceitful lusts. Of consequence, the "new man" must imply infinitely more

---

[1] *Journal*, Aug. 30, 1739. [2] Ibid., June 29, 1740.
[3] Cf. *The Principles of a Methodist*, § 5. [4] Warburton, *Works*, VIII. 328.
[5] *Journal*, Oct. 8, 1738. Wesley is quoting 2 Cor. 5: 17.
[6] Sermon, 'The New Birth', II. 5. Cf. Sermon, 'The Great Privilege of those that are Born of God', I. 1.
[7] Sermon, 'The Marks of the New Birth', IV. 1.

than outward good conversation; even "a good heart which after God is created in righteousness and true holiness"—a heart full of that faith which, working by love, produces all holiness of conversation. The change from the former to the latter of these states is what I call "the new birth".'[1] Wesley, who clearly distinguished between the various steps in the process of salvation, was careful to differentiate the new birth from both justification and sanctification. 'If any doctrines within the whole compass of Christianity may be properly termed "fundamental", they are doubtless these two,—the doctrine of justification, and that of the new birth: the former relating to that great work which God does *for us*, in forgiving our sins; the latter to the great work which God does *in us*, in renewing our fallen state.'[2] He was equally emphatic that 'the new birth is not the same with sanctification'. The one takes place instantaneously; the other is gradual and progressive.[3]

For Wesley sanctification involved the ethical transformation of the believer. The particular form which he gave to his doctrine was 'Christian Perfection'. To most Anglicans this savoured either of pride or of self-delusion. To Calvinists it clearly implied some form of works-righteousness. Wesley repudiated both imputations, but he did not find it easy to reduce his teaching to consistent and intelligible terms. He drew his inspiration partly from Greek patristic sources, partly from Thomas à Kempis, partly from Jeremy Taylor and William Law. He clearly interpreted 'perfection' in more relative terms than most of his critics assumed. He insisted that a Christian could be holy in this life and in this world, but he did not suggest that he would be free of all errors and imperfections.[4] 'What is Christian Perfection?' he asked. 'Answer: The loving God with all our heart, mind, soul, and strength. This implies that no wrong temper, none contrary to love, remains in the soul, and that all the thoughts, words and actions are governed by pure love. Q. 2. But do you affirm that this perfection excludes all infirmities, ignorance and mistake? A. I continually affirm quite the contrary, and always have done so.'[5] His contemporaries were puzzled: he seemed to

---

[1] *Journal*, July 31, 1739. The author to whom Wesley was replying was the Revd. Henry Stebbing, D.D., Chancellor of Salisbury and preacher to Gray's Inn.
[2] Sermon, 'The New Birth', § 1.
[3] Ibid. IV. 3. Wesley here attacked Law's view of conversion.
[4] Cf. Sermon, *Christian Perfection*, I. Also *A Plain Account of Christian Perfection; Brief Thoughts on Christian Perfection*; letter to Mrs. Maitland, May 12, 1763; *An Earnest Appeal*, § 55.   [5] 'Thoughts on Christian Perfection', Qu. 1–2.

modify his claims in ways that contradicted his doctrine. But on occasion he could be simple and convincing. In 1740 Wesley had an interview with Bishop Gibson of London. 'He asked me what I meant by perfection. I told him without any disguise or reserve. When I ceased speaking, he said, "Mr. Wesley, if this be all you mean, publish it to the world. If anyone then can confute what you say, he may have free leave".'[1] Many were willing to try.

The topics thus far discussed are not the only ones on which Wesley was involved in controversy, but the others are not represented in this volume, and consequently can be ignored.[2] In one respect Wesley's approach to theological debate requires further comment. Certain kinds of discussion he swept aside with impatience. In his own mind he drew a sharp distinction between essential doctrines and non-essential opinions. This was not original. His views had been anticipated by John Flavel, and expressed by him with admirable clarity. 'It is a pernicious evil to advance a mere opinion into the place and seat of an article of faith; and to lay as great stress upon it, as they ought to do upon the most clear and fundamental point.'[3] 'O that opinions should separate friends!' exclaimed Wesley, 'This is bigotry all over.' 'What can destroy the work of God in these parts', he asked, 'but zeal for and contending about opinions?'[4] Earnest men do not always agree as to where to draw the line that separates eternal truth from exploratory speculation; this explains why Wesley differed radically from his opponents as to which matters must be treated with the utmost seriousness and which might be regarded with some indifference. 'Orthodoxy, or right opinions', he said 'is at best but a very slender part of religion, if it can be allowed to be a part at all.'[5] 'On this [the Godhead of Christ]', he said, 'I *must* insist as the foundation of all our hope.'[6] 'But as to all opinions which do not strike at the root of Christianity,

---

[1] *A Plain Account of Christian Perfection*, § 12. In response to Gibson's encouragement, Wesley published 'to the world' his sermon on *Christian Perfection*.

[2] Conspicuous among these are the subjects which divided Wesley from Whitefield and the Calvinists. Wesley summarized them as, 1. Unconditional election. 2. Irresistible grace. 3. Final Perseverance. (*Journal*, Aug. 24, 1743.)

[3] John Flavel, *A Blow at the Root*, Obs. 9.

[4] *Journal*, Apr. 3, 1746; ibid., Aug. 28, 1750. Cf. ibid., May 29, 1745.

[5] *A Plain Account of the People Called Methodists*, § 2. Cf. *A Farther Appeal*, Pt. III, IV. 10; letter to 'John Smith', Dec. 30, 1745; letter to Dr. John Erskine, Apr. 24, 1765; *A Letter to the Bishop of Gloucester*, below, p. 477.

[6] *Journal*, Apr. 5, 1768.

we think and let think.'[1] This invited confusion; which beliefs were essentials and which were mere opinions? Some of Wesley's critics must have been surprised at the vigour with which he attacked them. In Wesley's mind an essential doctrine was one vital to salvation. Everything else represented speculative theory, and therefore held a very marginal place in his interest.

VI

The attacks on Wesley's methods were even more vehement than the protests against his teachings. Theological deviations are by their nature relatively subtle; the excitements of revivalism are blatantly obvious. Beyond question Wesley offended the religious proprieties of the period. He knew that to his contemporaries the strange circumstances surrounding his mission suggested, indeed proved, that 'the work is not of God'.[2] He himself was puzzled by what was happening; 'during this whole time I had many thoughts concerning the unusual manner of my ministering among' the people.[3] Friends were perplexed, and warned him against setting too much store by bizarre phenomena. He carefully sifted the evidence, tried to isolate the basic facts, and discussed with friends like Whitefield what was taking place. No one denied that astonishing things happened when Wesley preached. In the first couple of years after his conversion, the *Journal* is punctuated with accounts of these dramatic events. 'While I was speaking, several dropped down as dead; and among the rest, such a cry was heard, of sinners groaning for the righteousness of faith, as almost drowned my voice. But many of these soon lifted up their heads with joy.'[4] The popular explanation, seized on by Warburton, was that Wesley was driving people mad.[5] Wesley himself claimed that he was restoring them to true sanity. Others

---

[1] *The Character of a Methodist*, § 1. Cf. *A Farther Appeal*, Pt. III, IV. 9: 'But we do not lay the main store of our religion on any opinions, right or wrong; neither do we ever begin, or willingly join in, any dispute concerning them.'

[2] *Journal III*, Preface § 6.

[3] Ibid., June 11, 1739. It is curious feature of the revival that these spectacular phenomena accompanied it only for a relatively short period (at the beginning); chiefly in one place (Bristol); and largely under the preaching of one man (John Wesley). Yet when the reader studies the sermons of Wesley there seems little in them to account for these bizarre reactions.

[4] Ibid., June 12, 1742. Note the use made of such incidents in [Gibson], *Observations upon the Conduct and Behaviour of a Certain Sect usually distinguished by the Name of Methodists*, p. 10.

[5] Warburton, *Works*, VIII. 375-8, 385, 388, 400. Cf. *A Farther Appeal*, Pt. I, VII. 11.

insisted that the striking phenomena were a manifestation of demonic possession. Wesley was inclined to believe that Satan convulsed those on the point of yielding to Christ, since he was struggling to save his kingdom from destruction.[1] Warburton and those who agreed with him felt that Wesley's dramatic accounts deliberately exploited the suggestion of miracle—whereas every reasonable man knew that miracles had ceased many centuries ago. But Wesley did not invoke miracles to prove anything. 'We prove these [the doctrines we preach] by Scripture and reason', and the strange events connected with his mission must be interpreted by the same means.[2] Warburton, citing the episode when both Wesley and his horse were instantaneously healed of their disabilities, attacked it as a claim to miraculous powers.[3] But Wesley's account was purely factual, and his sole comment was, 'A very odd accident this also.'[4] He was inclined to accept what he could not explain. 'The question between us', he told a friendly critic, 'turns chiefly, if not wholly, on a matter of fact. You deny that God does now work these effects; at least that he works them in this manner. I affirm both; because I have heard these things with my ears, and seen them with my eyes.'[5] These events were a challenge to religious formalism, and reflection convinced Wesley that in the past unusual gifts had been withdrawn from the church because 'dry, formal, orthodox men began even then to ridicule whatever gifts they had not themselves, and to decry them all as either madness or imposture'.[6] With time the excitement moderated. People no longer swooned, and Wesley's preaching was not interrupted by screams. He himself denounced the manifestations which had once been so characteristic of the revival. When one of his preachers, Thomas Maxfield, 'did not put a stop' to those who 'had dreams, visions, or impressions, as they thought from God', 'I opposed them', said Wesley, 'with my might, and in a short time heard no more of them.'[7] A pattern less offensive to eighteenth-century tastes became characteristic of Methodism; but there was no question that in the first instance the dramatic accompaniments

---

[1] Cf. *Journal*, May 13, 1740, May 3, 1741, June 27, 1747.

[2] *The Principles of a Methodist Farther Explained*, V. 7. Cf. *A Farther Appeal*, Pt. III, III. 29: 'You seem to lie under an entire mistake, both as to the nature and use of miracles.'

[3] Warburton, *Works*, VIII. 332.
[4] *Journal*, Mar. 17, 1746.

[5] Ibid., May 20, 1739.
[6] Ibid., Aug. 15, 1750.

[7] Ibid., Apr. 23, 1763. For a late (and emphatic) expression of Wesley's dislike of the dramatic accompaniments of revivalism, see *Journal*, Apr. 3, 1786.

of Wesley's movement were the most controversial aspect of the revival.

Wesley's methods offended contemporary canons of good taste. In addition they invoked the spectre of 'enthusiasm', that gravest of all violations of propriety. Most educated people found any display of strong emotion deeply repugnant. The fear was extraordinarily widespread. Wesley records that in so remote a part of Ireland as Galway he heard 'a warm sermon against enthusiasts'. Whatever might be the explanation of the pyschic phenomena associated with his preaching, emotion was unquestionably stirred to a notable degree. Since the commonest fear of the age thus coincided with the most conspicuous feature of Wesley's work, it is scarcely surprising that he was widely accused of disseminating 'enthusiasm'.

The charge came from a variety of sources. When Wesley preached at Matins at St. Mary Arches at Exeter, he was told that he must not occupy the pulpit (as previously arranged) at Evensong. 'Not', added the rector, 'that you preach any false doctrine. I allow all that you have said is true; and it is the doctrine of the Church of England. But it is not guarded. It is dangerous. It might lead people into enthusiasm or despair.'[1] A number of clergymen denounced Methodist practices from the pulpit; frequently such sermons were subsequently published in pamphlet form. Some of the authors, like Thomas Church, were able and courteous, as Wesley himself acknowledged;[2] some were rude and abusive. Some, like Warburton and Lavington, were prominent figures. All of them attacked Wesley as an enthusiast.[3] The way these new prophets preached, said Warburton, might in itself do more harm than if they revived old heresies or invented new ones.[4] The serious feature of enthusiasm, as he saw it, was its anti-rational tendency. It generated fumes which obscured the understanding and depraved the judgement. It had corrupted Law's mind; it was destroying Wesley's.[5] Warburton regarded enthusiasm as 'a kind of ebullition or critical ferment of the mind'; its 'fervours . . . soon rise into madness when unchecked

---

[1] Ibid., Nov. 24, 1739.

[2] Wesley spoke of Church as 'a gentleman, a scholar, and a Christian' (*An Answer to Mr. Rowland Hill's Tract, Entitled* Imposture Detected, I. 14).

[3] e.g., Richard Smalbroke, *A Charge Delivered to the Clergy . . . of the Diocese of Lichfield and Coventry*; or the letter of Thomas Herring, then Archbishop of York, quoted in *A Farther Appeal*, Pt. I, III. 1.

[4] Warburton, *Works*, VIII. 353. [5] Ibid., p. 272 n.

by reason'.[1] He conceded that strong minds often survive the disorders caused by an inflamed imagination; in that case they merely surmount the disease and become highly 'successful impostors'. Having 'set out in all the blaze of fanaticism, [they] have completed their schemes amidst the cool depths and stillness of politics'.[2] Ignatius Loyola was 'the great example of this kind of enthusiast', and Wesley had obviously been his very diligent imitator.[3] When Warburton compared the founder of the Jesuits with the founder of the Methodists, he was using an incidental illustration. Lavington expanded the general theme into a large book. Wherever he could find in Catholic history an example of waywardness or fanaticism, he tried to prove that it could be exactly duplicated among the Methodists. The argument was not particularly cogent, and Lavington laboured it almost beyond endurance.

Wesley, then, was accused of enthusiasm. It was a serious charge, but he did not consider himself guilty, and consequently he felt obliged to refute it. Moreover, at this point he was engaged in a struggle on two fronts. On the one hand he was repelling the attacks of his fellow churchmen; on the other, he was trying to exclude fanatics from his societies.[4] He found it necessary to define the key term, especially since most people were so vague about its meaning. 'I believe thinking men mean by enthusiasm a sort of religious madness; a *false imagination* of being inspired by God. And by an *enthusiast*, one that *fancies* himself under the influence of the Holy Ghost, when, in fact, he is not. Let him prove me guilty of this who can.'[5] Wesley's teaching about the direct witness of the Holy Spirit undoubtedly encouraged the accusation of enthusiasm.[6] He admitted that those who 'think themselves inspired by God, and are not' can justly be accused of this fault, since 'false, imaginary

[1] Warburton, *Works*, VIII., p. 382. Note the elements Bishop Gibson identified in enthusiasm: a belief in 'an extraordinary presence of God', 'extraordinary communications from God', 'extraordinary emanations and assistances of the Holy Spirit', 'special directions from God' [Gibson], *Observations*, pp. 13–15.

[2] Ibid., p. 425.

[3] Ibid., p. 382. Note Wesley's comment on Ignatius Loyola: 'surely one of the greatest men that ever engaged in the support of so bad a cause! I wonder any man should judge him to be an enthusiast. No; but he knew the people with whom he had to do'. *Journal*, Aug. 16, 1742.

[4] *Journal*, Feb. 22, 1741.

[5] *A Farther Appeal*, Pt. I, I. 27. Cf. Ibid., Pt. III, II. 10, and III. 1. Wesley's fullest examination of enthusiasm is in his Sermon, 'The Nature of Enthusiasm'.

[6] Sermon, 'The Witness of the Spirit'. In *A Farther Appeal* he is concerned to correct misinterpretations of his teaching.

inspiration is enthusiasm'.[1] He believed, however, that it was much easier than most people imagined to distinguish between spurious claims and the genuine experience of personal fellowship with God. The attitude of his critics, it was clear, sprang from a disbelief 'that there is any extraordinary work now wrought on earth'.[2] Wesley, on the other hand, punctuated the record of his mission with incidents which clearly suggested that God's power was currently and consistently at work in the lives of men. He realized that this exposed him to the charge of being an enthusiast. On one occasion, when he found that a five-hour service had been superimposed upon his normal Sunday responsibilities, he feared that his strength might not be equal to the demand, 'but God looked to that: so I must think; and they that will call it enthusiasm may'.[3] He was aware that he was caught in an uncomfortable dilemma. 'If I ascribe anything to God, it is *enthusiasm*. If I do not (or if I do) it is *vanity and boasting*, . . . What then can I do to escape your censure?'[4] Against his critics Wesley defended himself with careful arguments.[5] In all possible ways he made it clear that, though he defined enthusiasm differently from his contemporaries, he disliked it as much as they. He resisted it in his own converts no less than in others.[6] And he kept reminding his readers that if the Methodists were guilty of enthusiasm, so were the authors of the *Homilies* and of the Book of Common Prayer.[7]

The eighteenth century held explicit views about the proper place to preach. Everyone believed that sermons belonged in churches; to preach outside them was certainly indecent and probably illegal.[8] Wesley himself came reluctantly to the position that it was permissible to preach in the open air. After his conversion, when the doors of one church after another were closed against him, he yielded to George Whitefield's prompting. 'At four o'clock in the afternoon', he noted, 'I submitted to be more vile, and proclaimed in the highways the glad tidings of salvation, speaking from a little eminence . . . to about three thousand people.'[9] This was a daring innovation on the part of a cleric who was very proper and no longer

---

[1] *Journal*, Jan. 17, 1739.   [2] *A Farther Appeal*, Pt. III, II. 2.
[3] *Journal*, May 29, 1743.
[4] *The Principles of a Methodist Farther Explained*, VI. 2.
[5] e.g. sermon, 'The Nature of Enthusiasm'.
[6] *Journal*, July 13, 1741.   [7] *A Farther Appeal*, Pt. III, III. 1.
[8] For the reaction of the Dean of Christ Church to preaching in the open air, see Charles Wesley, *Journal*, I. 137, 156. Cf. [Gibson], *Observations*, p. 4.
[9] *Journal*, Apr. 2, 1739.

young—'having been all my life (till very lately) so tenacious of every point relating to decency and order, that I should have thought the saving of souls almost a sin if it had not been done in a church'.[1] Having discovered the practical advantages of preaching in the open air, Wesley was prepared to defend them. He made short shrift of Lavington's remark that the excesses of both Papists and Methodists began with field-preaching.[2] Warburton's reflections on Wesley's manner of preaching were too vague to deserve serious attention, and Wesley quickly dismissed them.[3] In *A Farther Appeal* he addressed himself seriously to demolish the arguments of his critics. It was pointless for them to cite the provisions of the Act of Toleration: these applied to dissenters, while Wesley and his converts were members of the Church of England.[4] To argue that the gathering of great multitudes invited seditious tumults reflected ignorance both of the genuine hunger of the common people and of the power of the Gospel to satisfy it. It was irrelevant to emphasize the number of churches available for preaching; they were closed to Methodists, and the people who needed to hear the message never darkened their doors. Field-preaching had proved its efficacy. At Kingswood and Newcastle Wesley had shown that by preaching in the open air he could reach multitudes of miners hitherto untouched by religion and completely neglected by the regular ministrations of the Church.[5] He would neither apologize for his method nor abandon it.

The question, Who should preach? was closely related to the question, Where should they preach? Again, Wesley's contemporaries thought the answer was obvious: only men duly ordained and thus properly authorized might preach. Initially Wesley agreed. When he first accepted lay assistants he intended that their responsibilities should be strictly limited.[6] Conducting a fellowship class was one thing; preaching to a congregation was another. But Thomas Maxfield, one of his earliest helpers, revealed unusual aptitudes, and began to preach. When Wesley heard of this he hurried back to

---

[1] *Journal*, Mar. 29, 1739.

[2] *A Letter to the Author of the Enthusiasm of Methodists and Papists Compared*, § 4.

[3] *A Letter to the Bishop of Gloucester*, I. 17.

[4] Bishop Gibson argued that the Methodists could not invoke the provisions of the Act of Toleration, since they had not registered either their preachers or their meeting-houses. *The Case of the Methodists briefly stated* (1744), pp. 2–4; *Observations*, pp. 3–4.

[5] *A Farther Appeal*, Pt. I, VI. 4–10; Pt. III, III. 22–5. Cf. *An Earnest Appeal*, §§ 68–75; letter to Westley Hall, Dec. 30, 1745.

[6] Wesley intended to restrict his lay assistants to 'exhorting', i.e. they were to testify to their own spiritual experience, and exhort others to worthy conduct.

London, determined to check this irregularity. His mother warned him to proceed with caution: it might be that Maxfield was as truly called of God to preach as Wesley himself, but at least he must postpone action until he had listened to Maxfield. Wesley consented. The evidence convinced him that he had been wrong: clearly it was not contrary to the will of God that laymen should preach. The decision proved to be important. Few clergymen rallied to the movement; generally speaking, those who were not actively hostile stood aloof.[1] Without lay preachers to maintain the regular work in the emerging Methodist societies, the Wesleys could not have devoted so much of their time and energy to an itinerant ministry. But it was still necessary to justify this development. Many churchmen regarded it as a dangerous innovation. Wesley reported listening to a sermon, preached in a marvellously conciliatory spirit, on 'the unlawfulness of laymen's preaching'. On another occasion, a friendly clergyman, having commended one of Wesley's sermons in glowing terms, 'expressed the most rooted prejudice against lay preachers or preaching out of a church'.[2] His critics, said Wesley, appealed in vain to Biblical precedents. Under the old dispensation, many of the most effective preachers and teachers were not priests—partly because the priesthood was limited to the tribe of Levi. In any case, Wesley was careful to restrict his assistants to preaching; they never administered the sacraments. He pointed out that in New Testament times, Our Lord and his apostles were not ordained, but they certainly preached. Calvin was a layman and an indefatigable preacher.[3] As usually happened in such matters, Wesley relied in the last resort on the evidence of experience. When he compared the results of lay preaching with those achieved by many ordained ministers, he could only conclude that 'God is pleased with irregular even more than with regular preaching'.[4] 'Is not a lay preacher', he asked, 'preferable to a drunken preacher, to a cursing, swearing preacher?'[5] Wesley, however, was not satisfied with his lay preachers as he found them. He insisted that they improve their education in every way open

---

[1] For Wesley's explanation of this, see *A Farther Appeal*, Pt. III, III. 6; *Journal*, June 16, 1755; letter to Dorothy Furly, Jan. 18, 1761; letter to the Countess of Huntingdon, Mar. 20, 1763.

[2] *Journal*, Apr. 12, 1747; Aug. 10, 1747.

[3] Cf. *A Farther Appeal*, Pt. III, III. 10–15; *A Letter to a Clergyman* (1748).

[4] Letter to Thomas Adam, Oct. 31, 1755.

[5] Letter to James Clark, Sept. 18, 1756, § 7. Cf. letter to the Earl of Dartmouth, Apr. 10, 1761.

to them. But he could not alter the fact that many of them were of humble origin, and eighteenth-century society resented the suggestion that such men might speak with authority to those who were socially their betters.[1]

The Church of England set great store by right order, and many of Wesley's critics blamed him for transgressing the elementary canons of proper ecclesiastical behaviour. He was accused of failing in due obedience to the bishops and in proper courtesy toward his fellow clerics. He denied both charges. He did not use 'scurrilous invectives against the governors and pastors of the national church'. 'This', he added, 'is an entire mistake.'[2] His personal contacts with bishops were usually friendly. Many of the leaders of the eighteenth-century church were scholarly, dignified, and humane; by prevailing standards most of them were conscientious and hard-working. Wesley had a somewhat strained interview with Joseph Butler, perhaps the most distinguished of all the Hanoverian bishops, and one of Butler's comments is celebrated: 'Sir, the pretending to extraordinary revelations and gifts of the Holy Ghost is a horrid thing, a very horrid thing.'[3] The main thrust of Butler's criticism was that Wesley lacked proper authorization to preach in his diocese. By a number of other bishops Wesley was treated with marked courtesy. 'Mr. Wesley,' said Bishop Lowth, 'may I be found at your feet in another world.'[4] With Potter, Secker, and Gibson Wesley had numerous contacts, for the most part friendly in nature. This is the more surprising since the bishops usually heard about Wesley's activities from sources strongly prejudiced against him. Wesley also had other relations, less personal and direct, with the leaders of the church; at least five of his open letters were addressed to bishops who had publicly criticized him. In dealing with an avowed antagonist Wesley was respectful even though he was firm in maintaining his case. He disliked anonymous attacks; when he detected lawn sleeves behind a veiled onslaught, he was much more outspoken. His tone was sharpest in dealing with Lavington, who initially did not acknowledge his authorship of *The Enthusiasm of Methodists and Papists Compared*. With Warburton and Gibson he

---

[1] In some quarters in the Church of England suspicion of lay preaching persisted into the twentieth century. Cf. Owen Chadwick, *The Victorian Church*, II. 164.

[2] *A Letter to the Bishop of Gloucester*, I. 20.

[3] A full account of this famous interview is in John Whitehead, *Life of John Wesley*, II. 118–20.

[4] Luke Tyerman, *The Life and Times of the Rev. John Wesley, M.A.*, III. 253.

was also forthright and uncompromising. The degree of bluntness that appears in his open letters varied somewhat with the ability and honesty of his opponents, but even when he hit hardest he seldom forgot the deference due to a bishop.

When Wesley was accused of failing in proper respect to 'the bishops and governors of the Church', the real issue was insubordination. He denied the charge of disobedience: 'I both do and will obey them, in whatever I can with a clear conscience.'[1] He pointed out, however, that the bishops had reciprocal responsibilities, and they had often failed to discharge them. The hardships suffered by the Methodists could in large part be laid at the bishops' doors. On one occasion, having described the early stages of the revival, he continued: 'But now several bishops began to speak against us, either in conversation or in public. On this encouragement several of the clergy stirred up the people to treat us as outlaws and mad dogs. The people did so, both in Staffordshire, Cornwall and many other places.'[2]

Many of the inferior clergy resented Wesley's activities and abused him on account of them. Others, it is true, adopted a different attitude. Wesley repeatedly mentions courtesies and civilities which he received at the hands of his fellow ministers. When he heard a couple of helpful sermons in a single day, he remarked: 'I was much refreshed by both and united in love both to the two preachers and to the clergy in general.'[3] He tells us of 'a minister . . . of a truly moderate spirit' who said to Wesley, 'I have done all I can for this people; and I can do them no good. Now let others try: if they can do any, I will thank them with all my heart.'[4] In Cornwall a clergyman intervened when Wesley was being rabbled by a mob and rescued him.[5] Admittedly he often met with studied insults, and he knew that the clergy frequently attacked him behind his back.[6] On his part he never hesitated to express his contempt for the clergyman who was unworthy of his calling.[7] The question, however, was more than one of personal relationships. What right had

---

[1] *A Farther Appeal*, Pt. I, VI. 11. Cf. *An Earnest Appeal*, § 83; *Journal*, Dec. 30, 1745; *The Principles of a Methodist Farther Explained*, III. 4.
[2] *Journal*, Mar. 11, 1745. Cf. *A Farther Appeal*, Pt. III, III. 21.
[3] Ibid., Mar. 10, 1745.   [4] Ibid., July 23, 1748.
[5] Ibid., July 4, 1745.   [6] Cf. ibid., June 18, 1743.
[7] Wesley denied, however, that he had abused 'the regular clergy, not the highest or worthiest excepted', *The Principles of a Methodist Farther Explained*, VI. 11. Cf. *A Farther Appeal*, Pt. I, VI. 11; *A Letter to the Bishop of London*, § 13.

Wesley to constitute himself an evangelist at large? The Church had regulations, and he was breaking them. Wesley claimed that his ordination to a college fellowship was a general authorization and did not restrict him to a specific locality.[1] As a result, he remained (as he believed) within the letter of the law. Wesley, of course, never hesitated to break regulations when he felt subject to a higher constraint. When accused of 'invading other men's office',[2] he argued that he could not 'be said to "intrude into the labours" of those who do not labour at all, but suffer thousands of those for whom Christ died to "perish for lack of knowledge"'.[3] In writing to a friendly critic he was more explicit. 'But in the meantime, you think "I ought to sit still; because otherwise I should invade another's office if I interfered with other people's business, and intermeddled with souls that did not belong to me." Permit me to speak plainly. If by Catholic principles you mean any other than scriptural, they weigh nothing with me: I allow no other rule, whether of faith or practice, than the Holy Scriptures.' Even this was not sufficiently explicit. 'Suffer me now to tell you my principles in this matter', he added. 'I look upon all the world as my parish; thus far, I mean, that in whatever part of it I am, I judge it meet, right, and my bounden duty to declare unto all that are willing to hear the glad tidings of salvation.'[4]

VII

Attacks on the movement and its leader naturally led to assaults on the man and his character. The eighteenth century was an age of satire. In novels or on the stage Whitefield and the Wesleys appeared as fanatics and hypocrites; popular prints depicted them as unctuous defrauders of their flock. Rumour was rife, much of it malicious. Howell Harris told Wesley that 'he had been much dissuaded from either hearing or seeing me, by many who said all manner of evil

---

[1] Cf. Wesley's reply to Bishop Butler: 'Being ordained a fellow of a college, I was not limited to any particular cure, but have an indeterminate commission to preach the Word of God in any part of England. I do not therefore conceive that in preaching here by this commission, I break any human law.' (Whitehead, *Wesley*, II. 120.)

[2] e.g. by Warburton.

[3] *Journal*, July 31, 1739. Wesley was quoting from his letter in reply to the author of *A Caution against Religious Delusion*.

[4] *Journal*, June 11, 1739. Wesley is quoting a letter 'I had some time since wrote to a friend'—the Revd. James Hervey, a former pupil of his at Lincoln College, and subsequently an evangelical of decidedly Calvinistic views.

of me'.[1] The most prevalent report was that he was a Papist. It was reported that he harboured Spanish agents. At the time of the Jacobite rebellion of 1745 he was accused of being a French spy. Sometimes he was identified not only as a Catholic but as a Jesuit. Once he was described as a 'Presbyterian Papist'.[2] It was claimed that he was 'beside himself', and therefore should not be allowed to preach.[3] Wesley noted such rumours but otherwise ignored them. 'The more evil men say of me, for my Lord's sake, the more good will he do by me.'[4]

Printed attacks by responsible public figures were a more serious matter. In most of the pamphlets to which Wesley felt obliged to reply, personal aspersions mingled with criticisms of his methods. The notable example was Bishop Warburton's *The Doctrine of Grace*. No one else indulged in such comprehensive personal abuse. Yet this was a kind of backhanded compliment. Warburton regarded Wesley as a particularly dangerous enthusiast, 'because in parts and learning he is far superior to the rest, and formed of the best stuff that nature ever put into a fanatic to make a successful head and leader of a sect'.[5] Wesley, he felt, had the misfortune to bring great gifts to an age unresponsive to a fanatic's appeal: 'It hath been Mr. J. Wesley's mishap, with every other requisite of a skilful leader, to fall upon times very unpropitious to the fortunes of a new sect.'[6]

Warburton, of course, was not content with general reflections on Wesley as a sectarian leader. No one in the eighteenth century had established a record comparable with Warburton's for violent and abusive personal controversy,[7] and he was not likely to be lenient with a travelling evangelist. Towards Wesley he adopted a consistently supercilious attitude. He was offended by what he interpreted as Wesley's 'claim to almost every apostolic gift and grace'.[8] This confirmed Warburton's suspicion that he was dealing with an incorrigible fanatic. An infallible symptom of this aberration was to

[1] Ibid., June 18, 1739.

[2] *An Earnest Appeal*, § 75; *Journal*, Aug. 27, 1741, Aug. 26, 1741, Sept. 24, 1743, May 15, 1748, Feb. 5, 1749, Mar. 26 and 31, 1752. For the 'Presbyterian Papist' rumour, see *Journal*, Oct. 30, 1743.   [3] *Journal*, May 6, 1739.

[4] Ibid., June 11, 1739. Cf. *A Farther Appeal*, Pt. I, II. 1: 'As to what is personal, I leave it as it is. God be merciful to me, a sinner!'

[5] *Letters from the Rev. Dr. Warburton, Bishop of Gloucester, to the Hon. Charles Yorke, from 1752 to 1770* (1812), p. 51.   [6] Warburton, *Works*, VIII. 364.

[7] Cf. introduction to *A Letter to the Bishop of Gloucester*, below, p. 460.

[8] Warburton, *Works*, VIII. 322.

affirm 'as high a degree of divine communication' as in the days of the primitive church.[1] In Warburton's eyes Wesley's ardour confirmed the diagnosis: 'the zeal and the faith of a fanatic are such exact tallies to one another, that I have no conception how either can exist alone.'[2] It was consequently Warburton's aim 'to tear off the mask from the furious and deformed visage of fanaticism and seduction'.[3] Warburton regarded fanaticism as merely the least offensive of Wesley's faults. '*No heretic*', he declared, '*will ever be able to raise a sect, but he in whose constitution Nature has enabled fraud and fanaticism to act in concert.*'[4] Wesley was clearly an impostor, 'taking in as many as he could'.[5] Admittedly he was a skilful actor, intent on finding the most extensive stage on which to display his talents. Moreover he was a hypocrite. He was hopelessly biased. He was avid for martyrdom. He constantly complained of persecution, yet clearly he brought it upon himself. He was a prime disturber of the peace, himself the cause of all the tumults that punctuated his mission.[6]

VIII

Wesley usually wrote with his own followers in mind. The works in this volume, however, were primarily directed to a constituency outside his own societies. They form his most explicit defence of the movement which he had launched. At the time they constituted an effective apologia. Posterity finds them illuminated at many points by other works—his *Journal*, *Letters*, *Sermons*, and the pamphlets on Methodism.[7] In all of them there are moments when personal attacks focus attention on Wesley himself. He defended himself when necessary, but normally he made few claims on his own behalf. He was aware that an individual might prove to be a mighty instrument in the hands of God, and after discussing with a Lutheran minister the career of the great Pietist leader, A. H. Francke, he made a revealing comment: 'So can God, if it pleaseth him, enable one man to revive his work throughout a whole nation.'[8] The task,

---

[1] Warburton, *Works*, VIII., p. 318; also pp. 319, 360. [2] Ibid., p. 360.
[3] Ibid., p. 405. [4] Ibid., p. 380. [5] Ibid., p. 395.
[6] Ibid., pp. 364–6, 383, 355–60.
[7] Cf. *The Character of a Methodist; A Short History of Methodism; Advice to the People Called Methodists; The Principles of a Methodist; The Principles of a Methodist Farther Explained.*
[8] *Journal*, Apr. 20, 1748.

however, was more important than the agent, and Wesley's descriptions of his movement clarify his objectives and ideals. He believed that he was restoring, in life and witness, the standards of the apostolic church. Over against 'what is generally called Christianity' he set 'the true old Christianity, which, under the new name of Methodism, is everwhere spoken against'.[1] He believed that faith, hope, and love could be—and had been—awakened in the hearts of ordinary people. He insisted that right belief would inevitably lead to upright conduct, and so the familiar dichotomy of faith and works would disappear. 'By Methodists I mean a people who profess to pursue (in whatsoever measure they have attained) holiness of heart and life; inward and outward conformity in all things to the revealed will of God; who place religion in a uniform resemblance to the great object of it; in a steady imitation of him they worship, in all his imitable perfections; more particularly in justice, mercy, and truth, or universal love filling the heart and governing the life.'[2]

Wesley, it will be observed, stressed the interdependence of the inward and the outward elements of Christian obedience. In the eighteenth century formalism was a pervasive blight, and consequently he placed great emphasis on 'inward, vital religion', which he equated with the apostolic experience of 'righteousness, and peace, and joy in the Holy Ghost'.[3] The inner dynamic was the secret of all vigorous discipleship; those who lacked the one could not manifest the other. Wesley recognized the danger of confusing the vitality with its source. 'Inward impressions' could not be made a 'rule of action', though many critics 'either ignorantly or maliciously ascribe' this error 'to the body of the people called Methodists'.[4] He had no intention of leaving his followers to be the playthings of emotion. The only true source of insight, and so of vitality, was 'the written word' illuminated by the Spirit of Life. This conviction antedated his conversion, and he never doubted its entire soundness. 'In the year 1729 I began not only to read, but to study the Bible, as the one, the only standard of truth, and the only model of pure religion. Hence I saw, in a clearer and clearer light, the indispensable necessity of having "the mind which was in Christ", and of

[1] Ibid., Sept. 16, 1739.
[2] *Advice to the People Called Methodists*, § 2. Cf. the longer and more glowing account in *The Character of a Methodist*, §§ 5–6. Also, *An Earnest Appeal*, § 99.
[3] *Journal III*, Preface, § 4. The reference is to Rom. 14 :17. Cf. *An Earnest Appeal*, § 67: '. . . solid, inward, vital religion!'
[4] *Journal*, June 22, 1742.

"walking as Christ also walked".[1] 'I allow no other rule,' he declared, 'whether of faith or practice, than the Holy Scriptures.'[2]

Vital religion, inspired and guided by the Word of God, would inevitably result in the complete transformation of life. It was not enough to have 'the form of godliness'; men needed its power also, and through Wesley's preaching they found it. He pointed to results. 'The drunkard commenced sober and temperate; the whoremonger abstained from adultery and fornication; the unjust from oppression and wrong. He that had been accustomed to curse and swear for many years, now swore no more. The sluggard began to work with his hands, that he might eat his own bread. The miser learned to deal his bread to the hungry, and to cover the naked with a garment. Indeed, the whole form of their life was changed. They left off doing evil, and learned to do well.'[3] To this pragmatic test he was willing to submit. He pointed to the results of his message: could a diseased tree produce such fruits? In reporting on the societies in Yorkshire,

> I found them [he says] all alive, strong, and vigorous of soul, believing, loving, and praising God their Saviour . . . From the beginning they had been taught both the law and the Gospel. 'God loves *you*: therefore love and obey *him*. Christ died for you: therefore die to sin. Christ is risen: therefore rise in the image of God. Christ liveth evermore: therefore live to God, till you live with him in glory.' So we preached; and so you believed. This is the Scriptural way, the Methodist way, the true way. God grant we may never turn therefrom, to the right hand or to the left.[4]

---

[1] *A Plain Account of Christian Perfection*, § 5.

[2] Letter to the Revd. James Hervey, Mar. 20, 1739. Cf. *An Earnest Appeal*, § 27.

[3] *A Farther Appeal*, Pt. III, I. 4. A very similar account is given in *An Answer to the Rev. Mr. Church's Remarks on the Rev. Mr. John Wesley's Last Journal*, II. 18. Cf. *Journal III*, Preface, § 4; *A Letter to the Bishop of London*, § 21.

[4] Letter to Ebenezer Blackwell, Dec. 20, 1751. Cf. *Journal*, Apr. 8, 1750.

An Earnest Appeal to Men of Reason and Religion

Introduction

The Christianity of the Hanoverian Age had certain genuine virtues and many unquestioned faults. In combination they made the Church of England inhospitable to a movement like Methodism. Even in the days of the 'Holy Club' at Oxford, Wesley had found the university (a predominantly clerical society) strongly critical of what it dismissed as over-zealous piety. After his conversion the hostility of the clergy became more pronounced, and he found himself consistently excluded from churches in which he had preached his newly discovered message of forgiveness, justification, and the total transformation of the believer's life. This was disconcerting; actually it proved to be an advantage. Wesley was compelled to turn to open-air preaching, and he immediately found an immense audience which he would never have touched had he remained within church buildings.

Opposition to his mission now took new forms. The converse of popular support was the danger of popular hostility; with it came the threat of mob violence. A campaign of pamphlet abuse also began. Since Wesley had found a wider audience in the fields, his critics sought a wider audience through the press. Many of these early attacks were violent in temper and ill informed as to fact. Most of them required no answer. But some of those who represented the best side of the Hanoverian Church—its sober learning, its decent and orderly ways, its hatred of irrational extremes, its devotion to the parish system—felt outraged by what they heard about the teachings and the methods of the new evangelists. These critics could not be ignored. Many of them based their attacks on hearsay evidence; they needed to be correctly informed as to the facts. Even more important was the task of removing serious theological misconceptions. A fair evaluation of recent developments was badly needed. In an age which boasted of its rationality, reasonable men ought to look with candour and objectivity at a serious attempt to recover the vitality of faith. To help them Wesley embarked on his first major attempt to explain his movement to the men who

should have given it a sympathetic welcome: he published his
Appeals.

Wesley assigned the *Appeals* a distinctive and very important
place among his writings. Evidently he composed them with care.
He regarded them as a particularly effective statement of his position.
He cited them as a telling defence of his movement. He repeatedly
referred to them in his *Journal* and in his letters. 'I have', he wrote,
'again and again communicated my thoughts on most heads to all
mankind; I believe intelligibly; particularly in the *Appeals to Men
of Reason and Religion.*'[1] He noted with obvious pleasure cases in
which former critics had been brought to a better understanding of
his aims, his message, and his methods through reading the *Appeals*.[2]
In *A Letter to the Rev. Mr. Horne* he quoted at inordinate length
from *A Farther Appeal* in order to vindicate the orthodoxy of his
teaching on justification.[3] In writing to Bishop Warburton he made
extensive use of the same work to remove misconceptions about his
views on sanctification.[4] He expressed the hope that the Revd. John
Downes had not read the *Appeals*: only on that supposition could
Wesley absolve him of responsibility for culpably false statements
about Methodist teachings.[5] Moreover he regarded these works as
valuable instruments in promoting the intelligent goodwill without
which his mission could hardly prosper. 'At every new place', he
wrote to John Bredin, one of his preachers at work in Ireland, 'you
may give the *Earnest Appeal* to the chief man in the town.'[6]

An Earnest Appeal to Men of Reason and Religion is undoubtedly
more telling than its sequel.[7] It is much briefer, it is better organized,
and it achieves its purpose more effectively. At the very outset
Wesley described the kind of response with which he was prepared
to meet both critics and inquirers: he was always 'ready to give
any that are willing to hear a plain account both of our principles
and actions'.[8] He aimed to persuade 'either men of no religion at all
or men of a lifeless, formal religion' that 'there is a better religion
to be attained'.[9] Thus before embarking on his defence he has

---

[1] *Journal*, Jan. 5, 1761.
[2] Cf. ibid., Jan. 28, 1745, Jan. 8, 1746, Jan. 6, 1748, Sept. 20, 1748, Apr. 26, 1756.
[3] Cf. below, pp. 443-5.   [4] Cf. below, pp. 510, 519-25.
[5] *A Letter to the Reverend Mr. John Downes* (1759), § 1.
[6] Letter to John Bredin, Nov. 9, 1779.
[7] *A Farther Appeal* consists of three parts, and was published in two stages, but it is
clearly one work, and Wesley usually referred to it as such.
[8] § 1.   [9] § 2.

indirectly sketched the character of the critics whom he hoped to convince. The 'men of reason', self-assured because of their superior intelligence, felt no need of religion, though they were clearly ignorant both of its nature and of its power. On the other hand, 'the men of religion' were too often lulled into false security by the formal propriety of the faith they professed, and consequently they too knew little of true Christianity. Clearly the excellence of what he commended lay in its spiritual vitality rather than its dogmatic orthodoxy. Wesley never depreciated the importance of correct belief, but that was not his immediate concern. His first step was to establish the primacy of love; when our love of God responds to his love of us we discover that it is 'the fountain of all the good we have received and of all we ever hope to enjoy'. Wesley was describing a life inwardly enriched by every spiritual grace and therefore outwardly set free from the oppression of evil.[1] He was convinced that abstract patterns of theological thought are no substitute for the vibrancy of a transforming experience. Even when Wesley proceeded to offer a definition of faith, he related it as intimately as possible to life. 'Faith', he said, 'is that divine evidence whereby the spiritual man discerneth God and the things of God. It is with regard to the spiritual world what sense is with regard to the natural.'[2] With considerable care Wesley then developed the parallel between faith on the one hand and sight, hearing, taste, and feeling on the other.

The early paragraphs of the work reach a conclusion for which we are scarcely prepared. 'This', he said, 'is a short, rude sketch of the doctrine we teach. These are our fundamental principles; . . .'[3] Elsewhere in his works Wesley showed himself perfectly ready to discuss justification, sanctification, or any other major theological topic, but here he has attempted nothing of the kind. He was not providing a dogmatic system; he was indicating his approach to a simple but very basic question: what is the Christian religion? He was convinced of the essential soundness of his answer. The general character of his intellectual outlook, he thought, ought to win his message a wide acceptance. Why, then, was he so savagely attacked by those who should have encouraged his mission? Wesley was concerned to show that by their own principles his critics ought to have been his supporters. The hostility he encountered was so illogical that he could only conclude that his opponents were

[1] §§ 2, 3.   [2] § 6.   [3] § 12.

defending themselves against an attack which they anticipated but which he had never launched. 'Are you not enemies to *us* because you take it for granted we are so to *you*?'[1]

In few of his works did Wesley reveal himself so clearly as an eighteenth-century English divine. He appealed confidently to 'men of reason' because he was convinced that he himself was a man of reason. He was prepared to defend the essential rationality of true faith. To love God and our neighbour and as a result to do good to all men seemed so eminently sensible that he was amazed that anyone ventured to doubt it.[2] Unfortunately those who considered themselves enlightened did not understand what it means to be saved by faith and consequently they did not desire 'this truly reasonable religion'.[3] Wesley had no patience with zealots who profess to exalt faith by isolating it from 'the faculty of reasoning'. It was a disastrous mistake to believe that 'all reasoning concerning the things of God [is] utterly destructive of the true religion'. On this point he was emphatic: 'So far as [a man] departs from true genuine reason he departs from Christianity.'[4]

The man who insisted that he was religious without being so was in no better case than the man who claimed to be reasonable but was not. Both professed principles which they did not apply, and both attacked the Methodists, who in fact put into practice what the others merely honoured in words. The acid test of a religious man could be found in his submission to Biblical authority. But the Methodist doctrines to which their 'orthodox' critics objected were drawn straight from the Bible. 'Is it possible', asked Wesley, 'for any who believe the Scripture to deny one tittle of this? You cannot. You dare not.'[5] On controverted doctrines, like salvation by faith, Wesley claimed that he was on the side of St. Paul and the Anglican formularies; his critics agreed with the canons of the Council of Trent. Under these circumstances, who was the faithful son of the Church of England?[6]

The methods of the revival were as controversial as its doctrines. Field preaching was attacked as a dangerous innovation. The strict and disciplined practices of the early Methodists were treated as an offence. Wesley and his followers, it was claimed, disobeyed the constituted government of the church, and the new evangelism was clearly schismatic in its effects. But Wesley insisted that all these

[1] § 18.   [2] §§ 20–2.   [3] § 23.   [4] § 27.   [5] § 56.
[6] Cf. §§ 57–9.

accusations were at variance with the facts.[1] With equal emphasis he repudiated the insinuation that in his case godliness was great gain —financial gain. So he explained the way his societies functioned, and insisted that none of the funds they raised passed through his hands. He and his brother depended for their support on the dividends they drew from their college fellowships at Oxford.[2]

Wesley never underestimated the cogency of an appeal to experience. Consider, he urged, the actual results of his mission. Notable changes had taken place in English life. 'Behold, the day of the Lord is come. He is again visiting and redeeming his people.'[3] The results were beyond dispute. Why, then, did ostensibly reasonable and religious men feel constrained to question the reality of so beneficial a transformation? If they could not approve, at least they might forbear. Had the advice of Gamaliel lost its cogency?

This brief epitome of the argument of *An Earnest Appeal* makes clear its essential purpose. The work does not expound doctrine; it appeals for understanding. The reader interested in the refinements of Methodist theology must look for them elsewhere. The *Sermons*, for example, contain much detailed exposition of sin and salvation. The aim of *An Earnest Appeal* was to sweep away misconceptions. When men who ought to have been allies insisted on being enemies, the free course of the revival was impeded. Wesley was always willing to accept the hostility of those who rightly were his foes. He expected nothing but opposition from flagrant sinners. But the case was different with 'men of reason and religion'. They should have recognized the basic affinity between Wesley and themselves. Nor should they have allowed their common objectives to be obscured by groundless personal antipathies.

An Earnest Appeal admirably illustrates a quality common to all Wesley's works. He was the master of an unusually clear, simple, direct style. There are few redundant words in his writings. 'I do not love tautology', he said.[4] There is little straining after effect, though once he has found a telling statement of his case he is apt to repeat it.[5] In his controversial works he never lets his style get entangled in the complexities of his argument; he knows what he

---

[1] §§ 68–85.   [2] §§ 87–96, and note on § 93.
[3] § 99.
[4] *The Principles of a Methodist Farther Explained*, IV. 1.
[5] Cf. his description of the effects of his mission, *Journal III*, Preface, § 4; *A Farther Appeal*, Pt. III, I. 4; *An Answer to the Rev. Mr. Church's Remarks on the Rev. Mr. John Wesley's Last Journal*, II. 18; *A Letter to the Bishop of London*, § 21.

wants to say, and he says it in as forthright a fashion as possible.[1] 'The most obvious, easy, common words, wherein our meaning can be conveyed, we prefer before others, both on ordinary occasions and when we speak of the things of God. We never, therefore, willingly or designedly, deviate from the most usual way of speaking, unless when we express Scripture truths in Scripture words, which, we presume, no Christian will condemn.'[2]

For a summary of the ten editions published during Wesley's lifetime, a stemma illustrating the transmission of the text, and a list of the substantive variant readings from the edited text (based on the first edition, Newcastle, Gooding, 1743), see the appendix to this volume, pp. 543–7. For full bibliographical details see *Bibliography*, No. 74.

[1] This is as true of his translations as it is of his own writings. In the *Appeals*, his renderings of classical and patristic authors are far crisper and shorter than those of most nineteenth-century translators.

[2] *The Character of a Methodist*, § 2.

A N

EARNEST APPEAL

T O

Men of Reaſon and Religion.

B Y

JOHN WESLEY, M. A.

FELLOW of *Lincoln College, Oxford.*

JOHN, Chap. vii. Ver. 51.
*Doth our Law judge any Man, before it hear him,
and know what he doth?*

NEWCASTLE UPON TYNE,
Printed by JOHN GOODING, on the *Side.*
[Price Six-pence.]
MDCCXLIII.

An
Earnest Appeal

to

Men of Reason and Religion

1. Although it is with us 'a very small thing to be judged of you or of man's judgment',[1] seeing we know God will 'make our innocency as clear as the light, and our just dealing as the noonday';[2] yet are we ready to give any that are willing to hear a plain account both of our principles and actions: as having 'renounced the hidden things of shame', and desiring nothing more than 'by manifestation of the truth to commend ourselves to every man's conscience in the sight of God'.[3]

2. We see—and who does not?—the numberless follies and miseries of our fellow creatures. We see on every side either men of no religion at all or men of a lifeless, formal religion. We are grieved at the sight, and should greatly rejoice if by any means we might convince some that there is a better religion to be attained, a religion worthy of God that gave it. And this we conceive to be no other than love: the love of God and of all mankind; the loving God with all our heart and soul and strength, as having first loved *us*, as the fountain of all the good we have received, and of all we ever hope to enjoy; and the loving every soul which God hath made, every man on earth, as our own soul.

3. This love we believe to be the medicine of life, the never-failing remedy, for all the evils of a disordered world, for all the miseries and vices of men. Wherever this is, there are virtue and happiness, going hand in hand. There is humbleness of mind, gentleness, longsuffering, the whole image of God, and at the same time a 'peace

---

[1] Cf. 1 Cor. 4: 3.

[2] Cf. Ps. 37: 6 (Book of Common Prayer version, henceforth 'B.C.P.'), though Wesley has 'righteousness' from the Authorized Version ('A.V.') instead of the B.C.P.'s 'innocency'.

[3] Cf. 2 Cor. 4: 2 (cf. Wesley's *Explanatory Notes upon the New Testament*, henceforth '*Notes*').

that passeth all understanding',[1] and 'joy unspeakable and full of glory':[2]

> Eternal sunshine of the spotless mind;
> Each prayer accepted, and each wish resigned; . . .
> 5   Desires composed, affections ever even,
> Tears that delight, and sighs that waft to heaven.[3]

4. This is the religion we long to see established in the world, a religion of love and joy and peace, having its seat in the heart, in the inmost soul, but ever showing itself by its fruits, continually
10 springing forth not only in all innocence—for 'love worketh no ill to his neighbour'[4]—but likewise in every kind of beneficence, in spreading virtue and happiness all around it.

5. This religion have we been following after for many years, as many know, if they would testify. But all this time, seeking wisdom
15 we found it not; we were spending our strength in vain. And being now under full conviction of this, we declare it to all mankind. For we desire not that others should wander out of the way as we have done before them, but rather that they may profit by our loss, that they may go (though we did not, having then no man to guide us)
20 the strait way to the religion of love, even by faith.

6. Now faith (supposing the Scripture to be of God) is πραγμάτων ἔλεγχος οὐ βλεπομένων[5]—the demonstrative evidence of things unseen, the supernatural evidence of things invisible, not perceivable by eyes of flesh, or by any of our natural senses or faculties. Faith is
25 that divine evidence whereby the spiritual man discerneth God and the things of God. It is with regard to the spiritual world what sense is with regard to the natural. It is the spiritual sensation of every soul that is born of God.

7. Perhaps you have not considered it in this view. I will then
30 explain it a little farther.

Faith, according to the scriptural account, is the eye of the new-born soul. Hereby every true believer in God 'seeth him who is invisible'.[6] Hereby (in a more particular manner since life and immortality have been brought to light by the gospel)[7] he seeth 'the

---

[1] Phil. 4: 7.   [2] 1 Pet. 1: 8.
[3] Alexander Pope, 'Eloisa to Abelard', ll. 209–10, 213–14.   [4] Rom. 13: 10.
[5] Heb. 11: 1. The printer of the 1st ed. (John Gooding of Newcastle) transliterates into English italic, adding the footnote: 'The reader is desired to excuse our want of Greek types.'
[6] Cf. Heb. 11: 27.   [7] See 2 Tim. 1: 10.

light of the glory of God in the face of Jesus Christ,'[1] and 'beholdeth what manner of love it is which the Father hath bestowed upon us, that we' (who are born of the Spirit) 'should be called the sons of God'.[2]

It is the ear of the soul, whereby a sinner 'hears the voice of the Son of God and lives';[3] even that voice which alone wakes the dead, saying, 'Son, thy sins are forgiven thee.'[4]

It is (if I may be allowed the expression) the palate of the soul. For hereby a believer 'tastes the good word, and the powers of the world to come';[5] and hereby he both 'tastes and sees that God is gracious',[6] yea, and 'merciful to him a sinner'.[7]

It is the feeling of the soul, whereby a believer perceives, through the 'power of the Highest overshadowing him,'[8] both the existence and the presence of him in whom he 'lives, moves, and has his being',[9] and indeed the whole invisible world, the entire system of things eternal. And hereby, in particular, he feels 'the love of God shed abroad in his heart'.[10]

8. 'By this faith we are saved'[11] from all uneasiness of mind, from the anguish of a wounded spirit, from discontent, from fear, and sorrow of heart, from that inexpressible listlessness and weariness, both of the world and of ourselves, which we had so helplessly laboured under for many years, especially when we were out of the hurry of the world, and sunk into calm reflection. In this we find that love of God and of all mankind which we had elsewhere sought in vain. This we know and feel—and therefore cannot but declare— saves everyone that partakes of it both from sin and misery, from every unhappy and every unholy temper.

> Soft peace she brings, wherever she arrives
> She builds our quiet as she forms our lives;
> Lays the rough paths of peevish nature even,
> And opens in each breast a little heaven.[12]

9. If you ask, 'Why then have not all men this faith, all, at least, who conceive it to be so happy a thing? Why do they not believe immediately?'—we answer (on the Scripture hypothesis), 'It is the

---

[1] 2 Cor. 4: 6.   [2] 1 John 3:1.   [3] Cf. John 5: 25.
[4] Mark 2: 5 (Cf. *Notes*); 'saying' is added to the text in the 1786 edition only.
[5] Cf. Heb. 6: 5.   [6] Cf. Ps. 34: 8 (B.C.P.).   [7] Cf. Luke 18: 13.
[8] Cf. Luke 1: 35.   [9] Cf. Acts 17: 28.   [10] Cf. Rom. 5: 5.
[11] Cf. Luke 7: 50; 18: 42; Eph. 2: 8.
[12] Matthew Prior, 'Charity', lines 5–8.

gift of God.'[1] No man is able to work it in himself. It is a work of omnipotence. It requires no less power thus to quicken a dead soul than to raise a body that lies in the grave. It is a new creation; and none can create a soul anew but he who at first created the heavens
5 and the earth.

10. May not your own experience teach you this? Can *you* give yourself this faith? Is it now in your power to see, or hear, or taste, or feel God? Have you already, or can you raise in yourself, any perception of God or of an invisible world? I suppose you do not
10 deny that there is an invisible world: you will not charge it in poor old Hesiod to Christian prejudice of education when he says, in those well known words,

> Millions of spiritual creatures walk the earth
> Unseen, whether we wake, or if we sleep.[2]

15 Now is there any power in your soul whereby you discern either these or him that created them? Or can all your wisdom and strength open an intercourse between yourself and the world of spirits? Is it in your power to burst the veil that is on your heart and let in the light of eternity? You know it is not. You not only do not but
20 cannot (by your own strength) thus believe. The more you labour so to do, the more you will be convinced, 'it is the gift of God'.

11. It is the *free gift* of God, which he bestows not on those who are worthy of his favour, not on such as are previously holy, and so *fit* to be crowned with all the blessings of his goodness, but on the
25 ungodly and unholy, on those who till that hour were fit only for everlasting destruction, those in whom was no good thing, and whose only plea was, 'God, be merciful to me a sinner.'[3] No merit, no goodness in man, precedes the forgiving love of God. His pardoning mercy supposes nothing in us but a sense of mere sin and misery;
30 and to all who see, and feel, and own their wants, and their utter

---

[1] Eph. 2: 8.

[2] Cf. Milton, *Paradise Lost*, iv. 677-8. Cf. Hesiod, *Works and Days*, 166-73. Wesley was fond of using these lines of Milton to interpret this particular passage from Hesiod. Cf. his sermons, 'The Case of Reason Considered', II: 1; 'Of Good Angels', § 3; 'The Difference between Walking by Sight and Walking by Faith', § 5. In each case he mentions Hesiod by name and introduces the lines from Milton as though they were a translation of the Greek. In the last reference he quotes correctly the second line from Milton:

> Unseen both when we wake and when we sleep.

[3] Luke 18: 13.

inability to remove them, God freely gives faith, for the sake of him 'in whom he is always well pleased'.[1]

12. This is a short rude sketch of the doctrine we teach. These are our fundamental principles; and we spend our lives in confirming others herein, and in a behaviour suitable to them.

Now if you are a reasonable man, although you do not believe the Christian system to be of God, lay your hand upon your breast and calmly consider what it is that you can here condemn. What evil have we done to *you*, that you should join the common cry against us? Why should you say, 'Away with such fellows from the earth: it is not fit that they should live'?[2]

13. 'Tis true, your judgment does not fall in with ours. We believe the Scripture to be of God. This you do not believe. And how do you defend yourselves against them who urge you with the guilt of unbelief? Do you not say, 'Every man *must* judge according to the light he has', and that 'if he be true to this he ought not to be condemned'? Keep then to this, and turn the tables. Must not *we* also judge according to the light we have? You can in no wise condemn *us* without involving *yourselves* in the same condemnation. According to the light we have, we cannot but believe the Scripture is of God; and while we believe this we dare not turn aside from it to the right hand or to the left.[3]

14. Let us consider this point a little farther. You yourself believe there is a God. You have the witness of this in your own breast. Perhaps sometimes you tremble before him. You believe there is such a thing as right and wrong, that there is a difference between moral good and evil. Of consequence you must allow there is such a thing as conscience: I mean that every person capable of reflection is conscious to himself, when he looks back on anything he has done, whether it be good or evil. You must likewise allow that every man is to be guided by his own conscience, not another's. Thus far, doubtless, you may go without any danger of being a 'volunteer in faith'.[4]

15. Now, then, be consistent with yourself. If there be a God who, being just and good (attributes inseparable from the very idea of

---

[1] Cf. Matt. 3: 17; 17: 5, etc.

[2] Cf. Acts 22: 22.

[3] Deut. 5: 32, and (with slight variations) frequently elsewhere in the O.T.

[4] Wesley uses this phrase on several occasions (without indicating that it is a quotation) as implying gullibility, as in a letter to the *London Magazine*, Jan. 1, 1765: 'At present you are the volunteer in faith; you swallow what chokes my belief.'

God), is 'a rewarder of them that diligently seek him',[1] ought we not to do whatever we believe will be acceptable to so good a master? Observe: if we *believe*, if we are 'fully persuaded of this in our own mind',[2] ought we not thus to seek him, and that with all diligence? Else how should we expect any reward at his hands?

16. Again: ought we not to do what we believe is morally good, and to abstain from what we judge is evil? By good I mean conducive to the good of mankind, tending to advance peace and goodwill among men, promotive of the happiness of our fellow-creatures; and by evil what is contrary thereto. Then surely you cannot condemn our endeavouring, after our power, to make mankind happy (I now speak only with regard to the present world); our striving as we can to lessen their sorrows, and to teach them in whatsoever state they are, therewith to be content.[3]

17. Yet again: are we to be guided by our *own* conscience or by that of other men? You surely will not say that any man's conscience can preclude mine. You, at least, will not plead for robbing us of what you so strongly claim for yourselves: I mean, the right of private judgment, which is indeed inalienable from reasonable creatures. You well know that unless we faithfully follow the dictates of our own mind we cannot have 'a conscience void of offence toward God and toward man'.[4]

18. Upon your own principles, therefore, you must allow us to be at least *innocent*. Do you find any difficulty in this? You speak much of prepossession and prejudice: beware you are not entangled therein yourselves. Are you not prejudiced against *us*, because we believe and strenuously defend that system of doctrines which you oppose? Are you not enemies to us, because you take it for granted we are so to you? Nay, God forbid! I once saw one who, from a plentiful fortune, was reduced to the lowest extremity. He was lying on a sick bed, in violent pain, without even convenient food or one friend to comfort him: so that when his merciful landlord, to complete all, sent one to take his bed from under him, I was not surprised at his attempt to put an end to so miserable a life. Now when I saw that poor man, weltering in his blood, could I be angry at him? Surely no. No more can I at *you*. I can no more hate than I can envy you. I can only lift up my heart to God for you (as I did then for him) and with silent tears beseech the Father of mercies that he would look on you in your blood and say unto you, 'Live!'

---

[1] Heb. 11: 6.　　　[2] Cf. Rom. 14: 5.　　　[3] See Phil. 4: 11.　　　[4] Acts 24: 16.

19. 'Sir,' said that unhappy man,[1] at my first interview with him,
'I scorn to deceive you or any man. You must not tell *me* of your
Bible, for I don't believe one word of it. I know there is a God, and
believe he is all in all, the *anima mundi*, the

> . . . *vastam*   5
> *Mens agitans molem et magno se corpore miscens.*[2]

But farther than this I believe not. All is dark; my thought is lost.
But I hear', added he, 'you preach to a great number of people every
night and morning. Pray, what would you do with them? Whither
would you lead them? What religion do you preach? What is it good 10
for?' I replied, 'I *do* preach to as many as desire to hear, every night
and morning.' You ask what I would do with them. I would make
them virtuous and happy, easy in themselves, and useful to others.
Whither would I lead them? To heaven: to God the Judge, the
lover of all, and to Jesus the Mediator of the new covenant. What 15
religion do I preach? The religion of love: the law of kindness
brought to light by the gospel. What is this good for? To make all
who receive it enjoy God and themselves: to make them like God,
lovers of all, contented in their lives, and crying out at their death,
in calm assurance, 'O grave, where is thy victory? . . . Thanks be 20
unto God, who giveth *me* the victory, through *my* Lord Jesus
Christ.'[3]

20. Will you object to such a religion as this that it is not
reasonable? Is it not reasonable then to love God? Hath he not
given you life and breath and all things? Does he not still continue 25

---

[1] The identity of this 'unhappy man' is difficult to establish. Since Wesley did not
usually embellish his stories, it is probable that he was a man of education, able to
quote the classics for his purpose. It seems reasonable to assume that he was the 'Colonel
M——' mentioned in § 43 of this work. 'The horrid crime of self-murder', as Wesley
called it (*Thoughts on Suicide*), was deeply repugnant to him; as he grew older he regarded its prevalence in England as a national disgrace.

[2] In the 'Latin Sentences Translated' appended to volume 32 of his *Works* (1774)
Wesley noted the following: 'The *anima mundi*, the soul of the world, the

> *Vastam*
> *Mens agitans molem et magno se corpore miscens.*

> The all-informing soul
> Which spreads through the vast mass and moves the whole.'

Here he is quoting (inexactly) and translating from Virgil, *Aeneid*, vi. 726–7:

> *totamque infusa per artus*
> *Mens agitat molem et magno se corpore miscet.*

[3] Cf. 1 Cor. 15: 55, 57.

his love to you, 'filling your heart with food and gladness'?[1] What have you which you have not received of him? And does not love demand a return of love? Whether, therefore, you *do* love God or no, you cannot but own 'tis reasonable so to do; nay, seeing he is the
5 parent of all good, to love him with all your heart.

21. Is it not reasonable also to love our neighbour: every man whom God hath made? Are we not brethren? The children of one father? Ought we not then to love one another? And should we only love them that love us? Is that acting like our Father which is in
10 heaven? He causeth 'his sun to shine on the evil and on the good, and sendeth rain on the just and on the unjust.'[2] And can there be a more equitable rule of our love than, 'Thou shalt love thy neighbour as thyself'?[3] You will plead for the reasonableness of this, as also for that golden rule[4] (the only adequate measure of brotherly
15 love, in all our words and actions), 'Whatsoever ye would that men should do unto you, even so do unto them.'[5]

22. Is it not reasonable, then, that 'as we have opportunity' we should 'do good unto all men':[6] not only friends, but enemies; not only to the deserving, but likewise to the evil and unthankful? Is it
20 not right that all our life should be one continued labour of love? If a day passes without doing good, may one not well say with Titus: 'Amici, diem perdidi'?[a] And is it enough to feed the hungry, to clothe the naked, to visit those who are sick or in prison?[7] Should we have no pity for those

25   Who sigh beneath guilt's horrid stain,
            The worst confinement and the heaviest chain?[8]

Should we shut up our compassion toward those who 'are of all men most miserable'[9] because they are miserable by their own fault?

---

[a] 'My friends, I have lost a day.' [Cf. Suetonius, *The Lives of the Caesars*, Book VIII, 'The Deified Titus', section viii.]

---

[1] Cf. Acts 14: 17.   [2] Cf. Matt. 5: 45.   [3] Lev. 19: 18; Matt. 19: 19, etc.
[4] In Wesley's *Works*, XIV. 115, the compositor omitted the passage, 'of our love . . . golden rule', probably because his eye slipped from one 'rule' to the following. In the printed errata to that volume Wesley corrected the passage to read: 'And can there be a more equitable rule than this (the only . . .')', overlooking Leviticus 19: 18. In his own copy, later corrected in manuscript, he retained 'than this' and restored most of the original passage, 'thou shalt . . . that golden rule'.   [5] Cf. Matt. 7: 12.
[6] Gal. 6: 10.   [7] See Matt. 25: 35–6.
[8] Samuel Wesley, Jun., 'On the Death of Mr. William Morgan of Christ Church', in *Poems on Several Occasions* (1736), p. 109; reprinted as part of the introductory material to Wesley's *Journal*.   [9] 1 Cor. 15: 19.

If we have found a medicine to heal even that sickness, should we not, as 'we have freely received it, freely give'?[1] Should we not pluck them as brands out of the fire[2]—the fire of lust, anger, malice, revenge? Your inmost soul answers: 'It should be done: it is reasonable in the highest degree.' Well, this is the sum of our preaching and of our lives, our enemies themselves being the judges. If therefore you allow that it is reasonable to love God, to love mankind, and to do good to all men, you cannot but allow that religion which we preach and live to be agreeable to the highest reason.

23. Perhaps all this you can bear. It is tolerable enough, and if we spoke only of being 'saved by love' you should have no great objection: but you do not comprehend what we say of being 'saved by *faith*'. I know you do not. You do not in any degree comprehend what we mean by that expression. Have patience, then, and I will tell you yet again. By those words, 'we are saved by faith', we mean that the moment a man receives that faith which is above described he is saved from doubt and fear, and sorrow of heart, by a peace that passes all understanding;[3] from the heaviness of a wounded spirit, by joy unspeakable;[4] and from his sins, of whatsoever kind they were, from his vicious desires, as well as words and actions, by the love of God and of all mankind then shed abroad in his heart.[5]

24. We grant nothing is more unreasonable than to imagine that such mighty effects as these can be brought by that poor, empty, insignificant thing which the world *calls* 'faith'—and you among them. But supposing there be such a faith on the earth as that which the Apostle speaks of, such an intercourse between God and the soul: what is too hard for such a faith? You yourselves may conceive that 'all things are possible to him that *thus* believeth',[6] to him that thus 'walks with God',[7] that is now a citizen of heaven, an inhabitant of eternity. If therefore you will contend with us you must change the ground of your attack. You must flatly deny there is any faith upon earth. But perhaps this you might think too large a step. You cannot do this without a secret condemnation in your own breast. O that you would at length cry to God for that heavenly gift whereby alone this truly reasonable religion, this beneficent love of God and man, can be planted in your heart!

---

[1] Cf. Matt. 10: 8. [2] See Zech. 3: 2. [3] See Phil. 4: 7.
[4] 1 Pet. 1: 8. [5] See Rom. 5: 5. [6] Cf. Mark 9: 23.
[7] Cf. Gen. 5: 22, 24, etc.

25. If you say, 'But those that profess this faith are the most unreasonable of all men', I ask, 'Who are those that profess this faith?' Perhaps you do not personally know such a man in the world. Who are they that so much as profess to have *this* 'evidence of things not seen',[1] that profess to 'see him that is invisible',[2] to 'hear the voice of God',[3] and to have his spirit ever 'witnessing with their spirits, that they are the children of God'?[4] I fear you will find few that even profess *this* faith among the large numbers of those who are called believers.

26. 'However, there are enough that profess themselves Christians.' Yea, too many, God knoweth—too many that confute their vain professions by the whole tenor of their lives. I will allow all you can say on this head, and perhaps more than all. 'Tis now some years since I was engaged unawares in a conversation with a strong reasoner who at first urged the wickedness of the American Indians as a bar to our hope of converting them to Christianity. But when I mentioned their temperance, justice, and veracity (according to the accounts I had then received), it was asked: 'Why, if those heathens are such men as these, what will they gain by being made Christians? What would they gain by being such Christians as we see everywhere round about us?' I could not deny they would lose, not gain, by such a Christianity as this. Upon which she added: 'Why, what else do you mean by Christianity?' My plain answer was: 'What do you apprehend to be more valuable than good sense, good nature, and good manners? All these are contained, and that in the highest degree, in what I mean by Christianity. Good sense (so called) is but a poor, dim shadow of what Christians call faith. Good nature is only a faint, distant resemblance of Christian charity. And good manners, if of the most finished kind that nature assisted by art can attain to, is but a dead picture of that holiness of conversation which is the image of God visibly expressed. All these, put together by the art of God, I call Christianity.' 'Sir, if this be Christianity,' said my opponent in amaze, 'I never saw a Christian in my life.'

27. Perhaps it is the same case with you. If so, I am grieved for you, and can only wish, till you do see a living proof of this, that you would not say you see a Christian. For this is scriptural Christianity, and this alone. Whenever, therefore, you see an unreasonable man,

---

[1] Heb. 11:1.   [2] Cf. Heb. 11:27; John 5:25.
[3] Cf. Gen. 3:8; Deut. 5:25.   [4] Cf. Rom. 8:16.

you see one who perhaps calls himself by that name, but is no more a Christian than he is an angel. So far as he departs from true genuine reason, so far he departs from Christianity. Do not say this is only asserted, not proved. It is undeniably proved by the original charter of Christianity. We appeal to this, to the written Word. If any man's temper, or words, or actions, are contradictory to right reason, it is evident to a demonstration they are contradictory to this. Produce any possible or conceivable instance and you will find the fact is so. The lives therefore of those who are *called* Christians is no just objection to Christianity.

28. We join with you then in desiring a religion founded on reason, and every way agreeable thereto. But one question still remains to be asked: 'What do you mean by reason?' I suppose you mean the eternal reason, or the nature of things: the nature of God and the nature of man, with the relations necessarily subsisting between them. Why, this is the very religion *we* preach: a religion evidently founded on, and every way agreeable to, eternal reason, to the essential nature of things. Its foundation stands on the nature of God and the nature of man, together with their mutual relations. And it is every way suitable thereto. To the nature of God, for it begins in knowing him—and where but in the true knowledge of God can you conceive true religion to begin? It goes on in loving him and all mankind—for you cannot but imitate whom you love. It ends in serving him, in doing his will, in obeying him whom we know and love.

29. It is every way suited to the nature of man, for it begins in man's knowing himself: knowing himself to be what he really is— foolish, vicious, miserable. It goes on to point out the remedy for this, to make him truly wise, virtuous, and happy, as every thinking mind (perhaps from some implicit remembrance of what it origin- ally was) longs to be.

It finishes all by restoring the due relations between God and man, by uniting for ever the tender father and the grateful, obedient son; the great Lord of all and the faithful servant, doing not his own will but the will of him that sent him.[1]

30. But perhaps by reason you mean the faculty of reasoning, of inferring one thing from another.

There are many, it is confessed, particularly those who are styled 'mystic divines', that utterly decry the use of reason, thus

---

[1] See John 6: 38.

understood in religion—nay, that condemn all reasoning concerning the things of God as utterly destructive of true religion.

But we can in no wise agree with this. We find no authority for it in Holy Writ. So far from it that we find there both our Lord and his apostles continually reasoning with their opposers. Neither do we know, in all the productions of ancient or modern times, such a chain of reasoning or argumentation, so close, so solid, so regularly connected, as the Epistle to the Hebrews. And the strongest reasoner whom we have ever observed (excepting only Jesus of Nazareth) was that Paul of Tarsus, the same who has left that plain direction for all Christians: 'In malice (or wickedness) be ye children; but in understanding (or reason) be ye men.'[1]

31. We therefore not only allow, but earnestly exhort all who seek after true religion to use all the reason which God hath given them in searching out the things of God. But your *reasoning justly*, not only on this but on any subject whatsoever, presupposes *true judgments* already formed whereon to ground your argumentation. Else, you know, you will stumble at every step, because *ex falso non sequitur verum*—it is impossible, if your premisses are false, to infer from them true conclusions.[2]

32. You know, likewise that before it is possible for you to form a true judgment of them it is absolutely necessary that you have a *clear apprehension* of the things of God, and that your ideas thereof be all *fixed*, *distinct*, and *determinate*. And seeing our ideas are not innate, but must all originally come from our senses, it is certainly necessary that you have senses capable of discerning objects of this kind—not those only which are called 'natural senses', which in this respect profit nothing, as being altogether incapable of discerning objects of a spiritual kind, but *spiritual* senses, exercised to discern spiritual good and evil. It is necessary that you have the *hearing* ear and the *seeing* eye, emphatically so called; that you have a new class of senses opened in your soul, not depending on organs of flesh and blood, to be 'the *evidence* of things not seen'[3] as your bodily senses

---

[1] 1 Cor. 14: 20.

[2] The Latin expression which Wesley quotes is a proposition which regularly appears in traditional textbooks on logic. Wesley, it must be remembered, had been a college tutor and had drilled his pupils in the rules of logic. For this purpose he used Henry Aldrich's *Artis Logicae Compendium*. He valued accurate thought. He tried to practise it himself, and he encouraged others to do the same. Cf. his *Compendium of Logic*, which is in large measure a translation of Aldrich. As an interesting example of his application of the rules of logic, see his sermon on 'The Means of Grace'.

[3] Heb. 11: 1.

are of visible things, to be the avenues to the invisible world, to discern spiritual objects, and to furnish you with ideas of what the outward 'eye hath not seen, neither the ear heard'.[1]

33. And till you have these internal senses, till the eyes of your understanding are opened, you can have no apprehension of divine things, no idea of them at all. Nor consequently, till then, can you either judge truly or reason justly concerning them, seeing your reason has no ground whereon to stand, no materials to work upon.

34. To use the trite instance: as you cannot reason concerning colours if you have no natural sight—because all the ideas received by your other senses are of a different kind, so that neither your hearing nor any other sense can supply your want of sight, or furnish your reason in this respect with matter to work upon—so you cannot reason concerning spiritual things if you have no spiritual sight, because all your ideas received by your outward senses are of a different kind; yea, far more different from those received by faith or internal sensation than the idea of colour from that of sound. These are only different species of one genus, namely, sensible ideas received by external sensation, whereas the ideas of faith differ *toto genere* from those of external sensation. So that it is not conceivable that external sensation should supply the want of internal senses, or furnish your reason in this respect with matter to work upon.

35. What then will your reason do here? How will it pass from things natural to spiritual? From the things that are seen to those that are not seen? From the visible to the invisible world? What a gulf is here! By what art will reason get over the immense chasm? This cannot be till the Almighty come in to your succour, and give you that faith you have hitherto despised. Then, upborne as it were on eagles' wings, you shall soar away into the regions of eternity, and your enlightened reason shall explore even 'the deep things of God', God himself 'revealing them to you by his Spirit'.[2]

---

[1] Cf. 1 Cor. 2: 9. Wesley's interpretation of the senses is a part of the epistemology he derived from John Locke. He accepts the fact that innate ideas do not exist; all knowledge comes from sense impressions or reflection upon them. Sense impressions report on the physical world, and cannot transcend their own limitations. Wesley emphasizes this, because it clears the way for his interpretation of faith. The 'evidence of things not seen' has its appropriate way of registering on the soul an understanding of spiritual truths (cf. § 6). Wesley argues by analogy from our senses and knowledge based on their reports to faith and the assurance based on its testimony.

[2] Cf. 1 Cor. 2: 10.

36. I expected to have received much light on this head from a treatise lately published and earnestly recommended to me: I mean *Christianity Not Founded on Argument.*[1] But on a careful perusal of that piece, notwithstanding my prejudice in its favour, I could not
5 but perceive that the great design uniformly pursued throughout the work was to render the whole of the Christian institution both odious and contemptible. In order to this the author gleans up with great care and diligence the most plausible of those many objections that have been raised against it by late writers, and proposes them
10 with the utmost strength of which he was capable. To do this with the more effect he *personates* a Christian. He *makes a show* of defending an avowed doctrine of Christianity, namely the supernatural influence of the Spirit of God, and often for several sentences together (indeed in the beginning of almost every paragraph) speaks
15 so like a Christian that not a few have received him according to his wish. Meanwhile with all possible art and show of reason, and in the most laboured language, he pursues his point throughout, which is to prove 'that Christianity is contrary to reason'—or 'that no man acting according to the principles of reason can possibly be a
20 Christian'.

37. It is a wonderful proof of the power that smooth words may have even on serious minds, that so many have mistook such a writer as this for a friend of Christianity, since almost every page of his tract is filled with gross falsehood and broad blasphemy, and
25 these supported by such exploded fallacies and commonplace sophistry that a person of two or three years' standing in the university might give them a sufficient answer, and make the author appear as irrational and contemptible as he labours to make Christ and his apostles.

30 38. I have hitherto spoken to those, chiefly, who do not receive the

---

[1] Henry Dodwell 'the younger' (d. 1784) published his controversial work, *Christianity not founded on Argument*, in 1741 (2nd ed., 1742). His father had been a learned scholar of High Church—indeed, of Nonjuror—sympathies, and it was natural to assume that a book by his son which apparently advocated unquestioning faith meant what it seemed to say. But critics insisted that Dodwell was undermining the theological enterprise by making belief appear ridiculous in the eyes of intelligent men. The book was answered by William Dodwell (a brother) in *The Nature, Procedure, Extent, Value and Effects of Rational Faith Considered, in Two Sermons preached before the University of Oxford on March 11 and June 24, 1744* (Oxford, 1744). William admitted that his brother was a Deist, and that his position was really infidelity. A number of other replies were published, and when Wesley paused to discuss the implications of the work he was dealing with a highly topical subject.

Christian system as of God. I would add a few words to another sort of men, though not so much with regard to *our* principles or practice as with regard to *their own*. To you who *do* receive it, who believe the Scripture, but yet do not take upon you the character of *religious men*, I am therefore obliged to address myself to you likewise under the character of *men of reason*.

39. I would only ask: 'Are you such indeed? Do you answer the character under which you appear?' If so, you are consistent with yourselves: your principles and practice agree together.

Let us try whether this is so or not. Do you not take the name of God in vain?[1] Do you remember the sabbath day to keep it holy?[2] Do you not speak evil of the ruler of your people?[3] Are you not a drunkard, or a glutton, faring as sumptuously as you can every day? Making a god of your belly? Do you not avenge yourself? Are you not a whoremonger or adulterer? Answer plainly to your own heart, before God the judge of all.[4]

Why then do you say you believe the Scripture? If the Scripture is true, you are lost. You are in the broad way that leadeth to destruction.[5] Your 'damnation slumbereth not'.[6] You are 'heaping up to yourself wrath against the day of wrath and revelation of the righteous judgment of God'.[7] Doubtless, if the Scripture is true (and you remain thus), it had been good for you if you had never been born.[8]

40. How is it that *you* call yourselves men of reason? Is reason inconsistent with itself? You are the farthest of all men under the sun from any pretence to that character. A common swearer, a sabbath-breaker, a whoremonger, a drunkard, who says he believes the Scripture is of God, is a monster upon earth, the greatest contradiction to his own as well as to the reason of all mankind. In the name of God (that worthy name whereby you are called, and which you daily cause to be blasphemed) turn either to the right hand or to the left. Either *profess* you are an infidel, or *be* a Christian. Halt no longer thus between two opinions.[9] Either cast off the Bible or your sins. And in the mean time, if you have any spark of your boasted reason left, do not 'count us your enemies'[10]—as I fear you have done hitherto, and as thousands do wherever we have declared, 'they who

---

[1] See Exod. 20: 7.   [2] Exod. 20: 8.   [3] See Acts 23: 5.
[4] Heb. 12: 23.   [5] See Matt. 7: 13.   [6] 2 Pet. 1: 3.
[7] Cf. Rom. 2: 5.   [8] See Matt. 26: 24.   [9] See 1 Kgs. 18: 21.
[10] Cf. Ps. 139: 22.

do such things shall not inherit eternal life'[1]—because we tell you
the truth, seeing these are not our words, but the words of him that
sent us; yea, though in doing this 'we use great plainness of speech',[2]
as becomes the ministry we have received. 'For we are not as many
5 who corrupt (cauponize, soften, and thereby adulterate) the word
of God; but as of sincerity, but as of God, in the sight of God,
speak we in Christ.'[3]

41. But it may be you are none of these. You abstain from all such
things. You have an unspotted reputation. You are a man of honour,
10 or a woman of virtue. You scorn to do an unhandsome thing, and
are of an unblameable life and conversation. You are harmless (if
I understand you right) and useless from morning to night. You do
no hurt—and no good—to anyone, no more than a straw floating
upon the water. Your life glides smoothly on from year to year and
15 from one season to another; having no occasion to work

> . . . you waste away
> In gentle inactivity the day.[4]

42. I will not now shock the easiness of your temper by talking
about a future state. But suffer me to ask you a question about
20 present things: are you *now* happy?

I have seen a large company of 'reasonable creatures' called
Indians sitting in a row on the side of a river, looking sometimes at
one another, sometimes at the sky, and sometimes at the bubbles on
the water. And so they sat (unless in the time of war) for a great part
25 of the year, from morning to night.

These were doubtless much at ease, but can you think they were
happy? And how little happier are you than they?

43. You eat, and drink, and sleep, and dress, and dance, and sit
down to play. You are carried abroad. You are at the masquerade,
30 the theatre, the opera-house, the park, the levee, the drawing-room.
What do you do there? Why, sometimes you talk, sometimes you
look at one another. And what are you to do tomorrow? The next
day? The next week? The next year? You are to eat, and drink, and
sleep, and dance, and dress, and play again. And you are to be

---

[1] Cf. Gal. 5: 21.   [2] 2 Cor. 3: 12.   [3] 2 Cor. 2: 17.
[4] With slight modifications this is the translation which Wesley offers in his sermon
'On Spiritual Idolatry' (I. 4) of a couple of lines which he quotes from Horace, *Satires*,
II. vi. 61-2:

> Somno et inertibus horis
> Ducere sollicitae jucunda oblivia vitae.

carried abroad again, that you may again look at one another! And is this all? Alas, how little more happiness have you in this, than the Indians in looking at the sky or water!

Ah poor, dull round! I do not wonder that Col. M——[1] (or any man of reflection) should prefer death itself, even in the midst of his years, to such a life as this, and should frankly declare that he chose to go out of the world because he found nothing in it worth living for.

44. Yet 'tis certain there is business to be done, and many we find in all places (not to speak of the vulgar, the drudges of the earth) who are continually employed therein. Are you of that number? Are you engaged in trade or some other reputable employment? I suppose profitable, too, for you would not spend your time, and labour, and thought, for nothing. You are then making your fortune; you are getting money. True, but money is not your ultimate end. The treasuring up gold and silver for its own sake, all men own, is as foolish and absurd, as grossly unreasonable, as the treasuring up spiders or the wings of butterflies. You consider this but as a means to some farther end. And what is that? Why, the enjoying yourself, the being at ease, the taking your pleasure, the living like a gentleman. That is, plainly, either the whole or some part of the happiness above described.

Supposing then your end to be actually attained. Suppose you have your wish before you drop into eternity. Go and sit down with Thleeanowhee[2] and his companions on the river side—after you have toiled for fifty years you are just as happy as they.

45. Are you, can you, or any reasonable man, be *satisfied* with this? You are not. It is not possible you should. But what else can you do? You *would* have something better to employ your time, but you know not where to find it upon earth.

And indeed it is obvious that the earth as it is now constituted, even with the help of all European arts, does not afford sufficient employment to take up half the waking hours of half its inhabitants.

What then can you do? How can you employ the time that lies so heavy upon your hands? This very thing which you seek declare

---

[1] It is possible that Colonel M—— is identical with the educated man whose attempted suicide Wesley described in §§ 18, 19 above.

[2] Thleeanowhee or Thleeanouhee was the nephew of Tomo-chachi, the chief of some Creek Indians settled near Savannah in Georgia. See Wesley's *Journal* for Feb. 14, 1736.

we unto you.[1] The thing you want is the religion we preach. That
alone leaves no time upon our hands. It fills up all the blank spaces
of life. It exactly takes up all the time we have to spare, be it more
or less, so that 'he who hath much hath nothing over, and he that
has little has no lack'.[2]

46. Once more: can you or any man of reason think you was made
for the life you now lead? You cannot possibly think so: at least,
not till you tread the Bible under foot. The oracles of God bear thee
witness in every page (and thine own heart agreeth thereto) that
thou wast made in the image of God, an incorruptible picture of the
God of glory. And what art thou even in thy present state? An
everlasting spirit, going to God. For what end then did he create
thee but to dwell with him above this perishable world, to know
him, to love him, to do his will, to enjoy him for ever and ever!
O look more deeply into thyself, and into that Scripture which
thou professest to receive as the 'Word of God', as 'right concerning
all things'.[3] There thou wilt find a nobler, happier state described
than it ever yet entered into thy heart to conceive. But God hath
now revealed it to all those who 'rejoice evermore', and 'pray
without ceasing', and 'in everything give thanks',[4] and 'do his will
on earth as it is done in heaven'.[5] For this thou wast made. Hereunto
also thou art called. O be not disobedient to the heavenly calling![6]
At least, be not angry with those who would fain bring thee to be
a living witness of that religion 'whose ways are' indeed 'ways of
pleasantness, and all her paths, peace'.[7]

47. Do you say in your heart: 'I know all this already. I am not
barely a man of reason. I am a religious man, for I not only avoid
evil and do good, but use all the means of grace. I am constantly at
church, and at the Sacrament too. I say my prayers every day. I
read many good books. I fast—every Thirtieth of January,[8] and
Good Friday.' Do you indeed? Do you do all this? This you may do.

---

[1] See Acts 17: 23.   [2] Cf. Exod. 16: 18; 2 Cor. 8: 15.
[3] Cf. Ps. 119: 128.   [4] 1 Thess. 5: 16–18.   [5] Cf. Matt. 6: 10.
[6] See Acts 26: 19.   [7] Prov. 3: 17.
[8] After the Restoration of the monarchy in 1660, the anniversary of the execution of
King Charles I (Jan. 30, 1649) was included in the church calendar and an appropriate
service was provided in the Book of Common Prayer (1662). The cult of 'Charles, King
and Martyr' was popular, and was closely associated with the attempt to make non-
resistance and passive obedience the characteristic doctrines of the Anglican Church.
After 1688, when divine right and kindred doctrines were seriously discredited, the day
was less ardently observed, but Nonjurors, Jacobites, and Tory High Churchmen still
celebrated it—even linking it (so Wesley hints) with another famous execution.

You may go thus far, and yet have no religion at all—no such religion as avails before God. Nay, much farther than this, than you have ever gone yet, or so much as thought of going. For you may 'give all your goods to feed the poor', yea, 'your body to be burned', and yet very possibly, if St. Paul be a judge, 'have no charity',[1] no true religion.

48. This religion, which alone is of value before God, is the very thing you want. You want (and in wanting this, you want all) the religion of love. You do not love your neighbour as yourself, no more than you love God with all your heart.[2] Ask your own heart now if it be not so? 'Tis plain you do not love God. If you did you would be happy in him. But you know you are not happy. Your *formal* religion no more makes you happy than your neighbour's *gay* religion does him. O how much have you suffered for want of plain dealing! Can you now bear to hear the naked truth? You have the 'form of godliness', but not 'the power'.[3] You are a mere whited wall.[4] Before the Lord your God I ask you, 'Are you not?' Too sure. For your 'inward parts are very wickedness'.[5] You love 'the creature more than the Creator'.[6] You are 'a lover of pleasure more than a lover of God'.[7] A lover of God? You do not love God at all, no more than you love a stone. You cannot love God: for you love praise. You love the world: therefore the love of the Father is not in you.[8]

49. You are on the brink of the pit, ready to be plunged into everlasting perdition. Indeed you 'have a zeal for God, but not according to knowledge'.[9] O how terribly have you been deceived, posting to hell, and fancying it was heaven! See at length that outward religion without inward is nothing—is far worse than nothing, being indeed no other than a solemn mockery of God. And *inward religion you have not.* You have not the 'faith that worketh by love'.[10] Your faith (so called) is no living, saving principle. It is not the Apostle's faith, 'the substance (or subsistence) of things hoped for, the evidence of things not seen'.[11] So far from it, that this faith is the very thing which you call 'enthusiasm'.[12] You are not content with being

---

[1] Cf. 1 Cor. 13: 3.   [2] See Matt. 22: 37–9.   [3] 2 Tim. 3: 5.
[4] Acts 23: 3.   [5] Ps. 5: 9 (B.C.P.).   [6] Rom. 1: 25.
[7] Cf. 2 Tim. 3: 4.   [8] See 1 John 2: 15.   [9] Rom. 10: 2.
[10] Cf. Gal. 5: 6.   [11] Heb. 11: 1.
[12] In the eighteenth century 'enthusiasm' meant religious fanaticism, especially any suggestion of illumination by the Holy Spirit. It played a large part in anti-Methodist polemics, and appears frequently in this volume. Cf. Introduction (pp. 25–7) and the introduction to *A Farther Appeal* (pp. 97–8).

without it, unless you blaspheme it too. You even revile that 'life which is hid with Christ in God',[1] all seeing, tasting, hearing, feeling God. These things 'are foolishness unto *you*'. No marvel, for 'they are spiritually discerned'.[2]

5   50. O no longer shut your eyes against the light! Know you have a name that you live, but are dead.[3] Your soul is utterly dead in sin, dead in pride, in vanity, in self-will, in sensuality, in love of the world. You are utterly dead to God. There is no intercourse between your soul and God. 'You have neither seen him' (by faith, as our

10 Lord witnessed against them of old time) 'nor heard his voice at any time.'[4] You have no spiritual 'senses exercised to discern spiritual good and evil'.[5] You are angry at infidels, and are all the while as mere an infidel before God as they. You have 'eyes that see not and ears that hear not'.[6] You have a *callous, unfeeling* heart.

15   51. Bear with me yet a little longer: my soul is distressed for you. 'The god of this world hath blinded your eyes',[7] and you are 'seeking death in the error of your life'.[8] Because you do not commit gross sin, because you give alms and go to the church and sacrament, you imagine that you are serving God: yet in very deed you are serving

20 the devil. For you are doing still your own will, not the will of God your Saviour. You are pleasing yourself in all you do. Pride, vanity, and self-will (the genuine fruits of an earthly, sensual, devilish heart),[9] pollute all your words and actions. You are in darkness, in the shadow of death. O that God would say to you in thunder,

25 'Awake, thou that sleepest, and arise from the dead, and Christ shall give thee light!'[10]

   52. But, blessed be God, he hath not yet left himself without witness!

> All are not lost! There be who faith prefer,
30   Though few, and piety to God,[11]

who know the power of faith and are no strangers to that inward vital religion, 'the mind that was in Christ',[12] 'righteousness, and

---

[1] Cf. Col. 3: 3.   [2] Cf. 1 Cor. 2: 14.   [3] See Rev. 3: 1.
[4] Cf. John 5: 37.   [5] Cf. Heb. 5: 14.
[6] Cf. Pss. 115: 5–6; 135: 16–17; Mark 8: 18.
[7] Cf. 2 Cor. 4: 4.   [8] Cf. Wisd. 1: 12.   [9] See Jas. 3: 15.
[10] Eph. 5: 14—the text of Charles Wesley's sermon, preached before the University of Oxford on Apr. 4, 1742 (*Bibliography*, No. 59), later incorporated by John Wesley into his 'standard' sermons.   [11] Cf. Milton, *Paradise Lost*, vi. 142–7.
[12] Cf. Phil. 2: 5.

peace, and joy in the Holy Ghost'.[1] Of you who 'have tasted the good word of God, and the powers of the world to come',[2] would we be glad to learn if we have 'erred from the faith',[3] or walked con‑ trary to 'the truth as it is in Jesus'.[4] 'Let the righteous smite me friendly, and reprove me',[5] if haply that which is amiss may be done away, and what is wanting supplied, 'till we all come to the measure of the stature of the fulness of Christ'.[6]

53. Perhaps the first thing that now occurs to your mind relates to the doctrine which we teach. You have heard that we say, 'Men may live without sin.' And have you not heard that the Scripture says the same (we mean, without *committing* sin)? Does not St. Paul say plainly that those who believe do not 'continue in sin', that they cannot 'live any longer therein'?[a] Does not St. Peter say: 'He that hath suffered in the flesh hath ceased from sin, that he no longer should live . . . to the desires of men, but to the will of God'?[b] And does not St. John say most expressly: 'He that committeth sin is of the devil. . . . For this purpose the Son of God was manifested, that he might destroy the works of the devil. Whosoever is born of God doth not commit sin, for his seed remaineth in him, and he cannot sin, because he is born of God.'[c] And again: 'We know that whosoever is born of God sinneth not.'[d]

54. You see, then, it is not *we* that say this, but the Lord. These are not *our* words, but *his*. And who is he that replieth against God? Who is able to make God a liar? Surely he will be 'justified in his saying, and clear when he is judged'![7] Can you deny it? Have you not often felt a secret check when you was contradicting this great truth? And how often have you wished for what you was taught to deny? Nay, can you help wishing for it at this moment? Do you not now earnestly desire to cease from sin? To commit it no more? Does not your soul pant after this glorious liberty of the sons of God? And what strong reason have you to expect it? Have you not had a foretaste of it already? Do you not remember the time when God first lifted up the light of his countenance upon you?[8] Can it

[a] Rom. 6: 1–2.   [b] 1 Pet. 4: 1–2.
[c] 1 John 3: 8–9.   [d] 1 John 5: 18.

[1] Rom. 14: 17.   [2] Heb. 6: 5.
[3] 1 Tim. 6: 10.   [4] Cf. Eph. 4: 21.
[5] Cf. Ps. 141:5 (B.C.P.).   [6] Cf. Eph. 4: 13.
[7] Cf. Ps. 51: 4 (B.C.P.); Rom. 3: 4.   [8] See Ps. 4: 6.

ever be forgotten? The day when the 'candle of the Lord' first 'shone upon your head'?[1]

> Butter and honey did you eat,
>   And, lifted up on high,
> You saw the clouds beneath your feet,
>   And rode upon the sky.

> Far, far above all earthly things,
>   Triumphantly you rode;
> You soared to heaven on eagles' wings,
>   And found, and talked with God.[2]

You then had power not to commit sin. You found the Apostle's words strictly true: 'he that is begotten of God keepeth himself, and that wicked one toucheth him not'.[3] But those whom you took to be experienced Christians telling you this was only the time of your espousals, this could not last always, you must come down from the mount, and the like, shook your faith. You looked at men more than God, and so became weak and like another man.[4] Whereas had you then had any to guide you according to the truth of God, had you then heard the doctrine which now you blame, you had never fallen from your steadfastness, but had found that in this sense also 'the gifts and calling of God are without repentance'.[5]

55. Have you not another objection nearly allied to this, namely that we preach perfection? True, but what perfection? The term you cannot object to, because it is scriptural. All the difficulty is to fix the meaning of it according to the Word of God. And this we have done again and again, declaring to all the world that Christian perfection does not imply an exemption from ignorance, or mistake, or infirmities, or temptations, but that it does imply the being so 'crucified with Christ' as to be able to testify, 'I live not, but Christ liveth in me',[a] and 'hath purified my heart by faith'.[b] It does imply the 'casting down every high thing that exalteth itself against the knowledge of God, and bringing into captivity every thought to the

---

[a] [Cf.] Gal. 2: 20. [b] [Cf.] Acts 15: 9.

[1] Cf. Job 29: 3; Prov. 20: 27.
[2] John and Charles Wesley, *Hymns and Sacred Poems* (1742), p. 69. See *Bibliography*, No. 54, and G. Osborn (ed.), *The Poetical Works of John and Charles Wesley* (henceforth '*Poet. Wks.*'), II. 120–1. John Wesley has altered the first person of the original to the second person. [3] 1 John 5: 18.
[4] See Judg. 16: 7, 11, 17. [5] Rom. 11: 29.

obedience of Christ'.[a] It does imply the 'being holy as he that hath called us is holy, in all manner of conversation'.[b] And, in a word, the 'loving the Lord our God with all our heart, and serving him with all our strength'.[1]

56. Now is it possible for any who believe the Scripture to deny one tittle of this? You cannot. You dare not. You would not for the world. You know it is the pure Word of God. And this is the whole of what we preach. This is the height and depth of what we (with St. Paul) call perfection—a state of soul devoutly to be wished for by all who have tasted of the love of God. O pray for it without ceasing.[2] It is the one thing you want. 'Come with boldness to the throne of grace',[3] and be assured that when you ask this of God you shall have 'the petition you ask of him'.[4] We know indeed that 'to man'—to the natural man—'this is impossible'.[5] But we know also that as 'no work is impossible with God',[6] so 'all things are possible to him that believeth'.[7]

57. For 'we are saved by faith'.[8] But have you not heard this urged as another objection against us, that we preach salvation by faith alone? And does not St. Paul do the same thing? 'By grace', saith he, 'ye are saved through faith.'[9] Can any words be more express? And elsewhere, 'Believe in the Lord Jesus and thou shalt be saved.'[c]

What we mean by this (if it has not been sufficiently explained already) is that we are saved from our sins only by a confidence in the love of God. As soon as we 'behold what manner of love it is which the Father hath bestowed upon us',[10] 'we love him (as the Apostle observes) because he first loved us'.[11] And then is that commandment written in our heart, 'that he who loveth God love his brother also',[12] from which love of God and man, meekness, humbleness of mind, and all holy tempers spring. Now these are the very essence of salvation, of Christian salvation, salvation from sin. And from

---

[a] 2 Cor. 10: 5.   [b] [Cf.] 1 Pet. 1: 15.   [c] Acts 16: 31.

[1] Cf. Mark 12: 30, etc.   [2] See 1 Thess. 5: 17.   [3] Cf. Heb. 4: 16.
[4] Cf. 1 Sam. 1: 27.   [5] Matt. 19: 26.
[6] Cf. Luke 1:37, 'For with God nothing shall be impossible.'
[7] Mark 9: 23.
[8] This exact phrase occurs nowhere in the Bible, but in italicizing it Wesley seems to have had in mind Eph. 2: 8, which he quotes in a following sentence.
[9] Eph. 2: 8; see preceding note.   [10] Cf. 1 John 3: 1.
[11] 1 John 4: 19.   [12] 1 John 4: 21.

these outward salvation flows, that is, holiness of life and conversation. Well, and are not these things so? If you know in whom you have believed you need no further witnesses.

58. But perhaps you doubt whether that faith whereby we are
5 thus saved implies such a trust and confidence in God as we describe. You cannot think faith implies assurance, an assurance of the love of God to our souls, of his being now reconciled to us, and having forgiven all our sins. And this we freely confess, that if number of voices is to decide the question we must give it up at once, for you
10 have on your side not only some who desire to be Christians indeed, but all nominal Christians in every place, and the Romish Church, one and all. Nay, these last are so vehement in your defence that in the famed Council of Trent they have decreed: 'If any man hold *fiduciam* (trust, confidence, or assurance of pardon) to be essential
15 to faith, let him be accursed.'[1]

59. Thus does that Council anathematize the Church of England. For she is convict hereof by her own confession.[2] The very words in the Homily on Salvation are:

... Even the devils ... believe that Christ was born of a virgin; ...
20 that he wrought all kind of miracles, declaring himself very God; ...

---

[1] *Canones et Decreta Dogmatica Concilii Tridenti* (Rome, 1564), sessio Sexta, Canon XII: '... vel eam fiduciam solam esse, qua justificamur, anathema sit'. The author of *The Notions of the Methodists Farther Disproved* (Newcastle, 1743), p. 40, pointed out that Wesley's quotation was incorrect, and in *A Farther Appeal* (Pt. I, IV. 3) Wesley reproduced the English text of the twelfth canon as furnished by the anonymous author of *The Notions*. See further the following note.

[2] Wesley's original text has been modified as a result of a dispute about chronology. In the first edition of *An Earnest Appeal* § 59 began thus: 'If we consider the time when this decree was passed, namely just after the publication of our Homilies, it will appear more than probable that the very design of the Council was to anathematize the Church of England, as being now convict by her own confession of "that damnable and heretical doctrine".' The author of *The Notions of the Methodists Farther Disproved* not only pointed out that Wesley had misquoted the canons of the Council of Trent, but he also claimed that Wesley's dates were incorrect. The facts are as follows: the decree on the doctrine of justification was proclaimed at Trent on Jan. 13, 1547; the Book of Homilies was published on July 31 of that year. Therefore, argued Wesley's opponent, it could not have been the 'very design of the Council ... to anathematize the Church of England' (op. cit., pp. 39–40). In *A Farther Appeal* Wesley conceded that he had misquoted the Council, 'not having the book then by [him]' (Pt. I, IV. 3). Concerning chronology, he argued that Jan. 13, 1547 was the date on which the Council began to discuss justification, not that on which it published its report. Even if true, this would not have strengthened Wesley's case, since the next decree was issued on March 3, still well ahead of the date on which the Book of Homilies was published.

Wesley attempted, without complete success, to remove from future editions of *An Earnest Appeal* the statement about the 'very design' of the Council, though he still

that for our sakes he suffered a most painful death, to redeem us from death everlasting. . . . These articles of our faith the devils believe, and so they believe all that is written in the Old and New Testament. . . . And yet for all this faith they be but devils. They remain still in their damnable estate, lacking the very true Christian faith. 5

The right and true Christian faith is, not only to believe the Holy Scriptures and the articles of our faith are true; but also to have a sure *trust* and *confidence* . . . to be saved from everlasting damnation through Christ.[1]

Or (as it is expressed a little after), 'a sure trust and confidence 10 which a man hath in God, that by the merits of Christ his sins are forgiven, and he reconciled to the favour of God'.[2]

60. Indeed the Bishop of Rome saith, 'If any man hold this, let him be *anathema maranatha*.' But 'tis to be hoped papal anathemas do not move *you*. You are a member of the Church of England. 15 Are you? Then the controversy is at an end. Then hear the Church: faith is 'a sure trust which a man hath in God, that his sins are forgiven'. Or if you are not, whether you hear our church or no, at least hear the Scriptures. Hear believing Job declaring his faith: 'I know that my Redeemer liveth.'[3] Hear Thomas (when having 20 seen, he believed) crying out, 'My Lord and my God.'[4] Hear St. Paul clearly describing the nature of *his* faith: 'The life I now live I live by faith in the Son of God, who loved *me* and gave himself

insisted that what Trent had anathematized was authoritative Church of England doctrine. In the third edition (1744) the opening sentences were amended, but because the 1749 and 1765 editions stemmed mainly from the second rather than from the third edition, the original sentence continued therein—surprisingly in the case of the 1765 edition, so carefully edited by Charles Wesley, who was evidently not so sensitive about the error as his brother John.

The phrase 'that damnable and heretical doctrine' has a long ancestry. Something similar occurs in the pronouncement of the Fourth Lateran Council ('doctrina non tam haeretica quam insana'); of the Council of Constance ('articulos . . . haereticos . . . reprobatos . . . damnatos . . . illa perniciosa doctrina'); and in certain of the pronouncements of the Council of Trent. It was thoroughly domesticated in England during the Anglican–Roman Catholic controversies during the reigns of James I and James II. In the earlier part of the seventeenth century it occurs in Perkins and Ussher (as well as in a host of obscure pamphleteers on both sides). In the post-Restoration period it can be found in several of the works collected by Bishop Edmund Gibson (Wesley's opponent) in the massive series of anti-Roman pamphlets which he edited and reissued under the title, *A Preservative against Popery*.

[1] *Certain Sermons or Homilies appointed by the King's Majesty* (1547; henceforth '*Homilies*'), 'The Third Part of the Sermon of Salvation' (henceforth 'Salvation, 'Pt. III', etc.). A 'Second Book' was issued under Elizabeth I.

[2] Ibid. This is the definition of faith which Wesley quotes most frequently.

[3] Job 19: 25.   [4] Cf. John 20: 28–9.

for *me*.'[1] Hear (to mention no more) all the believers who were with Paul when he wrote to the Colossians, bearing witness: 'We give thanks unto the Father, . . . who *hath delivered* us from the power of darkness, and *hath translated* us into the kingdom of his dear Son:
5 in whom we have redemption through his blood, even *the forgiveness of sins*.'[a]

61. But what need have we of distant witnesses? You have a witness in your own breast. For am I not speaking to one that loves God? How came *you* then to love him at first? Was it not because
10 you knew that he loved you? Did you, could you love God at all, till you 'tasted and saw that he was gracious',[2] that he was merciful to you a sinner?[3] What avails then controversy or strife of words? 'Out of thy own mouth'![4] You own you had no love to God till you was sensible of his love to you. And whatever expressions any sinner
15 who loves God uses to denote God's love to him, you will always upon examination find that they directly or indirectly imply forgiveness. Pardoning love is still at the root of all. He who was offended is now reconciled. The new song which God puts in every mouth is always to that effect: 'O Lord, I will praise thee. Though thou wast
20 angry with me, thine anger is turned away. . . . Behold, God is my salvation. I will trust and not be afraid: for the Lord Jehovah is my strength and my song; he is also become my salvation.'[b]

62. A confidence then in a pardoning God is essential to a true faith. The forgiveness of sins is one of the first of those unseen
25 things whereof faith is the evidence. And if you are sensible of this, will you quarrel with us concerning an indifferent circumstance of it? Will you think it an important objection that we assert that this faith is usually given *in a moment*? First let me entreat you to read over that authentic account of God's dealings with men, the Acts
30 of the Apostles. In this treatise you will find how he wrought from the beginning on those who received remission of sins by faith. And can you find one of these (except perhaps St. Paul) who did not receive it in a moment? But abundance you find of those who did, besides Cornelius and the three thousand.[c] And to this also agrees
35 the experience of those who now receive the heavenly gift. Three or four exceptions only have I found in the course of several years.

---

[a] Col. 1: 12–14.   [b] Isa. 12: 1–2.   [c] Acts 2: 41.

---

[1] Cf. Gal. 2: 20.   [2] Cf. Ps. 34: 8 (B.C.P.).
[3] See Luke 18: 13.   [4] Cf. Luke 19: 22.

(Perhaps you yourself may be added to that number, and one or two more whom you have known.) But all the rest of those who from time to time among us have believed in the Lord Jesus were in a moment brought 'from darkness to light, and from the power of Satan unto God'.[1]

63. And why should it seem a thing incredible to you who have known 'the power of God unto salvation'[2]—whether he wrought thus in your soul or no (for 'there are diversities of operations, but the same spirit')[3]—that 'the dead should hear the voice of the Son of God',[4] and in that moment live? Thus he useth to act, to show that when he willeth, to do is present with him. 'Let there be light (said God), and there was light.'[5] 'He spake the word, and it was done.'[6] 'Thus the heavens and the earth were created, and all the hosts of them.'[7] And this manner of acting in the present case highly suits both his power and love. There is therefore no hindrance on God's part, since 'as his majesty is, so is his mercy'.[8] And whatever hindrance there is on the part of man, when God speaketh it is not. Only ask then, O sinner, 'and it shall be given thee',[9] even the faith that brings salvation; and that without any merit or good work of thine, for it is 'not of works, lest any man should boast'.[10] No; it is of *grace*, of grace alone. For 'unto him that worketh not, but believeth on him that justifieth the ungodly, his faith is counted to him for righteousness.'[11]

64. 'But by talking thus you encourage sinners.' I do encourage them—to repent. And do not you? Do not you know how many heap sin upon sin, purely for want of such encouragement? Because they think they can never be forgiven, there is no place of repentance left. Does not *your* heart also bleed for them? What would you think too dear to part with, what would you not do, what would you not suffer, to bring one such sinner to repentance? Could not your love 'endure all things'[12] for them? Yes—if you believed it would do them good, if you had any hope they would ever be better. Why do you not believe it would do them good? Why have you not a hope that they will be better? Plainly because you do not love them enough: because you have not that charity which not only endureth, but at the same time 'believeth and hopeth all things'.[13]

---

[1] Acts 26: 18. [2] Rom. 1: 16. [3] Cf. 1 Cor. 12: 4, 6.
[4] Cf. John 5: 25. [5] Gen. 1: 3. [6] Cf. Ps. 33: 9. [7] Cf. Gen. 2: 1.
[8] Ecclus. 2: 18. [9] Matt. 7: 7, etc. [10] Eph. 2: 9. [11] Cf. Rom. 4: 5.
[12] 2 Tim. 2: 10; cf. 1 Cor. 13: 7. [13] Cf. 1 Cor. 13: 7.

65. But that you may see the whole strength of this objection I will show you without any disguise or reserve how I encourage the very chief of sinners. My usual language to them runs thus:

O ye that deny the Lord that bought you, yet hear the word of the
5   Lord. Ye seek rest, but find none.[1] Even in laughter your heart is in heaviness.[2] How long spend ye your labour for that which is not bread, and your strength for that which satisfieth not?[3] You know your soul is not satisfied. It is still an aching void. Sometimes you find (in spite of your principles) a sense of guilt, an awakened conscience. That grisly
10 phantom religion (so you describe her) will now and then haunt you still. 'Righteousness looking down from heaven',[4] is indeed to *us* no unpleasing sight. But how does it appear to *you*?

Horribili super aspectu mortalibus instans?[5]

How often are you in fear of the very things you deny? How often in
15 racking suspense? 'What if there be an hereafter? A judgment to come? An unhappy eternity?' Do you not start at the thought? Can you be content to be always thus? Shall it be said of *you* also:

Here lies a dicer, long in doubt
If death could kill the soul, or not.
20 Here ends his doubtfulness, at last
Convinced—but O, the die is cast![6]

Or are you already convinced there is no hereafter? What a poor state then are you in now! Taking a few more dull turns upon earth, and then dropping into nothing! What kind of spirit must you be of if you
25 can sustain yourself under the thought! Under the expectation of being in a few moments swept away by the stream of time, and then for ever

. . . swallowed up, and lost
In the wide womb of uncreated night![7]

But neither indeed are you *certain* of this—nor of anything else: 'It may
30 be so; it may not. A vast scene is behind. But clouds and darkness rest upon it.' All is doubt and uncertainty. You are continually tossed to and fro,[8] and have no firm ground for the sole of your foot.[9] O let not

---

[1] See Matt. 12: 43.   [2] See Prov. 14: 13.
[3] Isa. 55: 2.   [4] Cf. Ps. 85: 11.
[5] Lucretius, *De Rerum Natura* (*On the Nature of Things*), i. 65—'Threatening mortals from on high with its horrible visage'. All contemporary editions of Wesley's text contain the error 'astans' for 'instans'.
[6] Samuel Wesley, 'Epitaph on a Gamester and Free Thinker', *Poems*, 1736, p. 92; the original has 'sceptic', not 'dicer'.   [7] Milton, *Paradise Lost*, ii. 149–50.
[8] See Eph. 4: 14.   [9] See Gen. 8: 9.

the poor wisdom of man any longer exalt itself against the wisdom of God. You have fled from him long enough: at length suffer your eyes to be opened by him that made them. You want rest to your soul. Ask it of him who 'giveth to all men liberally, and upbraideth not'.[1] You are now a mere riddle to yourself, and your condition full of darkness and perplexity. You are one among many restless inhabitants of a miserable, disordered world, 'walking in a vain shadow, and disquieting yourself in vain'.[2] But the light of God will speedily disperse the anxiety of your vain conjectures. By adding heaven to earth, and eternity to time, it will open such a glorious view of things as will lead you, even in the present world, to a 'peace which passeth all understanding'.[3]

66. O ye gross, vile, scandalous sinners, hear ye the word of the Lord. 'Turn ye, turn ye from your evil ways';[4] 'so iniquity shall not be your ruin'.[5] 'As I live, saith the Lord, I have no pleasure in the death of a sinner, but rather that he should turn and live.'[6] O make haste! Delay not the time! 'Come, and let us reason together. Though your sins be as scarlet, they shall be white as snow; though they be red as crimson, they shall be as wool.'[7] 'Who is this that cometh from Edom, with dyed garments, red in his apparel?'[8] It is he on whom 'the Lord hath laid the iniquities of us all'![9] 'Behold, behold the Lamb of God, that taketh away thy sins!'[10] See 'the only begotten Son of the Father, full of grace and truth'![11] He loveth *thee*. He gave himself for *thee*. Now his bowels of compassion yearn over *thee*! O believe in the Lord Jesus, and *thou* shalt be saved![12] 'Go in peace, sin no more!'[13]

67. Now cannot *you* join in all this? Is it not the very language of your heart? O when will you take knowledge that *our* whole concern, our constant labour, is to bring all the world to the religion which you feel, to solid, inward, vital religion! What power is it then that keeps us asunder? 'Is thine heart right, as my heart is with thy heart? . . . If it be, give me thy hand. . . . Come with me and see', and rejoice in, 'my zeal for the Lord'.[14] No difference between us (if thou art a child of God) can be so considerable as our agreement is. If we differ in smaller things, we agree in that which is greatest of all. How is it possible, then, that *you* should be induced to think or speak evil of us? How could it ever come into your mind to oppose us or weaken our hands? How long shall we complain of the wounds

---

[1] Jas. 1: 5.   [2] Cf. Ps. 39: 7 (B.C.P.).   [3] Phil. 4: 7.   [4] Ezek. 33: 11.
[5] Ezek. 18: 30.   [6] Cf. Ezek. 33: 11.   [7] Cf. Isa. 1: 18.
[8] Isa. 63: 1; cf. v. 2.   [9] Cf. Isa. 53: 6.   [10] Cf. John 1: 29.
[11] Cf. John 1: 14.   [12] See Acts 16: 31.   [13] Cf. John 8: 11.
[14] 2 Kgs. 10: 15–16. This furnished the text for Wesley's sermon, 'Catholic Spirit'.

which we receive in the house of our friends? Surely 'the children of this world' are still 'wiser in their generation than the children of light'.[1] Satan is not divided against himself! Why are they who are on the Lord's side? How is it that 'wisdom is' *not* 'justified of her 5 own children'?[2]

68. Is it because you have heard that we only make religion a cloak for covetousness,[3] and because you have heard abundance of particulars alleged in support of that general charge? 'Tis probable you may also have heard **how** much we have *gained* by preaching 10 already; and, to crown all, that we are only Papists in disguise, who are undermining and destroying the Church.

69. You 'have heard this'. Well: and can you believe it? Have you then never heard the fifth chapter of St. Matthew? I would to God you could believe this! 'What is written there? How readest thou?'[4] 15 'Blessed are ye when men shall revile you and persecute you, and say all manner of evil against you falsely for my name's sake. Rejoice, and be exceeding glad, for great is your reward in heaven; for so persecuted they the prophets that were before you'[5]—namely, by reviling them, and saying all manner of evil of them, falsely. Do not 20 you know that this (as well as all other Scriptures) must needs be fulfilled?[6] If so, take knowledge that this day also it is fulfilled in your ears.[7] For our Lord's sake, and for the sake of his gospel which we preach, men *do* revile us and persecute us, and (blessed be God who giveth us to rejoice therein), say all manner of evil of us, 25 falsely. And how can it be otherwise? 'The disciple is not above his master. It is enough for the disciple that he be as his master, and the servant as his Lord. If they have called the master of the house Beelzebub, how much more shall they call them of his household!'[8]

30 70. This only we confess, that 'we preach *inward* salvation, *now* attainable by *faith*'. And for preaching *this* (for no other crime was then so much as pretended) we were forbid to preach any more in any of those churches where, till then, we were gladly received. This is a notorious fact. Being thus hindered from preaching in the 35 places we should first have chosen, we now declare 'the grace of God which bringeth salvation'[9] 'in all places of his dominion',[10] as well knowing that God 'dwelleth not *only* in temples made with

---

[1] Cf. Luke 16: 8. [2] Cf. Matt. 11: 19. [3] 1 Thess. 2: 5.
[4] Cf. Luke 10: 26. [5] Matt. 5: 11–12. [6] See Mark 14: 49, etc.
[7] See Luke 4: 21. [8] Matt. 10: 24–5. [9] Titus 2: 11. [10] Ps. 103: 22.

hands'.[1] This is the real, and it is the only real, ground of complaint against us. And this we avow before all mankind—we *do* preach *this* salvation by *faith*. And not being suffered to preach it in the usual places, we declare it wherever a door is opened, either on a mountain or plain or by a river side (for all which we conceive we have suffi- cient precedent), or in a prison, or as it were in the house of Justus[2] or the school of one Tyrannus.[3] Nor dare we refrain. 'A dispensa- tion of the gospel is committed to me', and 'woe is me if I preach not the gospel'.[4]

71. Here we allow the fact but deny the guilt. But in every other point alleged we deny the fact, and call upon all the world to prove it if they can. More especially we call upon those who for many years saw our manner of life at Oxford. These well know that 'after the most straitest sect of our religion we lived Pharisees',[5] and that the grand objection to us for all those years was the being 'righteous overmuch':[6] the going to church and to the Lord's Table; the relieving the poor, visiting those that were sick and in prison; instructing the ignorant, and labouring to reclaim the wicked— *more than was necessary* for salvation. These were our open, flagrant crimes from the year 1729 to the year 1737, touching which our Lord shall judge in that day.

72. But, waiving the things that are past, 'which of you *now* convinceth us of sin?'[7] Which of you (I here more especially appeal to my brethren of the clergy) can personally convict us of any un- godliness or unholiness of conversation? Ye know in your own hearts (all that are candid men, all that are not utterly blinded with prejudice) that we 'labour to have a conscience void of offence both toward God and toward man'.[8] Brethren, I would to God that in this ye were even as we. But indeed (with grief I speak it) ye are not. There are among yourselves ungodly and unholy men, openly, undeniably such: drunkards, gluttons, returners of evil for evil, liars, swearers, profaners of the day of the Lord. Proof hereof is not wanting if ye require it. Where then is your zeal against these?

---

[1] Cf. Acts 7: 48; 17: 24.   [2] Acts 18: 7.   [3] Acts 19: 9.
[4] 1 Cor. 9: 17, 16.   [5] Cf. Acts 26: 5.
[6] Eccles. 7: 16. In 1739 Dr. Joseph Trapp preached a series of four sermons in various London churches against the Methodists, publishing them under the title of *The Nature, Folly, Sin, and Danger of being Righteous Overmuch*. This pamphlet was several times reprinted, and frequently attacked. See Richard Green, *Anti-Methodist Publications* (London, Kelly, 1902), Nos. 10, 14, 15, 93.
[7] Cf. John 8: 46.   [8] Cf. Acts 24: 16.

A clergyman so drunk he can scarce stand or speak may, in the presence of a thousand people, set upon another clergyman of the same church both with abusive words and open violence.ᵃ And what follows? Why, the one is still allowed to dispense the sacred
5 signs of the body and blood of Christ. But the other is not allowed to receive them—because he is a field preacher![1]

73. O ye pillars and fathers of the church, are these things well-pleasing to him who 'hath made you overseers over that flock which he hath purchased with his own blood'?[2] O that ye would suffer me
10 to boast myself a little![3] Is there not a cause? Have not ye compelled me? Which of your clergy are more unspotted in their lives, which more unwearied in their labours, than those whose 'names ye cast out as evil', whom ye count 'as the filth and offscouring of the world'?[4] Which of them is more zealous to 'spend and be spent'[5]
15 for the lost sheep of the house of Israel?[6] Or who amongst them is more ready to 'be offered up for their flock upon the sacrifice and service of their faith'?[7]

74. Will ye say, as the historian of Catiline: *Si sic pro patria!*[8] If this were done in defence of the Church, and not in order to
20 undermine and destroy it! That is the very proposition I undertake to prove: that 'we are now defending the Church, even the Church of England, in opposition to all those who either secretly undermine or openly attempt to destroy it'.

75. That we are Papists (we who are daily and hourly preaching
25 that very doctrine which is so solemnly anathematized by the whole Church of Rome) is such a charge that I dare not waste my time in industriously confuting it. Let any man of common sense only look on the title pages of the sermons we have lately preached at Oxford,[9]

ᵃ At Epworth, in Lincolnshire.

[1] On Sunday, January 2, 1743, Wesley preached at 8 a.m. from his father's tomb in Epworth churchyard. When some of his hearers asked if they should receive the sacrament at the communion service in the parish church, Wesley encouraged them to do so, but advised them first to ask leave of the curate, the Revd. John Romley. 'One did so in the name of the rest; to whom he said, "Pray tell Mr. Wesley I shall not give *him* the sacrament, for he is not *fit*."' *Journal*, Jan. 2, 1743.

[2] Cf. Acts 20: 28.   [3] See 2 Cor. 11: 16.   [4] Cf. 1 Cor. 4: 13.
[5] 2 Cor. 12: 15.   [6] Matt. 10: 6, etc.   [7] Cf. Phil. 2: 17.

[8] 'If only this were done for the fatherland.' L. Annaeus Florus, *Epitome of Roman History*, II. xii. 12.

[9] Wesley had published three Oxford sermons: one on Job 3: 17 (1735, *Bibliography* No. 6), *A Sermon on Salvation by Faith* (1738, *Bibliography* No. 10), and *The Almost Christian* (1741, *Bibliography* No. 50). Clearly he had the second in mind, though the contents (not the title-page) of the third also supported his claim.

and he will need nothing more to show him the weight of this senseless, shameless accusation—unless he can suppose the governors both of Christ Church and Lincoln College, nay, and all the university, to be Papists too.

76. You yourself can easily acquit us of this, but not of the other part of the charge. You still think we are secretly undermining, if not openly destroying, the Church.

What do you mean by the Church? A visible Church (as our Article defines it) is 'a company of faithful (or believing) people: *coetus credentium*'.[1] This is the essence of a Church, and the properties thereof are (as they are described in the words that follow), 'that the pure word of God be preached therein, and the sacraments duly administered'.[2] Now, then, according to this authentic account, what is the Church of England? What is it, indeed, but the *faithful people*, the *true believers* of England? It is true, if these are scattered abroad they come under another consideration. But when they are visibly joined by assembling together to hear 'the pure word of God preached' and to 'eat of one bread' and 'drink of one cup', they are then properly 'the visible Church of England'.

77. It were well if this were a little more considered by those who so vehemently cry out, 'The Church, the Church!' (as those of old, 'The Temple of the Lord, the Temple of the Lord!'),[3] not knowing what they speak, nor whereof they affirm. A provincial or national church, according to our Article, is the true believers of that province or nation. If these are dispersed up and down they are only a part of the invisible church of Christ. But if they are visibly joined by assembling together to hear his word and partake of his supper, they are then a visible church, such as the Church of England, of France, or any other.

78. This being premised I ask, 'How do we undermine or destroy the Church—the provincial, visible Church of England?' The

---

[1] No. XIX, 'Of the Church', of the Thirty-nine Articles, which reads: 'The visible Church of Christ is a congregation of faithful men, in the which the pure Word of God is preached, and the Sacraments be duly ministered, according to Christ's ordinance, in all those things that of necessity are requisite to the same. . . .' Cf. Wesley's sermon 'Of the Church' (§ 16): 'It may be observed that, at the same time our Thirty-nine Articles were compiled and published, a Latin translation of them was published by the same authority. In this the words were *coetus credentium*, "a congregation of believers". . . .' Actually the phrase was *coetus fidelium*. (*Articuli XXXIX Ecclesiae Anglicanae* (1562), Art. XIX, De Ecclesia.)

[2] This Wesley alters in Vol. 14 of his *Works* (1772) to: 'among whom the pure word of God is preached, and the sacraments duly administered'.   [3] Jer. 7: 4.

Article mentions three things as essential to a visible church: living faith, without which indeed there can be no church at all, neither visible nor invisible; secondly, preaching (and consequently hearing) the pure word of God, else that faith would languish and die; and
5 thirdly, a due administration of the sacraments, the ordinary means whereby God increaseth faith. Now come close to the question: in which of these points do we undermine or destroy the church?

Do we shut the door of faith? Do we lessen the number of believing people in England? Only remember what faith is, accord-
10 ing to our Homilies, viz. 'a sure trust and confidence in God, that through the merits of Christ *my* sins are forgiven, and *I* reconciled to the favour of God'.[1] And we appeal to all mankind, do we destroy this faith, which is the life and soul of the Church? Is there, in fact, less of this faith in England than there was before we went forth?
15 I think this is an assertion which the father of lies himself will scarce dare to utter or maintain.

With regard then to this first point it is undeniable we neither undermine nor destroy the Church. The second thing is, the preaching and hearing the pure word of God. And do we hinder
20 this? Do we hinder any minister from *preaching* the pure word of God? If any preach not at all, or not the pure word of God, is the hindrance in us or in themselves? Or do we lessen the number of those that *hear* the pure word of God? Are then the hearers thereof (whether read or preached) fewer than they were in times past?
25 Are the usual places of public worship less frequented by means of our preaching? Wheresoever our lot has been cast for any time are the churches emptier than they were before? Surely none that has any regard left either for truth or modesty will say that in this point we are enemies to, or destroyers of, the Church.

30 The third thing requisite, if not to the *being*, at least to the *well-being* of a Church, is the due administration of the sacraments, particularly that of the Lord's Supper. And are we in this respect underminers or destroyers of the Church? Do we either by our example or advice draw men away from the Lord's Table? Where
35 we have laboured most are there the fewest communicants? How does the fact stand in London, Bristol, Newcastle? O that you would no longer shut your eyes against the broad light which encompasses you on every side!

---

[1] See § 59 above. Wesley has altered the personal pronouns from the third to the first.

79. I believe you are sensible by this time not only how weak this objection is, but likewise how easy it would be terribly to retort every branch of it upon most of those that make it, whether we speak of *true* living faith, of preaching the *pure* word of God, or of the *due* administration of the sacraments, both of baptism and the Lord's Supper. But I spare you. It sufficeth that our God knoweth, and will make manifest in that day whether it be by reason of *us* or *you* that 'men abhor the offering of the Lord'.[1]

80. Others object that we do not observe the laws of the Church, and thereby undermine it. What laws? The rubrics or canons? In every parish where I have been curate yet, I have observed the rubrics with a scrupulous exactness, not for wrath, but for conscience' sake. And this, so far as belongs to an unbeneficed minister, or to a private member of the Church, I do now. I will just mention a few of them, and leave you to consider which of us has observed or does observe them most.

(1). Days of fasting or abstinence to be observed:

The forty days of Lent,
The Ember days at the four seasons,
The three Rogation days,
All the Fridays in the year, except Christmas Day.[2]

(2). So many as intend to be partakers of the Holy Communion shall signify their names to the curate at least some time the day before;
And if any of these be an open and notorious evil liver . . . the curate shall advertise him, that in any wise he presume not to come to the Lord's Table until he hath openly declared himself to have truly repented.[3]

(3). Then (after the Nicene Creed) the curate shall declare unto the people what holidays *or fasting-days* are in the week following to be observed.[4]

(4). The minister shall first receive the communion in both kinds himself, and *then proceed to deliver the same to the bishops, priests, and deacons*, in like manner, if any be present, and *after that* to the people.[5]

(5). In cathedral and collegiate churches and colleges, where there

[1] Cf. 1 Sam. 2: 17.   [2] B.C.P., Tables and Rules.
[3] Ibid., Communion, opening rubrics. Here and in his other quotations from the Prayer Book Wesley condenses to a greater extent than his single ellipsis would indicate.
[4] Ibid., Communion, opening sentence of rubric following the Nicene Creed. Here, as in the succeeding quotations, Wesley italicizes the points most often ignored by the clergy of his day.
[5] Ibid., Communion, rubric governing the distribution of the elements.

are many priests and deacons, they shall *all receive the communion with the priest every Sunday at the least*.[1]

(6). The children to be baptized must be ready at the font *immediately after the last Lesson*.[2]

5 (7). The curate of every parish shall warn the people that without great necessity they procure not their children to be baptized *at home in their houses*.[3]

(8). The curate of every parish shall diligently *upon Sundays and holidays, after the Second Lesson* at Evening Prayer, *openly in the church* instruct and examine so many children as he shall think convenient in some part of the catechism.[4]

(9). Whensoever the bishop shall give notice for children to be brought unto him for their confirmation, the curate of every parish shall either bring or *send in writing, with his hand subscribed thereunto, the names of all such persons* within his parish as he shall think fit to be presented to the bishop.[5]

81. Now the question is not whether these rubrics *ought* to be observed (you take this for granted in making the objection), but whether in fact they *have been* observed, by *you* or *me* most? Many can witness I have observed them punctually, yea, sometimes at the hazard of my life; and as many, I fear, that you have not observed them at all, and that several of them you never pretended to observe. And is it *you* that are accusing *me* for not observing the rubrics of the Church? What grimace is this! 'O tell it not in Gath! Publish it not in the streets of Askelon!'[6]

82. With regard to the canons, I would in the first place desire you to consider two or three plain questions:

First, have you ever read them over?

Secondly, how can these be called 'The Canons of the Church of England', seeing they were never legally established by the Church, never regularly confirmed in any full Convocation?[7]

---

[1] B.C.P., Communion, closing rubrics.
[2] Ibid., Baptism, opening rubrics.   [3] Ibid., Private Baptism, opening rubrics.
[4] Ibid., Catechism, closing rubrics.   [5] Ibid.   [6] 2 Sam. 1: 20.
[7] *The Constitutions and Canons Ecclesiastical* (1604) had a complex history. The work embraced rules drawn from a variety of sources—some medieval, some dating from the primacy of Archbishop Parker. The canons, 151 in number, were drafted by Richard Bancroft (Bishop of London, subsequently Archbishop of Canterbury). They were adopted by the Convocation of Canterbury in 1604, when the see of Canterbury was vacant—which is possibly the point of Wesley's comment. The Convocation of York adopted them in 1606. Only the Latin version has authority. An Act of Parliament of 1606 restricted their application at certain points. As with the rubrics, Wesley condenses the canons which he quotes, but he indicates the fact by an ellipsis only once. He italicizes when he wishes to arrest the attention of the reader.

Thirdly, by what right am I required to observe such canons as were never legally established?

And then I will join issue with you on one question more, viz. whether you or I have observed them most?

To instance only in a few:

Can. 29. No person shall be admitted godfather or godmother to any child . . . before the said person hath received the Holy Communion.

Can. 59. Every parson, vicar, or curate, upon every Sunday *and holiday before Evening Prayer, shall for half an hour or more* examine and instruct the youth and ignorant persons of his parish.

Can. 64. Every parson, vicar, or curate, shall declare to the people *every Sunday* whether there be any holidays *or fasting-days* the week following.

Can. 68. No minister shall *refuse or delay* to christen any child that is brought to the church to him upon Sundays or holidays to be christened, or to bury any corpse that is brought to the church or churchyard. (N.B. Inability to pay fees does not alter the case.)

Can. 75. No ecclesiastical persons shall spend their time idly, by day or by night, playing at *dice, cards,* or *tables.*

Now let the clergyman who has observed only these five canons for one year last past, and who has read over all the canons in his congregation (as the King's ratification straitly enjoins him to do once every year), let him, I say, cast the first stone at us for 'not observing the canons (so called) of the Church of England'.

83. However, we cannot be (it is said) friends to the Church, because we do not 'obey the governors' of it, and 'submit ourselves' (as at our ordination we promised to do) 'to all their godly admonitions and injunctions'.[a] I answer, in every individual point of an indifferent nature we do and will (by the grace of God) obey the governors of the Church. But the 'testifying the gospel of the grace of God'[1] is not a point of an indifferent nature. 'The ministry which we have received of the Lord Jesus'[2] we are at all hazards to fulfil.

---

[a] The author of a tract just published at Newcastle (entitled *The Notions of the Methodists fully disproved, in a letter to the Rev. Mr. John Wesley*) much insists upon this objection. I have read and believe it quite needless to take any farther notice of this performance, the writer being so utterly unacquainted with the merits of the cause, and showing himself so perfectly a stranger both to my life, preaching, and writing—and to the Word of God, and to the Articles and Homilies of the Church of England. [For a note on this publication see *A Farther Appeal*, Pt. I, II. 1.]

---

[1] Cf. Acts 20: 24.   [2] Ibid.

It is 'the burden of the Lord'[1] which is laid upon us here; and we are 'to obey God rather than man'.[2] Nor yet do we in any ways violate the promise which each of us made when it was said unto him, 'Take thou authority to preach the Word of God, in the name of the Father, and of the Son, and of the Holy Ghost.'[3] We then promised to 'submit' (mark the words) 'to the *godly* admonitions and injunctions of our ordinary'. But we did not, could not promise to obey such injunctions as we know are *contrary to the Word of God*.

84. 'But why then' (say some) 'do you leave the Church?' 'Leave the Church'! What can you mean? Do we leave so much as the *church walls*? Your own eyes tell you we do not. Do we leave the *ordinances* of the Church? You daily see and know the contrary. Do we leave the *fundamental doctrine* of the Church, namely salvation by faith? It is our constant theme, in public, in private, in writing, in conversation. Do we leave the *practice* of the Church, the standard whereof are the Ten Commandments—which are so essentially inwrought in her constitution (as little as you may apprehend it) that whosoever breaks one of the least of these is no member of the Church of England? I believe you do not care to put the cause on this issue. Neither do you mean this by 'leaving the Church'. In truth, I cannot conceive what you mean. I doubt you cannot conceive yourself. You have retailed a sentence from somebody else, which you no more understand than he. And no marvel, for it is a true observation:

Nonsense is never to be understood.[4]

85. Nearly related to this is that other objection, that we 'divide the Church'. Remember, the church is 'the faithful people', or true believers. Now how do we divide these? Why, by our societies. Very good. Now the case is plain. We 'divide them' (you say) 'by uniting them together'. Truly a very uncommon way of dividing! O, but we divide those who are thus united with each other from the rest of the Church. By no means. Many of them were before 'joined to all their brethren' of the Church of England (and many

---

[1] Jer. 23: 33–8.   [2] Acts 5: 29

[3] B.C.P., Ordering of Priests. Wesley has reversed and conflated sentences from the words of the bishop at the imposition of hands and the delivery of the Bible.

[4] John Dryden, *The Hind and the Panther*, i. 429, 'But nonsense never can be understood.'

were not, until they knew us)¹ by 'assembling themselves together'
to hear the Word of God, and to eat of one bread and drink of one
cup. And do they now 'forsake that assembling themselves together'?² You cannot, you dare not, say it. You know they are more
diligent therein than ever, it being one of the fixed rules of our   5
societies, that every member attend the ordinances of God, i.e. that
he do not divide from the Church.³ And if any member of the Church
does thus divide from or leave it he hath no more place among us.

86. I have considered this objection the more at large because it is
of most weight with sincere minds. And to all these, if they have   10
fairly and impartially weighed the answer as well as the objection,
I believe it clearly appears that we are neither *undermining* nor
destroying, neither *dividing* nor *leaving* the Church. So far from it
that we 'have great heaviness' on her account, yea, 'continual
sorrow in our hearts'.⁴ And our prayer to God is that he would   15
'repair the breaches of Zion',⁵ and 'build the walls of Jerusalem',⁶
that this our desolate Church may flourish again and be 'the praise
of the whole earth'.⁷

87. But perhaps you have heard that we in truth regard no church
at all: that *gain* is the true spring of all our actions; that I, in parti-   20
cular, am well paid for my work, having thirteen hundred pounds
a year (as a reverend author accurately computes it) at the Foundery
alone, over and above what I receive from Bristol, Kingswood,
Newcastle, and other places; and that whoever survives me will see
I have made good use of my time, for I shall not die a beggar.⁸   25

88. I freely own this is one of the best devised objections which
has ever yet been made, because it not only puts us upon proving
a negative (which is seldom an easy task), but also one of such a
kind as scarce admits of any demonstrative proof at all. But for such
proof as the nature of the thing allows I appeal to my manner of life   30
which hath been from the beginning. Ye who have seen it (and not
with a friendly eye) for these twelve or fourteen years last past, or

¹ The parenthetical comment was absent from the 1st ed.   ² Heb. 10: 25.
³ A few weeks earlier Wesley had published *The Nature, Design, and General Rules
of the United Societies* (*Bibliography*, No. 73), § 6 beginning: 'It is expected of all who
desire to continue in these societies that they should continue to evidence their desire of
salvation, *thirdly*, by attending upon all the ordinances of God. . . .'
⁴ Cf. Rom. 9: 2.   ⁵ Cf. 1 Kgs. 11: 27.
⁶ Cf. Neh. 2: 17; Ps. 51: 18.   ⁷ Jer. 51: 41; cf. Isa. 62: 7.
⁸ On the Foundery, see below, notes to § 90. For an estimate of Wesley's income at
this time and a discussion of the hostile pamphlets which raised the question, see
Luke Tyerman, *The Life and Times of the Rev. John Wesley, MA.*, I. 427–30.

for any part of that time, have ye ever seen anything like the love of gain therein? Did I not continually remember the words of the Lord Jesus: 'It is more blessed to give than to receive.'[1] Ye of Oxford, do ye not know these things are so? What gain did I seek
5 among you? Of whom did I take anything? From whom did I covet silver, or gold, or apparel? To whom did I deny anything which I had, even to the hour that I departed from you? Ye of Epworth and Wroot, among whom I ministered for (nearly) the space of three years, what gain did I seek among you? Or of whom
10 did I take or covet anything? Ye of Savannah and Frederica, among whom God afterwards proved me and showed me what was in my heart, what gain did I seek among *you*? Of whom did I take anything? Or whose food or apparel did I covet (for silver and gold had ye none,[2] no more than I myself for many months), even when
15 I was in hunger and nakedness? Ye yourselves, and the God and Father of our Lord Jesus Christ, know that I lie not.

89. But (it is said) things are fairly altered now. Now I cannot complain of wanting anything, having the yearly income of a bishop in London, over and above what I gain at other places. At what
20 other places, my friend? Inform yourself a little better, and you will find that both at Newcastle, Bristol, and Kingswood (the only places beside London where any collection at all is made)[3] the money collected is both received and expended by the stewards of those several societies, and never comes into my hands at all,
25 neither first nor last. And you, or any who desires it, shall read over the accounts kept by any of those stewards and see with your own eyes that by all these societies I gain just as much as you do.

90. The case in London stands thus. In November 1739 two gentlemen then unknown to me (Mr. Ball and Mr. Watkins) came
30 and desired me once and again to preach in a place called the Foundery near Moorfields.[4] With much reluctance I at length

---

[1] Acts 20: 35.   [2] See Acts 3: 6.

[3] The Bristol edition of 1765, edited by Charles Wesley, alters this to: 'Newcastle, Bristol, and Kingswood, and at all other places where any collection at all is made'; from this the version in *Works*, Vol. 14, omitted the first 'at' and the second 'at all'.

[4] The Foundery (originally the King's Foundery, predecessor to the Royal Woolwich Arsenal) had been severely damaged in 1716 during the recasting of cannon captured during Marlborough's campaigns. It was then abandoned. In 1739, when troubles at the Fetter Lane society made it necessary for the Methodists to part company with the Moravians, Wesley was invited by Messrs. Ball and Watkins to open work at the Foundery. Subsequently Wesley bought the derelict buildings and remodelled them to suit his needs. In addition to the meeting-house (seating 1,500 people on benches) there

complied. I was soon after pressed to take that place into my own hands. These who were most earnest therein lent me the purchase money, which was £115. Mr. Watkins and Mr. Ball then delivered me the names of several subscribers who offered to pay, some four or six, some ten shillings a year, toward the repayment of the purchase- money and the putting the buildings into repair. This amounted one year to near £200, the second to about £140, and so the last.

91. The United Society began a little after, whose weekly contribution (chiefly[1] for the poor) is received and expended by the stewards, and comes not into my hands at all. But there is also a quarterly subscription of many of the society which is nearly equal to that above mentioned.

92. The uses to which these subscriptions have been hitherto applied are: *first*, the payment of that £115; *secondly*, the repairing (I might almost say rebuilding) that vast, uncouth heap of ruins at the Foundery; *thirdly*, the building galleries both for men and women; *fourthly*, the enlarging the society room to near thrice its first bigness. All taxes and occasional expenses are likewise defrayed out of this fund. And it has hitherto been so far from yielding any overplus that it has never sufficed for these purposes yet. So far from it that I am still in debt on these accounts near £300. So much have I hitherto gained by preaching the gospel, besides a debt of £150 still remaining on account of the schools[2] built at Bristol and another

were various other facilities: a school room, a 'band-room', living quarters for Wesley, accommodation for his preachers, stabling, etc. This passage provides details about the purchase of the Foundery; the *Journal* shows what a vital role it played in Wesley's movement.

Both Ball and Watkins appear in Wesley's diaries and *Journal*. Wesley mentions Ball as 'a fresh instance of that strange truth, "The servants of God suffer nothing." His body was well-nigh torn asunder with pain; but God made all his bed in his sickness; so that he was continually giving thanks to God, and making his boast of his praise.' (*Journal*, Oct. 19, 1740.)

Samuel Watkins was responsible for introducing Wesley to the Revd. Vincent Perronet, vicar of Shoreham, Kent, and a lifelong friend and supporter of Wesley.

[1] Wesley's *Works* (1772) omits 'chiefly'.

[2] Wesley had built a school in the Horsefair, Bristol, in 1739, and one for colliers' children in Kingswood a short time later. Both also served as meeting-places for Methodist fellowship. In 1746 a new building was begun at Kingswood, and two years later the school there was completely reorganized. In that same year of 1748 the Bristol building was torn down and replaced by a larger building which served chiefly as a Methodist meeting-place. The new Kingswood School so outstripped Wesley's other educational ventures that it became known as 'the school'—a fact which possibly explains why the version of this passage in Wesley's *Works* (1772) reads 'school' instead of 'schools'.

of above £200 on account of that now building at Newcastle![1] I desire any reasonable man would now sit down and lay these things together, and let him see whether, allowing me a grain of common sense (if not of common honesty), he can possibly conceive that a view of gain would induce me to act in this manner.

93. You can never reconcile it with any degree of common sense that a man who wants nothing, who has already all the necessaries, all the conveniences, nay, and many of the superfluities of life, and these not only independent on anyone, but less liable to contingencies than even a gentleman's freehold estate;[2] that such an one should calmly and deliberately throw up his ease, most of his friends, his reputation, and that way of life which of all others is most agreeable both to his natural temper and education; that he should toil day and night, spend all his time and strength, knowingly destroy a firm constitution and hasten into weakness, pain, diseases, death—to gain a debt of six or seven hundred pounds!

94. But supposing the balance on the other side, let me ask you one plain question: 'For what gain (setting conscience aside) will *you* be obliged to act thus? To live exactly as I do? For what price will *you* preach (and that with all your might, not in an easy, indolent, fashionable way) eighteen or nineteen times every week? And this throughout the year? What shall I give *you* to travel seven or eight hundred miles, in all weathers, every two or three months? For what salary will *you* abstain from all other diversions than the doing good and the praising God?' I am mistaken if you would not prefer strangling to such a life, even with thousands of gold and silver.

95. And what is the comfort you have found out for me in these circumstances? Why, that I 'shall not die a beggar'. So now I am supposed to be heaping up riches—that I may leave them behind me. Leave them behind me? For whom? My wife and children? Who are they? They are yet unborn. Unless thou meanest the children of faith whom God hath given me. But my heavenly father

---

[1] The 'Orphan House', whose first stone was laid Dec. 20, 1742.

[2] As a fellow of Lincoln College, Oxford, Wesley did not receive a fixed annual stipend. When in residence he was entitled to certain allowances as well as to rooms in college. A special benefaction entitled each fellow to £10; in addition there was a 'dividend' (as it was called in many colleges), representing a share of the income the college derived from various sources—especially from the 'fines' payable when tenants renewed the leases of college estates. The sum which a fellow might receive fluctuated considerably. In an exceptional year Wesley received over £80; in a poor one, £18. Sums between £25 and £38 were more usual. Cf. V. H. H. Green, *The Young Mr. Wesley*, App. II.

feedeth them.[1] Indeed if I lay up riches at all it must be to leave
behind me, seeing my fellowship is a provision for life. But I cannot
understand this. What comfort would it be to my soul, now launched
into eternity, that I had left behind me gold as the dust, and silver
as the sand of the sea? Will it follow me over the great gulf? Or can [5]
I go back to it? Thou that liftest up thy eyes in hell, what do thy
riches profit thee now? Will all thou once hadst under the sun gain
thee a drop of water to cool thy tongue? O the comfort of riches left
behind to one who is tormented in that flame![2]—You put me in
mind of those celebrated lines (which I once exceedingly admired) [10]
addressed by way of consolation to the soul of a poor self-murderer:

> Yet shall thy grave with rising flowers be dressed,
> And the green turf lie light upon thy breast!
> Here shall the year its earliest beauties show:
> Here the first roses of the spring shall blow: [15]
> While angels with their silver wings o'ershade
> The place, now sacred by thy relics made.[3]

96. I will now simply tell you my sense of these matters, whether
you will hear or whether you will forbear. Food and raiment I have,
such food as I choose to eat, and such raiment as I choose to put on. [20]
I have a place where to lay my head.[4] I have what is needful for life
and godliness.[5] And I apprehend this is all the world can afford.
The kings of the earth can give me no more. For as to gold and
silver, I count it dung and dross: I trample it under my feet. I (yet
not I, but the grace of God that is in me)[6] esteem it just as the mire [25]
in the streets.[7] I desire it not. I seek it not. I only fear lest any of it
should cleave to me, and I should not be able to shake it off before
my spirit returns to God. It must indeed pass through my hands,
but I will take care (God being my helper) that the mammon of
unrighteousness[8] shall only pass through; it shall not rest there. [30]
None of the accursed thing shall be found in my tents[9] when the
Lord calleth me hence. And hear ye this, all you who have discovered
the treasures which I am to leave behind me: if I leave behind me

---

[1] See Matt. 6: 26.   [2] See Luke 16: 23–6.
[3] Pope, 'Elegy to the Memory of an Unfortunate Lady', lines 63–8. Wesley has made
a couple of slight verbal changes and altered line 65 drastically.
[4] See Matt. 8: 20.   [5] See 2 Pet. 1: 3.
[6] See 1 Cor. 15: 10.   [7] Mic. 7: 10, etc.
[8] Luke 16: 9.   [9] Josh. 6: 18, etc.

ten pounds (above my debts and the little arrears of my fellowship)[1]
you and all mankind bear witness against me that 'I lived and died
a thief and a robber.'[2]

97. Before I conclude, I cannot but entreat you who know God to
review the whole matter from the foundation. Call to mind what the
state of religion was in our nation a few years since. In whom did
you find the holy tempers that were in Christ: 'bowels of mercies,
lowliness, meekness, gentleness, contempt of the world, patience,
temperance, long-suffering';[3] burning love to God, rejoicing evermore, and in everything giving thanks;[4] and a tender love to all
mankind, covering, believing, hoping, enduring all things?[5] Perhaps
you did not know one such man in the world. But how many that
had all unholy tempers? What vanity and pride, what stubbornness
and self-will, what anger, fretfulness, discontent, what suspicion
and resentment, what inordinate affections,[6] what irregular passions,
what foolish and hurtful desires[7] might you find, in those who were
called the best of men, in those who made the strictest profession of
religion, who had even 'the form of godliness'?[8] Did you not
frequently bewail, wherever your lot was cast, the general want of
even *outward religion*? How few were seen at the public worship of
God? How much fewer at the Lord's Table? And was even this
little flock zealous of good works,[9] careful as they had time to do
good to all men? On the other hand, did you not with grief observe
outward irreligion in every place? Where could you be for one week
without being an eye- or an ear-witness of cursing, swearing, or
profaneness, of sabbath-breaking or drunkenness, of quarrelling or
brawling, of revenge or obscenity? Were these things done in a
corner? Did not gross iniquity of all kinds overspread our land as
a flood? Yea, and daily increase, in spite of all the opposition which
the children of God did or could make against it?

98. If you had then been told that the jealous God would soon
arise and maintain his own cause; that he would pour down his
Spirit from on high, and renew the face of the earth; that he would

---

[1] The 1765 Bristol edition adds after 'debts': 'and my books'; to this Wesley's *Works*
(1772) adds 'or what may happen to be due on account of them', but omits 'and the
little arrears of my fellowship'. 'Books', of course, means the income from Wesley's
publications; as required by the college statutes, Wesley resigned his Lincoln fellowship upon his marriage in 1751.

[2] Cf. John 10: 1.   [3] Cf. Col. 3: 12.   [4] See 1 Thess. 5: 16, 18.
[5] See 1 Cor. 13: 7.   [6] Col. 3: 5.   [7] 1 Tim. 6: 9 (cf. *Notes*).
[8] 2 Tim. 3: 5.   [9] Titus 2: 14.

shed abroad his love in the hearts of the outcasts of men, producing all holy and heavenly tempers, expelling anger, and pride, and evil desire, and all unholy and earthly tempers: causing outward religion, the work of faith, the patience of hope, the labour of love,[1] to flourish and abound, and wherever it spread abolishing outward 5 irreligion, destroying all the works of the devil;[2] if you had been told that this living knowledge of the Lord would in a short space of time overspread our land, yea, and daily increase, in spite of all the opposition which the devil and his children did or could make against it—would you not vehemently have desired to see that day, 10 that you might bless God and rejoice therein?

99. Behold, the day of the Lord is come. He is again visiting and redeeming his people. Having eyes, see ye not? Having ears, do ye not hear? Neither understand with your hearts?[3] At this hour the Lord is rolling away our reproach.[4] Love of all mankind, meekness, 15 gentleness, humbleness of mind, holy and heavenly affections, do take [the] place of hate, anger, pride, revenge, and vile or vain affections. Hence wherever the power of the Lord spreads, springs outward religion in all its forms. The houses of God are filled: the Table of the Lord is thronged on every side. And those who thus 20 show their love of God show they love their neighbour also, by being careful to maintain good works,[5] by doing all manner of good (as they have time) to all men. They are likewise careful to abstain from all evil. Cursing, sabbath-breaking, drunkenness, with all other (however fashionable) works of the devil, are not once named 25 among them. All this is plain, demonstrable fact. For this also is not done in a corner. Now, do you acknowledge the day of your visitation? Do you bless God and rejoice therein?

100. What hinders? Is it this, that men say all manner of evil of those whom God is pleased to use as instruments in his work? O ye 30 fools, did ye suppose the devil was dead? Or that he would not fight for his kingdom? And what weapons shall he fight with, if not with lies? Is he not a liar, and the father of it?[6] Suffer ye then thus far. Let the devil and his children say all manner of evil of us. And let them go on deceiving each other and being deceived. But *ye* need 35 not be deceived also—or if you are, if you *will* believe all they say,

---

[1] See 1 Thess. 1: 3.   [2] See 1 John 3: 8.
[3] See Isa. 6: 10; Acts 28: 27.   [4] See Josh. 5: 9.
[5] The 1786 London edition omits 'by being careful to maintain good works', but this is probably a printer's error.   [6] See John 8: 44.

be it so, that we are weak, silly, wicked men, without sense, without learning, without even a desire or design of doing good, yet I insist upon the fact: Christ is preached, and sinners are converted to God. This none but a madman can deny. We are ready to prove it by a 5 cloud of witnesses. Neither, therefore, can the inference be denied, that God is now visiting his people. O that all men may know in this their day the things that make for their peace!

101. Upon the whole, to men of the world I would still recommend the known advice of Gamaliel: 'Refrain from these men, and 10 let them alone; for if this work be of men it will come to nought: but if it be of God, ye cannot overthrow it; lest haply ye be found even to fight against God.'[1] But unto you whom God hath chosen out of the world I say: 'Ye are our brethren and of our father's house; it behoveth you, in whatsoever manner ye are able, to 15 "strengthen our hands in God."'[2] And this ye are all able to do: to wish us good luck in the name of the Lord, and to pray continually that 'none of these things may move us', and that we may 'not count our lives dear unto ourselves, so that we may finish our course with joy, and the ministry which we have received of the 20 Lord Jesus'.[3]

PRIMITIVE CHRISTIANITY[4]

PART I

1. Happy the souls who first believed,
   To Jesus and each other cleaved,
   Joined by the unction from above
   In mystic fellowship of love.

25
2. Meek, simple followers of the Lamb
   They lived, and spake and thought the same,
   Brake the commemorative bread,
   And drank the spirit of their Head.

---

[1] Acts 5: 38–9.   [2] Cf. 1 Sam. 23: 16.

[3] Cf. Acts 20: 24. Appended to the text in Wesley's *Works* (1772) is the information (incorrect): 'Written in the year 1744.'

[4] This poem was introduced by Wesley in the second edition, omitted from those of 1750 and 1765 (thus cutting the pamphlet down to the handy 48-page format) but restored for the collected *Works* in 1772, clearly because Wesley considered it an important illustration of *An Earnest Appeal*.

3. On God they cast their every care;
    Wrestling with God in mighty prayer
    They claimed the grace through Jesus given:
    By prayer they shut and opened heaven.

4. To Jesus they performed their vows,   5
    A little church in every house;
    They joyfully conspired to raise
    Their ceaseless sacrifice of praise.[1]

5. Propriety[2] was there unknown,
    None called what he possessed his own:[3]   10
    Where all the common blessings share,
    No selfish happiness was there.

6. With grace abundantly endued,
    A pure, believing multitude,
    They all were of one heart and soul,   15
    And only love inspired the whole.

7. O what an age of golden days!
    O what a choice, peculiar race!
    Washed in the Lamb's all-cleansing blood,
    Anointed kings, and priests to God!   20

8. Where shall I wander now to find
    The successors they left behind?
    The faithful, whom I seek in vain,
    Are 'minished from the sons of men.

9. Ye different sects, who all declare   25
    'Lo! here is Christ!' or 'Christ is there!'
    Your stronger proofs divinely give,
    And show me where the Christians live.

10. Your claim, alas! ye cannot prove;
    Ye want the genuine mark of love: 30
    Thou only, Lord, thine own canst show,
    For sure thou hast a church below.

---

[1] See Heb. 13: 15.   [2] i.e. 'property'.   [3] See Acts 4: 32.

11.   The gates of hell cannot prevail,
      The church on earth can never fail:
      Ah! join me to thy secret ones;
      Ah! gather all thy living stones.

12.   Scattered o'er all the earth they lie,
      Till thou collect them with thine eye,
      Draw by the music of thy name,
      And charm into a beauteous frame.

13.   For this the pleading Spirit groans
      And cries in all thy banished ones:
      Greatest of gifts, thy love impart,
      And make us of one mind and heart.

14.   Join every soul that looks to thee
      In bonds of perfect charity:
      Now, Lord, the glorious fulness give,
      And all in all for ever live.

PART II

15.   Jesus, from whom all blessings flow,
      Great builder of thy church below,
      If now thy spirit moves my breast,
      Hear, and fulfil thy own request.

16.   The few that truly call thee Lord
      And wait thy sanctifying word,
      And thee their utmost Saviour own,
      Unite, and perfect them in one.

17.   Gather them in on every side,
      And in thy tabernacle hide;
      Give them a resting-place to find,
      A covert from the storm and wind.[1]

18.   O find them out some calm recess,
      Some unfrequented wilderness!
      Thou, Lord, the secret place prepare,
      And hide, and feed *the woman*[2] there,

[1] See Isa. 4: 6.   [2] Apparently the church as the bride of Christ. See Rev. 12: 6.

19. Thither collect thy little flock,
    Under the shadow of their Rock:[1]
    The holy seed, the royal race,
    The standing monuments of thy grace.

20. O let them all thy mind express,   5
    Stand forth thy chosen witnesses!
    Thy power unto salvation show,
    And perfect holiness below:

21. The fulness of thy grace receive,
    And simply to thy glory live;   10
    Strongly reflect the light divine,
    And in a land of darkness shine.[2]

22. In them let all mankind behold
    How Christians lived in days of old;
    (Mighty their envious foes to move,   15
    A proverb of reproach—and love.)

23. O make them of one soul and heart,[3]
    The all-conforming mind impart,
    Spirit of peace and unity,
    The sinless mind that was in thee.   20

24. Call them into thy wondrous light,
    Worthy to walk with thee in white;[4]
    Make up thy jewels,[5] Lord, and show
    The glorious, spotless church below.

25. From every sinful wrinkle free,   25
    Redeemed from all iniquity,
    The fellowship of saints make known;
    And O my God, might I be one!

26. O might my lot be cast with these,
    The least of Jesu's witnesses!   30
    O that my Lord would count me meet
    To wash his dear disciples' feet!

---

[1] See Isa. 32: 2.   [2] See Isa. 9: 2.   [3] See Acts 4: 32.
[4] See Rev. 3: 4.   [5] See Mal. 3: 17.

27. This only thing do I require,
    Thou know'st 'tis all my heart's desire—
    Freely what I receive to give,[1]
    The servant of thy church to live.

28. After my lowly Lord to go,
    And wait upon thy saints below,
    Enjoy the grace to angels given,
    And serve the royal heirs of heaven.

29. Lord, if I now thy drawings feel,
    And ask according to thy will,
    Confirm the prayer, the seal impart,
    And speak the answer to my heart.

30. Tell me (or thou shalt never go)[2]
    'Thy prayer is heard; it shall be so:' . . .
    The word hath passed thy lips—and I
    Shall with thy people live and die.

[1] See Matt. 10: 8.   [2] See Gen. 32: 26.

A Farther Appeal to Men of Reason and Religion

Introduction

An Earnest Appeal owed much of its force to its relative brevity. Both Wesley and his followers, however, felt that a great deal still remained to be said. Wesley had, indeed, 'declared [his] principles and practice, and answered some of the most important as well as the most common, objections to each'. Nevertheless he insisted that he had 'not yet delivered [his] own soul'.[1] Attacks on the Methodist movement, so far from abating, were increasing in number, in virulence, and in importance. When the first Methodist conference met in June 1744, Wesley's associates urged him to 'write a farther appeal'. He agreed, and adopted the suggested title. Part I appeared in December 1744; the second and third parts were published together a year later.

Wesley's aim was frankly apologetic: he intended to meet objections that 'partly relate to the *doctrines* I teach, partly to my *manner* of teaching them, and partly to the effects which are supposed to follow from teaching these doctrines in this manner'.[2] The essentials of his message could be succinctly epitomized: 'Now all I teach respects either the nature and condition of justification, the nature and condition of salvation, the nature of justifying and saving faith, or the Author of faith and salvation.'[3] Wesley was well aware that in in many quarters his theology was regarded as novel and dangerous. With some care he defined exactly what he meant by the technical terms he used, and then proceeded to prove that in every instance his interpretation coincided exactly with that of the official pronouncements of the Church of England. By voluminous quotation he showed that The Book of Common Prayer, the Thirty-nine Articles, and the *Homilies* all supported his teachings. Then, in a brief summary, he epitomized his argument thus far: 'The doctrine of the Church of England appears to be this: (1). That no good work, properly so called, can go before justification. (2). That no degree of true sanctification can be previous to it. (3). That as the meritorious cause of justification is the life and death of Christ, so

---

[1] *A Farther Appeal*, Pt. I, initial paragraph.
[2] Ibid.   [3] Ibid. I. 1.

the condition of it is faith, faith alone. And, (4). That both inward and outward holiness are consequent on this faith, and are the ordinary stated condition of final justification.'[1] This sets forth with admirable succinctness his theological position; he defended, reiterated, or amplified it in many of his subsequent writings.

Wesley was replying to his critics, and eighteenth-century usage dictated that he should examine their writings in some detail. Naturally his response to his opponents varied with the seriousness of their challenge. He usually dismissed with dispatch the anonymous scribblers who peddled malicious gossip or scurrilous abuse. He passed over with a curt reference the first of two pamphlets on *The Notions of the Methodists . . . Disproved*; but the second of these required and received careful attention. It raised important questions, and these demanded a reply. Moreover, Wesley had recently opened in Newcastle a promising extension of his mission, and *The Notions* reflected the angry reaction of some of the clerics of that city. To ignore the attacks might suggest that they could not be met, and consequently his work might suffer.

In addition Wesley found that he had to answer far more important opponents. He realized that he was now facing a new phenomenon. His views and his methods had come under public attack from the highest dignitaries in the church. *Observations upon the Conduct of a Certain Sect usually distinguished by the Name of Methodists* was widely attributed to Bishop Gibson of London, the most formidable figure on the episcopal bench. In the northern province it was being circulated with and commended by a brief pamphlet written by Thomas Herring, Archbishop of York.[2] In addition Bishop Richard Smalbroke of Lichfield and Coventry had recently published a charge addressed to the clergy of his diocese;[3] in it he vigorously attacked Methodist 'enthusiasm'. To some churchmen this kind of episcopal response was decisive. Wesley had been condemned; he should obediently submit.

> Now the bishops and chief ministers of this Church, the Bishop of London especially in his excellent *Pastoral Letter*, have publicly declared themselves against your doctrines and practices, and yet you

---

[1] *A Farther Appeal*, Pt. I, II. 8. In the 1772 edition of his works he took care to indicate the importance he attached to this passage.

[2] This also was anonymous; only in the 1772 edition of his works did Wesley disclose the identity of the author to whom he replied.

[3] *A Charge delivered to the Reverend Clergy in the several parts of the Diocese of Lichfield and Coventry in a Triennial Visitation of the same in 1741* (1744).

stiffly disobey their directions, and with unparalleled obstinacy withstand and reject all their admonitions; you avowedly transgress the
laws both of church and state, and violate the canons which were made,
and are now executed by those who have the chief authority; and thus
you are manifestly guilty both of schism and rebellion, which are two
very grievous and damnable sins.[1]

For personal, no less than for ecclesiastical, reasons this was a serious
challenge. Wesley's parents and teachers had instilled in him a keen
awareness of the duty of submitting to constituted authorities; it was
therefore no light matter for him explicitly to criticize those whom
God had set over the household of faith. He believed that he had
no alternative. Having taken the initial step, he never felt obliged
to retreat. As can be seen, a considerable part of the present volume
consists of replies addressed to episcopal critics.

Certain charges had already become standard in anti-Methodist
polemics. Most of them are dealt with in *A Farther Appeal*. Some
(as we have already noted) concerned doctrine; others concerned
general methods; still others, the degree to which Methodist
practices were at variance with the ordered life of the Church of
England. As a churchman who believed that he was both loyal and
orthodox, Wesley was at some pains to refute charges of theological
deviation, but these probably aroused less general concern—
certainly their discussion engendered less emotional heat—than
other issues. 'Enthusiasm' was a phobia of the eighteenth century.
Archbishop Herring warned his readers of 'the great indiscretion' of
regarding 'the enthusiastic ardour' of the Methodists as 'the true and
only Christianity'. Bishop Smalbroke accused the Methodists of
'enthusiastical pretentions' in claiming that they could experience
the personal inspiration of the Holy Spirit.[2] The aspersion was as
serious as it was common. Wesley was well aware that 'Fanaticism,
if it means anything at all, means the same with enthusiasm, or
religious madness.'[3] He insisted, however, that the kind of religion
he encouraged was 'rational as well as scriptural; it is as pure from
enthusiasm as from superstition. It is true', he continued,

> the contrary has been continually affirmed. But to affirm is one thing,
> to prove another. Who will prove that it is enthusiasm to love God,
> even though we love him with all our heart? to rejoice in the sense of his

---

[1] *The Notions of the Methodists Fully Disproved*, pp. 19–20.
[2] Smalbroke, *Charge*, p. 1. Cf. ibid., p. 51: 'The Christian religion is no enthusiasm.'
[3] *A Farther Appeal*, Pt. III, III. 1.

love to us? to praise him, even with all our strength. Who is able to make good this charge against the love of all mankind? or, laying rhetorical flourishes aside, to come close to the question, and demonstrate that it is enthusiasm, in every state we are in, therewith to be content?[1]

It is important to remember that Wesley became a Methodist without ceasing to be a man of his own age. An evangelical did not necessarily capitulate to fanaticism or superstition. Reality in religion did not involve a collapse into irrationality. He consistently defended his position by an appeal to 'clear Scripture and cogent reason'.[2] Despite repeated charges from his critics, Wesley never wavered on this point.

In an established church a new movement inevitably disrupted old ways. Those who were comfortable in the existing system resented the suggestion of change. They bitterly attacked Wesley's innovations; he felt obliged to defend his methods. Field preaching and the use of laymen in religious work were the matters of most frequent complaint. With variations, these issues appear and reappear in the controversial works. Wesley insisted that laymen have played a vital part in the long history of the development of the faith. Look at many of the great figures in the Bible: the patriarchs, the prophets, the apostles were not priests, nor was our Lord himself. If the layman's right to participate in church reform is challenged, weigh the precedent provided by John Calvin. But the immediate justification of Wesley's policy was a crying need. No one else was attempting the work of religious renewal: could those who ignored the challenge condemn those who did what they could to meet it? The charges brought against the character of his assistants would not bear scrutiny. Nor, for that matter, would many of the parallel aspersions cast on the leaders of the revival. They were not young and inexperienced men. If they were too few in number was that their fault? They were accused of being deficient in learning: but look, cried Wesley, at the qualifications of some of the men who launched such charges!

As far as field preaching was concerned, it might be a novelty, but it was certainly not a threat to religion. The regular worship of the church did not reach the neediest of the people: was it a crime

---

[1] *A Farther Appeal*, Pt. III, II. 1.
[2] Ibid., Pt. III, III. 29. Cf. Pt. I, VII. 13.

to seek them where they could be found? Let those who envied the Methodists their hearers submit to the rigours the field preachers had to face!

At the end of Part I, Wesley pauses to recapitulate his argument. 'I have endeavoured to show, First, that the *doctrines* I teach are no other than the great truths of the gospel; Secondly, that though I teach them, not as I would, but as I *can*, yet it is in a *manner* not contrary to law; and Thirdly, that the *effects* of thus preaching the gospel have not been such as was weakly or wickedly reported.'[1]

Part I is much the longest section of *A Farther Appeal*, and it raises certain points which deserve consideration. The character of the work is largely determined by the standards and conventions of eighteenth-century controversy. It was assumed that the dissection of an opponent's work and the detailed refutation of his arguments constituted an effective form of debate. So Wesley examines point by point the case advanced in *The Notions, Observations*, and Smalbroke's *Charge*. This may have been effective at the time, and the situation of the Methodist movement may have required that Wesley adopt it. It does not heighten the interest of the work for the modern reader. But it does afford an illuminating insight both into the mentality of the age and into the mind of Wesley himself. We see the subjects that were considered worthy of serious discussion, and we can follow the debate, step by step, as it proceeds.

In other respects also the work provides interesting sidelights on Wesley. Few of his writings reflect so clearly his academic background. He was engaged in serious controversy with opponents who were only too ready to treat him as a raving 'enthusiast'. In writing for simple readers he laid aside the trappings of his education. Here he employed to the full the dialectical skill he had perfected as a college lecturer in logic. As fellow of Lincoln he had also been a lecturer in Greek, and his use of the learned languages was a reminder to his critics that he was quite at home in Greek and Latin, and that he knew Hebrew as well. He was ready and able to argue about the meaning of the Fathers, and for this purpose to cite their writings in the original.

More significant than this incidental display of learning is the evidence of his amazing knowledge of the Bible. Though he read widely in both ancient and modern languages as well as in English, he was quite content to be classified as *homo unius libri*—a man of

[1] Ibid., Pt. I, VII. 18.

one book. Scriptural language shaped his style; scriptural content governed his thought.

The three parts of *A Farther Appeal* represent different phases of a comprehensive argument. Part I is devoted to a detailed refutation of what Wesley regarded as unwarranted accusations levelled against his teachings and his methods. Part II is essentially an exposé of national apostasy. First Wesley examines the charges laid by the Hebrew prophets against their fellow countrymen; then he proves that in every respect the Englishmen of his own day were far more guilty of transgressing the law of God than were the Jews of old. But he was not content to denounce. The remedy lay in a recovery of the heritage of a Christian nation. Every segment of the religious spectrum had its place in his appeal. Presbyterians, Independents, Baptists, Quakers, Roman Catholics—each denomination had its distinctive traditions, and each had in some measure forsaken its heritage.

In this society, so flagrantly disobedient to the will of God, Wesley felt called to summon sinners to repentance. Where he looked for encouragement and support he encountered only hostility. But, as he makes clear in Part III, he believed that the attacks on his movement often came from men who were morally in no position to criticize. They did nothing to meet an acknowledged need; they merely abused those who did their utmost to rectify a deplorable situation. Yet the state of religion in England, Wesley argues, must be obvious to anyone whose eyes have not been blinded by crass complacency. 'Is there a nation under the sun which is so deeply fallen from the very first principles of religion? Where is the country in which is found so utter a disregard to even heathen morality; such a thorough contempt of justice and truth, and all that should be dear and honourable to rational creatures?'[1] Wesley believed that he knew his fellow countrymen well. Few of his contemporaries had travelled the highways of the land so extensively, or mingled so freely with all segments of society. He had experienced at first hand the violence bred of prejudice and ignorance, and he was ready to provide detailed accounts of the brutalities from which he and his followers had suffered.[2] The tragedy of the situation was that the worst excesses were instigated by those who should have been the leaders of the people. Wesley insisted that he was issuing no blanket condemnation. From many of the gentry he had received protection

[1] Pt. III, I. 1.   [2] Cf. Pt. III, II. 5–14.

and support; though he had some harsh things to say about some of the clerics, he never forgot that he was a clergyman himself.

Wesley was convinced that religious inertia and moral torpor were widespread; they were all the more tragic because the country was now confronted with a demonstration of the Christian faith in its authentic vitality. 'Just at this time, when we wanted little of "filling up the measure of our iniquities", two or three clergymen of the Church of England began vehemently to "call sinners to repentance". In two or three years they had sounded the alarm to the utmost borders of the land. Many thousands gathered together to hear them; and in every place where they came many began to show such a concern for religion as they never had done before.'[1] The immediate effect was a striking moral transformation. 'But this was not all. Over and above this outward change, they began to experience inward religion.'[2] In few of his writings has Wesley given such a vivid account of the change effected by his preaching. This is the truest apologia for his work. It was doubtless necessary to remove misunderstandings and discredit malicious rumours, but his consuming interest lay in quite other things. He was always at his best when recording the triumphs of redeeming grace. But Wesley was always more than a narrator. He always 'preached for a verdict'. He was doing so when he wrote *A Farther Appeal*. 'Surely you are without excuse, all who do not yet know the day of your visitation! the day wherein the great God, who hath been forgotten among us days without number, is arising at once to be avenged of his adversaries, and to visit and redeem his people.'[3]

For a summary of the five editions published during Wesley's lifetime, a stemma illustrating the transmission of the text, and a list of the substantive variant readings from the edited text (based on the first edition, London, Strahan, 1745), see the Appendix to this volume, pp. 547–54. For full bibliographical details of Part I see *Bibliography*, No. 95, and for Parts II and III, No. 96.

[1] Pt. III, I. 4.   [2] Pt. III, I. 5.   [3] Pt. III, IV. 1.

A

FARTHER APPEAL

To MEN of

REASON and RELIGION.

By *JOHN WESLEY*, M. A.
Fellow of *Lincoln College*, OXFORD.

Let the Righteous smite me friendly and reprove me.
PSA. CXLI. 5.

L O N D O N:
Printed by W. STRAHAN; and sold by T. TRYE
near *Gray's-Inn Gate, Holbourn*; HENRY BUTLER,
at the Corner of *Bow Church-Yard*; and at the
Foundery, near *Upper-Moorfields*, 1745.
(Price Bound One Shilling.)

A
FARTHER APPEAL
TO
Men *of* Reason *and* Religion

PART I

In a former treatise[1] I declared, in the plainest manner I could, both my principles and practice, and answered some of the most important as well as the most common objections to each. But I have not delivered my own soul.[2] I believe it is still incumbent upon me to answer other objections, particularly such as have been urged by those who are esteemed religious or reasonable men.

These partly relate to the *doctrines* I teach, partly to my *manner* of teaching them, and partly to the *effects* which are supposed to follow from teaching these doctrines in this manner.

I. 1. I will briefly mention what those doctrines are before I consider the objections against them. Now all I teach respects either the nature and condition of *justification*, the nature and condition of *salvation*, the nature of justifying and saving *faith*, or the *Author* of faith and salvation.[3]

2. First: the nature of justification. It sometimes means our acquittal at the last day.[a] But this is altogether out of the present question—that justification whereof our Articles and Homilies speak, meaning present forgiveness, pardon of sins, and consequently acceptance with God, who therein 'declares his righteousness' or mercy, by or 'for the remission of the sins that are past',[b] saying, 'I will be merciful to thy unrighteousness, and thine iniquities I will remember no more.'[4]

I believe the condition of this is faith:[c] I mean, not only that without faith we cannot be justified, but also that as soon as anyone has true faith, in that moment he is justified.

---

[a] Matt. 12: 37.   [b] Rom. 3: 25.   [c] Rom. 4: 5, etc.

[1] *An Earnest Appeal to Men of Reason and Religion*, above.
[2] See Ezek. 14: 14, 20.   [3] See Heb. 5: 9, 12: 2.   [4] Cf. Heb. 8: 12.

Good works follow this faith,[a] but cannot go before it: much less can sanctification, which implies a continued course of good works springing from holiness of heart. But it is allowed that entire sanctification goes before our justification at the last day.[b]

5 It is allowed also that repentance[c] 'and fruits meet for repentance'[d] go before faith. Repentance absolutely must go before faith; fruits meet for it, if there be opportunity. By repentance I mean conviction of sin producing real desires and sincere resolutions of amendment; and by 'fruits meet for repentance' forgiving our
10 brother,[e] ceasing from evil, doing good,[f] using the ordinances of God,[g] and in general obeying him according to the measure of grace which we have received.[h] But these I cannot as yet term 'good works', because they do not spring from faith and the love of God.

3. By salvation I mean, not barely (according to the vulgar notion)
15 deliverance from hell, or going to heaven, but a present deliverance from sin, a restoration of the soul to its primitive health, its original purity; a recovery of the divine nature; the renewal of our souls after the image of God in righteousness and true holiness, in justice, mercy, and truth. This implies all holy and heavenly tempers,
20 and by consequence all holiness of conversation.[1]

Now if by salvation we mean a present salvation from sin, we cannot say holiness is the condition of it: for it is the thing itself. Salvation, in this sense, and holiness, are synonymous terms. We must therefore say 'we are saved by faith.'[2] Faith is the sole condi-
25 tion of this salvation. For without faith we cannot be thus saved. But whosoever believeth is saved already.

Without faith we cannot be thus saved. For we can't rightly serve God unless we love him. And we can't love him unless we know him; neither can we know God, unless by faith. Therefore salvation
30 by faith is only, in other words, the love of God by the knowledge of God, or the recovery of the image of God by a true spiritual acquaintance with him.

4. Faith, in general, is a divine, supernatural ἔλεγχος[i] of things not seen,[3] not discoverable by our bodily senses, as being either

---

[a] Luke 6: 43.	[b] Heb. 12: 14.	[c] Mark 1: 15.	[d] Matt. 3: 8.
[e] Matt. 6: 14, 15.	[f] Luke 3: 4, 9, etc.	[g] Matt. 7: 7.	[h] Matt. 25: 29.

[i] Evidence or conviction.

---

[1] See 2 Pet. 1: 4; Gen. 1: 27; Eph. 4: 24; 1 Pet. 1: 15.
[2] Cf. Luke 7: 50; Eph. 2: 8.   [3] Heb. 11: 1.

past, future or spiritual. Justifying faith implies, not only a divine
ἔλεγχος that 'God was in Christ, reconciling the world unto himself',[1]
but a sure trust and confidence that Christ died for *my* sins, that he
'loved *me* and gave himself for *me*'.[2] And the moment a penitent
sinner believes this, God pardons and absolves him.

And as soon as his pardon or justification is witnessed to him by
the Holy Ghost, he is saved. He loves God and all mankind. He has
'the mind that was in Christ',[3] and power to 'walk as he also walked'.[4]
From that time—unless he 'make shipwreck of the faith'[5]—salvation gradually increases in his soul. For 'so is the kingdom of God,
as if a man should cast seed into the ground, and it springeth up,
first the blade, then the ear, after that the full corn in the ear'.[6]

5. The first sowing of this seed I cannot conceive to be other than
instantaneous—whether I consider experience, or the Word of God,
or the very nature of the thing. However, I contend not for a
circumstance, but the substance; if you can attain it another way,
do. Only see that you do attain it; for if you fall short, you perish
everlastingly.

This beginning of that vast, inward change is usually termed 'the
new birth'. Baptism is the outward sign of this inward grace[7] which
is supposed by our Church to be given with, and through that sign
to all infants, and to those of riper years, if they 'repent and believe
the Gospel'.[8] But how extremely idle are the common disputes on
this head! I tell a sinner, 'You must be born again.'[9] 'No', say you,
'He was born again in baptism. Therefore he cannot be born again
now.' Alas! What trifling is this? What if he was *then* a child of
God? He is *now* manifestly a 'child of the devil'.[10] For the works of
his father he doth. Therefore do not play upon words. He *must* go
through an entire change of heart. In one not yet baptised, you yourself would call that change 'the new birth'. In him, call it what you
will; but remember meantime that if either he or you die without
it, your baptism will be so far from profiting you that it will greatly
increase your damnation.

6. The Author of faith and salvation is God alone. It is he that
works in us both to will and to do.[11] He is the sole giver of every
good gift,[12] and the sole author of every good work. There is no more

---

[1] 2 Cor. 5: 19. [2] Gal. 2: 20. [3] Cf. Phil. 2: 5.
[4] Cf. 1 John 2: 6. [5] Cf. 1 Tim. 1: 19 (cf. *Notes*). [6] Mark 4: 26–8.
[7] See B. C. P., Catechism. [8] Mark 1: 15. [9] John 3: 7.
[10] Acts 13: 10. [11] See Phil. 2: 13.
[12] See B.C.P., Prayers, second for Ember Weeks.

of power than of merit in man; but as all merit is in the Son of God, in what he has done and suffered for us, so all power is in the Spirit of God. And therefore every man, in order to believe unto salvation, must receive the Holy Ghost. This is essentially necessary to every
5 Christian, not in order to his working miracles, but in order to faith, peace, joy, and love—the ordinary fruits of the Spirit.[1]

Although no man on earth can explain the *particular manner* wherein the Spirit of God works on the soul, yet whosoever has these fruits cannot but know and *feel* that God has wrought them
10 in his heart.

Sometimes he acts more particularly on the understanding, opening or enlightening it (as the Scripture speaks), and revealing, unveiling, discovering to us 'the deep things of God'.[2]

Sometimes he acts on the wills and affections of men; withdraw-
15 ing them from evil, inclining them to good, *inspiring* (breathing, as it were) good thoughts into them. So it has frequently been expressed by an easy, natural metaphor strictly analogous to רוח, πνεῦμα, *Spiritus*, and the words used in most modern tongues also, to denote the third person in the ever-blessed Trinity. But however
20 it be expressed, it is certain all true faith, and the whole work of salvation, every good thought, word, and work, is altogether by the operation of the Spirit of God.

II. 1. I come now to consider the principal objections which have lately been made against these doctrines.

25 I know nothing material which has been objected as to the nature of justification; but many persons seem to be very confused in their thoughts concerning it, and speak as if they had never heard of any justification antecedent to that of the last day. To clear up this, there needs only a closer inspection of our Articles and Homilies,
30 wherein justification is always taken for the present remission of our sins.

But many are the objections which have been warmly urged against the condition of justification, faith alone, particularly in two treatises—the former entitled, *The Notions of the Methodists* Fully
35 *Disproved*,[3] the second, *The Notions of the Methodists* Farther

---

[1] See Gal. 5: 22. [2] 1 Cor. 2: 10.

[3] *The Notions of the Methodists Fully Disproved, by setting the Doctrine of the Church of England concerning Justification and Regeneration in a true light* is an anonymous pamphlet of 24 pages, published at Newcastle upon Tyne in 1743. The author, who resented Wesley's aspersions on the clergy and his incursion into Newcastle, challenged both his motives and his methods. Ostensibly he was concerned to set right Wesley's

Disproved[1]—in both of which it is vehemently affirmed: (1). That this is not a scriptural doctrine, (2). That it is not the doctrine of the Church of England.

It will not be needful to name the former of these anymore, seeing there is neither one text produced therein to prove this doctrine unscriptural, nor one sentence from the Articles or Homilies to prove it contrary to the doctrine of the Church. But so much of the latter as relates to the merits of the cause I will endeavour to consider calmly. As to what is personal I leave it as it is. 'God be merciful to me, a sinner.'[2]

2. To prove this doctrine unscriptural, that 'faith alone is the condition of justification', you allege that 'sanctification, according to Scripture, must go before it', to evince which you quote the following texts, which I leave as I find them: 'Go, disciple all nations . . . teaching them to observe all things, whatsoever I have commanded them.'[a] 'He that believeth and is baptized shall be saved.'[b] 'Preach repentance and remission of sins.'[c] 'Repent and be baptized every one of you . . . for the remission of sins.'[d] 'Repent and be converted, that your sins may be blotted out.'[e] 'By one offering he hath perfected for ever them that are sanctified.'[f] You add, 'St. Paul taught "repentance toward God, and faith toward our Lord Jesus Christ";[g] and calls "repentance from dead works, and faith toward God",[h] first principles.'[3]

You subjoin, ' "But ye are washed (says he), but ye are sanctified, but ye are justified." '[4] By "washed" is meant their baptism, and by their baptism is meant, first their sanctification, and then their

---

| [a] Matt. 28: 19, 20. | [b] Mark 16: 16. | [c] Luke 24: 47. | [d] Acts 2: 38. |
| [e] Acts 3: 19. | [f] Heb. 10: 14. | [g] Acts 20: 21. | [h] Heb. 6: 1. |

---

theological aberrations, but his treatment of Justification, Regeneration, and the Holy Spirit is superficial. There is a vigorous personal attack on Wesley for his insubordination to church authorities and for his arrogant and disruptive spirit. It is not surprising that Wesley had a low opinion of the quality of this work.

[1] *The Notions of the Methodists Farther Disproved, in Answer to their Earnest Appeal, &c. With a Vindication of the Clergy of the Church of England from their Aspersions* (Newcastle, 1743) is a longer and much more competent work than its predecessor, and Wesley naturally felt that it deserved much more serious attention. The course of the author's argument can be inferred from Wesley's refutation. The tone of the pamphlet is often supercilious and sometimes bitter. Its calm assurance that it has demolished Wesley's theological position left Wesley with no alternative to replying in some detail. The two works were republished as a single pamphlet in London in 1744.

[2] Luke 18: 13.   [3] *Notions Farther Disproved*, p. 7.   [4] 1 Cor. 6: 11.

justification.'[1] This is a flat begging the question; you take for granted the very point which you ought to prove. 'St. Peter also', you say, 'affirms that "Baptism doth save us"[2] or justify us.'[3] Again you beg the question. You take for granted what I utterly deny, viz.
5 that 'save' and 'justify' are here synonymous terms. Till this is proved you can draw no inference at all, for you have no foundation whereon to build.

I conceive these, and all the Scriptures which can be quoted to prove sanctification antecedent to justification (if they do not relate
10 to our final justification), prove only (what I have never denied) that repentance or conviction of sin, and 'fruits meet for repentance', precede that faith whereby we are justified; but by no means that the love of God, or any branch of true holiness, must or can precede faith.

15 3. It is objected, secondly, that justification by faith alone is not the doctrine of the Church of England.

> You believe (says the writer above mentioned) that no good work can be previous to justification, nor consequently a condition of it. But, God be praised, . . . our church has nowhere delivered such abomin-
20 able doctrine.[a]

> The clergy . . . contend for inward holiness as previous to the first justification. This is the doctrine they universally inculcate, and which . . . you cannot oppose without contradicting the doctrine of our Church.[b]

25 > All your strongest persuasives to the love of God . . . will not blanch over the deformity of that doctrine . . . that men may be justified . . . by faith alone . . . Unless you publicly recant this horrid doctrine, your faith is vain.[c]

> If you will vouchsafe to purge out this venomous part of your prin-
30 ciples, in which the 'wide, essential, fundamental, irreconcilable difference',[4] as you very justly term it, mainly consists, then there will be found so far no disagreement between you and the clergy of the Church of England.[d]

---

[a] [*Notions Farther Disproved*], p. 14.

[b] [Ibid.,] pp. 25, 26 [The passage is even more varied and compressed than is revealed by the ellipses which we have added, and the same is true of others of these quotations, even though Wesley does no injustice to the meaning].

[c] [Ibid.,] p. 27.   [d] Ibid.

---

[1] *Notions Farther Disproved*, p. 8.   [2] Cf. 1 Pet. 3: 21.

[3] *Notions Farther Disproved*, p. 8.

[4] From Wesley's answer to 'a serious clergyman' in London who 'desired to know in what points we differ from the Church of England', *Journal*, Sept. 13, 1739.

4. In order to be clearly and fully satisfied what the doctrine of
the Church of England is (as it stands opposite to the doctrine of the
antinomians on the one hand, and to that of *justification by works* on
the other) I will simply set down what occurs on this head either in
her liturgy, Articles, or Homilies: 5

> Spare thou them, O God, which *confess their faults*. Restore thou
> them that are *penitent*; according to thy promises declared unto
> mankind in Christ Jesu our Lord.[1]
> He pardoneth and absolveth all them that *truly repent* and *un-
> feignedly believe* his holy gospel.[2]   10
> Almighty God, who dost forgive the sins of them that are *penitent*,
> create and make in us new and contrite hearts; that we, *worthily
> lamenting our sins* and *acknowledging our wretchedness*, may obtain of
> thee perfect remission and forgiveness, through Jesus Christ our
> Lord.[a]   15
> Almighty God . . . hath promised forgiveness of sins to all them that
> with *hearty repentance* and *true faith* turn unto him.[b]
> Our Lord Jesus Christ . . . hath left power . . . to absolve all sinners
> who *truly repent* and *believe* in him.[c]
> Give him unfeigned *repentance* and steadfast *faith*, that his sins may   20
> be blotted out.[d]
> He is a merciful receiver of all true, *penitent* sinners, and is ready to
> pardon us if we come unto him with *faithful repentance*.[e]

Infants indeed our Church supposes to be justified in baptism,
although they cannot then either *believe* or *repent*. But she expressly   25
requires both *repentance* and *faith* in those who come to be baptized
when they are of riper years.

As earnestly therefore as our Church inculcates justification by
faith alone, she nevertheless supposes repentance to be previous to
faith, and 'fruits meet for repentance'; yea, and unverisal holiness   30
to be previous to final justification, as evidently appears from the
following words:

> Let us beseech him . . . that the rest of our life may be pure and
> holy, so that at the last we may come to his eternal joy.[f]

[a] [B.C.P.,] Collect for Ash Wednesday.   [b] [Ibid.,] Communion Office.
[c] [Ibid.,] Visitation of the sick.
[d] Ibid.   [e] [Ibid.,] Commination Office.
[f] [Ibid., Morning and Evening Prayer,] Absolution.

---

[1] B.C.P., Morning Prayer, General Confession.
[2] Ibid., Morning Prayer, Absolution.

May we seriously apply our hearts to that holy and heavenly wisdom . . . here, which may in the end bring us to life everlasting.[a]

Raise us from the death of sin unto the life of righteousness, . . . that at the last day we may be found acceptable in thy sight.[b]

5   If we from henceforth walk in his ways, . . . seeking always his glory, . . . Christ . . . will set us on his right hand.[c]

5. We come next to the Articles of our Church. The former part of the ninth runs thus:

Of Original or Birth Sin

10   Original sin . . . is the fault and corruption of the nature of every man, . . . whereby man is very far gone from original righteousness, and is of his own nature inclined to evil, so that the flesh lusteth always contrary to the spirit: and therefore in every person born into this world it deserveth God's wrath and damnation.

Art. X. Of Free Will

15   The condition of man after the fall of Adam is such that he cannot turn and prepare himself by his own natural strength and good works to faith and calling upon God. Wherefore we have no power to do good works pleasant and acceptable to God, without the grace of God 20 by Christ preventing us that we may have a good will, and working with us when we have that good will.

Art. XI. Of the Justification of Man

We are accounted righteous before God only for the merit of our Lord and Saviour Jesus Christ, by faith, and not for our own works or 25 deservings. Wherefore that we are justified by faith only is a most wholesome doctrine, and very full of comfort, as more largely is expressed in the Homily of Justification.

I believe this Article relates to the *meritorious cause* of justification, rather than to the *condition* of it. On this therefore I do not build 30 anything concerning it, but on those that follow.

Art. XII. Of Good Works

Albeit that good works, which are the fruits of faith and follow after justification, cannot put away our sins; yet are they pleasing and acceptable to God in Christ, and do spring out necessarily of a true 35 and lively faith; insomuch that by them a lively faith may be as evidently known, as a tree may be know by the fruit.

[a] [B.C.P.,] Visitation of the Sick.   [b] [Ibid.,] Burial Office.
[c] [Ibid.,] Commination Office.

We are taught here, (1), that good works, in general, follow after justification; (2), that they spring out of a true and lively faith (that faith whereby we are justified); (3), that true, justifying faith may be as evidently known by them as a tree discerned by the fruit.

Does it not follow that the supposing any good work to go *before* 5 justification is full as absurd as the supposing an apple or any other fruit to grow before the tree?

But let us hear the Church speaking yet more plainly.

Art. XIII. Of Works done before Justification

Works done before the grace of Christ and the inspiration of his 10 Spirit (i.e. before justification, as the title expresses it), are not pleasant to God, forasmuch as they spring not of faith in Jesu Christ . . .: Yea rather, for that they are not done as God hath willed and commanded them to be done, we doubt not they have the nature of sin.

Now if all works done before justification have the nature of sin, 15 both because they spring not of faith in Christ, and because they are not done as God hath willed and commanded them to be done, what becomes of sanctification previous to justification? It is utterly excluded; seeing whatever is previous to justification is not good or holy, but evil and sinful. 20

Although therefore our Church does frequently assert that we ought to repent and bring forth fruits meet for repentance if ever we would attain to that faith whereby alone we are justified; yet she never asserts (and here the hinge of the question turns) that these are *good works* so long as they are previous to justification. Nay, she 25 expressly asserts the direct contrary, viz., that they have all the nature of sin. So that this 'horrid, scandalous, wicked, abominable, venomous, blasphemous doctrine'[1] is nevertheless the doctrine of the Church of England.

6. It remains to consider what occurs in the Homilies, first with 30 regard to the *meritorious cause* of our justification, agreeable to the eleventh, and then with regard to the *condition* of it, agreeable to the twelfth and thirteenth Articles.

These things must go together in our justification: upon God's part, his great mercy and grace; upon Christ's part, the satisfaction of 35

---

[1] Wesley has gathered together in a composite sentence adjectives which are scattered throughout *Notions Farther Disproved*, and which reflect the structure of the argument of the pamphlet.

God's justice; and upon our part, true and lively faith in the merits of Jesus Christ.[a]

So that the grace of God doth not shut out the justice (or righteousness) of God in our justification; but only shutteth out the righteousness of man . . . as to *deserving* our justification.

And therefore St. Paul declareth nothing on the behalf of man concerning his justification, but only a true faith.

And yet that faith doth not shut out repentance, hope, love, to be joined with faith (that is, *afterwards*; see below) in every man that is justified. . . . Neither doth faith shut out the righteousness of our good works, necessarily to be done afterwards; but it excludeth them, so that we may not do them to this intent, to be made just (or to be justified) by doing them.

That we are justified by *faith alone* is spoken to take away clearly all *merit* of our works, and wholly to ascribe the merit and deserving of our justification unto Christ only.[b]

The true meaning of this saying, 'we be justified by faith only', is this: we be justified by the merits of Christ only, and not of our own works.[c]

7. Thus far touching the *meritorious cause* of our justification, referred to in the eleventh Article. The twelfth and thirteenth are a summary of what now follows with regard to the *condition* of it.

Of (justifying) true faith three things are specially to be noted: (1), that it bringeth forth good works; (2), that without it can no good works be done; (3), what good works it doth bring forth.[d]

Without faith can no good work be done, accepted and pleasant unto God. For 'as a branch cannot bear fruit of itself (saith our Saviour Christ) except it abide in the vine, so cannot you, except you abide in me.'[1] Faith giveth life to the soul; and they be as much dead to God that lack faith, as they be to the world whose bodies lack souls. Without faith all that is done of us is but dead before God. Even as a picture is but a dead representation of the thing itself, so be the works of all unfaithful (unbelieving) persons before God. They be but shadows of lively and good things, and not good things indeed. For true faith doth give life to the works, and without faith no work is good before God.[e]

We must set no good works before faith, nor think that before faith a man may do any good works; for such works are as the course of an

---

[a] Homily on Salvation, Part I.   [b] Ibid., Part II.
[c] Ibid., Part III.   [d] [*Homilies*,] Sermon on Faith, Part I.
[e] Homily, 'Of Works annexed to Faith', Part I. [Wesley's original incorrectly reads 'ibid. Part III' here, but gives the correct citation three paragraphs later.]

[1] Cf. John 15: 4.

horse that runneth out of the way, which taketh great labour, but to no purpose.[a]

Without faith we have no virtues, but only the shadows of them. All 'the life of them that lack the true faith is sin'.[b]

As men first have life, and after be nourished, so must our faith go 5 before, and after be nourished with good works. And life may be without nourishment, but nourishment cannot be without life. . . .

I can show a man that by faith without works lived and came to heaven. But without faith never man had life. The thief on the cross only believed, and the most merciful God justified him. . . . Truth it is, 10 if he had lived and not regarded faith and the works thereof, he should have lost his salvation again. But this I say, faith by itself saved him. But works by themselves never justified any man.[c]

Good works go not before in him which shall afterward be justified. But good works do follow after, when a man is first justified.[d]   15

8. From the whole tenor then of her Liturgy, Articles and Homilies, the doctrine of the Church of England appears to be this:

(1). That no good work, properly so called, can go *before* justification;

(2). That *no degree* of true sanctification can be previous to it;   20

(3). That as the *meritorious cause* of justification is the life and death of Christ, so the *condition* of it is faith, faith alone; and

(4). That both inward and outward holiness are consequent on this faith, and are the ordinary, stated condition of final justification.

9. And what more can you desire, who have hitherto opposed 25 justification by faith alone, merely upon a principle of conscience, because you was zealous for holiness and good works? Do I not effectually secure these from contempt at the same time that I defend the doctrines of the Church? I not only allow, but vehemently contend, that none shall ever enter into glory who is not holy on 30 earth, as well in heart as 'in all manner of conversation'.[1] I cry aloud, 'Let all that have believed be careful to maintain good works';[2] and, 'Let every one that nameth the name of Christ depart from all iniquity.'[3] I exhort even those who are conscious they do not believe, 'Cease to do evil, learn to do well';[4] 'The kingdom of 35 heaven is at hand';[5] therefore repent, and 'bring forth fruits meet

---

[a] Ibid.   [b] Ibid.   [c] Ibid.
[d] Homily on Fasting, Part I. [Quoting Augustine, *De Fide et Operibus*, cap. 4.]

---

[1] 1 Pet. 1: 15.   [2] Cf. Titus 3: 8.   [3] 2 Tim. 2: 19.
[4] Isa. 1: 16, 17.   [5] Matt. 3: 2.

for repentance'.[1] Are not these directions the very same in substance which you yourself would give to persons so circumstanced? What means then this endless 'strife of words'?[2] Or 'what doth your arguing reprove?'[3]

5   10. Many of those who are perhaps as 'zealous of good works'[4] as you, think I have allowed you too much. Nay, my brethren, but how can we help allowing it, if we allow the Scriptures to be from God? For is it not written, and do not you yourselves believe: 'Without holiness no man shall see the Lord'?[5] And how, then, 10 without fighting about words, can we deny that holiness is a condition of final acceptance? And, as to the first acceptance or pardon, does not all experience as well as Scripture prove that no man ever yet truly 'believed the gospel'[6] who did not first *repent*? That none was ever yet truly 'convinced of righteousness' who was not first 15 'convinced of sin'?[7] Repentance therefore in this sense we cannot deny to be necessarily previous to faith. Is it not equally undeniable that the running back into known wilful sin (suppose it were drunkenness or uncleanness) stifles that repentance or conviction? And can that repentance come to any good issue in his soul, who 20 resolves not to forgive his brother? Or who obstinately refrains from what God convinces him is right, whether it be prayer or hearing his Word? Would you scruple yourself to tell one of these, 'Why, if you *will* thus drink away all conviction, how should you ever truly know your want of Christ? Or consequently, believe in 25 Him? If you *will* not forgive your brother his trespasses, neither will your heavenly Father forgive you your trespasses.[8] If you will not ask, how can you expect to receive?[9] If you will not hear, how can "faith come by hearing"?[10] It is plain, "you grieve the Spirit of God".[11] You *will not* have him to reign over you. Take care that 30 he do not utterly depart from you. For "unto him that hath shall be given; but from him that hath not (i.e. uses it not) shall be taken away even that which he hath"'.[12] Would you scruple on a proper occasion to say this? You could not scruple it if you believe the Bible. But in saying this you allow all which I have said, viz., that 35 previous to justifying faith there *must* be repentance, and if opportunity permit, 'fruits meet for repentance'.[13]

---

[1] Matt. 3: 8.   [2] Cf. 1 Tim. 6: 4.   [3] Job 6: 25.   [4] Titus 2: 14.
[5] Cf. Heb. 12: 14.   [6] Cf. Mark 1: 15.   [7] John 16: 8 (cf. *Notes*).
[8] See Matt. 6: 15.   [9] See Matt. 21: 22; John 16: 24; 1 John 3: 22.
[10] Rom. 10: 17.   [11] Cf. Eph. 4: 30.   [12] Cf. Matt. 25: 29.   [13] Matt. 3: 8.

11. And yet I allow you this, that although both repentance and the fruits thereof are in *some sense* necessary before justification, yet neither the one nor the other is necessary in the *same sense* or in the *same degree* with faith. Not in the *same degree*: for in whatever moment a man believes (in the Christian sense of the word) he is justified, his sins are blotted out, 'his faith is counted to him for righteousness'.[1] But it is not so at whatever moment he repents, or brings forth any or all the fruits of repentance. Faith alone therefore justifies, which repentance alone does not, much less any outward work. And consequently none of these are necessary to justification in the *same degree* with faith.

Nor in the *same sense*: for none of these has so direct, immediate a relation to justification as faith. This is *proximately* necessary thereto; repentance, *remotely*, as it is necessary to the increase or continuance of faith: and the fruits of repentance still more remotely, as they are necessary to repentance.[2] And even in this sense these are only necessary on supposition—if there be time and opportunity for them; for in many instances there is not, but God cuts short his work, and faith prevents the fruits of repentance. So that the general proposition is not overthrown, but clearly established by these concessions; and we conclude still, both on the authority of Scripture and the Church, that faith alone is the proximate condition of justification.[3]

III. 1. I was once inclined to believe that none would openly object against what I had anywhere said of the nature of salvation. How greatly then was I surprised some months ago when I was shown a kind of circular letter, which one of those whom 'the Holy Ghost hath made . . . overseers'[4] of his church, I was informed, had sent to all the clergy of his diocese.[5]

[1] Cf. Rom. 4: 5.
[2] In the first edition the compositor omitted the following from Wesley's manuscript: 'faith: and the fruits of repentance still more remotely, as they are necessary to'. An erratum slip was affixed to some copies, but unfortunately this was missed in preparing the next edition (called the 'fourth', Bristol, 1758), from which subsequent editions derived their text. Wesley removed the nonsense from these later editions by altering the second 'repentance' to 'faith', but by the error (and his failure to correct it fully) he lost the third element in the process of justification, viz. faith, repentance, fruits of repentance.
[3] Wesley used these opening pages, covering I. 1–II. 11, with minor alterations, as an outline of his teaching, in *A Letter to the Rev. Mr. Horne*—see below.
[4] Acts. 20: 28.
[5] In his *Works* (1772), Wesley added the footnote: 'The (then) Archbishop of York.' At the time this was Thomas Herring (1693–1757), who in 1747 became Archbishop of

Part of it ran (nearly, if not exactly) thus:

> There is great indiscretion in preaching up a sort of religion as the
> true and only Christianity which, in their own account of it, consists in
> an enthusiastic ardour, to be understood or attained by very few, and
> 5 not to be practised without breaking in upon the common duties of life.

O my Lord, what manner of words are these! Supposing candour
and love out of the question, are they words of truth? I dare stake
my life upon it there is not one true clause in all this paragraph.
The propositions contained therein are these:

10   (1). That the religion I preach consists in an enthusiastic
       ardour;
    (2). That it can be attained by very few;
    (3). That it can be understood by very few;
    (4). That it cannot be practised without breaking in upon the
15   common duties of life;
    (5). And that all this may be proved by my own account of it.

I earnestly entreat your Grace to review my own account of it
as it stands in any of my former writings; or to consider the short
account which is given in this. And if you can thence make good any
20 one of those propositions, I do hereby promise before God and the
world that I will never preach more.

At present I do not well understand what your Grace means by
'an enthusiastic ardour'. Surely you do not mean 'the love of God'!
No, not though a poor, pardoned sinner should carry it so far, as
25 to 'love the Lord his God with all his heart, and with all his soul,
and with all his strength'![1] But this alone is the ardour which I
preach up, as the foundation of 'the true and only Christianity'.
I pray God so to fill your whole heart therewith that you may praise
him for ever and ever.

30 But why should your Grace believe that the love of God 'can be
attained by very few'? Or that it 'can be understood by very few'?
All who attain it understand it well. And did not He who is loving
to every man design that every man should attain true love? O that
all would know in this their day, the things that make for their
35 peace![2]

Canterbury. This circular (no copy of which has so far been discovered) was a kind of
covering letter for Bishop Gibson's *Observations upon the* . . . *Methodists*, for which see
below, p. 329.

[1] Cf. Luke 10: 27.   [2] See Luke 19: 42.

And *cannot* the love both of God and our neighbour 'be practised without breaking in upon the common duties of life'? Nay, can any of the common duties of life be rightly practised without them? I apprehend, not. I apprehend I am then laying the true, the only foundation for all those duties, when I preach, 'Thou shalt love 5 the Lord thy God with all thy heart . . ., and thy neighbour as thyself.'[1]

2. With this letter was sent (I believe to every clergyman in the diocese) the pamphlet entitled *Observations on the Conduct and Behaviour of a Certain Sect, Usually Distinguished by the Name of* 10 *Methodists.* It has been generally supposed to be wrote by a person who is every way my superior.[2] Perhaps one reason why he did not inscribe his name was that his greatness might not make me afraid; and that I might have liberty to stand, as it were, on even ground, while I answer for myself.[3]   15

In considering, therefore, such parts of these *Observations* as naturally fall in my way, I will take that method which I believe that author desires, using no ceremony at all, but speaking as to an equal, that it may the more easily be discerned where the truth lies.

The first query relating to doctrine is this: 20

Whether notions in religion may not be heightened to such *extremes* as to lead *some* into a disregard of religion itself, through despair of attaining such exalted heights? And whether *others* who have imbibed those notions may not be led by them into a disregard and disesteem of the common duties and offices of life; to such a degree at least as is 25 inconsistent with that attention to them, and that diligence in them, which Providence has made necessary to the well-being of private families and public societies, and which Christianity does not only require in all stations and in all conditions, but declares at the same time[4] that the performance even of the lowest offices in life *as unto* 30 *God* (whose providence has placed people in their several stations) is truly a *serving of Christ*, and will not fail of its reward in the next world?[5]

---

[1] Luke 10: 27.

[2] This pamphlet appeared anonymously in 1744. From the first it was widely attributed to Edmund Gibson, Bishop of London. Gibson never admitted his authorship—though he never denied it—and Wesley's attempts to induce him to accept responsibility met with no success. Cf. *A Letter to the Bishop of London* below.

[3] The concluding part of this sentence is quoted by Wesley in the second paragraph of *A Letter to the Bishop of London.*

[4] Here the *Observations* cites Col. 3: 22 and Eph. 5: 6.

[5] *Observations*, p. 9, Query 1 of Part II.

You have interwoven so many particulars in this general question that I must divide and answer them one by one.

Q[uery] (1). Whether notions in religion may not be heightened to such *extremes* as to lead *some* into a disregard of religion itself?

5   A[nswer]: They may. But that I have *so* heightened them it lies upon you to prove.

Q. (2). Whether *others* may not be led into a disregard of religion through despair of attaining such exalted heights?

A. What heights? The loving God with all our heart? I believe
10   this is the most exalted height in man or angel. But I have not heard that any have been led into a disregard of religion through despair of attaining this.

Q. (3). Whether others who have imbibed these notions may not be led by them into a disregard and disesteem of the common duties
15   and offices of life?

A. My notions are: 'True religion is the loving God with all our heart, and our neighbour as ourselves; and in that love abstaining from all evil, and doing all possible good to all men.'[1] Now, it is not possible in the nature of things that any should be led by these
20   notions into either a disregard or disesteem of the common duties and offices of life.

Q. (4). But may they not be led by them into such a degree at least of disregard for the common duties of life, as is inconsistent with that attention to them, and diligence in them, which Providence
25   has made necessary?

A. No. Quite the reverse. They lead men to discharge all those duties with the strictest diligence and closest attention.

Q. (5). Does not Christianity require this attention and diligence in all stations and in all conditions?
30   *A.* Yes.

Q. (6). Does it not declare that the performance even of the lowest offices of life *as unto God* is truly *a serving of Christ*, and will not fail of its reward in the next world?

A. It does. But whom are you confuting? Not me. For this is the
35   doctrine I preach continually.

3. Query the second:

Whether the enemy of mankind may not find his account in their

---

[1] Cf. *An Earnest Appeal*, § 2.

carrying Christianity, which was designed for a rule to *all* stations and *all* conditions, to such *heights* as make it fairly practicable by a *very few*, in comparison, or rather by none?[1]

I answer: (1). The *height* to which we carry Christianity (as was but now observed) is this, 'Thou shalt love the Lord thy God with 5 all thy heart, and thy neighbour as thyself.' (2). The enemy of Christianity cannot find his account in our carrying it to this height. (3). You will not say, on reflection, that Christianity, even in this height, is practicable by *very few*, or rather *by none*. You yourself will confess, this is a rule (as God designed it should [be]) 10 for *all* stations and *all* conditions.

Query the third:

Whether, in particular, carrying the doctrine of justification by faith alone to such a height as not to allow that a careful and sincere observance of moral duties is so much as a *condition* of our acceptance with 15 God, and of our being justified in his sight; whether this, I say, does not naturally lead people to a *disregard* of those duties, and a low esteem of them; or rather to think them no part of the Christian religion?[2]

I trust justification by faith alone has been so explained above as to secure, not only a high esteem, but also a careful and sincere 20 observance of all moral duties.

4. Query the fourth:

Whether a due and regular attendance on the public offices of religion, paid by good men in a serious and composed way, does not better answer the true ends of devotion, and is not a better evidence of the 25 co-operation of the Holy Spirit, than those sudden agonies, roarings and screamings, tremblings, droppings down, ravings and madnesses, into which their hearers have been cast?[3]

I must answer this query likewise part by part.

Q. (1). Whether a due and regular attendance on the public 30 offices of religion, paid in a serious and composed way, by good (i.e. well meaning) men, does not answer the true ends of devotion?

A. I suppose by 'devotion' you mean public worship; by the 'true ends' of it, the love of God and man; and by 'a due and regular attendance on the public offices of religion, paid in a serious and 35 composed way', the going as often as we have opportunity to our parish church, and to the sacrament there administered. If so, the

---

[1] *Observations*, p. 9.   [2] *Ibid*.   [3] *Observations*, p. 10.

question is, 'Whether *this attendance* on *those offices* does not produce the love of God and man?' I answer: sometimes it does; and sometimes it does not. I myself thus attended them for many years, and yet am conscious to myself that during that whole time
5 I had no more of the love of God than a stone. And I know many hundreds, perhaps thousands, of serious persons, who are ready to testify the same thing.

Q. (2). But is not this a better evidence of the co-operation of the Holy Spirit than those *sudden agonies*?
10 *A*. All these persons, as well as I, can testify also that this is no evidence at all of the co-operation of the Holy Spirit. For some years I attended these public offices, *because I would not be punished* for non-attendance. And many of these attended them *because their parents did before them*, or *because they would not lose their character*.
15 Many more because they confounded the means with the end, and fancied this *opus operatum*[1] would bring them to heaven. How many thousands are now under this strong delusion? Beware you bring not their blood on your own head!

Q. (3). However, does not this attendance better answer those
20 ends than those roarings, screamings, etc.?
I suppose you mean, 'better than an attendance on that preaching which has often been accompanied with these'.
I answer: (1). There is no manner of need to set the one in opposition to the other, seeing we continually exhort all who attend on our
25 preaching to attend the offices of the Church. And they do pay a more regular attendance there than ever they did before. (2). Their attending the Church did not, in fact, answer those ends at all till they attended this preaching also. (3). It is the preaching remission of sins through Jesus Christ which alone answers the true ends of de-
30 votion. And this will always be accompanied with the co-operation of the Holy Spirit; though not always with sudden agonies, roarings, screamings, tremblings, or droppings down. Indeed, if God is pleased at any time to permit any of these I cannot hinder it. Neither can this hinder the work of his Spirit in the soul, which
35 may be carried on either with or without them. But, (4), I cannot

---

[1] *Opus operatum*, act done. The phrase has a long history in theological debate, especially in connection with sacramental doctrine. The teaching associated with the phrase was officially approved by the Council of Trent (Session VII, Of the Sacraments in General, Canon VIII); and this explicit association of Catholic teaching with the words increased Protestant antipathies to it.

apprehend it to be any reasonable proof that 'this is not the work of God' that a convinced sinner should 'fall into an extreme agony, both of body and soul';ᵃ that another should 'roar for the disquietness of her heart';ᵇ that others should scream or 'cry with a loud and bitter cry, "What must we do to be saved?"';ᶜ that others should 'exceedingly tremble and quake';ᵈ and others, in a deep sense of the majesty of God, 'should fall prostrate upon the ground'.ᵉ

Indeed by picking out one single word from a sentence, and then putting together what you had gleaned in sixty or seventy pages, you have drawn a terrible group[1] for them who look no farther than those two lines in the *Observations*. But the bare addition of half a line to each word, just as it stands in the place from which you quoted it, reconciles all both to Scripture and reason, and the spectre-form vanishes away.

You have taken into your account 'ravings and madnesses', too. As instances of the former you refer to the case of John Haydonᶠ and of Thomas Maxfield.ᵍ I wish you would calmly consider his reasoning on that head, who is not prejudiced in my favour: 'What influence sudden and sharp awakenings may have upon the body, I pretend not to explain. But I make no question Satan, so far as he gets power, may exert himself on such occasions, partly to hinder the good work in the persons who are thus touched with the sharp arrows of conviction, and partly to disparage the work of God, as if it tended to lead people to distraction.'[2]

For instances of madness you may refer to pages 88, 90, 91, 92, 93. The words in page 88 are these:

I could not but be under some concern with regard to one or two

---

ᵃ *Journal* 3, p. 26 [i.e. for Mar. 6, 1739, cited in *Observations*, p. 10].
ᵇ [Ibid.,] p. 40 [Apr. 17, 1739, cited *Observations*, p. 10; cf. Ps. 38: 8].
ᶜ [Ibid.,] p. 50 [i.e. May 21, 1739, cited *Observations*, p. 10; see Esther 4: 1, Acts 16: 30].
ᵈ [Ibid.,] p. 58 [i.e. June 15, 1739, cited *Observations*, p. 10; cf. Heb. 12: 21].
ᵉ [Ibid.,] p. 59 [i.e. June 16, 1739, cited *Observations*, p. 10].
ᶠ [Ibid.,] p. 44 [i.e. May 2, 1739, cited *Observations*, p. 10].
ᵍ [Ibid.,] p. 50 [i.e. May 21, 1739, cited *Observations*, p. 10; Maxfield was later employed by Wesley as his first full time lay preacher].

---

[1] The author of *Observations* cites 37 page references to this *Journal* (some of them more than once) as well as seven references to the sixth and seventh extracts from Whitefield's *Journal*. Wesley selects citations from several groups.
[2] See letter from the Revd. Ralph Erskine of the Associate Presbytery to Wesley, quoted in the latter's *Journal* for June 30, 1739. They were in correspondence about revival phenomena.

persons who were tormented in an unaccountable manner and seemed to be, indeed, *lunatic* as well as *sore vexed.*¹ . . . Soon after I was sent for to one of these who was so strangely 'torn of the devil'² that I almost wondered her relations did not say, 'Much religion hath made thee mad.'³ We prayed God to bruise Satan under her feet.⁴ Immediately 'we had the petition we asked of him'⁵ she cried out vehemently, 'He is gone! He is gone!' and was filled with the spirit of 'love, and of a sound mind'.⁶ I have seen her many times since, strong in the Lord. When I asked abruptly, 'What do you desire now?' she answered, 'Heaven.' I asked, 'What is in your heart?' She replied, 'God.' I asked, 'But how is your heart when anything provokes you?' She said, 'By the grace of God, I am not provoked at anything. All the things of this world pass by me as shadows.'⁷

Are these the words of one that is beside herself? Let any man of reason judge!

Your next instance (page 90) stands thus:

About noon I came to Usk, where I preached to a small company of poor people on 'The Son of man is come to save that which is lost.'⁸ One grey-headed man wept and trembled exceedingly, and another who was there (I have since heard), as well as two or three who were at The Ddefauden⁹ 'are gone quite distracted', that is (my express words, that immediately follow, specify what it was which some accounted distraction),¹⁰ they mourn and refuse to be comforted till they have 'redemption through his blood'.¹¹

If *you* think the case mentioned [on] pages 92, 93,¹² to be another instance of madness, I contend not. It was because I did not understand that uncommon case that I prefaced it with this reflection: 'The fact I nakedly relate, and leave every man to his own judgment upon it.' Only be pleased to observe that this 'madness', if such it was, is no more chargeable upon *me* than upon *you*. For the subject

---

¹ See Matt. 17: 15. ² Cf. Luke 9: 42. ³ Cf. Acts 26: 24.
⁴ See Rom. 16: 20. ⁵ Cf. 1 John 5: 15. ⁶ 2 Tim. 1: 7.
⁷ *Journal*, Oct. 12, 1739. ⁸ Matt. 18: 11.
⁹ 'A high hill, two or three miles beyond Chepstow'; see *Journal*, Oct. 15, 1739.
¹⁰ There is an error in the original text, where Wesley's editorial interpolation reads: 'my express words are that immediately follow, specifying what it was which *some accounted distraction*'. Possibly the original manuscript read 'my express words are those that. . .', but in his *Works* he attempts correction in another way, by omitting 'are'; we have completed this correction by altering 'specifying' to 'specify'.
¹¹ *Journal*, Oct. 17, 1739; Eph. 1: 7.
¹² Ibid., Oct. 23, 1739.

of it had no relation to, or commerce with me, nor had I ever seen her before that hour.

5. Query the fifth:

> Whether those exalted strains in religion, and an imagination of being already in a state of *perfection*, are not apt to lead men to spiritual pride and to a contempt of their fellow Christians, while they consider *them* as only going on in what they call the *low* and *imperfect way*, i.e. as growing in grace and goodness only *by degrees*; even though it appear by the lives of those who are considered by them as in that *low* and *imperfect* way, that they are persons who are gradually working out their salvation by their own honest endeavours, and through the ordinary assistances of God's grace, with an humble reliance upon the merits of Christ for the pardon of their sins, and the acceptance of their sincere, though imperfect services?[1]

I must divide this query, too. But first permit me to ask, 'What do you mean by "those exalted strains in religion"?' I have said again and again, I know no more exalted strain than 'I will love thee, O Lord my God';[2] especially, according to the propriety of David's expression אֶרְחָמְךָ יְהוָה. *Ex intimis visceribus diligam te, Domine.*[3] This premised, let us go on step by step.

---

[1] *Observations*, p. 10.

[2] Cf. Ps. 18: 1.

[3] The Hebrew means 'I will love thee, O Lord.' The Latin phrase includes the Vulgate form of the same words (*diligam te Domine*: Ps. 17: 2 in the Vulgate). The phrase *ex intimis visceribus* does not occur in the Psalm, though the identification of emotional states with physical organs is wholly in keeping with Hebrew psychology. Wesley must have supplied the phrase himself, and the association of ideas is clear. The word רחם (from which אֶרְחָמְךָ is derived) means 'womb'; Wesley may have felt that by extension it could indicate the viscera in general, so that *ex intimis visceribus diligam te* may have seemed a reasonable paraphrase of אֶרְחָמְךָ. In a manuscript footnote to his own copy of the *Works* (1772) Wesley added a translation of the Latin: 'I will love thee from my inmost bowels.'

This raises an interesting point. Wesley knew the language well enough to write *A Short Hebrew Grammar* (*Bibliography*, No. 190), but in each of the two places where he quotes Hebrew in *A Farther Appeal* there were typographical errors in the first edition. (The other example is in I. 6 above.) The mistakes may have been made by the printer, though this seems unlikely. In both cases the Hebrew, if read aloud, sounds correct, but has been incorrectly reduced to writing. If Wesley were responsible, he was right about the sounds, wrong about the letters. He very seldom quoted Hebrew in his works; here, presumably, he used it to show that (whatever his critics might say) he was not an unlearned man. He did not bother—or more likely he had not the opportunity—to check his quotation against the original. His memory was right in essentials, wrong about details. But behind his memory lay the discipline of study; at Oxford, he tells us, his 'manner was to spend several hours a day in reading the Scripture in the original tongues' (*The Principles of a Methodist*, § 16).

Q. (1). Whether the preaching of 'loving God from our inmost bowels' is not apt to lead men to spiritual pride, and to a contempt of their fellow Christians?

A. No: But so far as it takes place it will humble them to the dust.

Q. (2). Whether an imagination of being already in a state of *perfection* is not *apt to lead* men into this spiritual pride?

A. (1). If it be a *false* imagination, it *is* spiritual pride. (2). But *true* Christian perfection is no other than humble love.

Q. (3). Do not men who imagine they have attained this despise others as only going on in what they account the *low* and *imperfect* way, i.e. as growing in grace and goodness *by degrees*?

A. (1). Men who only *imagine* they have attained this may probably despise those that are going on in any way. (2). But the growing in grace and goodness by degrees is no mark of a low and imperfect way. Those who are fathers in Christ grow in grace by degrees as well as the new born babes.

Q. (4). Do they not despise those who are working out their salvation with an humble reliance upon the merits of Christ for the pardon of their sins, and the acceptance of their sincere though imperfect services?

A. (1). They who really love God despise no man. But, (2), they grieve to hear many talk of thus 'relying on Christ' who, though perhaps they are grave, honest, moral men, yet by their own words appear not to love God at all; whose souls cleave to the dust, who love the world, who have no part of the mind that was in Christ.[1]

6. Query the sixth:

Whether the same exalted strains and notions do not tend to weaken the *natural* and *civil* relations among men, by leading the inferiors, into whose heads those notions are infused, to a disesteem of their superiors; while they consider them as in a much *lower dispensation* than themselves; though those superiors are otherwise sober and good men, and regular attendants on the ordinances of religion?[2]

I have mentioned before what those exalted notions are. These do not tend to weaken either the *natural* or *civil* relations among men, or to lead inferiors to a disesteem of their superiors, even where those superiors are neither good nor sober men.

---

[1] See Ps. 119: 25; Phil. 2: 5.   [2] *Observations*, p. 10.

Query the seventh:

Whether a *gradual* improvement in grace and goodness is not a better
foundation of comfort and of an assurance of a gospel new birth, than
that which is founded on the doctrine of a *sudden* and *instantaneous*
change; which, if there be any such thing, is not easily distinguished 5
from fancy and imagination; the workings whereof we may well
suppose to be more *strong* and *powerful*, while the person considers
himself in the state of one who is admitted as a candidate for such
a change, and is taught in due time to expect it?[1]

Let us go one step at a time.   10

Q. (1). Whether a *gradual* improvement in grace and goodness is
not a good foundation of comfort?

A. Doubtless it is, if by grace and goodness be meant the knowledge and love of God through Christ.

Q. (2). Whether it be not a good *foundation* of an assurance of 15
a gospel new birth?

A. If we daily grow in this knowledge and love, it is a good *proof*
that we are born of the Spirit. But this does in no wise supersede
the previous witness of God's Spirit with ours, that we are the
children of God.[2] And this is properly the *foundation* of the assurance 20
of faith.

Q. (3). Whether this improvement is not a better foundation of
comfort and of an assurance of the gospel new birth than *that* which
is founded on the doctrine of a sudden and instantaneous change?

A. A better foundation than that—*that*? What? To what substan- 25
tive does this refer? According to the rules of grammar (for all the
other substantives are in the genitive case, and consequently to be
considered as only parts of that which governs them) you must
mean 'a better foundation than that foundation which is founded on
this doctrine'. As soon as I understand the question, I will endeavour 30
to answer it.

Q. (4). Can that *sudden* and *instantaneous* change be easily distinguished from fancy and imagination?

A. Just as easily as light from darkness, seeing it brings forth
with it a peace that passeth all understanding,[3] a joy unspeakable, 35

---

[1] *Observations*, p. 10.

[2] Rom. 8: 16. See below, V. 9, and Wesley's sermon, 'The Witness of the Spirit',
preached from this text.

[3] See Phil. 4: 7.

full of glory,[1] the love of God and all mankind filling the heart, and power over all sin.

_Q_. (5). May we not well suppose the workings of imagination to be more *strong* and *powerful* in one who is taught to expect such a change?

A. Perhaps we may. But still the tree is known by its fruits.[2] And such fruits as those above mentioned imagination was never yet *strong* enough to produce, nor any power save that of the Almighty.

7. There is only one clause in the eighth query which falls under our present inquiry:

> They make it their *principal* employ, wherever they go, to instil into people a few *favourite tenets* of their own; and this with such diligence and zeal as if the whole of Christianity depended upon them, and all efforts toward the true Christian life, without a belief of those tenets, were vain and ineffectual.[3]

I plead guilty to this charge. I do make it my principal, nay, my whole employ, and that wherever I go, to instil into the people a few 'favourite tenets'. (Only be it observed they are not *my own* but his that sent me.) And it is undoubtedly true that this I do (though deeply conscious of my want both of zeal and diligence) as if the whole of Christianity depended upon them, and all efforts without them were void and vain.

I frequently sum them all up in one: 'In Christ Jesus (i.e. according to his gospel) neither circumcision availeth anything, nor uncircumcision, but faith which worketh by love.'[4] But many times I instil them one by one, under these or the like expressions: 'Thou shalt love the Lord thy God with all thy heart, and with all thy mind, and with all thy soul, and with all thy strength. . . . Thou shalt love thy neighbour as thyself'[5]—as thy own soul, as Christ loved us; 'God is love; and he that dwelleth in love dwelleth in God, and God in him';[6] 'Love worketh no ill to his neighbour; therefore love is the fulfilling of the law';[7] 'While we have time let us do good unto all men, especially unto them that are of the household of faith';[8] 'Whatsoever ye would that men should do unto you, even so do unto them.'[9]

These are my 'favourite tenets', and have been for many years. O that I could instil them into every soul throughout the land!

---

[1] I Pet. I: 8.   [2] See Matt. 12: 33.   [3] *Observations*, p. 11.
[4] Gal. 5: 6.   [5] Cf. Mark 12: 30–1.   [6] I John 4: 16.
[7] Rom. 13: 10.   [8] Cf. Gal. 6: 10.   [9] Cf. Matt. 7: 12.

Ought they not to be instilled with such diligence and zeal as if the whole of Christianity depended upon them? For who can deny that all efforts toward a Christian life, without more than a bare belief, without a thorough *experience* and *practice* of these, are utterly vain and ineffectual?

8. Part of your ninth query is to the same effect:

> A few young heads . . . set up their own schemes as the great standard of Christianity, and . . . indulge their own notions to such a degree as to perplex, unhinge, terrify, and distract the minds of multitudes of people who have lived from their infancy under a gospel ministry and in the regular exercise of a gospel worship; and all this by persuading them that they . . . neither are nor can be true Christians, but by adhering to *their doctrines.*[1]

What do you mean by *their own* schemes? Their *own* notions? *Their* doctrines? Are they not *yours* too? Are they not the schemes, the notions, the doctrines of Jesus Christ? The great, fundamental truths of his gospel? Can you deny one of them without denying the Bible? 'It is hard for you to kick against the pricks'![2]

'They persuade (you say) multitudes of people that they cannot be true Christians but by adhering to their doctrines.' Why, who says they can? Whosoever he be, I will prove him to be an infidel. Do *you* say that any man can be a true Christian without loving God and his neighbour? Surely you have not so learned Christ! It is *your* doctrine as well as *mine* and St. Paul's: 'Though I speak with the tongues of men and angels; though I have all knowledge, and all faith; though I give all my goods to feed the poor, yea, my body to be burned, and have not love, I am nothing.'[3]

Whatever public worship, therefore, people may have attended, or whatever ministry they have lived under from their infancy, they must at all hazards be convinced of this, or they perish for ever: Yea, though that conviction at first 'unhinge' them ever so much; though it should, in a manner, 'distract' them for a season. For it is better that they should be 'perplexed' and 'terrified' now, than that they should sleep on and awake in hell.

9. In the tenth, twelfth, and thirteenth queries I am not concerned. But you include me also when you say in the eleventh: 'They absolutely deny that recreations of any kind, considered as such, are or can be innocent.'[4]

---

[1] *Observations*, p. 12.   [2] Acts 9: 5, 26: 14.
[3] Cf. 1 Cor. 13: 1–3.   [4] *Observations*, p. 13.

I cannot find any such assertion of mine, either in the place you refer to[1] or any other. But what kinds of recreation are innocent it is easy to determine by that plain rule: 'Whether ye eat or drink, or whatever ye do, do all to the glory of God.'[2]

5   I am now to take my leave of you for the present. But first I would earnestly entreat you to acquaint yourself what our doctrines are before you make any farther *Observations* upon them. Surely, touching the nature of salvation we agree that 'pure religion and undefiled is this, to visit the fatherless and widows in their affliction' 10 —to do all possible good from a principle of love to God and man; 'and to keep ourselves unspotted from the world'[3]—inwardly and outwardly to abstain from all evil.

10. With regard to the *condition* of salvation, it may be remembered that I allow not only faith, but likewise holiness or 15 universal obedience, to be the ordinary condition of *final* salvation. And that when I say faith alone is the condition of *present* salvation, what I would assert is this: (1), that without faith no man can be saved from his sins, can be either inwardly or outwardly holy; and (2), that at what time soever faith is given, holiness commences 20 in the soul; for that instant 'the love of God (which is the source of holiness) is shed abroad in the heart'.[4]

But it is objected by the author of *The Notions of the Methodists [Farther] Disproved*: 'St. James says, "Can faith save him?"'[5] I answer, 'Such a faith as is without works cannot *bring a man to* 25 *heaven*.' But this is quite beside the present question.

You object, (2), 'St. Paul says that "faith made perfect by love", St. James that "faith made perfect by works" is the condition of salvation.'[6] You mean final salvation. I say so too. But this also is beside the question.

30   You object, (3), that 'the belief of the Gospel'[7] is called 'the obedience of faith';[8] and (4), that what Isaiah terms 'believing'

----

[1] Gibson had cited 'Wesley's Journal II, p. 13'. It seems clear that Wesley consulted the second edition of 1743, finding nothing applicable. If he had turned to the first edition, however, he would have found the entry to which Gibson surely referred, under the date March 2, 1738, Wesley's resolutions about his personal behaviour, of which the second read: 'To labour after continual seriousness, not willingly indulging myself in any the least levity of behaviour, or in laughter; no, not for a moment.'

[2] Cf. 1 Cor. 10: 31.   [3] Cf. Jas. 1: 27.   [4] Cf. Rom. 5: 5.

[5] *Notions Farther Disproved*, p. 30: cf. Jas. 2: 14.

[6] Ibid., p. 31; cf. Gal. 5: 6, and Jas. 2: 22.   [7] Cf. Mark 1: 15.

[8] *Notions Farther Disproved*, p. 31. See Rom. 1: 5, cited by the author, and also in Wesley's text.

St. Paul terms 'obeying'.[1] Suppose I grant you both the one and the other, what will you infer?

You object, (5), that in one Scripture our Lord is styled 'the saviour of them that believe', and in another 'the author of eternal salvation to all them that obey him'.[2] (6). That to the Galatians St. Paul writes, 'Neither circumcision availeth anything, nor uncircumcision, but faith which worketh by love', and to the Corinthians, 'Circumcision is nothing, and uncircumcision is nothing, but the keeping the commandments of God.'[3] And hence you conclude, 'There are several texts of Scripture wherein unbelief and disobedience are equivalently used.'[4] Very true. But can you conclude from thence that we are not *saved by faith alone*?

11. You proceed to answer some texts which I had quoted. The first is Eph. 2. 8: 'By grace ye are saved through faith.' 'But (say you) faith does not mean here that grace especially so called, but includes also obedience.'[5] But how do you prove this? That circumstance you had forgot, and so run off with a comment upon the context, to which I have no other objection than that it is nothing at all to the question.

Indeed some time after you add, 'It is plain then that good works are always, in St. Paul's judgment, joined with faith' (so undoubtedly they are, that is, as an effect is always joined with its cause); 'and therefore we are not saved by faith alone'.[6] I cannot possibly allow the consequence.

You afterwards cite two more texts, and add, 'You see mere faith cannot be a condition of justification.'[7] You are out of your way. We are no more talking now of justification than of final salvation.

In considering Acts 16: 31, 'Believe in the Lord Jesus and thou shalt be saved', you say again: 'Here the word "believe" does not signify faith only . . . Faith necessarily produces charity and repentance; therefore these are expressed by the word "believe".'[8] I.e., faith necessarily produces holiness. Therefore holiness is a condition of holiness. I want farther proof. That Paul and Silas 'spake unto him the word of the Lord', and that his faith did in 'the same hour' work by love, I take to be no proof at all.[9]

---

[1] Ibid., p. 31. The author compares Isa. 53: 1, and Rom. 10: 16.
[2] Ibid., p. 31, comparing 1 Tim. 4: 10, and Heb. 5: 9.
[3] Ibid., pp. 31–2, comparing Gal. 5: 6, and 1 Cor. 7: 19 (mis-cited as 1 Cor. 7: 12).
[4] Ibid., p. 32.   [5] Ibid.   [6] Ibid., pp. 32–3.
[7] Ibid., p. 34; the texts were Acts 26: 20 and Acts 26: 18.
[8] Ibid., p. 33.   [9] Ibid., p. 34; cf. Acts 16: 32–3.

You then undertake to show that confessing our sins is a condition of justification, and that a confidence in the love of God is not a condition. Some of your words are: 'This, good sir, give me leave to say, is the greatest nonsense and contradiction possible. It is
5 impossible you can understand this jargon yourself, and therefore you labour in vain to make it intelligible to others. You soar aloft on eagle's wings, and leave the poor people to gape and stare after you.'[1]

This is very pretty and very lively. But it is nothing to the purpose,
10 for we are not now speaking of justification. Neither have I said one word of 'the condition of justification' in the whole tract to which you here refer.

'In the next place (say you) if we are saved (finally, you mean) only by a confidence in the love of God. . . .'[2] Here I must stop you
15 again; you are now running beside the question on the other hand. The sole position which I here advance is this: true believers are saved from inward and outward sin by faith. By faith alone the love of God and all mankind is shed abroad in their hearts,[3] bringing with it the mind that was in Christ, and producing all holiness of
20 conversation.

IV. 1. I am now to consider what has been lately objected with regard to the *nature* of saving faith.

The author last mentioned cannot understand how 'those texts of St. John are at all to the purpose':[4] 'Behold what manner of love
25 the Father hath bestowed upon us, that we should be called the sons of God.'[a] And, 'We love him, because he first loved us.'[b] I answer, (1), these texts were not produced in the [*Earnest*] *Appeal* by way of proof, but of illustration only. But, (2), I apprehend they may be produced as a proof, both that Christian faith implies a
30 confidence in the love of God, and that such a confidence has a direct tendency to salvation, to holiness both of heart and life.

'Behold what manner of love the Father hath bestowed upon us, that we should be called the sons of God!' Are not these words an expression of Christian faith? As direct an one as can well be
35 conceived? And I appeal to every man whether they do not express the strongest confidence of the love of God? Your own comment

[a] 1 John 3: 1.   [b] 1 John 4: 19.

[1] *Notions Farther Disproved*, p. 35.   [2] Ibid., p. 36.   [3] See Rom. 5: 5.
[4] *Notions Farther Disproved*, pp. 36–7, referring to Wesley's *An Earnest Appeal*, § 57.

puts this beyond dispute: 'Let us consider attentively and with grateful hearts the great love and mercy of God in calling us to be his sons, and bestowing on us the privileges belonging to such.'[1] Do you not perceive that you have given up the cause? You have yourself taught us that these words imply 'a sense of the great love 5 and mercy of God in bestowing upon us the privileges belonging to his sons'.

The Apostle adds, 'Beloved, now are we the sons of God; and it doth not yet appear what we shall be. But we know that when he shall appear, we shall be like him; for we shall see him as he is.'[2]   10

I suppose no one will say, either that these words are not expressive of Christian faith, or that they do not imply the strongest confidence in the love of God. It follows, 'And every man that hath this hope in him, purifieth himself, even as he is pure.'[3]

Hence it appears that this faith is a saving faith; that there is the 15 closest connexion between this faith and holiness. This text therefore is directly to the purpose in respect of both the propositions to be proved.

The other is: 'We love him, because he first loved us.' And here also, for fear I should fail in the proof, you have drawn it up ready to 20 my hands.

'God sent his only Son . . . to redeem us from sin by purchasing for us grace and salvation. By which grace we . . . through faith and repentance have our sins pardoned. . . . And therefore we are bound to return the tribute of our love and gratitude, and to obey him 25 faithfully as long as we live.'[4]

Now, that we have our sins pardoned, if we do not *know* they are pardoned, cannot bind us either to love or obedience. But if we do know it, and by that very knowledge or confidence in the pardoning love of God are both bound and enabled to love and obey 30 him, this is the whole of what I contend for.

2. You afterwards object against some other texts which I had cited to illustrate the nature of saving faith. My words were, 'Hear believing Job declaring his faith: "I know that my Redeemer liveth." '[5] I here affirm two things: (1), that Job was then a believer; 35 (2), that he declared his faith in these words. And all I affirm, you allow. Your own words are, 'God was pleased to bestow upon him

---

[1] Ibid.   [2] 1 John 3: 2.   [3] 1 John 3: 3.
[4] *Notions Farther Disproved*, p. 37.
[5] Job 19: 25. See *Notions Farther Disproved*, pp. 52–3, and *An Earnest Appeal*, § 60.

a strong assurance of his favour, . . . to inspire him with a prophecy
of the resurrection, and that he should have a share in it.'[1] I went
on, 'Hear Thomas (when having seen, he believed) crying out, "My
Lord and my God."' Hereon you comment thus: 'The meaning of
5 which is that St. Thomas . . . makes a confession both of his faith
and repentance.'[2] I agree with you. But you add, 'In St. Thomas's
confession there is not implied any assurance of pardon.' You
cannot agree with yourself in this, but immediately subjoin, 'If it
did imply such an assurance, he might well have it, since he had an
10 immediate revelation of it from God himself.'[3]

Yet a little before you endeavoured to prove that one who was not
a whit behind the very chief apostles had not such an assurance:
where, in order to show that faith does not imply this, you said,
'St. Paul methinks has fully determined this point, 1 Cor. 4: 4;
15 "I know nothing by myself", says he, "yet am I not hereby justified." . . . And if an apostle so illuminated don't think himself
justified'[4], then, I grant, he has fully determined the point. But
before you absolutely fix upon that conclusion, be pleased to remember your own comment that follows, on those other words of
20 St. Paul: 'The life I now live, I live by faith in the Son of God, who
loved me, and gave himself for me.' Your words are, 'And no
question a person endowed with such extraordinary gifts, might
arrive at a very eminent degree of assurance.'[5] So he *did* 'arrive at
a very eminent degree of assurance', though he *did not* 'think him-
25 self justified'!

I can scarce think you have read over that chapter to the Colossians; else surely you would not assert that those words on which
the stress lies, viz., 'Who hath delivered us from the power of darkness, and hath translated us into the kingdom of his dear Son: In
30 whom we have redemption through his blood, even the forgiveness of
sins'[6] 'do not relate to Paul and Timothy who wrote the epistle, but
to the Colossians to whom they wrote'.[7] I need be at no pains to
answer this; for presently after your own words are, 'He hath made
us, meaning the Colossians as well as himself, meet to be inheritors.'[8]

35   3. You may easily observe that I quoted the Council of Trent by
memory, not having the book then by me. I own, and thank you for

---

[1] *Notions Farther Disproved*, p. 54.
[2] Ibid., p. 55; cf. *An Earnest Appeal*, § 60, and John 20: 28.
[3] Ibid., p. 55.   [4] Ibid., p. 51.
[5] Ibid., pp. 55–6; see Gal. 2: 20.   [6] Col. 1: 13, 14.
[7] *Notions Farther Disproved*, p. 56.   [8] Ibid.; cf. Col. 1: 12.

correcting my mistake; but in correcting one you make another, for
the Decrees of the Sixth Session were not 'published on the thirteenth of January', but the session itself began on that day.[1]

I cannot help reciting your next words, although they are not
exactly to the present question. 'The words of the twelfth Canon of
the Council of Trent are: "If any man shall say that justifying faith
is nothing else but a confidence in the divine mercy, remitting sins
for Christ's sake, and that this confidence is that alone by which we
are justified, let him be accursed".' You add, 'This, sir, I am sure
is true doctrine, and perfectly agreeable to the doctrine of our
Church. . . . And so you are not only anathematized by the Council
of Trent, but also condemned by our own Church. . . . Our Church
holds no such scandalous and disgraceful opinion. . . . According to
our Church, no man can have the true faith who has not a loving
heart. . . . Therefore faith is not a confidence that any man's sins
are actually forgiven, and he reconciled to God.'[2] (What have the
the premises to do with the conclusion?)

4. To decide this, let our Church speak for herself whether she
does not suppose and teach that *every particular believer* knows that
his sins are forgiven, and *he himself* is reconciled to God.

First then, our Church supposes and teaches every particular
believer to say concerning himself, 'In my baptism I was made
a member of Christ, a child of God, and an inheritor of the kingdom
of heaven. . . . And I thank God who hath called me to that state of
salvation. And I pray God that I may continue in the same to my
life's end.'[3]

Now does this person *know* what he says to be true? If not, it is
the grossest hypocrisy. But if he does, then he knows that *he in
particular* is reconciled to God.

The next words I shall quote may be a comment on these; may
God write them in our hearts!

A true Christian man is not afraid to die, who is the very member of
Christ, the temple of the Holy Ghost, the son of God, and the very
inheritor of the everlasting Kingdom of Heaven. But plainly contrary,

---

[1] Ibid., pp. 39-40. Wesley had claimed that the decrees of the sixth session of the
Council of Trent were published just after the Homilies, making it 'more than probable
that the very design of the Council was to anathematize the Church of England'. (*An
Earnest Appeal*, §§ 58, 59.) As a result of this criticism he revised the passage for the
third edition of 1744.

[2] *Notions Farther Disproved*, pp. 40-3.

[3] B.C.P., Catechism, second and fourth answers, somewhat paraphrased.

he not only puts away the fear of death, but wishes, desires, and longs heartily for it.[a]

Can this be, unless he has a sure confidence that he, in particular, is reconciled to God?

5 Men commonly fear death, first because of leaving their worldly goods and pleasures; (2). For fear of the pains of death; and, (3). For fear of perpetual damnation. But none of these causes trouble good men, because they stay themselves by true faith, perfect charity, and sure hope of endless joy and bliss everlasting.[b]

10 All these therefore have great cause to be full of joy, and not to fear death nor everlasting damnation. For death cannot deprive them of Jesus Christ; death cannot take him from us, nor us from him. Death not only cannot harm us, but also shall profit us and join us to God more perfectly. And thereof a Christian heart may surely be certified.

15 'It is God', saith St. Paul, 'which hath given us an earnest of his Spirit.'[1] As long as we be in the body, we are in a strange country. But we have a desire rather to be at home with God.[c]

He that runneth may read in all these words the confidence which our Church supposes every particular believer to have that he him-
20 self is reconciled to God. To proceed:

The only instrument of salvation required on our parts is faith, that is, a sure trust and confidence that God both hath and will forgive our sins, that he hath accepted us again into his favour, for the merits of Christ's death and passion.[d]

25 But here we must take heed that we do not halt with God through an unconstant, wavering faith. Peter coming to Christ upon the water, because he fainted in faith, was in danger of drowning. So we, if we begin to waver or doubt, it is to be feared lest we should sink as Peter did; not into the water, but into the bottomless pit of hell-fire. There-
30 fore I say unto you, that we must apprehend the merits of Christ's death by faith, and that with a strong and steadfast faith, nothing doubting but that Christ by his own oblation hath taken away our sins, and hath restored us again to God's favour.[e]

5. If it be still said that the Church speaks only of men in general,

---

[a] [*Homilies*,] Sermon against the Fear of Death, Part I.
[b] Ibid., Part II.   [c] Ibid.
[d] [*Homilies*,] Second Sermon on the Passion.   [e] Ibid.

---

[1] Cf. 2 Cor. 5: 5.

but not of the confidence of this or that particular person, even this last poor subterfuge is utterly cut off by the following words:

> *Thou*, O man, hast received the body of Christ which was once broken, and his blood which was shed for the remission of *thy* sin. Thou hast received his body, to have within *thee* the Father, the Son, and the Holy Ghost, for to endow *thee* with grace, and to comfort *thee* with their presence. Thou hast received his body to endow *thee* with everlasting righteousness, and *to assure thee* of everlasting bliss.[a]

I shall add but one passage more, from the first part of the Sermon on the Sacrament.

> Have a sure and constant faith, not only that the death of Christ is available for all the world, but that he hath made a full and sufficient sacrifice for *thee*, a perfect cleansing of *thy* sins, so that thou mayest say with the Apostle, he loved thee and gave himself for *thee*.[1] For this is to make Christ *thine own*, and to apply his merits unto *thyself*.[2]

Let every reasonable man now judge for himself what is the sense of our Church as to the *nature* of *saving faith*. Does it not abundantly appear that the Church of England supposes every particular believer to have a sure confidence that *his* sins are forgiven and *he himself* reconciled to God?[3] Yea, and how can the absolute necessity of this faith, this unwavering confidence, be more strongly or peremptorily asserted than it is in those words: 'If we begin to waver or doubt, it is to be feared lest we sink as Peter did, not into the water, but into the bottomless pit of hell-fire.'[4]

6. I would willingly dismiss this writer here. I had said in the *Earnest Appeal* (what I am daily more and more confirmed in) that this faith is usually given in a moment. This you greatly dislike. Your argument against it, if put into form, will run thus:

> They who first apprehended the meaning of the words delivered, then gave their assent to them, then had confidence in the promises to which they assented, and lastly, loved God, did not receive faith in a moment.

---

[a] [*Homilies*,] Sermon on the Resurrection [the italics are Wesley's].

---

[1] See Gal. 2: 20.
[2] *Homilies*, Concerning the Sacrament, Pt. I; the italics are Wesley's.
[3] Ibid., Of Salvation, Pt. II; see *An Earnest Appeal*, § 59.
[4] Ibid., Of the Passion, Pt. II.

But the believers mentioned in the Acts first apprehended the meaning of the words, then gave their assent, then had confidence in the promises, and lastly, loved God: therefore,

The believers mentioned in the Acts did not receive faith in a
5   moment.[1]

I deny the major. They might first apprehend, then assent, then confide, then love, and yet receive faith in a moment—in *that* moment wherein their general confidence became particular, so that each could say, '*My* Lord, and *my* God.'[2]

10   One paragraph more I will be at the pains to transcribe. 'You insinuate that the sacraments are only requisite to the well-being of a visible church, whereas the Church declares that the due administration of them is an essential property thereof. . . . I suppose you hinted this to gratify your loving disciples the Quakers.'[3]

15   This is flat and plain. Here is a fact positively averred, and a reason also assigned for it. Now do you take yourself to be a man of candour? I had almost said, of common honesty? My very words in the place referred to, are: 'A visible church is a company of faithful people. This is the essence of it. And the properties thereof are that
20   the pure word of God be preached therein, and the sacraments duly administered.'[4]

7. Before I take my leave, I cannot but recommend to you that advice of a wise and good man:

Be calm in arguing; for fierceness makes
25   Error a fault, and truth discourtesy.[5]

I am grieved at your extreme warmth. You are in a thorough ill-humour from the very beginning of your book to the end. This cannot hurt *me*, but it may *yourself*. And it does not at all help your cause. If you denounce against me all the curses from Genesis to the
30   Revelation they will not amount to one argument. I am willing (so far as I know myself) to be reproved either by you or any other. But whatever you do, let it be done in love, in patience, in meekness of wisdom.

V. 1. With regard to the Author of faith and salvation abundance
35   of objections have been made, it being a current opinion that 'Christians are not *now* to receive the Holy Ghost.'

---

[1] *Notions Farther Disproved*, pp. 57–8; cf. *An Earnest Appeal*, § 62.
[2] John 20: 28.   [3] *Notions Farther Disproved*, p. 59.
[4] *An Earnest Appeal*, § 76.   [5] George Herbert, 'The Church Porch', st. 52.

Accordingly, whenever we speak of the Spirit of God, of his operations in the souls of men, of his revealing unto us the things of God, or inspiring us with good desires or tempers, whenever we mention the feeling his mighty power working in us according to his good pleasure, the general answer we have to expect is: 'This is all rank *enthusiasm*. So it was with the apostles and first Christians. But only *enthusiasts* pretend to this now.'

Thus all the Scriptures, abundance of which might be produced, are set aside at one stroke, and whoever cites them as belonging to all Christians is set down for an enthusiast.

The first tract I have seen wrote expressly on this head is remarkably entitled, *The Operations of the Holy Spirit Imperceptible, and How Men may Know when they are under the Guidance and Influence of the Spirit.*[1]

You begin: 'As we have some among us who pretend to a more than ordinary guidance by the Spirit . . . (indeed I do not: I pretend to no other guidance than is ordinarily given to all Christians) it may not be improper to discourse on the operations of God's Holy Spirit. . . . To this end, be thou pleased, O gracious fountain of truth, to assist me with thy heavenly direction in speaking of thee.'[2]

Alas, sir, what need have you to speak any more? You have already granted all I desire, viz., that 'we may all now enjoy, and know that we do enjoy, the heavenly direction of God's Spirit'.

However, you go on, and observe that the *extraordinary gifts* of the Holy Ghost were granted to the first Christians only, but his *ordinary graces* to all Christians in all ages, both which you then attempt to enumerate—only suspending your discourse a little when 'some conceited enthusiasts' come in your way.

2. You next inquire, 'after what manner these graces are raised in our souls'? And answer, 'How to distinguish these heavenly motions from the natural operations of our minds we have no light to discover, the Scriptures . . . declaring that the operations of the Holy

---

[1] According to the sub-title this was 'A sermon preached at St. Nicolas Church in Newcastle upon Tyne, on Whitsunday, May 22, 1743.' Although Wesley leaves the work anonymous it was 'by Thomas Dockwray, M.A., Lecturer of the said church'. It was published by John White of Newcastle in a pamphlet of 23 pages, dedicated to the Mayor and Aldermen of the city. Wesley first visited Newcastle in May 1742, and awakened a remarkable popular response. Dockwray's sermon, like the two pamphlets by the author of *The Notions*, reflects the clerical reaction.

[2] Dockwray, *Operations*, pp. 5–6.

Spirit are not subject to any sensible *feelings* or perceptions. For what communications can there be between feelings which are properties peculiar to matter, and the suggestions of the Spirit . . . All reasonable Christians believe that he works his graces in us in an 5 imperceptible manner, and that there is no sensible difference between his and the natural operations of our minds.'¹

I conceive this to be the strength of your cause. To support that conclusion, that the operations of the Spirit are imperceptible, you here allege: (1). 'That all reasonable Christians believe this.' So you 10 say: but I want proof. (2). 'That there can be no communications (I fear you mistook the word) between the suggestions of the Spirit, and feelings which are properties peculiar to matter.' How? Are the feelings now in question, 'properties peculiar to matter'? The feeling of peace, joy, love? Or any feelings at all? I can no more understand 15 the philosophy than the divinity of this. (3). 'That the Scriptures declare, the operations of the Spirit are not subject to any sensible feelings.' You are here disproving, as you suppose, a proposition of mine. But are you sure you understand it? By 'feeling' I mean being inwardly conscious of. By 'the operations of the Spirit', I do 20 not mean the *manner* in which he operates, but the *graces* which he operates in a Christian. Now be pleased to produce those Scriptures which declare that a Christian cannot feel or perceive these operations.

3. Are you not convinced, sir, that you have laid to my charge 25 things which I know not? I do not 'gravely tell you (as much an enthusiast as you over and over affirm me to be) that I sensibly feel (in your sense) the motions of the Holy Spirit'.² Much less do I make this, any more than 'convulsions, agonies, howlings, roarings, and violent contortions of the body', either 'certain signs of men's 30 being in a state of salvation', or necessary in order thereunto.³ You might with equal justice and truth inform the world, and the worshipful the magistrates of Newcastle,⁴ that I make 'seeing the wind' or 'feeling the light' necessary to salvation.

Neither do I 'confound the extraordinary with the ordinary 35 operations of the Spirit'.⁵ And as to your last inquiry, 'What is the best proof of our being led by the Spirit?' I have no exception to

---

¹ Dockwray, *Operations*, pp. 11–12.   ² Cf. Ibid., p. 14.   ³ Ibid., pp. 14–15.
⁴ The sermon was dedicated to these men, apparently assembled officially in their regalia for a special Whit Sunday service.
⁵ Dockwray *Operations*, pp. 15–16.

that just and scriptural answer, which you your self have given
'A thorough change and renovation of mind and heart, and the
leading a new and holy life.'[1]

4. That I confound the *extraordinary* with the *ordinary* operations
of the Spirit, and therefore am an enthusiast, is also strongly urged 5
in a *Charge* delivered to his clergy and lately published by the Lord
Bishop of Lichfield and Coventry.[2]

An extract of the former part of this I subjoin in his Lordship's
words:

> I cannot think it improper to obviate the contagion of those *enthu-* 10
> *siastical* pretensions that have lately betrayed whole multitudes, either
> into presumption or melancholy. *Enthusiasm* indeed, when detected, is
> apt to create infidelity; and infidelity is so shocking a thing that many
> rather run into the other extreme, and take refuge in enthusiasm. But
> infidelity and enthusiasm seem now to act in concert against our 15
> established religion. As infidelity has been sufficiently opposed, I shall
> now lay before you the weakness of those enthusiastical pretensions.[a]
>
> Now to confute effectually, and strike at the root of those enthu-
> siastical pretensions . . .,
>
> First, I shall show that it is necessary to lay down some method for 20
> distinguishing real from pretended inspiration.[b]
>
> Many expressions occur in the New Testament concerning the
> operations of the Holy Spirit. But men of an enthusiastical temper have
> confounded passages of a quite different nature, and have jumbled
> together those that relate to the extraordinary operations of the Spirit 25
> with those that relate only to his ordinary influences. . . . It is therefore
> necessary to use some method for separating those passages relating to
> the operations of the Spirit that have been so misapplied to the service
> of enthusiastical pretenders.[c]
>
> I proceed therefore to show, Secondly, that a distinction is to be made 30
> between those passages of Scripture about the blessed Spirit that

---

[a] [Smalbroke, *Charge,*] pp. 1-2.   [b] [Ibid.,] p. 3.   [c] [Ibid.,] pp. 5-7.

---

[1] Ibid., pp. 17-19.

[2] See Richard Smalbroke, *A Charge deliver'd to the Reverend the Clergy in several
Parts of the Diocese of Lichfield and Coventry, in a Triennial Visitation of the same in
1741*, published by J. and P. Knapton of London in 1744, pp. (iv), 64. The bishop did
not name Wesley, but claimed that 'men of an enthusiastical temper . . . have confounded those passages . . . that relate to the extraordinary operations of the Spirit with
those that relate only to his ordinary influence' (p. 6; see Wesley's quotation below).
Wesley's quotations from the *Charge* are frequently little more than a précis of the
argument rather than an abridgment, though he picks up key words and phrases here
and there.

peculiarly belong to the primitive church, and those that relate to Christians in all ages.ᵃ

The exigencies of the apostolical age required the *miraculous* gifts of the Spirit. But these soon ceased. When therefore we meet in the
5   Scripture with an account of those extraordinary gifts, and likewise with an account of his ordinary operations, we must distinguish the one from the other. And that not only for our own satisfaction, but as a means to stop the growth of enthusiasm.ᵇ

And such a distinction ought to be made by the best methods of
10   interpreting the Scriptures; which most certainly are an attentive consideration of the occasion and scope of those passages, in concurrence with the general sense of the primitive church.ᶜ

I propose, Thirdly, to specify some of the chief passages of Scripture that are misapplied by modern enthusiasts, and to show that they are
15   to be interpreted chiefly, if not only, of the apostolical church, and that they very little, if at all, relate to the present state of Christians.ᵈ

I begin (says your lordship) with the original promise of the Spirit as made by our Lord a little before he left the world.

I must take the liberty to stop your lordship on the threshold.
20   I deny that this is the 'original promise of the Spirit'. I expect his assistance in virtue of many promises, some hundred years prior to this.

If you say, 'However, this is the original or first promise of the Spirit in the New Testament'—No, my Lord; those words were
25   spoken long before: 'He shall baptize you with the Holy Ghost, and with fire.'¹

Will you reply, 'Well, but this is the original promise made by our Lord,' I answer, Not so, neither. For it was before this Jesus himself 'stood and cried, If any man thirst, let him come unto me
30   and drink. He that believeth on me, as the Scripture hath said, out of his belly shall flow rivers of living water. And this he spake of the Spirit, which they should receive who believed on him.' (Οὗ ἔμελλον λαμβάνειν οἱ πιστεύσαντες εἰς αὐτόν.²) If I mistake not, this may more justly be termed our Lord's 'original promise of the Spirit'.
35   And who will assert that this is 'to be interpreted chiefly, if not only, of the apostolic church'?

5. Your lordship proceeds: 'It occurs in the fourteenth and

ᵃ [Smalbroke, *Charge*,] p. 7.   ᵇ [Ibid.,] pp. 7–10.   ᶜ [Ibid.,] p. 11.
ᵈ [Ibid.,] pp. 11–12.

---

¹ Matt. 3: 11.   ² Cf. John 7: 37–9.

sixteenth chapters of St. John's Gospel, in which he uses these words':—In what verses, my Lord? Why is not this specified?[a] Unless to furnish your Lordship with an opportunity of doing the very thing whereof you before complained, of 'confounding passages of a quite contrary nature, and jumbling together those that relate to the extraordinary operations of the Spirit with those that relate to his ordinary influences'?

You cite the words thus: 'When the Spirit of truth is come, he will guide you into all truth, and he will show you things to come.' (These are nearly the words that occur, chapter sixteen, verse thirteen.)

'And again, "The Comforter, which is the Holy Ghost, whom the Father will send in my name, he shall teach you all things, and bring all things to your remembrance, whatsoever I have said unto you."' These words occur in the fourteenth chapter at the twenty-sixth verse.

But, my Lord, I want the original promise still: the original (I mean) of those made in this very discourse. Indeed your margin tells us where it is (chapter fourteen, verse sixteen)—but the words appear not. Taken together with the context they [there] run thus:

> If ye love me, keep my commandments.
> And I will pray the Father, and he will give you another Comforter, that he may abide with you for ever:
> Even the Spirit of truth, whom the world cannot receive, because it seeth him not, neither knoweth him.[b]

My Lord, suffer me to inquire why you slipped over this text? Was it not (I appeal to the Searcher of your heart!) because you was conscious to yourself that it would necessarily drive you to that unhappy dilemma, either to assert that 'for ever', εἰς τὸν αἰῶνα, meant only sixty or seventy years, or to allow that the text must be interpreted of the *ordinary* operations of the Spirit in all future ages of the church?

And indeed that the promise in this text belongs to all Christians evidently appears, not only from your lordship's own concession, and from the text itself (for who can deny that this Comforter or Paraclete is now given to all them that believe?), but also from the

---

[a] I take it for granted that the citation of texts in the margin, which is totally wrong, is a blunder of the printer's. [The marginal citations were of John 14: 16 (instead of 16: 13) and of John 16: 13 (instead of 14: 26).]

[b] John 14: 15–17.

preceding, as well as following, words. The preceding are, 'If ye love me, keep my commandments. And I will pray the Father.' None surely can doubt but these belong to all Christians in all ages. The following words are, 'Even the Spirit of truth, whom the world cannot receive.' True, the *world* cannot; but *all Christians* can and will receive him *for ever*.

6. The second promise of the Comforter made in this chapter, together with its context, stands thus:

Judas saith unto him (not Iscariot), Lord, how is it that thou wilt manifest thyself unto us, and not unto the world?

Jesus answered and said unto him, If any man love me, he will keep my word. And my Father will love him, and we will come unto him, and make our abode with him.

He that loveth me not, keepeth not my word: and the word which ye hear is not mine, but the Father's which sent me.

These things have I spoken unto you, being yet with you.

But the Comforter, which is the Holy Ghost, whom the Father will send in my name, he will teach you all things, and bring all things to your remembrance, whatsoever I have said unto you.[a]

Now, how does your lordship prove that this promise belongs only to the primitive church? Why, (1), you say, 'It is very clear from the bare recital of the words.'[1] I apprehend not. But this is the very question, which is not to be begged, but proved. (2). You say, 'The Spirit's "bringing all things to their remembrance, whatsoever he had said unto them", cannot possibly be applied to any other persons but the apostles.'[2] 'Cannot be applied'! This is a flat begging the question again, which I cannot give up without better reasons. (3). 'The gifts of prophecy, and of being "guided into all truth, and taught all things", can be applied only to the apostles, and those of that age who were immediately inspired.'[3] Here your lordship, in order the more plausibly to beg the question, again 'jumbles together the extraordinary with the ordinary operations of the Spirit'.[4] The gift of prophecy, we know, is one of his extraordinary operations; but there is not a word of it in this text. Nor therefore ought it to be 'confounded with his ordinary operations', such as the being 'guided into all truth'[5] (all that is necessary to salvation), and

[a] John 14: 22–6.

[1] Smalbroke, *Charge*, p. 12.   [2] Ibid., p. 13.   [3] Ibid., p. 13.
[4] Ibid., p. 6: cf. § 4 above.   [5] John 16: 13.

'taught all (necessary) things', in a due use of the means he hath ordained.[a]

In the same manner, namely, in a serious and constant use of proper means, I believe the assistance of the Holy Ghost is given to all Christians, to 'bring all things *needful* to their remembrance, whatsoever Christ hath spoken to them'[1] in his Word. So that I see no occasion to grant, without some kind of proof (especially considering the occasion of this, and the scope of the preceding verses) that even 'this promise cannot possibly be applied to any other persons but the apostles'.

7. In the same discourse of our Lord we have a third promise of the Comforter. The whole clause runs thus:

> If I go not away, the Comforter will not come unto you; but if I go, I will send him unto you.
> And when he is come, he will reprove (or convince) the world of sin, and of righteousness, and of judgment:
> Of sin, because they believe not on me:
> Of righteousness, because I go to my Father, and ye see me no more:
> Of judgment, because the prince of this world is judged.
> I have yet many things to say unto you, but ye cannot bear them now. But when he shall come, the Spirit of truth, he will guide you into all truth: . . . And he will show you things to come.[b]

There is only one sentence here which has not already been considered: 'He will show you things to come.'

And this, it is granted, relates to the gift of prophecy—one of the *extraordinary* operations of the Spirit.

The general conclusion which your lordship draws is expressed in these words: 'Consequently all pretensions to the Spirit, in the proper sense of the words of this promise (i.e. of these several texts of St. John) are vain and insignificant, as they are claimed by modern enthusiasts.'[2] And in the end of the same paragraph you add: 'None but the ordinary operations of the Spirit are to be now expected, since those that are of a miraculous or extraordinary kind are . . . *not pretended to*, even by modern enthusiasts.'[3]

My Lord, this is surprising. I read it over and over, before I could credit my own eyes. I verily believe this one clause, with

[a] John 14: 26.   [b] John 16: 7–13.

Cf. John 14: 26.   [2] Smalbroke, *Charge*, p. 13.   [3] Ibid., pp. 14–15.

unprejudiced persons, will be an answer to the whole book. You
have been vehemently crying out all along against those enthusiastical pretenders; nay, the very design of your book, as you openly
declare, was to stop the growth of their enthusiasm who 'have had
5 the assurance (as you positively affirm, page six) to claim to themselves the extraordinary operations of the Holy Spirit'. And here
you as positively affirm that those extraordinary operations 'are
not pretended to by them at all'!

8. Yet your lordship proceeds: 'The next passage of Scripture
10 I shall mention as peculiarly belonging to the primitive times,
though misapplied to the present state of Christians by modern
enthusiasts, is what relates to the "testimony of the Spirit", and
"praying by the Spirit", in the eighth chapter of the Epistle to the
Romans.'ᵃ

15 I believe it incumbent upon me thoroughly to weigh the force of
your lordship's reasoning on this head. You begin, 'After St. Paul
had treated of that spiritual principle in Christians, which enables
them "to mortify the deeds of the body",¹ he says, "if any man have
not the Spirit of Christ, he is none of his".² This makes the distinc-
20 tion of a true Christian, particularly in opposition to the Jews.'³
I apprehend it is just here that your lordship turns out of the way,
when you say, 'Particularly in opposition to the Jews.' Such a
particular opposition I cannot allow, till some stronger proof is
produced than St. Paul's occasionally mentioning six verses before
25 'the imperfection of the Jewish law'.⁴

Yet your lordship's mind is so full of this that after repeating the
fourteenth and fifteenth verses— 'as many as are led by the Spirit of
God, they are the sons of God: For ye have not received the spirit
of bondage again to fear; But ye have received the spirit of adoption,
30 whereby we cry, Abba, Father!'—you add: 'In the former part of
this verse the Apostle shows again the imperfection of the Jewish
law.'⁵ This also calls for proof. Otherwise, it will not be allowed that
he here speaks of the *Jewish* law at all—not though we grant that
'the Jews were subject to the fear of death, and lived in consequence
35 of it in a state of bondage'.⁶ For are not all unbelievers, as well as
the Jews, more or less in the same fear and bondage?

ᵃ [Smalbroke, *Charge*,] p. 16 [Cf. Rom. 8: 26, 27].

¹ Rom. 8: 13; cf. verses 4-8.   ² Rom. 8: 9.
³ Smalbroke, *Charge*, pp. 16-17.   ⁴ Ibid., p. 17. The bishop cited 'v. 2, 3, etc.'.
⁵ Ibid., p. 17.   ⁶ Ibid., pp. 17-18.

Your lordship goes on: 'In the latter part of the verse he shows the superiority of the Christian law to that of the Jews.'[a] Where is the proof, my Lord? How does it appear that he is speaking either of the Christian or Jewish law in those words, 'Ye have received the spirit of adoption, whereby we cry, Abba, Father'? However, you infer 'Christians then are the adopted sons of God, in contradistinction to the Jews, as the former had the gifts of the Holy Ghost, which none of the latter had at that time, and the body of the Jews never had.'[1] No, nor 'the body of the Christians' neither. So that if this be a proof against the Jews, it is the very same against the Christians.

I must observe farther on the preceding words: (1), that your lordship begins here to take the word 'Christians' in a new and peculiar sense, for the whole body of the then Christian church; (2), that it is a bad inference, 'as, or because they had the gifts of the Holy Ghost, therefore they were the sons of God'. On the one hand, if they were the children of God it was not because they had those gifts. On the other, a man may have all those gifts, and yet be a child of the devil.

9. I conceive, not only that your lordship has proved nothing hitherto, not one point that has any relation to the question; but that strictly speaking you have not attempted to prove anything, having taken for granted whatever came in your way. In the same manner you proceed: 'The Apostle goes on, "the Spirit itself beareth witness with our spirit, that we are the children of God".[2] This passage, as it is connected with the preceding one, relates to the general adoption of Christians, or their becoming the sons of God instead of the Jews.'[3] 'This passage relates'—How is that proved? By its connection with the preceding? In no wise, unless it be good arguing to prove *ignotum per ignotius*.[4] It has not yet been proved that the preceding passage itself has any relation to this matter.

Your lordship adds: 'But what was the ground of this preference that was given to Christians? It was plainly the (miraculous) *gifts of the Spirit* which they had, and which the Jews had not.'[5] This

[a] [Ibid.,] p. 18.

---

[1] Ibid., p. 18.   [2] Rom. 8: 16.   [3] Smalbroke, *Charge*, p. 18.
[4] 'The unknown explained by the more unknown'; a proverbial expression. Cf. Chaucer, *The Canon's Yeoman's Tale*, 1457, and Wesley, Sermon 72, 'Of Evil Angels', II. 12, where he furnishes a translation.
[5] Smalbroke, *Charge*, pp. 18–19.

preference given to Christians was just before expressed by their becoming the sons of God instead of the Jews. Were the gifts of the Spirit then the ground of this preference? The ground of their becoming the sons of God? What an assertion is this! And how little
5 is it mended, though I allow that 'these miraculous gifts of the Spirit were a testimony that God acknowledged the Christians to be his people and not the Jews, since the Christians who worked miracles did it not "by the works of the law", but "by the hearing of faith"!'[1]

Your lordship concludes, 'From these passages of St. Paul, com-
10 pared together, it clearly follows that the forementioned testimony of the Spirit . . . was the *public* testimony of miraculous gifts . . . And, consequently, "the witness of the Spirit that we are the children of God" cannot possibly be applied to the *private* testimony of the Spirit given to our own consciences, as is pretended by modern
15 enthusiasts.'[2]

If your conclusion, my lord, will stand without the premises, it may; but that it has no manner of connection with them I trust does partly, and will more fully, appear when we view the whole passage to which you refer. And I believe that passage, with very little
20 comment, will prove in direct opposition to that conclusion, that the testimony of the Spirit there mentioned is not the public testimony of miraculous gifts, but must be applied to the private testimony of the Spirit given to our own consciences.

10. St. Paul begins the eighth chapter of his Epistle to the Romans
25 with the great privilege of every Christian believer (whether Jew or Gentle before): 'There is now no condemnation for them that are in Christ Jesus', engrafted into him by faith, 'who walk not after the flesh, but after the Spirit'. For now every one of them may truly say 'The law (or power) of the spirit of life in Christ Jesus (given
30 unto me for his sake) hath made me free from the law (or power) of sin and death. For that which the law could not do, in that it was weak through the flesh, God sending his own Son in the likeness of sinful flesh, and for sin' did; when he 'condemned (crucified, put to death, destroyed) sin in the flesh: that the righteousness of the
35 law might be fulfilled in us, who walk not after the flesh, but after the Spirit. For they that are after the flesh mind the things of the flesh; but they that are after the Spirit, the things of the Spirit.'[a]

[a] Rom. 8: 1–5.

[1] Smalbroke, *Charge*, p. 19, quoting Gal. 3: 2, 5.
[2] Ibid., p. 20, quoting Rom. 8: 16.

Is it not evident that the Apostle is here describing a true
Christian, a holy believer? In opposition, not particularly to a Jew,
much less to the Jewish law, but to every unholy man, to all,
whether Jews or Gentiles, 'who walk after the flesh'? He goes on:
'For to be carnally minded is death; but to be spiritually minded is 5
life and peace. Because the carnal mind is enmity against God; for
it is not subject to the law of God, neither indeed can be. So then
they that are in the flesh cannot please God.'[a]

The opposition between a holy and an unholy man is still glaring
and undeniable. But can any man discern the least glimmering of 10
opposition between the Christian and the Jewish law?

The Apostle goes on:

> But ye are not in the flesh, but in the Spirit, if so be that the Spirit of
> God dwell in you. Now if any man have not the Spirit of Christ, he is
> none of His. But if Christ be in you, the body is dead because of (or 15
> with regard to) sin, but the Spirit is life because of righteousness. But
> if the Spirit of him that raised up Jesus from the dead dwell in you, he
> that raised up Christ from the dead shall also quicken your mortal
> bodies by his Spirit which dwelleth in you. Therefore, brethren, we
> are debtors, not to the flesh, to live after the flesh. For if ye live after 20
> the flesh ye shall die: but if ye through the Spirit do mortify the
> deeds of the body, ye shall live. For as many as are led by the Spirit of
> God, they are the sons of God.[b]

Is there one word here, is there any the least intimation, of
miraculous gifts, or of the Jewish law? 25

It follows, 'For ye have not received the spirit of bondage again,
to fear'; (such as all sinners have when they are first stirred up to
seek God, and begin to serve him from a slavish fear of punishment)
'but ye have received the spirit of adoption (of free love) whereby
we cry, Abba, Father! The Spirit itself' (which 'God hath sent 30
forth into our hearts, crying Abba, Father')[1] 'beareth witness with
our spirit, that we are the children of God'.[c]

I am now willing to leave it, without farther comment, to the
judgment of every impartial reader, whether it does not appear from
the whole scope and tenor of the text and context taken together 35
that this passage does not refer to the Jewish law nor to the public
testimony of miracles; neither of which can be dragged in without

---

[a] Rom. 8: 6–8.   [b] Rom. 8: 9–14.   [c] Rom. 8: 15–16.

[1] Cf. Gal. 4: 6.

putting the utmost force on the natural meaning of the words. And if so, it will follow that this witness of the Spirit is the private testimony given to our own consciences, which, consequently, all sober Christians may claim without any danger of enthusiasm.

5   11. 'But I go on (says your lordship, page twenty-one) to the consideration of the other passages in the same chapter, relating to our "praying by the Spirit", namely at verses twenty-six and twenty-seven, which run thus: "Likewise the Spirit also helpeth our infirmities: For we know not what we should pray for as we ought;
10 but the Spirit itself maketh intercession for us with groanings which cannot be uttered. And he that searcheth the hearts knoweth what is the mind of the Spirit, because he maketh intercession for the saints, according to the will of God."'

Here is a circumstance highly needful to be observed before we
15 enter upon this question. Your lordship undertakes to fix the meaning of an expression used by St. Paul in the fourteenth chapter of his first Epistle to the Corinthians. And in order thereto you laboriously explain part of the eighth chapter to the Romans. My lord, how is this? Will it be said, 'Why, this is often alleged to prove the wrong
20 sense of that Scripture'? I conceive, this will not salve the matter at all. Your lordship had before laid down a particular method as the only sure one whereby to distinguish what Scriptures belong to all Christians, and what do not. This method is, the considering the occasion and scope of those passages by comparing the text and
25 context together. You then propose, by the use of this method, to show that several texts have been misapplied by enthusiasts. One of these is the fifteenth verse of the fourteenth chapter of the first Epistle to the Corinthians. And to show that enthusiasts have misapplied this, you comment on the eighth chapter to the Romans.[1]
30   However, let us weigh the comment itself. The material part of it begins thus: 'Now he adds another proof of the truth of Christianity: "Likewise the Spirit helpeth our infirmities" or our "distresses", for ἀσθενείαις signifies both.' (I doubt that; I require authority for it.) 'And then he mentions in what instances he does so, viz., in prayers
35 to God about afflictions.' (In nothing else, my lord? Did he 'help

---

[1] Smalbroke's definition of his method has been epitomized by Wesley in V. 4 (pp. 141–2). The present section of *A Farther Appeal* clearly reflects Wesley's academic background. He had been lecturer in logic at Lincoln College (1726–30), and the rigorous dissection of an opponent's arguments came to him quite naturally. He is, of course, engaged in a detailed demonstration of the slipshod reasoning which he detected in Smalbroke's *Charge*.

their infirmities' in no other instance than this?) '"We know not (says he) what we should pray for as we ought"; that is, whether it be best for us to bear afflictions, or to be delivered from them. But the Spirit, or the gift of the Spirit, instructs us how to pray in a manner agreeable to the will of God.'ᵃ The Spirit, *or the gift of the* Spirit! What marvellous reasoning is this? If these 'are often put for each other', what then? How is that evinced to be the case here?

12. 'The Apostle goes on, "The Spirit itself maketh intercession for us, with groanings which cannot be uttered"; that is, the spiritual or inspired person prayed in that capacity for the whole assembly.'ᵇ 'That is'! Nay, that is again the very point to be proved; else we get not one step farther.

'The Apostle goes on thus (verse twenty-seven): "And he that searcheth the hearts knoweth what is the mind of the Spirit (that is, of the spiritual or inspired person), because he maketh intercession for the saints according to the will of God"; that is, God knows the intention of the spiritual person who has the gift of prayer, . . . which he uses for the benefit of the whole assembly. He, I say, leaves it entirely to God, whether it be best that they should suffer afflictions, or be delivered from them.'ᶜ

My lord, this is more astonishing than all the rest! I was expecting all along in reading the preceding pages (and so, I suppose, was every thinking reader) when your lordship would mention that the person miraculously inspired for that intent, and praying κατὰ Θεόν[1] either for the support or deliverance of the people, should 'have the very petition which he asked of him'.[2] Whereas you intended no such thing! But shut up the whole with that lame and impotent conclusion, 'He leaves it to God, whether it be best they should suffer afflictions, or be delivered from them.'

Had he then that miraculous gift of God, that he might do what any common Christian might have done without it? Why, any person in the congregation might have prayed thus. Nay, could not pray otherwise if he had the ordinary grace of God: 'Leaving it to God whether he should suffer afflictions still, or be delivered from them.' Was it *only* in the apostolical age that 'the Spirit instructed Christians *thus* to pray'? Cannot a man pray *thus*, either for himself or others, unless he have the *miraculous* gift of prayer? So, according

---

ᵃ [Smalbroke, *Charge*,] pp. 22-3.   ᵇ [Ibid.,] pp. 23-4.   ᶜ [Ibid.,] pp. 24-5.

---

[1] 'According to (the will of) God', Rom. 8: 27.   [2] Cf. 1 John 5: 15.

to your lordship's judgment, 'to pray in such a manner as in the event to leave the continuance of our sufferings or our deliverance from them, with a due submission, to the good pleasure of God', is one of those 'extraordinary operations of the Spirit' which none now
5 pretend to but 'modern enthusiasts'!

I beseech your lordship to consider. Can you coolly maintain that 'the praying with a due submission to the will of God', even in heavy affliction, is a miraculous gift? An extraordinary operation of the Holy Ghost? Is *this* peculiar to the primitive times? Is it what
10 none but enthusiasts now pretend to? If not, then your lordship's own account of 'praying by the Spirit' indisputably proves that this is one of the ordinary privileges of all Christians, to the end of the world.

13. 'I go on (your lordship adds) to another passage of Scripture
15 that has been entirely misapplied by modern enthusiasts. "And my speech and my preaching were not with enticing words of man's wisdom, but in demonstration of the Spirit and of power; that your faith should not stand in the wisdom of man, but in the power of God."[a] It is only necessary to evince that by the "demonstration
20 of the Spirit and of power" is meant the demonstration of the truth of Christianity, that arises from the prophecies of the Old Testament and the miracles of Christ and his apostles.'[b] Yet it is necessary farther to evince that these words have *no other* meaning. But first, how will you evince that they bear this? In order thereto your
25 lordship argues thus: 'The former *seems to be* the "demonstration of the Spirit" with regard to the prophetical testimonies of him. . . . And the "demonstrations of power" *must signify* the power of God exerted in miracles.'[c] 'Must'? Why so? That δύναμις often signifies miraculous power, is allowed. But what follows? That it *must mean*
30 so in this place? That still remains to be proved.

Indeed your lordship says this 'appears from the following verse, in which is assigned the reason for using this method of proving Christianity to be true, viz., "that your faith should not stand in the wisdom of man, but in the power of God". By the power of God,
35 *therefore*, must necessarily be understood the miracles performed by Christ and his apostles.'[1] By the illative particle, 'therefore', this proposition should be an inference from some other: but what other

---

[a] 1. Cor. 2: 4–5.   [b] [Smalbroke, *Charge*,] pp. 27, 29.   [c] [Ibid.,] pp. 29–30.

[1] Smalbroke, *Charge*, p. 30.

I cannot yet discern. So that for the present I can only look upon it as a fresh instance of begging the question.

'He goes on in the seventh, tenth, and following verses to explain this "demonstration of the Spirit and of power".'[1] But he does not say one syllable therein either of the ancient prophecies or of miracles. Nor will it be easily proved that he speaks either of one or the other, from the beginning of the chapter to the end.

After transcribing the thirteenth verse, 'which things also we speak, not in the words which man's wisdom teacheth, but which the Holy Ghost teacheth, comparing spiritual things with spiritual',[2] your lordship adds: 'From which last passage it appears that the words which the Holy Ghost is said to teach must be the prophetical revelations of the Old Testament, which were discovered to the apostles by the same Spirit.'[a] I cannot apprehend how this appears. I cannot as yet see any connection at all between the premisses and the conclusion.

Upon the whole I desire any calm and serious man to read over this whole chapter, and then he will easily judge what is the natural meaning of the words in question. And whether (although it be allowed that they were *peculiarly* fulfilled in the apostles, yet) they do not manifestly belong, in a lower sense, to every true minister of Christ? For what can be more undeniable than this, that *our* preaching also is vain unless it be attended with the power of that Spirit who alone pierceth the heart? And that your hearing is vain unless the same 'power be present to heal'[3] your soul, and to give *you* a faith which 'standeth not in the wisdom of man, but in the power of God'?

14. Another passage that your lordship thinks has been misapplied by enthusiasts, but was really peculiar to the times of the apostles, is 1 John 2: 20 and 27. 'Ye have an unction from the Holy One, and ye know all things. . . . But the anointing which ye have received of him abideth in you; and ye need not that any man teach you, but as the same anointing teacheth you of all things, and is truth, and is no lie. And even as it hath taught you, ye shall abide in him.'[b] 'Here the Apostle arms the true Christians against seducers by an argument drawn from the "unction from the Holy One", that was *in* or rather *among* them; that is, from the immediate inspiration of some of their teachers.'[c]

| [a] [Ibid.,] pp. 31–32. | [b] [Ibid.,] p. 35. | [c] [Ibid.,] p. 37. |

[1] Ibid.   [2] 1 Cor. 2: 13.   [3] Cf. Luke 5:17.

Here it rests upon your lordship to prove, as well as affirm, (1). That ἐν should be translated 'among'; (2). That this 'unction from the Holy One' means 'the inspiration of some of their teachers'.

The latter your lordship attempts to prove thus: 'The inspired
5 teachers of old were set apart for that office by an extraordinary effusion of the Holy Ghost: therefore "the unction from the Holy One" here means such an effusion.'[a] I deny the consequence, so the question is still to be proved.

Your lordship's second argument is drawn from the twenty-
10 sixth verse of the fourteenth chapter of St. John's gospel.

Proposed in form, it will stand thus:

If those words, 'He shall teach you all things', relate only to a miraculous gift of the Holy Ghost, then these words, 'The same anointing teacheth you of all things', relate to the same miraculous gift:
15 But those words relate only to a miraculous gift:
Therefore, these relate to the same.[b]

I conceive it will not be very easy to make good the consequence in the first proposition. But I deny the minor also, the contradictory whereto, I trust, has appeared to be true.
20 I grant indeed that these words were more *eminently* fulfilled in the age of the apostles. But this is altogether consistent with their belonging *in a lower sense* to all Christians, in all ages; seeing they have all need of an 'unction from the Holy One', a supernatural assistance from the Holy Ghost, that they may know, in the due use
25 of all proper means, all things needful for their souls' health. Therefore it is no enthusiasm to teach that the 'unction from the Holy One' belongs to all Christians in all ages.

15. There is one topic of your lordship's yet untouched; that is, authority—one you have very frequently made use of, and wherein,
30 probably, the generality of readers suppose your lordship's great strength lies.[1] And indeed when your lordship first mentioned 'the general sense of the primitive church',[c] I presumed you would have produced so numerous authorities that I should not easily be able

[a] [Smalbroke, *Charge*,] p. 38.   [b] [Ibid.,] pp. 38-40.   [c] [Ibid.,] p. 9.

[1] Richard Smalbroke was the author of a number of works on the New Testament and the early history of the Church—e.g. *The Pretended Authority of the Clementine Constitutions Confuted* (1714); *An Enquiry into the Authority of the . . . Complutensian Edition of the New Testament* (1722); *A Vindication of the Miracles of Our Saviour* (2 vols., 1729, 1731).

to consult them all. But I soon found my mistake, your lordship naming only Chrysostom, Jerome, Origen, and Athanasius.

However, though these four can no more be termed the primitive church than the church universal, yet I consent to abide by their suffrage. Nay, I will go a step farther still. If any two of these affirm 5 that those seven texts belong *only* to the apostolical age, and *not* to the Christians of succeeding times, I will give up the whole cause.

But let it be observed: if they should affirm that these primarily belong to the Christians of the apostolical age, that does not prove the point, because they may in a *secondary* sense belong to others, 10 notwithstanding; nor does any of them speak home to the question unless he maintain in express terms that these texts refer *only* to the miraculous gifts of the Spirit, and *not at all* to the state of *ordinary* Christians.

16. Concerning those three texts: John fourteen, verse sixteen 15 and twenty-six, and John sixteen, verse thirteen, 'I could easily add (says your lordship) the authorities of Chrysostom and the other ancient commentators.'ᵃ St. Chrysostom's authority I will consider now, and that of the others when they are produced.

It is granted that he interprets not only John 16: 13, but also both 20 the passages in the fourteenth chapter, as *primarily* belonging to the apostles. Yet part of his comment on the twenty-sixth verse is as follows:

> Such is that grace (of the Comforter) that if it finds sadness, it takes it away; if evil desire, it consumes it. It casts out fear, and suffers him 25 that receives it to be a man no longer, but translates him, as it were, into heaven. Hence 'none of them counted anything his own', but 'continued in prayer, with gladness and singleness of heart'.¹ For this chiefly is there need of the Holy Ghost. For the fruit of the Spirit is joy, peace, faith, meekness.² Indeed spiritual men often grieve; but that 30 grief is sweeter than joy. For whatever is of the Spirit is the greatest gain, as whatever is of the world is the greatest loss. Let us therefore in keeping the commandments (according to our Lord's exhortation, verse 15) secure the unconquerable assistance of the Spirit, and we shall be nothing inferior to angels.³   35

St. Chrysostom, here, after he had shown that the promise of the Comforter *primarily* belonged to the apostles (and whoever

---

ᵃ [Ibid.,] p. 15.

¹ Cf. Acts 2: 44, 46.   ² See Gal. 5: 22–3.
³ Chrysostom, *In Joannem*, lxxv (lxxiv). 5.

questioned it?) undeniably teaches that in a *secondary* sense it belongs to all Christians; to all spiritual men, all who keep the commandments. I appeal therefore to all mankind, whether his authority touching the promise of our Lord in these texts does not overthrow
5 the proposition it was cited to prove?

Although your lordship names no other author here, yet [on] page 42 you say: 'The assigned sense of these passages was confirmed by the authority of Origen.' It is needful therefore to add what occurs in his works with regard to the present question.

10 He occasionally mentions this promise of our Lord, in four several places. But it is in one only that he speaks pertinently to the point in hand, where his words are these: '"When the Spirit of truth is come, he will guide you into all truth", and "he will teach you all things". . . . The sum of all good things consists in this, that
15 a man be found worthy to receive the grace of the Holy Ghost. Otherwise, nothing will be accounted perfect in him who hath not the Holy Spirit.'ᵃ

Do these words confirm that 'sense of those passages' which your lordship had 'assigned'? Rather do they not utterly overturn it?
20 And prove (as above) that although this promise of our Lord primarily belongs to the apostles, yet in the secondary sense it belongs (according to Origen's judgment) to all Christians in all ages?

17. The fourth text mentioned as belonging to the first Christians
25 only is Rom. 8: 15, 16; and [on] page 26 it is said, 'This interpretation is confirmed by the authority of the most eminent Fathers.' The reader is particularly referred to Origen and Jerome *in locum*. But here seems to be a mistake of the name. 'Jerome *in locum*' should mean, Jerome 'upon the place', upon Rom. 8: 15, 16. But I cannot
30 perceive that there is one word upon that place in all St. Jerome's works.[1]

Nor indeed has Origen commented upon it, any more than Jerome. But he occasionally mentions it in these words:

He is a babe who is fed with milk; . . . but if he seeks the things that

---

ᵃ [Origen, *In Librum Jesu Nave* (*On the Book of Joshua*), iii. 2, in *Opera*,] Vol. II, p. 403, Edit. Bened. [ed. Charles Delarue, 4 vols., Paris, 1733–59.]

[1] The footnote in the *Charge*, p. 26, reads: 'See Origen, Jerome, etc., in loc.' Smalbroke may have been misled by the fact that a commentary on Romans (*Expositio in Epistolam ad Romanos*) was attributed to Jerome, but the work is spurious, and was apparently written by Pelagius. Cf. Migne, *Patrologia Latina*, XXX. 708c.

are above, . . . without doubt he will be of the number of those, who 'receive not the spirit of bondage again unto fear, but the spirit of adoption', through whom they 'cry Abba, Father'.[a]

Again:

> The fullness of time is come, . . . when they who are willing receive 5
> the adoption, as Paul teaches in these words, 'Ye have not received the spirit of bondage again unto fear; but ye have received the spirit of adoption whereby we cry, Abba, Father!' And it is written in the Gospel according to St. John,[1] to 'as many as received him, to them gave he power to become the sons of God, even to them that believe in his 10 name'.[b]

Yet again,

> Every one that is born of God, and doth not commit sin, by his very actions saith, 'Our Father which art in heaven', 'the Spirit itself bearing witness with their Spirit, that they are the children of God'.[c] 15

According to Origen therefore, this testimony of the Spirit is not any *public* testimony by miracles, peculiar to the first times, but an *inward* testimony, belonging in common to all that are born of God. And consequently the authority of Origen does not 'confirm that interpretation' neither; but absolutely destroys it. 20

18. The last authority your lordship appeals to on this text is 'that of the great John Chrysostom, who reckons the testimony of the "Spirit of adoption by which we cry, Abba, Father", . . . among the miraculous gifts of the Spirit. . . . I rather choose (your lordship adds, page 26) to refer you to the words of St. Chrysostom, than to 25 transcribe them here, as having almost translated them in the present account of the "testimony of the Spirit".'

However, I believe it will not be labour lost to transcribe a few of those words. It is in his comment on the fourteenth verse that he first mentions St. Paul's comparison between a Jew and 30

---

[a] [Ibid.,] Vol. I, p. 79. [In Delarue's edition of Origen, which on the basis of his own statement and the other citations Wesley would seem to have used here, the quotation is not found at this point, which embraces *De Principiis*, i. 2, 3. Perhaps a misprint is to blame.]

[b] [Ibid., *De Oratione (On Prayer)*, xxii. 2,] Vol. I, pp. 231, 232.

[c] Ibid. [op. cit., xxii. 3; the closing quotation is from Rom. 8: 16.]

---

[1] John 1: 12.

a Christian. How fairly your lordship has represented this, let every reader judge:

'As many as are led by the Spirit of God, they are the sons of God' . . . Whereas the same title had been given of old to the Jews also . . ., he shows in the sequel how great a difference there is between that honour and this. For though, says he, the titles are the same, yet the things are not. And he plainly proves it by comparing both what they had received, and what they looked for. And first he shows what they had received, viz., 'a spirit of bondage'. Therefore he adds, 'Ye have not received the spirit of bondage again unto fear: but ye have received the spirit of adoption.' What means 'the spirit of fear'? Observe their whole life, and you will know clearly. For punishments were at their heels, and much fear was on every side, and before their face. . . . But with us it is not so. For our mind and conscience are cleansed, . . . so that we do all things well, not for fear of present punishment, but through our love of God, and an habit of virtue. . . . They, therefore, though they were called sons, yet were as slaves; but we, being made free, have received the adoption, and look not for a land of milk and honey, but for heaven. . . .

He brings also another proof 'that we have the spirit of adoption, by which, (says he) we cry, Abba, Father'. . . . This is the first word we utter, μετὰ τάς θαυμαστάς ὠδῖνας εκείνας, καὶ τὸν ξένον καὶ παράδοξον λοχεθμάτων νόμον: after those amazing throes (or birth-pangs) and that strange and wonderful manner of bringing forth. . . .[1]

He brings yet another proof of the superiority of those who had 'this Spirit of adoption'. 'The Spirit itself beareth witness with our spirit that we are the children of God.' I prove this, says he, not only from the voice itself, but also from the cause whence that voice proceeds. For the Spirit suggests the words while we thus speak, which he hath elsewhere expressed more plainly: 'God hath sent forth the Spirit of his Son into our hearts, crying, Abba, Father!'[2] But what is 'The Spirit beareth witness with our spirit'? He means the Paraclete, by the gift given unto us. . . . (But that this was an extraordinary gift we have no intimation at all, neither before nor after). And when 'the Spirit beareth witness', what doubt is left? If a man or an angel spake, some might doubt. But when the Most High beareth witness to us, who can doubt any longer?[3]

---

[1] Chrysostom, *In Epistolam ad Romanos*, Homilia XIV, § 2. Presumably Wesley reproduced the Greek to indicate that he had consulted the original—which apparently he felt that Smalbroke had not done. His translation is clear and direct.

[2] Gal. 4: 6.

[3] Chrysostom, Homily 14 on Romans. (The bishop's *Charge* had cited Edit. Savil., Tom. 2, pp. 115, 120).

Now let any reasonable man judge how far your lordship has 'translated' the words of St. Chrysostom, and whether he 'reckons the testimony of the Spirit among the miraculous gifts of the Holy Ghost', or among those ordinary gifts of the Spirit of Christ, which if a man have not he is none of his.[1]

19. The fifth text your lordship quotes as describing a miraculous gift of the Spirit is First Corinthians, 2: 14, 15.[2] To prove which you comment on the eighth chapter to the Romans, particularly the twenty-sixth verse. And here again it is said, 'that the interpretation assigned is confirmed by several of the most eminent Fathers, more especially the great John Chrysostom, as well as by Origen and Jerome "upon the place".'

I cannot find St. Jerome to have writ one line 'upon the place'. And it is obvious that St. Chrysostom supposes the whole context from the seventeenth to the twenty-fifth verses to relate to all Christians in all ages. How this can be said to 'confirm the interpretation assigned' I cannot conjecture. Nay, it is remarkable that he expounds the former part of the twenty-sixth verse as describing the ordinary privilege of all Christians. Thus far, therefore, he does not confirm, but overthrow 'the interpretation before assigned'. But in the middle of the verse he breaks off, and expounds the latter part as describing one of the miraculous gifts.

Yet I must do the justice to this venerable man to observe: he does not suppose that miraculous gift was given only that the inspired might do what any ordinary Christian might have done without it—this interpretation, even of the latter part of the verse, he does in no wise confirm—but that he might ask in every particular circumstance the determinate thing which it was the will of God to give.

20. The third Father by whom it is said this interpretation is confirmed is Origen. The first passage of his which relates to Romans 8: 26 runs thus:

> Paul, perceiving how far he was, after all these things, from knowing to pray for what he ought as he ought, says, 'We know not what we should pray for as we ought.'[3] But he adds, whence what is wanting may be had by one who indeed does not know, but labours to be found worthy of having the defect supplied. For he says, 'Likewise the

---

[1] See Rom. 8: 9.
[2] The bishop does not in fact refer to this text, but simply speaks about 'praying by the Spirit'.   [3] Rom. 8: 26.

Spirit also helpeth our infirmities: for we know not what we should pray for as we ought; but the Spirit itself maketh intercession for us, with groanings which cannot be uttered. And he that searcheth the hearts knoweth what is the mind of the Spirit; because he maketh
5 intercession for the saints according to the will of God.'[1] The Spirit which crieth Abba, Father, in the hearts of the saints, knowing well our groanings in this tabernacle, 'maketh intercession for us to God with groanings which cannot be uttered'. . . . To the same effect is that Scripture, 'I will pray with the Spirit, I will pray with the understand-
10 ing also.'[a] For our understanding (or mind, ὁ νοῦς) cannot pray if the Spirit do not pray before it, and the understanding, as it were, listen to it.[b]

Again:

I would know how the saints cry to God without a voice. The
15 Apostle shows, 'God hath sent forth the Spirit of his Son into our hearts, crying, Abba, Father!' And he adds, 'The Spirit itself maketh intercession for us, with groanings which cannot be uttered.' And again, 'He that searcheth the hearts knoweth what is the mind of the Spirit, because he maketh intercession for the saints, according to the will of
20 God.' Thus, therefore, the Spirit making intercession for us with God, the cry of the saints is heard without a voice.[c]

Once more in his homily on Joshua:

Jesus, our Lord, doth not forsake us; but although when we would pray 'we know not what to pray for as we ought, yet the Spirit itself
25 maketh intercession for us with groanings which cannot be uttered'. Now the Lord is that Spirit. The Spirit assists our prayers and offers them to God with groanings which we cannot express in words.[d]

I believe all rational men will observe from hence that Origen is so far from confirming that he quite overturns your lordship's
30 interpretation of the sixteenth as well as the twenty-sixth verse of this chapter; seeing, in his judgment, both that testimony of the Spirit and this prayer belong to all Christians in all ages.

21. The sixth Scripture which your lordship has undertaken to show relates only to the apostolical times, is First Corinthians 2: 4, 5.

[a] 1 Cor. 14: 15.
[b] [Origen, *De Oratione* (*On Prayer*), ii. 3, 4, in *Opera* (ed. Delarue),] Vol. I, p. 199.
[c] [Ibid., *In Exodum* (*On Exodus*), v. 4,] Vol. II, p. 146.
[d] [Ibid., *In Librum Jesu Nave* (*On the Book of Joshua*), ix. 2,] Vol. II, p. 419.

[1] Rom. 8: 26–7.

And 'this interpretation also (it is said), is confirmed by the authority of Chrysostom, Origen, and other ancient writers'.[a] With those other 'ancient writers' I have no concern yet. St. Chrysostom so far confirms this interpretation as to explain that whole phrase, 'the demonstration of the Spirit and of power', of 'the power of the Spirit shown by miracles'. But he says not one word of any 'proof of the Christian religion arising from the types and prophecies of the Old Testament'.[1]

Origen has these words:

> Our word has a certain peculiar demonstration, more divine than the Grecian logical demonstration. This the Apostle terms 'the demonstration of the Spirit and of power': of the Spirit, because of the prophecies, sufficient to convince any one, especially of the things that relate to Christ; of power, because of the miraculous powers, some footsteps of which still remain.[b]

Hence we may doubtless infer that Origen judged this text to relate in its primary sense to the apostles. But can we thence infer that he did not judge it to belong, in a lower sense, to all true ministers of Christ?

Let us hear him speaking for himself in the same treatise:

> 'And my speech and my preaching were not with enticing words of man's wisdom, but in demonstration of the Spirit and of power; that your faith should not stand in the wisdom of men, but in the power of God'. . . . Those who hear the Word preached with power are themselves filled with power (N.B. Not the power of working miracles), which they demonstrate both in their disposition, and in their life, and in their striving for the truth unto death. But some, although they profess to believe, have not this power of God in them, but are empty thereof.[c]

(Did Origen then believe that the power mentioned in this text belonged *only* to the apostolical age?)

> See the force of the Word, conquering believers by a persuasiveness attended with the power of God! . . . I speak this to show the meaning of them that said, 'And my speech and my preaching were not with the

[a] [*Charge*,] pp. 32–3.
[b] [Origen, *Contra Celsum* (*Against Celsus*), i. 2, in *Opera* (ed. Delarue),] Vol. I, p. 321.   [c] [Ibid., i. 62,] p. 377.

---

[1] *Charge*, p. 29.

enticing words of man's wisdom, but in demonstration of the Spirit and of power; that your faith should not stand in the wisdom of men, but in the power of God.' This divine saying means that what is spoken is not sufficient of itself (although it be true and most worthy to be
5 believed) to pierce a man's soul, if there be not also a certain power from God given to the speaker, and grace bloom upon what is spoken, and this grace cannot be but from God.[1]

After observing that this is the very passage which your lordship mentions at the close of the other (but does not cite) I desire every
10 unprejudiced person to judge whether Origen does not clearly determine that the power spoken of in this text is in some measure given to all true ministers in all ages.

22. The last Scripture which your lordship affirms 'to be peculiar to the times of the apostles' is that in the first Epistle of St. John,
15 concerning 'the unction of the Holy One'.[2]

To confirm this interpretation we are referred to the authority of Origen and Chrysostom, on the parallel passages in St. John's Gospel.[a]

But it has appeared that both these Fathers suppose those passages
20 to belong to all Christians; and consequently their authority (if these are parallel passages) stands full against this interpretation.

Your lordship subjoins: 'I shall here only add that of the great Athanasius, who (in his *Epistle to Serapion*) interprets the "unction from the Holy One" not *merely* of divine grace, but of the extra-
25 ordinary gifts of the Holy Spirit.'

Nay, it is enough if he interprets it at all of ordinary grace, such as is common to all Christians.

And this your lordship allows he does. But I cannot allow that he interprets it of anything else. I cannot perceive that he interprets it
30 at all 'of the extraordinary gifts of the Holy Spirit'.

His words are:

The Holy Spirit is called, and is, the unction and the seal. For John writes: 'The anointing which ye have received of him abideth in you; and ye need not that any man should teach you, but as his Anointing
35 (his Spirit) teacheth you of all things.'[3] Again, it is written in the prophet Isaiah, 'The Spirit of the Lord is upon me, because he hath

---

[a] [*Charge*,] p. 42.

---

[1] Origen, *Contra Celsum*, vi. 2. The opening sentence is carried over from i. 62.
[2] Cf. 1 John 2: 20. [3] 1 John 2: 27.

anointed me.'[1] And Paul writes thus: 'In whom also ye were sealed.'[2] And again, 'Grieve not the Holy Spirit of God, whereby ye are sealed unto the day of redemption.' . . .[3] This anointing is the breath of the Son, so that he who hath the Spirit may say, 'We are the sweet-smelling savour of Christ.'. . .[4] Because we are partakers of the Holy Spirit, we have the Son: and having the Son, we have 'the Spirit, crying in our hearts, Abba, Father'.[5]

And so, in his *Oration against the Arians*:

He sendeth the Spirit of his Son into our hearts, crying Abba, Father.'[6] His Son in us, invoking the Father, makes him to be called our Father. Certainly God cannot be called their Father, who have not the Son in their hearts.[7]

Is it not easy to be observed here, (1), that Athanasius makes that *testimony of the Spirit* common to all the children of God; (2), that he joins 'the anointing of the Holy One' with that seal of the Spirit wherewith all that persevere are 'sealed to the day of redemption';[8] and (3), that he does not, throughout this passage, speak of the extraordinary gifts at all?

Therefore, upon the whole, the sense of the primitive church, so far as it can be gathered from the authors above cited, is that 'although some of these Scriptures *primarily* refer to those extraordinary gifts of the Spirit which were given to the apostles and a few other persons in the apostolical age; yet they refer also, in a *secondary* sense, to those ordinary operations of the Holy Spirit which all the children of God do and will experience, even to the end of the world'.

23. What I mean by 'the ordinary operations of the Holy Ghost' I sum up in the words of a modern writer:[9]

Sanctification being opposed to our corruption, and answering fully to the latitude thereof, whatsoever of holiness and perfection is wanting in our nature must be supplied by the Spirit of God. Wherefore, being by nature we are totally void of all saving truth, and under an impossibility

---

[1] Cf. Isa. 61: 1.   [2] Cf. Eph. 1: 13.   [3] Eph. 4: 30.   [4] Cf. Eph. 5: 2.
[5] Athanasius, *Epistolae IV ad Serapionem* (*Four Letters to Serapion*), iii. 3; iv. 4. The final sentence only is from Letter IV. For the closing quotation cf. Gal. 4: 6.
[6] Cf. Gal. 4: 6.
[7] Athanasius, *Orationes contra Arianos* (*Speeches against the Arians*), iv. 22.
[8] Cf. Eph. 4: 30.
[9] John Pearson (1613–83), master of Trinity College, Cambridge, bishop of Chester, and author of *An Exposition of the Creed* (1659), from which Wesley here quotes. He deliberately withholds Pearson's name until the end of the lengthy extract—see p. 166 below.

of knowing the will of God; . . . this 'Spirit searcheth all things, yea, even the deep things of God',[1] and revealeth them unto the sons of men; so that thereby the darkness of their understanding is expelled, and they are enlightened with the knowledge of God. . . . The same
5 Spirit which revealeth the object of faith generally to the universal church, . . . doth also illuminate the understanding of such as believe, that they may receive the truth. For 'faith is the gift of God',[2] not only in the object, but also in the act. . . . And this gift is a gift of the Holy Ghost working within us. . . . And as the increase [and] perfection,[3]
10 so the original of faith is from the Spirit of God . . . by an internal illumination of the soul. . . .

The second part of the office of the Holy Ghost is the renewing of man in all the parts and faculties of his soul. For our natural corruption consisting in an aversation[4] of our wills, and a depravation of our affec-
15 tions, an inclination of them to the will of God is wrought within us by the Spirit of God. . . .

The third part of his office is to lead, direct, and govern us in our actions and conversations. . . . 'If we live in the Spirit', quickened by his renovation, we must 'also walk in the Spirit',[5] following his direction,
20 led by his manuduction. We are also animated and acted[6] by the Spirit of God, who giveth 'both to will and to do';[7] and 'as many as are *thus* led by the Spirit of God, are the Sons of God'.[a] Moreover, that this direction may prove more effectual, we are guided in our prayers by the same Spirit, according to the promise, 'I will pour upon the house of
25 David, and upon the inhabitants of Jerusalem, the spirit of grace and supplication.'[b] Whereas then 'this is the confidence which we have in Him, that if we ask anything according to his will, he heareth us';[8] and whereas 'we know not what we should pray for as we ought, the Spirit itself maketh intercession for us with groanings which cannot be uttered;
30 and he that searcheth the hearts knoweth what is the mind of the Spirit, because he maketh intercession for the saints according to the will of God.'[c] From which intercession (made for all true Christians) he hath the name of the 'Paraclete' given him by Christ, who said, 'I will pray the Father, and he will give you another Paraclete.'[d] For 'if any man

---

[a] Rom. 8: 14.   [b] Zech. 12: 10.   [c] Rom. 8: 26-7.   [d] John 14: 16.

[1] 1 Cor. 2: 10.   [2] Eph. 2: 8.
[3] Instead of Pearson's 'increase and perfection', which is here restored, Wesley reads 'increase of perfection', possibly a printer's error for 'increase or perfection'.
[4] In Pearson's day this meant 'estrangement', but by the time Wesley wrote it was almost synonymous with 'aversion', which gradually replaced it, and is found in the *Works* (1772).   [5] Gal. 5: 25.
[6] Pearson has 'acted', in the sense of 'actuated', which replaced the original in the 1778 edition.
[7] Phil. 2: 13.   [8] 1 John 5: 14.

sin, we have a Paraclete with the Father, Jesus Christ the righteous',
saith St. John;[1] 'Who maketh intercession for us', saith St. Paul.[a] And
we have 'another Paraclete',[b] saith our Saviour; 'Which also maketh
intercession for us'[c], saith St. Paul. A Paraclete then, in the notion of
the Scriptures, is an intercessor. . . .'[2]   5

It is also the office of the Holy Ghost to 'assure us of the adoption of
sons',[3] to create in us a sense of the paternal love of God toward us,
to give us an earnest of our everlasting inheritance. 'The love of God is
shed abroad in our hearts by the holy Ghost which is given unto us.'[4]
'For as many as are led by the Spirit of God, they are the sons of God.'[5] 10
'And because we are sons, God hath sent forth the Spirit of his Son
into our hearts, crying Abba, Father.'[6] 'For we have not received the
spirit of bondage again to fear, but we have received the spirit of
adoption, whereby we cry Abba, Father: the Spirit itself bearing witness with our spirit, that we are the children of God.'[d]   15

As therefore we are born again by the Spirit, and receive from him
our regeneration, so we are also by the same Spirit 'assured of our
adoption'.[7] Because being 'sons, we are also heirs, heirs of God, and
joint-heirs with Christ',[8] by the same Spirit we have the pledge or
rather the 'earnest of our inheritance'.[9] For 'he which establisheth us in 20
Christ, and hath anointed us, is God; who hath also sealed us, and
hath given us the earnest of his Spirit in our hearts';[10] so that we are
'sealed with that Holy Spirit of promise, which is the earnest of our
inheritance'.[11] The Spirit of God, as given unto us in this life, . . . is
to be looked upon as an earnest, being part of that reward which is 25
promised, and upon performance of the covenant which God hath
made with us, certainly to be received.[12]

Your lordship observed that 'the interpretation of those passages
which relate to the "unction from the Holy One"[13] depends on the
sense of those other passages of Holy Scripture, particularly those in 30
St. John's Gospel'.[14] Now if so, then these words fix the sense of six out

---

[a] Cf. Rom. 8: 34.   [b] John 14: 16.   [c] Rom. 8: 27.   [d] Rom. 8: 15–16.

---

[1] Cf. 1 John 2: 1.
[2] Wesley omits Pearson's fourth office: 'to join us unto Christ, and make us members
of that one body of which our Saviour is the head.'
[3] Cf. Gal. 4: 5.   [4] Rom. 5:5.   [5] Rom. 8: 14.
[6] Cf. Gal. 4: 6.   [7] Cf. Gal. 4: 5.   [8] Cf. Rom. 8: 17.
[9] Eph. 1: 14.   [10] Cf. 2 Cor. 1: 21–2.   [11] Eph. 1: 13–14.
[12] John Pearson, *An Exposition of the Creed*, 4th ed., enlarged, London, J. M., 1676,
folio, pp. 327–30, (ed. E. Burton, Oxford University Press, 1833, I. 550–5)—the section
on the offices of the Holy Spirit from Pearson's exposition of 'I believe in the Holy
Ghost.' Cf. Wesley's use of this same passage in *A Letter to the Bishop of Gloucester*,
pp. 519–21 below.   [13] 1 John 2: 20.   [14] Smalbroke, *Charge*, p. 42.

of the seven texts in question; and every one of them, in the judgment of this writer, describes the ordinary gifts bestowed on all Christians.

It now rests with your lordship to take your choice; either to condemn or to acquit both. Either your lordship must condemn 5 Bishop Pearson for an enthusiast—a man no ways inferior to Bishop Chrysostom—or you must acquit me: for I have his express authority on my side concerning every text which I affirm to belong to all Christians.

24. But I have greater authority than his, and such as I reverence 10 only less than that of the oracles of God. I mean, that of our own Church. I shall close this head by setting down what occurs in her authentic records concerning either our 'receiving the Holy Ghost', or his ordinary operations in all true Christians.

In her daily service she teaches us all to beseech God 'to grant 15 us . . . his Holy Spirit, that those things may please him which we do at this present, and that the rest of our life may be pure and holy';[1] to pray for our sovereign lord the king, that God would 'replenish him with the grace of his Holy Spirit';[2] for all the royal family, that they may be 'endued with his Holy Spirit, and enriched with his 20 heavenly grace';[3] for all the clergy and people, that he would 'send down upon them the healthful Spirit of his grace';[4] for the catholic Church, that 'it may be guided and governed by his good Spirit':[5] and for all therein who at any time 'make their common supplication unto him',[6] that 'the fellowship or communication of the Holy 25 Ghost may be with them all evermore'.[7]

Her collects are full of petitions to the same effect: 'Grant that we . . . may daily be renewed by thy Holy Spirit.'[a] Grant that in all our sufferings here for the testimony of thy truth, we may . . . by faith behold the glory that shall be revealed, and being filled with 30 the Holy Ghost may love and bless our persecutors.'[b] 'Send thy Holy Ghost, and pour into our hearts that most excellent gift of charity.'[c] 'O Lord, from whom all good things do come, grant to us thy humble servants, that by thy holy inspiration we may think those

---

[a] [B.C.P., Collects,] Collect for Christmas Day.
[b] [Ibid.,] Saint Stephen's Day. [c] [Ibid.,] Quinquagesima Sunday.

[1] B.C.P., Morning Prayer, Absolution. [2] Ibid., Prayer for the King's Majesty.
[3] Ibid., Prayer for the Royal Family. [4] Ibid., Prayer for the Clergy and People.
[5] Ibid., Prayers, For all Conditions of Men.
[6] Ibid., Morning Prayer, etc., Prayer of St. Chrysostom.
[7] Ibid., Benediction (2 Cor. 13: 14).

things that are good, and by thy merciful guidance may perform the same.'ᵃ 'We beseech thee, leave us not comfortless, but send to us the Holy Ghost to comfort us.'ᵇ 'Grant us by the same Spirit to have a right judgment in all things, and evermore to rejoice in his holy comfort.'ᶜ (N.B. The Church here teaches all Christians to claim the Comforter, in virtue of the promise made John fourteen.¹) 'Grant us, Lord, we beseech thee, the Spirit, to think and do always such things as be rightful.ᵈ 'O God, forasmuch as without thee we are not able to please thee, mercifully grant that thy Holy Spirit may in all things direct and rule our hearts.'ᵉ 'Cleanse the thoughts of our hearts by the inspiration of thy Holy Spirit, that we may perfectly love thee, and worthily magnify thy holy name.'ᶠ

'Give thy Holy Spirit to this infant (or this person) that *he* may be born again.'² 'Give thy Holy Spirit to these persons (N.B. already baptized) that they may continue thy servants.'³

'Almighty God, who hast vouchsafed to regenerate these persons by water and the Holy Ghost, . . . strengthen them with the Holy Ghost, the Comforter, and daily increase in them the manifold gifts of thy grace.ᵍ

From these passages it may sufficiently appear for what purposes every Christian, according to the doctrine of the Church of England, does now 'receive the Holy Ghost'.⁴ But this will be still more clear from those that follow; wherein the reader may likewise observe a plain, rational sense of God's revealing himself to us, of the *inspiration* of the Holy Ghost, and of a believer's *feeling* in himself the mighty working of the Spirit of Christ.

25.

God gave them of old grace to be his children, as he doth us now. But now, by the coming of our Saviour Christ, we have received more abundantly the Spirit of God in our hearts.ʰ

He died to destroy the rule of the devil in us, and he rose again to send down his Holy Spirit to rule in our hearts.ⁱ

ᵃ [Ibid.,] Fifth Sunday after Easter.   ᵇ [Ibid.,] The Sunday after Ascension Day.
ᶜ [Ibid.,] Whitsunday.   ᵈ [Ibid.,] Ninth Sunday after Trinity.
ᵉ [Ibid.,] Nineteenth Sunday after Trinity.
ᶠ [Ibid.,] Communion Office.   ᵍ [Ibid.,] Office of Confirmation.
ʰ Homily on Faith, Part II.   ⁱ Homily on the Resurrection.

---

¹ See John 14: 26.   ² B.C.P., Baptism, Baptism of Adults.
³ Ibid., Baptism of Adults.   ⁴ Acts 8: 15, 19.

We have the Holy Spirit in our hearts as a seal and pledge of our everlasting inheritance.[a]

The Holy Ghost sat upon each of them, like as it had been cloven tongues of fire; . . . to teach . . . that it is he which giveth eloquence and
5   utterance in preaching the gospel, which engendereth a burning zeal towards God's Word, and giveth all men a tongue, 'yea a fiery tongue'. (N.B. Whatever occurs in any of the *Journals* of God's 'giving me utterance' or 'enabling me to speak with power' cannot therefore be quoted as enthusiasm, without wounding the Church through my side.)
10   'So that if any man be a dumb Christian, not professing his faith openly,. . . he giveth men occasion to doubt . . . lest he have not the grace of the Holy Ghost within him.'[b]

It is the office of the Holy Ghost to sanctify; which, the more it is hid from our understanding, (i.e. the particular manner of his working)
15   the more it ought to move all men to wonder at the secret and mighty workings of God's Holy Spirit which is within us. For it is the Holy Ghost that doth *quicken* the minds of men, *stirring up* godly motions in their hearts. . . . Neither doth he think it sufficient inwardly to work the new birth of man, unless he do also dwell and abide in him. 'Know
20   ye not', saith St. Paul, 'that ye are the temple of God, and that his Spirit dwelleth in you?'[1] 'Know ye not that your bodies are the temples of the Holy Ghost which is in you?'[2] Again he saith, 'Ye are not in the flesh, but in the Spirit.'[3] For why? 'The Spirit of God dwelleth in you.'[4] To this agreeth St. John: 'The anointing which ye have received
25   (he meaneth the Holy Ghost) abideth in you.'[c] And St. Peter saith the same: 'The Spirit of Glory and of God resteth upon you.'[5] O what comfort is this to the heart of a true Christian, to think that the Holy Ghost dwelleth in him! 'If God be with us', as the Apostle saith, 'who can be against us?' . . .[6] He giveth patience and joyfulness of heart in
30   temptation and affliction, and is therefore worthily called 'the Comforter'. . . .[d] He doth instruct the hearts of the simple in the knowledge of God and his Word; therefore he is justly termed 'The Spirit of truth.' . . .[e] And 'where the Holy Ghost doth instruct and teach, there is no delay at all in learning'.[f]

35   From this passage I learn, (1), that every true Christian now receives the Holy Ghost, as the Paraclete or Comforter promised by

---

[a] Homily on the Resurrection.   [b] Homily on Whitsunday, Part I.
[c] 1 John 2: 27.   [d] John 14: 16.   [e] John 16: 13.
[f] Ibid. [i.e., Homily on Whit Sunday, Part I, citing at end Bede, Hom. 9 upon Luke].

---

[1] 1 Cor. 3: 16.   [2] Cf. 1 Cor. 6: 19.   [3] Rom. 8: 9.
[4] 1 Cor. 3: 16.   [5] 1 Pet. 4: 14.   [6] Cf. Rom. 8: 31.

our Lord;[a] (2), that every Christian receives him as 'the Spirit of truth' (promised John sixteen) to 'teach him all things';[1] and, (3), that the anointing mentioned in the first Epistle of St. John 'abides in every Christian'.[2]

26.   5

In reading of God's word, he profiteth most . . . that is most inspired with the Holy Ghost.[b]

Human and worldly wisdom is not needful to the understanding of Scripture, but the revelation of the Holy Ghost, who inspireth the true meaning unto them that with humility and diligence search for it.[c]   10

Make him know and feel that there is no other name under heaven given unto men, whereby we can be saved.[3]

If we feel our conscience at peace with God through remission of our sin, . . . all is of God.[d]

If you feel such a faith in you, rejoice in it, . . . and let it be daily   15 increasing by well working.[e]

The faithful may feel wrought tranquillity of conscience, the increase of faith and hope, with many other graces of God.[f]

Godly men feel inwardly God's Holy Spirit inflaming their hearts with love.[g]   20

God give us grace to know these things, and to feel them in our hearts! This knowledge and feeling is not of ourselves. . . . Let us therefore meekly call upon the bountiful Spirit, the Holy Ghost, . . . to inspire us with his presence, that we may be able to hear the good-ness of God to our salvation. For without his lively inspiration can we   25 not so much as speak the name of the Mediator: 'No man can say that Jesus is the Lord, but by the Holy Ghost.'[4] Much less should we be able to believe and know these great mysteries that be opened to us by Christ. . . . But 'we have received', saith St. Paul, 'not the spirit of the world, but the Spirit which is of God'; for this purpose, 'that we may   30 know the things which are freely given to us of God'.[5] In the power of the Holy Ghost resteth all ability to know God and to please him. . . . It is he that purifieth the mind by his secret working. . . . He enlighteneth the heart to conceive worthy thoughts of Almighty God. He sitteth in the tongue of man to stir him to speak his honour. He only ministereth   35

---

[a] John 14: [16, 16:] 13.   [b] Homily on reading the Scripture, Part I.
[c] Ibid., Part II [quoting Chrysostom].   [d] Homily on Rogation Week, Part III.
[e] Homily on Faith, Part III.   [f] Homily on the Sacrament, Part I.
[g] Homily on certain places of Scripture, Part I.

---

[1] i.e. John 14: 26.   [2] Cf. 1 John 2: 27.
[3] Cf. Acts 4: 12; Homilies, Of the Passion.   [4] 1 Cor. 12: 3.
[5] Cf. 1 Cor. 2: 12.

spiritual strength to the powers of the soul and body. . . . And if we have any gift whereby we may profit our neighbour, all is wrought by this one and the selfsame Spirit.[a]

27. Every proposition which I have anywhere advanced concern-
5 ing those operations of the Holy Ghost which I believe are common to all Christians in all ages is here clearly maintained by our own Church.

Under a full sense of this, I could not well understand for many years how it was that on the mentioning any of these great truths,
10 even among men of education, the cry immediately arose, 'An enthusiast, an enthusiast!' But I now plainly perceive this is only an old fallacy in a new shape. To object 'enthusiasm' to any person or doctrine is but a decent method of begging the question. It generally spares the objector the trouble of reasoning, and is a shorter
15 and easier way of carrying his cause.

For instance, I assert that 'till a man "receives the Holy Ghost"[1] he is without God in the world; that he cannot know the things of God unless God reveal them unto him by his Spirit; no, nor have even one holy or heavenly temper, without the inspiration of the
20 Holy One'.[2] Now should one who is conscious to himself that he has experienced none of these things attempt to confute these proposi-tions, either from Scripture or antiquity, it might prove a difficult task. What then shall he do? Why, cry out, 'Enthusiasm! Enthu-siasm!' And the work is done.

25 But what does he mean by 'enthusiasm'? Perhaps nothing at all: few have any distinct idea of its meaning. Perhaps 'something very bad', or 'something I never experienced and do not understand'. Shall I tell you then what that 'terrible something' is? I believe thinking men mean by enthusiasm a sort of religious madness,
30 a *false imagination* of being inspired by God; and by an enthusiast one that *fancies* himself under the influence of the Holy Ghost, when in fact is he not.

---

[a] Homily for Rogation Week, Part III.

---

[1] Cf. John 20: 22; Acts 8: 15.
[2] The comment faithfully reflects a characteristic strain in Wesley's thought (cf. sermon, *Scriptural Christianity*, §§ 3, 4, 5). Wesley quotes the words in a way which implies previous publication; the fact that they are repeated in *A Letter to the Bishop of Gloucester* (II. 25) strengthens the impression. However, they do not seem to be in the works published before 1745. He may be quoting from a sermon or spoken comment, or reproducing a statement contained in a letter which has not survived.

Let him prove me guilty of this who can. I will tell you once more the whole of my belief on these heads. And if any man will show me (by arguments, not hard names) what is wrong, I will thank God and him.

28. Every good gift is from God, and is given to man by the Holy 5 Ghost. By nature there is in us no good thing. And there can be none, but so far as it is wrought in us by that good Spirit. Have we any true knowledge of what is good? This is not the result of our natural understanding. 'The natural man discerneth not the things of the Spirit of God',[1] so that we never can discern them until 'God 10 reveals them unto us by his Spirit'.[2] 'Reveals', that is, unveils, uncovers; gives us to know what we did not know before. Have we love? It is 'shed abroad in our hearts by the Holy Ghost which is given unto us'.[3] He *inspires*, breathes, infuses into our soul, what of ourselves we could not have. Does our spirit rejoice in God our 15 Saviour? It is 'joy in (or by) the Holy Ghost'.[4] Have we true inward peace? It is 'the peace of God'[5] wrought in us by the same Spirit. Faith, peace, joy, love, are all his fruits. And as we are figuratively said to *see* the light of faith, so by a like figure of speech we are said to *feel* this peace and joy and love; that is, we have an inward ex- 20 perience of them, which we cannot find any fitter word to express.

The reasons why in speaking of these things I use those terms ('inspiration' particularly) are, (1), because they are scriptural; (2), because they are used by our Church; (3), because I know none better. The word 'influence' of the Holy Ghost, which I suppose 25 you use, is both a far stronger and a less natural term than 'inspiration'. It is far stronger, even as far as 'flowing into the soul' is a stronger expression than 'breathing upon it'. And less natural, as 'breathing' bears a near relation to spirit, to which 'flowing in' has only a distant relation. 30

But you thought I had meant 'immediate inspiration'. So I do, or I mean nothing at all. Not indeed such inspiration as is *sine mediis*.[6] But all inspiration, though by means, is immediate. Suppose, for instance, you are employed in private prayer, and God pours his love into your heart. God then acts *immediately* on your soul; and 35 the love of him which you then experience is as immediately breathed into you by the Holy Ghost as if you had lived seventeen hundred years ago. Change the term: say, God then *assists* you to love him?

---

[1] 1 Cor. 2: 14. [2] 1 Cor. 2: 10. [3] Rom. 5: 5.
[4] Rom. 14: 17. [5] Phil. 4: 7; Col. 3: 15. [6] 'Without means.'

Well, and is not this immediate assistance? Say, his spirit *concurs* with yours. You gain no ground. It is immediate concurrence, or none at all. God, a spirit, acts upon your spirit. Make it out any otherwise if you can.

5   I cannot conceive how that harmless word 'immediate' came to be such a bugbear in the world. 'Why, I thought you meant such inspiration as the apostles had; and such a receiving the Holy Ghost as that was at the day of Pentecost.' I do, in part. Indeed I do not mean that Christians now receive the Holy Ghost in order to
10 work miracles; but they do doubtless now receive, yea, are 'filled with the Holy Ghost',[1] in order to be filled with the fruits of that blessed Spirit. And he *inspires* into all true believers now a degree of the same peace and joy and love which the apostles felt in themselves on that day when they were first 'filled with the Holy Ghost'.

15 29. I have now considered the most material objections I know which have been lately made against the great doctrines I teach. I have produced, so far as in me lay, the strength of those objections, and then answered them, I hope, in the spirit of meekness. And now I trust it appears that these doctrines are no other than the doctrines
20 of Jesus Christ; that they are all evidently contained in the Word of God, by which alone I desire to stand or fall; and that they are fundamentally the same with the doctrines of the Church of England, of which I do and ever did profess myself a member.

But there remains one objection, which though relating to the
25 head of doctrine, yet is independent on all that went before. And that is: 'You cannot agree in your doctrines among yourselves. One holds one thing, and one another. Mr. Whitefield anathematizes Mr. Wesley; and Mr. Wesley anathematizes Mr. Whitefield. And yet each pretends to be led by the Holy Ghost, by the infallible
30 Spirit of God! Every reasonable man must conclude from hence that neither one nor the other is led by that Spirit.'

I need not say how continually this has been urged, both in common conversation and from the press. (I am grieved to add, and from the pulpit too; for if the argument were good it would over-
35 turn the Bible.) Nor, how great stress has been continually laid upon it; whoever proposes it proposes it as demonstration, and generally claps his wings, as being quite assured it will admit of no answer.

And indeed I am in doubt whether it does admit (I am sure it

[1] Acts 2: 14.

does not *require*) any other answer than that coarse one of the countryman to the Romish champion—'Bellarmine, thou liest.'[1] For every proposition contained herein is grossly, shamelessly false: (1). 'You cannot agree in your doctrines among yourselves.' Who told you so? All our fundamental doctrines I have recited 5 above. And in every one of these we do and have agreed for several years. In these we hold one and the same thing. In smaller points each of us thinks and lets think. (2). 'Mr. Whitefield anathematizes Mr. Wesley.' Another shameless untruth. Let any one read what Mr. Whitefield wrote, even in the heat of controversy, and he will 10 be convinced of the contrary. (3). 'And Mr. Wesley anathematizes Mr. Whitefield.' This is equally false and scandalous. I reverence Mr. Whitefield, both as a child of God and a true minister of Jesus Christ. (4). 'And yet each pretends to be led by the Holy Ghost, by the infallible Spirit of God.' Not in our private opinions; nor 15 does either of us pretend to be any farther led by the Spirit of God than every Christian must pretend to be, unless he will deny the Bible. For only 'as many as are led by the Spirit of God are the sons of God'.[2] Therefore if you do not pretend to be led by him too, yea, if it be not so in fact, 'you are none of his'.[3] 20

And now what is become of your demonstration? Leave it to the carmen and porters, its just proprietors; to the zealous apple-women that cry after me in the street, 'This is he that rails at the *whole dutiful* of man.'[4] But let everyone that pretends to learning or reason be ashamed to mention it any more. 25

30. The first inference, easily deduced from what has been said, is that we are not 'false prophets'. In one sense of the word we are no prophets at all; for we do not foretell things to come. But in another (wherein every minister is a prophet) we are. For we do speak in the name of God. Now a false prophet (in this sense of the 30 word) is one who declares as the will of God what is not so. But we declare (as has been shown at large) nothing else as the will of God

---

[1] One of many stories told to illustrate Bellarmine's humility when rebuked or resisted. Cf. James Brodrick, *The Life and Work of Blessed Robert Francis Cardinal Bellarmine*, II. 410; X. M. Le Bachelet, *Bellarmin avant son cardinalat*, pp. 354-8, 375-6.

[2] Cf. Rom. 8: 14.   [3] Cf. Rom. 8: 9.

[4] A double error unworthy of the intelligent men for whom Wesley wrote; the apple-women did not realize that Whitefield, not Wesley, had become notorious for his criticism of the religious classic, *The Whole Duty of Man*, nor could they remember its title correctly. (The 1786 edition alters 'dutiful' to 'duty', surely through a compositor's mistaken zeal.)

but what is evidently contained in his written Word, as explained by our own Church. Therefore, unless you can prove the Bible to be a false book, you cannot possibly prove us to be false prophets.

5 The text which is generally cited on this occasion is Matthew seven, verse fifteen.[1] But how unhappily chosen! In the preceding chapters our Lord had been describing that 'righteousness which exceeds the righteousness of the Scribes and Pharisees', and without which we cannot 'enter into the Kingdom of Heaven'[2]—even the life of God in the soul, holiness of heart producing all holiness
10 of conversation. In this he closes that rule which sums up the whole with those solemn words, 'Enter ye in at the strait gate' (such indeed is that of universal holiness); 'for wide is the gate, and broad is the way, that leadeth to destruction'. The gate of hell is wide as the whole earth; the way of unholiness is broad as the great deep. 'And
15 many there be which go in thereat'; yea, and excuse themselves in so doing, 'because strait is the gate and narrow is the way that leadeth unto life, and few there be that find it'.[3] It follows, 'Beware of false prophets';[4] of those who speak as from God what God hath not spoken, those who show you any other way to life than that
20 which I have now shown. So that the false prophets here spoken of are those who point out any other way to heaven than this, who teach men to find a wider gate, a broader way than that described in the foregoing chapters. But it has been abundantly shown that we do not. Therefore (whatever we are beside) we are not false
25 prophets.

Neither are we (as has been frequently and vehemently affirmed) 'deceivers of the people'.[5] If we teach 'the truth as it is in Jesus',[6] if we 'speak as the oracles of God',[7] it follows that we do not deceive those that hear, though they should believe whatever we speak.
30 'Let God be true and every man a liar'[8]—every man that contradicts his truth. But he will 'be justified in his saying, and clear when he is judged'.[9]

31. One thing more I infer: 'That we are not enthusiasts.' This accusation has been considered at large, and the main arguments
35 hitherto brought to support it have been weighed in the balance and found wanting: particularly this, 'That none but enthusiasts

---

[1] 'Beware of false prophets, which come to you in sheep's clothing, but inwardly they are ravening wolves'.
[2] Cf. Matt. 5: 20.   [3] Matt. 7: 13-14.   [4] Matt. 7: 15.   [5] Cf. John 7: 12.
[6] Cf. Eph. 4: 21.   [7] 1 Pet. 4: 11.   [8] Cf. Rom. 3: 4.   [9] Ibid.

suppose either that "promise of the Comforter",[a] or the "witness of the Spirit",[b] or that "unutterable prayer",[c] or the "unction from the Holy One",[d] to belong, in common, to all Christians.'[1] O my Lord, how deeply have you condemned the generation of God's children! Whom have you represented as rank, dreaming enthu- 5 siasts? As either deluded or *designing* men? Not only Bishop Pearson, a man hitherto accounted both sound in heart and of good understanding; but likewise Archbishop Cranmer, Bishop Ridley, Bishop Latimer, Bishop Hooper, and all the venerable compilers of our liturgy and Homilies;[2] all the members of both the Houses of Con- 10 vocation, by whom they were revised and approved; yea, King Edward [the Sixth], and all his lords and commons together, by whose authority they were established? And with these modern enthusiasts Origen, Chrysostom, and Athanasius are comprehended in the same censure! 15

I grant a deist might rank both us and them in the number of 'religious madmen'; nay, ought so to do on *his* supposition that the gospel is but a 'cunningly-devised fable'.[3] And on this ground some of them have done so in fact. One of them was asking me several years since: 'What! Are *you* one of the knight-errants? How, I 20 pray, got this quixotism into *your* head? You want nothing; you have a good provision for life; and are in a fair way of preferment; and must you leave all to fight windmills, to convert savages in America?' I could only reply: 'Sir, if the Bible is a lie, I am as very a madman as you can conceive. But if it be true, I am in my senses. 25 I am neither madman nor enthusiast. For "there is no man who hath left father, or mother, or wife, or house, or land for the gospel's sake, but he shall receive an hundredfold in this world, with persecutions; and in the world to come eternal life."'[4]

[a] John 14: 16, 26; 16: 13.   [b] Rom. 8: 15, 16.
[c] Rom. 8: 26, 27.   [d] 1 John 2: 20, 27.

[1] Wesley is recapitulating Smalbroke's argument by citing the scriptural texts on which the bishop had chiefly relied.

[2] Thomas Cranmer was primarily responsible for The Book of Common Prayer, and he contributed several sermons to the First Book of Homilies. In both enterprises Ridley, Latimer, and Hooper played a minor and unrecorded part. They are included here as fellow martyrs with Cranmer in the Marian persecution. Among the unspecified 'venerable compilers' of 'our homilies' were Jewel, Grindal, and Parker (in the 'Second Tome'). Wesley is stressing the authentic Anglican heritage, though it might be thought that to a High-Churchman those responsible for the 1662 revision of the B.C.P. would be more congenial figures.

[3] Cf. 2 Pet. 1: 16.   [4] Cf. Mark 10: 29–30.

Nominal, outside Christians, too, men of form, may pass the same judgment. For we give up all our pretensions to what they account happiness, for what they (with the deists) believe to be a mere dream. We expect, therefore, to pass for enthusiasts with
5 these also: 'But wisdom is justified of all her children.'[1]

32. I cannot conclude this head without one obvious remark. Suppose we really were enthusiasts; suppose our doctrines were false and unsupported either by reason, Scripture or authority: then why hath not someone 'who is a wise man, and endued with
10 knowledge among you', attempted, at least, to show us our fault 'in love and meekness of wisdom'?[2] Brethren, 'if ye have bitter zeal in your hearts, your wisdom descendeth not from above. The wisdom that is from above is pure, peaceable, gentle, easy to be entreated, full of mercy or pity.'[3] Does this spirit appear in one
15 single tract of all those which have been published against us? Is there one writer that has reproved us in love? Bring it to a single point. 'Love hopeth all things.'[4] If you had loved us in any degree you would have hoped that God would some time give us the knowledge of his truth. But where shall we find even this slender instance
20 of love? Has not everyone who has wrote at all (I do not remember so much as one exception) treated us as *incorrigible*? Brethren, how is this? Why do ye labour to teach us an evil lesson against yourselves? O may God never suffer others to deal with you as ye have dealt with us!

25 VI. 1. Before I enter upon the consideration of those objections which have been made to the manner of our preaching, I believe it may be satisfactory to some readers if I relate how I began to preach in this manner.

I was ordained Deacon in 1725, and Priest in the year following.[5]
30 But it was many years after this before I was convinced of the great truths above recited. During all that time I was utterly ignorant of the nature and condition of *justification*. Sometimes I confounded it with sanctification—particularly when I was in Georgia. At other times I had some confused notion about the forgiveness of sins, but
35 then I took it for granted the time of this must be either the hour of death, or the day of judgment.

I was equally ignorant of the nature of *saving faith*, apprehending

---

[1] Luke 7: 35.   [2] Cf. Jas. 3: 13.
[3] Jas. 3: 14, 15, 17.   [4] Cf. 1 Cor. 13: 7.
[5] Wesley's memory here fails him. He was not priested until 1728.

it to mean no more than a 'firm assent to all the propositions contained in the Old and New Testament'.[1]

2. As soon as, by the great blessing of God, I had a clearer view of these things, I began to declare them to others also. 'I believed, and therefore I spake.'[2] Wherever I was now desired to preach, salvation by faith was my only theme. My constant subjects were: 'Believe in the Lord Jesus Christ, and thou shalt be saved.'[3] 'Him hath God exalted to be a Prince and a Saviour, to give repentance and remission of sins.'[4] These I explained and enforced with all my might, both in every church where I was asked to preach, and occasionally in the religious societies of London and Westminster, to some or other of which I was continually pressed to go by the stewards or other members of them.

Things were in this posture when I was told I must preach no more in this, and this, and another church.[5] The reason was usually added without reserve: 'Because you preach such doctrines.' So much the more those who could not hear me there flocked together when I was at any of the societies, where I spoke more or less, though with much inconvenience, to as many as the room I was in would contain.

3. But after a time, finding those rooms could not contain a tenth part of the people that were earnest to hear, I determined to do the same thing in England which I had often done in a warmer climate; namely, when the house would not contain the congregation, to preach in the open air. This I accordingly did, first at Bristol, where the society rooms were exceeding small, and at Kingswood, where we had no room at all; afterwards in or near London.[6]

And I cannot say I have ever seen a more awful sight than when on Rose Green, or the top of Hanham Mount, some thousands of people were calmly joined together in solemn waiting upon God, while

> They stood and under open air adored
> The God who made both air, earth, heaven and sky.[7]

---

[1] Cf. B.C.P., Ordering of Deacons.   [2] Cf. Ps. 116: 10; 2 Cor. 4: 13.
[3] Acts 16: 31.   [4] Cf. Acts 5: 31.
[5] Frequent occasions on which Wesley was informed that he would not be permitted to return to churches where he had just preached are noted in his *Journal*, Oct. 1738 to Mar. 1739.
[6] See the account given by Wesley of the beginnings of field preaching, *Journal*, Mar. 29 to Apr. 2, 1739. Rose Green and Hanham Mount, which he goes on to mention, were among the sites where Wesley preached when he began his open-air ministry in the Bristol area.
[7] Cf. Milton, *Paradise Lost*, iv. 720–2:

> both stood,
> Both turn'd, and under open sky adored
> The God that made both sky, air, earth, and heaven.

And whether they were listening to his Word, with attention still as night, or were lifting up their voice in praise, as the sound of many waters, many a time have I been constrained to say in my heart, 'How dreadful is this place. This also is no other than the house of God! This is the gate of heaven!'[1]

Be pleased to observe: (1). That I was forbidden, as by a general consent, to preach in any church (though not by any judicial sentence) 'for preaching such doctrine'. This was the open, avowed cause. There was at that time no other, either real or pretended (except that the people crowded so). (2). That I had no desire or design to preach in the open air till after this prohibition. (3). That when I did, as it was no matter of choice, so neither of premeditation. There was no scheme at all previously formed which was to be supported thereby; nor had I any other end in view than this, to save as many souls as I could. (4). Field preaching was therefore a sudden expedient, a thing submitted to rather than chosen, and therefore submitted to because I thought preaching even thus better than not preaching at all. First, in regard to my own soul, because 'a dispensation of the gospel being committed to me' I did not dare 'not to preach the gospel';[2] Secondly, in regard to the souls of others, whom I everywhere saw 'seeking death in the error of their life'.[3]

4. But the author of the *Observations* and of *The Case of the Methodists Briefly Stated, More Particularly in the Point of Field Preaching*,[4] thinks field preaching worse than not preaching at all, 'because it is illegal'.

Your argument, in form, runs thus:

That preaching which is contrary to the laws of the land is worse than not preaching at all:
But field preaching is contrary to the laws of the land:
Therefore, it is worse than not preaching at all.

The first proposition is not self-evident, not indeed universally true—for the preaching of all the primitive Christians was contrary to the whole tenor of the Roman law, the worship of their devil gods being established by the strongest laws then in being. Nor is it ever true, but on supposition that the preaching in question is an indifferent thing.

---

[1] Cf. Gen. 28: 17.   [2] Cf. 1 Cor. 9: 16, 17.
[3] Cf. Wisd. 1: 12.   [4] See note to III. 2 above, p. 119.

But waiving this, I deny the second proposition: I deny that field preaching is contrary to the laws of our land.

To prove which you begin thus: 'It does not appear that any of the preachers among the Methodists have qualified themselves and the places of their assembling, according to the Act of Toleration.'[1]

I answer: (1). That Act grants toleration to those who *dissent* from the established Church. But we do not dissent from it; therefore we *cannot* make use of that Act; (2). That Act exempts Dissenters from penalties consequent on their breach of preceding laws. But we are not conscious of breaking any law at all; therefore we *need not* make use of it.

In the next section you say: They 'have broken through all these provisions, . . . in open defiance of government, . . . and have met not only in houses, but in the fields, . . . notwithstanding the statute (22 Car. II, c. 1) which forbids this by name'.[2]

I answer: (1). We do nothing *in defiance* of government. We reverence magistrates, as the ministers of God. (2). Although we have met in the fields, yet we do not conceive that statute at all affects us: not only because that Act points wholly at Dissenters, whereas we are members of the established Church, but also because (they are your own words) 'it was evidently intended to suppress and prevent sedition',[3] whereas no sedition, nor any the least approach thereto, can with any colour be laid to our charge.

In your third section you affirm that the Act of Toleration itself cannot secure us in field preaching from the penalties of former laws.[4] We have no desire it should; as not apprehending ourselves to be condemned by any former law whatever. Nor does what you add, that 'the Act of Toleration . . . forbids any assembly of persons dissenting from the Church of England to meet with the doors locked',[5] affect us at all; because we do not dissent from it.

5. In *The Case of the Methodists Briefly Stated*, your first observation is: 'The Act of Toleration . . . leaves them liable to the penalties of several statutes made against unlawful assemblies.'[6]

I suppose then these several statutes specify what those 'unlawful assemblies' are; and whether unlawful as being condemned by previous laws, or made unlawful by those statutes.

---

[1] *Observations*, p. 3.   [2] Cf. *Observations*, pp. 3, 4.
[3] *The Case of the Methodists Briefly Stated*, p. 2. Cf. below, § 5.
[4] See *Observations*, p. 4.   [5] *Observations*, p. 4.
[6] *Case*, p. 1.

And it still remains to be proved that our assemblies are *unlawful*, in one or other of these senses.

You next observe, that 'the Dissenters of all denominations qualify themselves according to the Act of Toleration; otherwise they are
5 liable to the penalties of all the laws recited in this Act'.[1]

I answer, as before, all this strikes wide. It relates wholly to 'persons *dissenting* from the Church'. But we are not the men. We do not dissent from the Church. Whoever affirms it, we put him to the proof.

10 You go on: 'One of those laws so recited (viz., 22 Car. II, c. 1) is that which forbids field preaching by name; and was evidently intended, not only to *suppress*, but also to *prevent* sedition; as the title of the Act declares,[2] and as the preamble expresses it, "to provide further and more speedy remedies against it".'[3]

15 Was this, then, in your own judgment, the *evident intention* of that Act, viz., *to provide remedies against sedition*? Does the very title of the Act declare this? And the preamble also express it? With what justice then, with what ingenuity or candor, with what shadow of truth or reason, can any man cite this Act against us? Whom you
20 yourself no more suspect of a design to raise sedition (I appeal to your own conscience in the sight of God) than of a design to blow up the city of London.

6. Hitherto, therefore, it hath not been made to appear that field preaching is contrary to any law in being. However, 'It is dangerous.'
25 This you strongly insist on. 'It may be attended with mischievous consequences. It may give advantages to the enemies of the established government. It is big with mischief.'[a]

With what mischief? Why,

evil-minded men, by meeting together *in the fields* under pretence
30 of religion, may raise riots and tumults; or by meeting *secretly*, may carry on *private* cabals against the state.[b]

And if the *Methodists* themselves are a *harmless* and *loyal* people, it is nothing to the point in hand, for disloyal and seditious persons may use such an opportunity of getting together in order to execute any
35 private design. Mr. Whitefield says thirty, fifty, or eighty thousand

---

[a] *Observations*, sections I and II [pp. 3, 4].   [b] *The Case of the Methodists*, p. 2.

[1] Cf. *Case*, pp. 1–2.
[2] 22 Car. II, c. 1 is entitled 'An Act to Prevent and Suppress Seditious Conventicles'; it is commonly known as 'The Conventicle Act, 1670'. Cf. *Statutes of the Realm*, V. 648–51.   [3] *Case*, p. 2.

have attended his preaching at once. Now, (1), he cannot know one
tenth part of such a congregation; (2), all people may come and carry
on what designs they will; therefore (3), this is a great opportunity put
into the hands of seditious persons to raise disturbances. . . . With what
safety to the public these field preachings may be continued, let the 5
world judge.ᵃ

May I speak without offence? I cannot think you are in earnest.
You do not mean what you *say*. Do you *believe* Mr. Whitefield had
eighty thousand hearers at once?¹ No more than you believe he
had eighty millions. Is not all this talk of danger mere finesse, 10
thrown in purely *ad movendam invidiam*?² You know governments
generally are suspicious, especially in time of war; and therefore
apply, as you suppose, to their weak side, in hopes, if possible, to
deliver over these heretics to the secular arm. However, I will
answer *as if* you spoke from your heart. For I am in earnest, if you 15
are not.

First, 'The preacher cannot know a tenth part of his congregation.'
Let us come to the *present* state of things. The largest congregations
that *now* attend the preaching of any Methodist are those (God be
merciful to me!) that attend mine. And cannot I know a tenth part 20

ᵃ Ibid., pp. 2, 3, 4.

¹ In challenging the attendance statistics of the Methodist revival, Gibson unquestionably raises a complicated question. In quoting Whitefield's *Journal* he is careful
to give exact page references: the figures are Whitefield's, not his. Estimating crowds is
notoriously difficult (as modern reporting constantly illustrates), and there is often
present a desire (conscious or unconscious) to use the statistics to prove a point. It is
clear from the round figures given by Whitefield that we are dealing with rough estimates.
In his *Journal* Wesley repeatedly reports that many thousands (three, ten, twenty, even
thirty thousand) gathered to hear him preach. Whitefield, a more flamboyant character,
put the figures in his own case even higher. Wesley's defence, only partially convincing,
must rest on a distinction between two kinds of audience. The congregations which
gathered in his preaching houses were often large, but his pastoral activity was such
that he must soon have gained personal knowledge of a large proportion of them. But
this leaves untouched the problem of the crowds to which he preached in the course of
his travels. Less than two days after arriving in Bristol in 1739 he preached to 'about
three thousand people' (*Journal*, Apr. 2, 1739), almost all of whom must have been total
strangers. As the range of his itinerancy extended, he must have been preaching regularly to vast crowds in which there were no familiar faces. By concentrating his reply on
his regular congregations (as I believe he does here) he evades Gibson's point. Whether
that point is really a valid criticism of evangelism in the open air is a different question.
² 'To provoke hostility.' The phrase is good classical Latin, though apparently it does
not occur in classical authors. A number of close approximations can be found (e.g.
Cicero, *Philippics*, III. xviii; Livy, *History*, XXXVIII. xliii. 2). This particular con-
junction of words was probably due to Wesley himself. Cf. the similar use of the phrase
in *An Answer to the Rev. Mr. Church's Remarks* (1745), II. 15.

of one of these congregations, either at Bristol, Kingswood, New-castle, or London? As strange as it may seem, I generally know two thirds of the congregation in every place even on *Sunday* evening, and nine in ten of those who attend at most other times. (2). 'All
5 people may come and carry on what designs they will.' Not so. All field preaching is now in the open day. And were only ten persons to come to such an assembly with arms, it would soon be inquired with what design they came. This is therefore, (3), no 'great opportunity put into the hands of seditious persons to raise disturbances'.
10 And if ever any disturbance has been raised it was quite of another kind.

The public then is entirely safe, if it be in no other danger than arises from field preaching.

7. There is one other sentence belonging to this head, in the
15 eighth section of the *Observations*. 'The religious societies', you say, 'in London and Westminster, for many years past, . . . have received no discouragements, but on the contrary have been *countenanced* and *encouraged* both by the bishops and clergy.'[1] How is this? Have *they* then 'qualified themselves and the places of their assembling
20 according to the Act of Toleration'? Have *they* 'embraced the protection which that Act might give them, in case they complied with the conditions of it'? If not, are they not all 'liable to the penalties of the several statutes made before that time against unlawful assemblies'?[2]

25 How can they escape? Have they 'qualified themselves for holding these separate assemblies according to the tenor of that Act'? Have then the several 'members thereof taken the oaths to the government'? And are the 'doors of the places wherein they meet always open at the time of such meeting'? I presume you know they are
30 not; and that neither 'the persons nor places are so qualified as that Act directs'.

8. How then come 'the bishops and clergy to *countenance* and *encourage*' unlawful assemblies? If it be said, 'they meet in a private, inoffensive way',[3] that is nothing to the point in hand. If those
35 meetings are *unlawful* in themselves, all their inoffensiveness will not make them lawful. 'O, but they behave "with modesty and decency".'[4] Very well; but the law! What is that to the law? There can be no solid defence but this: they are not *Dissenters* from the

---

[1] *Observations*, p. 8.   [2] Ibid., pp. 3-4; *Case*, p. 1; cf. §§ 4-5 above.
[3] *Observations*, p. 8.   [4] Ibid.

Church; therefore they *cannot use*, and they do *not need* the Act of Toleration. And their meetings are not seditious; therefore the statute against seditious meetings does not affect them.

The application is obvious. If our meetings are illegal, so are theirs also. But if this plea be good (as doubtless it is) in the one case, it is good in the other also.

9. You propose another objection to our *manner* of preaching, in the second part of the *Observations*. The substance of it I will repeat, and answer as briefly as I can.

They 'run up and down from place to place, and from county to county';[1] that is, *they preach in several places*. This is undoubtedly true. They 'draw after them confused multitudes of people';[2] that is, *many come to hear them*. This is true also. 'But they would do well to remember, God is not the author of *confusion* or of *tumult*, but of peace.'[3] I trust we do; nor is there any *confusion* or *tumult* at all in our largest congregations—unless at some rare times when sons of Belial mix therewith on purpose to disturb the peaceable worshippers of God.

'But our Church has provided against this preaching up and down in the ordination of a priest, by expressly limiting the exercise of the powers then conferred upon him to "the congregation where he shall be lawfully appointed thereunto".'[4]

I answer, (1). Your argument proves too much. If it be allowed just as you propose it, it proves that no priest has authority either to preach or minister the sacraments in any other than his own congregation.

(2). Had the powers conferred been *so limited* when I was ordained priest my ordination would have signified just nothing. For I was not *appointed to any congregation* at all, but was ordained as a member of the 'College of Divines' (so our statutes express it) 'founded to overturn all heresies, and defend the catholic faith'.

(3). For many years after I was ordained priest this limitation was never heard of. I heard not one syllable of it, by way of objection, to my preaching up and down in Oxford or London or the parts adjacent; in Gloucestershire or Worcestershire; in Lancashire, Yorkshire, or Lincolnshire. Nor did the strictest disciplinarian scruple suffering me to exercise those powers wherever I came.

(4). And, in fact, is it not universally allowed that every priest,

---

[1] *Observations*, p. 11.   [2] Ibid.
[3] Ibid., footnote.   [4] Ibid., pp. 11–12.

as such, has a power, in virtue of his ordination, either to preach or to administer the sacraments in any congregation, wherever the rector or curate desires his assistance? Does not everyone, then, see through this thin pretence?

5 10. 'The bishops and universities, indeed have power to grant licences to *itinerants*. But the Church has provided in that case, they are not to preach in any church (Canon 50) till they show their licence.'[1] .

The Church has well provided in that case. But what has *that* case to do with the case of common clergymen? Only so much as to show how grossly this Canon has been abused, at Islington in particular, where the churchwardens were instructed to hinder, by main force, the priest whom the vicar himself had appointed, from preaching, and to quote this Canon, which, as you plainly show, belongs to quite another thing.[2]

In the note you add: 'Mr. Wesley, being asked by what authority he preached, replied, "By the authority of Jesus Christ, conveyed to me by the (now) Archbishop of Canterbury, when he laid his hands upon me and said, 'Take thou authority to preach the gospel.'" In this reply he thought fit, for a plain reason, to leave out *this latter part* of the commission; for that would have shown his reader the *restraint* and *limitation* under which the exercise of the power is granted.'[3] Nay, I did not *print* the latter part of the words for a plainer reason—because I did not *speak* them. And I did not speak them then, because they did not come into my mind. Though probably if they had I should not have spoken them; it being my only concern to answer the question proposed, in as few words as I could.

But before those words, which you suppose to imply such a restraint as would condemn all the bishops and clergy in the nation, were those spoken without any restraint or limitation at all, which I apprehend to convey an indelible character: 'Receive the Holy Ghost for the office and work of a Priest in the Church of God,

---

[1] *Observations.* p. 12.

[2] The Revd. George Stonehouse, M.A., vicar of St. Mary's, Islington, was 'convinced of "the truth as it is in Jesus"' shortly before John Wesley's own conversion (cf. Wesley, *Journal*, May 10, 1738). Thereafter he showed himself very willing to have George Whitefield or the Wesleys occupy his pulpit. The congregation became restive, the churchwardens consulted the bishop, and Gibson (it was believed) abetted them in their opposition to the vicar. The churchwardens turned the canons to an unusual use, one which only an expert in church law (such as Gibson) could have suggested.

[3] *Observations*, p. 11, footnote.

now committed unto thee by the imposition of our hands. Whose sins thou dost forgive, they are forgiven; and whose sins thou dost retain, they are retained. And be thou a faithful dispenser of the Word of God, and of his Holy Sacraments; in the name of the Father, and of the Son, and of the Holy Ghost.'[1]

You proceed: 'In the same journal he declares . . . that he looks upon all the world as his parish, and explains his meaning as follows: "In whatever part of it I am, I judge it meet, right, and my bounden duty, to declare unto all that are willing to hear, the glad tidings of salvation. This is the work which I know God hath called me to." '[2] Namely, by 'the laying on of the hands of the presbytery',[3] which directs me how to obey that general command, 'while we have time, let us do good unto all men'.[4]

11. You object farther: 'That the Methodists do not observe the rubric before the Communion service; which directs so many as desire to partake of the Holy Communion to signify their names to the curate the day before.'[5] What curate desires they should? Whenever any minister will give but one week's notice of this, I undertake all that have any relation to me shall signify their names within the time appointed.

You object also that they break through the twenty-eighth Canon, which requires that 'if strangers come often to any church from other parishes, they should be remitted to their own churches, there to receive the communion with their neighbours'.[6]

But what if there be no communion there? Then this Canon does not touch the case, nor does any one break it by coming to another Church purely because there is no Communion at his own.

As to your next advice, 'to have a greater regard to the rules and orders of the Church',[7] I *cannot*; for I now regard them next to the Word of God. And as to your last: 'to renounce communion with the Church',[8] I *dare not*. Nay, but let them thrust us out. We *will not* leave the ship: if you *cast us* out of it, then our Lord will take us up.

12. To the same head may be referred the objection sometime urged by a friendly and candid man, viz., 'that it was unlawful to use extemporary prayer, because there was a Canon against it'.[9]

---

[1] B.C.P., Ordering of Priests.   [2] *Observations*, p. 11, footnote.
[3] 1 Tim. 4: 14.   [4] Cf. Gal. 6: 10.   [5] Cf. *Observations*, pp. 4–5.
[6] Ibid., p. 5.   [7] Ibid., p. 6.   [8] Ibid., p. 6.
[9] In the *Journal* for Nov. 28, 1740 Wesley recounts how 'a gentleman came to me full of good will, to exhort me not to leave the Church; or (which was the same thing in his

It was not quite clear to me that the Canon he cited was against extemporary prayer. But supposing it were, my plain answer would be: 'That Canon I dare not obey; because the law of man binds only so far as it is consistent with the Word of God.'

5   The same person objected my not obeying the bishops and governors of the Church. I answer, I both do and will obey them, in whatsoever I can with a clear conscience. So that there is no just ground for that charge that I *despise* either the rules or the governors of the Church. I obey them in all things where I do not apprehend
10 there is some particular law of God to the contrary. Even in that case I show all the deference I can; I endeavour to act as inoffensively as possible; and am ready to submit to any penalty which can by law be inflicted upon me. Would to God every minister and member of the Church were herein altogether as I am!

15   VII. 1. I have considered the chief objections that have lately been urged against the *doctrines* I teach. The main arguments brought against this *manner of teaching* have been considered also. It remains to examine the most current objections concerning *the effects* of this teaching.

20   Many affirm, 'that it does abundance of hurt; that it has had very bad effects; insomuch that if any good at all has been done, yet it bears no proportion to the evil'.

But come to particulars: 'First, then, you are disturbers of the public peace.'

25   What, do we either teach or raise sedition? Do we speak evil of the ruler of our people? Or do we stir them up against any of those that are put in authority under him? Do we directly or indirectly promote faction, mutiny, or rebellion? I have not found any man in his senses yet that would affirm this.

30   'But it is plain, peace is broke and disturbances do arise in consequence of your preaching.' I grant it. But what would you infer? Have you never read the Bible? Have you not read that the Prince

---

account) to use extempore prayer'. He argued that you cannot do two things at once; but extemporary prayer presupposes that you simultaneously think what to say, and pray; therefore it is impossible. Wesley's diary shows that the man was Mr. Allen of Kettering. It was natural for Wesley to challenge the relevance of the appeal to the canons, since there is no specific reference in them to extempore prayer. His critic may have had in mind Canon 36, which requires in worship 'illam prorsus formam, quae in dicto libro praescribitur, et non aliam, sit observaturus' (*Constitutions and Canons Ecclesiastical, 1604*, ed. J. V. Bullard, p. 41). But this concerns the use of the B.C.P. in public worship, requiring that the minister 'will use the form in the said book prescribed . . . and none other'.

of Peace himself was, in *this* sense, a disturber of the public peace?
'When he came into Jerusalem all the city was moved',[a] shaken as
with an earthquake. And the disturbance arose higher and higher,
till the whole multitude cried out together, 'Away with him, away
with him; crucify him, crucify him; and Pilate gave sentence it   5
should be done.'[1] Such another disturber of the public peace was
that Stephen, even from the time he began 'disputing with the
Libertines and Cyrenians' till the people 'stopped their ears, and
ran upon him with one accord, and cast him out of the city and
stoned him'.[2] Such disturbers of the peace were all those ringleaders   10
of the sect of the Nazarenes (commonly called apostles) who, where-
ever they came, 'turned the world upside down'.[3] And above all the
rest that Paul of Tarsus, who occasioned so much disturbance at
Damascus,[b] at Antioch of Pisidia,[c] at Iconium,[d] at Lystra,[e] at
Philippi,[f] at Thessalonica,[g] and particularly at Ephesus. The con-   15
sequence of his preaching there was that 'the whole city was filled
with confusion'. And 'they all ran together with one accord, . . .
some crying one thing, some another'; inasmuch as 'the greater part
of them knew not wherefore they were come together'.[4]

2. And can we expect it to be any otherwise *now*? Although what   20
we preach is the gospel of peace, yet if you will violently and
illegally hinder our preaching, must not this create disturbance? But
observe, the disturbance begins on *your* part. All is peace till you
raise that disturbance. And then you very modestly impute it to *us*,
and lay your *own* riot at *our* door!   25

But of all this our Lord had told us before: 'Think not that I am
come to send peace upon earth' (that this will be the immediate
effect wherever my gospel is preached with power): 'I am not come
to send peace, but a sword.'[5] This (so far as the wisdom of God
permits, by whom 'the hairs of your head are all numbered')[6] will be   30
the first consequence of my coming, whenever my word turns
sinners 'from darkness to light, from the power of Satan unto God'.[7]

I would wish all you who see this Scripture fulfilled, by disturbance following the preaching the gospel, to remember the behaviour

---

[1] Cf. Luke 23: 21, 24; John 19: 15.   [2] Cf. Acts 6: 9; 7: 57–8.
[3] Acts 17: 6.   [4] Acts 19: 29, 32.   [5] Matt. 10: 34.
[6] Cf. Matt. 10: 30.   [7] Acts 26: 18.

of that wise magistrate at Ephesus on the like occasion. He did not lay the disturbance to the preacher's charge, but 'beckoned to the multitude . . ., and said, Ye men of Ephesus, . . . ye ought to be quiet, and to do nothing rashly. For ye have brought these men, who
5 are neither robbers of temples, nor yet blasphemers of your Goddess.' (Not convicted of any such notorious crime as can at all excuse this lawless violence.) 'But if Demetrius hath a matter against any, the law is open, and there are deputies' (or proconsuls, capable of hearing and deciding the cause); 'let them implead one another. But
10 if ye inquire any thing concerning other things, it shall be determined in a lawful assembly.'[1]

3. 'But you create divisions in private families.' Accidentally, we do. For instance, suppose an entire family to have the form but not the power of godliness;[2] or to have neither the form nor the power—
15 in either case they may in some sort agree together. But suppose, when these hear the plain Word of God, one or two of them are convinced, 'This is the truth. And I have been all this time in the broad way that leadeth to destruction.'[3] These then will begin to mourn after God, while the rest remain as they were. Will they not
20 therefore of consequence divide, and form themselves into separate parties? Must it not be so in the very nature of things? And how exactly does this agree with the words of our Lord? 'Suppose ye that I came to send peace upon earth? I tell you nay; but rather division. For from henceforth there shall be five divided in one
25 house, three against two, and two against three. The father shall be divided against the son, and the son against the father; the mother against her daughter, and the daughter against the mother; the mother-in-law against the daughter-in-law, and the daughter-in-law against the mother-in-law.'[a] 'And the foes of a man shall be
30 they of his own household.'[b]

Thus it was from the very beginning. For is it to be supposed that a *heathen* parent would long endure a *Christian* child? Or that a *heathen* husband would agree with a *Christian* wife? Unless either the believing wife could gain her husband; or the unbelieving
35 husband prevailed on the wife to renounce *her way* of worshipping God; at least, unless she would obey him in going no more to those

[a] Luke 12: 51–3.   [b] Matt. 10: 36.

---

[1] Cf. Acts 19: 33–9.   [2] See 2 Tim. 3: 5.   [3] Cf. Matt. 7: 13.

societies or *conventicles* (ἑταιρίαι),[1] as they termed the Christian assemblies.

4. Do you think now I have an eye to *your* case? Doubtless I have; for I do not fight as one that beateth the air.[2] 'Why have not I a right to hinder my own wife or child from going to a conventicle? 5 And is it not the duty of wives to obey their husbands? And of children to obey their parents?' Only set the case seventeen hundred years back, and your own conscience gives you the answer. What would St. Paul have said to one whose husband forbade her to follow 'this way'[3] any more? What directions would our Saviour 10 have given to him whose father enjoined him not to hear the gospel? His words are extant still: 'He that loveth father or mother more than me, is not worthy of me. And he that loveth son or daughter more than me, is not worthy of me.'[a] Nay more, 'If any man cometh to me, and hateth not (in comparison of me) his father and mother 15 and wife and children, yea, and his own life, he cannot be my disciple.'[b]

'O, but this is not a parallel case. For they were *heathens*; but I am a *Christian*.' A Christian! Are you so? Do you understand the word? Do you know what a Christian is? If you are a Christian, 20 you have the mind that was in Christ, and you so walk as he also walked.[4] You are holy as he is holy, both in heart, and in all manner of conversation.[5] Have you then the mind that was in Christ? And do you walk as Christ walked? Are you inwardly and outwardly holy? I fear, not even outwardly. No, you live in known sin. Alas! 25 How then are you a Christian? What, a railer a Christian? A common swearer a Christian? A sabbath-breaker a Christian? A drunkard or whoremonger a Christian? Thou art a heathen, barefaced; the wrath of God is on thy head, and the curse of God upon thy back. Thy damnation slumbereth not.[6] By reason of such 30 Christians it is that the holy name of Christ is blasphemed.[7] Such as thou they are that cause the very savages in the Indian woods to cry out, 'Christian much drunk, Christian beat men, Christian tell lies, devil Christian! Me no Christian.'

---

[a] Matt. 10: 37, 38.   [b] Luke 14: 26.

---

[1] ἑταιρίαι, a term found in some late patristic writers, but not in classical Greek nor in the New Testament. Cf. John of Damascus, Migne, *Patrologia Graeca*, XCIV. 768c.

[2] See 1 Cor. 9: 26.   [3] Acts 9: 2, 22: 4.   [4] See Phil. 2: 5; 1 John 2: 6.
[5] See 1 Pet. 1: 15.   [6] See 2 Pet. 2: 3.   [7] See Rom. 2: 24.

And so *thou* wilt direct thy wife and children in the way of salvation! Woe unto thee, thou 'devil Christian'! Woe unto thee, thou blind leader of the blind![1] What wilt thou make them? Twofold more the children of hell than thyself?[2] Be ashamed. Blush, if thou canst blush. Hide thy face. Lay thee in the dust. Out of the deep cry unto God,[3] if haply he may hear thy voice. Instantly smite upon thy breast. Who knoweth but God may take thee out of the belly of hell?[4]

5. 'But you are not one of these. You fear God, and labour to have a conscience void of offence.[5] And it is from a principle of *conscience* that you restrain your wife or children from hearing *false doctrine*.' But how do you know it is false doctrine? Have you heard for yourself? Or, if you have not heard, have you carefully read what we have occasionally answered for ourselves? A man of conscience cannot condemn any one unheard. This is not common humanity. Nor will he refrain from hearing what *may be* the truth, for no better reason than fear of his reputation. Pray observe. I do not say every man (or any man) is obliged in conscience to hear us. But I do say every man in England who condemns us is obliged to hear us first. This is only common justice, such as is not denied to a thief or a murderer. Take your choice, therefore. Either hear us, or condemn us not. Either speak nothing at all, or hear before you speak.

But suppose you have both read and heard *more than you liked*? Did you read and hear fairly? Was not you loaden with prejudice? Did you not read or hear, *expecting no good*; perhaps *desiring* to find fault? If so, what wonder you judge as you do! What a poor mock trial is this! You had decided the cause in your own breast before you heard one word of the evidence. And still do *you* talk of acting out of conscience? Yea, a conscience void of offence?

We will put the case farther yet. Suppose your censure was just, and this was actually false doctrine. Still everyone must give an account of himself to God; and you cannot *force* the conscience of any one. You cannot *compel* another to see as you see. You ought not to attempt it. Reason and persuasion are the only weapons you ought to use, even toward your own wife and children. Nay, and it is impossible to *starve* them into conviction, or to *beat* even truth into

---

[1] Matt. 15: 14. [2] See Matt. 23: 15.
[3] See Ps. 130: 1. [4] Jonah 2: 2.
[5] Acts 24: 16.

their head. You may *destroy* them in this way, but cannot *convert* them. Remember what our own poet has said:

> By force beasts act, and are by force restrained;
> The human mind by gentle means is gained. . . .
> Thou canst not take what I refuse to yield: 5
> Nor reap the harvest, though thou spoilst the field.[1]

6. Every reasonable man is convinced of this. And perhaps you do not concern yourself so much about the doctrine, but the mischief that is done. 'How many poor families are starved, ruined, brought to beggary!' By what? Not by *contributing* a penny a week (the usual 10 contribution in our societies) and *letting that alone* when they please, when there is any shadow of reason to suppose they cannot afford it. You will not say any are brought to beggary by this—nor[2] by gifts to me, for I receive none save (sometimes) the food I eat. And public collections are nothing to me. That it may evidently appear 15 they are not, when any such collection is made to clothe the poor, or for any other determinate purpose, the money is both received and expended before many witnesses, without ever going through my hands at all. And then likewise all possible regard is had to the circumstances of those who contribute anything. And they are told 20 over and over, 'if there . . . be a willing mind, it is accepted according to that a man hath'.[3]

But where are all these families that have been brought to beggary? How is it that none of them is forthcoming? Are they all *out of town*? Then indeed I am in no danger of clearing myself from *their* 25 indictment. It is the easiest thing of a thousand for one at Newcastle to say that I have beggared him and all his kindred. If one of the long-bearded men on Tyne Bridge were to say so just now, I could not readily confute him. But why will you not bring a few of these to tell me so to my face? I have not found one that would do this 30 yet. They pray you would have them excused.

I remember a man coming to me with a doleful countenance, putting himself into many lamentable postures, gaping as wide as he could, and pointing to his mouth, as though he would say he could not speak. I inquired of his companion what was the matter, 35

---

[1] Prior, *Solomon*, ii. 257–8, 261–2. Line 261 reads: 'Thou shalt not gain what I deny to yield.'

[2] The contemporary editions read 'not', probably an uncorrected misprint.

[3] 2 Cor. 8: 12.

and was informed, 'he had fallen into the hands of the Turks, who had used him in a barbarous manner, and cut out his tongue by the roots'. I believed him. But when the man had had a cheerful cup, he could find his tongue as well as another. I reflected, 'How is it that
5 I could so readily believe that tale?' The answer was easy: 'Because it was told of a Turk.' My friend, take knowledge of your own case. If you had not first took me for a Turk or something equally bad, you could not so readily have believed that tale!

7. 'But can it be that there is no ground at all for a report which is
10 in everyone's mouth?' I will simply tell you all the ground which I can conceive. I believe many of those who attend on my ministry have less of this world's goods than they had before, or at least might have had if they did not attend it. This fact I allow; and it may be easily accounted for in one or other of the following ways.
15 First: I frequently preach on such texts as these: 'Having food and raiment, let us be content therewith. They who desire to be rich fall into temptation, and a snare, and many foolish and hurtful lusts, which drown men in destruction and perdition.'[1] 'Lay not up for yourselves treasures upon earth, where the rust and moth doth
20 corrupt, and where thieves break through and steal. But lay up for yourselves treasures in heaven, where neither rust nor moth doth corrupt, and where thieves do not break through and steal.'[2]

Now should any of those who are labouring by all possible means 'to lay up treasure upon earth' *feel* these words, they would not
25 'enlarge their desires as hell',[3] but be 'content with such things as they had'.[4] They then probably might not heap up so much for their heirs as otherwise they would have done. These would therefore *have less* than if they had not heard me; because they would *grasp at less*.
30 Secondly: Wherever the gospel takes effect, 'the foes of a man will be those of his own household'.[5] By this means, then, some who hear and receive it with joy will be poorer than they were before. Their domestic foes will in many cases hinder, embroil, and disturb the course of their affairs. And their relations, who assisted them before,
35 or promised at least so to do, will probably withdraw or deny that assistance, *unless they will be advised by them.* Perhaps their nearest relations, it being no new thing for parents to disown their children, if 'after the way which they call heresy, these worship the God of

---

[1] Cf. 1 Tim. 6: 8, 9.   [2] Matt. 6: 19-20.   [3] Cf. Hab. 2: 5.
[4] Cf. Heb. 13: 5.   [5] Cf. Matt. 10: 36.

their fathers'.[1] Hence therefore some *have less* of this world's goods than they had in times past, either because they *earn less*, or because they *receive less* from them on whom they depend.

Thirdly: It is written that 'those who received not the mark of the beast, either on their foreheads, or in their right hands',[2] either openly or secretly, were not permitted 'to buy or sell any more'.[3] Now whatever the mystery contained herein may be, I apprehend the plain mark of the beast is wickedness, inward and outward unholiness—whatever is secretly or openly contrary to justice, mercy, or truth. And certain it is, the time is well nigh come when those who have not this mark can neither buy nor sell, can scarce follow any profession so as to gain a subsistence thereby. Therefore many of those who attend on my ministry are by this means poorer than before. They will not receive the mark of the beast either on their forehead or in their hand; or if they had received it before, they rid themselves of it as soon as possible. Some cannot follow their former way of life *at all* (as pawnbrokers, smugglers, buyers or sellers of uncustomed goods). Others cannot follow it *as they did before*. For they cannot oppress, cheat or defraud their neighbour; they cannot lie, or say what they do not mean; they *must* now speak the truth from their heart. On all these accounts they *have less* of this world's goods, because they *gain less* than they did before.

Fourthly: 'All that will live godly in Christ Jesus shall suffer persecution';[4] if in no other way, yet at least in this, that 'men will by reviling persecute them, and say all manner of evil against them falsely for his sake'.[5] One unavoidable effect of this will be that men whose subsistence depends on their daily labour will be often in want, for few will care to employ those of so 'bad a character'. And even those who did employ them before, perhaps for many years, will employ them no more, so that hereby some may indeed be brought to beggary.

8. What! Does this touch *you*? Are *you* one of those who will 'have nothing to do with those scandalous wretches'? Perhaps you will say: 'And who can blame me for it. May I not employ whom I please?' We will weigh this. You employed A. B. for several years. By your own account he was an honest, diligent man. You had no objection to him but his following 'this way'. For this reason you turn him off. In a short time, having spent his little all, and having

---

[1] Cf. Acts 24: 14.   [2] Cf. Rev. 20: 4.   [3] Cf. Rev. 13: 17.
[4] 2 Tim. 3: 12.   [5] Cf. Matt. 5: 11.

no supply, he wants bread; so does his family, too, as well as himself. Before he can get into other business to procure it, through want of convenient food to eat and raiment to put on, he sickens and dies. This is not an imaginary scene. I have known the case;
5 though too late to remedy it.

'And what then?' Why then *you* are a murderer. 'O earth, cover not thou his blood!'[1] No, it doth not. 'The cry thereof hath entered into the ears of the Lord God of Sabaoth.'[2] And God requireth it at *your* hands; and will require it in an hour when you think not.
10 For *you* have as effectually murdered that man as if you had stabbed him to the heart.

It is not I, then, who ruin and starve that family, it is *you*. *You* who call yourself a Protestant! *You* who cry out against the persecuting spirit of the *Papists*! Ye fools and blind![3] What! Are ye better
15 than they? Why, Edmund Bonner[4] would have *starved* the heretics in *prison*; whereas *you starve* them in their *own houses*.

And all this time you talk of 'liberty of conscience'! Yes, liberty for such a conscience as your own—a conscience *past feeling* (for sure it had some once); a conscience seared with a hot iron.[5] Liberty
20 to serve the devil according to your poor, hardened conscience, you allow; but not liberty to serve God.

Nay, and what marvel? Whosoever thou art that readest this and feelest in thy heart a real desire to serve God, I warn thee, expect no liberty for thy conscience from him that hath no conscience at all.
25 All ungodly, unthankful, unholy men, all villains of whatever denomination, will have liberty indeed all the world over, as long as their master is 'god of this world'.[6] But expect not liberty to worship God in spirit and in truth,[7] to practise pure and undefiled religion[8] (unless the Lord should work a new thing in the earth),
30 from any but those who themselves love and serve God.

9. 'However, 'tis plain you make men idle. And this tends to beggar their families.' This objection having been continually urged for some years, I will trace it from the foundation.

---

[1] Cf. Job 16: 18.   [2] Cf. Jas. 5: 4.   [3] Matt. 23: 17, 19.
[4] Edmund Bonner (*c.* 1500–69), Bishop of London from 1539 until his deprivation in 1559, was one of the foremost champions in the Tudor period of the dependence of the English Church on the papacy. Under Queen Mary he played an important part in reconciling England with Rome, and on him fell a major share of the responsibility for attempting to stamp out Protestantism. The immense popularity of John Foxe's *Acts and Monuments* ('The Book of Martyrs') permanently branded Bonner as a cruel and implacable persecutor.
[5] 1 Tim. 4: 2.   [6] 2 Cor. 4: 4.   [7] See John 4: 23, 24.   [8] See Jas. 1: 27.

Two or three years after my return from America one Captain Robert Williams of Bristol made affidavit before the (then) mayor of the city that 'it was a common report in Georgia Mr. Wesley took people off from their work and *made them idle* by preaching so much'.[1]   5

The fact stood thus: At my first coming to Savannah the generality of the people rose at seven or eight in the morning. And that part of them who were accustomed to work usually worked till six in the evening. A few of them sometimes worked till seven, which is the time of sunset there in midsummer.   10

I immediately began reading prayers and expounding the Second Lesson, both in the morning and evening. The morning service began at five, and ended at or before six; the evening service began at seven.

Now supposing all the grown persons in the town had been present   15 every morning and evening, would this have 'made them idle'? Would they hereby have had *less*, or considerably *more time for working*?

10. The same rule I follow now, both at London, Bristol, and Newcastle upon Tyne, concluding the service at every place, winter   20 and summer, before six in the morning, and not ordinarily beginning to preach till near seven in the evening.

Now do you who make this objection work longer throughout the year than from six to six? Do you desire that the generality of people should? Or can you count them idle that work so long?   25

Some few are indeed accustomed to work longer. These I advise not to come on weekdays. And it is apparent that they take this advice, unless on some rare and extraordinary occasion.

But I hope none of *you* who turn them out of their employment have the confidence to talk of *my* making them idle! Do you (as the   30 homely phrase is) cry wh—— first?[2] I admire your cunning, but not your modesty.

So far am I from either *causing* or *encouraging* idleness that an idle person, known to be such, is not suffered to remain in any of our

---

[1] The circulation of this affidavit in broadsheet form was the immediate cause of Wesley's publication of the first extract from his *Journal* in 1740. For a full discussion of the circumstances see *Methodist History*, Vol. VIII, No. 2 (Jan. 1970), pp. 25–32.

[2] An allusion to John 8: 7. For other echoes of this saying see Aphra Behn, *The Town Fop* (1676), Act iv., sc. 3: 'She cries whore first, brings him upon his knees for her fault; and a piece of plate, or a new petticoat, makes his peace again'; also Swift, *Polite Conversation* (1738), Dial. i: 'You cried whore first, when you talked of the knapsack.'

societies; we drive him out as we would a thief or murderer. 'To show all possible diligence' (as well as frugality) is one of our standing rules; and one concerning the observance of which we continually make the strictest inquiry.[1]

5 11. 'But you drive them out of their senses. You *make them mad.*' Nay, then they are idle with a vengeance. This objection, therefore, being of the utmost importance, deserves our deepest consideration.

And first, I grant, it is my earnest desire to drive all the world into what you probably call 'madness'—I mean, inward religion—to 10 make them just as mad as Paul was when he was so accounted by Festus.[2]

The counting all things on earth but dung and dross, so we may win Christ;[3] the trampling under foot all the pleasures of the world; the seeking no treasure but in heaven;[4] the having no desire of the 15 praise of men,[5] a good character, a fair reputation; the being exceeding glad when men revile us, and persecute us, and say all manner of evil against us falsely;[6] the giving God thanks when our father and mother forsake us,[7] when we have neither food to eat, nor raiment to put on, nor a friend but what shoots out bitter words,[8] nor a place 20 where to lay our head:[9] this is utter *distraction* in *your* account; but in God's it is sober, rational religion, the genuine fruit, not of a distempered brain, not of a sickly imagination, but 'of the power of God in the heart, of victorious love, and of a sound mind'.[10]

12. I grant, secondly, it is my endeavour to drive all I can into 25 what *you* may term another species of 'madness', which is usually preparatory to this, and which I term 'repentance' or 'conviction'.

I cannot describe this better than a writer of our own has done. I will therefore transcribe his words:

When men *feel* in themselves the heavy burden of sin, see damnation 30 to be the reward of it, and behold with the eye of their mind the horror of hell; they tremble, they quake, and are inwardly touched with sorrowfulness of heart, and cannot but accuse themselves, and open their grief unto Almighty God, and call unto him for mercy. This being done seriously, their mind is so occupied, partly with sorrow and heavi- 35 ness, partly with an earnest desire to be delivered from this danger of hell and damnation, that all desire of meat and drink is laid apart, and

---

[1] See *The Nature, Design, and General Rules of the United Societies* (1743), § 5, in Vol. 9 of this edition, *The Methodist Societies: History, Nature, and Design.*
[2] See Acts 26: 24.   [3] See Phil. 3: 8.   [4] See Matt. 6: 20, etc.
[5] See John 12: 43.   [6] See Matt. 5: 11.   [7] See Ps. 27: 10.
[8] See Ps. 64: 3.   [9] See Matt. 8: 20.   [10] Cf. 2 Tim. 1: 7.

loathsomeness (or loathing) of all worldly things and pleasure cometh in place. So that nothing then liketh them more than to weep, to lament, to mourn, and both with words and behaviour of body to show themselves weary of life.[1]

Now what if your wife, or daughter, or acquaintance, after hearing 5 one of these field preachers, should come and tell you, that they 'saw damnation' before them and 'beheld with the eye of their mind the horror of hell'? What if they should 'tremble and quake', and be so taken up 'partly with sorrow and heaviness, partly with an earnest desire to be delivered from this danger of hell and damnation', as 10 'to weep, to lament, to mourn, and both with words and behaviour to show themselves weary of life'? Would you scruple to say that they were *stark mad*? That these fellows had driven them *out of their senses*? And that whatever writer it was that talked *at this rate*, he was fitter for Bedlam than any other place? 15

You have overshot yourself now to some purpose. These are the very words of our own Church. You may read them, if you are so inclined, in the first part of the Homily on Fasting. And consequently, what you have peremptorily determined to be 'mere lunacy and distraction' is that 'repentance unto life'[2] which, in the judgment 20 both of the Church and of St. Paul, is 'never to be repented of'.[3]

13. I grant, thirdly, that *extraordinary* circumstances have attended this conviction in some instances. A particular account of these I have frequently given. While the Word of God was preached, some persons have dropped down as dead; some have been, as it 25 were, in strong convulsions; some roared aloud, though not with an articulate voice; and others spoke the anguish of their souls.

This, I suppose, you believe to be perfect madness. But it is easily accounted for, either on principles of reason or Scripture.

First, on principles of reason. For how easy is it to suppose that 30 a strong, lively, and sudden apprehension of the heinousness of sin, the wrath of God, and the bitter pains of eternal death, should affect the body as well as the soul during the present laws of vital union; should interrupt or disturb the ordinary circulations, and put nature out of its course! Yea, we may question whether, while 35 this union subsists, it be possible for the mind to be affected in so

---

[1] *Homilies*, Of Fasting, Pt. I, quoted also in *The Principles of a Methodist Farther Explained*, VI. 4, and *A Letter to the Bishop of Gloucester*, II. 28.
[2] Acts 11: 18.   [3] Cf. 2 Cor. 7: 10.

violent a degree without some or other of those bodily symptoms following.

It is likewise easy to account for these things on principles of Scripture. For when we take a view of them in this light, we are to
5 add to the consideration of natural causes the agency of those spirits who still excel in strength, and as far as they have leave from God, will not fail to torment whom they cannot destroy; to *tear* those *that are coming* to *Christ*.[1] It is also remarkable that there is plain Scripture precedent of every symptom which has lately appeared. So that
10 we cannot allow even the *conviction* attended with these to be *madness*, without giving up both reason and Scripture.

14. I grant, fourthly, that touches of extravagance, bordering on madness, may sometimes attend severe conviction. And this also is easy to be accounted for by the present laws of the animal economy.
15 For we know fear or grief, from a temporal cause, may occasion a fever, and thereby a delirium.

It is not strange, then, that some, while under strong impressions of grief or fear from a sense of the wrath of God, should for a season *forget* almost all things else, and scarce be able to answer a common
20 question; that some should *fancy* they see the flames of hell, or the devil and his angels around them; or that others for a space should be *afraid*, like Cain, 'whosoever meeteth me will slay me'.[2] All these, and whatever less common effects may sometimes accompany this conviction, are easily known from the natural distemper of madness,
25 were it only by this one circumstance, that whenever the person convinced tastes the pardoning love of God they all vanish away in a moment.

Lastly, I have seen one instance (I pray God I may see no more such!) of real, lasting madness.

30 Two or three years since, I took one with me to Bristol who was under deep convictions, but of as sound an understanding in all respects as ever he had been in his life. I went a short journey, and when I came to Bristol again, found him really distracted. I inquired particularly at what time and place and in what manner this
35 disorder began. And I believe there are at least threescore witnesses alive and ready to testify what follows. When I went from Bristol he contracted an acquaintance with some persons who were not of the same judgment with me. He was soon prejudiced against me. Quickly after, when our society were met together in Kingswood

---

[1] See Mark 9: 20.   [2] Cf. Gen. 4: 14.

house, he began a vehement invective both against my person and doctrines. In the midst of this he was struck raving mad. And so he continued till his friends put him into Bedlam; and probably laid *his* madness too to *my* charge.[1]

15. I fear there may also be some instances of real madness proceeding from a different cause.

Suppose, for instance, a person hearing me is strongly convinced that a liar cannot enter into the Kingdom of Heaven. He comes home and relates this to his parents or friends, and appears to be very uneasy. These *good Christians* are disturbed at this, and afraid he is running mad too. They are resolved he shall never hear any of those fellows more; and keep to it in spite of all his entreaties. They will not suffer him, when at home, to be alone, for fear he should read or pray. And perhaps in a while they will constrain him, at least by repeated importunities, to do again the very thing for which he was convinced the wrath of God cometh upon the children of disobedience.[2]

What is the event of this? Sometimes the Spirit of God is quenched, and departs from him. Now you have carried the point. The man is easy as ever, and sins on without any remorse. But in other instances, where those convictions sink deep, and the arrows of the Almighty stick fast in the soul,[3] you will drive that person into real, settled madness, before you can quench the Spirit of God. I am afraid there have been several instances of this. You have forced the man's conscience till he is stark mad. But then, pray, do not impute that madness to me. Had you left him to my direction, or rather to the direction of the Spirit of God, he would have been filled with love and a sound mind.[4] But you have taken the matter out of God's hand. And now you have brought it to a fair conclusion!

16. How frequent this case may be, I know not. But doubtless most of those who make this objection, of our driving men mad, have never met with such an instance in their lives. The common cry is occasioned either by those who are *convinced* of sin, or those who are inwardly *converted* to God: mere madness both (as was observed before) to those who are without God in the world. Yet

---

[1] An incident during the troubled period when the Methodist societies were seriously disturbed by tensions, primarily between the Wesleys and the Moravians, but also between Wesley and Whitefield. In the *Journal* for Aug. 15, 1744 Wesley identifies the man as 'Mr. S——'. For another reference to this incident see Wesley's second letter to Thomas Church, *The Principles of a Methodist Farther Explained*, IV. 9.

[2] Col. 3: 6.   [3] See Ps. 38: 2; Job 6: 4.   [4] See 2 Tim. 1: 7.

I do not deny but you may have seen one in Bedlam who *said* he had followed *me*. But observe, a madman's saying this is no proof of the fact. Nay, and if he really had, it should be farther considered that his being in Bedlam is no sure proof of his being mad. Witness
5 the well-known case of Mr. Periam;[1] and I doubt more such are to be found. Yea, it is well if some have not been sent thither for no other reason but because they followed me: their kind relations either concluding that they must be distracted before they could do this; or perhaps hoping that Bedlam would *make* them mad, if it
10 did not *find* them so.

17. And it must be owned a confinement of such a sort is as fit to *cause* as to *cure* distraction. For what scene of distress is to be compared to it? To be separated at once from all who are near and dear to you; to be cut off from all reasonable conversation, to be secluded
15 from all business, from all reading, from every innocent entertainment of the mind, which is left to prey wholly upon itself, and day and night to pore over your misfortunes; to be shut up day by day in a gloomy cell, with only the walls to employ your heavy eyes, in the midst either of melancholy silence, or horrid cries, groans, and
20 laughter intermixed; to be forced by the main strength of those

Who laugh at human nature and compassion[2]

to take drenches of nauseous, perhaps torturing medicines, which you know you have no need of now, but know not how soon you may, possibly by the operation of these very drugs on a weak or tender
25 constitution. Here is distress! It is an astonishing thing, a signal proof of the power of God, if any creature who has his senses when that confinement begins does not lose them before it is at an end!

How must it heighten the distress if such a poor wretch, being deeply convinced of sin, and growing worse and worse (as he
30 probably will, seeing there is no medicine here for *his* sickness, no such physician as his case requires) be soon placed among the *incurables*! Can imagination itself paint such a hell upon earth? Where even 'Hope never comes, that comes to all'![3] For what remedy? If a man of sense and humanity should happen to visit
35 that house of woe, would he give the hearing to a madman's tale?

---

[1] Joseph Periam, an attorney's clerk, was converted (in part, at least) by reading Whitefield's sermon on the new birth. His friends committed him to a madhouse, because (1) he had fasted for nearly a fortnight; (2) he prayed so fervently that he could be heard 'several storeys high'; (3) he had sold his clothes and given the proceeds to the poor. Cf. *The Life of the Rev. Mr. George Whitefield*, by an Impartial Hand (1739).
[2] Source of quotation unidentified.   [3] Milton, *Paradise Lost*, i. 66–7.

Or if he did, would he credit it? 'Do we not know', might he say, 'how well any of these will talk in their lucid intervals?' So that a thousand to one he would concern himself no more about it, but leave the weary to wait for rest in the grave!

18. I have now answered most of the current objections, particu- 5 larly such as have appeared of weight to religious or reasonable men. I have endeavoured to show, First, that the *doctrines* I teach are no other than the great truths of the gospel; Secondly, that though I teach them, not as I would, but as I *can*, yet it is in a *manner* not contrary to law; and Thirdly, that the *effects* of thus preaching the 10 gospel have not been such as was weakly or wickedly reported, those reports being mere artifices of the devil to hinder the work of God. Whosoever therefore ye are who look for God to 'revive his work in the midst of the years',[1] cry aloud that he may *finish* it nevertheless, may 'cut it short in righteousness'.[2] Cry to 'Messiah the 15 Prince' that he may soon 'end the transgression';[3] that he may 'lift up his standard'[4] upon earth, sending by whom he will send, and working his own work, when he pleaseth, and as he pleaseth, till 'all the kindreds of the people worship before him',[5] and the earth 'be full of the knowledge of the glory of the Lord'![6] 20

An
Act of Devotion

1. Behold the servant of the Lord!
   I wait thy guiding hand to feel,
   To hear and keep thine every word,
   To prove and do thy perfect will:
   Joyful from all my works to cease, 25
   Glad to fulfil all righteousness.

2. Me if thy grace vouchsafe to use,
   Meanest of all thy creatures, me,
   The deed, the time, the manner choose;
   Let all my fruit be found of thee, 30
   Let all my works in thee be wrought,
   By thee to full perfection brought.

[1] Cf. Hab. 3: 2.   [2] Rom. 9: 28.   [3] Cf. Dan. 9: 24, 25.
[4] Isa. 59: 19.   [5] Cf. Ps. 22: 27.   [6] Cf. Hab. 2: 14.

3. My every weak, though good, design
    O'errule or change as seems thee meet;
Jesus, let all the work be thine;
    Thy work, O lord, is all-complete,
5 And pleasing in thy Father's sight;
Thou only hast done all things right.

4. Here then to thee thine own I leave;
    Mould as thou wilt the passive clay:
But let me all thy stamp receive,
10   But let me all thy words obey,
Serve with a single heart and eye,
And to thy glory live, and die.

To the Reverend Mr. Thomas Church

Rev. Sir,
15 Since this was in the press I have seen your *Remarks* upon my
last *Journal.* I will endeavour, as you desire, 'attentively to consider
the points' therein 'objected to me'. In the meantime, I am,
                Reverend Sir,
                      Your servant for Christ's sake,
20   John Wesley
London,
    Dec. 22, 1744[1]

[1] *Remarks on the Rev. Mr. John Wesley's Last Journal . . . By Thomas Church, A.M.,
Vicar of Battersea,* London, for M. Cooper, 1745. It was a common practice for a
publication to be dated for the following year if (as in this instance) it appeared in the
closing months. Church's *Remarks* were dated at the end November 3, 1744. Wesley's
reply was completed in February 1745, and appeared as *An Answer to the Rev. Mr.
Church's Remarks on the Rev. Mr. Wesley's Last Journal,* for which see Vol. 9 of this
edition: *The Methodist Societies: History, Nature, and Design* and *Bibliography,* No. 97.
Wesley omitted this letter from the reprint of *A Farther Appeal* in his *Works,* Vol. 14,
transposing its date to the end of the prose section of the treatise.

A

FARTHER APPEAL

To MEN of

REASON and RELIGION

PART II[1]

I. 1. It is not my present design to touch on any particular *opinions*, whether they are right or wrong; nor on any of those smaller points of practice which are variously held by men of different persuasions; but First, to point out some things which on *common* principles are condemned by men of every denomination, 5 and yet found in all; and Secondly, some wherein those of each denomination are more particularly inconsistent with *their own* principles.

And first it is my design, abstracting from opinions of every kind, as well as from disputable points of practice, to mention such of 10 those things as occur to my mind which are on common principles condemned, and notwithstanding found, more or less, among men of every denomination.

2. But before I enter on this unpleasing task, I beseech you, brethren, by the mercies of God[2]—by whatever love you bear to 15 God, to your country, to your own souls—do not consider who speaks, but what is spoken. If it be possible, for one hour lay prejudice aside; give what is advanced a fair hearing. Consider simply on each head, Is this true, or is it false? Is it reasonable, or is it not?

---

[1] Parts II and III were from the outset published as a unit distinct from Part I, but paginated continuously with each other, although Part III was presented with a separate title-page. 'Part II' first appeared on the title page of the so-called 'Third Edition' of 1746, which also introduced a new scriptural motto, Isa. 58: 1; this replaced Ps. 141: 5, copied (perhaps inadvertently) from the title-page of Part I. Part III was described as such in the internal title-pages from the first edition onwards, and for its motto employed Luke 19: 41–2. For full bibliographical details see *Bibliography*, No. 96, and for a summary of the seven editions published during Wesley's lifetime, a stemma illustrating the transmission of the text, and a list of substantive variant readings, see the Appendix, pp. 549–54.   [2] Rom. 12: 1.

If you ask, 'But in whose judgment?' I answer, In your own: I appeal to the light of your own mind. Is there not a faithful witness in your own breast? By this you must stand or fall. You cannot be judged by another man's conscience. Judge for yourself by the best
5 light you have. And the merciful God teach me and thee whatsoever we know not!

Now as I speak chiefly to those who believe the Scriptures, the method I propose is this: first to observe what account is given therein of the Jews, the ancient church of God, inasmuch as 'all
10 these things were written for our instruction',[1] who say we are *now* the visible church of the God of Israel; secondly to appeal to all who profess to be members thereof, to everyone who is called a Christian, how far in each instance the parallel holds, and how much *we* are better than *they*.

15 3. First I am to observe what account the Scriptures give of the Jews, the ancient church of God. I mean, with regard to their moral character, their tempers, and outward behaviour.

No sooner were they brought out of Egypt than we find them 'murmuring against God'.[a] Again, when he had just brought them
20 through the Red Sea 'with a mighty hand and a stretched out arm'.[b] And yet again, quickly after, in the wilderness of Zin, 'your murmurings (saith Moses) are not against us, but against the Lord'.[c] Nay, even while he was 'giving them bread from heaven'[2] they were still 'murmuring and tempting God',[d] and their amazing language
25 at that very season was, 'Is the Lord among us or not?'[e]

The same spirit they showed during the whole forty years that he 'bore their manners in the wilderness'.[3] A solemn testimony whereof 'Moses spake in the ears of all the congregation of Israel'[4] when God was about to take him away from their head: 'They
30 have corrupted themselves', saith he; 'their spot is not of his children; they are a perverse and crooked generation. . . . The Lord led Jacob about, he instructed him, he kept him as the apple of his eye.'[f] 'He made him ride on the high places of the earth, that he might eat the increase of the fields. . . . Then he forsook God which
35 made him, and lightly esteemed the rock of his salvation.'[g]

---

[a] Exod. 14: 12. [Cf. Exod. 16: 7, 8.]
[b] Exod. 15: 24. [Cf. Deut. 5: 15; Ezek. 20: 34.]   [c] Exod. 16: 8.
[d] Exod. 17: 2, 3.   [e] Exod. 17: 7.   [f] Deut. 32: 5, 10.   [g] Deut. 32: 13, 15.

---

[1] See Rom. 15: 4 (cf. *Notes*).   [2] Cf. Exod. 16: 4; John 6: 32.
[3] Cf. Acts 13: 18.   [4] Deut. 31: 30.

In like manner God complains long after this: 'Hear, O heavens, and give ear, O earth!... I have nourished and brought up children, and they have rebelled against me. The ox knoweth his owner, and the ass his master's crib: but Israel doth not know, my people doth not consider. Ah sinful nation, a people laden with iniquity, a seed 5 of evil-doers, children that are corrupters; they have forsaken the Lord, they have provoked the Holy One of Israel.'ᵃ 'Can a maid forget her ornaments, and a bride her attire? Yet my people have forgotten me, days without number.'ᵇ

4. And 'as they did not like to retain God in their knowledge',[1] so 10 they had small regard to the ordinances of God. 'Even from the days of your fathers', saith God by his prophets, 'ye are gone away from mine ordinances, and have not kept them.'ᶜ 'Ye have said, It is vain to serve God; and what profit is it that we have kept his ordinances?'ᵈ 'Thou hast not called upon me, O Jacob; but thou 15 hast been weary of me, O Israel. Thou hast not brought me my burnt offerings, neither hast thou honoured me with thy sacrifices.'ᵉ And so the prophet himself confesses, 'Thou meetest... those that remember thee in thy ways.... But there is none that calleth upon thy name, that stirreth up himself to take hold of thee.'ᶠ 20

5. But they called upon his name by vain oaths, by perjury, and blasphemy. So Jeremiah: 'Because of swearing the land mourneth';ᵍ 'and though they say, The Lord liveth, surely they swear falsely'.ʰ So Hosea: 'They have spoken words, swearing falsely in making a covenant.'[2] So Ezekiel: 'They say, The Lord seeth us not, the 25 Lord hath forsaken the earth.'[3] So Isaiah: 'Their tongue and their doings are against the Lord, to provoke the eyes of his glory';ⁱ 'They say, Let him make speed, and hasten his work that we may see it; and let the counsel of the Holy One draw nigh, and come, that we may know it.'ʲ And so Malachi: 'Ye have wearied the Lord 30 with your words;... Ye say, Everyone that doeth evil is good in the sight of the Lord, and he delighteth in them; and, Where is the God of judgment?'ᵏ

6. And as they 'despised his holy things', so they 'profaned his sabbaths'.ˡ Yea, when God sent unto them, saying, 'Take heed unto 35

ᵃ Isa. 1: 2–4.   ᵇ Jer. 2: 32.   ᶜ Mal. 3: 7.   ᵈ Mal. 3: 14.
ᵉ Isa. 43: 22–3.   ᶠ Isa. 64: 5, 7.   ᵍ Jer. 23: 10.   ʰ Jer. 5: 2.
ⁱ Isa. 3: 8.   ʲ Isa. 5: 19.   ᵏ Mal. 2: 17.   ˡ Ezek. 22: 8.

---

[1] Rom. 1: 28.   [2] Hos. 10: 4.   [3] Ezek. 8: 12.

yourselves, and bear no burden on the sabbath day . . ., neither do ye any work, but hallow ye the sabbath day, as I commanded your fathers': yet 'they obeyed not, neither inclined their ear, but made their neck stiff, that they might not hear, nor receive instruction'.[a]

5 Neither did they honour their parents, or those whom God from time to time appointed to be rulers over them. 'In thee' (in Jerusalem, saith the prophet) 'they have set light by father and mother.'[b] And from the very day when God brought them up out of the land of Egypt their murmurings, chiding, rebellion, and disobedience
10 against those whom he had chosen to go before them make the most considerable part of their history. So that had not Moses 'stood in the gap',[1] he had even then destroyed them from the face of the earth.

7. How much more did they afterwards provoke God by drunken-
15 ness, sloth, and luxury? 'They have erred through wine', saith the prophet Isaiah, 'and through strong drink they are out of the way';[c] which occasioned those vehement and repeated warnings against that reigning sin: 'Woe to the drunkards of Ephraim, . . . them that are overcome with wine![d] 'The drunkards of Ephraim shall be
20 trodden under foot';[e] 'Woe unto them that rise up early . . . that they may follow strong drink; that continue until night, till wine inflame them! . . . But they regard not the work of the Lord, neither consider the operation of his hands';[f] 'Woe unto them that are mighty to drink wine, and men of strength to mingle strong drink!'[g]
25 'Woe to them that are at ease in Zion, . . . that lie upon beds of ivory, and stretch themselves upon their couches, and eat the lambs out of the flock, and the calves out of the midst of the stall; that chant to the sound of the viol, and invent to themselves instruments of music; . . . that drink wine in bowls, and anoint themselves with
30 the chief ointments! But they are not grieved for the affliction of Joseph.'[h] 'Behold this', saith Ezekiel to Jerusalem, 'was the iniquity of thy sister Sodom; . . . fullness of bread, and abundance of idleness was in her and in her daughters.'[i]

8. From sloth and 'fullness of bread' *lewdness* naturally followed.
35 It was even while Moses was with them that 'the people began to commit whoredom with the daughters of Moab'.[2] Yea, of the

---

[a] Jer. 17: 21–3. [b] Ezek. 22: 7. [c] Isa. 28: 7.
[d] Isa. 28: 1. [e] Isa. 28: 3. [f] Isa. 5: 11, 12.
[g] Isa. 5: 22. [h] Amos 6: 1, 4–6. [i] Ezek. 16: 49.

[1] Cf. Ezek. 22: 30. [2] Num. 25: 1.

daughters of Zion Isaiah complains, they 'walk with stretched forth necks and wanton eyes'.[a] And of his people in general God complains by Jeremiah: 'When I had fed them to the full, they . . . assembled themselves by troops in the harlots' houses. They were as fed horses in the morning: every one neighed after his neighbour's wife.'[b] 'They be all adulterers, an assembly of treacherous men.'[c] 'The land is full of adulterers.'[d]

Yea, and some of them were given up to *unnatural lusts*. Thus we read: the men of Gibeah 'beset the house' wherein the stranger was, 'and beat at the door, and spake to the master of the house, saying, Bring forth the man that came into thine house, that we may know him'.[e] 'And there were also' long after 'Sodomites in the land',[1] in the days of Rehoboam and of the following kings, 'the very show of whose countenance witnessed against them, and they declare their sin as Sodom, they hid it not'.[f]

9. This was accompanied with injustice in all its forms. Thus all the prophets testify against them: 'The Lord . . . looked for judgment, but behold *oppression*; for righteousness, but behold a cry.'[g] 'Thou hast taken *usury* and increase; thou hast greedily gained of thy neighbour by *extortion*. . . . Behold, I have smitten my hand at thy *dishonest gain* which thou hast made.'[h] 'The balances of deceit are in Jacob's hand; he loveth to oppress.'[i] 'Are there not yet the *scant measure* that is abominable; the wicked balances, and the bag of *deceitful weights*?'[j] 'He that departeth from evil maketh himself a prey: and the Lord saw it, and it displeased him that there was no judgment.'[k] 'The wicked devoureth the man that is more righteous than he. . . . They take up all of them with the angle, they catch them in their net, and gather them in their drag.'[l] 'They covet fields and take them by *violence*; and houses, and take them away.'[m] 'They pull off the robe with the garment from them that pass by securely.'[n] 'They have dealt by oppression with the stranger; they have vexed the fatherless and the widow.'[o] 'The people of the land have used *oppression* and exercised *robbery*, and have vexed the poor and needy; yea, they have oppressed the stranger wrongfully.'[p] 'Their

[a] Isa. 3: 16.	[b] Jer. 5: 7, 8.	[c] Jer. 9: 2.	[d] Jer. 23: 10.
[e] Judg. 19: 22.	[f] [Cf.] Isa. 3: 9.	[g] Isa. 5: 7.	[h] Ezek. 22: 12, 13.
[i] Hos. 12: 7.	[j] Mic. 6: 10, 11.	[k] Isa. 59: 15.	[l] Hab. 1: 13–15.
[m] Mic. 2: 2.	[n] Mic. 2: 8.	[o] Ezek. 22: 7.	[p] Ezek. 22: 29.

[1] 1 Kgs. 14: 24.

works are works of iniquity, and the act of *violence* is in their hands.'ᵃ
'Judgment is turned away backward, and justice standeth afar off;
for truth is fallen in the street, and equity cannot enter.'ᵇ

10. Truth indeed was fallen, as well as justice. 'Every mouth
5 (saith Isaiah) speaketh folly.'ᶜ 'This is a rebellious people, lying
children.'ᵈ 'Their lips have spoken lies and muttered perverseness.
None calleth for justice, nor any pleadeth for truth; they trust in
vanity and speak lies.'ᵉ This occasioned that caution of Jeremiah:
'Take ye heed every one of his neighbour, and trust ye not in any
10 brother: for every brother will utterly supplant, and every neighbour will walk with slanders. And they will deceive every one his
neighbour, and will not speak the truth: they have taught their
tongue to speak lies, and weary themselves to commit iniquity.'ᶠ

11. And even those who abstained from these gross outward sins
15 were still inwardly corrupt and abominable. 'The whole head was
sick, and the whole heart was faint'; yea, 'from the sole of the foot
even unto the head there was no soundness, but wounds, and
bruises, and putrifying sores'.ᵍ 'All these nations (saith God) are
uncircumcised, and all the house of Israel are uncircumcised in
20 heart.'ʰ 'Their heart is divided.'ⁱ 'They have set up their idols in
their heart; . . . they are all estranged from me through their idols.'ʲ

Their soul still 'clave unto the dust'.¹ They 'laid up treasures
upon earth'.² 'From the least of them (saith Jeremiah) even unto the
greatest, every one is given to covetousness.'ᵏ 'They panted after
25 the dust of the earth.'ˡ They 'laded themselves with thick clay'.ᵐ
They 'joined house to house and laid field to field, until there was
no place'.ⁿ Yea, they 'enlarged their desires as hell'; they were 'as
death, and could not be satisfied'.ᵒ

12. And not only for their covetousness, but for their *pride* of
30 heart were they an abomination to the Lord. 'The pride of Israel
(saith Hosea) doth testify to his face.'ᵖ 'Hear ye, give ear (saith
Jeremiah), be not proud. . . . Give glory to the Lord your God.'�q
But they would not be reproved; they were still 'wise in their own
eyes and prudent in their own sight',ʳ and continually saying to

---

ᵃ Isa. 59: 6.   ᵇ Isa. 59: 14.   ᶜ Isa. 9: 17.   ᵈ Isa. 30: 9.
ᵉ Isa. 59: 3, 4.   ᶠ Jer. 9: 4, 5.   ᵍ Isa. 1: 5, 6.   ʰ Jer. 9: 26.
ⁱ Hos. 10: 2.   ʲ Ezek. 14: 3, 5.   ᵏ Jer. 6: 13.   ˡ Amos 2: 7.
ᵐ Hab. 2: 6.   ⁿ Isa. 5: 8.   ᵒ Hab. 2: 5.   ᵖ Hos. 7: 10.
q Jer. 13: 15, 16.   ʳ Isa. 5: 21.

---

¹ Cf. Ps. 119: 25.   Cf. Matt. 6: 19.

their neighbour, 'Stand by thyself, come not near to me; for I am holier than thou!'ᵃ

They added *hypocrisy* to their pride. 'This people (saith God himself) draw near me with their mouth, and with their lips do honour me, but have removed their hearts far from me.'ᵇ 'They have not cried unto me with their heart, when they howled upon their beds.'ᶜ 'They return, but not to the Most High; they are like a deceitful bow.'ᵈ 'They did but flatter him with their mouth and dissembled with him in their tongue.'ᵉ So that herein they only 'profaned the holiness of the Lord. . . . And this have ye done again (saith Malachi), covering the altar of the Lord with tears, with weeping and with crying out, insomuch that he regardeth not the offering any more.'ᶠ

13. This God continually declared to those formal worshippers—that their outside religion was but vain. 'To what purpose is the multitude of your sacrifices? saith the Lord; I am full of the burnt offerings of rams, . . . and I delight not in the blood of bullocks, or of lambs, or of he goats. . . Bring no more vain oblations; incense is an abomination unto me; the new moons and sabbaths, the calling of assemblies, I cannot away with; it is iniquity, even the solemn meeting. . . . When you spread forth your hands, I will hide mine eyes from you; yea, when ye make many prayers, I will not hear.'ᵍ 'He that killeth an ox is as if he slew a man; he that sacrificeth a lamb, as if he cut off a dog's neck.'ʰ 'When they fast, I will not hear their cry; and when they offer an oblation, I will not accept it.'ⁱ 'Go ye, serve your idols, if ye will not hearken unto me; but pollute ye my holy name no more with your gifts.'ʲ

14. Yet all this time were they utterly *careless* and *secure*; nay, *confident* of being in the favour of God. They were 'at ease'; they 'put far away the evil day'.ᵏ 'Even when God had poured his anger upon Israel, it set him on fire round about, yet he knew it not: it burned him, yet he laid it not to heart.'ˡ 'A deceived heart had turned him aside, that he could not say, Is there not a lie in my right hand?'ᵐ So far from it that at this very time they said, 'We are innocent; we have not sinned.'ⁿ 'We are wise, and the law of the Lord is with us.'ᵒ 'The temple of the Lord! The temple of the Lord are we.'ᵖ

ᵃ Isa. 65: 5.	ᵇ Isa. 29: 13.	ᶜ Hos. 7: 14.	ᵈ Hos. 7: 16.
ᵉ Ps. 78: 36 [B.C.P.]	ᶠ Mal. 2: 11, 13.	ᵍ Isa. 1: 11, 13, 15.	ʰ Isa. 66: 3.
ⁱ Jer. 14: 12.	ʲ Ezek. 20: 39.	ᵏ Amos 6: 3.	ˡ [Cf.] Isa. 42: 25.
ᵐ Isa. 44: 20.	ⁿ Jer. 2: 35.	ᵒ Jer. 8: 8.	ᵖ Jer. 7: 4.

15. Thus it was that they hardened themselves in their wickedness. 'They are impudent children (saith God) and stiff hearted.'[a] 'Were they ashamed when they had committed abomination? Nay, they were not at all ashamed, neither could they blush.'[b] 'I have spread out my hand all the day to a rebellious people . . . that provoketh me to answer continually to my face.'[c] 'They will not hearken unto me: (saith the Lord), for all the house of Israel are impudent and hard hearted.'[d] 'Since the day that their fathers came forth out of the land of Egypt unto this day, I have sent unto them all my servants the prophets, rising up early and sending them; yet they hearkened not unto me, nor inclined their ear, but hardened their neck; they did worse than their fathers.'[e]

They were equally hardened against mercies and judgments. When he 'gave them rain, both the former and the latter in his season'; when 'he reserved unto them the appointed weeks of the harvest', filling their hearts with food and gladness,[1] still none of this 'revolting and rebellious people said, Let us now fear the Lord our God'.[f] Nor yet did 'they turn unto him' when 'he smote them'.[g] 'In that day did the Lord call to weeping and to mourning; . . . and behold joy and gladness, . . . eating flesh and drinking wine; let us eat and drink, for tomorrow we shall die.'[h] Although 'he consumed them, yet they refused to receive instruction; they made their faces harder than a rock. . . . None repented him, but every one turned to his course, as a horse rusheth into the battle.'[i] 'I have given you want of bread in all your places, yet have ye not returned unto me, saith the Lord. I have also withholden the rain from you, when there were yet three months unto the harvest; . . . I have smitten you with blasting and mildew; . . . your gardens and your vineyards . . . the palmer-worm devoured; . . . I have sent among you the pestilence after the manner of Egypt; your young men have I slain with the sword; . . . I have overthrown some of you as God overthrew Sodom and Gomorrah, and ye were as a firebrand plucked out of the burning; yet have ye not returned unto me, saith the Lord.'[j]

16. In consequence of their resolution not to return, they would not endure sound doctrine or those that spake it. They 'said to the

---

[a] Ezek. 2: 4.   [b] Jer. 6: 15.   [c] Isa. 65: 2, 3.   [d] Ezek. 3: 7.
[e] Jer. 7: 25, 26.   [f] Jer. 5: 23, 24.   [g] Isa. 9: 13.   [h] Isa. 22: 12, 13.
[i] Jer. 5: 3; 8: 6.   [j] Amos 4: 6–11.

---

[1] See Acts 14: 17.

seers, See not; and to the prophets, Prophesy not unto us right things; speak unto us smooth things; . . . cause the Holy One of Israel to cease from before us'.[a] But 'they hated him that rebuked in the gate, and they abhorred him that spake uprightly'.[b] Accordingly, 'Thy people (saith God to Ezekiel) still are talking against thee, by the walls, and in the doors of the houses'.[c] 'And Amaziah the priest sent to Jeroboam, king of Israel, saying: Amos hath conspired against thee in the midst of the house of Israel; the land is not able to bear all his words. . . . Also Amaziah said unto Amos, . . . Go, flee thee away into the land of Judah, and prophesy there; but prophesy not again any more at Bethel, for it is the king's chapel, and it is the king's court.'[d] From the same spirit it was that they said of Jeremiah, 'Come, and let us devise devices against him. . . . Come, and let us smite him with the tongue, and let us not give heed to any of his words.'[e] Hence it was that he was constrained to cry out, 'O Lord, I am in derision daily; every one mocketh me. Since I spake, the word of the Lord was made a reproach unto me, and a derision, daily; . . . for I heard the defaming of many, fear on every side. Report, say they, and we will report it. All my familiars watched for my halting, saying, Peradventure he will be enticed, and we shall prevail against him, and we shall take our revenge on him.'[f] And elsewhere: 'Woe is me, my mother, that thou hast borne me a man of strife and a man of contention to the whole earth! I have neither lent on usury, nor men have lent to me on usury; yet every one of them doth curse me.'[g]

17. But 'if a man walking in the spirit of falsehood do lie (saith the prophet Micah) saying, I will prophesy unto thee of wine and strong drink; he shall even be the prophet of this people'.[h] And God gave them pastors after their own heart; such were those sons of Eli, 'sons of Belial, who knew not the Lord',[i] rapacious, covetous, violent men,[j] by reason of whom 'men abhorred the offering of the Lord';[k] who not only 'made themselves vile',[l] but also 'made the Lord's people to transgress',[m] while they 'made themselves fat with the chiefest of all the offerings of Israel'.[n] Such were those of whom Isaiah says, 'The priest and the prophet have erred through strong drink; they are swallowed up of wine.'[o] 'Come ye, say they, I will

[a] Isa. 30: 10, 11. [b] Amos 5: 10. [c] Ezek. 33: 30. [d] Amos 7: 10, 12, 13.
[e] Jer. 18: 18. [f] Jer. 20: 7, 8, 10. [g] Jer. 15: 10. [h] Mic. 2: 11.
[i] 1 Sam. 2: 12. [j] Ibid., vv. 14–16. [k] ibid., v. 17, [l] 1 Sam. 3: 13.
[m] 1 Sam. 2: 24. [n] Ibid., v. 29. [o] Isa. 28: 7.

fetch wine, and we will fill ourselves with strong drink; and to-morrow shall be as this day, and much more abundant.'ᵃ Therefore, saith he, 'the Lord hath poured out upon you the spirit of deep sleep, and hath closed your eyes: the prophets and the seers hath
5 he covered, and the vision of all is become unto you as the words of a book that is sealed'.ᵇ Such also were those of whom he saith, 'His watchmen are blind; they are all ignorant; they are all dumb dogs, they cannot bark, sleeping, lying down, loving to slumber. Yea, they are greedy dogs, which can never have enough; and they are
10 shepherds that cannot understand. They all look to their own way, every one for his gain, from his quarter.'ᶜ

Little better were those of whom the prophets that followed have left us so dreadful an account: 'Both prophet and priest are profane; yea, in my house have I found their wickedness, saith the Lord. . . .
15 And from the prophets of Jerusalem is profaneness gone forth into all the land.'ᵈ 'Her priests have violated my law, and have profaned my holy things; they have put no difference between the holy and the profane, . . . and I am profaned among them.'ᵉ 'If I be a father, where is mine honour? And if I be a master, where is
20 my fear? saith the Lord of Hosts unto you, O priests, that despise my name.'ᶠ

Yea, some of them were fallen into the grossest sins. 'The company of priests (saith Hosea) commit lewdness. . . . There is [the] whoredom of Ephraim; Israel is despised.'ᵍ 'I have seen also in the
25 prophets of Jerusalem (saith God by Jeremiah) an horrible thing: they commit adultery, and walk in lies.'ʰ

18. And those who were clear of this were deeply covetous. 'Who is there among you that would shut the doors for nought? Neither do ye kindle fire on my altar for nought. I have no pleasure in you,
30 saith the Lord of Hosts.'ⁱ 'The priests of Zion preach for hire, and the prophets thereof divine for money: yet will they lean upon the Lord, and say, Is not the Lord among us?'ʲ 'Thus saith the Lord: . . . the prophets bite with their teeth, and cry, Peace: and he that putteth not into their mouths, they even prepare war against him.'ᵏ
35 Therefore 'the word of the Lord came unto Ezekiel, saying, Pro-phesy against the shepherds of Israel, and say: Woe be to the shepherds of Israel that do feed themselves! Should not the shepherds

---

ᵃ Isa. 56: 12. ᵇ Isa. 29: 10, 11. ᶜ Isa. 56: 10, 11. ᵈ Jer. 23: 11, 15.
ᵉ Ezek. 22: 26. ᶠ Mal. 1: 6. ᵍ Hos. 6: 9, 10. ʰ Jer. 23: 14.
ⁱ Mal. 1: 10. ʲ Mic. 3: 11. ᵏ Mic. 3: 5

feed the flocks? Ye eat the fat, and ye clothe you with the wool; but ye feed not the flock. The diseased have ye not strengthened, neither have ye healed that which was sick, neither have ye bound up that which was broken, neither have ye brought again that which was driven away, neither have ye sought that which was lost; 5 but with force and with cruelty have ye ruled them. And they were scattered, because there is no shepherd; and they became meat to all the beasts of the field. . . . Yea, my flock was scattered upon all the face of the earth, and none did search or seek after them.'[a]

19. To the same effect do the other prophets declare: 'Ye are 10 departed out of the way; ye have caused many to stumble. . . . Therefore have I also made you contemptible and base before all the people.'[b] 'From the prophet even unto the priest, every one dealeth falsely. They have healed also the hurt of the daughter of my people slightly, saying, Peace, peace, when there is no peace.'[c] 15 'They prophesy lies in my name.'[d] 'They say still unto them that despise me, The Lord hath said, ye shall have peace; and they say unto every man that walketh after the imagination of his own heart, No evil shall come upon you.'[e] 'The prophets of Jerusalem . . . strengthen the hands of the evil-doers, that none doth return from 20 his wickedness.'[f] 'They have seduced my people . . .; and one built up a wall, and, lo, others daubed it with untempered mortar.'[g] 'With lies they have made the hearts of the righteous sad, whom I have not made sad; and strengthened the hands of the wicked, that he should not return from his wicked way, by promising him life.'[h] 'Many 25 pastors have destroyed my vineyard, they have trodden my portion under foot; they have made my pleasant portion a desolate wilderness.'[i] 'There is a conspiracy of her prophets in the midst of her, like a roaring lion ravening the prey. They have devoured souls.'[j] 'Thus saith the Lord: Feed the flock of the slaughter; whose 30 possessors slay them and hold themselves not guilty, and they that sell them say, Blessed be the Lord, for I am rich; and their own shepherds pity them not.'[k]

II. 1. Such is the general account which the Scriptures give of the Jews, the ancient church of God. And since all these things were 35 'written for our instruction',[1] who are now the visible church of the

[a] Ezek. 34: 1–6.	[b] Mal. 2: 8, 9.	[c] Jer. 6: 13, 14.	[d] Jer. 14: 14.
[e] Jer. 23: 17.	[f] Jer. 23: 14.	[g] Ezek. 13: 10.	[h] Ezek. 13: 22.
[i] Jer. 12: 10.	[j] Ezek. 22: 25.		[k] Zech. 11: 4, 5.

[1] Rom. 15: 4 (cf. *Notes*).

God of Israel, I shall in the next place appeal to all who profess this—to every one who calls himself a Christian—how far in each instance the parallel holds, and how much we are better than they?

And first, were they *discontented*? Did they *repine* at the provi-
5 dence of God? Did they say, 'Is the Lord among us or not?'[1] when they were in imminent *danger*, or pressing *want*, and saw no way to escape? And which of us can say, *I am clear* from this sin; I have washed my hands and my heart in innocency? Have not we who 'judge others, done the same things'?[2] *Murmured* and *repined* times
10 without number? Yea, and that when we were not in pressing *want*, nor distressed with imminent *danger*. Are we not in general (our own writers being the judges), have we not ever been from the earliest ages, a *repining, murmuring, discontented* people, never long satisfied either with God or man? Surely in this we have great need
15 to humble ourselves before God, for we are in no wise better than they.

But Jeshurun 'forsook God which made him, and lightly esteemed the rock of his salvation'.[3] And did not England too? Ask ye of the generations of old, inquire 'from the rising of the sun to the going
20 down thereof',[4] whether there was ever a people called by his name which had less of 'God in all their thoughts',[5] who in the whole tenor of their behaviour showed so 'light an esteem for the rock of their salvation'.

Could there ever be stronger cause for God to cry out, 'Hear,
25 O heavens, and give ear, O earth!' For hath he not 'nourished and brought us up as his children'? And yet, how have we 'rebelled against him'! If Israel of old 'did not know' God; if his ancient people 'did not consider';[6] was this peculiar to them? Are not we also under the very same condemnation? Do we as a people know
30 God? Do we consider him as God? Do we tremble at the presence of his power? Do we revere his excellent majesty? Do we remember at all times, God is here! He is now reading my heart; he spieth out all my ways; there is not a word in my tongue but he knoweth it altogether.[7] Is this the character of us English Christians, the mark
35 whereby we are known from the heathen? Do we thus know God? Thus consider this power, his love, his all-seeing eye? Rather, are we not likewise a 'sinful nation'[8] who 'have forgotten him days

---

[1] Exod. 17: 7.   [2] Cf. Rom. 2: 1.   [3] Deut. 32: 15.
[4] Ps. 50: 1.   [5] Cf. Ps. 10: 4.   [6] Cf. Isa. 1: 2, 3.
[7] Ps. 139: 4.   [8] Isa. 1: 4.

without number'?[1] 'A people laden with iniquity', continually 'forsaking the Lord, and provoking the Holy One of Israel'.[2]

2. There is indeed a wide difference, in this respect, between the Jews and us: they *happened* (if I may so speak) to forget God because other things came in their way; but we *design* to forget him; we do it of set purpose, because we do not like to remember him. From the accounts given by Jeremiah we have reason to believe that when that people was most deeply corrupted, yet the greatest men in the nation—the ministers of state, the nobles and princes of Judah— talked of God sometimes, perhaps as frequently as upon any other subject. But is it so among us? Rather, is it not a point of good breeding to put God far away, out of our sight? Is he talked of at all among the great—the nobles or ministers of state in England? Among any persons of rank or figure in the world? Do they allow God any place in their conversation? From day to day, from year to year, do *you* discourse one hour of the wonders he doth for the children of men?[3] If one at a gentleman or a nobleman's table was to begin a discourse of the wisdom, greatness, or power of God, would it not occasion (at least) as much astonishment as if he had begun to talk blasphemy? And if the *unbred* man persisted therein would it not put all the company in confusion? And what do you sincerely believe the more favourable part would say of him when he was gone? But that, 'He is a little touched in his head!' or 'Poor man! he has not seen the world.'

You know this is the naked truth. But how terrible is the thought to every serious mind! Into what a state is this Christian nation fallen! Nay, the men of eminence, of fortune, of education! Would not a thinking foreigner who should be present at such an interview be apt to conclude that the men of quality in England were atheists? That they did not believe there was any God at all—or at best but an Epicurean God, who sat at ease upon the circle of the heavens,[4] and did not concern himself about us worms of the earth?[5] Nay, but he understands every thought now rising in your heart. And how long can you put him out of your sight? Only till this veil of flesh is rent in sunder. For your *pomp* will not then follow you.[6] Will not your body be mingled with common dust? And your soul stand naked before God? O that you would 'now acquaint yourself with God',[7] that you may then be clothed with glory and immortality!

---

[1] Cf. Jer. 2: 32.   [2] Cf. Isa. 1: 4.   [3] See Ps. 107: 8, 15, 21, 31
[4] See Isa. 40: 22.   [5] Mic. 7: 17.   [6] See Isa. 14: 11.   [7] Cf. Job 22: 21.

3. Did God complain of the Jews, 'Even from the days of your fathers ye are gone away from mine ordinances, and have not kept them'?[1] And how justly may he make the same complaint of us? For how exceeding small a proportion do we find of those in any
5 place who call themselves Christians that make a conscience of attending them? Does one third of the inhabitants in any one parish throughout this great city constantly attend *public prayer* and the *ministry of his Word*, as of conscience towards God? Does one tenth of those who acknowledge it as an institution of Christ duly attend
10 *the Lord's Supper*? Does a fiftieth part of the *nominal* members of the Church of England observe the *fasts* of the Church, or so much as the forty days of *Lent*, and all *Fridays* in the year? Who of these then can cast the first stone[2] at the Jews for neglecting the ordinances of God?

Nay, how many thousands are found among us who have never
15 partook of the Supper of the Lord? How many thousands are there that live and die in this unrepented disobedience? What multitudes, even in this Christian city, do not attend any public worship at all? No, nor spend a single hour from one year to another in privately pouring out their hearts before God?[3] Whether God 'meeteth him
20 that remembereth *him* in his ways'[4] or not is no concern of theirs; so the man eats and drinks, and 'dies as a beast dieth':[5]

> Drops into the dark and disappears.[6]

It was not therefore of the children of Israel alone that the messenger of God might say, 'There is none (comparatively) that
25 calleth upon thy name, that stirreth himself up to take hold of thee.'[7]

4. Ye have heard that it was said to them of old time, 'Because of *swearing* the land mourneth.'[8] But if this might be said of the land of Canaan, how much more of *this* land? In what city or town, in what market or exchange, in what street or place of public resort, is
30 not the holy 'name whereby we are called'[9] taken in vain, day by day? From the noble to the peasant, who fails to call upon God in this, if in no other way? Whither can you turn, where can you go, without hearing some praying to God for damnation either on his neighbour or himself? Cursing those, without either fear or remorse, whom
35 Christ hath bought to 'inherit a blessing'![10]

Are *you* one of these stupid, senseless, shameless wretches, that call so earnestly for damnation on your own soul? What if God

---

[1] Mal. 3: 7.　　　[2] See John 8: 7.　　　[3] See Ps. 62: 8.　　　[4] Cf. Isa. 64: 5.
[5] Cf. Eccles. 3: 19.　　[6] Source of quotation unidentified.　　[7] Isa. 64: 7.
[8] Jer. 23: 10.　　　[9] Cf. Jer. 23: 6.　　　[10] 1 Pet. 3: 9; cf. Acts 20: 28.

should take you at your word? Are you able to 'dwell with everlasting burnings'?[1] If you are, yet why should you be in haste to be
in the 'lake of fire burning with brimstone'?[2] God help you, or you
will be there soon enough, and long enough—for that 'fire is not
quenched', but 'the smoke thereof ascendeth up' 'day and night, for 5
ever and ever'.[3]

And what is that important affair concerning which you was but
now appealing to God? Was you 'calling God to record upon your
soul',[4] touching your everlasting salvation? No; but touching the
beauty of your horse, the swiftness of your dog, or the goodness of 10
your drink! How is this? What notion have you of God? What do
you take him to be?

Idcirco stolidam praebet tibi vellere barbam Jupiter?[5]

What stupidity, what infatuation is this! Thus without either pleasure
or profit or praise, to set at nought him that hath 'all power both in 15
heaven and earth'![6] Wantonly to 'provoke the eyes of his glory'![7]

Are you a man of letters who are sunk so low? I will not then
send you to the inspired writers (so called)—perhaps you may dis-
dain to receive instruction by them—but to the old, blind, heathen.
Could you only fix in your mind the idea he had of God (though it 20
is not strictly just, unless we refer it to God made man) you would
never thus affront him more:

Ἦ, καὶ κυανέῃσιν ἐπ' ὀφρύσι νεῦσε Κρονίων
Ἀμβρόσιαι δ' ἄρα χαῖται ἐπερρώσαντο Ἄνακτος
Κρατὸς ἀπ' ἀθανάτοιο, μέγαν δ' ἐλέλιξεν Ὄλυμπον.[8] 25

---

[1] Isa. 33: 14.   [2] Rev. 19: 20.
[3] Cf. Isa. 34: 10; Mark 9: 43–8; Rev. 14: 11; 20: 10.   [4] Cf. 2 Cor. 1: 23.
[5] Persius, *Satires*, ii. 28–9: 'Will Jupiter therefore offer you his foolish beard to
pluck?' In the appendix to Vol. 32 of his *Works* (1774) Wesley thus paraphrases:
'Thinkest thou that God is mocked?'   [6] Cf. Matt. 28: 18.   [7] Isa. 3: 8.
[8] Homer, *Iliad*, i. 528–30. On Dec. 7, 1764 Wesley wrote to his brother Charles:
'Translate for me into good English the Latin verses that occur in the *Earnest Appeal*;
and why not those three Greek ones?—

Ἦ, καί κυανέῃσιν ἐπ' ὀφρύσι νεῦσε Κρονίων,

Charles's version did not appear. Alexander Pope's paraphrase runs thus:

Jove spoke, and awful bends his sable brows,
Shakes his ambrosial curls, and gives the nod,
The stamp of fate and sanction of the god:
High heaven with trembling the dread signal took,
And all Olympus to the centre shook.

In Vol. 32 of his *Works* (1774) Wesley adds a brief translation which seems to derive
from Pope's:

Jove spake, and nodded with his sable brow,
And huge Olympus to his centre shook.

Shall not the very heathen then 'rise up in judgment against this
generation and condemn it'?[1] Yea, and not only the learned heathens
of Greece and Rome, but the savages of America. For I never
remember to have heard a wild Indian name the name of *Sootalei-*
5 *cātee*[2] (Him that sitteth in heaven) without either laying his hand
upon his breast, or casting his eyes down to the ground. And are you
a Christian! O how do you cause the very name of Christianity to
be blasphemed among the heathen![3]

5. But is it *light* swearing only (inexcusable as that is) because of
10 which our 'land mourneth'?[4] May it not also be said of us, 'Though
they say the Lord liveth, surely they swear *falsely*?'[5] Yea, to such
a degree that there is hardly the like in any nation under heaven;
that almost every corner of the land is filled with wilful, deliberate,
perjury.

15 I speak not now of the perjuries which every common swearer
cannot but run into day by day. (And indeed common swearing
'notoriously contributes to the growth of perjury. For oaths are
little minded when common use has sullied them, and every
minute's repetition has made them cheap and vulgar'.[6]) Nor of
20 those which are continually committed and often detected in our
open courts of justice. Only with regard to the latter I must remark,
that they are a natural consequence of that monstrous, shocking,
manner where in oaths are usually administered therein—without
any decency or seriousness at all, much less with that awful solemnity
25 which a rational heathen would expect in an immediate appeal to
the great God of heaven.

---

[1] Matt. 12: 41.

[2] Wesley went to Georgia for the sole purpose of converting the Indians. He was to
be a missionary, not a chaplain to the settlers. Because of disciplinary problems in the
colony, the authorities were anxious to keep him in Savannah, and his contacts with the
Indians were few. But he was always a shrewd observer of what went on about him, and
his comments show that he was quite aware of Indian customs and practices.

[3] See Rom. 2: 24.

[4] Jer. 23: 10.   [5] Jer. 5: 2.

[6] John Disney, *An Essay upon the Execution of the Laws against Immorality and
Prophaneness*, 'the second edition, enlarged', London, for Joseph Downing, 1710, p. 7.
(N.B. This was the edition used by Wesley, not the first edition of 1708.) John Disney
(1677–1730), after training at the Middle Temple, earned considerable local fame in
Lincolnshire (Wesley's native county) as a particularly effective justice of the peace.
He was deeply interested in the societies for the reformation of manners, and his *Essays*
(the second, which Wesley also quotes, was published in 1710) were written in part to
emphasize the needs which these societies were formed to meet, and to answer objections to their activities. In 1719 Disney was ordained by Edmund Gibson, then bishop
of Lincoln.

I had once designed to consider all the oaths which are customarily taken by any set of men among us. But I soon found this was a work too weighty for me; so almost *in infinitum*[1] are oaths multiplied in England—I suppose to a degree which is not known in any other nation in Europe.   5

What I now propose is to instance only in a few (but those not of small importance) and to show how amazingly little regard is had to what is solemnly promised or affirmed before God.

6. This is done, in part, to my hands by a late author. So far as he goes, I shall little more than transcribe his words.[a]   10

When a Justice of Peace is sworn into the commission he makes oath, 'That . . . he shall do equal right to the poor and to the rich, after his cunning, wit, and power, and after the laws and customs of the realm and statutes thereof made', in all articles in the King's commission to him directed. What those articles are you will find in the first *assignavi-*   15 *mus* of the commission: 'We have assigned you and every one of you, jointly and severally . . . to keep and cause to be kept all ordinances and statutes' made for . . . the quiet rule and government of our people 'in all and every the articles thereof', . . . according to the force, form, and effect of the same; and to 'chastise and punish all persons, offending   20 against' . . . any of them, . . . 'according to the form of those statutes and ordinances.' So that he is solemnly sworn to the execution of all such statutes as the legislative power of the nation has thought fit to throw upon his care. Such are all those (among others) made against 'drunkenness, tippling, profane swearing, blasphemy, lewd and dis-   25 orderly practices, and profanation of the Lord's Day'. And 'tis hard to imagine how a Justice of Peace can think himself more concerned to suppress riots or private quarrels than he is to levy twelvepence on a profane swearer, five shillings on a drunkard, ten shillings on the public house that suffers tippling, or any other penalty which the law exacts on   30 vice and immorality. The same oath . . . binds him both to one and the other, laying an equal obligation upon his conscience. How a magistrate who neglects to punish excess, profaneness, and impiety, . . . can excuse himself from the guilt of *perjury*, I don't pretend to know. If he reasons fairly he will find himself as much forsworn as an evidence who, being   35 upon his oath to declare 'the whole truth', nevertheless conceals the most considerable part of it. And his perjury is so much the more infamous, as the ill example and effects of it will be mischievous.

[a] [John] Disney, First *Essay*, p. 30 [i.e. pp. 30–2, greatly abridged.]

---

[1] *In infinitum*, a form less common than *ad infinitum*, but in the eighteenth century considered equally correct.

7. The same author (in the preface to his *Second Essay*)[1] goes on:

You, gentlemen of the Grand Juries, take a solemn oath that you will '*diligently inquire*, and true *presentment* make, of *all* such articles, matters, and things *as shall be given you in charge*; as also, that you will
5 (not only present no person for envy, hatred, or malice, but) not leave any *unpresented*, for fear, favour, or affection'. Now are not the laws against immorality and profaneness 'given you in charge', as well as those against riots, felony, and treason? Are not presentment and indictment *one* method expressly appointed by the statute for the
10 punishment of *drunkenness* and *tippling*?[2] Are not houses of *bawdry* and *gaming* punishable in the same courts, and consequently presentable by you? Is not the Proclamation for the punishing of vice, profaneness, and immorality, always read before you as soon as you are sworn?[3] . . . And does not the Judge of Assize, or Chairman of the
15 Bench, in the charge given immediately after the reading it, either recite to you the particular laws against such offences, or refer you for them to that Proclamation? 'Tis plain from all this that you are bound upon your oaths to present all vice and immorality, as well as other crimes, that fall within your knowledge, because they are expressly
20 'given you in charge'. And this you are to do, not only when *evidence* is offered before you by the *information of others*, but with regard to all such offences as you or any of you are able of your *own personal knowledge* to present. All which you have sworn to do impartially, without 'fear, favour, or affection'.[4]

25 I leave it now with all reasonable men to consider, how few Grand Jurors perform this? And consequently, what multitudes of them throughout the nation fall under the guilt of *wilful perjury*!

8. The author proceeds:

I shall next address myself to you that are *Constables*. And to you I
30 must needs say that if you know your duty, 'tis no thanks to us that are *Justices*. For the oath we usually give you is so *short*, and in such *general* terms, that it leaves with you no manner of instruction in the particulars of the office to which you are sworn. . . . But that which ought to be given you recites part of your duty in the following words: 'You shall do
35 your best endeavour that rogues, vagabonds, and night-walkers be apprehended; and that the statutes made for their punishment be duly put in execution. You shall have a *watchful eye* to such as shall keep

---

[1] John Disney, *A Second Essay upon the Execution of the Laws against Immorality and Prophaneness*, London, Joseph Downing, 1710.

[2] Disney cites 4 Jas. I, c. 5, s. 5.   [3] 23 Eliz., c. 1, s. 9 (Disney).

[4] Disney, *Second Essay*, pp. v–vii.

any house or place where any *unlawful game* is used; as also to such as
shall *frequent* such places, or shall *use* any *unlawful games* there or
elsewhere. . . . You shall *present all* and *every* the offences contrary to
the statutes made to restrain the *tippling in inns, ale-houses,* and other
victualling houses; and for repressing of *drunkenness.* You shall once in 5
the year, during your office, present all popish recusants. . . . You shall
well and duly execute all precepts and warrants to you directed. . . .
And you shall well and duly, according to your knowledge, power, and
ability, do and execute all other things belonging to the office of a constable, so long as you shall continue therein.'   10

Upon this I would observe first, that *actors of plays* are expressed by
name within the statute to be taken up for vagabonds, and punished
accordingly; and that though a statute of Queen Elizabeth's excepts
such companies as have a licence under the hand and seal of a nobleman, yet a later statute in the reign of King James I has taken away that 15
protection from them, by declaring that 'from thenceforth no authority
to be given by any peer of the realm shall be available to free or discharge them from the pains and punishments of that former statute'. . . .
Every Constable therefore in those parishes where any of these strolling
players come is bound by his oath to seize upon, correct, and send them 20
packing without delay.

The next part of your oath obliges you to keep a watchful eye on
such houses as keep, and such persons as use, unlawful gaming.
The statute directs you weekly, or at least monthly, to search within
your liberties all houses or places suspected of this offence, and upon 25
discovering to bring them to punishment. Upon this article I would
observe, (1). That the law makes some allowance for artificers, husband-
men, apprentices, labourers, and servants, 'to play in Christmas', but
at no other time of the year; and (2). That 'all sports and pastimes'
whatsoever are made unlawful upon the Lord's Day by a statute of 30
King Charles II. . . . You are therefore bound upon oath to bring to
punishment such as are guilty of profaning that day by any sports or
pastimes whatsoever.

The following parts of your oath are, (1). That you shall present all
and every the offences of tippling and drunkenness that come to your 35
knowledge; . . . (2). That you shall once in the year present all popish
recusants. . . . Nay, and by the statute on which your oath is grounded,
you are obliged once a year to present in session all those within your
parishes who (not being Dissenters) come not once in a month, at least,
to Church; and (3), that you shall well and duly execute all precepts and 40
warrants to you directed. I believe no Constable will pretend to be
ignorant of this. How is it then that when we send out warrants to
levy on offenders for swearing, drunkenness, and the like, those

warrants are so ill obeyed? . . . Are you not sworn to execute *these* as well as any other, and that duly too, according to the tenor of your precept? Your precept tells you, you shall demand such a sum, and if the offender will not pay, you shall 'levy it by distress of his goods'; and

5   'if no distress can be taken' you are then only to set him in the stocks— otherwise you have no authority so to do. Nor is the setting him in the stocks, when you might have distrained, any execution of your precept. . . .

The last part of your oath is, in general terms, that you shall well and

10   duly, according to your knowledge, power, and ability, do and execute 'all other things' belonging to the office of a Constable. . . . I shall instance in some things which certainly belong to your office, because you, and none else, can do them: (1). A Constable may, without a warrant, apprehend any persons, and carry them before a Justice, who

15   are driving carts, horses, or cattle on the Lord's Day.[1] (2). He may do the same, without a warrant, to such as he shall find at any sports or pastimes on that day;[2] (3), to such as he shall find tippling in public houses;[3] (4), to shopkeepers selling or exposing goods for sale on the Lord's Day;[4] and lastly, to such as he shall find drunk, or blaspheming,

20   or profanely swearing or cursing.[5]

Thus I have shown you, in part, what belongs to your office. It is well if according to the tenor of your oath you 'duly, to the best of your knowledge and ability, do and execute all these things'. But remember that if you do not, if you neglect any of them, you are forsworn.

25   Now let all men judge how many *Constables* in England are clear of wilful perjury![6]

9.

I will now (he goes on) address myself to churchwardens. . . . Your oath is, that 'you shall well and truly execute the office of a church-

30   warden for the ensuing year; and to the best of your skill and know-ledge, present such persons and things as are presentable by the ecclesiastical laws of the realm'. . . . (I shall set down only a few of these.)

The statute of King James I obliges you to present once a year all

35   monthly *absenters* from church. . . .

The ninetieth Canon enjoins you . . . first to *admonish*, and then, if they reform not, to *present* all your parishioners who do not duly resort to church on Sundays, and there continue the 'whole time of divine service'. On this article observe: (1). That a person's being

---

[1] Disney cites 29 Chas. II, c. 7.   [2] 1 Chas. I, c. 1 (Disney).
[3] 21 Jas. I, c. 7 (Disney).   [4] 1 Jas. I, c. 22, s. 28; 29 Chas. II, c. 7 (Disney).
[5] 4 Jas. I, c. 5, s. 9; 10 Wm. III, c. 32, s. 6; 7 Wm. III, c. 11 (Disney).
[6] Disney, *Second Essay*, pp. viii–xviii, xxi–xxiii.

absent from church . . . is ground sufficient for you to proceed . . .; (2).
That you are not only to present those who do not come to church,
but also those that behave *irreverently* or *indecently* there, either
walking about or talking; all who do not '*abide there orderly and
soberly*' the whole time of service and sermon, . . . and all that loiter 5
away any part of that time in the churchyard or in the fields.

The one hundred and twelfth Canon enjoins you within forty days
after Easter to exhibit to the bishop or his chancellor the names of all
above the age of sixteen within your parish that did not receive the
communion.   10

Other statutes oblige you to present drunkenness, tippling, and
public houses suffering persons to tipple in them.

And the one hundred and ninth Canon binds you to present all
manner of vice, profaneness, and debauchery, 'requiring you faithfully
to present all and every the offenders in adultery, whoredom, drunken- 15
ness, profane swearing, or any other uncleanness and wickedness of
life . . .'. It is therefore a part of that office to which you are solemnly
sworn, to present not only all drunkenness and tippling, but profane
swearing, lewdness, and whatsoever else is contrary to Christian piety.
So that if you know any of your parishioners, be his quality or circum- 20
stances what they will, that is guilty of any of these, you are obliged
to 'present him at the next Visitation', or you are yourselves guilty of
perjury. . . . And the twenty-sixth Canon expresses such an abhorrence
of a churchwarden's neglect in this matter that it forbids the minister
in any wise to admit you to the Holy Communion, 'who', as the words 25
of the Canon are, 'having taken your oaths to present all such offences in
your several parishes, shall notwithstanding your said oaths, either in
neglecting or refusing to present, wittingly and willingly, desperately
and irreligiously incur the horrid guilt of perjury'.[1]

And who is clear? I appeal to every minister of a parish, from one 30
end of England to the other: how many churchwardens have you
known in twenty, thirty, forty years, who did not thus 'desperately
and irreligiously incur the horrid guilt of perjury'?

10. I proceed to perjuries of another kind. The oath taken by all
captains of ships, every time they return from a trading voyage, 35
runs in these terms:

> I do swear that the entry above written, now tendered and sub-
> scribed by me, is a just report of the name of my ship, its burthen,
> built,[2] property, number, and country of mariners, the present master

[1] Disney, *Second Essay*, pp. xxiii–xxix.
[2] Throughout Wesley's lifetime this was the correct substantive, though we would
now use 'build'.

and voyage; and that it doth farther contain a true account of my lading, with the particular marks, numbers, quantity, quality, and consignment, of all the goods and merchandises in my said ship, to the best of my knowledge; and that I have not broke bulk, or delivered any
5 goods out of my said ship, since her loading in. So help me God.

These words are so clear, express and unambiguous, that they require no explanation. But who takes this plain oath, without being 'knowingly and deliberately forsworn'? Does one captain in fifty? Does one in five hundred? May we not go farther yet? Are there
10 five captains of vessels now in London who have not at one time or another by this very oath, which they knew to be false when they took it, incurred the guilt of wilful perjury?

11. The oath which all officers of His Majesty's Customs take at their admission into their office runs thus:

15 I do swear to be true and faithful in the execution, to the best of my knowledge and power, of the trust committed to my charge and inspection in the service of His Majesty's Customs; and that I will not take or receive any reward or gratuity, directly or indirectly, other than my salary or what is or shall be allowed me from the Crown, or the regular
20 fees established by law, for any service done or to be done in the execution of my employment in the Customs, on any account whatsoever. So help me God.

On this it may be observed, (1), that there are 'regular fees established by law' for some of these officers; (2), that the rest do
25 hereby engage, not to take or receive 'any reward or gratuity, directly or indirectly', other than their salary or allowance from the Crown, 'on any account whatsoever'.

How do the former keep this solemn engagement? They whose fees *are* 'established by law'? Do they take those established fees, and
30 no more? Do they not 'receive any *farther* gratuity'? Not 'on any account whatsoever'? If they do, they are undeniably guilty of wilful perjury.

And do the latter take *no fees at all*? Do they receive 'no reward or gratuity, . . . for any service done, or to be done, in the execution
35 of their employment'? Do they not take any money 'directly or indirectly . . . on any account whatsoever'? Every time they do receive either more or less, they also are flatly *forsworn*.

Yet who scruples either the one or the other? Either the taking *a larger fee* than the law appoints? Or the taking *any fee*, large or
40 small, which is offered, even where the law appoints none at all?

What innumerable *perjuries* then are here committed, over and over, day by day! And without any remorse; without any shame! Without any fear either of God or man!

12. I will produce but one instance more. The oath of one who votes for a Member of Parliament is this: 5

> I do swear I have not received or had, by myself, or of any person whatsoever in trust for me, or for my use and benefit, directly or indirectly, any sum or sums of money, office, place or employment, gift or reward, or any promise or security for any money, office, employment, or gift, in order to give my vote at this election, and that   10
> I have not before been polled at this election. So help me God.

We may observe here, (1), that this oath is taken once in seven years (if required) by all the freeholders in every county throughout England and Wales, as well as by all the freemen in every city and borough town; and (2), that hereby every voter swears, in   15
words liable to no evasion, that he has not received, 'directly or indirectly, any . . . gift or reward, or . . . promise' of any.

But—to pass over those godless and shameless wretches who frequently vote twice at one election—how few are there who can take this oath with a conscience void of offence?[1] Who have not   20
received directly or indirectly, any gift or promise of any? No? Have not *you*? If you have received nothing else, have not you received meat or drink? And did you pay for the meat or drink you received? If not, that was *a gift*; and consequently, you are as really perjured as the man that has received an hundred pounds.   25

What a melancholy prospect is then before us! Here are almost all the common people of any substance throughout the land, both in the city and country, calling God to record to a *known, wilful falsehood*!

13. I shall conclude this head in the weighty words of the author   30
before cited.

> Most of these, I am afraid, look upon their oaths as *things of course*, and little to be regarded. . . . But can there be anything in the world more sacred than an *oath*? Is it not a solemn appeal to God for your sincerity? And is not that very appeal an acknowledgment that he will   35
> surely punish falsehood? Nay farther, is it not a *calling down* the vengeance of God upon yourselves if you are false? Do you not, by laying your hand upon the gospel, declare that *you hope for no salvation*

---

[1] Acts 24: 16.

by Christ if you perform not what you then promise, or if what you
then affirm is not true? And do not the words, 'So help me God!'
sufficiently prove that the intention of your oath is so? And that if you
swear false, you are to expect no mercy from God, either in this world
5 or the next? And do you not *personally* and expressly give your consent to this heavy curse by *kissing the Book*? How then dare any of you
venture to play with so awful an engagement? Is it that you think the
oath of a *Grand Juryman*, or *parish officer*, (of a *captain*, an *officer of the
Customs*, or a *voter* in elections) is not as sacred and binding as that of
10 an *evidence at the bar*? What is it can make the difference? . . . Both
of them are equally appeals to God, and imprecations of his vengeance
upon *wilful perjury*.[1]

14. If there be then a God that is not mocked, what a weight of
sin lies on this nation! And sin of no common dye, for perjury has
15 always been accounted one of the deepest stain. And how will
anyone attempt to excuse this? By adding blasphemy thereto? So
indeed some have done, saying like those of old, 'Tush, thou God
carest not for it.'[2] 'The Lord seeth (i.e. regardeth) us not. The Lord
hath forsaken the earth.'[3] He has left second causes to take their
20 course, and man 'in the hand of his own counsel'.[4]

How many are they who now speak thus? According to whose
minute philosophy[5] the *particular* providence of God is utterly
exploded, 'the hairs of our head are no longer numbered', and not
only a sparrow but a city, an empire, may 'fall to the ground, without
25 the will or care of our heavenly Father'.[6] You allow then only a
general providence. I do not understand the term. Be so kind as to
let me know what you mean by 'a *general* providence, contradistinguished from a *particular* one'. I doubt you are at a loss for an
answer; unless you mean some huge unwieldy thing—I suppose
30 resembling the *primum mobile* in the Ptolemaic system[7]—which

---

[1] Disney, *Second Essay*, pp. xxxv–xxxvi. [2] Ps. 10: 14 (B.C.P.).
[3] Ezek. 9: 9. [4] Ecclus. 15: 14.
[5] An allusion to George Berkeley's *Alciphron: or, The Minute Philosopher*. In this
work Berkeley explicitly criticized the rationalism of the deists from the standpoint of
his distinctive spiritual interpretation of reality. In the first four dialogues he argued that
natural religion can be supported by very powerful arguments; in the final three sections
of the work he showed that his basic principles can be invoked to defend the doctrines of
traditional Christianity.
[6] Cf. Matt. 10: 29, 30.
[7] *Primum mobile*, the supposed outermost sphere of the universe, added in the Middle
Ages to the Ptolemaic system of astronomy. It was supposed to revolve round the earth
from east to west every 24 hours, carrying within it the other spheres, variously estimated
at eight or nine.

continually whirls the whole universe round, without affecting one thing more than another. I doubt this hypothesis will demand more proof than you are at present able to produce; beside that it is attended with a thousand difficulties such as you cannot readily solve. It may be therefore your wisest way for once to think with the vulgar; to acquiesce in the plain, scriptural account. This informs us that although God dwelleth in heaven, yet he still 'ruleth over all';[1] that his providence extends to every individual in the whole system of beings which he hath made; that all *natural causes* of every kind depend wholly upon his will, and he increases, lessens, suspends, or destroys their efficacy according to his own good pleasure; that he uses *preternatural causes* at his will—the ministry of good or or evil angels; and that he hath never yet precluded himself from exerting his own immediate power, from *speaking* life or death into any of his creatures, from *looking* a world into being, or into nothing.

'Thinkest thou then, O man, that thou shalt escape the judgment of this great God?'[2] O no longer 'treasure up unto thyself wrath against the day of wrath'![3] Thou canst not recall what is past; but now 'keep thyself pure',[4] even were it at the price of all that thou hast; and acknowledge the goodness of God in that he did not long since cut thee off, and send thee to thy own place.[5]

15. The Jews of old were charged by God with 'profaning his sabbaths'[6] also. And do we Christians come behind them herein? (I speak of those who acknowledge the obligation.) Do we 'call the sabbath a delight, holy of the Lord, honourable; not doing our own ways, nor finding our own pleasure, nor speaking our own words'?[7] Do our man-servant and maid-servant rest thereon? And the 'stranger that is within our gates'?[8] Is no business but what is really necessary done within our house? You know in your own conscience, and God knoweth, that the very reverse of this is true.

But setting aside these things which are done as it were by stealth, whether by mean or honourable men; how many are they in every city, as well as in this, who profane the sabbath with a high hand? How many in this that openly defy both God and the king, that break the laws both divine and human, by working at their trade, delivering their goods, receiving their pay, or following their

---

[1] Ps. 103: 19.   [2] Cf. Rom. 2: 3.   [3] Rom. 2: 5.   [4] 1 Tim. 5: 22.
[5] See Rom. 11: 22; Acts 1: 25.   [6] Cf. Ezek. 22: 8, etc.
[7] Cf. Isa. 58: 13.   [8] Cf. Exod. 20: 10; Deut. 5: 14.

ordinary business in one branch or another, and 'wiping their mouth, and saying, I do no evil'?[1] How many buy and sell on the day of the Lord, even in the open streets of this city? How many open or (with some modesty) *half open* their shops? Even when they
5 have not the pretence of perishable goods; without any pretence at all—money is their God, and gain their godliness.[2] But what are all these droves in the skirts of the town that wellnigh cover the face of the earth? Till they drop one after another into the numerous receptacles prepared for them in every corner.[3] What are these to
10 gain by profaning the day of the Lord? Nothing at all. They 'drink in iniquity like water'.[4] Nay, many of them *pay* for their sin—perhaps great part of what should sustain their family the ensuing week. I know not what is 'finding our own pleasure, or doing our own ways',[5] if this is not. What then shall we plead in *your* excuse?
15 That 'many others do it as well as you'? Nay, number is so far from extenuating your fault that it aggravates it above measure. For this is open war against God. A whole army of you joins together, and with one consent, in the face of the sun, 'runs upon the thick bosses of his buckler'.[6]

20 16. It is once mentioned in the prophets: 'In thee (Jerusalem) they have set light by father and mother.'[7] But frequent mention is made of their setting light by their civil parents, of their murmurings and rebellions against their governors. Yet surely our boasting against them is excluded, even in this respect. For do not all our
25 histories witness such a series of mutinies, seditions, factions, and rebellions, as are scarce to be paralleled in any other kingdom since the world began? And has not the wild, turbulent, ungovernable spirit of our countrymen been continually acknowledged and lamented (as abundance of their writings testify to this day) by the
30 cool, rational part of the nation? Terrible effects whereof have been seen and felt, more or less, in every generation.

But did this spirit exist only in times past? Blessed be God, it is now restrained; it does not break out; but the traces thereof are still easy to be found.[a] For whence springs this continual 'speaking evil
35 of dignities'?[8] Of all who are at the helm of public affairs? Whence

---

[a] N.B. This was wrote a year ago.

[1] Cf. Prov. 30: 20.   [2] See 1 Tim. 6: 5
[3] Presumably the 'pleasure gardens' that proliferated in the suburbs.
[4] Job 15: 16.   [5] Cf. Isa. 58: 13.   [6] Cf. Job 15: 26.
[7] Ezek. 22: 7.   [8] Cf. 2 Pet. 2: 10; Jude 8.

this 'speaking evil of the ruler of our people',[1] so common among all orders of men? I do not include those whose province it is to inspect all the public administrations. But is not almost every private gentleman in the land, every clergyman, every tradesman—yea every man or woman that has a tongue—a politician, a settler of the state? Is not every carman and porter abundantly more knowing than the King, Lords, and Commons together? Able to tell you all their foibles, to point out their faults and mistakes, and how they ought to proceed if they will save the nation? Now all this has a natural, undeniable tendency to mutiny and rebellion. O what need have we, above any nation on earth, of his continual care and protection, who alone is able to 'rule the raging of the sea' and 'still the madness of the people'.[2]

17. But to proceed. Were there 'drunkards in Ephraim',[3] 'mighty to drink wine, men of strength to mingle strong drink'?[4] And are there not in England? Are they not the growth of every county, city, and town therein? These do not indeed, or not often 'rise up early . . . that they may follow strong drink', and so 'continue till night, till wine inflame them'.[5] They have found a readier way; namely, to begin at night, and continue following their wine or strong drink till the morning. And what numbers are there of these throughout the land? Lost to reason and humanity, as well as to religion? So that no wonder 'they regard not the works of the Lord, neither consider the operation of his hands'.[6]

Nor indeed have *our* drunkards need to continue from morning to night, until wine inflame them, seeing *they* have found a far more compendious method of casting aside all sense and reason, and disencumbering themselves of all remains either of conscience or understanding. So that whatever work of darkness is speedily to be done, and that without any danger of being interrupted either by fear, compassion, or remorse, they may be in a few moments, by one draught, as effectually qualified for it as if they could swallow a legion of devils. Or (if that be all their concern) they may at a moderate expense destroy their own body as well as soul, and plunge through this *liquid fire* into that 'prepared for the devil and his angels'.[7]

Friend! Stop! You have the form of a man still. And perhaps some remains of understanding. O may the merciful God lay hold

---

[1] Cf. Acts 23: 5.   [2] Ps. 65: 7 (B.C.P.); cf. Ps. 89: 9.   [3] Cf. Isa. 28: 1, 3.
[4] Isa. 5: 22.   [5] Cf. Isa. 5: 11.   [6] Isa. 5: 12.   [7] Matt. 25: 41.

of that! Unto him all things are possible.[1] Think a little, for once.
What is it you are doing? Why should you destroy yourself? I could
not use the worst enemy I have in the world as you use yourself.
Why should you murder yourself inch by inch? Why should you
5 burn yourself alive? O spare your own body, at least, if you have no
pity for your soul! But have you a soul, then? Do you really believe
it? What, a soul that must live for ever? O spare thy soul! Do not
destroy thy own soul with an everlasting destruction! It was made
for God. Do not give it into the hands of that old murderer of men!
10 Thou canst not stupefy it long. When it leaves the body it will
awake and sleep no more. Yet a little while, and it launches out into
the great deep, to live and think and feel for ever. And what will
cheer thy spirit there, if thou hast not 'a drop of water to cool thy
tongue'?[2] But the die is not yet cast. Now cry to God, and 'iniquity
15 shall not be thy ruin'.[3]

18. Of old time there were also those that 'were at ease in Zion;
. . . that lay upon beds of ivory, and stretched themselves upon their
couches; that ate the lambs out of the flock and calves out of the
stall'.[4] But how inelegant were these ancient epicures! 'Lambs out
20 of the flock, and calves out of the stall'? Were these the best dainties
they could procure? How have we improved since Jeroboam's
time! Who can number the varieties of our tables? Or the arts we
have 'to enlarge the pleasure of tasting'.[5] And what are their couches,
or beds of ivory, to the furniture of our apartments? Or their 'chains
25 and bracelets', . . . and 'mantles, and changeable suits of apparel',[6]
to the ornaments of our persons? What comparison is there between
their diversions and ours? Look at Solomon in all his glory;[7] and yet
may we not question whether he was not an utter stranger to *the
pleasures of the chase*? And notwithstanding his four thousand horses,
30 did he ever see a *race* in his life? He 'made gardens and orchards',
and 'pools of water'; he 'planted vineyards and built houses'.[8] But
had he one *theatre* among them all? No. This is the glory of later
times. Or had he any conception of a *ball*, an *assembly*, a *masquerade*,
or a *ridotto*?[9] And who imagines that all his instruments of music

---

[1] See Matt. 19: 26.   [2] Cf. Luke 16: 24.   [3] Cf. Ezek. 18: 30.   [4] Cf. Amos 6: 1, 4.
[5] Source of quotation unidentified, but cf. Sermons, 'The Danger of Riches', I. 13,
and 'On the Education of Children', § 19.
[6] Isa. 3: 19, 22.   [7] Matt. 6: 29.   [8] Cf. Eccles. 2: 4–6.
[9] Masquerades, in particular, represented a form of festivity at the English court
which had recently given great offence to those anxious to safeguard public morality.
(Cf. Introduction to *A Letter to the Bishop of London*, and Edward Young, *The Love of*

put together were any more to be compared to ours than his or his father's rumbling Hebrew verses

To the soft sing-song of Italian lays.[1]

In all these points our pre-eminence over the Jews is much every way.   5

Yea, and over our own ancestors as well as theirs. But is this our glory or our shame? Were Edward the Third, or Henry the Fifth to come among us now, what would they think of the change in their people? Would they applaud the elegant variety at the Old Baron's table?[2] Or the costly delicacy of his furniture and apparel? Would 10
they listen to these instruments of music? Or find pleasure in those diversions? Would they rejoice to see the nobles and gentry of the land lying 'at ease, stretching themselves on beds' of down? Too delicate to use their own limbs, even in the streets of the city; to bear the touch of the people, the blowing of the wind, or the shining 15
of the sun! O how would their hearts burn within them![3] What indignation, sorrow, shame must they feel to see the ancient hardiness lost; the British temperance, patience, and scorn of super-fluities, the rough, indefatigable industry exchanged for softness, 'idleness, and fullness of bread'![4] Well for them that they were 20
gathered unto their fathers[5] before this exchange was made!

19. To prove at large that the luxury and sensuality, the sloth and indolence, the softness and idleness, the effeminacy and false delicacy of our nation are without a parallel, would be but lost labour. I fear we may say the *lewdness* too: for if the Jews, as the prophet speaks, 25
'assembled themselves by troops in the harlots' houses',[6] so do the English, and much more abundantly. Indeed, where is *male chastity* to be found? Among the nobility? Among the gentry? Among the tradesmen? Or among the common people of England? How few lay any claim to it at all? How few desire so much as the 30
reputation of it? Would you yourself account it an honour or a reproach to be ranked among those of whom it is said, 'These are

---

Fame, iii. 227–30.) A ridotto was a social assembly devoted to music and dancing. Gatherings of this kind were a marked feature of London social life in the eighteenth century.

[1] Cf. Samuel Wesley, Jun., 'The Bondsmen', in *Poems on Several Occasions* (1736), p. 258 (line 287)—'To tempt Italian sing-song to our shore'.

[2] The Old Baron, a well known eating house and place of entertainment. Cf. *London and its Environs described* (1761).

[3] See Luke 24: 32.   [4] Cf. Ezek. 16: 49.   [5] Judg. 2: 10.   [6] Jer. 5: 7.

they which were not defiled with women; for they are virgins'?[1] And how numerous are they now, even among such as are accounted men of honour and probity, who 'are as fed horses, every one neighing after his neighbour's wife'?[2]

5　　But as if this were not enough, is not the sin of Sodom, too, more common among us than ever it was in Jerusalem? Are not our streets beset with those monsters of uncleanness who 'burn in their lust one toward another', whom God hath 'given up to a reprobate mind, to do those things which are not convenient'?[3] O Lord, thy

10　compassions fail not; therefore we are not consumed.

　　20. Neither do we yield to them in *injustice* any more than *uncleanness*. How frequent are open robberies among us? Is not the act of *violence* even in our streets? And what laws are sufficient to prevent it? Does not *theft* of various kinds abound in all parts of

15　the land, even though death be the punishment of it? And are there not among us, who 'take usury and increase', who 'greedily gain of their neighbour by *extortion*'?[4] Yea, whole trades which subsist by such extortion as was not named either among the Jews or heathens? Is there not yet 'the scant measure', 'the wicked balances, and the

20　bag of deceitful weights'?[5] Beside the thousand nameless ways of overreaching and defrauding, the *craft* and *mystery* of every trade and profession. It were an endless task to descend to particulars, to point out in every circumstance how not only *sharpers* and *gamesters*—those public nuisances, those scandals to the English

25　nation—but high and low, rich and poor, men of character and men of none, in every station of public or private life, 'have corrupted themselves',[6] and generally applaud themselves, and count it *policy* and wisdom so to do. So that if *gain* be at hand, they care not though 'justice stand afar off'; so that 'he which departeth from evil', which

30　cometh not into their secret, still 'maketh himself a prey',[7] and the wicked still 'devoureth the man that is more righteous than he'.[8]

　　And what redress? Suppose a great man to oppress the needy; suppose the rich grinds the face of the poor. What remedy against such *oppression* can he find in this Christian country? If the one is

35　rich and the other poor, doth not 'justice stand afar off'? And is not the poor under the utmost improbability (if not impossibility) of

---

[1] Rev. 14: 4.　　　　　　[2] Cf. Jer. 5: 8.
[3] Cf. Rom. 1: 27–8.　　　[4] Cf. Ezek. 22: 12.
[5] Cf. Mic. 6: 10–11.　　　[6] Exod. 32: 7; Deut. 9: 12.
[7] Isa. 59: 14–15.　　　　　[8] Hab. 1: 13.

obtaining it? Perhaps the hazard is greater among us than either among Jews, Turks, or heathens.

For example: suppose a great man, with or without form of law, does wrong to his poor neighbour. What will you do? Sue his lordship at common law? Have the cause tried at the next sessions or assizes? Alas! Your own neighbours, those who know the whole case, will tell you, 'You are out of your senses.' 'But twelve good men and true will do me justice.' Very well; but where will you find them—men unbiased, incapable of corruption, superior both to fear and favour, to every view whether of gain or loss? But this is not all; they must not only be good and true, but wise and understanding men. Else how easy is it for a skilful pleader to throw a mist before their eyes? Even supposing, too, the judge to be quite impartial, and proof against all corruption. And should all these circumstances concur—of which, I fear, there are not many precedents—supposing a verdict is given in your favour, still you have gained nothing. The suit is removed into a higher court, and you have all your work to begin again. Here you have to struggle with all the same difficulties as before, and perhaps many new ones too. However, if you have money enough, you *may* succeed; but if that fails, your cause is gone. Without *money* you can have no more *law*; *poverty* alone utterly shuts out *justice*.

'But cannot an honest *attorney* procure me justice?' An *honest* attorney! Where will you find one? Of those who are called *exceeding honest* attorneys, who is there that makes any scruple:

(1). To promote and encourage *needless suits*, if not *unjust* ones too;
(2). To *defend a bad cause*, knowing it so to be:
By making a *demur*, and then withdrawing it;
By pleading some *false plea* to the plaintiff's declaration;
By putting in an *evasive answer* to his bill;
By *protracting* the suit, if possible, till the plaintiff is ruined;
(3). To *carry a cause* not amounting to ten shillings into Westminster Hall, by laying it in his declaration as above forty;
(4). To *delay* his own client's suit knowingly and wilfully, in order to gain more thereby;
(5). To *draw himself* the pleadings or conveyances of his client, instead of giving them to be drawn by able counsel;
(6). To *charge* his client with the fees which should have been given to such counsel, although they were not given;

(7) To *charge* for drawing fair copies where none were drawn;

(8). To charge *fees for expedition* given to clerks, when not one farthing has been given them;

(9). To send his clerk a journey (longer or shorter) to do business
5 with or for different persons, and to *charge the* horse-hire and *expense* of the journey to *every* person severally;

(10). To send his clerk to Westminster on the business of ten (it may be) or twenty persons, and to charge *each of these twenty* for his attendance, as if he had been sent on account of one only;

10 (11). To charge *his own attendance* in like manner; and

(12). To fill up his bill with *attendances*, *fees*, and *term-fees*, though his client is no whit forwarder in his cause.

This is he that is called an '*honest attorney*'! How much honester is a pickpocket!

15 But there is a magistrate whose peculiar office it is to redress the injured and oppressed. Go then and make trial of this remedy. Go and tell your case to the Lord Chancellor. Hold! You must go on regularly. You must tell him your case *in form of law*, or not at all. You must therefore *file a bill* in Chancery, and *retain* a lawyer
20 belonging to that court. 'But you have already spent all you have; you have *no money*.' Then I fear you will have *no justice*. You stumble at the threshold. If you have either lost or spent all, your cause is naught; it will not even come to a hearing. So, 'if the oppressor has secured all that you had, he is as safe as if you was under
25 the earth.

21. Now what an amazing thing is this! The very *greatness* of the villainy makes it beyond *redress*! But suppose he that is oppressed has some substance left, and can go through all the courts of justice, what parallel can we find among Jews, Turks, or heathens, for
30 either the *delays* or the *expense* attending it? With regard to the former, how monstrous is it that in a suit relating to that inheritance which is to furnish you and your family with food and raiment you must wait month after month, perhaps year after year, before it is determined whether it be yours or not? And what are you to *eat* or
35 to *wear* in the meantime? Of that the court takes no cognizance! Is not this very *delay*—suppose there were no other grievance attending the English course of law—wrong beyond all expression? Contrary to all sense, reason, justice, and equity? A *capital* cause is tried in one day, and finally decided at once. And 'is the life less

than meat? Or the body of less concern than raiment'?[1] What a shameless mockery of justice then is this putting off *pecuniary* causes from term to term, yea, from year to year!

With regard to the latter. A man has wronged me of a hundred pounds. I appeal to a judge for the recovery of it. How astonishing 5 is it that this judge himself cannot give me what is my right, and what evidently appears so to be, unless I first give perhaps one half of the sum to men I never saw before in my life!

22. I have hitherto supposed that all causes, when they are decided, are decided according to justice and equity. But is it so? 10 Ye learned in the law, is no *unjust sentence* given in your courts? Have not the same causes been decided quite opposite ways? One way this term, just the contrary the next? Perhaps one way in the morning (this I remember an instance of), and another way in the afternoon. How is this? Is there no *justice* left on earth? No regard 15 for right or wrong? Or have causes been puzzled so long that you know not now what is either wrong or right, what is agreeable to law or contrary to it? I have heard some of you frankly declare that it is in many cases next to impossible to know what is law, and what is not. So are your *folios* of law multiplied upon you that no human 20 brain is able to contain them; no, nor any consistent scheme or abstract of them all.

But is it really owing to *ignorance* of the law—this is the most *favourable* supposition—that so few of you scruple *taking fees* on either side of almost any cause that can be conceived? And that you 25 generally plead in the manner you do on any side of any cause? Rambling to and fro in a way so abhorrent from common sense, and so utterly foreign to the question? I have been amazed at hearing the pleadings of some eminent counsel. And when it has fallen out that the pleader on the other side understood only the common rules of 30 logic, he has made those eminent men appear either such egregious knaves, if they could help it, or such egregious blockheads, if they could not, that one would have believed they would show their face there no more. Meantime, if there be a God that judgeth righteously,[2] what horrid insults upon him are these! 'Shall I not visit for these 35 things, saith the Lord? Shall not my soul be avenged of such a nation as this!'[3]

23. There is one instance more of—I know not what to term it— injustice, oppression, sacrilege, which hath long cried aloud in the

[1] Cf. Matt. 6: 25.   [2] Jer. 11: 20; 1 Pet. 2: 23.   [3] Jer. 5: 9, 29; 9: 9.

ears of God. For among men who doth hear? I mean the manage-
ment of many of those who are entrusted with our *public charities.*
By the pious munificence of our forefathers we have abundance of
these, of various kinds. But is it not glaringly true (to touch only on
5 a few generals) that the managers of many of them either: (1). Do
not apply the benefaction to *that use* for which it was designed by
the benefactor; or (2). Do not apply it with such *care* and *frugality*
as in such a case are indispensably required; or (3). Do not apply
the whole of the benefaction to any charitable use at all, but *secrete*
10 part thereof from time to time for the use of themselves and their
families; or, lastly, by plain, barefaced oppression, *exclude* those
from having any part in such benefaction who dare (though with
all possible tenderness and respect) set before them the things that
they have done.

15   Yet Brutus is an honourable man:
               So are they all; all honourable men![1]

And some of them had in esteem for religion, accounted patterns
both of honesty and piety! But God 'seeth not as man seeth'.[2] He
'shall repay them to their face'.[3] Perhaps even in the present world.
20 For that Scripture is often still fulfilled: 'This is the curse that goeth
forth over the face of the whole earth. . . . I will bring it forth, saith
the Lord of Hosts, and it shall enter into the house of the thief . . .'
(such he is and no better, in the eyes of God, no whit honester than
a highwayman) 'and it shall remain in the midst of the house, and
25 shall consume it, with the timber thereof, and the stones thereof.'[4]
     24. And is not 'truth, as well as justice, fallen in our streets'?[5]
For who 'speaketh the truth from his heart'?[6] Who is there that
makes a conscience of speaking the thing as it is, whenever he speaks
at all? Who scruples the telling of *officious lies*? The varying from
30 truth in order to do good? How strange does that saying of the
ancient Father sound in modern ears: 'I would not tell a lie, no,
not to save the souls of the whole world.'[7] Yet is this strictly agreeable to the Word of God, to that of St. Paul in particular: if any say
'let us do evil that good may come', their 'damnation is just'.[8]

---

[1] Shakespeare, *Julius Caesar*, III. ii. 87–8.   [2] 1 Sam. 16: 7.
[3] Cf. Deut. 7: 10.   [4] Zech. 5: 3–4.
[5] Cf. Isa. 59: 14.   [6] Ps. 15: 2 (B.C.P.).
[7] Augustine, *Contra Mendacium* (*Against Lying*), cap. 15 (Migne, *Patrologia Latina*,
XL. 540).   [8] Rom. 3: 8.

But how many of us do this evil without ever considering whether good will come or no? Speaking what we do not mean merely out of *custom*, because it is *fashionable* so to do? What an immense quantity of falsehood does this ungodly fashion occasion day by day! For hath it not overrun every part of the nation? How is all 5 our language swollen with *compliment*? So that a well-bred person is not *expected* to speak as he thinks. We do not look for it at his hands. Nay, who would thank him for it? How few would suffer it? It was said of old, even by a warrior and a king, 'He that telleth lies shall not tarry in my sight.'¹ But are not we of another mind? 10 Do not we rather say, 'He that telleth not lies shall not tarry in my sight'? Indeed the trial seldom comes; for both speakers and hearers are agreed that form and ceremony, flattery and compliment, should take place, and truth be banished from all that 'know the world'.   15

And if the rich and great have so small regard to truth as to lie, even for lying sake, what wonder can it be that men of lower rank will do the same thing *for gain*? What wonder that it should obtain, as by common consent, in all kinds of *buying and selling*? Is it not an adjudged case that it is no harm to tell lies *in the way of trade*? 20 To say that is the *lowest price* which is not the lowest; or that you *will not take* what you *do take* immediately? Insomuch that it is a proverb even among the Turks, when asked to abate of their price, 'What! do you take me to be a Christian?' So that never was that caution more seasonable than it is at this day: 'Take ye heed every 25 one of his neighbour, and trust ye not in any brother; for every brother will utterly supplant, . . . and they will deceive every one his neighbour.'²

25. And as for those few who abstain from outward sins, is their heart right with God?³ May he not say of us also (as of the Jews), 30 'This people is uncircumcised in heart'?⁴ Are not *you*? Do you then 'love the Lord your God with all your heart, and with all your strength'?⁵ Is he *your* God and your all? The desire of your eyes? The joy of your very heart? Rather, do you not 'set up your idols in your heart'?⁶ Is not your 'belly your God'?⁷ Or your diversion? 35 Or your fair reputation? Or your friend? Or wife? Or child? That is, plainly, do not you delight in some of these earthly goods more than in the God of heaven? Nay, perhaps you are one of those

¹ Ps. 101: 7.   ² Jer. 9: 4-5.   ³ See 2 Kgs. 10: 15.   ⁴ Cf. Jer. 9: 26.
⁵ Cf. Mark 12: 30.   ⁶ Cf. Ezek. 14: 4, 7.   ⁷ Cf. Phil. 3: 19.

grovelling souls that 'pant after the dust of the earth'.[1] Indeed, who does not? Who does not get as much as he can? Who of those who are not accounted covetous, yet does not gather all the money he can fairly, and perhaps much more? For are they those only whom 5 the world ranks among misers that use every art to increase their fortune? Toiling early and late, spending all their strength in 'loading themselves with thick clay? How long?'[2] Until the very hour when God calleth them; when he saith unto each of them, 'Thou fool! this night shall thy soul be required of thee! And whose 10 shall those things be which thou hast prepared?'[3]

26. And yet doth not our *pride*, even the pride of those whose 'soul cleaves to the dust',[4] 'testify against us'?[5] Are 'they not wise in their own eyes, and prudent in their own conceit'?[6] Have not writers of our own remarked that there is not upon earth a more 15 *self-conceited* nation than the English; more opiniated[7] both of their own national and personal wisdom, and courage and strength. And indeed, if we may judge by the inhabitants of London, this is evident to a demonstration; for what inhabitant of the metropolis does not suppose himself to have a *metropolitical* understanding? 20 Are not the very meanest of them able to instruct both the king and all his counsellors? What cobbler in London is not wiser than the principal Secretary of State? What coffee-house disputant is not an abler divine than his Grace of Canterbury? And how deep a contempt of others is joined with this high opinion of ourselves! 25 I know not whether the people of all other nations are greater masters of dissimulation; but there does not *appear* in any nation whatever such a proneness to despise their neighbour; to despise not foreigners only (near two thousand years ago they remarked, *Britannos hospitibus feros*)[8] but their own countrymen—and that 30 very often for such surprising reasons as nothing but undeniable fact could make credible. How often does the gentleman in his coach despise those 'dirty fellows that go afoot'? And these, on the other hand, despise full as much those 'lazy fellows that loll in their coaches'. No wonder then that those who have the 'form of godli-

---

[1] Amos 2: 7.   [2] Cf. Hab. 2: 6.   [3] Cf. Luke 12: 20.
[4] Cf. Ps. 119: 25.   [5] Isa. 59: 12; Jer. 14: 7.   [6] Cf. Isa. 5: 21.
[7] An earlier form of 'opinionated', which was still current throughout the eighteenth century, though in the 1786 edition this better known form replaced 'opiniated', which had been retained through six editions during Wesley's lifetime, and indeed appears in Jackson's edition of Wesley's *Works*.
[8] Horace, *Odes*, III. iv. 33: 'The Britons, no friends to strangers'.

ness'[1] should despise them that have not; that the saint of the world[2] so frequently says to the gross sinner, in effect if not in terms, 'Stand by thyself; come not near unto me; for I am holier than thou!'[3]

27. Yet what kind of holiness is this? May not God justly declare of us also, 'This people draw near me with their mouth, but they have removed their hearts far from me.'[4] 'They do but flatter me with their mouth, and dissemble with me in their tongue.'[5] Is it not so with *you*? When you speak to God, do your lips and your heart go together? Do you not often utter words by which you mean just nothing? Do not you say and unsay? Or say one thing to God, and another to man? For instance, you say to God, 'Vouchsafe, O Lord, to keep me this day without sin.'[6] But you say to man, 'This cannot be done; it is all folly and madness to expect it.' You ask of God that you 'may perfectly love him, and worthily magnify his holy name':[7] but you tell man there is no perfect love upon earth; it is only a madman's dream. You pray God to 'cleanse the thoughts of your heart by the inspiration of his Holy Spirit':[8] but you assure your neighbour there is no such thing as *inspiration* now, and that none pretend to it but enthusiasts. What gross *hypocrisy* is this! Surely, you think, there is no 'knowledge in the Most High'.[9] O 'be not deceived; God is not mocked. But whatsoever ye sow, that also shall ye reap'![10]

28. Such at present is the religion of this Christian nation! So do we honour him by whose name we are called. And yet was there ever a nation more careless and secure? More unapprehensive of the wrath of God! How can a man more effectually expose himself to the ridicule of those who are esteemed men of understanding than by showing any concern, as if the judgments of God were hanging over our heads?[a] Surely then 'a deceived heart hath turned us aside, that we cannot say: Is there not a lie in my right hand?'[11] Surely this our confidence is not of God: it is rather a judicial infatuation, a stupid insensibility, a deep sleep, the forerunner of heavy vengeance.

Ruin behind it stalks, and empty desolation.[12]

[a] This was wrote a year ago, but I am afraid it is too true, even at this day.

[1] 2 Tim. 3: 5.   [2] See *A Farther Appeal*, Part III, III. 35.   [3] Isa. 65: 5.
[4] Cf. Isa. 29: 13.   [5] Ps. 78: 36 (B.C.P.).   [6] B.C.P., Morning Prayer, Te Deum.
[7] Cf. B.C.P., Communion, Collect for Purity.
[8] Ibid.   [9] Ps. 73: 11.   [10] Cf. Gal. 6: 7.   [11] Cf. Isa. 44: 20.
[12] Cf. Abraham Cowley, *Pindarique Odes*, 'Isaiah 34', IV. line 19, referring to 'the Destroying Angel': Ruin behind him stalks, and empty desolation.

Surely never was any people more fitted for destruction! 'Impudent children are they, and stiff-hearted.'[1] 'Are they ashamed when they have committed abomination?'[2] When they have openly profaned the day of the Lord? When they have committed lewd-
5 ness? Or when they have uttered such curses and blasphemies as are not heard of among the heathens? Nay, 'They are not at all ashamed, neither can they blush.'[3] And though God send unto them all his servants, rising up early and sending them, 'yet will they not hear; they harden their neck; they do worse than their fathers'.[4]
10 What then can God 'do more for his vineyard which he hath not done'?[5] He hath long tried us with mercies, 'giving rain and fruitful seasons',[6] 'filling us with the flour of wheat'.[7] We have had plenty of all things, and while war roared around, 'peace has been in all our borders'.[8] But still 'this revolting and rebellious people said not,
15 Let us now fear the Lord our God'.[9] Nay, they gave him no thanks for all his mercies; they did not even acknowledge them to be his gift. They did not see the hand of God in any of these things; they could *account for them* another way. O ye unwise, when will ye understand? Know ye not yet there is a God that ruleth the world? What did ye
20 see with your eyes? Was the 'race to the swift, or the battle to the strong'?[10] Have ye forgotten Dettingen[11] already? Does not England know that God was there? Or suppose your continuance in peace, or success in war, be the mere result of your own wisdom and strength; do ye command the sun and the clouds also? Can ye
25 pour out or 'stay the bottles of heaven'?[12] But let it all be nature, chance, anything—so God may have no hand in governing the earth!

29. Will his judgments bring us to a better mind? Do we 'hear the rod and him that has appointed it'?[13] Let us observe: What fruit
30 do we find in those who are 'even consumed by means of his heavy hand'?[14] Let any that desires to be clearly satisfied herein visit the

---

[1] Cf. Ezek. 2: 4.   [2] Cf. Jer. 6: 15; 8: 12.   [3] Ibid.
[4] Cf. Jer. 7: 25–6, etc.   [5] Cf. Isa. 5: 4.   [6] Cf. Acts 14: 17.
[7] Cf. Ps. 147: 14 (B.C.P.).   [8] Ibid.   [9] Cf. Jer. 5: 23–4.
[10] Cf. Eccles. 9: 11.
[11] Dettingen, a village on the river Main, in Bavaria, was the scene on June 27, 1743 of a battle between the French forces and the 'Pragmatic Army' (English, Hanoverians, and Austrians). The French, though numerically superior, were decisively defeated by the allies, led by King George II of England. In his *Journal* (Feb. 1 and Nov. 12, 1744) Wesley includes letters from converts who fought in the battle. Handel commemorated the victory with his *Dettingen Te Deum*.
[12] Job 38: 37.   [13] Cf. Mic. 6: 9.   [14] Cf. Ps. 39: 11 (B.C.P.).

hospitals of this city. Let him judge for himself how the patients there receive God's fatherly visitation; especially *there*, because mercy also is mixed with judgment; so that it is evident 'the Lord loveth whom he chasteneth'.[1] Go then into any *ward*, either of men or women. Look narrowly from one end to the other. Are they humbling themselves under the hand of God? Are they trembling under a sense of his anger? Are they praising him for his love? Are they exhorting one another not to faint when they are rebuked of him? How do nine in ten of them spend the time, that important time from morning to evening? Why, in such a manner that you would not easily learn from thence whether they were Christians, pagans, or Mahometans.

Is there any deeper distress than this to be found? Is there a greater affliction than the loss of health? Perhaps there is; the loss of liberty, especially as it is sometimes circumstanced. You may easily be convinced of this by going into either Ludgate or Newgate.[2] What a scene appears as soon as you enter! The very place strikes horror into your soul. How dark and dreary! How unhealthy and unclean! How void of all that might minister comfort! But this is little compared to the circumstances that attend the being confined in this shadow of death. See that poor wretch, who was formerly in want of nothing, and encompassed with friends and acquaintance, now cut off, perhaps by an unexpected stroke, from all the cheerful ways of men; ruined, forsaken of all, and delivered into the hands of such masters and such companions! I know not if to one of a thinking, sensible turn of mind, there could be anything like it on this side hell.

What effect then has this heavy visitation of God on those who lie under it for any time? There is, perhaps, an exception here and there; but in general, they are abandoned to all wickedness, utterly divested of all fear of God, and all reverence to man; insomuch that they commonly go out of that school completely fitted for any kind

---

[1] Cf. Heb. 12: 6.

[2] Newgate and Ludgate were two London prisons with particularly noisome reputations. In the late seventeenth century the records of nonconformist persecution are full of descriptions of the fearful conditions in Newgate, the chief prison of the City. John Howard's *The State of the Prisons in England and Wales* (1777) described the terrible situation which still prevailed. Wesley's account is intermediate between these two in point of date; what he says can be confirmed in detail by reference to these other witnesses. As an indefatigable prison visitor, Wesley knew at first hand the conditions he describes.

or degree of villany, perfectly brutal and devilish, thoroughly furnished for every evil word and work.

30. Are our countrymen more effectually reclaimed when danger and distress are joined? If so, the *army*, especially in time of war, must be the most religious part of the nation. But is it so indeed? Do the soldiery walk as those who see themselves on the brink of eternity? *Redeeming* every opportunity of glorifying God, and doing good to men, because they know not the hour in which their Lord will require their souls of them?[1] So far from it that a 'soldier's religion' is a byword, even with those who have no religion at all; that vice and profaneness in every shape reign among them without control; and that the whole tenor of their behaviour speaks, 'Let us eat and drink, for tomorrow we die.'[2]

Have those who are exposed to still more danger, the English *sea forces*, more religion than those at land? It is said they were once remarkable for this. And it is certain Sir Francis Drake feared God, as did most of his commanders, and, we have reason to believe, his mariners and sailors too. But what shall we say of the *navy* that now is, more particularly of the ships of war? Is religion there? Either the power or the form? Is not almost every single man-of-war a mere floating hell? Where is there to be found more consummate wickedness, a more full, daring contempt of God and all his laws, except in the bottomless pit? But here description fails: And 'the goodness of God endureth yet daily'![3] But 'shall I not visit for these things, saith the Lord? . . . Shall not my soul be avenged on such a nation as this?'[4] O that the *prospect* of national judgments may suffice! That we may remember ourselves and turn unto the Lord our God before his long-suffering mercy is at an end, and he pours out the vials of his wrath upon us![5]

But how small ground have we as yet to hope for this? For who will now 'suffer the word of exhortation'?[6] How few will 'endure sound doctrine',[7] and the honest, close application of it? Do they not 'say unto the seers: See not; and unto the prophets: Prophesy smooth things'?[8] And if a man will do thus, if he will 'sew pillows to all arm-holes',[9] and 'cause the Holy One of Israel to cease from before them';[10] if he will 'prophesy . . . of wine and strong drink, he shall even be the prophet of this people'.[11]

[1] See Luke 12: 20   [2] 1 Cor. 15: 32.   [3] Ps. 52: 2 (B.C.P.).   [4] Jer. 5: 9, 9: 9.
[5] See Rev. 16: 1.   [6] Heb. 13: 22.   [7] 2 Tim. 4: 3.   [8] Cf. Isa. 30: 10.
[9] Ezek. 13: 18.   [10] Cf. Isa. 30: 11.   [11] Mic. 2: 11.

31. I am sensible how nice a subject this is, and how extremely difficult it is so to speak as neither to say too little nor too much, neither more nor less than the cause of God requires. I know also that it is absolutely impossible so to speak as not to give offence. But whosoever is offended I dare not be silent; neither may I refrain from plainness of speech. Only I will endeavour to use all the tenderness I can, consistently with that plainness.

In tender love then I ask, are there none among us—I speak to you, my brethren, who are priests and prophets of the Lord, set apart to 'minister in holy things',[1] and to 'declare the word of the Lord'[2]—are there none among us who commit *lewdness*, as did those by whom 'Israel was defiled'?[3] Hath not the Lord seen an horrible thing in some of the prophets of this land also, even that 'they commit adultery, and (to conceal it) walk in lies'?[4] God forbid that I should affirm this. I only propose (not maintain) the question. If there be such a wretch, I pray God to strike him to the heart and to say, 'Thou art the man!'[5]

Are there none of you, like them, 'mighty to drink wine, . . . men of strength to mingle strong drink'?[6] Yea, are there none that 'err through strong drink, that are swallowed up of wine?'[7] Are there not found those who say, 'I will fetch wine, and we will fill ourselves with strong drink; and tomorrow shall be as this day, and much more abundant'?[8]

Alas, my brother! Is this the voice of a 'minister of Christ? A steward of the mysteries of God'?[9] Suppose you find at any time trouble and heaviness, 'is there no help for you in your God'?[10] Is not the God whom you serve able to deliver you from any plague or trouble? Is the being 'drunk with wine' a better relief than the being 'filled with his Spirit'?[11] Do you not understand this? Do you 'not know the Lord'?[12] Take heed you do not destroy both your own soul and them that hear you! O beware! If you know not his love, fear his power! Make haste to flee from the wrath to come,[13] lest he smite you with a curse great as your sin, and sweep you away from the face of the earth.

32. Can such as you be said to honour or fear God, any more than those spoken of by Malachi?[14] May not God complain, 'These

---

[1] Cf. 1 Cor. 9: 13.   [2] Cf. Ps. 118: 17; Acts 20: 27.   [3] Hos. 5: 3; 6: 10.
[4] Jer. 23: 14.   [5] 2 Sam. 12: 7.   [6] Isa. 5: 22.
[7] Cf. Isa. 28: 7.   [8] Isa. 56: 12.   [9] Cf. 1 Cor. 4: 1.
[10] Cf. Ps. 3: 2 (B.C.P.).   [11] Cf. Eph. 5: 18.   [12] Cf. Judg. 2: 10, etc.
[13] Matt. 3: 7.   [14] See Mal. 1: 6-2: 17.

priests have violated my law and profaned my holy things.'[1] Yea,
whensoever you presume with those unhallowed hands to touch the
mysteries of God;[2] whensoever you utter his name or his Word
with those unhallowed lips! But is it on this account only that God
5 may say, 'Both prophet and priest are profane'?[3] May he not add,
'They have put no difference between the holy and the profane;
therefore I am profaned among them.'[4] For is it not so? Do *you*
put a 'difference between the holy and the profane', him that feareth
God, and him that feareth him not? Do you put an effectual dif-
10 ference between them even in the most solemn office of our religion?
At the table of the Lord, do you take care to 'separate the precious
from the vile'?[5] To receive all those who (as you may reasonably
believe) 'draw near with penitent hearts and lively faith';[6] and
utterly to reject those who testify against themselves that they are
15 without hope and without God in the world?[7]

Nay, who dares repel one of the greatest men in his parish from
the Lord's table? Even though he be a drunkard or a common
swearer? Yea, though he openly deny the Lord that bought him?
Mr. Stonehouse[8] *did* this once. But what was the event? The
20 gentleman brought an action against him, for the terror of all such
insolent fellows in succeeding times. And who was able and willing
to espouse the cause? He alone who took it into his own hand, and
before the day when it should have been tried here, called the
plaintiff to answer at a higher bar.[9]

25 33. O my brethren, is it not for want of your making this difference, as well as for many other abominations, that with regard to
some among us (how many God knoweth) that Scripture is now
also fulfilled: 'His watchmen are blind; they are ignorant; . . . they
are shepherds that cannot understand.'[10] 'The Lord hath poured out
30 upon them the spirit of deep sleep, and hath closed their eyes; the
prophets and the seers hath he covered. And the vision of all is

---

[1] Cf. Ezek. 22: 26.   [2] 1 Cor. 4: 1.   [3] Jer. 23: 11.   [4] Cf. Ezek. 22: 26.
[5] Cf. Jer. 15: 19.   [6] B.C.P., Communion, Exhortation.   [7] See Eph. 2: 12.
[8] Revd. George Stonehouse, vicar of St. Mary's, Islington. Charles Wesley was at
one time his curate, and was probably responsible for his conversion. Cf. also note to
Pt. I, VI. 10.
[9] Wesley omitted the last two sentences from his collected *Works*, 1772. This was
because a letter published in the *London Magazine* charged Wesley with 'some false
facts affirmed by him in his *Farther Appeal*'. Wesley explained and slightly modified
his position in a letter to the editor of the *London Magazine*, dated June 18, 1746, but
the erring text nevertheless continued to appear in the editions of the *Farther Appeal*
published in 1765 and 1781.   [10] Isa. 56: 10, 11.

become unto you as the words of a book that is sealed, which men deliver to one that is learned, saying, Read this, I pray thee: and he saith, I cannot; for it is sealed.'[1]

If you ask what those other abominations are I will speak 'in love and in the spirit of meekness'.[2] There are found among us *covetous* men, men 'who mind earthly things';[3] who seek themselves and not Christ crucified, who 'love the world and the things of the world':[4] men in whom those words are still fulfilled: 'Who is there among you that would shut the doors for nought? Neither do ye kindle fire on my altar for nought. I have no pleasure in you, saith the Lord of Hosts.'[5] Yea, are there not those at this day—O that I might be found to fear where no fear is!—who 'make themselves fat with the chiefest of all the offerings of Israel'?[6] Are there not those who now 'enlarge their desire as hell, who are as death and cannot be satisfied'?[7] Who, though they want neither food to eat nor raiment to put on, yet seek more and more *preferment*? Who are continually studying to 'join house to house, and to lay field to field'?[8] To grow rich in the service of that Master who himself 'had not where to lay his head'?[9] Is it not to these that those dreadful words belong, enough to cause the ears of him that heareth to tingle, 'They are greedy dogs which can never have enough; . . . they all look to their own way' (not the way of their Lord), 'everyone for his gain, from his quarter.'[10]

Is it strange if among these there should be some who are cruel, *oppressive* men? Inasmuch as covetousness knows no mercy, nor can a lover of money be a lover of his neighbour. Have not some been known even to 'grind the face of the poor'?[11] To strip, rather than clothe the naked? Some who while they cried out as 'the horse-leech, . . . give, give',[12] would take if it was not given; like those of old who said, 'Thou shalt give it me now, and if not, I will take it by force';[13] or those spoken of by Micah, 'The prophets . . . bite with their teeth and cry, peace; and he that putteth not into their mouths, they even prepare war against him.'[14] Very great is the sin of these men before the Lord. If there be ten such now in the land, may God smite them this day with terror and astonishment, that they may have no rest in their bones till their sin is done away![15]

---

[1] Cf. Isa. 29: 10–11.   [2] 1 Cor. 4: 21.   [3] Phil. 3: 19.
[4] Cf. 1 John 2: 15.   [5] Mal. 1: 10.   [6] 1 Sam. 2: 29.
[7] Cf. Hab. 2: 5.   [8] Cf. Isa. 5: 8.   [9] Cf. Matt. 8: 20.
[10] Isa. 56: 11.   [11] Isa. 3: 15.   [12] Prov. 30: 15.
[13] 1 Sam. 2: 16.   [14] Mic. 3: 5.   [15] See Ps. 38: 3.

34. Are *you* as watchful and zealous to gain souls as those are to gain the gold that perisheth?[1] Do you know by experience what that meaneth, 'the zeal of thine house hath eaten me up'?[2] Or, are you one of those watchmen who do not watch at all?[3] Who neither know
5 nor care when the sword cometh? Of whom the prophet saith, 'They are dumb dogs that cannot bark—sleeping, lying down, loving to slumber.'[4]

Can it be supposed that such shepherds will *feed the flock*,[5] will 'give to every one his portion of meat in due season'?[6] Will these
10 'warn every man, and exhort every man, that they may present every man perfect in Christ Jesus'?[7] Will they take care to 'know all their flock by name, not forgetting the men-servants and women-servants'?[8] Will they inquire into the state of every soul committed to their charge? And watch over each with all tenderness and long-
15 suffering, 'as they that must give account'?[9] Marking how they either fall or rise? How these wax 'weary and faint in their mind',[10] and those 'grow in grace and in the knowledge of our Lord and Saviour Jesus Christ'?[11] Who can do this unless his whole heart be in the work? Unless he desire nothing but to 'spend and be spent
20 for them';[12] and 'count not his life dear unto himself',[13] so he may 'present them blameless in the day of the Lord Jesus'.[14]

Can any shepherd do this—and if he do not, he will never 'give an account with joy'[15]—who imagines he has little more to do than to *preach* once or twice a week; that this is the main point, the chief
25 part of that office which he hath taken upon himself before God? What gross ignorance is this! What a total mistake of the truth! What a miserable blunder touching the *whole nature* of his office! It is indeed a very great thing to speak in the name of God; it might make him that is the stoutest of heart tremble if he considered
30 that every time he speaks to others his own soul is at stake. But great, inexpressibly great as this is, it is perhaps the least part of our work. To 'seek and save that which is lost';[16] to bring souls from Satan to God; to instruct the ignorant; to reclaim the wicked; to

---

[1] 1 Pet. 1: 7.   [2] Ps. 69: 9; John 2: 17.   [3] See Isa. 56: 10.
[4] Cf. Isa. 56: 10.   [5] 1 Pet. 5: 2, etc.   [6] Cf. Luke 12: 42.
[7] Cf. Col. 1: 28.
[8] Ignatius of Antioch, *To Polycarp*, § 4. Wesley also quotes this advice in the *Journal*, Jan. 24, 1743.
[9] Heb. 13: 17.   [10] Heb. 12: 3.   [11] 2 Pet. 3: 18.
[12] Cf. 2 Cor. 12: 15.   [13] Cf. Acts 20: 24.   [14] 1 Cor. 1: 18.
[15] Cf. Heb. 13: 17.   [16] Cf. Luke 19: 10.

convince the gainsayer;[1] to direct their feet into the way of peace,[2] and then keep them therein; to follow them step by step lest they turn out of the way, and advise them in their doubts and temptations; to lift up them that fall; to refresh them that are faint, and to comfort the weak-hearted; to administer various helps as the variety of occasions require, according to their several necessities: these are parts of our office—all this we have undertaken at the peril of our own soul. A sense of this made that holy man of old cry out, 'I marvel if any ruler in the church shall be saved';[3] and a greater than him say, in the fullness of his heart, 'Who is sufficient for these things?'[4]

35. But who is *not* sufficient for these things, for the taking care of a parish—though it contain twenty thousand souls—if this implies no more than the taking care to preach there once or twice a week; and to procure one to read prayers on the other days, and do what is called 'the parish duty'? Is any trade in the nation so easy as this? Is not any man sufficient for it, without any more talents either of nature or grace than a small degree of common understanding? But O! what manner of shepherds are those who look no farther into the nature of their office, who sink no deeper into the importance of it than this! Were they not such as these concerning whom 'the word of the Lord came unto Ezekiel, saying, . . . Woe be to the shepherds that do feed themselves! Should not the shepherds feed the flocks? Ye eat the fat, and ye clothe you with the wool; but ye feed not the flock. The diseased have ye not strengthened, neither have ye healed that which was sick, neither have ye bound up that which was broken, neither have ye brought again that which was driven away, neither have ye sought that which was lost. . . . And they were scattered because there was no shepherd, and they became meat to all the beasts of the field. . . . Yea, my flock was scattered upon all the face of the earth, and none did search or seek after them.'[5]

I conjure you, brethren, in the name of the Lord Jesus, the great shepherd of the sheep, who hath bought them and us with his own

---

[1] Titus 1: 9.   [2] See Luke 1: 79.

[3] Cf. Chrysostom, *In Epistolam ad Hebraeos* (*On the Epistle to the Hebrews*), Homily xxxiv. 1 (on Heb. 13: 17): 'Miror an fieri possit ut aliquis ex rectoribus sit salvus' (Migne, *SG*, LXIII. 254), of which Wesley's quotation is an almost exact translation. Charles Wesley's Journal for July 22, 1739 also quotes the sentence, in Latin, but changes 'rulers' to 'preacher'—'Miror aliquem praedicatorem salvari'.

[4] 2 Cor. 2: 16.   [5] Ezek. 34: 1–6.

blood, apply this each to his own soul! Let every man look unto God, and say, 'Lord, is it I?'[1] Am I one of these idle, careless, indolent shepherds that feed myself, not the flock? Am I one that cannot bark—slothful, sleeping, lying down, loving to slumber?[2]
5 Those who have not strengthened that which was diseased, neither healed that which was sick?[3] Search me, O Lord, and prove me; try out my reins and my heart.[4] Look well if there be any way of wickedness in me, and lead me in the way everlasting.'[5]

36. Have I not at least 'healed the hurt of thy people slightly'?
10 Have I not said, 'Peace, peace; when there was no peace'?[6] How many are they also that do this? Who do not study to speak what is *true*, especially to the rich and great, so much as what is *pleasing*? Who flatter *honourable* sinners, instead of telling them plain, 'How can ye escape the damnation of hell?'[7] O what an account have you
15 to make, if there be 'a God that judgeth the earth'.[8] Will he not require at *your* hands the blood of all these souls,[9] of whom 'ye are the betrayers and murderers'?[10] Well spake the prophets of your fathers, in whose steps ye now tread: 'They have seduced my people, and one built up a wall, and another daubed it with un-
20 tempered mortar.'[11] 'They strengthen the hands of the evil-doers, that none doth return from his wickedness.'[12] 'They prophesy lies in my name, saith the Lord.'[13] 'They say unto them that despise me: Ye shall have peace; and unto them that walk after the imagination of their own heart: No evil shall come upon you.'[14]

25 How great will your damnation be, who destroy souls instead of saving them? Where will you appear, or how will you stand, in that 'great and terrible day of the Lord'![15] How will ye lift up your head when 'the Lord descends from heaven'[16] 'in flaming fire, to take vengeance on his adversaries'![17] More especially on those who have
30 so betrayed his cause, and done Satan's work under the banner of Christ! With what voice wilt thou say, 'Behold me, Lord, and the sheep whom thou hadst given me, whom I gave to the devil, and told them they were in the way to heaven, till they dropped into hell'?

Were they not just such shepherds of souls as you are concerning
35 whom God spake by Jeremiah, 'Many pastors have destroyed my

---

[1] Matt. 26: 22.   [2] See Isa. 56: 10.   [3] See Ezek. 34: 4.
[4] See Ps. 26: 2.   [5] Ps. 139: 24 (B.C.P.).   [6] Cf. Jer. 6: 14, 8: 11.
[7] Matt. 23: 33.   [8] Ps. 58: 10 (B.C.P.)   [9] See Jer. 2: 34.
[10] Cf. Acts 7: 52.   [11] Cf. Ezek. 13: 10.   [12] Jer. 23: 14.
[13] Cf. Jer. 14: 14.   [14] Cf. Jer. 23: 17.   [15] Joel 2: 31.
[16] Cf. 1 Thess. 4: 16.   [17] Cf. 2 Thess. 1: 8.

vineyard; they have trodden my portion under foot; they have made my pleasant portion a desolate wilderness';[1] by Ezekiel, 'There is a conspiracy of her prophets; . . . like a roaring lion ravening the prey, they have devoured souls';[2] and by Zechariah, 'Thus saith the Lord: Feed the flock of the slaughter, whose possessors slay them, and hold themselves not guilty; and they that sell them say: Blessed be the Lord, for I am rich; and their own shepherds pity them not.'[3]

37. Is not this the *real ground*, the principal *reason*, of the present *contempt of the clergy*?[4] And long since was it assigned as such, by him who cannot lie. The same men of old who 'made the Lord's people to transgress',[5] thereby 'made themselves vile'.[6] They were *despised* both as the natural effect and the judicial punishment of their *wickedness*. And the same cause the prophet observes to have produced the same effect many hundred years after this. 'Ye are departed out of the way (saith the Lord); ye have caused many to stumble. . . . Therefore have I also made you *contemptible* and base before all the people.'[7]

I have now, brethren, 'delivered mine own soul',[8] and in so doing I have (as I proposed at first) 'used great plainness of speech',[9] as not studying 'to please men, but the Lord'.[10] The event I leave to him in whose name I have spoken, and who hath the hearts of all men in his hand.

'I have brought you heavy tidings'[11] this day, and yet I cannot but be persuaded that some of you will not 'count me your enemy, because I tell you the truth'.[12] O that all of us may *taste* the good word which we declare![13] May *receive* that knowledge of salvation, which we are commanded to *preach* unto every creature, through the remission of sins! My heart's desire is that all of us to whom 'is committed the ministry of reconciliation'[14] may ourselves be

---

[1] Jer. 12: 10.   [2] Ezek. 22: 25.   [3] Zech. 11: 4–5.

[4] 'The contempt of the clergy' had become almost a colloquial phrase as a result of of John Eachard's *The Grounds and Occasions of the Contempt of the Clergy*. It was published in 1670, and passed through repeated editions. Its biting wit made it extremely popular, but it was bitterly resented in the circles (both nonconformist and High Church) in which Wesley's parents and grandparents moved. It formed the basis of Macaulay's account of the condition of the clergy on the eve of James II's accession, and again stirred up controversy.

[5] Cf. 1 Sam. 2: 24.   [6] 1 Sam. 3: 13.   [7] Mal. 2: 8–9.

[8] Cf. Ezek. 14: 14, 20.   [9] Cf. 2 Cor. 3: 12.   [10] Cf. Gal. 1: 10.

[11] Cf. 1 Kgs. 14: 6.   [12] Cf. Gal. 4: 16.   [13] See Heb. 6: 5.

[14] Cf. 2. Cor. 5: 18, 19.

reconciled to God 'through the blood of the everlasting covenant';[1] that he may be henceforth unto us a God, and we may be unto him a people; that we may all *know* as well as *preach* the Lord, 'from the least unto the greatest',[2] even by that token, 'I am merciful to thy
5 unrighteousness: thy sins I remember no more!'[3]

III. 1. I have hitherto spoken more immediately to those who profess themselves members of the Church of England. But inasmuch as I am a debtor also to those who do not, my design is now to apply to them also; and briefly to show wherein (I fear) they are
10 severally inconsistent with *their own principles.*

I begin with those who are at the smallest distance from us, whether they are termed Presbyterians or Independents; of whom in general I cannot but have a widely different opinion from that I entertained some years ago, as having since then conversed with
15 many among them 'in whom the root of the matter is undeniably found',[4] and who labour 'to keep a conscience void of offence both toward God and toward man'.[5] I cannot therefore doubt but every serious man, of either one or the other denomination, does utterly condemn all that inward as well as outward unholiness which has
20 been above described.

But do you as a people avoid what you condemn? Are no whoremongers or adulterers found among you? No children disobedient to their parents? No servants that are slothful or careless? That 'answer again'?[6] That do not 'honour their masters'[7] as is meet in
25 the Lord? Are there none among you that censure or 'speak evil of the ruler of their people'?[8] Are there no drunkards, no gluttons, no luxurious men, no regular epicures, none 'whose belly is their God',[9] who, as their fortune permits, 'fare sumptuously every day'?[10] Have you no dishonest dealers, no unfair traders, no usurers or extor-
30 tioners? Have you no liars, either for gain or for good manners, so called? Are you clear of ceremony and compliment? Alas, you are sensible in most, if not all these respects, you have now small preeminence over us.

How much more sensible must you be of this if you do not rest
35 on the surface, but inquire into the bottom of religion, the religion of the heart? For what inward unholiness, what evil tempers are among us, which have not a place among you also? You likewise

---

[1] Heb. 13: 20.　　[2] Jer. 6: 13.　　[3] Cf. Heb. 8: 12.　　[4] Cf. Job 19: 28.
[5] Cf. Acts 24: 16.　　[6] Titus 2: 9.　　[7] Cf. 1 Tim. 6: 1.
[8] Cf. Acts 23: 5.　　[9] Cf. Phil. 3: 19.　　[10] Cf. Luke 16: 19.

bewail that ignorance of God, that want of faith and of the love of God and man, that inward idolatry of various kinds, that pride, ambition, and vanity, which rule in the hearts even of those who still have 'the form of godliness'.[1] You lament before God the deep covetousness that 'eats so many souls as doth a gangrene';[2] and perhaps are sometimes ready to cry out, 'Help, Lord, for there is *scarce* one godly man left. Lay to thine hand, for the faithful are minished from . . . the children of men!'[3]

2. And yet you retain 'the truth that is after godliness',[4]—at least as to the substance of it. You own what is laid down in Scripture both touching the *nature* and *condition* of *justification* and *salvation*. And with regard to the 'author of faith and salvation',[5] you have always avowed, even in the face of your enemies, that 'it is God which worketh in us, both to will and to do of his good pleasure';[6] that it is his Spirit alone who 'teacheth us all things',[7] all we know of 'the deep things of God';[8] that every true believer has 'an unction from the Holy One'[9] to 'lead him into all necessary truth';[10] that 'because we are sons, God sendeth forth the Spirit of his Son into our hearts, crying, Abba, Father';[11] and that 'this Spirit beareth witness with our spirit that we are the children of God'.[12]

How is it then, my brethren—so I can call you now, although I could not have done it heretofore[13]—how is it that the generality of you also are fallen from your steadfastness? In the times of persecution ye stood as a rock, though 'all the waves and storms went over'[14] you. But who can bear ease and fullness of bread![15] How are you changed since these came upon you! Do not many of you now (practically, I mean) put something else in the room of 'faith that worketh by love'?[16] Do not some of you suppose that gravity and composedness of behaviour are the main parts of Christianity? Especially provided you neither swear, nor take the name of God in vain. Do not others imagine that to abstain from idle songs and those fashionable diversions commonly used by persons of their

---

[1] 2 Tim. 3: 5. [2] Cf. 2 Tim. 2: 17—see Wesley's *Notes* for 'gangrene'.
[3] Cf. Ps. 12: 1 (B.C.P.) [4] Cf. Titus 1: 1. [5] Cf. Heb. 5: 9; 12: 2.
[6] Cf. Phil. 2: 13. [7] Cf. John 14: 26. [8] 1 Cor. 2: 10.
[9] 1 John 2: 20. [10] John 16: 13. [11] Cf. Gal. 4: 6. [12] Cf. Rom. 8: 16.
[13] As a young man, Wesley's increasing religious seriousness had been accompanied by a corresponding High Church inflexibility, to which he refers more than once in his works. Dissenters were regarded as guilty of schism, and their orthodoxy was suspect. It was a new experience for him to realize that a charitable attitude to nonconformists did not involve disloyalty to his Anglican principles.
[14] Ps. 42: 9 (B.C.P.). [15] Ezek. 16: 49. [16] Cf. Gal. 5: 6.

fortune is almost the whole of religion? To which if they add family prayer and a strict observation of the sabbath, then doubtless all is well! Nay, my brethren, this is well so far as it goes. But how little a way does it go toward Christianity? All these things, you cannot

5 but see, are merely *external*; whereas Christianity is an *inward* thing; without which the most beautiful outward form is lighter than vanity.[1]

Do not others of you rest in *convictions*? Or good *desires*? Alas, what do these avail? A man may be *convinced* he is sick, yea deeply

10 convinced, and yet never recover. He may *desire* food, yea with earnest desire, and nevertheless perish with hunger. And thus I may be *convinced* I am a sinner—but this will not justify me before God. And I may *desire* salvation—perhaps by fits and starts for many years—and yet be lost for ever. Come close then to the point,

15 and keep to your principles. Have *you* received the Holy Ghost? The Spirit which is of God, and is bestowed by him on all believers 'that we may know the things which are freely given to us of God'?[2] The time is short. Do you experience now that 'unction from the Holy One'?[3] Without which [that] you confess *outward* religion,

20 whether negative or positive, is nothing. Nay, and inward *conviction* of our wants is nothing, unless those wants are in fact supplied. Good *desires* also are nothing, unless we actually attain what we are stirred up to desire. For still, 'if any man have not the Spirit of Christ', whatever he desires, 'he is none of his'.[4] O my brother,

25 beware you stop not short! Beware you never account yourself a Christian, no, not in the lowest degree, till God 'hath sent forth the Spirit of Christ into your heart',[5] and that 'Spirit bear witness with your spirit, that you are a child of God'.[6]

3. One step farther from us are you who are called (though not

30 by your own choice) Anabaptists. The smallness of your number, compared to that of either the Presbyterians or those of the Church, makes it easier for you to have an exact knowledge of the behaviour of all your members, and to put away from among you every one that 'walketh not according to the doctrine you have received'.[7]

35 But is this done? Do all *your* members adorn the gospel? Are they all 'holy as he which hath called us is holy'?[8] I fear not. I have known some instances to the contrary; and doubtless you know many more. There are unholy, outwardly unholy men, in *your*

---

[1] Ps. 62: 9. [2] 1 Cor. 2: 12. [3] 1 John 2: 20. [4] Rom. 8: 9.
[5] Cf. Gal. 4: 6. [6] Cf. Rom. 8: 16. [7] Cf. Rom. 16: 17. [8] 1 Pet. 1: 15.

congregations also; men that profane either the name or the day of the Lord; that do not honour their natural or civil parents; that know not how to possess their bodies in sanctification and honour;[1] that are intemperate either in meat or drink, gluttonous, sensual, luxurious; that variously offend against justice, mercy, or truth, in their intercourse with their neighbour, and do not walk by that 'royal law, . . . Thou shalt love thy neighbour as thyself.'[2]

But how is this consistent with your leading principles: 'That no man ought to be admitted to baptism till he has that repentance whereby we forsake sin, and living faith in God through Christ'?[3]

For if no man ought to be *admitted* into a church or congregation who has not actual faith and repentance, then neither ought any who has them not to *continue* in any congregation. And consequently, an open sinner cannot remain among *you*, unless you practically renounce your main principle.

4. I refer it to your own serious consideration whether one reason why unholy men are still suffered to remain among you may not be this—that many of you have unawares put *opinion* in the room of *faith* and *repentance*? But how fatal a mistake is this! Supposing your opinion to be true, yet a *true opinion* concerning *repentance* is wholly different from the thing itself. And you may have a true opinion concerning faith all your life, and yet die an unbeliever.

Supposing therefore the *opinion* of *particular redemption* true, yet how little does it avail toward salvation? Nay, were we to suppose that *none can be saved* who do not hold it, it does not follow that *all will be saved* who do. So that if the one proved a man to be in ever so *bad a state*, the other would not prove him to be *in a good one*. And consequently, whosoever leans on this opinion, 'leans on the staff of a broken reed'.[4]

Would to God that ye would mind this one thing, 'to make your own calling and election sure'![5] That every one of you (leaving the rest of the world to him that made it) would himself 'repent, and believe the gospel'![6] Not repent alone—for then you know only the baptism of John—but believe and be 'baptized with the Holy Ghost and with fire'.[7] Are you still a stranger to that inward baptism wherewith all true believers are baptized? May the Lord constrain you to

---

[1] See 1 Thess. 4: 4.   [2] Jas. 2: 8.
[3] Cf. *A Confession of Faith* (1677), Ch. XXIX; *An Orthodox Creed, or a Protestant Profession of Faith* (1679). Wesley, while not quoting exactly, is faithful to the sense of both these famous Baptist confessions.   [4] Cf. Isa. 36: 6.
[5] 2 Pet. 1: 10.   [6] Cf. Mark 1: 15.   [7] Cf. Matt. 3: 11.

cry out, 'How am I straitened till it be accomplished!'¹ Even till the love of God inflame your heart and consume all your vile affections.² Be not content with anything less than this! It is this loving faith alone which opens our way into 'the general church of the first-
5 born, whose names are written in heaven',³ which giveth us to 'enter in within the veil, where Jesus our forerunner is gone before us'!⁴

5. There is still a wider difference in *some* points between us and the people usually termed Quakers.⁵ But not in *these* points. You, as well as we, condemn 'all ungodliness and unrighteousness of men';⁶
10 all those *works* of the devil which were recited above, and all those *tempers* from which they spring.

You agree that we are 'all to be taught of God',⁷ and to be 'led by his Spirit';⁸ that the Spirit alone *reveals* all truth, and *inspires* all holiness; that by his inspiration men attain *perfect love*, the love
15 which 'purifies them as he is pure';⁹ and that through this knowledge and love of God they have power to 'do always such things as please him';¹⁰ to worship God, a Spirit, according to his own will, that is, 'in spirit and in truth'.¹¹

Hence you infer that *formal worship* is not acceptable to God, but
20 that alone that springs from God in the heart. You infer also that they who are led by him will 'use great plainness of speech'¹² and great plainness of dress, seeking no 'outward adorning', but only 'the ornament of a meek and quiet spirit'.¹³

I will look no farther now than simply to inquire whether you
25 are consistent with these principles?

To begin with the latter: 'He that is led by the Spirit will use great plainness of speech.'

You would have said, 'will use the plain language'.¹⁴ But that term leads you into a grand mistake. That term, '*the* plain language',
30 naturally leads you to think of *one particular* way of speaking, as if

---

¹ Luke 12: 50. ² Rom. 1: 26. ³ Cf. Heb. 12: 23. ⁴ Cf. Heb. 6: 19-20.

⁵ Wesley's courteous attitude to the Quakers is the more significant because prudence might have suggested a more reserved approach. His opponents attacked him for being particularly susceptible to Quaker blandishments. (Cf. *Notions Fully Disproved*, p. 59.) But as he proceeds, Wesley speaks to Quaker problems with true Quaker directness.

⁶ Rom. 1: 18. ⁷ Cf. Isa. 54: 13; John 6: 45.

⁸ Cf. Rom. 8: 14. ⁹ Cf. 1 John 3: 3. ¹⁰ Cf. John 8: 29.

¹¹ John 4: 23, 24. ¹² 2 Cor. 3: 12. ¹³ 1 Pet. 3: 3, 4.

¹⁴ From the beginnings of Quakerism, 'plain language' was one of the characteristic testimonies of Friends. George Fox felt that customary usage regarding second personal pronouns was based on unchristian social distinctions, and encouraged hypocrisy and toadyism. The use of *thee* and *thou* became a distinguishing mark of Quakers, and as time passed it unquestionably sometimes degenerated into a conventional practice.

'plainness of speech' implied no more than the use of that *particular form*.

Alas! my brethren! Know ye not that your ancestors designed this only as a *specimen* of 'plain language'. And is it possible that you should mistake the sample for the whole bale of cloth? 5

Consult the light God has given you, and you must see that 'plainness of speech' does not lie in *a single point*, but implies an open undisguised sincerity, a childlike simplicity *in all we speak*.

I do not desire you to refrain from saying 'Thou' or 'Thee'. I would not spend ten words about it. But I desire you, whenever 10 you speak at all, to speak the truth, and nothing but the truth. I desire your words may be always the picture of your heart. This is truly 'plain language'.

Either do not pretend to 'plain speech' at all, or be *uniformly plain*. Are you so? I pray, consider. Do you never *compliment*? I do not 15 suppose you say, 'Sir, your very humble servant.' But do you say no *civil things*? Do you never *flatter*? Do you not *commend* any man or woman to their face? Perhaps farther than you do behind their back? Is this 'plainness of speech'? Do you never dissemble? Do you speak to all persons, high or low, rich or poor, just what you 20 think, neither more nor less, and in the shortest and clearest manner you can? If not, what a mere jest is your 'plain language'? You carry your condemnation in your own breast.

6. You hold also that 'he which is led by the Spirit will use great *plainness of dress*, seeking no outward adorning, but only the orna- 25 ment of a meek and quiet spirit'.[1] And that in particular 'he will leave "gold and costly apparel"[2] to those who know not God'.

Now I appeal to every serious, reasonable man among you, do your people act consistently with this principle? Do not many of your women wear *gold* upon their very feet? And many of your men 30 use 'ornaments of gold'?[3] Are you a stranger to these things? Have you not seen with your eyes (such triflings as will scarce bear the naming) their *canes* and *snuff-boxes* glitter, even in your solemn assembly, while ye were waiting together upon God? Surely they are not yet so lost to modesty as to pretend that they do not use 35 them by way of *ornament*. If they do not, if it be only out of neces- sity, a *plain oaken stick* will supply the place of the one, and a piece of *horn* or *tin* will unexceptionally answer all the reasonable ends of the other.

[1] 1 Pet. 3: 3, 4.   [2] Cf. Zech. 14: 14; 1 Tim. 2: 9.   [3] 2 Sam. 1: 24; Jer. 4: 30.

To speak freely (and do not count me your enemy for this) you cannot but observe, upon cool reflection, that you retain just so much of your *ancient* practice as leaves your *present* without excuse; as makes the inconsistency between the one and the other glaring
5 and undeniable. For instance: this woman is too strict a Quaker to lay out a *shilling* in a *necklace*. Very well; but she is not too strict to lay out *fourscore guineas* in a repeating *watch*. Another would not for the world wear any *lace*, no, not an *edging* round her cap. But she will wear point[1]—and sees no harm in it at all, though it should
10 be of twelve times the price. In one kind of *apron* or *handkerchief* she dares not lay out twenty shillings; but in another sort lays out twenty pounds. And what multitudes of you are very jealous as to the *colour* and *form* of your apparel (the least important of all the circumstances that relate to it), while in the most important, the
15 expense,[2] they are without any concern at all? They will not put on a *scarlet* or *crimson* stuff, but the richest *velvet*, so it be black or grave. They will not touch a coloured *ribbon*, but will cover themselves with a *stiff silk* from head to foot. They cannot bear *purple*, but make no scruple at all of being clothed in *fine linen*; yea, to such
20 a degree that the 'linen of the Quakers' is grown almost into a proverb.

Surely you cannot be ignorant that the sinfulness of *fine apparel* lies chiefly in the *expensiveness*. In that it is robbing God and the poor: it is defrauding the fatherless and widow; it is wasting the
25 food of the hungry, and withholding his raiment from the naked, to consume it on our own lusts.

7. Let it not be said that this affects only *a few* among you, and those of the *younger* and *lighter* sort. Yes, it does—your whole body. For why do you, who are *elder* and *graver*, suffer such things?
30 Why do ye not vehemently reprove them? And if they repent not, in spite of all worldly considerations expel them out of your Society? In conniving at their sin you make it your own; *you*, especially, who are Preachers.[3] Do you say, 'They cannot bear it; they will not hear'? Alas, into what state then are ye fallen! But whether they will bear it
35 or not, what is that to thee? Thou art to speak, 'whether they will

---

[1] *Point*, thread lace made wholly with a needle. Cf. *point-lace, needle-point*.

[2] 'the expense' is missing from the London editions of 1745 and 1746, but is included in the third edition, Bristol, 1746, and those stemming from it.

[3] The first edition and the 1746 London edition use the Quaker term 'Speakers', altered in the third edition, Bristol, to that more familiar to Methodists.

hear, or whether they will forbear'.[1] To say the very truth, I am afraid you rather strengthen their hands in their wickedness. For you not only do not testify against it (their expensiveness of dress) in the congregation, but even sit at their table and reprove them not.[a] Why then, thou also art one of 'the dumb dogs that cannot bark; 5 sleeping, lying down, loving to slumber'.[2]

I fix this charge upon every Preacher[3] in particular who saw a young woman, daughter to one of the Quakers in London, going to be married in apparel suitable to her diamond buckle, which cost a hundred guineas. Could you see this, and not call heaven and 10 earth to witness against it? Then I witness against thee in the name of the Lord, thou art a 'blind leader of the blind':[4] thou 'strainest a gnat, and swallowest a camel'![5]

Verily the sin both of teachers and hearers is herein exceeding great. And the little attempts toward plainness of apparel which are 15 still observable among you (I mean, in the colour and form of your clothes, and the manner of putting them on) only testify against you that you were once what you know in your hearts you are not now.

8. I come now to your main principle: 'We are all to be "taught of God";[6] to be *inspired* and "led by his Spirit".[7] And then we 20

[a] [All editions from the third, Bristol, 1746, add the following footnote:]

You say you do 'testify against it in the congregation'. Against what? 'Against gay and gaudy apparel.' I grant it. But this is not the thing I speak of. You quite mistake my mark. Do you testify against the *costliness* of their apparel, however plain and grave it may be? Against the *price* of the velvet, the linen, the silk, or raiment of whatever 25 kind? If you do this frequently and explicitly, you are clear. If not, own and amend the fault.

It is easy to discern how your people fell into this snare of the devil. You were at first a poor, despised, afflicted people. Then what some of you had to spare was little enough to relieve the needy members of your own society. In a few years you increased in goods, 30 and were able to relieve more than your own poor. But you did not bestow what was more than enough for your own, on the poor belonging to *other* societies. It remained either to lay it up, or to expend it in superfluities. Some chose one way, and some the other.

Lay this deeply to heart, ye who are now a poor, despised, afflicted people [i.e. the 35 Methodists]. Hitherto ye are not able to relieve your own poor. But if ever *your* substance increase, see that ye be not straitened in your own bowels [2 Cor. 6: 12], that ye fall not into the same snare of the devil. Before any of you either lay up treasures on earth, or indulge needless expense of any kind, I pray the Lord God to scatter you to the corners of the earth, and blot out your name from under heaven [Cf. Deut. 9. 14, 40 29: 20]!

---

[1] Ezek. 2: 5, 7; 3: 11.   [2] Cf. Isa. 56: 10.
[3] The first and 1746 London editions have 'Speaker'; cf. p. 256 n. 3 above.
[4] Cf. Matt. 15: 14.   [5] Cf. Matt. 23: 24.
[6] John 6: 45, etc.   [7] Cf. Rom. 8: 14; Gal. 5: 18.

shall worship him not with dead form, but "in spirit and in truth".[1]

These are deep and weighty words. But many hold fast the words, and are utterly ignorant of their meaning. Is not this an exceeding 5 common case? Are you not conscious abundance of your friends have done so? With whom the being 'taught of God' and 'led by his Spirit' are mere words of course, that mean just nothing. And their *crude* and *indigested* accounts, of the things they did not understand, have raised that deep prejudice against these great truths which we 10 find in the generality of men.

Do some of you ask: 'But dost thou acknowledge *the inward principle?*' I do, my friends; and I would to God every one of you acknowledged it as much. I say, all religion is either *empty show*, or *perfection by inspiration*; in other words, the obedient love of God by 15 the supernatural knowledge of God. Yea, and that all which 'is not of faith is sin';[2] all which does not spring from this loving knowledge of God, which knowledge cannot begin, or subsist[3] one moment, without *immediate inspiration*; not only all public worship, and all private prayer, but every thought, in common life, and word and 20 work. What think you of this? Do you not stagger? Dare you carry *the inward principle* so far? Do you acknowledge it to be the very truth? But alas! what is the acknowledging it? Dost thou experience this principle in thyself? What saith thy heart? Does God dwell therein? And doth it now echo to the voice of God? Hast 25 thou the *continual inspiration* of his Spirit filling thy heart with his love, as with 'a well of water springing up into everlasting life'?[4]

9. Art thou acquainted with the 'leading of his Spirit',[5] not by notion only, but by living experience? I fear very many of you talk of this who do not so much as know what it means. How does the 30 Spirit of God *lead* his children to this or that particular action? Do you imagine it is by *blind impulse* only? By *moving* you to do it, you know not why? Not so. He leads us by our *eye* at least as much as by the *hand*; and by *light* as well as by *heat*. He *shows* us the way wherein we should go, as well as *incites* us to walk therein. For 35 example. Here is a man ready to perish with hunger. How am I 'led by the Spirit' to relieve him? First, by his *convincing* me it is the will of God I should, and secondly, by his filling my heart with *love*

---

[1] John 4: 23.　　　　　　　　　　　　　　　　[2] Rom. 14: 23.
[3] As was then normal, Wesley used the verb transitively, implying 'support'.
[4] John 4: 14.　　　　　　　　　　　　　　　　[5] Cf. Gal. 5: 18.

toward him. Both this *light* and this *heat* are the gift of God; are wrought in me by the same Spirit who *leads* me by this *conviction*, as well as *love*, to go and feed that man. This is the plain, rational account of the *ordinary* leading of the Spirit. But how far from that which some have given!

Art *thou* thus led by the Spirit to every good word and work? Till God hath thereby made thy faith perfect? Dost thou know what *faith* is? It is a loving, obedient sight of a present and reconciled God. Now where this is, there is no *dead form*; neither can be, so long as it continues. But all that is said or done is full of God, full of spirit and life and power.

10. But perhaps, as much as you talk of them, you do not know the difference between *form* and *spirit*, or between worshipping God in a *formal* way, and worshipping him 'in spirit and in truth'.

The Lord is that Spirit.¹ The seeing and feeling and loving him is spiritual *life*. And whatever is said or done in the sight and love of God, that is full of 'spirit and life'.² All beside this is *form*, mere *dead form*; whether it be in our public addresses to God, or in our private; or in our worldly business, or in our daily conversation.

But if so, how poor and mean and narrow have your views and conceptions been! You was afraid of *formality* in public worship. And reason good. But was you afraid of it nowhere else? Did not you consider that formality in *common life* is also an abomination to the Lord? And that it can have no place in anything we say or do but so far as we forget God! O watch against it in every place, every moment, that you may every moment see and love God; and consequently, at all times and in all places, worship him 'in spirit and in truth'.³

My brethren, permit me to add a few words, in tender love to your souls. Do not you lean too much on the spirit and power which you believe rested upon your *forefathers*? Suppose it did; will that avail *you* if you do not drink into the same Spirit? And how evident is this, that whatever ye once were, ye are now 'shorn of your strength'.⁴ Ye are weak and become like other men. The Lord is well nigh departed from you. Where is now the spirit, the life, the power? Be not offended with my plain dealing, when I beseech you who are able to weigh things calmly to open your eyes and see multitudes even in the church pursuing, yea, and attaining the *substance* of spiritual life, and leaving unto you the *shadow*. Nay,

---

¹ 2 Cor. 3: 17.   ² Cf. John 6: 63.   ³ John 4: 24.   ⁴ Cf. Judg. 16: 17.

a still greater evil is before you. For if ye find not some effectual means to prevent it, your rising generation will utterly cast off the *shadow* as well as the *substance*.

11. There is abundantly greater difference still, according to your own account, between us who profess ourselves members of the Church of England and you who are members of the Church of Rome. But notwithstanding this, do you not agree with us in condemning the vices above recited—profaneness, drunkenness, whoredom, adultery, theft, disobedience to parents, and such like? And how unhappily do you agree with us in *practising* the very vices which you *condemn*?

And yet you acknowledge (nay and frequently contend for this with a peculiar earnestness) that every Christian is called to be 'zealous of good works',[1] as well as to 'deny himself, and take up his cross daily'.[2] How then do you depart from your own principles, when you are gluttons, drunkards, or epicures? When you live at your ease in all the elegance and voluptuousness of a plentiful fortune! How will you reconcile the being adorned with gold, arrayed in purple and fine linen, and faring sumptuously every day,[3] with the 'denying yourself and taking up your cross daily'? Surely while you indulge the desire of the flesh, the desire of the eye, and the pride of life,[4] the excellent rules of self-denial that abound in your own writers leave you of all men most inexcusable.

12. Neither can this self-indulgence be reconciled with the being 'zealous of good works'. For by this needless and continual expense you disable yourself from doing good. You bind your own hands. You make it impossible for you to do that good which otherwise you might, so that you injure the poor in the same proportion as you poison your own soul. You might have clothed the naked; but what was due to them was thrown away on your own costly apparel. You might have fed the hungry, entertained the stranger, relieved them that were sick or in prison;[5] but the superfluities of your own table swallowed up that whereby they should have been profited. And so this wasting of thy Lord's goods is an instance of complicated wickedness; since hereby thy poor brother perisheth, for whom Christ died.

I will not recommend to you either the writings or examples of those whom you account *heretics*—although some of these, if you

---

[1] Titus 2: 14.　　[2] Luke 9: 23.　　[3] See Luke 16: 19.
[4] 1 John 2: 16.　　[5] See Matt. 25: 35–6.

could view them with impartial eyes, might 'provoke you to jealousy'.[1] But O! that God would write in your hearts the rules of self-denial and love laid down by Thomas a Kempis![2] Or that you would follow both in this and in good works that burning and shining light[3] of your own church, the Marquis de Renty![4] Then would all who knew and loved the Lord rejoice to acknowledge you as 'the church of the living God'.[5] When ye were zealous of every good word and work, and abstained from all appearance of evil; when it was hereby shown that you were filled with the Holy Ghost and delivered from all unholy tempers; when ye were all 'unblameable and unrebukeable, without spot, or wrinkle, or any such thing',[6] 'a chosen generation, a royal priesthood, an holy nation, a peculiar people, showing forth' to all Jews, infidels and heretics, by your active, patient, spotless love of God and man, 'the praises of him who had called you out of darkness into his marvellous light'.[7]

13. Men and brethren, 'children of the stock of Abraham',[8] suffer me to speak a few words to you also; you who do not allow that 'Messiah, the Prince, is already come and cut off'.[9] However, you so far hear Moses and the prophets as to allow, (1), that it is 'the inspiration of the Holy One which giveth man understanding',[10] and that all the true children of God 'are taught of God';[11] (2), that the substance both of the law and the prophets is contained in that one word, 'Thou shalt love the Lord thy God with all thy heart, and with all thy soul, and with all thy strength: and thy neighbour as thyself';[12] and (3), that the sure fruit of love is obedience, 'ceasing from evil, and doing good'.[13]

---

[1] Rom. 10: 19.

[2] See Thomas à Kempis, *De Imitatio Christi*, I. xvi, III. xxxii. Wesley's first 'conversion' (about the time of his ordination) owed a great deal to this work and Jeremy Taylor's *Holy Living* and *Holy Dying*. As a result of reading à Kempis, he says, 'I began to see that true religion was seated in the heart, and that God's law extended to all our thoughts as well as words and actions' (*Journal*, May 24, 1738). To Wesley's contemporaries the *Imitatio* was best known in English translations entitled *The Christian's Pattern*—a title used also for Wesley's own editions of the work, both with the full text and in his more popular abridgment. (See *Bibliography*, Nos. 4, 45; cf. Nos. 55, 154).

[3] See John 5: 35.

[4] Wesley was deeply impressed by *The Holy Life of Monr. de Renty, a late Nobleman of France, and sometime Councellor to King Lewis the 13th*. Its author was John Baptist S. Jure, and it was published in an English translation (with the above title) in 1658. Wesley issued an abridgement of this work, which passed through six editions during his lifetime, for which see below, *A Second Letter to the Author of the Enthusiasm of Methodists, etc.*, § 47 and note.   [5] 1 Tim. 3: 15.   [6] Cf. Eph. 5: 27.

[7] Cf. 1 Pet. 2: 9.   [8] Acts 13: 26.   [9] Cf. Dan. 9: 26.   [10] Cf. Job 32: 8.

[11] John 6: 45; 1 Thess. 4: 9.   [12] Luke 10: 27, etc.   [13] Cf. Isa. 1: 16, 17.

And do *you* walk by this rule? Have *you yourself* that 'inspiration of the Holy One'? Are *you* 'taught of God'? Hath he opened your understanding? Have you the inward knowledge of the Most High? I fear not. Perhaps you know little more, even of the meaning of the
5 words, than a Mahometan.

Let us go a little farther. Do you 'love the Lord your God with all your heart, with all your soul, with all your strength'? Can *you* say, 'Whom have I in heaven but thee; and there is none upon earth that I desire besides thee'?[1] Do you desire God at all? Do
10 you desire to have anything to do with him, till you can keep the world no longer? Are you not content, so you enjoy the good things of earth, to let God stand afar off? Only calling upon him now and then, when you can't well do without him. Why then you do not *love* God at all, though you will sometimes condescend
15 to *use* him. You *love* the world. This possesses your *heart*. This therefore is your God. You renounce the God of your fathers, the God of Israel; you are still 'uncircumcised in heart'.[2] Your own conscience bears witness, you no more hear Moses and the prophets than you do Jesus of Nazareth.

20 14. From Moses and the prophets it has been shown that your forefathers were 'a faithless and stubborn generation; a generation which set not their hearts aright, and whose spirit cleaved not steadfastly unto God'.[3] And this you acknowledge yourselves. If you are asked, 'How is it that the promise is not fulfilled? Seeing "the sceptre
25 is long since departed from Judah",[4] why is not Shiloh come?' your usual answer is, 'Because of the sins of our fathers, God hath delayed his coming.' Have *you* then reformed from the sins of your fathers? Are *you* turned unto the Lord your God? Nay; do ye not tread in the same steps? Bating[5] that single point of outward
30 idolatry, what abomination did *they* ever commit, which *you* have not committed also? Which the generality of you do not commit still, according to your power? If therefore the coming of the Messiah was hindered by the sins of your forefathers, then by the same rule your continuance therein will hinder his coming to the end of the
35 world.

'Brethren, my heart's desire and prayer to God' is, that he would

---

[1] Ps. 73: 25. [2] Ezek. 44: 7, 9; Acts 7: 51.
[3] Ps. 78: 9 (B.C.P.). [4] Cf. Gen. 49: 10.
[5] This use of 'bate' in the sense of 'omit' seems to have been somewhat uncommon even in Wesley's day. The 1765 edition reads 'baring', which may have been a misprint for 'barring' rather than for 'bating'; the 1781 and 1786 editions change to 'except'.

'gather the outcasts of Israel'.[1] And I doubt not but when 'the fullness of the Gentiles is come in', then 'all Israel shall be saved'.[2] But meantime is there not great cause that ye should say with Daniel, 'O Lord, righteousness belongeth unto thee, but unto us confusion of face, as at this day; to the men of Judah, and unto all Israel. . . . O Lord, we have sinned, . . . we have rebelled against thee; neither have we obeyed the voice of the Lord our God. . . . Yet, O our God, incline thine ear, and hear; open thine eyes, and behold our desolations; . . . for we do not present our supplications before thee for our righteousnesses, but for thy great mercies. O Lord, hear. O Lord, forgive! O Lord, hearken and do; defer not, for thine own sake; for thy city and thy people are called by thy name.'[3]

15. I cannot conclude without addressing myself to you also who do not admit either the Jewish or Christian revelation. But still you desire to be happy. You own the essential difference between vice and virtue, and acknowledge (as did all the wiser Greeks and Romans) that vice cannot consist with happiness. You allow likewise that gratitude and benevolence, self-knowledge and modesty, mildness, temperance, patience, and generosity, are justly numbered among virtues; and that ingratitude and malice, envy and ill-nature, pride, insolence and vanity, gluttony and luxury, covetousness and discontent, are vices of the highest kind.

Now let us calmly inquire how far *your* life is consistent with your principles.

You seek happiness; but you find it not. You come no nearer it with all your labours. You are not happier than you was a year ago. Nay, I doubt you are more unhappy. Why is this, but because you look for happiness there, where you own it cannot be found? Indeed, what is there on earth which can long satisfy a man of understanding? His soul is too large for the world he lives in. He wants more room:

> *Aestuat infelix angusto limite mundi,*
> *Ut brevibus clausus Gyaris, parvaque Scripho.*[4]

---

[1] Rom. 10: 1; Ps. 147: 2 (B.C.P.).   [2] Rom. 11: 25, 26.
[3] Cf. Dan. 9: 7-10, 18-19.
[4] Juvenal, *Satires*, x. 169-70: 'He frets uneasily within the narrow limits of the world, as though he were cooped up within the rocks of Gyara or the diminutive Scriphos.' The second line of the original reads, 'Ut gyarae clausus scopulis parvaque Scripho.' The appendix to Wesley's *Works* (1774) adds a translation in verse:

> Frets at the narrow prison of the world
> As in a prison pent.

He has already travelled through all which is called pleasure—diversions and entertainments of every kind. But among these he can find no enjoyment of any depth; they are empty, shallow, superficial things; they pleased for a while, but the gloss is gone; and now they 5 are dull and tasteless. And what has he next? Only the same things again. For this world affords nothing more. It can supply him with no change. Go, feed again; but it is upon one dish still. Thus

Occidit miseros crambe repetita.[1]

Yet what remedy under the sun!

10   16. The sounder judgment, the stronger understanding you have, the sooner are you sated with the world; and the more deeply convinced, all that cometh is vanity[2]—foolish, insipid, nauseous. You see the foibles of men in so much clearer a light, and have the keener sense of the emptiness of life. Here you are, a poor, un-15 satisfied inhabitant of an unquiet world, turning your weary eyes on this side and on that side, seeking rest, but finding none.[3] You seem to be out of your place—neither the persons nor things that surround you are such as you want. You have a confused idea of *something* better than all this, but you know not where to find it. You are always 20 gasping for *something* which you cannot attain; no, not if you range to the uttermost parts of the earth.

But this is not all. You are not only *negatively* unhappy, as finding nothing whereon to stay the weight of your soul; but *positively* so, because you are unholy. You are miserable because you are vicious. 25 Are you not vicious? Are you then full of gratitude to him who giveth you life and breath, and all things? Not so; you rather spurn his gifts, and murmur at him that gave them. How often has your heart said, God did not use you well? How often have you questioned either his wisdom or goodness? Was this well done? What kind of 30 gratitude is this? It is the best you are master of. Then take knowledge of yourself. Black ingratitude is rooted in your inmost frame. You can no more love God than you can see him; or than you can be happy without that love.

Neither (how much soever you may pique yourself upon it) are 35 you a lover of mankind. Can love and malice consist? Benevolence

---

[1] Cf. Juvenal, *Satires*, vii. 154, 'Occidit miseros crambe repetita magistros'—'Served up again and again, the cabbage is the death of the unhappy master' (Loeb). The appendix to Wesley's *Works* (1774) adds the paraphrase: 'They are surfeited with the dull repetition.'

[2] Eccles. 11: 8.   [3] See Matt. 12: 43.

and envy? O do not put out your own eyes. And are not these horrid tempers in you? Do not you envy one man, and bear malice or ill will to another? I know you call these dispositions by softer names; but names change not the nature of things. You are pained that one should enjoy what you cannot enjoy yourself. Call this what 5 you please, it is rank envy. You are grieved that a second enjoys even what you have yourself; you rejoice in seeing a third unhappy. Do not flatter yourself; this is malice, venomous malice, and nothing else. And how could you ever think of being happy with malice and envy in your heart? Just as well might you expect to be at ease 10 while you held burning coals in your bosom.

17. I entreat you to reflect whether there are not other inhabitants in your breast which leave no room for happiness there. May you not discover, through a thousand disguises, pride? Too high an opinion of yourself? Vanity, thirst of praise, even (who would believe 15 it?) of the applause of knaves and fools? Unevenness or sourness of temper? Proneness to anger or revenge? Peevishness, fretfulness, or pining discontent? Nay, perhaps even covetousness. And did you ever think happiness could dwell with these? Awake out of that senseless dream. Think not of reconciling things incompatible. All 20 these tempers are essential misery. So long as any of these are harboured in your breast you must be a stranger to inward peace. What avails it you if there be no other hell? Whenever these fiends are let loose upon you you will be constrained to own:

> Hell is where'er I am; myself am hell![1]   25

And can the Supreme Being love those tempers which you yourself abhor in all but yourself? If not, they imply guilt as well as misery. Doubtless they do. Only inquire of your own heart. How often in the mid career of your vice have you felt a secret reproof, which you knew not how to bear, and therefore stifled as soon as 30 possible?

18. And did not even *this* point at an hereafter, a future state of existence? The more reasonable among you have no doubt of this; you do not imagine the whole man dies together: although you hardly suppose the soul, once disengaged, will dwell again in an house of 35 clay.[2] But how will *your* soul subsist without it? How are *you*

---

[1] Wesley is apparently thinking of Milton, *Paradise Lost*, iv. 75: 'Which way I fly is Hell; myself am Hell.'

[2] See Job 4: 19.

qualified for a separate state? Suppose this earthly covering, this vehicle of organized matter, whereby you hold commerce with the material world, were now to drop off! Now, what will you do in the regions of immortality? You cannot eat or drink there. You cannot
5 indulge either the desire of the flesh, the desire of the eye, or the pride of life.[1] You love only worldly things; and they are gone, fled as smoke, driven away for ever. Here is no possibility of sensual enjoyments; and you have a relish for nothing else. O what a separation is this, from all that you hold dear! What a breach is
10 made, never to be healed!

But beside this, you are unholy, full of evil tempers; for you did not put off these with the body. You did not leave pride, revenge, malice, envy, discontent behind you when you left the world. And now you are no longer cheered by the light of the sun, nor diverted
15 by the flux of various objects; but those dogs of hell are let loose to prey upon your soul with their whole, unrebated strength. Nor is there any hope that your spirit will now ever be restored to its original purity; not even that poor hope of a purging fire so elegantly described by the *heathen* poet some ages before the notion was
20 revived among the doctrines of the Romish church:

> —*Aliae tenduntur inanes*
> *Suspensae ad ventos; aliis sub gurgite vasto*
> *Infectum eluitur scelus, aut exuritur igni—*
> *Donec longa dies, exacto temporis orbe,*
25 > *Concretam exemit labem, purumque reliquit*
> *Aethereum sensum atque aurai simplicis ignem.*[2]

19. What a great gulf then is fixed between you and happiness, both in this world and that which is to come! Well may you shudder at the thought! More especially when you are about to enter on that
30 untried state of existence. For what a prospect is this when you stand on the verge of life, ready to launch out into eternity? What can you then think? You see nothing before you. All is dark and

---

[1] 1 John 2: 16.
[2] Virgil, *Aeneid*, vi. 740–2, 745–7. In the appendix to Vol. 32 of his *Works* (1774) Wesley himself supplied a translation of this passage:

> Some to the piercing winds are stretched abroad;
> Some plunged beneath the wat'ry gulf: the fire
> In some burns out the deep imprinted stain,
> Till the long course of slowly-rolling years
> Has purged out every spot, and pure remains
> Th'ethereal spirit, and simple heavenly fire.

dreary. On the very best supposition, how well may you address your parting soul in the words of dying Adrian:

> Poor, little, pretty, fluttering thing,
>   Must we no longer live together?
> And dost thou prune thy trembling wing,   5
>   To take thy flight thou know'st not whither?
>
> Thy pleasing vein, thy hum'rous folly
>   Is all neglected, all forgot;
> And pensive, wavering, melancholy,
>   Thou hop'st, and fear'st thou know'st not what.[1]   10

'Thou know'st not what'! Here is the sting, suppose there were no other. To be 'thou know'st not what'! Not for a month, or a year, but through the countless ages of eternity! What a tormenting uncertainty must this be! What racking unwillingness must it occasion to exchange even this known vale of tears for the unknown 15 valley of the shadow of death![2]

'And is there no cure for this?' Indeed there is an effectual cure; even the knowledge and love of God. There is a knowledge of God which *unveils* eternity, and a love of God which *endears* it. That knowledge makes the great abyss *visible*; and all *uncertainty* vanishes 20 away. That love makes it *amiable* to the soul, so that *fear* has no more place; but the moment God says, by the welcome angel of death, 'Come thou up hither', she

> Claps the glad wing, and towers away,
> And mingles with the blaze of day.[3]   25

20. See ye not what advantage every way a Christian has over *you*? Probably the reason you saw it not before was because you knew none but *nominal* Christians; men who professed to believe more (in *their* way of believing) but had no more of the knowledge or love of God than yourselves. So that with regard to real, *inward religion*, 30 you stood upon even ground. And perhaps in many branches of *outward* religion the advantage was on *your* side.

---

[1] Matthew Prior's translation (slightly misquoted) of Hadrian, *Morientis, Ad Animam Suam* (cf. Aelius Spartianus, *De Vita Hadriani*, § xxv).

[2] Ps. 23: 4.

[3] Cf. Thomas Parnell, 'A Night-Piece on Death', ll. 89–90:

> Clap the glad wing, and tow'r away,
> And mingle with the blaze of day.

See also Wesley, *A Collection of Moral and Sacred Poems* (1744), I. 264.

May the Lord, the God of the Christians, either reform these wretches, or take them away from the earth! That lay this grand stumbling-block in the way of those who desire to know the will of God!

5 O ye who desire to know his will, regard them not! If it be possible, blot them out of your remembrance.

They neither *can* nor *will* do you any good. O suffer them not to do you harm. Be not prejudiced against Christianity by those who know nothing at all of it. Nay, they condemn it, all *real, substantial* 10 Christianity; they speak evil of the thing they know not. They have a kind of *cant* word for the whole religion of the heart. They call it 'enthusiasm'.

I will briefly lay before you the ground of the matter, and appeal to you yourselves for the reasonableness of it.

15 21. What a miserable drudgery is the service of God unless I love the God whom I serve! But I cannot love one whom I know not. How then can I love God till I know him? And how is it possible I should know God, unless he make himself known unto me? By *analogy* or proportion? Very good. But where is that proportion to 20 be found? What proportion does a creature bear to its creator? What is the proportion between finite and infinite?

I grant, the *existence* of the creatures demonstratively shows the *existence* of their Creator. The whole creation speaks that there is a God. But that is not the point in question. I know there is a God. 25 Thus far is clear. But who will show me what that God is? The more I reflect, the more convinced I am that it is not possible for any or all the creatures to take off the veil which is on my heart, that I may discern this unknown God; to draw the curtain back which now hangs between, that I may see him which is 30 invisible.[1]

This veil of flesh[2] now hides him from my sight. And who is able to make it transparent, so that I may perceive 'through this glass' God always before me, till I see him 'face to face'?[3]

I want to know this great God who filleth heaven and earth;[4] who 35 is above, beneath, and on every side, in all places of his dominion; who just now besets me behind and before, and lays his hand upon me.[5] And yet I am no more acquainted with him than with one of the inhabitants of Jupiter or Saturn.

---

[1] Heb. 11: 27.   [2] See Heb. 10: 20.   [3] Cf. 1 Cor. 13: 12.
[4] See Jer. 23: 24.   [5] See Ps. 139: 5.

O my friend, how will you get one step farther unless God reveal himself to your soul?

22. And why should this seem a thing incredible to you? That God, a spirit, and the Father of the spirits of all flesh, should discover himself to your spirit, which is itself the breath of God, *Divinae particula aurae*?[1] Any more than that material things should discover themselves to your material eye? Is it any more repugnant to reason that spirit should influence spirit, than that matter should influence matter? Nay, is not the former the more intelligible of the two? For there is the utmost difficulty in conceiving how matter should influence matter at all; how that which is totally *passive* should *act*. Neither can we rationally account either for gravitation, attraction, or any natural motion whatsoever, but by supposing in all the finger of God, who alone conquers that *vis inertiae*[2] which is essential to every particle of matter, and worketh all in all.

Now if God should ever open the eyes of your understanding,[3] must not the love of God be the immediate consequence? Do you imagine you can see God without loving him? Is it possible, in the nature of things? *Si virtus conspiceretur oculis* (said the old heathen) *mirabiles amores excitaret sui.*[4] How much more if you see him who is the original fountain, the great archetype of all virtue, will that sight raise in you a love that is wonderful, such as the gay and busy world know not of!

23. What benevolence also, what tender love to the whole of human kind, will you drink in, together with the love of God, from the unexhausted source of love? And how easy is it to conceive that more and more of his image will be then transfused into your soul? That from disinterested love all other divine tempers will, as it were, naturally, spring? Mildness, gentleness, patience, temperance, justice, sincerity, contempt of the world; yea, whatsoever things are venerable and lovely, whatsoever are justly of good report.[5]

---

[1] 'A bit of the divine breath', or impetus; commonly used to indicate the divine spirit in man.

[2] 'The power of inertness.' This had become widely used as a proverbial expression; it indicated the property of matter by which, if left to itself, it will never change its state.

[3] Eph. 1: 18.

[4] Cf. Cicero, *De Officiis* (*On Moral Obligations*), I. 15: 'Formam quidem ipsam . . . et tamquam faciam honesti vides, "quae si oculis cerneretur, mirabiles amores", ut ait Plato, "excitaret sapientiae".' Addison's translation is as follows: 'If virtue could be made the object of sight, she would (as Plato says) excite in us a wonderful love.'

[5] See Phil. 4: 8.

And when you thus love God and all mankind, and are transformed into his likeness, then the commandments of God will not be grievous; you will no more complain that they destroy the comforts of life. So far from it, that they will be the very joy of your
5 heart—ways of pleasantness, paths of peace![1] You will experience here that solid happiness which you had elsewhere sought in vain. Without servile fear or anxious care so long as you continue on earth, you will gladly do the will of God here as the angels do it in heaven. And when the time is come that you should depart hence, when God
10 says, 'Arise and come away', you will pass with joy unspeakable out of the body into all the fullness of God.[2]

Now does not your own heart condemn you if you call *this* religion 'enthusiasm'? O leave that to those blind zealots who tack together a set of opinions and an outside worship, and call this
15 poor, dull, lifeless thing by the sacred name of 'Christianity'. Well might you account such Christianity as this a mere piece of empty pageantry, fit indeed to keep the vulgar in awe, but beneath the regard of a man of understanding.

But in how different a light does it now appear! If there be such
20 a religion as I have sketched out, must not every reasonable man see there is nothing on earth to be desired in comparison of it? But if any man desire this, let him ask of God; he giveth to all men liberally and upbraideth not.[3]

24. May you not ask, quite consistently with your principles, in
25 some manner resembling this:

'O thou Being of beings, thou Cause of all, thou seest my heart; thou understandest all my thoughts. But how small a part of thy ways do I understand! I know not what is above, beneath, on every side. I know not my own soul. Only this I know, I am not what I
30 ought to be. I see and approve the virtue which I have not. I do not love thee, neither am I thankful. I commend the love of mankind; but I feel it not. Thou hast seen hatred, malice, envy in my heart. Thou hast seen anger, murmuring, discontent. These uneasy passions harrow up my soul. I cannot rest while I am under this yoke. Nor
35 am I able to shake it off. I am unhappy, and that thou knowest.

'Have compassion upon me, thou whose years do not fail! On me, who have but a short time to live. I rise up, and am cut down as a flower. I flee as it were a shadow. Yet a little while, and I return to dust, and have no more place under the sun.

---

[1] See Prov. 3: 17.   [2] Eph. 3: 19.   [3] Jas. 1: 5.

'Yet I know thou hast made my soul to live for ever. But I know not where; and I am unwilling to try. I tremble, I am afraid to go thither, whence I shall not return. I stand quivering on the edge of the gulf; for clouds and darkness rest upon it. O God! *Must* I go always "creeping with terrors, and plunge into eternity with a peradventure"?'[1]

'O thou Lover of men, is there no help in thee? I have heard (what indeed *my* heart cannot conceive) that thou revealest thyself to those that seek thee, and pourest thy love into their hearts; and that they who know and love thee walk through the shadow of death and fear no evil.[2] O that this were so! That there were such an unspeakable gift, given to the children of men! For then might *I* hope for it. O God, if there be, give it unto *me*! Speak, that *I* may see thee! Make thyself known unto *me* also, in the manner that thou knowest! In any wise let me know thee and love thee, that I may be formed after thy likeness! That I may be love, as thou art love; that I may now be happy in thee; and, when thou wilt, fall into the abyss of thy love, and enjoy thee through the ages of eternity!'

---

[1] Cf. Sir Thomas Browne, *Christian Morals* (1682), i. 8, 'Covetousness, . . . only affected with the certainty of things present, makes a peradventure of things to come.'
[2] See Ps. 23: 4.

A
FARTHER APPEAL
To MEN of
REASON and RELIGION

PART III

I. 1. Now what can an impartial person think concerning the present state of religion in England? Is there a nation under the sun which is so deeply fallen from the very first principles of all religion? Where is the country in which is found so utter a disregard
5 to even heathen morality? Such a thorough contempt of justice, and truth, and all that should be dear and honourable to rational creatures?

What species of vice can possibly be named—even of those that nature itself abhors—of which we have not had, for many years,
10 a plentiful and still increasing harvest? What sin remains either in Rome or Constantinople which we have not imported long ago (if it was not of our native growth) and improved upon ever since? Such a complication of villainies of every kind, considered with all their aggravations, such a scorn of whatever bears the face of virtue, such
15 injustice, fraud, and falsehood; above all, such perjury, and such a method of law, we may defy the whole world to produce.

What multitudes are found throughout our land who do not even profess any religion at all? And what numbers of those who profess much confute their profession by their practice? Yea, and perhaps
20 by their exorbitant pride, vanity, covetousness, rapaciousness, or oppression, cause the very name of religion to stink in the nostrils of many (otherwise) reasonable men?

2. 'However, we have many thousands still of truly virtuous and religious men.' Wherein does their religion consist? In righteous-
25 ness and true holiness?[1] In love stronger than death? Fervent gratitude to God? And tender affection to all his creatures? Is their

[1] Eph. 4: 24.

religion the religion of the heart? A renewal of the soul in the image of God?[1] Do they resemble him they worship? Are they free from pride, from vanity, from malice and envy; from ambition and avarice, from passion and lust; from every uneasy and unlovely temper? Alas! I fear neither they (the greater part at least) nor you know what this religion means; or have any more notion of it than the peasant that holds the plough of the religion of a gymnosophist.[2]

'Tis well if the genuine religion of Christ has any more alliance with what you *call* religion than with the Turkish pilgrimages to Mecca, or the popish worship of our Lady of Loretto.[3] Have not you substituted in the place of the religion of the heart something (I do not say equally *sinful*, but) equally vain and foreign to the worshipping of God 'in spirit and in truth'?[4] What else can be said even of *prayer* (public or private) in the manner wherein you generally perform it? As a thing of course, running round and round in the same dull track, without either the knowledge or love of God? Without one heavenly temper, either attained or improved? O what mockery of God is this!

And yet even *this* religion, which can do you no good, may do you much harm. Nay, 'tis plain it does: it daily increases your *pride*, as you measure your goodness by the number and length of your performances. It gives you a deep *contempt* of those who do not come up to the full tale of your virtues. It inspires men with a zeal which is the very fire of hell—furious, bitter, implacable, unmerciful; often to a degree that extinguishes all compassion, all good nature and humanity. Insomuch that the execrable *fierceness* of spirit which is the natural fruit of such a religion hath many times, in spite of all ties, divine and human, broke out into open violence, into

---

[1] Gen. 1: 27; 9: 6. The 'image of God' (*imago Dei*) has had an important place in theological debate. In what does it consist? To what extent has it been obscured (or destroyed) by the Fall? How can it be restored? Such subjects were eagerly debated by the Greek Fathers and by St. Augustine. But here Wesley, though familiar with the debate, is content with the echo of the phrase, and clearly intends no profound theological implications.

[2] Gymnosophist, a member of a sect of ancient Hindu philosophers of ascetic tendency. They wore little clothing, ate no meat, and devoted themselves entirely to mystical contemplation; hence, a mystic or ascetic.

[3] Loreto, near Ancona, Italy, was the site of the 'Holy House', the alleged residence of the Virgin Mary at the time of the Annunciation. The house, a famous place of pilgrimage, was reputedly transported by angels from Nazareth to Dalmatia, and thence to Loreto.

[4] John 4: 24.

rapine, murder, sedition, rebellion, civil war, to the desolation of whole cities and countries.

Tantum haec religio potuit suadere malorum![1]

3. Now if there be a God, and one that is not a mere idle spectator of the things that are done upon earth, but a rewarder of men and nations according to their works, what can the event of these things be? It was reasonable to believe that he would have risen long ago and maintained his own cause, either by sending the famine or pestilence among us, or by pouring out his fury in blood.[2] And many wise and holy men have frequently declared that they daily expected this; that they daily looked for the patience of God to give place, and judgment to rejoice over mercy.

4. Just at this time, when we wanted little of 'filling up the measure of our iniquities',[3] two or three clergymen of the Church of England began vehemently to 'call sinners to repentance'.[4] In two or three years they had sounded the alarm to the utmost borders of the land. Many thousands gathered together to hear them; and in every place where they came many began to show such a concern for religion as they never had done before. A stronger impression was made on their minds of the importance of things eternal, and they had more earnest desires of serving God than they had ever had from their earliest childhood. Thus did God begin to draw them toward himself with the cords of love, with the bands of a man.[5]

Many of these were in a short time deeply convinced of the number and heinousness of their sins. They were also made thoroughly sensible of those tempers which are justly hateful to God and man, and of their utter ignorance of God, and entire inability either to know, love, or serve him. At the same time they saw in the strongest light the insignificancy of their *outside religion*. Nay, and often confessed it before God as the most abominable *hypocrisy*. Thus did they sink deeper and deeper into that repentance which must ever precede faith in the Son of God.

And from hence sprung 'fruits meet for repentance'.[6] The drunkard commenced sober and temperate. The whoremonger

---

[1] Lucretius, *De Rerum Natura* (*On the Nature of Things*), i. 101. In the appendix to his *Works*, Vol. 32 (1774), Wesley translates: 'So much mischief *this* religion does!'
[2] See Ezek. 14: 19. [3] Cf. Isa. 65: 7; Matt. 23: 32.
[4] Cf. Matt. 9: 13, etc. [5] See Hos. 11: 4. [6] Matt. 3: 8.

abstained from adultery and fornication, the unjust from oppression and wrong. He that had been accustomed to curse and swear for many years now swore no more. The sluggard began to work with his hands, that he might eat his own bread. The miser learned to deal his bread to the hungry, and to cover the naked with a garment. Indeed the whole form of their life was changed. They had 'left off doing evil and learned to do well'.[1]

5. But this was not all. Over and above this outward change they began to experience *inward* religion. 'The love of God was shed abroad in their hearts',[2] which they continue to enjoy to this day. They 'love him, because he first loved us',[3] and withheld not from us his Son, his only Son. And this love constrains them to love all mankind, all the children of the Father of heaven and earth, and inspires them with every holy and heavenly temper, the whole mind that was in Christ. Hence it is that they are now uniform in their behaviour, unblameable in all manner of conversation.[4] And in whatsoever state they are, they have learned therewith to be content.[5] Insomuch that now they can 'in everything give thanks'.[6] They more than patiently acquiesce: they rejoice and are exceeding glad[7] in all God's dispensations toward them. For as long as they love God (and that love no man taketh from them)[8] they are always happy in God. Thus they calmly travel on through life, being never weary nor faint in their minds, never repining, murmuring, or dissatisfied, casting all their care upon God,[9] till the hour comes that they should drop this covering of earth and return unto the great Father of spirits. Then especially it is that they 'rejoice with joy unspeakable and full of glory'.[10] You who credit it not, come and see. See these living and dying Christians:

> Happy while on earth they breathe;
> Mightier joys ordained to know,
> Trampling on sin, hell, and death,
> To the third heaven they go.[11]

Now if these things are so, what reasonable man can deny (supposing the Scriptures to be true) that God is now visiting this

---

[1] Cf. Isa. 1: 16, 17.   [2] Cf. Rom. 5: 5.   [3] 1 John 4: 19.
[4] See 1 Pet. 1: 15.   [5] See Phil. 4: 11.   [6] 1 Thess. 5: 18.
[7] Matt. 5: 12.   [8] See John 16: 22.   [9] See 1 Pet. 5: 7.   [10] 1 Pet. 1: 8.
[11] John and Charles Wesley, *Hymns and Sacred Poems* (1742), p. 128, the closing quatrain of st. 6 in a funeral hymn beginning 'Let the world lament their dead' (*Poet. Wks.*, II. 188), slightly altered; line 3 reads 'Trampling upon sin and death'.

nation, in a far other manner than we had cause to expect? Instead of pouring out his fierce displeasure upon us he hath made us yet another tender of mercy; so that even when 'sin did most abound, grace hath much more abounded'.[1]

5   6. Yea, 'the grace of God which bringeth salvation'[2]—present salvation from inward and outward sin—hath abounded of late years in such a degree as neither we nor our fathers had known. How *extensive* is the change which has been wrought on the minds and lives of the people! Know ye not that the sound is gone forth into

10 all the land?[3] That there is scarce a city or considerable town to be found where some have not been roused out of the sleep of death, and constrained to cry out, in the bitterness of their soul, 'What must I do to be saved?'[4] That this religious concern has spread to every age and sex, to most orders and degrees of men? To abundance

15 of those in particular who in time past were accounted monsters of wickedness, 'drinking in iniquity like water',[5] and committing 'all uncleanness with greediness'?[6]

     7. In what age has such a work been wrought, considering the *swiftness* as well as the *extent* of it? When have such numbers of

20 sinners in so short a time been recovered from the error of their ways?[7] When hath religion—I will not say since the Reformation, but since the time of Constantine the Great—made so large a progress in any nation within so small a space? I believe, hardly can either ancient or modern history supply us with a parallel instance.

25   8. Let understanding men observe also the *depth* of the work, so *extensively* and *swiftly* wrought. It is not a slight or superficial thing: but multitudes of men have been so thoroughly 'convinced of sin'[8] that their 'bones were smitten asunder, as it were with a sword',[9] 'dividing the very joints and marrow'.[10] Many of these have been

30 shortly after so filled with 'peace and joy in believing'[11] that whether they were in the body or out of the body they could scarcely tell.[12] And in the power of this faith they have trampled under foot whatever the world accounts either terrible or desirable; having evidenced in the severest trials so fervent a love to God, so in-

35 variable and tender a goodwill to mankind, particularly to their enemies, and such a measure of all the fruits of holiness, as were not

---

[1] Cf. Rom. 5: 20.   [2] Titus 2: 11.   [3] See Rom. 10: 18.
[4] Acts 16: 30.   [5] Cf. Job 15: 16.   [6] Eph. 4: 19.
[7] See Jas. 5: 20.   [8] Cf. John 8: 46.   [9] Cf. Ps. 42: 12 (B.C.P.).
[10] Cf. Heb. 4: 12.   [11] Cf. Rom. 15: 13.   [12] See 2 Cor. 12: 2.

unworthy the apostolic age. Now so deep a repentance, so firm a faith, so fervent love and unblemished holiness, wrought in so many persons, within so short a time, the world has not seen for many ages.

9. No less remarkable is the *purity* of the religion which has 5 extended itself so *deeply* and *swiftly*. I speak particularly with regard to the doctrines held by those among whom it is so extended. Those of the Church of England, at least, must acknowledge this. For where is there a body of people in the realm who, number for number, so closely adhere to what our Church delivers as pure 10 doctrine? Where are those who have approved and do approve themselves more *orthodox*, more sound in their opinions? Is there a Socinian or Arian among them all? Nay, were you to recite the whole catalogue of *heresies* enumerated by Bishop Pearson[1] it might be asked, 'Who can lay any one of these to their charge?'[2]   15

Nor is their religion more *pure* from *heresy* than it is from *superstition*. In former times, wherever an unusual concern for the things of God hath appeared, on the one hand *strange and erroneous* opinions continually sprung up with it; on the other, a *zeal* for things which were no part of religion, as though they had been 20 essential branches of it. And many have laid as great (if not greater) stress on trifles, as on the weightier matters of the law. But it has not been so in the present case. No stress has been laid on anything as though it were necessary to salvation but what is undeniably contained in the Word of God. And of the things contained therein the 25 stress laid on each has been in proportion to the nearness of its relation to what is there laid down as the sum of all—the love of God and our neighbour. So pure from superstition, so thoroughly *scriptural* is that religion which has lately spread in this nation.

10. It is likewise *rational*, as well as scriptural; it is as pure from 30 enthusiasm as from superstition. It is true the contrary has been continually affirmed. But to affirm is one thing, to prove is another. Who will prove that it is enthusiasm to love God? Even though we love him with all our heart? To rejoice in the sense of his love to us? To praise him, even with all our strength? Who is able to make good 35

---

[1] John Pearson (1612–86), Bishop of Chester and author of *An Exposition of the Creed* (1659), provides a vast amount of information about heresies rather than a formal catalogue of them. The footnotes of this famous and influential work are a mine of erudition, full of recondite information on the history of Christian doctrine. To a lesser extent the same is true of the thirty pieces collected in the *Minor Theological Works*, ed. by E. Churton (Oxford, 1844).   [2] Cf. Acts 7: 60.

this charge against the love of all mankind? Or, laying rhetorical flourishes aside, to come close to the question and demonstrate that it is enthusiasm, in every state we are in therewith to be content?[1] I do but just touch on the general heads. Ye men of reason, give me
5 a man who, setting raillery and ill names apart, will maintain this by dint of argument. If not, own this religion is the thing you seek—sober, manly, rational, divine—however exposed to the censure of those who are accustomed to revile what they understand not.

11. It may be farther observed, the religion of those we now
10 speak of is entirely clear from *bigotry*. (Perhaps this might have been ranked with *superstition*, of which it seems to be only a particular species.) They are in no wise bigoted to *opinions*. They do indeed hold right opinions. But they are peculiarly cautious not to rest the weight of Christianity there. They have no such overgrown
15 fondness for any opinions as to think those alone will make them Christians, or to confine their affection or esteem to those who agree with them therein. There is nothing they are more fearful of than this, lest it should steal upon them unawares. Nor are they bigoted to any particular branch, even of practical religion. They desire
20 indeed to be exact in every jot and tittle,[2] in the very smallest points of Christian practice. But they are not attached to one point more than another; they aim at uniform, universal obedience. They contend for nothing *trifling* as if it was important; for nothing *indifferent* as if it were necessary; for nothing *circumstantial* as if it
25 were essential to Christianity; but for everything in its own order.

12. Above all let it be observed that this religion has no mixture of *vice* or *unholiness*. It gives no man of any rank or profession the least licence to sin. It makes no allowance to any person for ungodliness of any kind. Not that all who follow after have attained this,
30 either are already perfect;[3] but however that be, they *plead* for no sin, either inward or outward. They condemn every kind and degree thereof, in themselves as well as in other men. Indeed, most in themselves; it being their constant care to bring those words home to their own case, 'Whosoever shall keep the whole law, and yet
35 offend in one point, he is guilty of all.'[4]

13. Yet there is not found among them that *bitter zeal*, in points either of small or of great importance, that spirit of *persecution*, which has so often accompanied the spirit of reformation. 'Tis an

[1] See Phil. 4: 11.   [2] See Matt. 5: 18.
[3] See Phil. 3: 12.   [4] Jas. 2: 10.

idle conceit that the spirit of persecution is among the Papists only; it is wheresoever the devil, that old murderer, works—and he still 'worketh in all the children of disobedience'.[1] Of consequence, all the children of disobedience will on a thousand different pretences, and in a thousand different ways, so far as God permits, persecute 5 the children of God. But what is still more to be lamented is that the children of God themselves have so often used the same weapons and persecuted others, when the power was in their own hands.

Can we wholly excuse those venerable men, our great Reformers themselves, from this charge? I fear not, if we impartially read over 10 any history of the Reformation. What wonder is it then that when the tables were turned, Bishop Bonner or Gardiner should make reprisals? That they should measure to others (indeed 'good measure, shaken together')[2] what had before been measured to them? Nor is it strange, when we consider the single case of Joan 15 Bocher, that God should suffer those (otherwise) holy men, Archbishop Cranmer, Bishop Ridley, and Bishop Latimer, to drink of the same cup with her.[3]

14. But can you find any tincture of this in the case before us? Do not all who have lately known the love of God know 'what 20 Spirit they are of'?[4] And that 'the Son of Man is not come to destroy men's lives, but to save them'?[5] Do they approve of the using any kind or degree of violence, on any account or pretence whatsoever, in matters of religion? Do they not hold the right every man has to judge for himself to be sacred and inviolable? Do they allow any 25 method of bringing even those who are farthest out of the way, who are in the grossest errors, to the knowledge of the truth, except the methods of reason and persuasion, of love, patience, gentleness, long-suffering? Is there anything in their *practice* which is inconsistent with this their constant *profession*? Do they in fact hinder 30 their own relations or dependants from worshipping God according

---

[1] Cf. Eph. 2: 12.   [2] Luke 6: 38.
[3] Edmund Bonner (cf. note on Pt. I, VII. 8) and Stephen Gardiner (Bishop of Winchester) were prominent figures in the Catholic reaction under Queen Mary; both had been deprived of their sees under Edward VI, and were popularly held responsible for the persecution of Protestants during Mary's reign. Joan Bocher (better known as Joan of Kent) was an Anabaptist; she distributed Tyndale's New Testament, and was condemned to death in 1550 for denying that Christ was incarnate of the Virgin Mary. After a great deal of hesitation, Cranmer reluctantly acquiesced in her death. Cranmer (burned at the stake at Oxford in 1556) and Latimer and Ridley (burned together at Oxford in 1555) were the most famous of the Marian martyrs.
[4] Cf. Luke 9: 55.   [5] Luke 9: 56.

to their *own conscience*? When they believe them to be in error, do
they use force of any kind in order to bring them out of it? Let the
instances, if there are such, be produced. But if no such are to be
found, then let all reasonable men who believe the Bible own that
5 a work of God is wrought in our land. And such a work (if we
survey in one view the *extent* of it, the *swiftness* with which it has
spread, the *depth* of that religion which was so swiftly diffused, and
its *purity* from all corrupt mixtures) as it must be acknowledged
cannot easily be paralleled, in all these concurrent circumstances,
10 by anything that is found in the English annals since Christianity
was first planted in this island.

II. 1. And yet those 'who can discern the face of the sky cannot
discern the signs of the times'.[1] Yet those who are esteemed wise
men do not know that God is now reviving his work upon earth.
15 Indeed concerning some of these the reason is plain; they *know* not,
because they *think* not of it. Their thoughts are otherwise employed;
their minds are taken up with things of quite a different nature. Or
perhaps they may think of it a *little* now and then, when they have
nothing else to do; but not seriously or deeply; not with any close-
20 ness or attention of thought. They are too much in haste to *weigh* the
facts whereof we speak, and to draw the just inferences therefrom.
Nor is the conviction which they may sometimes feel suffered to
sink into their hearts; but things that have a larger share in their
affections soon destroy the very traces of it.

25 2. True it is that there are some who think more deeply, who are
accustomed to consider things from the foundation, and to lay
circumstances together, that they may judge of nothing before
they have full evidence. And yet even some of these appear to be
in doubt concerning the present work. Now supposing it to be a work
30 of God, how can this be accounted for? That they who so diligently
inquire concerning it do not know the time of their visitation?
Perhaps because of the deeply rooted *prejudice* which they brought
with them to the inquiry, and which still hanging on their minds
makes it scarce possible for them to form an impartial judgment.
35 Perhaps even a slight *prepossession* might occasion their stumbling
on some of those rocks of offence[2] which, by the wise permission of
God, always did and always will attend any revival of his work.
Nay, it may be their very caution was carried to excess. They would

---

[1] Matt. 16: 3.
[2] See Isa. 8: 14; Rom. 9: 33; 1 Pet. 2: 8.

not judge before they had such evidence as the nature of the thing would not admit, or at least God did not see fit to give.

3. All this is very easy to conceive. But it may at first appear surprising to find men of renown, men supposed to be endowed with knowledge, and with abilities of every kind, flatly, openly, peremptorily *denying* that there has been any unusual work of God at all! Yea, a late eminent writer goes farther yet, accounts it an instance of downright enthusiasm to imagine that there is any extraordinary work now wrought upon the earth.[a]

It avails not to say, 'No, he does not deny this, but he denies it to be the work of God.' This is palpably trifling; for the work under consideration is of such a nature (namely, the conversion of men from all manner of sin, to holiness of heart and life) that if it be at any time wrought at all, it must be the work of God: seeing it is God alone, and not any child of man, who is able to 'destroy the works of the devil'.[1]

Yet neither is this difficult to be accounted for if we consider things more closely. For the same prejudice which keeps some *in doubt* may easily be conceived so to influence others as to make them wholly *deny* the work of God. And this it may do in several ways: it may either bring them to question the facts related, and hinder their endeavouring to be more fully informed; or prevent their drawing such inferences from those facts as they would otherwise see to be plain and undeniable. Yea, and it will give tenfold weight to the offences which must come, so as to overbalance all evidence whatsoever.

4. This also may account for the behaviour of those who, not content to suspend their judgment, or to *deny* the work of God, go farther still, even to the length of *contradicting* and *blaspheming*. Nay, some of these have expressed a deeper abhorrence, and shown a stronger enmity against this than they were ever known to do against popery, infidelity, or any heresy whatsoever. Some have persecuted the *instruments* whom it pleased God to use herein, only not to the death; and others have treated in the same manner all

---

[a] [Edmund Gibson,] *Observations*, Part III. [Wesley here puts his finger on one of the fundamental points at issue between him and his critics. They dismissed as 'enthusiasm' the suggestion that any unusual manifestations of God's presence and power could be expected in the modern world; Wesley insisted that it was of the essence of the gospel that such experiences were possible.]

---

[1] 1 John 3: 8.

those whom they termed their *followers*. A few instances of this it may
be proper to mention, out of very many which might be recited.

5. On the twentieth of June 1743 a great multitude of people
gathered together—chiefly from Walsall, Darlaston, and Bilston—
5 in Wednesbury churchyard, Staffordshire.¹ They went from thence
(after by sounding a horn they had gathered their whole company
together) to Mr. Eaton's house in the middle of the town, who was
at that time Constable.² He went to the door with his constable's
staff and began reading the Act of Parliament against riots,³ but the
10 stones flew so thick about his head that he was forced to leave off
reading and retire. They broke all his windows, the door of his
house, and a large clock in pieces. They went then to above fourscore other houses, in many of which there were not three panes of
glass left.

15 6. About Whitsuntide, 1743, a mob arose at Darlaston (near
Wednesbury) and broke all the windows (besides spoiling many of
their goods) of Joshua Constable, John Cotterell, Thomas Butler,
Thomas Wilkinson, Aaron Longmore, William Powell, Ann Evans,
Walter Carter, Samuel Carter, and Thomas Wilks.

20 Edward Martin, Ann Low, Joan Fletcher, Edward Horton,
Mumford Wilks, Jos. Yardly, and Robert Deacon had all their
windows broken twice.⁴

James Foster, Widow Hires, and Jonathan Jones had their
windows broken, and money extorted to save their houses.

25 John Foster and Joyce Wood had their windows broken, and
their goods broken and spoiled.

Jos. Spittle had his windows broken, his house broken open,
some goods spoiled, and some taken away.

---

¹ II. 5–14 contain extracts from Wesley's pamphlet, *Modern Christianity exemplified
at Wednesbury*, published at Newcastle in the autumn of 1745 (see *Bibliography*, No. 110,
and Vol. 9 of this edition), followed by an account of his own visit to the troubled area—
an account similar to, but independent of, that in his *Journal* for Oct. 20, 1743. The
later and more familiar spelling has been preferred where more than one are found in
Wesley or in contemporary documents, as with Stubs/Stubbs, Oniens/Onions.

² John Eaton, the Wednesbury Constable, was a Methodist, and about fifty at this
time. He died in 1753.

³ The Riot Act (1 Geo. I, stat. 2, c. 5) provided that if twelve or more persons should
unlawfully or riotously assemble and refuse to disperse within an hour after the reading
of a specified portion of the Act by a competent authority, they should be considered
felons. It was prompted by the many disturbances in the early months of 1715.

⁴ In the following depositions the form 'broke' is most common in the first edition,
but in many cases (not all) is changed to 'broken' in later editions. Here we have uniformly printed 'broken'.

William Woods had his windows broken twice, and was himself compelled to go along with the rabble.

Elizabeth Lingham, a widow with five children, had her goods spoiled, her spinning-wheel (the support of her family) broken; and her parish allowance reduced from two shillings and sixpence to one shilling and sixpence a week.

Valentine Amberley had his windows broken twice, his wife, big with child, beaten with clubs.

George Wynn had his windows and goods broken, and to save his house was forced to give them drink.

Thomas Day had his windows and goods broken, and was forced to remove from the town.

Joseph Stubbs had his windows broken twice, and his wife so frightened that she miscarried.[1]

7. On June 20, 1743, John Baker,[2] at the head of a large mob, came to the house of Jonas Turner at West Bromwich,[3] near Wednesbury, and asked him whether he would 'keep from these men' that went preaching about, and go to the church? He answered, 'I do go to the church. But I never see any of you there.' Presently one Daniel Onions with a great club broke great part of the window at one blow. Others laid hold of him and dragged him about sixty yards before he could get loose from them. Afterwards they broke all his windows and threw into the house abundance of stones to break his goods.

About four in the afternoon they came to the house of Widow Turner of West Bromwich. They threw in bricks and stones so fast that she was forced to open the door and run out among them. One of her daughters cried out, 'My mother will be killed!' On which they fell to throwing stones at her. She ran into a neighbour's house, but before she could shut the door they broke the bottom off with a brick end. They followed her other daughter with stones, and one with a great stake. She ran into another house, much frightened, expecting to be murdered. The widow asked, 'How can you come and abuse us thus?' On which one came with a large club, and swore if she spoke another word he would knock her on the head,

---

[1] Wesley omitted the preceding paragraph and several other later sections from the version incorporated in his *Works*, Vol. 15 (1772), in which he was followed by Thomas Jackson's well known third edition.

[2] John or 'Jack' Baker was known as 'the man who whacked his father'; he seems to have drowned himself a year or two later (Charles Wesley, *Journal*, II. 442).

[3] Spelt 'West Bramwick' in the original.

and bury her in the ditch. Then he went and broke all the glass that was left. The same they did to many of the neighbouring houses.

8. On the nineteenth of June James Yeoman of Walsall saw Mary
5 Bird in her father's house at Wednesbury, and swore, 'By G—, you are there now; but we will kill you tomorrow.' Accordingly he came with a mob the next day, and after they had broken all the windows, he took up a stone and said, 'Now, by G—, I will kill you.' He threw it, and struck her on the side of the head. The blood
10 gushed out, and she dropped down immediately.

The same day they came to John Turner's house. And after they had broken all the windows, casements, and ceiling, one of them cried out, 'I suppose now you will go to your dear Jesus's wounds, and see them opened for you.'

15 Another of them took Mr. Hands of Wednesbury by the throat, swore he would be the death of him, gave him a great swing round, and threw him upon the ground. As soon as he arose one Equal Baker gave him a blow on the eye and knocked him down again. In about half an hour the mob came to his house and broke all the
20 windows, except about twenty panes. The kitchen windows they cleared, lead, bars, and all, broke the window posts, and threw them into the house. The shop was shut up (he being an apothecary); but they quickly broke it open, broke all the pots and bottles in pieces, and destroyed all his medicines. They broke also the shelves and
25 drawers in the shop to pieces, and many of his household goods.

In the latter end of June, John Griffiths[1] of Wednesbury, and Francis Ward,[2] went to Mr D[olphin], Justice of the Peace.[3] They told him the condition they and their neighbours were in—their houses broken, and their goods spoiled. He replied: 'I suppose you
30 follow these parsons that come about. I will neither meddle nor make.'

9. On January 13, 1743-4, the mob rose again at Darlaston, broke all the windows of all who 'followed this way'[4] (except two or three who bought themselves off) broke open several houses, and took
35 what they liked, the people belonging to them being fled for their lives.

---

[1] Brother-in-law of John Eaton.
[2] Francis Ward (1707-82) was at this time churchwarden at Wednesbury, and also a prominent Methodist.
[3] John Dolphin became Sheriff in 1760.   [4] Cf. Acts 22: 4.

About the same time, the Reverend Mr. E[gginton][1] came to Darlaston; and meeting some others at Thomas Forshew's, they drew up a writing, and Nicholas Winspur, the crier of the town, gave public notice that all the people of the Society must come to Mr. Forshew's and sign it; or else their houses would be pulled 5 down immediately. It was to this effect: that they would never read, or sing, or pray together, or hear these parsons any more.

Several signed this through fear. They made everyone who did lay down a penny—'to make the mob drink'.

10. About Candlemas the wife of Joshua Constable of Darlaston 10 was going to Wednesbury when a mob met her in the road, threw her down several times, and abused her in a manner too horrible to write. A warrant was procured for some of these. But one of them only was carried before Mr. [William] G[ough], who came back and told his companions that the Justice said that they might go home 15 about their business. On this the mob rose again, came to Joshua's house, and destroyed all the necessary goods therein. They likewise broke and spoiled all his shop tools, threw the tiles off of the roof of the house, and pulled down one room, the joist of which they carried away with them. All his gunlocks they took away; and they tore in 20 pieces all his wife's linen, cut the bed and bedstead so that it was good for nothing, and tore her Bible and Common Prayer Book all to pieces. She and her husband retired to another house. But one telling the mob they were there, they swore they would tear it down immediately if the man let them stay any longer. So they went out in 25 the frost and snow, not knowing where to lay their head.

11. On Tuesday, January 31, 1743/4, Henry Old came to John Griffith's house, saying if he did not leave 'following this way' he had a hundred men at his command who should come and pull his house down. Soon after he brought some with him; but the neigh- 30 bours gave him money, and sent him away for that time.

Monday, February 6, between seven and eight at night, came part of the same company. Hearing them afar off, John and his wife fastened the door and left the house. Some of the neighbours going in soon after found them destroying all they could. Two chairs and 35 several bundles of linen were laid upon the fire. After they had destroyed what they could, they loaded themselves with clothes and meat and went their way.

---

[1] The Revd. Edward Egginton, vicar of Wednesbury, for whom see Wesley, *Journal*, Jan. 9 and Apr. 15–17, 1743, and his letter to 'John Smith', June 25, 1746, § 10.

The same day public notice was given at Walsall, by a paper fixed up there, that all who designed to assist in breaking the windows and plundering the houses of the Methodists at Wednesbury should be ready at ten o'clock the next morning on the Church
5 Hill.

12. The next morning, February 7 (being Shrove Tuesday), about half an hour after ten, great numbers of men were gathered together on the Church Hill. Thence they marched down, some armed with swords, some with clubs, and some with axes. They
10 first fell upon Benjamin Watson's house, and broke many of the tiles and all the windows. Next they came to Mr. Addinbrook's, broke a fine clock, with many of his goods, and stole all the things they could carry away. The next house was Jane Smith's, whose windows they broke, with what little goods she had. The next was
15 Mr. Bird's, where they destroyed everything they found, except what they carried away; cutting the beds in pieces, as they did all the beds which they could anywhere find. Thence they went to Mr. Edge's house; he was ill of a fever, so, for a sum of money, they passed it over. The next house was Mr. Hand's. They broke
20 all his counter, boxes, and drawers, and all (except some bedsteads) that axe or hammer could break. They spilled all his drugs and chemical medicines, and stole everything they could carry, even all his wife's wearing apparel, beside what they had on.

13. Mr. Eaton's house was next. They broke all his windows, and
25 all his inside doors in pieces, cut the lead off his house, destroyed or stole whatever they could lay their hands on. Some gentlemen offered to stop them if he would sign a paper implying that he would never hear those parsons more. But he told them he had felt already what a wounded conscience was; and by the grace of God he would
30 wound his conscience no more.

After they had done at Mr. Eaton's they plundered several other houses in Wednesbury and West Bromwich. It is scarce possible to describe the outrages they committed. Only they left them they plundered alive.

35 While they were plundering John Turner's house he waded through the brook to try if he could save some of his goods, which one David Garrington was carrying away. Upon which Garrington told him it would be the same here as it was in Ireland, for there would be a *massacre* very quickly. And he wished it was now.[1]

---

[1] In Oct.–Nov. 1641, after Strafford's strong rule had ended in Ireland, a rising

14. About eleven o'clock Sarah, the wife of John Sheldon,[1] being told the mob was coming to her house, went and met them at the gate. She asked John Baker, their captain, what they were come for. He answered, if she would have nothing more to do with these people not a pennyworth of her goods should be hurt. She made no reply. Then they broke the door open, and began breaking and plundering the goods. One coming out with a fire-shovel, she begged him not to take it away. He swore if she spoke another word, he would beat her brains out.

John Sheldon was this while helping Thomas Parkes to hide his goods, though he knew by the noise they were breaking his own to pieces. Between two and three he came to his house with William Sitch. William asked Sarah how she did, saying, for his part he took joyfully the spoiling of his goods. She answered that seeing so much wickedness she could not rejoice; but she blessed God she could bear it patiently, and found not the least anger in her. John Sheldon, seeing the spoil they had made, smiled and said, 'Here is strange work.' His wife told him if she had complied with their terms, not one pennyworth would have been hurt. He replied that if she had complied to deny the truth, and he had found his goods whole on that account, he should never have been easy as long as he lived; but he blessed God that she had rather chosen to suffer wrong.

The mob continued to rise for six days together. The damage they did in and about Wednesbury, at the very lowest computation, amounted to five hundred and four pounds, seventeen shillings.

Wednesday, October 18, 1743, I came to Birmingham, in my way to Newcastle. Thursday, October 20, several persons from Wednesbury earnestly desired me to call there. I yielded to their importunity, and went. I was sitting and writing at Francis Ward's in the afternoon, when the cry arose that the Darlaston mob had beset the house. I called together those that were in the house, and prayed that God would 'scatter the people that delight in war'.[2] And it was so. One went one way, and one another, so that in half an hour the house was clear on every side. But before five they

took place during which Roman Catholics massacred some four to five thousand Protestants. Many others died from cold, hunger, or ill-treatment. Reports reaching England profoundly moved public feeling, and the Irish massacre became part of the anti-Catholic mythology of the English people.

[1] John Sheldon was married to Sarah, the sister of Francis Ward.

[2] Ps. 68: 30.

returned with greater numbers. The cry of all was, 'Bring out the minister.'

I desired one to bring the captain of the mob into the house. After a few words interchanged, the lion was as a lamb. I then de-
5 sired him to bring in one or two more of the most angry of his companions. He did so; and in two minutes their mind was changed too. I then bade them who were in the room make way, that I might go out among the people. As soon as I was in the midst of them, I said, 'Here I am: what do you want with me?' Many cried out, 'We
10 want you to go with us to the Justice.' I told them, 'That I will, with all my heart.' So I walked before, and two or three hundred of them followed, to Bentley Hall, two miles from Wednesbury. But a servant came out and told them Justice Lane[1] was not to be spoken with. Here they were at a stand till one advised to go to Justice
15 Persehouse[2] at Walsall. About seven we came to his house. But he also sent word that he was in bed, and could not be spoken with.

All the company were now pretty well agreed to make the best of their way home. But we had not gone a hundred yards when the mob of Walsall came pouring in like a flood. The Darlaston mob
20 stood against them for a while; but in a short time, some being knocked down, and others much hurt, the rest ran away and left me in their hands.

To attempt to speak was vain, the noise being like that of taking a city by storm. So they dragged me along till they came to the town,
25 at a few hundred yards distance; where, seeing the door of a large house open, I endeavoured to go in. But a man, catching me by the

---

[1] John Lane (1699–1748). In the slightly fuller account of the riot given in the *Journal*, Mr. Lane's first response to the mob was the message, 'What have I to do with Mr. Wesley? Go and carry him back.' When his son came out and asked what was the matter, a man in the mob complained that Wesley got people up at five o'clock in the morning. The son's advice to the crowd was 'to go home and be quiet' (*Journal*, Oct. 20, 1743). Charles Wesley, reporting what his brother told him a few days later, states that another member of the mob added, 'To be plain, sir, if I must speak the truth, all the fault I find with him is that he preaches better than our parsons' (C. Wesley, *Journal*, Oct. 25, 1743).

[2] William Persehouse (1691–1749), of Reynolds Hall, Walsall, belonged to an old Staffordshire family, which had held the Reynolds Hall estates for a couple of centuries. Wesley includes in the *Journal* a document which he considered 'as great a curiosity in its kind as, I believe, was ever yet seen in England': an order to all officers of the peace in Staffordshire 'to make diligent search after the said Methodist preachers, and to bring him or them before some of us his said Majesty's Justices of the Peace, to be examined concerning their unlawful doings'. This was dated Oct. 12, 1743, and was signed by J. Lane and W. Persehouse—'the very justices to whose houses I was carried, and who severally refused to see me!' (*Journal*, Oct. 20, 1743).

hair (my hat having been caught away at the beginning) pulled me back into the middle of the mob, who were as so many ramping and roaring lions. They hurried me from thence, through the main street, from one end of the town to the other. I continued speaking all the time to those within hearing, feeling no pain or weariness. 5

At the west end of the town, seeing a door half open, I made towards it, and would have gone in; but a gentleman in the shop would not suffer me, saying they would pull the house down if I did. However, here I stood, and asked, 'Are you willing to hear me speak?' Many cried out, 'No, no! Knock his brains out.' Others 10 said, 'Nay, but we *will* hear him speak first.' I began asking, 'What hurt have I done you? Whom among you have I wronged in word or deed?' And continued speaking till my voice failed. Then the floods lifted up their voice again;[1] many crying out, 'Bring him away, bring him away.' 15

Feeling my strength renewed, I spoke again, and broke out aloud into prayer. And now one of the men who had headed the mob before turned, and said, 'Sir, follow me. Not a man shall touch a hair of your head.' Two or three more confirmed his words. At the same time the Mayor[2] (for it was he that stood in the shop) cried out, 20 'For shame, for shame; let him go.' An honest butcher spoke to the same effect, and seconded his words by laying hold of four or five one after another, who were running on the most fiercely. The people then dividing to the right and left, those three or four men who had spoken before took me between them, and carried me 25 through the midst; bitterly protesting they would knock down any that touched him. But on the bridge the mob rallied again. We therefore went on one side, over a mill dam, and thence through the meadows, till a little after ten God brought me safe to Wednesbury, having lost only a part of my waistcoat and a little skin from one of 30 my hands.

I believe every reasonable man will allow that nothing can possibly excuse these proceedings; seeing they are open, barefaced violations both of justice and mercy, and of all laws divine and human. 35

III. 1. I suppose no Protestant will undertake to defend such proceedings, even toward the vilest miscreants. But abundance of

---

[1] See Ps. 93: 3.
[2] Apparently William Haslewood, a chandler, who at Michaelmas had succeeded Martin Pashley, a grocer, in that office.

excuses have been made, if not for opposing it thus, yet for denying this work to be of God, and for not acknowledging the time of our visitation.

Some allege that the doctrines of these men are false, erroneous, and enthusiastic; that they are new and unheard of till of late; that they are Quakerism, fanaticism, popery.

This whole pretence has been already cut up by the roots; it having been shown at large that every branch of this doctrine is the plain doctrine of Scripture, interpreted by our own Church. Therefore it cannot be either false or erroneous, provided the Scripture be true. Neither can it be enthusiastic, unless the same epithet belongs to our Articles, Homilies, and liturgy. Nor yet can these doctrines be termed new. No newer, at least, than the reign of Queen Elizabeth; not even with regard to the way of expression, the manner wherein they are proposed. And as to the substance, they are more ancient still; as ancient not only as the gospel, as the times of Isaiah, or David, or Moses, but as the first revelation of God to man. If therefore they were unheard of till of late in any that is termed a Christian country, the greater guilt is on those who, as ambassadors of Christ, ought to publish them day by day.

'Fanaticism', if it means anything at all, means the same with 'enthusiasm', or religious madness, from which (as was observed before)[1] these doctrines are distant as far as the east from the west. However, it is a convenient word to be thrown out upon anything we do not like, because scarce one reader in a thousand has any idea of what it means. If any part of this doctrine is held by the Quakers, there is the more reason to rejoice. I would to God they held it all—though the doctrine itself would be neither better nor worse for this.

'Popery', in the mouth of many men, means just nothing; or at most 'something very horrid and bad'. But popery, properly speaking, is the distinguishing doctrines of the Church of Rome. They are summed up in the Twelve Articles which the Council of Trent added to the Nicene Creed.[2] Now who can find the least connexion between any of these and the doctrines whereof we are speaking?

---

[1] See above, I. 10–11.

[2] The Council of Trent reaffirmed the Niceno-Constantinopolitan Creed as the basis of faith (Sessio III, Feb. 4, 1546). Subsequently, Pope Pius IV published a short conspectus of the articles of faith as determined at Trent, in the Bull *Injunctum nobis* Nov. 13, 1564. This is the so-called *Professio fidei tridentinae*.

2. Others allege, 'Their doctrine is too strict. They make the way to heaven too narrow.' And this is in truth the original objection (as it was almost the only one for some time) and is secretly at the bottom of a thousand more which appear in various forms. But do they make the way to heaven any narrower than our Lord and his apostles made it? Is their doctrine stricter than that of the Bible? Consider only a few plain texts: 'Thou shalt love the Lord thy God with all thy heart, and with all thy mind, and with all thy soul, and with all thy strength.'[1] 'For every idle word which men shall speak, they shall give an account in the day of judgment.'[2] 'Whether ye eat or drink, or whatever ye do, do all to the glory of God.'[3] If their doctrine is stricter than this, they are to blame. But you know in your conscience it is not. And who can be one jot less strict without 'corrupting the Word of God'?[4] Can any steward of the mysteries of God[5] be found faithful if he change any part of that sacred depositum? No. He can abate nothing, he can soften nothing. He is constrained to declare to all men, 'I may not *bring down* the Scripture to your taste. You must *come up* to it, or perish for ever.'

3. This is the real ground of that other popular cry, concerning 'the uncharitableness of these men'. Uncharitable, are they? In what respect? Do they not feed the hungry, and clothe the naked?[6] 'No, that is not the thing. They are not wanting in this. But they are so uncharitable in judging! They think none can be saved but those of their own way. They damn all the world besides themselves.'

What do you mean? 'They think none can be saved but those of their own way'? Most surely they do. For as there is but one heaven, so there is but one way to it—even the way of faith in Christ (for we speak not of opinions, or outward modes of worship), the way of love to God and man, the 'highway of holiness'.[7] And is it uncharitable to think or say that none can be saved but those who walk in this way? Was he then uncharitable who declared, 'He that believeth not shall be damned'?[8] Or he that said, 'Follow holiness, without which no man shall see the Lord'?[9] And again: 'Though I bestow all my goods to feed the poor, and though I give my body to be burned', yet if I 'have not ἀγάπην (charity, love) all this profiteth me nothing.'[10]

---

[1] Cf. Deut. 6: 5; Mark 12: 30, etc.   [2] Cf. Matt. 12: 36.   [3] 1 Cor. 10: 31.
[4] Cf. 2 Cor. 2: 17.   [5] 1 Cor. 4: 1.   [6] See Matt. 25: 35, 36.
[7] Cf. Isa. 35: 8.   [8] Mark 16: 16.   [9] Heb. 12: 14.   [10] Cf. 1 Cor. 13: 3.

'But they damn all', you say, 'beside themselves'. 'Damn' all? What kind of word is this? They damn no man. None is able to damn any man but the Lord and Judge of all. What you probably mean by that strange expression is, 'They declare that God con-
5 demns all beside those who believe in Jesus Christ and love him and keep his commandments.' And so must *you* also, or you sin against God and your neighbour and your own soul. But is there any *uncharitableness* in this? In warning sinners to flee from the wrath to come?[1] On the contrary, not to warn a poor, blind, stupid wretch
10 that he is hanging over the mouth of hell would be so inexcusable a want of charity as would bring his blood upon our own head.

4. But there is no room for dispute touching these *doctrines* in general, seeing our Lord gives you so plain a rule by which you may easily and infallibly know whether they be of God. 'The tree is
15 known by its fruit.' 'Either therefore make the tree good, and its fruit good; or else make the tree corrupt, and its fruit corrupt.'[a] Now what fruit does the tree before us bring forth? Look and see; believe your own eyes and ears. Sinners leave their sins. The servants of the devil become the servants of God. Is this good or
20 evil fruit? That vice loses ground, and virtue, practical religion, gains? O dispute no more. Know the tree by its fruit. Bow and own the finger of God.[2]

5. But many who own these doctrines to be of God yet cannot be reconciled to the *instruments* he hath made use of. A very common
25 exception taken against these is (and was from the beginning) that 'they are so *young*'. Therefore (abundance of men have readily inferred) 'this work cannot be of God'.

Perhaps they are not so young as you conceive. Mr. Whitefield is now upwards of thirty; my brother is thirty-seven years of age;
30 I have lived above forty-two years;[3] and a gentleman in Cornwall for whom I often preach has the merit of having lived threescore and seventeen years.[4]

But supposing the antecedent true, what a consequence is this?

---

[a] Matt. 12: 33.

---

[1] Matt. 3: 7.   [2] See Luke 11: 20.
[3] George Whitefield was born Dec. 27, 1714, Charles Wesley Dec. 28, 1707, John Wesley June 28, 1703.
[4] Wesley undoubtedly refers to the Revd. John Bennet, curate of North Tamerton, Tresmere, and Laneast, for whom he had preached at least as early as Apr. 16, 1744 (see *Journal*).

What shadow of Scripture have you to support it? Doth not God 'send by whom he *will* send'?[1] And who shall say to him, 'What dost thou?[2] These are too young; send elder men.' What shadow of reason? Is it not possible that a person of thirty or forty may have as true a judgment in the things of God, and as great a blessing 5 attending his preaching, as one of fifty or fourscore?

I wish you would explain yourself a little on this head:

Scire velim, verbo *pretium quotus arroget annus*?[3]

How old do you require a man to be before God should have leave to speak by his mouth? O my brethren, who could have believed 10 any serious man would once have named such an argument as this? Seeing both Scripture and reason teach that God herein 'giveth account to none of his ways'.[4] But he worketh by whomsoever he *will* work; he showeth mercy by whom he will show mercy.

6. 'But there are only a *few* young heads.' I cannot but observe 15 here what great pains have been taken, what diligence shown, to make and to keep them few. What arts have not been used to keep back those, of the clergy in particular, who have been clearly convinced from time to time that they ought to join hearts and hands in the work? On this occasion it has been accounted meritorious 20 to 'say all manner of evil of us falsely';[5] to *promise* them whatever their hearts desired if they would refrain from these men; and, on the other hand, to *threaten* them with heavy things if ever they went among them more. So that how fully soever they were convinced, they could not act according to their conviction unless they could 25 give up at once all thought of preferment, either in Church or State; nay, all hope of even a fellowship or poor scholarship in either university. Many also have been threatened that if they went on in this way what little they had should be taken from them. And many have, on this very account, been disowned by their dearest 30 friends and nearest relations. So that there was no possibility the number of these labourers should ever be increased at all, unless by those who could break through all these ties, who desired nothing in the present world, who counted neither their fortunes, nor friends,

---

[1] Cf. Exod. 4: 13.   [2] Cf. Job 9: 12; Dan. 4: 35.
[3] Horace, *Epistles*, II. i. 35. Wesley himself supplies a good translation in Vol. 32 of his *Works* (1774): 'How old must a book be before it is good for anything?' In his quotation he substituted *verbo* (word) for Horace's *chartis* (book). He quotes the last four words in his 'Brief Thoughts on Christian Perfection' (1783), for which see Vol. 12 of this edition.
[4] Cf. Job 33: 13.   Cf. Matt. 5: 11.

nor lives dear unto themselves, so they might only 'keep a conscience void of offence toward God and toward men'.[1]

7. But what do you infer from their fewness? That because they
are few, therefore God cannot work by them? Upon what Scripture
do you ground this? I thought it was the same to him, 'to save by
many or by few'.[2] Upon what reason? Why cannot God save ten
thousand souls by one man, as well as by ten thousand? How little,
how inconsiderable a circumstance is number before God! Nay,
is there not reason to believe that whensoever God is pleased to
work a great deliverance, spiritual or temporal, he may first say, as
of old, 'The people . . . are too many for me to give the Midianites
into their hands'?[3] May he not purposely choose few as well as
inconsiderable instruments, for the greater manifestation of his own
glory? Very few, I grant, are the instruments now employed; yet
a great work is wrought already. And the fewer they are by whom
this large harvest hath hitherto been gathered in, the more evident
must it appear to unprejudiced minds that the work is not of man,
but of God.

8. 'But they are not only few, but *unlearned* also.' This is a grievous
offence; and is by many esteemed a sufficient excuse for not acknowledging the work to be of God.

The ground of this offence is partly true. Some of those who now
preach are unlearned. They neither understand the ancient languages nor any of the branches of philosophy. And yet this objection
might have been spared by many of those who have frequently made
it; because *they* are unlearned too (though accounted otherwise).
They have not themselves the very thing they require in others.

Men in general are under a great mistake with regard to what is
called 'the learned world'. They do not know, they cannot easily
imagine, how little learning there is among them. I do not speak of
abstruse learning, but of what all divines, at least of any note, are
supposed to have, viz., the knowledge of the tongues, at least Latin,
Greek, and Hebrew, and of the common arts and sciences.

How few men of learning, so called, understand Hebrew? Even
so far as to read a plain chapter in Genesis? Nay, how few understand Greek? Make an easy experiment. Desire that grave man who
is urging this objection only to tell you the English of the first
paragraph that occurs in one of Plato's *Dialogues*. I am afraid we
may go farther still. How few understand Latin? Give one of them

---

[1] Cf. Acts 24: 16. [2] 1 Sam. 14: 6. [3] Judg. 7: 2.

an *Epistle* of Tully,[1] and see how readily he will explain it, without his dictionary. If he can hobble through that, 'tis odds but a *Georgic* in Virgil or a *Satire* of Persius sets him fast.

And with regard to the arts and sciences: how few understand so much as the general principles of logic? Can one in ten of the clergy (O grief of heart!) or of the Masters of Arts in either university, when an argument is brought, tell you even the mood and figure wherein it is proposed? Or complete an enthymeme?[2] Perhaps you do not so much as understand the term: supply the *premiss* which is wanting in order to make it a full categorical syllogism. Can one in ten of them demonstrate a problem or theorem in Euclid's *Elements*? Or define the common terms used in metaphysics? Or intelligibly explain the first principles of it? Why then will they pretend to that learning which they are conscious to themselves they have not? Nay, and censure others who have it not and do not pretend to it? Where are sincerity and candour fled?

It will easily be observed that I do not depreciate learning of any kind. The knowledge of the languages is a valuable talent; so is the knowledge of the arts and sciences. Both the one and the other may be employed to the glory of God and the good of men. But yet I ask, where hath God declared in his Word that he cannot or will not make use of men that have it not? Has Moses or any of the prophets affirmed this? Or our Lord? Or any of his apostles? You are sensible all these are against you. You know the apostles themselves, all except St. Paul, were ἄνδρες ἀγράμματοι καὶ ἰδιῶται,[3] common, unphilosophical, unlettered men.

9. 'What! then you make yourselves *like the apostles*.' Because this silly objection has so often been urged, I will for once spend a few words upon it, though it does not deserve that honour. Why, must not every man, whether clergyman or layman, be in some respects 'like the apostles', or go to hell? Can any man be saved if he be not holy like the apostles? A follower of them, as they were of Christ? And ought not every preacher of the gospel to be in a *peculiar* manner like the apostles, both in holy tempers, in exemplariness of life, and in his indefatigable labours for the good of souls?

---

[1] Tully, still commonly used in the eighteenth century for Cicero.

[2] Enthymeme, a technical term used in both rhetoric and logic. In logic (as Wesley indicates) it is a syllogism with one premiss unexpressed—e.g., *Cogito, ergo sum*. Wesley, it will be remembered, had been a lecturer at Lincoln College in logic, in Greek, and in philosophy, and the charge of lack of learning has challenged his professional competence.

[3] Acts 4: 13, where the original reads ἄνθρωποι, not ἄνδρες.

Woe unto every ambassador of Christ who is not like the apostles in this: in holiness; in making full proof of his ministry;[1] in spending and being spent for Christ.[2] We *cannot*, and therefore we *need not* be like them in working outward miracles. But we may and ought
5 in 'working together with God'[3] for the salvation of men. And the same God who was always ready to help *their* infirmities is ready to help *ours* also. He who made them 'workmen that need not to be ashamed' will teach us also 'rightly to divide the word of truth'.[4] In this respect likewise, in respect of his 'having . . . help from God'[5]
10 for the work whereunto he is called, every preacher of the gospel is like the apostles. Otherwise he is of all men most miserable.[6]

10. And I am bold to affirm that these unlettered men 'have help from God' for that great work, the saving of souls from death;[7] seeing he hath enabled, and doth enable them still, to 'turn many
15 to righteousness'.[8] Thus hath he 'destroyed the wisdom of the wise, and brought to nought the understanding of the prudent'.[9] When they imagined they had effectually shut the door, and blocked up every passage whereby any help could come to two or three preachers, weak in body as well as soul, who they might reasonably believe
20 would, humanly speaking, wear themselves out in a short time; when they had gained their point by securing (as they supposed) all the men of learning in the nation—'He that sitteth in heaven laughed them to scorn',[10] and came upon them by a way they thought not of. 'Out of the stones he raised up those who should beget
25 children to Abraham.'[11] We had no more foresight of this than you. Nay, we had the deepest prejudices against it; until we could not but own that God gave 'wisdom from above'[12] to these unlearned and ignorant men, so that the work of the Lord prospered in their hand,[13] and sinners were daily converted to God.

30 Indeed in the one thing which they profess to know they are not ignorant men. I trust there is not one of them who is not able to go through such an examination in substantial, practical, experimental divinity, as few of our candidates for holy orders, even in the university (I speak it with sorrow and shame, and in tender love) are able
35 to do. But O! what manner of examination do most of those candidates go through! And what proof are the *testimonials* commonly

---

[1] See 2 Tim. 4: 5. [2] 2 Cor. 12: 15. [3] Cf. 1 Cor. 3: 9.
[4] Cf. 2 Tim. 2: 15. [5] Cf. Acts 26: 22. [6] 1 Cor. 15: 19.
[7] See Jas. 5: 20. [8] Dan. 12: 3. [9] Cf. 1 Cor. 1: 19.
[10] Cf. Ps. 2: 4. [11] Cf. Matt. 3: 9. [12] Cf. Jas. 3: 15, 17.
[13] See Ezra 5: 8; Isa. 53: 10.

brought (as solemn as the form is wherein they run) either of their piety or knowledge, to whom are entrusted those sheep which God hath purchased with his own blood![1]

11. 'But they are *laymen*. You seem to be sensible yourself of the strength of this objection. For as many as you have answered, I observe you have never once so much as touched on this.'

I have not. Yet it was not distrust of my cause, but tenderness to you which occasioned my silence. I had something to advance on this head also, but I was afraid you could not bear it. I was conscious to myself that some years since to touch this point was to touch the apple of my eye.[2] And this makes me almost unwilling to speak now, lest I should *shock* the prejudices I cannot *remove*.

Suffer me, however, just to intimate to you some things which I would leave to your farther consideration. The scribes of old, who were the ordinary preachers among the Jews, were not priests; they were no better than laymen. Yea, many of them were incapable of the priesthood, being of the tribe of Simeon, not of Levi.

Hence probably it was that the Jews themselves never urged it as an objection to our Lord's preaching (even those who did not acknowledge or believe that he was sent of God in an extraordinary character) that he was no priest after the order of Aaron. Nor indeed could be; seeing he was of the tribe of Judah.

Nor does it appear that any objected this to the apostles. So far from it that at Antioch in Pisidia we find 'the rulers of the synagogue sending unto' Paul and Barnabas, strangers just come into the city, 'saying, Men and brethren, if ye have any word of exhortation for the people, say on'.[a]

If we consider these things, we shall be the less surprised at what occurs in the eighth chapter of the Acts. 'At that time there was a great persecution against the Church . . .; and they were all scattered abroad' (i.e. all the church, all the believers in Jesus) 'throughout the regions of Judea and Samaria'.[b] 'Therefore they that were scattered abroad went everywhere preaching the word.'[c] Now what shadow of reason have we to say or think that all these were ordained before they preached?

12. If we come to later times—was Mr. Calvin ordained? Was he either priest or deacon? And were not most of those whom it pleased

---

[a] Acts 13: 15.   [b] Acts 8: 1.   [c] Ibid., v. 4.

[1] See Acts 20: 28.   [2] See Introduction, pp. 28–9. See also Zech. 2: 8.

God to employ in promoting the Reformation abroad laymen also? Could that great work have been promoted at all in many places if laymen had not preached? And yet how seldom do the very Papists urge this as an objection against the Reformation? Nay, as rigorous
5 as they are in things of this kind, they themselves appoint, even in some of their strictest *orders*, that 'if any lay brother believes himself called of God to preach as a missionary, the superior of the order, being informed thereof, shall immediately send him away'.[1]

In all Protestant churches it is still more evident that ordination
10 is not held a necessary prerequisite of preaching. For in Sweden, in Germany, in Holland, and I believe in every reformed Church in Europe it is not only permitted but required that before anyone is *ordained* (before he is admitted even into deacon's orders, wherever the distinction between priests and deacons is retained), he should
15 publicly preach a year or more *ad probandam facultatem*.[2] And for this practice they believe they have the authority of an express command of God: 'Let these first be proved; then let them use the office of a deacon, being found blameless.'[a]

13. 'In England, however, there is nothing of this kind, no lay-
20 man permitted to speak in public.' No! Can you be ignorant that in an hundred churches they do it continually? In how many (particularly in the West of England) does the *parish clerk* read one of the Lessons? In some he reads the whole service of the Church, perhaps every Lord's day. And do not other laymen constantly do
25 the same thing, yea, in our very *cathedrals*? Which, being under the more immediate inspection of the bishops, should be patterns to all other churches.

Perhaps it will be said, 'But this is not *preaching*.' Yea, but it is essentially such. For what is it to preach but *praedicare Verbum*
30 *Dei*—to publish the Word of God? And this *laymen* do all over England; particularly under the eye of every bishop in the nation.

---

[a] 1 Tim. 3: 10.

---

[1] Cf. *Bullarium Magnum Romanum* (1733), II. 361–2.

[2] 'To demonstrate capability.' Cf. The Form of Church Government, adopted by the Westminster Assembly of Divines, and approved by the General Assembly of the Church of Scotland, Feb. 10, 1645; the Belgic Confession, Art. XXXI. Wesley was appealing to the example of the Reformed churches, but he was unquestionably aware of the use of *facultas* in churches of the Catholic tradition: 'a privilege granted by the favour and indulgence of the ordinary to do that which by the letter of the general law he may not legally do without such a licence.'

Nay, is it not done in the universities themselves? Who ordained that singing man at Christ Church? Who is likewise utterly un-qualified for the work, murdering every Lesson he reads? Not even endeavouring to read it as the Word of God, but rather as an old song? Such a layman as this meddling at all with the Word of God, 5 I grant is a scandal to the English nation.

To go a step farther. Do not the fundamental constitutions of the University of Oxford—the *Statutes*, even as revised by Archbishop Laud—require every Bachelor of Arts, nine in ten of whom are laymen, to read three public lectures in moral philosophy, on what- 10 ever subject he chooses? My subject, I well remember, was the love of God. Now what was this but preaching?

Nay, may not a man be a Doctor of Divinity even in Oxford, though he never was ordained at all? The instance of Dr. Atwell, (late) Rector of Exeter College,[1] is fresh in everyone's memory. 15

These are a few of the considerations that may readily occur to any thinking man on this head. But I do not rest the cause on these. I believe it may be defended a shorter way.

14. It pleased God by two or three ministers of the Church of England to call many sinners to repentance,[2] who in several parts 20 were undeniably turned from a course of sin to a course of holiness.

The ministers of the places where this was done ought to have received those ministers with open arms, and to have taken them who had just begun to serve God into their peculiar care; watching over them in tender love, lest they should fall back into the snare 25 of the devil.[3]

Instead of this, the greater part spoke of those ministers as if the devil, not God, had sent them. Some repelled them from the Lord's table; others stirred up the people against them, representing them, even in their public discourses, as fellows not fit to live—Papists, 30 heretics, traitors, conspirators against their King and country.

And how did they watch over the sinners lately reformed? Even as a leopard watcheth over his prey. They drove some of them also from the Lord's table; to which till now they had no desire to approach. They preached all manner of evil concerning them, openly 35

---

[1] Joseph Atwell (*c*. 1696–*c*. 1768), fellow of Exeter College, Oxford, 1718; rector of the college, 1733–7; priest's orders, 1736; D.D., 1738. Exeter College is next door to Lincoln College; Wesley became a fellow of Lincoln in 1726, and consequently observed the case at close quarters. In eighteenth-century Oxford it was an extraordinary anomaly for the Head of a House to be a layman.

[2] See Matt. 9: 13, etc.   [3] 1 Tim. 3: 7; 2 Tim. 2: 26.

cursing them in the name of the Lord. They turned many out of their work; persuaded others to do so, too, and harassed them all manner of ways.

The event was that some were wearied out, and so turned back to
5 their vomit again.[1] And then these good pastors gloried over them, and endeavoured to shake others by their example.

15. When the ministers by whom God had helped them before came again to those places, great part of their work was to begin again—if it could be begun again. But the relapsers were often so
10 hardened in sin that no impression could be made upon them.

What could they do in a case of so extreme necessity? Where so many souls lay at stake?

No clergyman would assist at all. The expedient that remained was to find someone among themselves who was upright of heart,
15 and of sound judgment in the things of God, and to desire him to meet the rest as often as he could, in order to confirm them, as he was able, in the ways of God, either by reading to them, or by prayer, or by exhortation.

God immediately gave a blessing hereto. In several places, by
20 means of these plain men, not only those who had already begun to run well were hindered from drawing back to perdition, but other sinners also from time to time were converted from the error of their ways.

This plain account of the whole proceeding I take to be the best
25 defence of it. I know no Scripture which forbids making use of such help in a case of such necessity. And I praise God who has given even this help to those poor sheep when 'their own shepherds pitied them not'.[2]

[16.] 'But does not the Scripture say, "No man taketh *this honour*
30 to himself, but he that is called of God, as was Aaron"?'[3] Nor do these. The 'honour' here mentioned is the priesthood. But they no more take upon them to be priests than to be kings. They take not upon them to administer the sacraments, an honour peculiar to the priests of God. Only according to their power they exhort their
35 brethren to continue in the grace of God.[4]

'But for these *laymen* to exhort at all is a violation of all *order*'.

What is this 'order' of which you speak? Will it serve instead of the knowledge and love of God? Will this order rescue those from

---

[1] See Prov. 26: 11; 2 Pet. 2: 22.   [2] Cf. Zech. 11: 5.
[3] Heb. 5: 4.   [4] Acts 13: 43.

the snare of the devil who are not taken captive at his will? Will it
keep them who are escaped a little way from turning back into
Egypt? If not, how should I answer it to God, if rather than violate
I know not what order I should *sacrifice* thousands of souls thereto?
I dare not do it. It is at the peril of my own soul.   5

Indeed if by 'order' were meant *true Christian discipline*, whereby
all the living members of Christ are knit together in one, and all that
are putrid and dead immediately cut off from the body; this order
I reverence, for it is of God. But where is it to be found? In what
diocese, in what town or parish, within England or Wales? Are you   10
rector of a parish? Then let us go no farther. Does this order
obtain there? Nothing less. Your parishioners are a rope of sand.
As few (if any) of them are alive to God, so they have no connexion
with each other, unless such as might be among Turks or heathens.
Neither have *you* any power to cut off from that body, were it alive, 15
the dead and putrid members. Perhaps you have no desire; but all
are jumbled together, without any care or concern of yours.

It is plain, then, that what order is to be found is not among you
who so loudly contend for it, but among that very people whom you
continually blame for their violation and contempt of it. The little 20
flock you condemn is united together in one body, by one Spirit;
so that if 'one member suffers, all the members suffer with it; if
one be honoured, all rejoice with it'.[1] Nor does any dead member
long remain; but as soon as the hope of recovering it is past, it is
cut off.   25

[17.] Now suppose we were willing to relinquish our charge, and
to give up this flock into *your* hands, would *you* observe the same
order as we do now with them and the other souls under your care?
You *dare* not; because you have respect of persons. You fear the
faces of men. You *cannot*; because you have not 'overcome the   30
world'.[2] You are not above the desire of earthly things. And it is
impossible you should ever have any *true order*, or exercise any
Christian discipline, till you are wholly 'crucified to the world',[3] till
you desire nothing more but God.

Consider this matter, I entreat you, a little farther. Here are seven 35
thousand persons (perhaps somewhat more) of whom I take care,
watching over their souls as he that must give account. In order
hereto it lies upon me (so I judge), at the peril of my own salvation,
to know not only their names but their outward and inward states,

[1] Cf. 1 Cor. 12: 26.   [2] John 16: 33.   [3] Cf. Gal. 6: 14.

their difficulties and dangers; otherwise how can I know either how to guide them aright, or to commend them to God in prayer? Now if I am willing to make these over to *you*, will *you* watch over them in the same manner? Will *you* take the same care (or as much more
5 as you please) of each soul as I have hitherto done? Not such *curam animarum*[1] as you have taken these ten years in your own parish. Poor empty name! Has not your parish been in fact as much a *sinecure* to you as your prebend? O what an account have *you* to give to the great Shepherd and Bishop of souls![2]

10   18. There is one more excuse for denying this work of God, taken from the instruments employed therein; that is, that they are *wicked* men. And a thousand stories have been handed about to prove it.

But you may observe, their *wickedness* was not heard of till after they 'went about doing good'.[3] Their reputation for *honesty* was
15 till then unblemished. But it was impossible it should continue so when they were publicly employed in 'testifying of the world that its deeds were evil'.[4] It could not be but the Scripture should be fulfilled: 'The servant is not above his master. . . . If they have called the master of the house Beelzebub, how much more them of his
20 household?'[5]

Yet I cannot but remind considerate men in how remarkable a manner the wisdom of God has for many years guarded against this pretence, with respect to my brother and me in particular. Scarce any two men in Great Britain of our rank have been so held
25 out, as it were, to all the world; especially of those who from their childhood had always loved and studiously sought retirement. And I had procured what I sought. I was quite safe, as I supposed, in a little country town, when I was required to return to Oxford without delay to take the charge of some young gentlemen, by
30 Dr. Morley,[6] the only man then in England to whom I could deny nothing. From that time both my brother and I (utterly against our will) came to be more and more observed and known, till we were more spoken of than perhaps two so inconsiderable persons ever

---

[1] 'Cure [i.e. *care*] of souls'; cf. William Caxton, *Art and Craft to know well How to Die* (1490), 15, 'Euery persone hauing the cure of soules'.

[2] See 1 Pet. 2: 25.   [3] Acts 10: 38.   [4] Cf. John 3: 19.

[5] Cf. Matt. 10: 24–5.

[6] Dr. John Morley was rector of Lincoln College, Oxford, when Wesley was elected a fellow. He was a Lincolnshire man, and held the college living of Scotton, Lincs.; consequently when in residence at his rectory he was a neighbour of the Wesleys at Epworth. Wesley, who liked and admired him, upon his death spoke of him as 'one of the best friends I had in the world' (*Letters*, June 17, 1731).

were before in the nation. To make us more public still, as *honest* madmen at least, by a strange concurrence of providences over-turning all our preceding resolutions we were hurried away to America. However, at our return from thence we were resolved to retire out of the world at once, being sated with noise, hurry, and 5 fatigue, and seeking nothing but to be at rest. Indeed for a long season the greatest pleasure I had desired on this side eternity was

> Tacitum sylvas inter reptare salubres,
> Quaerentem quicquid dignum sapiente bonoque.¹

And we had attained our desire. We wanted nothing. We looked 10 for nothing more in this world, when we were dragged out again, by earnest importunity, to preach at one place and another, and another, and so carried on, we knew not how, without any design but the general one of saving souls, into a situation which, had it been named to us at first, would have appeared far worse than 15 death.

19. What a surprising apparatus of providence was here! And what stronger demonstrations could have been given of men's acting from 'a zeal for God', whether it were 'according to knowledge'² or no? What persons could in the nature of things have been 20 (antecedently) less liable to exception, with regard to their *moral character* at least, than those the all-wise God hath now employed? Indeed I cannot devise what manner of men could have been more unexceptionable on all accounts. Had God endued us with greater natural or acquired abilities, that very thing might have been 25 turned into an objection. Had we been remarkably defective, it would have been matter of objection of the other hand. Had we been Dissenters of any kind, or even Low-Churchmen³ (so called),

---

¹ Horace, *Epistles*, I. iv. 4–5. In the 'Latin Sentences Translated' appended to Vol. 32 of his *Works* (1774) Wesley gives the following translation:
> Creeping silent through the sylvan shades
> Exploring what is wise and good in man.

² Cf. Rom. 10: 2.

³ Wesley is pointing to one of the consequences of the Revolution of 1688 and the succeeding developments. A bitter partisan spirit developed in the Church of England. It was acute during the reign of Queen Anne, and the accession of the House of Hanover left the Church sadly divided between the Whigs, who supported the new dynasty, and the Tory High Churchmen, who tended to be Jacobite in sympathy. Wesley's impres-sionable early years coincided with the reign of Anne; as a young man at the University of Oxford (a Tory stronghold) he found the atmosphere entirely congenial.

it would have been a great stumbling-block in the way of those who are 'zealous for the Church'.[1] And yet had we continued in the impetuosity of our *High Church zeal*, neither should we have been willing to converse with dissenters, nor they to receive any good at
5 our hands. Some objections were kept out of the way by our known *contempt* of money and preferment; and others by that rigorous strictness of life which we exacted, not of others, but ourselves only. Insomuch that twelve or fourteen years ago the censure of one who had narrowly observed us (*me* in particular) went no farther
10 than this:

> Does J[ohn] beyond his strength persist to go,
> To his frail carcase literally foe?
> Careless of health, as if in haste to die,
> And lavish time t'insure eternity.[2]

15 So that upon the whole I see not what God could have done more in this respect which he hath not done; or what instruments he could have employed in such a work who would have been less liable to exception.

20. Neither can I conceive how it was possible to do that work,
20 the doing of which we are still under the strongest conviction is bound upon us at the peril of our own souls, in a less exceptionable manner. We have, by the grace of God, behaved not only with meekness but with all tenderness towards all men; with all the tenderness which we conceived it was possible to use without betraying
25 their souls. And from the very first it has been our especial care to deal tenderly with our brethren of the clergy. We have not willingly provoked them at any time; neither any single clergyman. We have not *sought* occasion to publish their faults; we have not *used* a thousand occasions that offered. When we were constrained to speak some-
30 thing, we spake *as little* as we believed we could without offending God; and that little, though in plain and strong words, yet as *mildly* and *lovingly* as we were able. And in the same course we have steadily persevered (as well as in earnestly advising others to tread

---

[1] Cf. Acts 21: 20.

[2] Samuel Wesley, Jun., in a poetical epistle to Charles Wesley, dated Apr. 20, 1732 (see John Whitehead, *The Life of the Rev. John Wesley, M.A.*, London, Couchman, 1793, I. 446). In the original the closing couplet reads:

> Lavish of health, as if in haste to die,
> And shorten time, t'ensure eternity.

in our steps) even though we saw that with regard to them by all this we profited nothing; though we knew we were still continually represented as implacable enemies to the clergy, as railers against them, as slanderers of them, as seeking all opportunities to blacken and asperse them. When a clergyman himself has vehemently 5 accused me of doing this, I bless God he could not provoke me to do it. I still 'kept my mouth as it were with a bridle',[1] and committed my cause to a higher hand.

21. The truth is, you impute that hatred to us which is in *your own breast*. (I speak not this of all the clergy—God forbid! But 10 let it fall on whom it concerns.) *You*, it is certain, have shown the utmost hatred to *us*, and in every possible way—unless you were actually to beat us (of which also we are not without precedent) or to shoot us through the head. And if you could prevail upon others to do this, I suppose you would think you did God service.[2] I do not 15 speak without ground. I have heard with my own ears such sermons (in Staffordshire particularly) that I should not have wondered if as soon as we came out of the church the people had stoned me with stones. And it was a natural consequence of what that poor minister had lately heard at the Bishop's visitation, as it was one 20 great cause of the miserable riots and outrages which soon followed.

It is this, my brethren, it is your own preaching, and not ours, which sets the people against you. The very same persons who are diverted with those sermons cannot but despise you for them in their hearts; even those who on your authority believe most of the asser- 25 tions which you advance. What then must they think of you who know the greatest part of what you assert to be utterly false? They may pity and pray for you, but they can esteem you no other than false witnesses against God and your brethren.

22. 'But what need is there (say even some of a milder spirit) 30 of this preaching in fields and streets? Are there not churches enough to preach in?' No, my friend, there are not; not for *us* to preach in. You forget: we are not suffered to preach there; else we should prefer them to any places whatever. 'Well, there are ministers enough without you.' Ministers enough, and churches enough— 35 for what? To reclaim all the sinners within the four seas?[3] If there were, they would all be reclaimed. But they are not reclaimed. Therefore it is evident there are not churches enough. And one plain reason why, notwithstanding all these churches, they are no

---

[1] Ps. 39: 2 (B.C.P.).   [2] See John 16: 2.   [3] See note 10 on p. 347.

nearer being reclaimed, is this: they never come into a church—perhaps not once in a twelvemonth, perhaps not for many years together. Will you say (as I have known some 'tender-hearted Christians'):[1] 'Then it is *their own* fault; let them die and be
5 damned.' I grant it is their own fault. And so it was *my* fault and *yours* when we went astray like sheep that were lost. Yet the Shepherd of Souls[2] sought after *us*, and went after us into the wilderness. And 'oughtest not thou to have compassion on thy fellow-servants, as he had pity on thee?'[3] Ought not we also 'to seek', as
10 far as in us lies, 'and to save that which is lost'?[4]

Behold the amazing love of God to the outcasts of men! His tender condescension to their folly! They would regard nothing done *in the usual way*. All this was lost upon them. The *ordinary* preaching of the Word of God they would not even deign to hear.
15 So the devil made sure of these careless ones. For who should pluck them out of his hand? Then God was moved to jealousy, and went *out of the usual way* to save the souls which he had made. Then over and above what was ordinarily spoken in his name in all the houses of God in the land, he commanded a voice to cry in the
20 wilderness: 'Prepare ye the way of the Lord. The time is fulfilled. The kingdom of heaven is at hand. Repent ye and believe the gospel.'[5]

23. Consider coolly if it was not highly expedient that something of this kind should be? How expedient, were it only on the account
25 of those poor sinners against their own souls, who (to all human appearance) were utterly inaccessible every other way? And what numbers of these are still to be found, even in or near our most populous cities? What multitudes of them were some years since both in Kingswood and the fells about Newcastle, who week after
30 week spent the Lord's day either in the alehouse or in idle diversions, and never troubled themselves about going to church or to any public worship at all! Now would you really have desired that these poor wretches should have sinned on till they dropped into hell? Surely you would not. But by what other means was it possible
35 they should have been plucked out of the fire?[6] Had the minister of the parish preached like an angel, it had profited them nothing; for they heard him not. But when one came and said, 'Yonder is a man preaching on the top of the mountain', they ran in droves to hear

---

[1] Cf. Eph. 4: 32.   [2] See 1 Pet. 2: 25.   [3] Cf. Matt. 18: 33.
[4] Luke 19: 10.   [5] Cf. Matt. 3: 3.   [6] Zech. 3: 2.

what he would say. And God spoke to their hearts. It is hard to conceive anything else which could have reached them. Had it not been for *field preaching*, the uncommonness of which was the very circumstance that recommended it, they must have run on in the error of their way, and perished in their blood.

24. But suppose *field preaching* to be, in a case of this kind, ever so *expedient*, or even *necessary*, yet who will contest with us for *this province*? May we not enjoy this quiet and unmolested? Unmolested, I mean, by any competitors. For who is there among you, brethren, that is willing (examine your own hearts) even to save souls from death at this price? Would not *you* let a thousand souls perish rather than you would be the instrument of rescuing them thus? I do not speak now with regard to conscience, but to the inconveniences that must accompany it. Can you sustain them, if you *would*? Can you bear the summer sun to beat upon your naked head? Can you suffer the wintry rain or wind, from whatever quarter it blows? Are you able to stand in the open air, without any covering or defence, when God casteth abroad his snow like wool, or scattereth his hoar-frost like ashes?[1] And yet these are some of the smallest inconveniences which accompany *field preaching*. Far beyond all these are the contradiction of sinners, the scoffs both of the great vulgar, and the small; contempt and reproach of every kind; often more than verbal affronts—stupid, brutal violence, sometimes to the hazard of health, or limbs, or life. Brethren, do you envy us *this honour*? What, I pray, would buy you to be a field preacher? Or what, think you, could induce any man of common sense to continue therein one year, unless he had a full conviction in himself that it was the will of God concerning him?

Upon this conviction it is (were we to submit to these things on any other motive whatsoever it would furnish you with a better proof of our *distraction* than any that has yet been found) that we now do, for the good of souls, what you cannot, will not, dare not do. And we desire not that you should. But this one thing we may reasonably desire of you: do not increase the difficulties which are already so great that without the mighty power of God we must sink under them. Do not assist in trampling down a little handful of men who for the present stand in the gap between ten thousand poor wretches and destruction, till you find some others to take their places.

[1] See Ps. 147: 16.

25. Highly needful it is that some should do this, lest those poor souls be lost without remedy. And it should rejoice the hearts of all who desire the kingdom of God should come that so many of them have been snatched already from the mouth of the lion[1] by an un-
5 common (though not unlawful) way. This circumstance therefore is no just excuse for not acknowledging the work of God. Especially if we consider that whenever it has pleased God to work any great work upon the earth, even from the earliest times, he hath stepped more or less out of the *common* way; whether to excite the atten-
10 tion of a greater number of people than might otherwise have regarded it, or to separate the proud and haughty of heart from those of an humble, childlike spirit: the former of whom, he fore-saw, trusting in their own wisdom, would fall on that stone and be broken; while the latter, inquiring with simplicity, would soon
15 know of the work that it was of God.

26. 'Nay (say some), but God is a God of wisdom. And it is his work to give understanding. Whereas this man is one of them, and he is a *fool*. You see the *fruits* of their *preaching*.' No, my friend, you don't. That is your mistake. A fool very possibly he may be.
20 So it appears by his talking, perhaps writing too. But this is none of the fruits of our preaching. He was a fool before ever he heard us. We found and are likely to leave him so. Therefore his folly is not to be imputed to us, even if it continue to the day of his death. As we were not the cause, so we undertake not the cure of disorders
25 of this kind. No fair man therefore can excuse himself thus, from acknowledging the work of God.

Perhaps you will say, 'He is not a natural fool neither. But he is so ignorant! He knows not the first principles of religion.' It is very possible. But have patience with him, and he will know them by and
30 by. Yea, if he be in earnest to save his soul, far sooner than you can conceive. And in the meantime, neither is this an objection of any weight. Many when they begin to hear us may, without any fault of ours, be utter strangers to the whole of religion. But this is no incurable disease. Yet a little while and they may be wise unto
35 salvation.

Is the ignorance you complain of among this people (you who object to the *people* more than to their *teachers*) of another kind? Don't they 'know how in meekness to reprove or instruct those that oppose themselves'?[2] I believe what you say. Many of them do not;

---

[1] See Amos 3: 12; 2 Tim. 4: 17.   [2] Cf. 2 Tim. 2: 25.

they have not put on gentleness and long-suffering.¹ I wish they had. Pray for them that they may; that they may be mild and patient toward all men. But what if they are not? Sure you do not make this an argument that God hath not sent us? Our Lord came, and we come, 'not to call the righteous, but sinners to repentance':² *passionate* sinners (such as these whereof you complain) as well as those of every other kind. Nor can it be expected they should be wholly delivered from their sin as soon as they begin to hear his word.

27. A greater stumbling-block than this is laid before you by those that 'say and do not'.³ Such I take it for granted will be among us, although we purge them out as fast as we can: persons that *talk much* of religion, that *commend* the preachers, perhaps are diligent in hearing them; it may be, read all their books, and sing their hymns; and yet no change is wrought in their hearts. Were they of old time as lions in their houses?⁴ They are the same still. Were they (in low life) slothful or intemperate? Were they tricking or dishonest, overreaching or oppressive? Or did they use to borrow and not pay? 'The Ethiopian hath not changed his skin.'⁵ Were they (in high life) delicate, tender, self-indulgent? Were they nice in furniture or apparel? Were they fond of trifles, or of their own dear persons? 'The leopard hath not changed her spots.'⁶ Yet their being with us for a time proves no more than that we have not the miraculous discernment of spirits.

Others you may find in whom there was a real change. But it was only for a season. They are not turned back, and are twofold more the children of hell than before.⁷ Yet neither is this any manner of proof that the former work was not of God. No, not though these apostates should with the utmost confidence say all manner of evil against us.⁸ I expect they should. For every other injury hath been forgiven, and will be to the end of the world. But hardly shall anyone forgive the intolerable injury of 'almost persuading him to be a Christian'.⁹ When these men therefore who were with us, but went out from among us, assert things that may cause your ears to tingle, if you consider either the Scripture or the nature of man it

---

¹ See Gal. 5: 22.   ² Matt. 9: 13, etc.   ³ Matt. 23: 3.
⁴ See 'lions at home, and foxes abroad', in Plutarch, *Lives of the noble Grecians and Romans* (trans. Sir Thos. North, ed. 1595), p. 522. Cf. also the English proverb, 'Every dog is a lion at home.'   ⁵ Cf. Jer. 13: 23.   ⁶ Ibid.
⁷ See Matt. 23: 15.   ⁸ See Matt. 5: 11.   ⁹ Cf. Acts 26: 28.

will not stagger you at all. Much less will it excuse you for not acknowledging the work in general to be of God.

28. But to all this it may possibly be replied, 'When you bring your credentials with you, when you prove by *miracles* what you assert, then we will acknowledge that God hath sent you.'

What is it you would have us *prove* by miracles? That the *doctrines* we preach are true? This is not the way to prove that— as our first Reformers replied to those of the Church of Rome who, you may probably remember, were continually urging them with this very demand. We prove the doctrines we preach by Scripture and reason; and, if need be, by antiquity.

What else is it then we are to prove by miracles?

Is it, (1), that A. B. was for many years without God in the world, a common swearer, a drunkard, a sabbath-breaker?

Or, (2), that he is not so now?

Or, (3), that he continued so till he heard us preach, and from that time was another man?

Not so. The proper way to prove these facts is by the testimony of competent witnesses. And these witnesses are ready, whenever required, to give full evidence of them.

Or would you have us prove by miracles:

(4). That this was not done 'by our own power or holiness'?[1] That God only is able to raise the dead; those who are dead in trespasses and sins?[2] Nay, 'if you hear not Moses and the prophets' and apostles on this head, 'neither would you believe though one rose from the dead'.[3]

It is therefore utterly unreasonable and absurd to require or expect the proof of *miracles* in questions of such a kind as are always decided by proofs of quite another nature.

29. 'But you relate them yourself.' I relate just what I saw from time to time: and this is true, that some of those circumstances seem to go beyond the ordinary course of nature. But I do not peremptorily determine whether they were supernatural or no. Much less do I rest upon them either the proof of other facts, or of the doctrines which I preach. I prove these in the *ordinary* way; the one by testimony, the other by Scripture and reason.

'But if you can work miracles when you please, is not this the surest way of proving them? This would put the matter out of dispute at once, and supersede all other proof.'

---

[1] Acts 3: 12.   [2] Eph. 2: 1.   [3] Cf. Luke 16: 31.

You seem to lie under an entire mistake both as to the nature and use of miracles. It may reasonably be questioned whether there ever was that man living upon earth, except the man Christ Jesus, that could work miracles 'when he pleased'. God only, *when he pleased*, exerted that power, and by whomsoever it pleased him.

But if a man could work miracles when he pleased, yet is there no Scripture authority, nor even example, for doing it in order to satisfy such a demand as this. I do not read that either our Lord or any of his apostles wrought any miracle on such an occasion. Nay, how sharply does our Lord rebuke those who made a demand of this kind? When 'certain of the scribes and of the Pharisees answered, saying: Master, we would see a sign from thee'; (Observe, this was their method of answering the strong reasons whereby he had just proved the works in question to be of God!) 'He answered and said to them, An evil and adulterous generation seeketh after a sign. But there shall no sign be given to it, but the sign of the prophet Jonas.'ᵃ 'An evil and adulterous generation'! Else they would not have needed such a kind of proof. Had they been willing to do his will, they would without this have known that the doctrine was of God.[1]

Miracles therefore are quite needless in such a case. Nor are they so conclusive a proof as you imagine. If a man could and did work them in defence of any doctrine, yet this would not *supersede other proof*. For there may be τέρατα ψεύδους, 'lying wonders',[2] miracles wrought in support of falsehood. Still therefore his doctrine would remain to be proved from the proper topics of Scripture and reason. And those even without miracles are sufficient. But miracles without these are not. Accordingly our Saviour and all his apostles, in the midst of their greatest miracles, never failed to prove every doctrine they taught by clear Scripture and cogent reason.

30. I presume by this time you may perceive the gross absurdity of demanding miracles in the present case; seeing one of the propositions in question (over and above our general doctrines) viz., 'That sinners are reformed', can only be proved by testimony; and the other, 'This cannot be done but by the power of God', needs no proof, being self evident.

'Why, I did once myself rejoice to hear (says a grave citizen, with an air of great importance) that so many sinners were reformed,

---

ᵃ Matt. 12: 38–9.

[1] See John 7: 17.   [2] 2 Thess. 2: 9.

till I found they were only turned from one wickedness to another;
that they were turned from cursing or swearing, or drunkenness,
into a no less damnable sin, that of schism.'

Do you know what you say? You have, I am afraid, a confused
5 huddle of ideas in your head. And I doubt, you have not *capacity* to
clear them up yourself; nor *coolness* enough to receive help from
others.

However, I will try. What is 'schism'? Have you any determinate
idea of it? I ask the rather because I have found, by repeated ex-
10 periments, that a common English tradesman receives no more light
when he hears or reads 'this is schism', than if he heard or read:

Bombalio, stridor, clangor, taratantara, murmur.[1]

Honest neighbour, don't be angry. Lay down your hammer, and
let us talk a little on this head.
15 You say, 'We are in the damnable sin of schism, and therefore in
as bad a state as adulterers or murderers.'

I ask once more, 'What do you mean by *schism*?' 'Schism!
Schism! Why, it is separating from the Church.' Ay, so it is. And
yet *every* separating from the church to which we once belonged is
20 not schism. Else you will make all the English to be schismatics in
separating from the Church of Rome. 'But we had just cause.' So
doubtless we had; whereas schism is a *causeless* separation from the
church of Christ. So far so good. But you have many steps to take
before you can make good that conclusion, that a separation from
25 a *particular national* church, such as the Church of England is,
whether with sufficient cause or without, comes under the scriptural
notion of *schism*.

However, taking this for granted, will you aver in cool blood that
all who die in such a separation, that is, every one who dies a
30 Quaker, a Baptist, an Independent or a Presbyterian, is as infallibly
damned as if he died in the act of murder or adultery? Surely you
start at the thought! It makes even nature recoil. How then can you
reconcile it to the love that 'hopeth all things'?[2]

---

[1] This line is composed of words for noise, arranged in a hexameter line. *Taratantara*
is found in Ennius, *Annales*, frag. 140 (Vahlens ed.); also in Virgil (who had it from
Ennius), *Aeneid*, ix. 503. *Bombalio* is a Greek loan word, the preferred spelling for which
is *bambalio*. The line is possibly the work of a humanist of the Renaissance, who knew
Ennius, indirectly, through the tradition of the grammarians.

[2] 1 Cor. 13: 17.

31. But whatever state they are in who *causelessly separate* from the Church of England, it affects not those of whom we are speaking; for they do not separate from it at all.

You may easily be convinced of this if you will only weigh the particulars following.

(1). A great part of these went to *no church* at all before they heard us preach. They no more pretended to belong to the Church of England than to the Church of Muscovy. If therefore they went to *no church* now, they would be no farther from the Church than they were before.

(2). Those who did *sometimes* go to church before, go three times as often now. These therefore *do not separate* from the Church. Nay, they are united to it more closely than before.

(3). Those who *never* went to church at all before, do go now *at all opportunities*. Will common sense allow any one to say that these are 'separated from the Church'?

(4). The main question is, are they turned from doing the works of the devil to do the works of God? Do they now live soberly, righteously, and godly in the present world?[1] If they do, if they live according to the *directions* of the Church, believe her *doctrines*, and join in her *ordinances*—with what face can you say that these men *separate* from the Church of England?

32. But in what state are they whom the clergy and gentry (and perhaps *you* for one) have successfully laboured to preserve from this damnable sin of schism? Whom you have kept from hearing these men, and 'separating from the Church'?

Is not the drunkard that was, a drunkard still? Inquire of his poor wife and family. Is not the common swearer still horribly crying to God for damnation upon his soul? Is not the sinner in every other kind exactly the same man still? Not better at least, if he be not worse, than he was ten years ago?

Now consider, (1). Does the Church of England gain either honour, or strength, or blessing, by such wretches as these calling themselves her members? By ten thousand drunkards, or whoremongers, or common swearers? Nay, ought she not immediately to spew them out? To renounce all fellowship with them? Would she not be far better without them than with them? Let any man of reason judge.

(2). Is the drunkard's *calling* himself of the Church of England

[1] See B.C.P., Morning Prayer, General Confession.

of any more use to him than to the Church? Will this save him from hell, if he die in his sin? Will it not rather increase his damnation?

(3). Is not a drunkard of any other church just as good as a drunk-
5 ard of the Church of England? Yea, is not a drunken *Papist* as much in the favour of God as a drunken *Protestant*?

(4). Is not a cursing, swearing *Turk* (if there be such an one to be found) full as acceptable to God as a cursing, swearing Christian?

Nay, (5), if there be any advantage, does it not lie on the side of
10 the former? Is he not the less inexcusable of the two—as sinning against less light?

O why will you sink these poor souls deeper into perdition than they are sunk already? Why will you prophesy unto them peace, peace; when there is no peace?[1] Why, if you do it not yourself
15 (whether you cannot, or will not, God knoweth) should you hinder us from 'guiding them into the way of peace'?[2]

33. Will you endeavour to excuse yourself by saying, 'There are not *many* who are the better for your preaching; and these by and by will be as bad as ever, as such and such an one is already'?

20 I would to God I could set this in a just light! But I cannot. All language fails.

God begins a glorious work in our land. You set yourself against it with all your might; to prevent its beginning where it does not yet appear, and to destroy it wherever it does. In part you prevail.
25 You keep many from hearing the word that is able to save their souls. Others who had heard it you induce to turn back from God, and to list under the devil's banner again. Then you make the success of your own wickedness an excuse for not acknowledging the work of God! You urge that not *many* sinners were reformed; and that
30 *some* are now as bad as ever!

Whose fault is this? Is it ours? Or your own? Why have not thousands more been reformed? Yea, for every one who is now turned to God, why are there not ten thousand? Because you and your associates laboured so heartily in the cause of hell; because you
35 and they spared no pains either to prevent or to destroy the work of God! By using all the power and wisdom you had you hindered thousands from hearing the gospel, which they might have found to be the power of God unto salvation.[3] Their blood is upon *your* heads.[4] By inventing, or countenancing, or retailing lies, some

---

[1] Jer. 6: 14, 8: 11.   [2] Cf. Luke 1: 79.   [3] Rom. 1: 16.   [4] See Acts 18: 6.

refined, some gross and palpable, you hindered others from profiting by what they did hear. *You* are answerable to God for these souls also. Many who began to taste the good word, and run the way of God's commandments, you by various methods prevailed on to hear it no more. So they soon drew back to perdition. But know that for every one of these also God will require an account of you in the day of judgment![1]

34. And yet, in spite of all the malice, and wisdom, and strength, not only of men, but of 'principalities and powers', of 'the rulers of the darkness of this world', of the 'wicked spirits in high places',[2] there are thousands found who are turned from 'dumb idols, to serve the living and true God'.[3] What a harvest then might we have seen before now, if all who say they are 'on the Lord's side'[4] had come, as in all reason they ought, 'to the help of the Lord against the mighty'?[5] Yea, had they only *not opposed* the work of God, had they only *refrained from* his messengers, might not the trumpet of God have been heard long since in every corner of our land? And thousands of sinners in every county been brought to 'fear God and honour the King'.[6]

Judge of what immense service we might have been, even in this single point, both to our king and country. All who hear and regard the Word we preach, 'honour the king' for God's sake. They 'render unto Caesar the things that are Caesar's', as well as 'unto God the things that are God's'.[7] They have no conception of *piety* without *loyalty*, knowing 'the powers that be are ordained of God'.[8] I pray God to strengthen all that are of this mind, how many soever they be. But might there not have been at this day an hundred thousand in England thus minded more than are now? Yea, verily, even by *our* ministry, had not they who should have strengthened us weakened our hands.

35. Surely you are not wise! What advantages do you throw away! What opportunities do you lose! Such as another day you may earnestly seek, and nevertheless may not find them. For if it please God to remove *us*, whom will you find to supply our place? We are in all things 'your servants for Jesus' sake';[9] though the more we love *you*, the less we are loved. Let *us* be employed, not in the highest but in the meanest, and not in the easiest but the

---

[1] See Matt. 12: 36.   [2] Eph. 6: 12; cf. *Notes*.
[3] Cf. 1 Cor. 12: 2; 1 Thess. 1: 9.   [4] Exod. 32: 26.   [5] Judg. 5: 23.
[6] 1 Pet. 2: 17.   [7] Cf. Matt. 22: 21, etc.   [8] Rom. 13: 1.   [9] 2 Cor. 4: 5.

hottest, service—ease and plenty we leave to those that want them. Let us go on in toil, in weariness, in painfulness, in cold or hunger, so we may but testify the gospel of the grace of God.[1] The rich, the honourable, the great, we are thoroughly willing (if it be the will of our Lord) to leave to you. Only let us alone with the poor, the vulgar, the base, the outcasts of men. Take also to yourselves 'the saints of the world';[2] but suffer us 'to call sinners to repentance';[3] even the most vile, the most ignorant, the most abandoned, the most fierce and savage of whom we can hear. To these we will go forth in the name of our Lord, desiring nothing, receiving nothing of any man (save the bread we eat while we are under his roof), and let it be seen whether God has sent us. Only let not *your* hands, who fear the Lord, be upon us. Why should we be stricken of *you* any more?

IV. 1. Surely ye are 'without excuse',[4] all who do not yet know the day of your visitation! The day wherein the great God, who hath been forgotten among us days without number, is arising at once to be avenged of his adversaries, and to visit and redeem his people. Are not his judgments and mercies both abroad? And still will ye not learn righteousness? Is not 'the Lord passing by'? Doth not 'a great and strong wind' already begin to 'rend the mountains', and to 'break in pieces the rocks before the Lord'? Is not the 'earthquake' also felt already? And 'a fire' hath begun to burn in his anger. Who knoweth what will be the end thereof? But at the same time he is speaking to many in 'a still, small voice'.[5] 'He that hath ears to hear, let him hear',[6] lest he be suddenly destroyed, and that without remedy!

2. What excuse can possibly be made for those who are regardless of such a season as this? Who are at such a crisis stupid, senseless, unapprehensive, caring for none of these things? Who do not give themselves the pains to think about them, but are still easy and unconcerned? What! Can there ever be a point on which it more behoves you to think? And that with the coolest and deepest

---

[1] Acts 20: 24.

[2] A phrase which Wesley took into his vocabulary from George Herbert's translation of a work by Juan de Valdes (*c.* 1500–*c.* 1541), *The Hundred and Ten Considerations of Signior John Valdesso; entreating of those things which are most profitable, most necessary, and most perfect in a Christian profession* (see Consideration 76). This he had read in October, 1733. Dec. 10, 1734, he wrote to his father: 'I never come from among these "saints of the world" (as J. Valdesso calls them) faint, dissipated, and shorn of all my strength, but I say, "God deliver me from an half-Christian." ' Cf. *A Farther Appeal*, Part II, II. 26.

[3] Matt. 9: 13.   [4] Rom. 1: 20.   [5] 1 Kgs. 19: 11–12.   [6] Matt. 11: 15, etc.

attention? As long as the heaven and the earth remain, can there be anything of so vast importance as God's last call to a guilty land just perishing in its iniquity!

You, with those round about you, deserved long ago to have 'drunk the dregs of the cup of trembling';¹ yea, to have been 5 'punished with everlasting destruction from the presence of the Lord, and from the glory of his power'.² But he hath not dealt with you according to your sins, nor rewarded you after your iniquities.³ And once more he is mixing mercy with judgment. Once more he is crying aloud, 'Turn ye, turn ye from your evil ways; for why will ye 10 die, O house of Israel?'⁴ And will you not deign to give him the hearing? If you are not careful to answer him in this matter, do you still shut your eyes, and stop your ears, and harden your stubborn heart? O beware, lest God laugh at your calamity, and mock when your fear cometh!⁵ 15

3. Will you plead that you have other concerns to mind? That other business engages your thoughts? It does so indeed; but this is your foolishness; this is the very thing that leaves you without excuse. For what business can be of equal moment? The mariner may have many concerns to mind, and many businesses to engage 20 his thoughts; but not when the ship is sinking. In such a circumstance (it is your own) you have but one thing to think of. Save the ship and your own life together! And the higher post you are in, the more deeply intent should you be on this one point. Is this a time for diversions? For eating and drinking, and rising up to play?⁶ 25 Keep the ship above water. Let all else go, and mind 'this one thing'!⁷

4. Perhaps you will say, 'So I do. I do mind this one thing—how to save the sinking nation. And therefore now I must think of *arms* and *provisions*. I have no time now to think of religion.' This is 30 exactly as if the mariner should say, 'Now I must think of my *guns* and *stores*. I have no time now to think of the *hold*.' Why, man, you must think of this or perish. It is *there* the leak is sprung. Stop that, or you and all your *stores* will go together to the bottom of the sea.

Is not this your very case? Then, whatever you do, *stop the leak*. 35 Else you go to the bottom! I do not speak against your stores. They are good in their kind, and it may be well they are laid in. But all your stores will not save the sinking ship, unless you can stop the

---

¹ Cf. Isa. 51: 17.   ² 2 Thess. 1: 9.   ³ See Ps. 103: 10.   ⁴ Ezek. 33: 11.
⁵ Prov. 1: 26.   ⁶ See Exod. 32: 6; 1 Cor. 10: 7.   ⁷ Phil. 3: 13.

leak. Unless you can some way keep out these 'floods of ungodliness'[1] that are still continually pouring in, you must soon be swallowed up in the great deep, in the abyss of God's judgments. This, this is the destruction of the English nation. It is *vice*, bursting
5 in on every side, that is just ready to sink us, into slavery first, and then into the nethermost hell. 'Who is a wise man, and endued with knowledge among you?'[2] Let him think of this. Think of this, all that love your country, or that care for your own souls. If now especially you do not think of 'this one thing', you have no excuse
10 before God or man.

5. Little more excuse have you who are still in doubt concerning this day of your visitation. For you have all the proof that you can reasonably expect or desire, all that the nature of the thing requires. That in many places abundance of notorious sinners are totally
15 reformed is declared by a thousand eye- and ear-witnesses, both of their present and past behaviour. And you are sensible the proof of such a point as this must, in the nature of things, rest upon testimony. And that God alone is able to work such a reformation you know all the Scriptures testify. What would you have more?
20 What pretence can you have for doubting any longer? You have not the least room to expect or desire any other, or any stronger evidence.

I trust you are not of those who *fortify* themselves against conviction; who are '*resolved* they will never believe this'. They ask, 'Who
25 are these men?' We tell them plainly; but they credit us not. Another and another of their own friends is convinced, and tell them the same thing. But their answer is ready, 'Are *you* turned Methodist too?' So *their* testimony likewise goes for nothing. Now how is it possible these should ever be convinced? For they will believe none
30 but those who speak on *one* side.

6. Do you delay fixing your judgment till you see a work of God without any stumbling-blocks attending it? That neither is yet, nor ever will [be]. 'It must needs be that offences will come.'[3] And scarce ever was there such a work of God before with so few as have
35 attended this.

When the Reformation began, what mountainous offences lay in the way of even the sincere members of the Church of Rome! They saw such failings in those great men, Luther and Calvin: their vehement *tenaciousness* of their own opinions; their *bitterness*

---

[1] Ps. 18: 4 (cf. B.C.P.).　　　[2] Jas. 3: 13.　　　[3] Cf. Matt. 18: 7.

toward all who differed from them; their *impatience* of contradiction, and utter want of *forbearance*, even with their own brethren.

But the grand stumbling-block of all was their open avowed separation from the Church; their rejecting so many of the *doctrines* and *practices* which the others accounted the most sacred; and their continual *invectives* against the Church they separated from—so much sharper than Michael's reproof of Satan.[1]

Were there fewer stumbling-blocks attending the Reformation in England? Surely no. For what was Henry the Eighth? Consider either his *character*, his *motives* to the work, or his *manner* of pursuing it! And even King Edward's ministry we cannot clear of persecuting in their turns, yea, and burning heretics. The main stumbling block also still remained, viz., open *separation* from the Church.

7. Full as many were the offences that lay in the way of even the sincere members of the Church of England when the people called Quakers first professed that they were sent of God to reform the land. Whether they were or no is beside our question. It suffices for the present purpose to observe that over and above their open, avowed, total separation from the Church, and their vehement invectives against many of her doctrines and the whole frame of her discipline, they spent their main strength in disputing about *opinions* and externals, rather than in preaching about faith, mercy, and the love of God.

In these respects, the case was nearly the same when the Baptists first appeared in England. They immediately commenced a warm dispute, not concerning the vitals of Christianity, but concerning the manner and time of administering one of the external ordinances of it. And as their opinion hereof totally differed from that of all the other members of the Church of England, so they soon openly declared their separation from it, not without sharp censures of those that continued therein.

8. The same occasion of offence was, in a smaller degree, given by the Presbyterians and Independents; for they also spent great part of their time and strength in opposing the commonly received opinions concerning some of the circumstantials of religion, and for the sake of these separated from the Church.

But I do not include that venerable man Mr. Philip Henry,[2]

---

[1] See Jude 9.

[2] Philip Henry (1631–96), son of a royalist courtier, was educated at Westminster School and Christ Church, Oxford. He was ordained a Presbyterian minister during the

nor any that were of his spirit, in this number. I know they abhorred contending about externals. Neither did they separate themselves from the Church. They continued therein till they were driven out whether they would or no. I cannot but tenderly sympathize with
5 these; and the more because this is, in part, our own case. Warm men spare no pains at this very day to *drive us* out of the Church. They cry out to the people, wherever one of us comes, 'A mad dog, a mad dog!'—if haply we might fly for our lives, as many have done before us. And sure it is we should have complied with their desire,
10 we should merely for peace and quietness have left the Church long before now, but that we could not in conscience do it. And it is on this single motive, it is for conscience sake that we still continue therein; and shall continue (God being our helper) unless they by violence thrust us out.

15 9. But to return. What are the stumbling-blocks in the present case compared to those in any of the preceding?

We do not dispute concerning any of the *externals* or *circumstantials* of religion. There is no room; for we agree with you therein. We approve of and adhere to them all: all that we learned together
20 when we were children, in our Catechism and Common Prayer Book. We were born and bred up in your own Church, and desire to die therein. We always were, and are now, zealous for the Church; only not with a blind, angry zeal. We hold, and ever have done, the same *opinions* which you and we received from our fore-
25 fathers. But we do not lay the main stress of our religion on any opinions, right or wrong; neither do we ever begin, or willingly join in, any dispute concerning them. The weight of all religion, we apprehend, rests on holiness of heart and life. And consequently, wherever we come we press this with all our might. How wide then
30 is the difference between our case and the case of any of those that are above mentioned? They avowedly separated from the Church: we utterly disavow any such design. They severely, and almost continually, inveighed against the doctrines and discipline of the Church they left: we approve both the doctrines and discipline of

---

Interregnum, and was one of the ministers ejected in 1662. He experienced imprisonment and the despoiling of his goods under the terms of the Clarendon Code. As his *Diaries* prove, he was a man of profoundly irenical spirit, deeply concerned about the unity of the church. He was highly respected by his contemporaries as a man of holy life. His son Matthew Henry (the celebrated biblical commentator) wrote a *Life* of his father which reflects the same temper. Wesley read this work with great appreciation (*Journal*, Nov. 7, 1741) and published extracts in Vol. 50 of his *Christian Library*.

our Church, and inveigh only against ungodliness and unrighteousness. They spent great part of their time and strength in contending
about externals and circumstantials: we agree with you in both; so
that having no room to spend any time in such vain contention, we
have our desire of spending and being spent in promoting plain, 5
practical religion. How many stumbling-blocks are removed out of
your way? Why do not you acknowledge the work of God?

10. If you say, 'Because you hold opinions which I cannot believe
are true', I answer: believe them true or false; I will not quarrel
with you about any *opinion*. Only see that your heart be right 10
toward God;[1] that you know and love the Lord Jesus Christ; that
you love your neighbour, and walk as your Master walked; and I
desire no more. I am sick of opinions. I am weary to bear them.
My soul loathes this frothy food. Give me solid and substantial
religion. Give me an humble, gentle lover of God and man; a man 15
full of mercy and good fruits, without partiality, and without hypocrisy; a man laying himself out in the work of faith, the patience of
hope, the labour of love. Let my soul be with these Christians,
wheresoever they are, and whatsoever opinion they are of. 'Whosoever *thus* doth the will of my Father which is in heaven, the same is 20
my brother, and sister, and mother.'[2]

11. Inexcusably infatuated must you be if you can even *doubt*
whether the propagation of this religion be of God! Only more
inexcusable are those unhappy men who *oppose, contradict*, and
blaspheme it. 25

How long will you stop your ears against him that still crieth,
'Why persecutest thou me? It is hard for thee to kick against the
pricks';[3] for a man to 'contend with his Maker'.[4] How long will you
despise the well known advice of a great and learned man: 'Refrain
from these men, and let them alone. If this work be of man, it will 30
come to nought, But if it be of God, ye cannot overthrow it.' And
why should you 'be found even to fight against God'?[5] If a man
fight with God, shall he prevail? 'Canst thou thunder with a voice
like him?'[6] Make haste. Fall down. Humble thyself before him, lest
he put forth his hand, and thou perish! 35

12. How long will you fight under the banner of the great enemy
of God and man? You are now in his service. You are *taking part
with the devil* against God. Even supposing there were no other

---

[1] See Ps. 78: 37.   [2] Cf. Matt. 12: 50.   [3] Acts 26: 14.
[4] Cf. Isa. 45: 9.   [5] Cf. Acts 5: 38–9.   [6] Job 40: 9.

proof, this would undeniably appear from the goodly company among whom you are enlisted, and who war one and the same warfare. I have heard some affirm that the most bitter enemies to the present work of God were *Pharisees*. They meant men who had the *form*
5 of godliness, but denied the *power* of it.¹ But I cannot say so. The sharpest adversaries thereof whom I have hitherto known (unless one might except a few honourable men whom I may be excused from naming) were the scum of Cornwall, the rabble of Bilston and Darlaston, the wild beasts of Walsall, and the turnkeys of
10 Newgate.²

13. Might not the very sight of these troops show any reasonable man to what *general* they belonged? As well as the weapons they never fail to use; the most horrid oaths and execrations, and lawless violence, carrying away as a flood whatsoever it is which stands
15 before it; having no eyes, nor ears, no regard to the loudest cries of reason, justice, or humanity. Can *you* join heart or hands with these any longer? With such an infamous, scandalous rabble rout, roaring and raging as if they were just broke loose with their Captain Apollyon from the bottomless pit?³ Does it not rather concern
20 you—and that in the highest degree, as well as every friend to his king and country, every lover of peace, justice and mercy—immediately to join and stop any such godless crew, as they would join to stop a fire just beginning to spread, or an inundation of the sea?

14. If on the contrary you join with that godless crew, and
25 strengthen their hands in their wickedness, must not you in all reason be accounted (like them) *a public enemy of mankind*? And indeed such must everyone appear in the eye of unprejudiced reason who opposes, directly or indirectly, the reformation of mankind. By *reformation* I mean, the bringing them back (not to
30 this or that system of opinions, or to this or that set of rites and ceremonies, how decent and significant soever; but) to the calm love of God and one another; to an uniform practice of justice, mercy, and truth.⁴ With what colour can you lay any claim to humanity, to benevolence, to public spirit, if you can once open
35 your mouth, or stir one finger, against such a reformation as this?

¹ See 2 Tim. 3: 5.

² Bilston, Darlaston, and Walsall were the scenes in Staffordshire of violent riots against the Methodists (cf. above, Pt. III, II. 5–14). In Cornwall also Wesley had experienced mob violence (e.g., *Journal*, Sept. 16, 1743, July 4, 1745). Newgate was the name of prisons in London, Bristol, and Dublin.

³ See Rev. 9: 11.   ⁴ Ps. 89: 14

'Tis a poor excuse to say, 'O, but the people are brought into several erroneous opinions.' It matters not a straw whether they are or no (I speak of such opinions as do not touch the foundation); 'tis scarce worthwhile to spend ten words about it. Whether they embrace this religious opinion or that is no more concern to me than whether they embrace this or that system of astronomy. Are they brought to holy tempers and holy lives? This is mine, and should be your inquiry; since on this both social and personal happiness depend—happiness temporal and eternal. Are they brought to the love of God and the love of their neighbour? Pure religion and undefiled is this.[1] How long then will you 'darken counsel by words without knowledge'?[2] The plain religion now propagated is love. And can you oppose this without being an enemy to mankind?

15. No; nor without being an enemy to your king and country; especially at such a time as this.[3] For however men of no thought may not see or regard it, or hectoring cowards may brave it out, it is evident to every man of calm reflection that our nation stands on the very brink of destruction. And why are we thus, but because 'the cry of our wickedness is gone up to heaven'?[4] Because we have so exceedingly, abundantly, beyond measure, 'corrupted our ways before the Lord'.[5] And because to all our other abominations we have added the open fighting against God; the not only rejecting, but even denying, yea, blaspheming his last offers of mercy; the hindering others who were desirous to close therewith; the despitefully using his messengers, and the variously troubling and oppressing those who did accept of his grace, break off their sins, and turn to him with their whole heart.

16. I cannot but believe it is chiefly on this account that God hath now 'a controversy with our land'.[6] And must not any considerate man be inclined to form the same judgment if he reviews the state

---

[1] See Jas. 1: 27.   [2] Cf. Job 38: 2.

[3] Dec. 18, 1745 (the date which Wesley appended to this work) had been proclaimed a national fast day in view of the advance of the Jacobite invaders. Prince Charles Edward ('The Young Pretender') reached Derby on Dec. 5, 1745, and there proclaimed his father (James Edward, 'The Old Pretender') King of England. When Wesley was writing, the northward retreat of the rebels had begun, but fear was still widespread. Wesley, who preached three times on the 18th, noted that 'such a solemnity and seriousness everywhere appeared as had not been lately seen in England' (*Journal*, Dec. 18, 1745). On the consternation created earlier that year in Newcastle by the anticipated approach of the Highland host, cf. *Journal*, Sept. 18, 1745 and succeeding entries. Culloden, the final battle of the Rebellion, did not take place until Apr. 16, 1746.

[4] Cf. 1 Sam. 5: 12; 1 Macc. 5: 31.

[5] Cf. Gen. 6: 12.   [6] Cf. Hos. 4: 1.

of public affairs for only a few years last past? I will not enter into particulars. But, in general, can you possibly help observing that whenever there has been anything like a public attempt to suppress 'this new sect' (for so it was artfully represented) another and

5 another public trouble arose? This has been repeated so often that it is surprising any man of sense can avoid taking notice of it. May we 'turn at length to him that smiteth us',[1] 'hearing the rod and him that appointeth it'![2] May we 'humble ourselves under the mighty hand of God',[3] before the great deep swallow us up!

10   17. Just now, viz., on the fourth of this instant December, the Reverend Mr. Henry Wickham, one of his Majesty's Justices of Peace for the West Riding of Yorkshire, writes an order—'To the Constable of Keighley', commanding him 'to convey the body of Jonathan Reeves[4] (whose real crime is the calling sinners to re-

15 pentance)[5] to his Majesty's jail and castle of York; suspected (saith the precept) of being a spy among us, and a dangerous man to the person and government of his Majesty King George.'

God avert the omen! I fear this is no presage either of the repentance or deliverance of our poor nation!

20   18. If we will not turn and repent, if we will harden our hearts, and acknowledge neither his judgments nor mercies; what remains but the fulfilling of that dreadful word which God spake by the prophet Ezekiel: 'Son of Man, when the land sinneth against me by trespassing grievously, then will I stretch forth my hand upon

25 it, and break the staff of the bread thereof . . . Though these three men, Noah, Daniel, and Job, were in it, they should deliver but their own souls. . . . Or if I bring a sword upon that land, and say, Sword, go through the land; . . . Or if I send a pestilence into that land, and pour out my fury upon it in blood; . . . though Noah,

30 Daniel, and Job were in it, as I live, saith the Lord God, they shall deliver neither son nor daughter; they shall but deliver their own souls by their righteousness.'[a]

---

[a] Ezek. 14: 13, 14, 17, 19, 20.

[1] Cf. Isa. 9: 13.   [2] Cf. Mic. 6: 9.   [3] 1 Pet. 5: 6.

[4] Jonathan Reeves was one of Wesley's early helpers. As a Methodist preacher he had a strenuous and sometimes dangerous career in Ireland and Wales, as well as in Yorkshire and the north. Ultimately he sought episcopal ordination, and was successively chaplain at the Magdalen Hospital and a curate in Whitechapel. His arrest on this occasion was a reflection of the belief (inspired by the prevailing panic) that Wesley and his preachers were spies for the Jacobites and the French.

[5] Cf. Matt. 9: 13, etc.

'Yet, behold, therein shall be left a remnant that shall be brought forth, both sons and daughters. . . . And ye shall be comforted concerning the evil that I have brought upon Jerusalem. . . . And ye shall know that I have not done without cause all that I have done in it, saith the Lord God.'[a]   5

London, Dec. 18,
  1745

[a] Ezek. 14: 22-3.

A Letter to the Right Reverend the Lord Bishop of London

Introduction

Edmund Gibson (1669–1748) was a distinguished member of the bench of bishops. In this respect he resembled another of Wesley's critics, Bishop Warburton of Gloucester. In certain circles, Warburton's name was probably as familiar as Gibson's. When Wesley replied to Warburton's *The Doctrine of Grace* in 1762, the Bishop of Gloucester was still the acknowledged arbiter of literary taste, whereas in 1747 Gibson had lived beyond his days of greatest influence. As a national figure, however, Edmund Gibson had played a far more significant role than Warburton. With William Wake (subsequently Archbishop of Canterbury) and White Kennett (subsequently Bishop of Peterborough) he had demolished Francis Atterbury's case in the Convocation Controversy. He had established himself as the greatest living expert on English ecclesiastical law, and his *Codex Juris Ecclesiastici Anglicani* (1713) ranked as the undisputed authority in its specialized and technical sphere, and does so still. As bishop, first of Lincoln, then of London (1720–48) he showed himself to be much more than a capable church administrator. He was deeply concerned about the prevailing laxity in morals. The masquerades held at Court had perceptibly lowered the tone of high society. Gibson opposed them, intervened with King George I, and succeeded in curbing the practice. The increasing consumption of gin was debauching the poor; he did his best to check it. His *Earnest Dissuasive from Intemperance* passed through fifteen editions in less than twenty years. He wrote on the need for a proper observance of the Sabbath. He published a very popular book of *Family Devotions*. To the people of his diocese he issued four letters warning them against Deists and freethinkers. Having early established a reputation for learning in literature and the law, he spent his later years in producing works marked by a strong pastoral concern.

Gibson, however, was a great deal more than the earnest and devoted head of an important diocese. For many years he was Sir Robert Walpole's chief adviser on religious affairs, and this gave

him a measure of influence which no other churchman of the period
could rival. In particular Gibson (a High Churchman but a Whig)
was determined to reconcile the clergy (overwhelmingly Tory) to the
House of Hanover. People jestingly referred to him as a pope;
when the comment reached Walpole's ears, he remarked that Gibson
was a very good pope indeed. The close association between the
prime minister and the bishop was broken in 1736 by a clash about
the Quakers' Relief Bill. Walpole supported the measure. Gibson
opposed it, and he was largely responsible for its defeat in the House
of Lords. Walpole did not forgive him. When the archbishopric
of Canterbury fell vacant in 1737, Gibson was passed over in favour
of Bishop Potter of Oxford. A decade later, after Walpole's fall from
power, Gibson was offered the primatial see; he declined it on the
grounds of age and infirmity.

Gibson was obviously a man whom Wesley was bound to respect.
Their concerns were similar. On many issues they thought alike.
Their personal contacts had been friendly. Gibson had ordained
Charles Wesley to the priesthood in 1735. On a number of occasions
he had granted the Wesley brothers long and serious interviews.[1]
When Wesley appeared before him in 1740 to explain what he
meant by 'perfection', the bishop agreed that such doctrine was
perfectly orthodox, and that Wesley should 'publish it to the world'.[2]
But Gibson was an eighteenth-century cleric, and occasions of
friction soon emerged. The Revd. George Stonehouse, curate of
St. Mary's, Islington, had been generous in welcoming Whitefield
and the Wesleys to his pulpit. When the parishioners objected,
Gibson (it was believed) had encouraged them in their protests,
and the Methodists resented what they felt they had good reason
to suspect. Whitefield was a more flamboyant character than the
Wesleys, less tactful in his dealings with authorities, less reserved
in describing his own emotional states, and much more eager to
proclaim to all the world the bizarre phenomena which marked the
early days of the revival. Like all Hanoverian bishops, Gibson was
suspicious of anything that smacked of 'enthusiasm', and in Whitefield he detected many of its most objectionable symptoms. *The
Bishop of London's Pastoral Letter to the people of his diocese, . . . by
way of caution against lukewarmness on the one hand and enthusiasm on*

---

[1] Charles Wesley, *Journal*, I. 81, 133, 135–6, 143–4.

[2] Wesley, *A Plain Account of Christian Perfection*, § 12. Cf. Introduction, above,
p. 22.

the other (1739), one of his first attacks on the new evangelism, was directed primarily against Whitefield. But Gibson never distinguished very sharply between Whitefield, the Wesleys, and the Moravians, and he was ready to attribute to each what he regarded as the excesses of the others. In 1744 there appeared anonymously a pamphlet entitled *Observations upon the Conduct and Behaviour of a Certain Sect usually distinguished by the Name of Methodists.* The illustrative material included some extracts from Wesley's *Journal*, but it was clearly directed chiefly against Whitefield. The work was commonly attributed to Gibson; on this assumption Wesley replied to it, though he did not mention Gibson by name.[1] The pamphlet attacked the Methodists on a variety of scores. They had transgressed the terms of the Acts of both Uniformity and Toleration, and so had forfeited any claim to official countenance. In the second and third parts of the work, Gibson posed a series of questions. He inquired 'whether the doctrines they teach, and the lengths they run, beyond what is practised in our religious societies, or in any other Christian church, be a service or a disservice to religion?'[2] On justification by faith, in particular, he believed that the Methodists had adopted extreme views, and these encouraged both a depreciation of good works and a dangerous tendency to 'enthusiasm'. One by one all the usual charges against the revivalists appear—field preaching, lay leadership, and violation of the basic order of the Church of England. Gibson never acknowledged that he wrote the *Observations*, but there was no doubt whatever that he was the author of *The Charge of the Right Reverend Father in God, Edmund, Lord Bishop of London, at the visitation of his diocese in the years 1746 and 1747*. This was the kind of publication with which Wesley was sadly familiar. It carried great weight because of its author's eminence; consequently it could not be ignored, yet it repeated accusations which Wesley had refuted publicly and at length. Like the *Observations* (and many other works) Gibson's charge not only attacked the theology and the methods of the new revivalism, but also discredited the leaders of the movement. 'There is', said Gibson, 'another species of enemies, who for some time past have been breaking in upon the peace and good order of the Church, and giving shameful disturbances to the parochial clergy, and using very unwarrantable methods.' Gibson recognized differences between the Moravians and the Methodists (though

---

[1] Cf. *A Farther Appeal*, pp. 119 ff.   [2] Gibson, *Observations*, p. 9.

apparently not between Wesley and Whitefield), but dismissed them as unimportant, since both groups were agreed in 'annoying the established ministry and drawing over to themselves the lowest and most ignorant of the people, by pretences to greater sanctity and more orthodox preaching'.[1] Gibson disliked their 'busy and schismatical spirit'; he was offended at their practice of gathering their followers 'in small bands under the teaching and direction, for the most part, of common mechanics and ignorant women'.[2]

The body of Gibson's charge was devoted to a critique of six 'doctrines big with pernicious influences upon practice'.[3] It is superfluous to enumerate them here, since Wesley deals with them one by one in his *Letter*. It is necessary to note, however, the consistently contemptuous terms in which Gibson spoke of the Methodists and their leaders.[4] By referring to 'the wild and indigested effusions of enthusiastical teachers'[5] he raised the spectre of the fanaticism which the eighteenth century so deeply abhorred. He implied that the Methodists were marked, to a pre-eminent degree, by a censorious and self-righteous spirit. He touched Wesley at a very sensitive point when he suggested that the Methodist leaders demanded of their converts 'punctual attendances upon their performances, though to the neglect of the business of their stations'.[6] On the duty of fulfilling the demands of one's calling, Wesley always laid the strongest possible emphasis, and Gibson's concluding innuendo seemed one further indication of the willingness of great churchmen to attack a movement which they would not bother to understand.

Wesley's *Letter to the Right Reverend the Lord Bishop of London* represents his controversial style at its best. It combines complete candour with genuine respect. It is direct, but always courteous. He feels obliged to expostulate with the bishop, but he never forgets that he is addressing a 'father in God' whose character and career have earned him the gratitude of his people. It was a part of early Methodist tradition that the closing appeal of this letter ('My lord, the time is short . . .') had a profound effect on Gibson, 'so a vulgar report got abroad that the Bishop of London had turned Methodist!'[7] In the following year Gibson died. Wesley always spoke of him with deference. In his sermon on 'The Signs of the Times', he referred to

---

[1] Gibson, *Charge*, p. 4. [2] Ibid., p. 6. [3] Ibid., p. 8.
[4] Cf. ibid., pp. 22 ff. [5] Ibid., p. 24. [6] Ibid., p. 26.
[7] Henry Moore, *Life of Wesley*, II. 415.

him as 'a person of considerable learning, as well as eminence in the church'. Nearly thirty years after writing the present letter, when preaching at the laying of the cornerstone of the City Road Chapel, Wesley described Gibson as 'a great man indeed who, I trust, is now in a better world'.[1]

For a summary of the four editions published during Wesley's lifetime, a stemma illustrating the transmission of the text, and a list of the substantive variant readings from the edited text (based on the first edition, London, Strahan, 1747), see the Appendix to this volume, pp. 555–6. For full bibliographical details see *Bibliography*, No. 137.

[1] Wesley, *Sermons*, 'The Signs of the Times', II. 2; *A Sermon on Numbers, xxiii. 23* (1777), § 2.

Á

LETTER

To the Right Reverend the

Lord Bifhop of *London*:

Occafioned by his Lordfhip's

Late Charge to his CLERGY.

By *JOHN WESLEY*, M. A.
Fellow of *Lincoln College, Oxford.*

---

*Let me not, I pray you, accept any Man's Perfon,
neither let me give flattering Titles unto Man.
For I know not to give flatering Titles. In fo
doing my Maker would foon take me away.*
JOB xxxiii. 21, 22.

LONDON:

Printed by W. STRAHAN. ~~Sold by B. There,~~
~~near Stay the Green all money and the~~
~~Book my Hawkor fifth.~~ MDCCXLVII.
(Price ~~Two~~ Pence.)
Three

[N.B. The text is in fact Job 32: 21-2.]

A
LETTER
To the Right Reverend the
Lord Bishop of London

My Lord,

1. When abundance of persons have for several years laid to my charge things that I knew not, I have generally thought it my duty to pass it over in silence, to be 'as one that heard not'.[1] But the case is different when a person of your lordship's character calls me forth 5 to answer for myself. Silence now might be interpreted contempt. It might appear like a sullen disregard, a withholding honour from him to whom honour is due, were it only on account of his high office in the Church. More especially, when I apprehend so eminent a person as this to be under considerable mistakes concerning me. 10 Were I now to be silent, were I not to do what was in my power for the removal of those mistakes, I could not have 'a conscience void of offence, either toward God or toward man'.[2]

2. But I am sensible how difficult it is to speak in such a manner as I ought and as I desire to do. When your lordship published 15 those queries under the title of *Observations*[3] I did not lie under the same difficulty; because, as your name was not inscribed, I had 'the liberty to stand, as it were, on even ground'.[4] But I must now always remember to whom I speak. And may the God 'whom I serve in the gospel of his Son'[5] enable me to do it with deep seriousness of 20 spirit, with modesty and humility; and at the same time with the

---

[1] Cf. John 8: 6. [2] Cf. Acts 24: 16.

[3] *Observations upon the Conduct and Behaviour of a Certain Sect usually distinguished by the Name of Methodists* (1744). The work was published anonymously; it was generally attributed to Gibson, though the bishop never either admitted or denied that he was the author. In the *Appeals*, as well as here, Wesley assumed that Gibson wrote the pamphlet.

[4] Wesley is quoting his own words from *A Farther Appeal*, Pt. I, III. 2, where he was discussing the anonymous *Observations* (see previous note). By repeating his previous comment and placing it within quotation marks, Wesley subtly reminds the bishop that this is not the first time he has raised the issue.

[5] Rom. 1: 9.

utmost plainness of speech, seeing we must both 'stand before the judgment seat of Christ'.[1]

3. In this then I entreat your lordship to bear with me. And in particular when I speak of myself (how tender a point!) just as
5 freely as I would of another man. Let not this be termed boasting. Is there not a cause? Can I refrain from speaking and be guiltless? And if I speak at all, ought I not to speak (what appears to me to be) the whole truth? Does not your lordship desire that I should do this? I will then, 'God being my helper'.[2] And you will bear with
10 me in my folly (if such it is), with my speaking in the simplicity of my heart.

4. Your lordship begins: 'There is another species of enemies who ... give shameful disturbance to the parochial clergy, and use very unwarrantable methods to prejudice their people against them, and
15 to seduce their flocks from them'—the Methodists and Moravians, who 'agree in annoying the established ministry, and in drawing over to themselves the lowest and most ignorant of the people by pretences to greater sanctity'.[a]

But have no endeavours been used to show them their error?
20 Yes. Your lordship remarks: 'Endeavours have not been wanting. . . . But though these endeavours have caused some abatement in the *pomp* and *grandeur* with which these people for some time acted' (truly, one would not have expected it from them!) 'yet they do not seem . . . to have made any impression upon their leaders.'[b]

25 Your lordship adds: 'Their innovations in points of discipline I do not intend to enter into at present', but 'to inquire what the doctrines are which they spread'[c]—doctrines 'big with pernicious influences upon practice'.[d]

Six of these your lordship mentions, after having premissed: 'It is
30 not at all needful to the end of guarding against them, to charge the particular tenets upon the particular persons among them.'[e] Indeed, my lord, it is needful in the highest degree. For if the minister who

---

[a] [*The Charge of the Right Reverend Father in God, Edmund, Lord Bishop of London, at the visitation of his diocese in the years 1746 and 1747* (no place, no printer, no date)], p. 4. [N.B. Here, as elsewhere, Wesley varies the syntax of his quotations from Gibson, though without altering their import.]
[b] [Ibid.,] p. 6.   [c] [Ibid.,] p. 7.   [d] [Ibid.,] p. 8.
[e] [Ibid.,] p. 7 [After 'persons' Gibson had added 'or sect'].

---

[1] Rom. 14: 10.
[2] B.C.P. Baptism of Adults, response to fourth question.

is to guard his people, either against Peter Böhler,[1] Mr. Whitefield, or me, does not know what our particular tenets are, he must needs 'run, as uncertainly, and fight, as one that beateth the air'.[2]

I will fairly own which of these belong to me. The *indirect practices* which your lordship charges upon me may then be con- 5 sidered, together with the *consequences* of these doctrines, and your lordship's instructions to the clergy.

5. 'The first that I shall take notice of (says your lordship) is the Antinomian doctrine.'[a] The second: 'That Christ has done all, and left nothing for us to do but to believe.'[b] These belong not to me. 10 I am unconcerned therein. I have earnestly opposed, but did never teach or embrace them.

'There is another notion (your lordship says) which we find propagated throughout the writings of those people, and that is the making *inward*, *secret*, and sudden *impulses* the guides of their 15 actions, resolutions, and designs.'[c] Mr. Church[3] urged the same objection before: 'Instead of making the Word of God the rule of his actions, he follows only his *secret impulse*.' I beg leave to return the same answer: 'In the whole compass of language there is not a proposition which less belongs to me than this. I have declared 20 again and again that I make the Word of God the rule of all my actions, and that I no more follow any *secret impulse* instead thereof than I follow Mahomet or Confucius.'[d]

---

[a] [Ibid.,] p. 8.   [b] [Ibid.,] p. 9.   [c] [Ibid.,] p. 14.
[d] *Answer to Mr. Church*, p. 38 [III. 5].

[1] Peter Böhler was a German Moravian who, more than any other man, was the human agent responsible for John Wesley's conversion (cf. *Journal*, Feb. to May, 1738). Wesley always acknowledged his debt to Böhler and felt strongly drawn to him as a man of faith, but the Methodists and the Moravians rapidly drifted apart on the implications of justification by faith. Wesley claimed that Moravian 'quietism' (the 'stillness' advocated by Philip Molther) had dangerous Antinomian tendencies, and the controversy became intense and prolonged. Cf. *Journal* (especially Nov. 1, 1739–Sept. 3, 1741); *A Short View of the Difference between the Moravian Brethren lately in England and the Rev. Mr. John and Charles Wesley* (1745). Other works on the subject were published intermittently till 1762.

[2] Cf. 1 Cor. 9: 26.

[3] The Revd. Thomas Church, M.A., Vicar of Battersea and Prebendary of St. Paul's, published his *Remarks on the Reverend Mr. John Wesley's Last Journal* in 1744. Early the following year Wesley replied with a long letter, which prompted Church to write *Some Farther Remarks on the Reverend Mr. John Wesley's Last Journal, Together with a few Considerations on his Farther Appeal*. Wesley's answer, entitled *The Principles of a Methodist Farther Explained*, appeared in 1746. Wesley always spoke of Church with respect, and regarded him as a courteous and scholarly opponent. See also Vol. 9 of this edition: *The Methodist Societies: History, Nature, and Design*.

6. Before I proceed, suffer me to observe, here are three grievous errors charged on the Moravians, Mr. Whitefield, and me conjointly, in none of which I am any more concerned than in the doctrine of the metempsychosis! But it was 'not needful to charge particular tenets on particular persons'. Just as needful, my lord, as it is not to put a stumbling-block in the way of our brethren; not to lay them under an almost insuperable temptation of condemning the innocent with the guilty. I beseech your lordship to answer in your own conscience before God, whether you did not foresee how many of your hearers would charge these tenets upon *me*? Nay, whether you did not design they should?[1] If so, my lord, is this Christianity? Is it humanity? Let me speak plain. Is it honest heathenism?

7. I am not one jot more concerned in instantaneous justification, as your lordship explains it, viz., 'a sudden instantaneous justification, by which the person receives from God a certain seal of his salvation, or an absolute assurance of being saved at the last'.[a] 'Such an instantaneous working of the Holy Spirit as finishes the business of salvation once for all'[b] I neither teach nor believe, and am therefore clear of all the consequences that may arise therefrom. I believe 'a gradual improvement in grace and goodness'[2]—I mean in the knowledge and love of God—is a good 'testimony of our present sincerity towards God';[3] although I dare not say it is 'the only true ground of humble assurance',[4] or the only foundation on which a Christian builds his 'hopes of acceptance and salvation'.[5] For I think 'other foundation' of these 'can no man lay, than that which is laid, even Jesus Christ'.[6]

8. To the charge of holding 'sinless perfection',[7] as your lordship

---

[a] [*Charge*,] p. 11.   [b] Ibid.

[1] The preceding sentence is inked through in some copies of the 1st ed., and omitted from the Dublin edition, Powell, 1748. Clearly doubt had arisen about the wisdom of some of Wesley's comments, and he had pondered halting distribution of the first edition. On Oct. 29, 1747 Charles Wesley wrote to his brother from Dublin: 'Your answer to the bishop should not be lost. Let the three passages be corrected with a pen, and then sell it privately.' This sentence was one of the offending passages, though it was continued—perhaps inadvertently, perhaps not—in the later editions. Another was at the end of § 11. The third may have been the title-page, from which the name of the booksellers (including Wesley's Foundery) are in some copies erased in ink, but more probably the word 'any' in § 19, where the context might imply that Gibson was one of Wesley's 'bitterest adversaries' and a hypocrite to boot.

[2] *Observations*, p. 10; cf. *A Farther Appeal*, Pt. I, III. 6 (above, p. 127).

[3] *Charge*, p. 12.   [4] Ibid., p. 11.   [5] Ibid., p. 14.

[6] Cf. 1 Cor. 3: 11.   [7] *Charge*, p. 15.

states it, I might likewise plead, 'Not guilty'; seeing one ingredient thereof, in your lordship's account, is 'freedom from temptation',[a] whereas I believe: 'There is no such perfection in this life as implies an entire deliverance from manifold temptations.'[1] But I will not decline the charge. I will repeat once more my coolest thoughts 5 upon this head; and that in the very terms which I did several years ago, as I presume your lordship cannot be ignorant:

What, it may be asked, do you mean by 'one that is perfect', or one that is 'as his Master'?[2] We mean, one in whom is 'the mind which was in Christ',[3] and who 'so walketh as he walked';[4] a man that 'hath clean 10 hands and a pure heart',[5] or that is 'cleansed from all filthiness of flesh and spirit';[6] one 'in whom there is no occasion of stumbling',[7] and who accordingly 'doth not commit sin'.[8] To declare this a little more particularly, we understand by that scriptural expression 'a perfect man'[9] one in whom God hath fulfilled his faithful word: 'From 15 all your filthiness, and from all your idols will I cleanse you';[10] 'I will also save you from all your uncleannesses.'[11] We understand hereby one whom God hath 'sanctified throughout', even in 'body, soul, and spirit';[12] one who 'walketh in the light, as he is in the light', in whom 'is no darkness at all, the blood of Jesus Christ his son' having 'cleansed 20 him from all sin'.[13]

This man can now testify to all mankind: 'I am crucified with Christ; nevertheless I live; yet I live not, but Christ liveth in me.'[14] He is 'holy, as God who called him is holy', both in life and 'in all manner of conversation'.[15] He 'loveth the Lord his God with all his 25 heart, and serveth him with all his strength'.[16] He 'loveth his neighbour (every man) as himself';[17] yea, 'as Christ loved us'[18]—them in particular that 'despitefully use him and persecute him',[19] because 'they know not the Son, neither the Father'.[20] Indeed his soul is all love, filled with 'bowels of mercies, kindness, meekness, gentleness, long-suffering'.[21] 30 And his life agreeth thereto, full of the 'work of faith, the patience of hope, the labour of love'.[22] And 'whatsoever he doth, either in word or

---

[a] Ibid., p. 17.

---

[1] *Hymns and Sacred Poems* (1742) (*Bibliography*, No. 54), Preface, § 3. This preface Wesley goes on to quote at length below.

[2] Luke 6: 40.   [3] Cf. Phil. 2: 5.   [4] Cf. 1 John 2: 6.   [5] Ps. 24: 4.
[6] Cf. 2 Cor. 7: 1.   [7] Cf. 1 John 2: 10.   [8] 1 John 3: 9.
[9] Job 8: 20; Eph. 4: 13; Jas. 3: 2.   [10] Ezek. 36: 25.   [11] Ezek. 36: 29.
[12] Cf. 1 Thess. 5: 23.   [13] 1 John 1: 5, 7.   [14] Cf. Gal. 2: 20.
[15] Cf. 1 Pet. 1: 15, 16.   [16] Cf. Mark 12: 30.   [17] Cf. Mark 12: 33.
[18] Cf. Eph. 5: 2.   [19] Cf. Matt. 5: 44.   [20] Cf. John 8: 19.
[21] Cf. Col. 3: 12.   [22] 1 Thess. 1: 3.

deed', he doth it 'all in the name', in the love and power, 'of the Lord
Jesus'.[1] In a word, he doth the will of God 'on earth, as it is in heaven'.[2]

    This it is to be 'a perfect man', to be 'sanctified throughout', 'created
anew in Jesus Christ',[3] even 'to have a heart so all-flaming with the
5   love of God' (to use Archbishop Ussher's words) 'as continually to
offer up every thought, word, and work, as a spiritual sacrifice, acceptable unto God through Christ.'[4] In every thought of our hearts, in every
word of our tongues, in every work of our hands, to 'show forth his
praise who hath called us out of darkness into his marvellous light'.[5]
10   O that both we, and all who seek the Lord Jesus in sincerity, may thus
'be made perfect in one'.[6]

    9. I conjure you, my lord, by the mercies of God, if these are not
the words of truth and soberness, point me out wherein I have erred
from the truth. Show me clearly wherein I have spoken either
15 beyond or contrary to the Word of God. But might I not humbly
entreat that your lordship, in doing this, would abstain from such
expressions as these: 'if they will but put themselves under their
direction and discipline', 'after their course of discipline is once
over',[a] as not suitable either to the weight of the subject or the
20 dignity of your lordship's character. And might I not expect something more than these loose assertions that this is a 'delusion
altogether groundless',[b] 'a notion contrary to the whole tenor both
of the Old and New Testament'; that 'the Scriptures forbid all
thought of it, as vain, arrogant, and presumptuous'; that they
25 'represent all mankind, without distinction, as subject to sin and
corruption' (subject to sin and corruption! Strong words!) 'during
their continuance in this world; . . . and require no more than an
honest *desire* and *endeavour* . . . to find ourselves less and less in
a state of imperfection' ?[c]
30   Is it not from your lordship's entirely mistaking the question—
not at all apprehending what perfection I teach—that you go on
to guard against the same imaginary consequences as your lordship

---

    [a] [*Charge*,] p. 15.   [b] [Ibid.,] p. 15.   [c] [Ibid.,] p. 16.

---

   [1] Cf. Col. 3: 17.   [2] Matt. 6: 10.   [3] Cf. Eph. 2: 10.
   [4] James Ussher, Archbishop of Armagh (1581–1656) was a prolific author both in
English and in Latin. There are a number of passages in his works which parallel this
quotation; the one which does so most closely seems to be in *A Body of Divinity* (1645),
p. 176.   [5] 1 Pet. 2: 9.
   [6] John 17: 23. N.B. The lengthy quotation is from the Preface, §§ 4–5, of Wesley's
Hymns and Sacred Poems of 1742, for which see *Bibliography*, No. 54, and Volume 12
of this edition, *Doctrinal Writings: Theological Treatises*.

did in the *Observations*? Surely, my lord, you never gave yourself the trouble to read the answer given in the *Farther Appeal*[1] to every objection which you now urge afresh! Seeing you do not now appear to know any more of my sentiments than if you had never proposed one question nor received one answer upon the subject! 5

10. If your lordship designed to show my real sentiments concerning the last doctrine which you mention, as one would imagine by your adding, 'these are his own words',[a] should you not have cited all my own words, at least all the words of that paragraph, and not have mangled it, as Mr. Church did before?[2] 10

It runs thus: 'Saturday, 28 [June, 1740]. I showed at large' (in order to answer those who taught that none but they who are full of faith and the Holy Ghost ought ever to communicate):

1. That the Lord's Supper was ordained by God to be a means of conveying to men either preventing, or justifying, or sanctifying grace, 15 according to their several necessities.

2. That the persons for whom it was ordained are all those who know and feel that they want the grace of God, either to restrain them from sin, or to show their sins forgiven, or to renew their souls in the image of God. 3. That inasmuch as we come to his table, not to *give* him 20 anything, but to *receive* whatsoever he sees best for us, there is no previous preparation indispensably necessary but a *desire* to receive whatsoever he pleases to give. And, 4, that no fitness is required at the time of communicating but a sense of our state, of our utter sinfulness and helplessness; everyone who knows he is fit for hell being just fit 25 to come to Christ, in this as well as all other ways of his appointment.[b]

In the *Second Letter* to Mr. Church (p. 26), I explain myself farther on this head:

I am sorry to find you still affirm that with regard to the Lord's Supper also I 'advance many injudicious, false, and dangerous things, 30

---

[a] [Ibid.,] p. 18.
[b] *Journal IV*, p. 47. [N.B. In the original edition of this *Journal* Wesley's italics were prolific, apparently in this instance indicating neither a quotation nor important emphases. These italics were followed in the passage as printed in the *Letter*, but in reproducing this most of the italics have been removed, following Wesley's own practice when later he used quotations in *The Principles of a Methodist Farther Explained*—see the following paragraph.]

---

[1] Wesley found himself obliged to answer repeatedly the staple accusations of his critics. In *A Farther Appeal* he had dealt one by one with objections Gibson had raised; in addition he explicitly cited *Observations* as a work which he was refuting. (*A Farther Appeal*, Pt. III, II. 3.)   [2] See below, third paragraph of § 10.

such as, (1), that a man ought to communicate without a sure trust in God's mercy through Christ'. (p. 117). You mark these as my words; but I know them not. (2). 'That there is no previous preparation *indispensably* necessary but a desire to receive whatsoever God pleases
5 to give.' But I include abundantly more in that 'desire' than you seem to apprehend; even a willingness to know and do the whole will of God. (3). 'That no fitness is required at the time of communicating' (I recite the whole sentence) 'but a sense of our state, of our utter sinfulness and helplessness; everyone who knows he is fit for hell being
10 just fit to come to Christ, in this as well as in all other ways of his appointment.' But neither can this sense of our utter sinfulness and helplessness subsist without earnest desires of universal holiness.[1]

And now what can I say?[2] Had your lordship never seen this? That is hardly to be imagined. But if you had, how was it possible
15 your lordship should thus explicitly and solemnly charge me, in the presence of God and all my brethren—only the person so charged was not present—with *meaning* by those words 'to *set aside* self-examination, and repentance for sins past, and resolutions of living better for the time to come, as things no way necessary to make
20 a worthy communicant'![a]

If an evidence at the bar should swerve from truth, an equitable judge may place the thing in a true light. But if the judge himself shall bear false witness, where then can we find a remedy?

Actual preparation was here entirely out of the question. It might
25 be *absolutely* and *indispensably* necessary, for anything I had either said or *meant* to the contrary. For it was not at all in my thoughts. And the habitual preparation which I had in terms declared to be indispensably necessary was 'a willingness to know and do the whole will of God', and 'earnest desires of universal holiness'.[3] Does your
30 lordship think this is 'meant to set aside all repentance for sins past, and resolutions of living better for the time to come'?

---

[a] [*Charge*,] p. 18.

---

[1] *The Principles of a Methodist Farther Explained*, II. 7. (See *Bibliography*, No. 123, and Volume 9 of this edition, *The Methodist Societies: History, Nature, and Design*.)

[2] In Wesley's original edition this formed the beginning of a new section numbered in error '10.' like its predecessor. The sections were similarly numbered 1–10, 10–22 in all four editions published during Wesley's lifetime. Instead of renumbering them 1–23 it seemed wiser to leave the familiar section numbers undisturbed, simply dropping the second '10', as did Thomas Jackson in his edition of Wesley's *Works*.

[3] Cf. the above extract from *Principles*, from which these quotations are taken. Wesley was writing to the Revd. Thomas Church, who, like Gibson, insisted on ignoring Wesley's teaching on many of the themes central to the Methodist revival.

11. Your lordship next falls with all your might upon that strange assertion, as you term it: 'We come to his table, not to *give* him anything, but to *receive* whatsoever he sees best for us.' 'Whereas (says your lordship) in the exhortation at the time of receiving the people are told that they must *give* "most humble and hearty thanks", 5
. . . and immediately after receiving both minister and people join "in *offering* and *presenting* themselves unto God".'ᵃ O God! In what manner are the most sacred things here treated! The most venerable mysteries of our religion! What quibbling, what playing upon words is here! 'Not to *give* him anything.'—'Yes, to *give* him thanks.' O 10
my lord, are these the words of a father of the Church?[1]

12. Your lordship goes on: 'To the foregoing account of these modern principles and doctrines . . . it may not be improper to subjoin a few observations upon the indirect *practices* of the same people in gaining proselytes.'ᵇ 15

(I). 'They persuade the people that the *established* worship, with a regular attendance upon it, is not sufficient to answer the ends of devotion.'

Your lordship mentioned this likewise in the *Observations*. In your fourth query it stood thus: 'Whether a due and regular attendance 20
on the public offices of religion, paid in a serious and composed way, does not answer the true ends of devotion?' Suffer me to repeat part of the answer then given:

> I suppose by 'devotion' you mean public worship, by the 'true ends' of it the love of God and man, and by 'a due and regular attendance on 25
> the public offices of religion, paid in a serious and composed way', the going as often as we have opportunity to our parish church and to the sacrament there administered. If so, the question is, 'Whether this attendance on those offices does not produce the love of God and man?' I answer: Sometimes it does; and sometimes it does not. I myself thus 30
> attended them for many years; and yet am conscious to myself that during that whole time I had no more of the love of God than a stone. And I know many hundreds, perhaps thousands, of serious persons who are ready to testify the same thing.[2]

ᵃ [Ibid.,] pp. 20–1.   ᵇ [Ibid.,] pp. 23–4.

---

[1] Wesley originally wrote: 'are these the words of a father of the Church, or of a boy in the third class of Westminster School?' He thought better of this latter innuendo, and apparently ordered it to be erased in ink from all copies of the first edition; it was dropped from later editions. Cf. note 1 on p. 338.

[2] *A Farther Appeal*, Pt. I, III. 4.

I subjoined, (1). We continually exhort all who attend on our preaching to attend the offices of the Church. And they do pay a more regular attendance there than ever they did before. (2). Their attending the Church did not in fact answer those ends at all, till they attended
5 this preaching also. (3). It is the preaching remission of sins through Jesus Christ which alone answers the true ends of devotion.[1]

13. (II). 'They . . . censure the clergy (says your lordship) as less zealous than themselves in the several branches of the ministerial function.' For this 'they are undeservedly reproached by these
10 noisy itinerant leaders'.[a]
My lord, I am not conscious to myself of this. I do not willingly compare myself with any man; much less do I reproach my brethren of the clergy, whether they deserve it or not. But it is needless to add any more on this head than what was said above a year ago.

15   I must explain myself a little on that practice which you so often term 'abusing the clergy'. I have many times great sorrow and heaviness in my heart on account of these my brethren. And this sometimes constrains me to speak to them in the only way which is now in my power, and sometimes (though rarely) to speak of them—of a few, not
20 all, in general. In either case I take an especial care: (1), to speak nothing but the truth; (2), to speak this with all plainness; and (3), with love, and in the spirit of meekness. Now if you will call this 'abusing', 'railing', or 'reviling', you must. But still I dare not refrain from it. I must thus rail, thus abuse, sinners of all sorts and degrees, unless
25 I will perish with them.[b]

14. (III). 'They value themselves upon extraordinary strictnesses and severities in life, and such as are beyond what the rules of Christianity require. . . . They captivate the people by such professions and appearances of *uncommon* sanctity. . . . But that
30 which can never fail of a general respect . . . is a quiet and exemplary life, free from many of the *follies* and *indiscretions* which those restless and vagrant teachers are apt to fall into.'[c]
By 'extraordinary strictnesses and severities' I presume your lordship means the abstaining from wine and animal food; which, it
35 is sure, Christianity does not require. But if you do, I fear your

---

[a] [*Charge*,] pp. 24–5.
[b] *Second Letter* to Mr. Church, p. 78 [i.e. *The Principles of a Methodist Farther Explained*, VI. 11 (see above, p. 342)].   [c] [*Charge*,] p. 25.

---

[1] *A Farther Appeal*, Pt. I, III. 4.

lordship is not thoroughly informed of the matter of fact. I began to
do this about twelve years ago, when I had no thought of 'annoying
parochial ministers', or of 'captivating any people' thereby, unless
it were the Chicasaw or Choctaw Indians. But I resumed the use of
them both about two years after, for the sake of some who thought   5
I made it a point of conscience, telling them, 'I *will* eat flesh while
the world standeth', rather than 'make my brother to offend'. Dr.
Cheyne[1] advised me to leave them off again, assuring me, 'Till you
do you will never be free from fevers.' And since I have taken his
advice I have been free (blessed be God) from all bodily disorders.[a] 10
Would to God I knew any method of being equally free from all
'follies and indiscretions'. But this I never expect to attain till my
spirit returns to God.

  15. But in how strange a manner does your lordship represent
this! What a construction do you put upon it!—'appearances of an   15
uncommon sanctity' in order to 'captivate the people'; 'pretensions
to more exalted degrees of strictness', 'to make their way into weak
minds and fickle heads';[b] 'pretences to greater sanctity' whereby
'they draw over to themselves the most ignorant of the people'.[c] If
these are 'appearances of an uncommon sanctity' (which indeed   20
might bear a dispute), how does your lordship know that they are
only 'appearances', that they do not spring from the heart? Suppose
these were 'exalted degrees of strictness', is your lordship absolutely
assured that we practise them only 'to make our way into weak
minds and fickle heads'? Where is the proof that these 'pretences   25
to greater sanctity' (as your lordship is pleased to phrase them) are
mere 'pretences', and have nothing of reality or sincerity in them?

  My lord, this is an accusation of the highest nature. If we are
guilty, we are not so much as moral heathens. We are monsters, not
only unworthy of the Christian name, but unfit for human society.   30
It tears up all 'pretences' to the love of God or man, to 'justice,
mercy, or truth'.[2] But how is it proved? Or does your lordship read

---

[a] I continued this about two years. [Added in *Works*, Vol. 16 (1772).]
[b] [*Charge*,] p. 25.   [c] [Ibid.,] p. 4.

[1] Dr. George Cheyne, M.D., F.R.S. (1671-1743), was a well-known pioneer in
dietetics and hygiene. His *Essay of Health and Long Life* reached its 6th edition in 1725.
His *Natural Method of Curing the Diseases of the Body and the Disorders of the Mind
Depending on the Body* (1742) strongly influenced Wesley's views on medical matters.
Cf. his comments on this work, *Journal*, Mar. 12, 1742.
[2] Cf. Ps. 89: 14.

the heart, and so pass sentence without any proof at all? O my lord, ought an accusation of the lowest kind to be thus received, even against the lowest of the people? How much less can this be reconciled with the apostolical advice to the Bishop of Ephesus: 'Against 5 a presbyter receive not an accusation but before two or three witnesses'—and those, face to face. When it is thus proved, 'them that sin rebuke before all'. Your lordship doubtless remembers the words that follow (how worthy to be written in your heart!): 'I charge thee, before God and the Lord Jesus Christ, and the elect 10 angels, that you observe these things without preferring one before another, doing nothing by partiality.'[a]

16. (IV). They 'mislead the people into an opinion of the *high merit* of punctual attendances on their performances, to the neglect of the business of their stations'.[b] My lord, this is not so. You 15 yourself, in this very *Charge*, have cleared us from one part of this accusation. You have borne us witness (p. 10), that we disclaim all *merit*, even in (really) good works. How much more in such works as we continually declare are not good, but very evil, such as the attending sermons, or any public offices whatever, 'to the neglect of 20 the business of our stations'!

When your lordship urged this before, in the *Observations*, I openly declared my belief (*Farther Appeal*, Part I, p. 18): 'That true religion cannot lead into a disregard or disesteem of the common duties and offices of life; that on the contrary it leads men to 25 discharge all those duties with the strictest diligence and closest attention; that Christianity requires this attention and diligence in all stations and in all conditions; that the performance of the lowest offices of life *as unto God* is truly *a serving of Christ*; and that this is the doctrine I preach continually'[1]—a fact whereof any man may 30 easily be informed. Now if after all this your lordship will repeat the charge, as if I had not once opened my mouth concerning it, I cannot help it. I can say no more. I commend my cause to God.

17. Having considered what your lordship has advanced concerning dangerous doctrines and indirect practices, I come now to the 35 instructions your lordship gives to the clergy of your diocese.

How awful a thing is this! The very occasion carries in it a solemnity not to be expressed. Here is an angel of the church of Christ,

---

[a] 1 Tim. 5: 19–21.   [b] [*Charge*,] p. 26.

[1] *A Farther Appeal*, Pt. I, III. 2, highly compressed. (See above, pp. 119–20.)

one of the stars in God's right hand, calling together all the subordinate pastors, for whom he is to give an account to God; and
directing them—in the name and by the authority of 'the great
shepherd of the sheep',[1] 'Jesus Christ, the first begotten from the
dead, the prince of the kings of the earth'[2]—how to 'make full proof   5
of their ministry',[3] that they may be 'pure from the blood of all
men';[4] how to 'take heed unto themselves and to all the flock over
which the Holy Ghost hath made them overseers', how to 'feed the
flock of God which he hath purchased with his own blood'![5] To this
end they are all assembled together. And what is the substance of all   10
his instructions? 'Reverend brethren, I charge you all, lift up your
voice like a trumpet! And *warn* and *arm* and *fortify* all mankind—
against a people called Methodists!'[6]

True it is, your lordship gives them several advices—but all in
order to this end. You direct them to 'inculcate . . . the excellency of   15
our liturgy, as a wise, grave, and serious service';[7] to show 'their
people that a diligent attendance on their business is a serving of
God'[8]; 'punctually to perform both the public offices of the Church
and all other pastoral duties';[7] and to 'engage the esteem of their
parishioners by a constant regularity of life'.[9] But all these your   20
lordship recommends *eo nomine*, as means to that great end, 'the
arming and *fortifying* their people against the Moravians or Methodists and their doctrines'.

Is it possible! Could your lordship discern no other enemies of the
gospel of Christ? Are there no other heretics or schismatics on   25
earth? Or even within the four seas?[10] Are there no Papists,[11] no
deists left in the land? Or are their errors of less importance?
Or are their numbers in England less considerable, or less likely to
increase? Does it appear then that they have lost their zeal for
making proselytes? Or are all the people so *guarded* against them   30
already that their labour is in vain? Can your lordship answer these
few plain questions to the satisfaction of your own conscience?

Have the Methodists (so called) already monopolized all the sins,
as well as errors, in the nation? Is Methodism the only sin, or the

---

[1] Heb. 13: 20.   [2] Rev. 1: 5 (cf. *Notes*).   [3] Cf. 2 Tim. 4: 5.
[4] Acts 20: 26.   [5] Cf. Acts 20: 28.   [6] Cf. *Charge*, pp. 7–8.
[7] Ibid., p. 24.   [8] Ibid., p. 26.   [9] Ibid., p. 25.
[10] 'The four seas' were the seas bounding Great Britain on the four sides; in popular
usage, 'within the four seas' meant 'in Great Britain' (*O.E.D.*). Cf. *A Farther Appeal*,
Pt. III, III. 22.
[11] The Dublin edition omits 'no Papists'.

only fatal or spreading sin, to be found within the Bills of Mortality?[1] Have two thousand (or more) 'ambassadors of Christ'[2] and 'stewards of the mysteries of God'[3] no other business than to 'guard', 'warn', 'arm', and 'fortify' their people against this? O my lord, if this
5 engrosses their time and strength—as it must if they follow your lordship's instructions—they will not give an account with joy,[4] either of themselves or of their flock, in that day!

18. Your lordship seems in some measure sensible of this when you very gently condemn their opinion, who think the Methodists
10 'might better be disregarded and despised than taken notice of and opposed, if it were not for the disturbance they give to the parochial ministers, and their unwarrantable endeavours to seduce the people from their lawful pastors'[a]—the same complaint with which your lordship opened your *Charge*: 'They give shameful disturbances to
15 the parochial clergy, they annoy the established ministry, using very unwarrantable methods, first to prejudice their people against them, and then to seduce their flocks from them.'[b]

Whether we seduce them or no (which will be presently considered) I am sorry your lordship should give any countenance to
20 that low, senseless, and now generally exploded slander, that we do it for a maintenance. This your lordship insinuates by applying to us those words of Bishop Sanderson:[5] 'And all this . . . "to serve their own belly",[6] to make a prey of their poor deluded proselytes; for by this means "the people fall unto them, and thereout suck
25 they no small advantage".'[c] Your lordship cannot but know that my fellowship, and my brother's studentship, afford us more than sufficient for life and godliness; especially for that manner of life which we choose, whether out of ostentation or in sincerity.

19. But do we willingly 'annoy the established ministry', or 'give
30 disturbance to the parochial clergy'? My lord, we do not. We trust,

---

[a] [*Charge*,] p. 22.   [b] [Ibid.,] p. 4.
[c] [Ibid.,] p. 5 [Sanderson quotes Ps. 73: 10 (B.C.P.)].

[1] 'Bills of mortality' were returns of the deaths in a given district. In 1592 they began to appear weekly for the area in and around London.
[2] Cf. 2 Cor. 5: 20.   [3] 1 Cor. 4: 1.   [4] See Heb. 13: 17.
[5] Robert Sanderson (1587–1663) was a fellow of Lincoln College; Regius professor of divinity, Oxford (1642); bishop of Lincoln (1660). The passage quoted by Gibson (*Charge*, p. 5) is from *Ad Aulam*, Sermon XV, § 28, reprinted in *The Works of Robert Sanderson* (6 vols., Oxford, 1854), I. 394. Both Gibson and Wesley were successors of Sanderson—Gibson as a former bishop of Lincoln, Wesley as a fellow of Lincoln College.   [6] Rom. 16: 18.

herein, to have 'a conscience void of offence'.[1] Nor do we designedly 'prejudice their people against them'. In this also our heart condemneth us not. 'But you "seduce their flocks from them".' No, not even from those who feed themselves, not the flock. All who hear us attend the service of the Church at least as much as they 5 did before. And for this very thing are we reproached as 'bigots to the Church' by those of most other denominations.

Give me leave, my lord, to say you have mistook and misrepresented this whole affair from the top to the bottom. And I am the more concerned to take notice of this, because so many have fallen 10 into the same mistake. It is indeed, and has been from the beginning, the πρῶτον ψεῦδος,[2] the capital blunder of our bitterest adversaries— though how they can advance it I see not, without 'loving' if not 'making, a lie'.[3] It is not our care, endeavour, or desire, to *proselyte* any from one man to another, or from one church (so called), from 15 one congregation or society, to another (we would not move a finger to do this, to make ten thousand such proselytes); but 'from darkness to light', from Belial to Christ, 'from the power of Satan unto God'.[4] Our one aim is to proselyte sinners to repentance, the servants of the devil to serve the living and true God. If this be not 20 done in fact, we will stand condemned; not as well-meaning fools, but as devils incarnate. But if it be, if the instances glare in the face of the sun, if they increase daily, maugre all the power of earth and hell; then, my lord, neither you nor any man beside—let me use great plainness of speech—can *oppose* and 'fortify people against us' 25 without being 'found even to fight against God'![5]

20. I would fain set this point in a clearer light. Here are, in and near Moorfields,[6] ten thousand poor souls for whom Christ died, rushing headlong into hell. Is Dr. Bulkeley,[7] the parochial minister,

[1] Acts 24: 16.

[2] Both words in this Greek phrase can be rendered in a variety of ways—'first lie', 'initial falsehood', etc. Wesley's rendering ('capital blunder') is free but not inexact. Cf. Ussher's use of the phrase, *The Whole Works of the Most Rev. James Ussher* (17 vols., Dublin, 1847), XI. 329.

[3] Cf. Rev. 22: 15; for the tactical alteration from 'any' to 'that' see above, p. 338, note 1.   [4] Acts 26: 18.   [5] Acts 5: 39.

[6] Moorfields, an open space just outside the City of London which gave its name to the district in which the Foundery (Wesley's headquarters) was located.

[7] Benjamin Bulkeley, D.D. (Oxon.) was assistant preacher at St. Luke's, Old Street (which Wesley calls 'our parish church', *Journal*, Aug. 3, 1740), and so not technically the 'parochial minister'. He was also rector of Chingford and canon of St. Paul's. The rector of St. Luke's was William Nichols, vicar of St. Giles, Cripplegate, and president of Magdalene College, Cambridge. Bulkeley's name is spelt 'Bulkely' in the *Letter*.

both willing and able to stop them? If so, let it be done, and I have no place in these parts. I go, and call other sinners to repentance. But if after all he has done, and all he can do, they are still in the broad way to destruction, let me see if God will put a word even in
5 my mouth. True, I am a poor worm that of myself can do nothing. But if God sends, by whomsoever he will send, his word shall not return empty. All the messenger of God asks, is Δός ποῦ στῶ (no help of man!) καὶ γῆν κινήσω.¹ The arm of the Lord is revealed. The lion roars, having the prey plucked out of his teeth. And 'there is
10 joy in the presence of the angels of God over' more than 'one sinner that repenteth'.²

21. Is this any *annoyance* to the parochial minister? Then what manner of spirit is he of? Does he look on this part of his flock as lost, because they are found of the Great Shepherd? My lord, great
15 is my boldness toward you. You speak of the 'consequences' of our doctrines. You seem well pleased with the success of your 'endeavours' against them because (you say) they 'have pernicious consequences, are big with pernicious influences upon practice', 'dangerous to religion and the souls of men'.ᵃ In answer to all this
20 I appeal to plain fact. I say once more: 'What have been the 'consequences' (I would not speak, but I dare not refrain) of the doctrines I have preached for nine years last past? By the fruits shall ye know those of whom I speak—even the cloud of witnesses who at this hour experience the gospel which I preach to be the power of God
25 unto salvation. The habitual drunkard, that was, is now temperate in all things. The whoremonger now flees fornication. He that stole steals no more, but works with his hands.³ He that cursed or swore, perhaps at every sentence, has now learned to serve the Lord with fear, and rejoice unto him with reverence. Those formerly enslaved
30 to various habits of sin are now brought to uniform habits of holiness. These are demonstrable facts. I can name the men, with their places of abode. One of them was an avowed atheist for many years; some

---

ᵃ [*Charge,*] pp. 8, 22.

---

¹ See *Journal*, May 20, 1739: '. . . methought I could have cried out (in another sense than poor vain Archimedes), "Give me where to stand, and I will shake the earth." ' Wesley refers to this passage in two of his other letters: *A Second Letter to the Author of the Enthusiasm of Methodists and Papists Compar'd*, § 3; *A Letter to the Bishop of Gloucester*, below, p. 472. For the source of this exclamation by Archimedes (287–212 B.C.) see *Pappus, Alexandr., Collectio*, lib. viii, prop. 10, xi.
² Luke 15: 10.   ³ See Eph. 5: 28.

were Jews, a considerable number Papists; the greatest part of them as much strangers to the form as to the power of godliness.'

My lord, can you deny these facts? I will make whatever proof of them you shall require. But if the facts be allowed, who can deny the doctrines to be (in substance) the gospel of Christ? 'For is there any other name under heaven given to men, whereby they may thus be saved?'[1] Or is there any other word that thus 'commendeth itself to every man's conscience in the sight of God'?[2]

22. But I must draw to a conclusion. Your lordship has without doubt had some success in *opposing* this doctrine. Very many have, by your lordship's unwearied endeavours, been deterred from hearing it at all, and have thereby probably escaped the being *seduced* into holiness, have lived and died in their sins. My lord, the time is short. I am past the noon of life, and my remaining years flee away as a shadow. Your lordship is old and full of days, having passed the usual age of man. It cannot therefore be long before we shall both drop this house of earth, and stand naked before God; no, nor before we shall 'see the great white throne coming down from heaven, and him that sitteth thereon'.[3] On his left hand shall be those who are shortly to dwell in 'everlasting fire, prepared for the devil and his angels'.[4] In that number will be all who died in their sins. And among the rest, those whom you *preserved* from repentance. Will you then rejoice in your success? The Lord God grant it may not be said in that hour: 'These have perished in their iniquity; but their blood I require at thy hands.'[5]   I am,

Your lordship's dutiful
Son and servant,
John Wesley[6]

London,
June 11, 1747

---

[1] Cf. Acts 4: 12.   [2] Cf. 2 Cor. 4: 2.   [3] Cf. Rev. 20: 11.
[4] Matt. 25: 41.   [5] Cf. Ezek. 3: 18.
[6] Appended is a poem by Charles Wesley setting forth by means of a prayer the basic message of Methodist preaching. In the original edition this had no title. The Dublin edition of 1748 supplied the title 'For a Preacher of the Gospel', and the Bristol edition of 1749 the title 'For a Person called forth to bear his Testimony'. The poem was also appended to the 3rd edition of *An Earnest Appeal* (1749), with this latter title. Wesley incorporated stanzas 5–7 and 8–9 as hymns 427 and 428 in his *Collection of Hymns*, for which see Volume 7 of this edition. The poem was omitted, however, from the edition of the *Letter* which he prepared for his collected *Works*.

Open Letters to Dr. George Lavington
Bishop of Exeter

Introduction

When bishops attacked the Methodists, Wesley usually felt obliged to reply. This volume contains open letters to Gibson and to Warburton, who were both men of outstanding importance. Bishop Lavington was in a very different category, yet he required more attention than either of his more eminent colleagues.

George Lavington (1684–1762) was a product of Winchester and New College, Oxford. He became a fellow of his college, and in due course began to accumulate preferments. As a young man he had been a Whig in the Tory University of Oxford. This did not encourage academic promotion, but it won him influential friends in the world of politics. He was appointed a chaplain to King George I. He was successively prebendary of Worcester and of St. Paul's. He held several desirable livings, and in 1747, through the good offices of the Duke of Newcastle and the Earl of Hardwicke, he was appointed to the see of Exeter.

Lavington was not one of the more distinguished churchmen of the period. He had few claims to scholarship. He was neither an author nor a preacher of note. When elevated to the bench of bishops, he could not be regarded as an outstanding figure in any respect. Early in his episcopate he found himself involved in a controversy which rapidly became a *cause célèbre*. In 1748 there appeared, anonymously, what purported to be an extract from a visitation charge delivered by Lavington. The statement was brief; the wording was ambiguous, but the implication was clear: at heart the bishop was a Methodist. An unidentified clergyman was inspired to publish a pamphlet which also assumed that Lavington favoured the Methodists.[1] Lavington was furious, and issued a disclaimer which hinted that the Methodist leaders had deliberately perpetrated the hoax. The charge, of course, was groundless, but it was too serious to be ignored. The stewards of Wesley's London meeting-house, the Foundery, promptly issued a disclaimer. A number of

[1] *A Letter to the Right Reverend Father in God George, Lord Bishop of Exeter, occasioned by his Lordship's late Charge to the Clergy of his Diocess* [sic] (1748).

other protests appeared. The Countess of Huntingdon wrung from Lavington a somewhat reluctant retraction, and made it public. The bishop nursed his resentment, and in March 1749 he published anonymously the first instalment of a massive attack on the Methodists. The aim of *The Enthusiasm of Methodists and Papists Compar'd* was 'to draw a comparison between the wild and pernicious enthusiasms of some of the most eminent saints of the popish communion, and those of Methodists in our own country'. The author dismissed the Methodists as 'a set of pretended reformers—a dangerous and presumptuous sect, animated with an enthusiastical and fanatical spirit'.[1]

The tone of the work was scurrilous. Its effects might easily have proved serious. It was widely assumed that Catholic practices presupposed submission to papal domination; many people believed that both pointed to Jacobite sympathies. To link Methodists with Papists was therefore a serious imputation when the rebellion of 1745 was a very recent memory. Indeed, in some parts of the country the Methodists had been mobbed on the grounds that they were secret agents of the Young Pretender. In any case, 'enthusiasm' by itself was a very serious accusation; it was the all-inclusive charge always hurled at zeal in religion or intensity of spiritual experience. Two replies to Lavington appeared at once, one by Whitefield, the other by Vincent Perronet. In the same year Lavington published a second part of his work, with a long preface addressed to Whitefield. In 1751 a third part appeared. Wesley was in no immediate hurry to join the fray. Only after the appearance of Lavington's second part did he compose and publish *A Letter to the Author of The Enthusiasm of Methodists and Papists Compar'd* (1750). In due course he added a much lengthier contribution to the controversy, *A Second Letter to the Author of The Enthusiasm of Methodists and Papists Compar'd* (1751), to which he prefixed a letter 'To the Right Reverend the Lord Bishop of Exeter'. This was apparently designed to flush him out of his shelter of anonymity by discussing a specific reference to him in Part III of *Enthusiasm*. To this particular point Lavington replied in *The Bishop of Exeter's Answer to Mr. J. Wesley's late Letter to his Lordship*. Wesley concluded the exchange with *A Second Letter to the Lord Bishop of Exeter*, a relatively brief response written from Newcastle-upon-

---

[1] George Lavington, *The Enthusiasm of Methodists and Papists Compar'd*, Pt. I, Preface.

Tyne on May 8, 1752. They never really came to grips over Lavington's charges; the bishop merely insisted in his *Letter* that the remainder of Wesley's *Second Letter to the Author of the Enthusiasm of Methodists*, etc., was 'mere rant and declamation' which he would not demean himself to answer.

As we have seen, Wesley engaged in this controversy with considerable reluctance. 'I began writing a letter to the "Comparer" of the Papists and the Methodists. Heavy work, such as I should never choose, but sometimes it must be done. Well might the ancient say: "God made practical divinity necessary, the devil controversial." But it *is* necessary. We must "resist the devil", or he will not "flee from us".'[1] Wesley felt that he could not ignore the book; it might be a slanderous attack, obviously prompted by malice, but it was also apparent that it was being widely used to discredit the Methodists. Indeed, for some years Wesley continued to encounter its effects. At the parish church at Cullompton, Devon, he heard 'by way of sermon, part of *Papists and Methodists Compared*', but he added that it did not diminish his own outdoor congregation immediately after the service.[2] At York he discovered that a justice of the peace was distributing widely certain parts of Lavington's *Enthusiasm*, and was apparently doing so as a means of stirring up hostility against the Methodists.[3] Even those who shared Lavington's position considered his performance mediocre, though they thought it likely to accomplish his purpose. Bishop Warburton, writing to his friend Richard Hurd, admitted that the work was 'on the whole composed well enough—though it be a bad copy of Stillingfleet's famous book of "The Fanaticism of the Church of Rome"—to do the execution he intended'. But even Warburton, who was certainly no friend of the Methodists, could not suppress a sneer at Lavington's obvious attempt to equate Methodism with everything that was discreditable.[4]

Lavington launched his attack by propounding the thesis that enthusiasm has been consistently uniform in character, 'operating in much the same manner in all sects and professions of religion, and discovering itself in similar peculiarities of notions and behaviours'.[5] He did not directly accuse the Methodists of popery, though he

[1] Wesley, *Journal*, Nov. 19, 1751.
[2] Ibid., Aug. 25, 1751.   [3] Ibid., Apr. 25, 1752.
[4] Warburton, *Letters from a late Eminent Prelate*, Letter xlvii (2nd ed., London, 1809), pp. 117–18.
[5] Lavington, *The Enthusiasm of Methodists and Papists Compar'd*, Pt. I, § 1.

insisted 'that they are doing the Papists' work for them and agree with them in some of their principles'.[1] Wesley and Whitefield undoubtedly attracted to their cause some unstable people; Lavington argued that the Methodists were well aware that these and all their other disciples would quickly melt away unless mesmerized by startling phenomena. He contended that simple austerities were merely the prelude to more spectacular types of appeal. 'The first necessary point for drawing followers is to put on a sanctified appearance; by a demure look, precise behaviour in discourse or silence, apparel, and food; and other marks of external piety.'[2] Such elementary displays of piety soon gave way to the dramatic manifestations characteristic of the Revival—to 'the struggles and pangs of the new birth'; to 'inspirations, revelations, illuminations, and all the extraordinary and immediate actions of all the persons in the sacred Trinity'; to 'special directions, missions and calls, by immediate revelation'; to 'ecstasies and raptures, apparitions and visions'.[3] In every case, Lavington found that the claims of the Methodists were precisely parallel to the most extravagant pretensions of St. Francis, St. Dominic, St. Ignatius, St. Teresa. 'From all this,' he insisted, 'and from more in the sequel, it has appeared and will appear, that this new dispensation is a composite of enthusiasm, superstition, and imposture.'[4]

In the second and third parts of the work the direct attacks on Methodist practices tend to thrust into the background the comparisons with popish aberrations. The irony is often heavy-handed, but Lavington consistently isolated the elements in Wesley's *Journal* which readers are still apt to find disconcerting. In many of the Methodist preachers he detected a lurking strain of pride, and he believed that this ministered to 'the affectation of prophesying and other miraculous gifts and operations'.[5] He objected to the habit of attributing all favourable developments to the special providence of God and all misfortunes to the activity of the devil.[6] He was deeply disturbed by the phenomena which accompanied the revival. Wesley seemed to be driving his people 'into direct madness and distraction'.[7] Consider, he said, 'their cryings out, screamings, shriekings, roarings, groanings, tremblings, gnashings, yellings, foamings, convulsions, swoonings, dropping, blasphemies, curses,

---

[1] Lavington, *The Enthusiasm of Methodists and Papists Compar'd*, Pt. I, § 2.
[2] Ibid., Pt. I, § 7.   [3] Ibid., Pt. I, §§ 15–30.   [4] Ibid., Pt. I, § 31.
[5] Ibid., Pt. II, § 5.   [6] Ibid., Pt. II, § 7.   [7] Ibid., Pt. II, § 4.

dying and despairing agonies, varieties of tortures in body and mind'.[1] He was sceptical about healings and exorcisms.[2] About many of these features Wesley himself had his own perplexities.[3] The matter on which Wesley was entitled to protest was the way Lavington used the *Journal* as a quarry for material. He ignored the change in Wesley's life which followed his conversion, and discredited developments subsequent to it by citing difficulties and uncertainties previous to it. He treated all incidents alike; he overlooked the rather fundamental distinction between persons who had been converted to Methodism and those who had not. Even when Wesley clearly specified that he was recounting the troubles and perplexities of a total stranger, Lavington invoked the case in order to discredit the Methodists. Sometimes he twisted the evidence so grossly that it is difficult to attribute the distortion to carelessness or haste.

Wesley felt, with some reason, that he was dealing with an unprincipled controversialist. Initially *The Enthusiasm* appeared anonymously. The disguise was somewhat transparent, but it meant that the bishop was evading responsibility for the attacks he launched against the Methodists. He was claiming the right to ridicule and denigrate by name men who were placed at a serious disadvantage because they could not identify their assailant. Consequently the tone of Wesley's first reply was unusually severe. In his mind anonymity aggravated all the other faults of an opponent. As soon as Lavington acknowledged his authorship, Wesley changed his mode of address and modified his tone.

In 1754 the three parts of *The Enthusiasm* were republished as a two-volume work. The following year Lavington launched a similar attack on the Moravians.[4] It attracted little attention, and in no respect can it be regarded as a success. It is worth observing that seventy years after its first appearance, *The Enthusiasm* was resurrected to serve the ends of nineteenth-century religious feuds. The Revd. Richard Polwhele edited the work and contributed a long introduction full of bitter aspersions on nonconformists and Anglican evangelicals.

The final word, however, should concern not the polemics of controversialists but the relationships of churchmen. Wesley was

---

[1] Ibid., Pt. III, § 5. Cf. § 20.
[2] Ibid., Pt. III, §§ 9–17, §§ 30–6.
[3] Cf. Introduction, above, p. 23.
[4] *The Moravians Compared and Detected* (1755).

not a vindictive man and seldom harboured resentment. On August 29, 1762 he worshipped in Exeter Cathedral. 'I was well pleased', he recorded, 'to partake of the Lord's Supper with my old opponent, Bishop Lavington. O may we sit down together in the Kingdom of our Father!'[1] Fifteen days later Lavington was dead.

[1] Wesley, *Journal*, Aug. 29, 1762.

A
LETTER

To the A U T H O R of the

ENTHUSIASM

O F

METHODISTS

A N D

P A P I S T S

C O M P A R'D

Agedum ! Pauca accipe contrà
H O R.

L O N D O N:
Printed by H. C o c k, and Sold by G. *Wood-fall,* near *Charing-Crofs* ; *A. Dodd,* at the *Peacock,* in the *Strand* ; *J. Robinfon,* in *Ludgate-Street* ; *T. Trye,* near *Gray's Inn* ; and *T. James,* under the *Royal-Exchange.*

[Price Four-Pence.]

[N.B. The motto is from Horace, *Satires*, I. iv. 38—'Come now, listen to a few words in answer' (Loeb).]

A

LETTER

To the AUTHOR of the

ENTHUSIASM

OF

METHODISTS, &c.[1]

Sir,

1. In your late pamphlets you have undertaken to prove that Mr. Whitefield and I are gross enthusiasts; and that our 'whole conduct is but a counterpart of the most wild fanaticism of the most abominable communion in its most corrupt ages'.[a]   5

You endeavour to support this charge against us by quotations from our writings, compared with quotations from celebrated writers of the Romish communion.

2. It lies upon me to answer for one. But I must not burden you with too long an answer, lest ('for want either of leisure or inclina-   10 tion')[b] you should not give this, any more than my other tracts, a reading. In order therefore to spare both you and myself I shall at present consider only your first Part; and that as briefly as possible. Accordingly I shall not meddle with your other quotations; but leaving them to whom they may concern shall only examine   15 whether those you have made from my writings prove the charge of enthusiasm or no.

This, I conceive, will be abundantly sufficient to decide the question between you and me. If these do prove the charge, I am

---

[a] [George Lavington, *The Enthusiasm of Methodists and Papists Compar'd*, London, Knapton, 1749,] Preface, p. 3. [Actually the pages of the preface are not numbered, but Wesley supplies numbers, counting the first page of the preface as p. 1.]

[b] [Ibid.,] Preface, p. 5.

---

[1] For a summary of the three editions published during Wesley's lifetime, and a list of the substantive variant readings from the edited text (based on the first edition, London, Cock, [1750]), see the appendix to this volume, p. 556. For full bibliographical details see *Bibliography*, No. 177.

cast.[1] If they do not, if they are the words of truth and soberness, it will be an objection of no real weight against sentiments just in themselves, though they should also be found in the writings of Papists—yea, of Mahometans or pagans.

5   3. Let the eight pages you *borrow*[2] stand as they are. I presume they will do neither good nor harm. In the tenth, you say the Methodists 'act on the same plan' with the Papists, 'not perhaps from compact and design; but a similar configuration and texture of brain, or the fumes of imagination producing similar effects. From
10 a commiseration, or horror, arising from the grievous corruptions of the world, perhaps from a real motive of sincere piety, they both set out with warm pretences to a reformation.'[3] Sir, this is an uncommon thought: that sincere piety should arise from the 'configuration and texture of the brain'; as well as that 'pretences to
15 a reformation' should spring from a 'real motive of sincere piety'!

4. You go on, 'both commonly begin their adventures with field preaching'.[a] Sir, do you condemn field preaching *toto genere*, as evil in itself? Have a care! Or you (I should say, the gentleman that assists you) will speak a little too plain, and betray the *real* motive
20 of his *sincere* antipathy to the people called Methodists.

Or do you condemn the preaching on Hanham Mount, in particular, to the colliers of Kingswood?[4] If you doubt whether this has 'done any real good',[5] it is a very easy thing to be informed. And I leave it with all impartial men, whether the good which has
25 in fact been done by preaching there, and which could not possibly have been done any other way, does not abundantly 'justify the irregularity'[b] of it.

5. But you think I am herein *inconsistent* with myself. For I say, 'the uncommonness is the very circumstance that recommends it',
30 (I mean, that recommended it to the colliers in Kingswood) and

---

[a] [Lavington,] *Enthusiasm, etc.*, p. 11.   [b] [Ibid.,] p. 15.

---

[1] Among the various shades of meaning of 'cast' are, to defeat in a competition, to declare guilty, to condemn, to defeat in an action at law.

[2] From Francis Lee, *The History of Montanism* (1709).

[3] Lavington, *Enthusiasm*, p. 10.

[4] Hanham Mount was in Kingswood, about four miles east of Bristol, and one of the locations where Wesley first began to preach in the open air. In a letter dated Apr. 29, 1739 he wrote: 'Between 10 and 11 I began preaching the gospel there in a meadow, on the top of the hill.' Hanham Mount is still used on occasion as an open-air preaching place. Cf. *A Letter to the Bishop of Gloucester*, I. 20 and note.

[5] Lavington, *Enthusiasm*, p. 15.

yet I said but a page or two before, 'We are not suffered to preach in the churches; else we should prefer them to any places whatsoever.'[1]

Sir, I still aver both the one and the other. I do *prefer* the preaching in a church when I am suffered. And yet, when I am not, the wise providence of God overrules this very circumstance for good; many coming to hear because of the uncommonness of the thing, who would otherwise not have heard at all.

6. Your second charge is that I 'abuse the clergy', 'throw out so much gall of bitterness' against them, and 'impute this black art of calumny to the Spirit and power given from God'.[a]

Sir, I plead not guilty to the whole charge. And you have not cited one line to support it. But, if you could support it, what is this to the point in hand? I presume calumny is not enthusiasm. Perhaps you will say, 'But it is something as bad.' True; but it is nothing to the purpose. Even the 'imputing this to the Spirit of God', as you here represent it, is an instance of *art*, not of *enthusiasm*.

7. You charge me, thirdly, with 'putting on a sanctified appearance, in order to draw followers by a demure look, precise behaviour, and other marks of external piety. For which reason (you say) Mr. Wesley made and renewed that noble resolution, not willingly to indulge himself in the least levity of behaviour, or in laughter—no, not for a moment. To speak no word not tending to the glory of God; and not a tittle of worldly things.'[b]

Sir, you miss the mark again. If this 'sanctified appearance' was 'put on' to 'draw followers', if it was 'for this reason' (as you flatly affirm it was) that 'Mr. Wesley made and renewed that noble resolution' (it was made eleven or twelve years before, about the time of my removal to Lincoln College) then it can be no instance of enthusiasm, and so does not fall within the design of your present work—unless your title-page does not belong to your book, for that confines you to the enthusiasm of the Methodists.

8. But consider this point in another view. You accuse me of 'putting on a sanctified appearance, a demure look, precise behaviour, and other marks of external piety'. How are you assured, sir, this was barely *external*? And that it was a bare *appearance* of sanctity? You affirm this as from personal knowledge. Was you

---

[a] [Ibid.,] p. 15 [= 17].   [b] [Ibid.,] pp. 18, 19.

[1] *A Farther Appeal*, Pt. III, III. 22, 23.

then acquainted with me three or four and twenty years ago? 'He
made and renewed that noble resolution' in order to 'draw followers.'
Sir, how do you know that? Are you in God's place, that you take
upon you to be the searcher of hearts? 'That noble resolution, not
5 willingly to indulge himself in the least levity of behaviour'. Sir,
I acquit you of having any concern in this matter. But I appeal to
all who have the love of God in their hearts whether this is not
a rational, scriptural resolution worthy of the vocation wherewith
we are called.[1] 'Or in laughter—no, not for a moment.' No, nor
10 ought I to indulge it at all if I am conscious to myself it hurts my
soul. In which let every man judge for himself. 'To speak no word
not tending to the glory of God.' A *peculiar* instance of enthusiasm
this! 'And not a tittle of worldly things.' The words immediately
following are: 'Others may, nay must. But what is that to me?'
15 (words which in justice you ought to have inserted)—who was then
entirely disengaged from worldly business of every kind. Notwithstanding which, I have often since engaged therein when the order
of Providence plainly required it.

9. Though I did not design to meddle with them, yet I must here
20 take notice of three of your instances of popish enthusiasm. The
first is: 'that Mechtildis tortured herself for having spoken an idle
word'. (The point of comparison lies not in torturing herself, but
in her doing it on such an occasion.) The second: 'that not a word
fell from St. Catherine of Siena that was not religious and holy'.
25 The third, 'that the lips of Magdalen di Pazzi were never opened but
to chant the praises of God'.[a] I would to God the comparison
between the Methodists and Papists would hold in this respect!
Yea, that you, and all the clergy in England, were guilty of just such
enthusiasm.

30   10. You cite as a fourth instance of my enthusiasm that I say
a Methodist (a real Christian), 'cannot adorn himself, on any pretence, with gold or costly apparel'.[b] If this be enthusiasm, let the
Apostle look to it.[2] His words are clear and express. If *you* can
find a *pretence* to set them aside, do. I cannot; nor do I desire it.

35   11. My 'seeming contempt of money'[c] you urge as a fifth instance
of my enthusiasm. Sir, I understand you. You was obliged to call it
'seeming' lest you should yourself confute the allegation you brought

---

[a] [*Enthusiasm*,] p. 19.   [b] [Ibid.,] p. 21.   [c] [Ibid.,] p. 26.

[1] See Eph. 4: 1.   [2] See Jas. 2: 2–4.

in your title-page. But if it be only 'seeming', whatever it prove beside, it cannot prove that I am an enthusiast.

12. Hitherto you have succeeded extremely ill. You have brought five accusations against me; and have not been able to make one good. However, you are resolved to throw dirt enough that some may stick. So you are next to prove upon me, 'a restless impatience and insatiable thirst of travelling, and undertaking dangerous voyages for the conversion of infidels; together with a declared contempt of all dangers, plains, and sufferings; and the designing, loving, and praying for ill usage, persecution, martyrdom, death, and hell.'[a]

In order to prove this uncommon charge you produce four scraps of sentences which you mark as my words, though as they stand in your book they are neither sense nor grammar.[b] But you do not refer to the page or even the treatise where any one of them may be found. Sir, 'tis well you hide your name; or you would be obliged to hide your face from every man of candour, or even common humanity.

13. 'Sometimes indeed', you say, Mr. Wesley 'complains of the scoffs both of the great vulgar and the small'; to prove which, you disjoint and murder (as your manner is) another of my sentences: 'But at other times the note is changed, and "till he is despised, no man is in a state of salvation".'[c] The note is changed! How so? When did I say otherwise than I do at this day, viz. 'That none are children of God but those who are hated or despised by the children of the devil.'

I must beg you, sir, in your Third Part to inform your reader that whenever any solecism or mangled sentences appear in the quotations from my writings, they are not chargeable upon *me*; that if the sense be mine (which is not always—sometimes you do me too much honour even in this) yet I lay no claim to the manner of expression: the English is all your own.

14. 'Corporal severities, or mortification by tormenting the flesh'[d] is the next thing you charge upon me. Almost two sentences you bring in proof of this. The one, 'Our bed being wet (it was in a storm at sea) I laid me down on the floor and slept sound till morning. And I believe I shall not find it needful to go to bed, as 'tis called,

---

[a] [Ibid.,] p. 27 [i.e. 26; 'designing' represents Lavington's 'desire'].
[b] [Ibid.,] p. 31 [i.e. pp. 26–7].   [c] [Ibid.,] p. 32 [i.e. p. 28].
[d] [Ibid.,] p. 31.

any more.'ᵃ But whether I do or not, how will you prove that my motive is to 'gain a reputation for sanctity'?¹ I desire (if it be not too great a favour) a little evidence for this.

5 The other fragment of a sentence speaks 'of bearing cold on the naked head, rain and wind, frost and snow'.ᵇ True; but not as matter of 'mortification by tormenting the flesh'. Nothing less. These things are not spoken of there as voluntary instances of mortification (you yourself know perfectly well they are not; only you *make free* with your friend) but as some of the unavoidable inconveniences which
10 attend preaching in the open air.

Therefore you need not be so 'sure that the Apostle condemns that ἀφειδία σώματος,² "not sparing the body", as useless and superstitious'; and that it is a 'false show of humility'.ᶜ *Humility* is entirely out of the question, as well as *chastity*, in the case of hardships
15 endured (but not properly chosen) out of *love* to the souls for which Christ died.

15. You add a 'word or two' of my 'ardent desire of going to hell', which you think I 'adopted' from the Jesuit Nieremberg.ᵈ Sir, I know not the man. I am wholly a stranger both to his person and to his
20 doctrine. But if this is his doctrine, I disclaim it from my heart. I ardently desire that both you and I may go to heaven.

But Mr. Wesley says, 'A poor old man decided the question of disinterested love.—He said, . . . "I do not care what place I am in. Let God put me where he will, or do with me what he will, so I may
25 set forth his honour and glory." 'ᵉ

He did say so. And what then? Do these words imply 'an ardent desire of going to hell'? I do not suppose the 'going to hell' ever entered into his thoughts. Nor has it any place in my notion of 'disinterested love'. How you may understand that term I know not.
30 But you will prove I have this desire whether I will or no. You are sure this was my '*original meaning*', in the words cited by Mr. Church:³

Doom if thou canst to endless pains,
Or drive me from thy face;

ᵃ [*Enthusiasm*,] p. 32.   ᵇ [Ibid.,] p. 32.   ᶜ [Ibid.,] p. 33
ᵈ [Ibid.,] pp. 34-5 [J. E. Nieremberg (1595–1658), a Spanish Jesuit of German origin and a prolific writer on Scripture, theology, natural history, the devotional life, etc.].
ᵉ [Ibid.,] p. 35.

---

¹ Lavington, *Enthusiasm*, p. 31.   ² Col. 2: 23.
³ See Wesley, *An Answer to the Rev. Mr. Church's Remarks*, III. 4, in Vol. 9 of this edition.

'God's power or justice', you say, 'must be intended; because he speaks of God's love in the very next lines:

> But if thy stronger love constrains,
> Let me be saved by grace.'[a]

Sir, I will tell you a secret. Those lines are not mine. However, I will once more venture to defend them, and to aver that your consequence is good for nothing: 'If this love is spoken of in the latter lines, then it is not in the former.' No? Why not? I take it to be spoken of in both. The plain meaning of which is: If thou art not love, I am content to perish. But if thou art, let me find the effects thereof—let me be saved by grace.

16. You next accuse me of maintaining 'a stoical insensibility'.[1] This objection also you borrow from Mr. Church. You ought likewise to have taken notice that I had answered it, and openly disowned that doctrine; I mean, according to the rules of common justice. But that is not your failing.

17. Part of your thirty-ninth page runs thus: 'With respect to all this patient enduring hardships, etc., it has been remarked by learned authors, that some persons by *constitutional* temper have been fond of bearing the worst that could befall them; . . . that others from a *sturdy humour* and the force of education have made light of the most exquisite tortures; that when *enthusiasm* comes in, in aid of this natural or acquired sturdiness, and men fancy they are upon *God's work*, and entitled to his *rewards*, they are immediately all on fire for rushing into sufferings and pain.'

I take knowledge of your having faithfully abridged your own book, shall I say? Or the *learned* Dr. Middleton's?[2] But what is it you are endeavouring to prove?

Quorsum haec tam putida tendunt?[3]

---

[a] [Ibid.,] pp. 35–6 [The quotation borrowed by Lavington from Church is from Charles Wesley, 'The Means of Grace'; see *Bibliography*, Nos. 17, 40, and *Poet. Wks.*, I. 236].

[1] Lavington, *Enthusiasm*, p. 36.

[2] Wesley implies that Lavington's purported quotation from 'learned authors' was in fact merely an epitome of his own argument. Apart from a couple of sermons, Lavington published nothing except his attacks on the Methodists and on the Moravians. The book by Conyers Middleton (fellow of Trinity College, Cambridge, and librarian of the University), is *A Free Inquiry into the Miraculous Powers which are supposed to have subsisted in the Christian Church* (1748). This created a great stir, and was answered by Wesley (among others); see *Bibliography*, No. 160, and Vol. 13 of this edition, and cf. Warburton, *The Doctrine of Grace*, Bk. I.

[3] 'Whither tends this putrid stuff?' Horace, *Satires*, II. vii. 21.

The paragraph *seems* to point at me. But the plain, natural tendency of it is to invalidate that great argument for Christianity which is drawn from the constancy of the martyrs. Have you not here also spoken a little too plain? Had you not better have kept the
5 mask on a little longer?

Indeed you lamely add, 'The solid and just comforts which a true martyr receives from above are groundlessly applied to the counterfeit.'[1] But this is not enough even to save appearances.

18. You subjoin a truly surprising thought: 'It may moreover be
10 observed that both ancient and modern enthusiasts always take care to secure some advantage by their sufferings.'[a] O rare enthusiasts! So they are not such fools neither as they are vulgarly supposed to be. This is just of a piece with the 'cunning epileptic demoniacs'[2] in your other performance. And don't you think (if you would but
15 speak all that is in your heart, and let us into the whole secret) that there was a compact likewise between Bishop Hooper and his executioner, as well as between the ventriloquist and the exorcist?[3]

But what 'advantage' do they 'take care to secure'? A good salary? A handsome fortune? No, quite another matter: 'free com-
20 munications with God', and 'fuller manifestations of his goodness'.[b] I dare say you do not envy them; no more than you do those self-interested enthusiasts of old, who 'were tortured, not accepting deliverance, that they might obtain a better resurrection'.[4]

19. You proceed to prove my enthusiasm from my notions of
25 conversion. And here great allowances are to be made, because you are talking of things quite out of your sphere. You are got into an unknown world! Yet you still talk as magisterially as if you was only running down the Fathers of the primitive church.

And, first, you say, I 'represent conversion as sudden and in-
30 stantaneous'.[c] Soft and fair! Do you know what *conversion* is? (A term, indeed, which I very rarely use, because it rarely occurs in the New Testament.) 'Yes; it is to "start up perfect men at once".'[d]

---

[a] [*Enthusiasm*,] p. 40.   [b] [Ibid.,] p. 40.   [c] [Ibid.,] p. 40.   [d] [Ibid.,] p. 41.

[1] Lavington, *Enthusiasm*, p. 39.   [2] Ibid., Pt. II, § 7.

[3] On the execution during the Marian persecutions of Bishop John Hooper of Gloucester, see John Foxe, *Acts and Monuments*, I. xi. On the compact between the ventriloquist and the exorcist, see Conyers Middleton, op. cit., p. 92: 'If we suppose, then, that there were artists of this kind among the ancient Christians, how easily, by a correspondence between the ventriloquist and the exorcist, might they delude the most sensible of the audience!' (Cf. Wesley, *A Letter to Conyers Middleton*, IV. iii. 9.)

[4] Heb. 11: 35.

Indeed, sir, it is not. A man is usually converted long before he is a perfect man. 'Tis probable most of those Ephesians to whom St. Paul directed his epistle were converted. Yet they were not 'come (few, if any) to a perfect man; to the measure of the stature of the fullness of Christ'.[1]

20. I do not, sir, indeed, I do not undertake to make you understand these things. I am not so vain as to think it is in my power. 'Tis the utmost of my hope to convince you, or at least those who read your works, that you understand just nothing about them.

To put this out of dispute, you go on: 'Thus faith, and being born of God, are said to be an instantaneous work, at once, and in a moment, as lightning. Justification, the same as regeneration, and having a lively faith—this always in a moment.'[a] I know not which to admire most, the English or the sense, which you here father upon me. But in truth 'tis all your own: I do not thus confound faith and 'being born of God'. I always speak of them as different things: 'tis you that thus jumble them together. 'Tis you who discover justification also to be 'the same as regeneration and having a lively faith'; I take them to be three different things—so different as not ever to come under one *genus*. And yet 'tis true that each of these, 'as far as I know',[2] is at first experienced suddenly; although two of them (I leave you to find out which) gradually increase from that hour.

21. 'After these sudden conversions', say you, 'they receive their assurances of salvation.'[b] Sir, Mr. Bedford's ignorance in charging this doctrine upon me might be *involuntary*, and I am persuaded was *real*. But yours cannot be so. It must be *voluntary*; if it is not rather *affected*. For you had before you, while you wrote, the very tract wherein I corrected Mr. Bedford's mistake, and explicitly declared, 'The assurance whereof I speak is not an assurance of salvation.'[3] And the very passages you cite from me

---

[a] [Ibid.,] p. 41.   [b] [Ibid.,] p. 43.

[1] Cf. Eph. 4: 13.   [2] Cf. Lavington, *Enthusiasm*, p. 41.

[3] On Aug. 13, 1738 the Revd. Arthur Bedford, chaplain to the Prince of Wales, preached a sermon at St. Lawrence Jewry, London, on *The Doctrine of Assurance*, publishing it shortly afterwards. In the third instalment of his *Journal* (which Lavington used) Wesley stated under the date Oct. 6, 1738: 'I went to the Rev. Mr. Bedford, to tell him, between me and him alone, of the injury he had done both to God and his brother by preaching and printing that very weak sermon on assurance, which was an *ignoratio elenchi* from beginning to end; seeing the assurance we preach is of quite another kind from what he writes against. We speak of an assurance of our *present pardon*, not, as he does, of our *final perseverance*.'

prove the same; every one of which (as you yourself know in your own conscience) relates wholly and solely to present pardon, not to future salvation.

Of *Christian perfection* I shall not say anything to *you*, till you have
5 learned a little heathen honesty.[a]

22. That this is a lesson you have not yet learned appears also from your following section, wherein you roundly affirm: 'Whatever they think, say, or do (i.e. the Methodists, according to their own account), is from God; and whatever opposeth, is from the
10 devil.'[1] I doubt not but Mr. Church believed this to be true when he asserted it. But this is no plea for *you*, who having read the *Answer* to Mr. Church, still assert what you know to be false.[2]

'Here we have', say you, 'the true spirit and very essence of enthusiasm, . . . which sets men above carnal reasoning, and all
15 conviction of plain Scripture.'[b] It may, or may not; that is nothing to me. I am not above either reason or Scripture. To either of these I am ready to submit. But I cannot receive scurrilous invective instead of Scripture; nor pay the same regard to low buffoonery as to clear and cogent reasons.

20 23. With your two following pages I have nothing to do. But in the fifty-second, I read as follows: 'A Methodist, says Mr. Wesley, went to receive the Sacrament . . ., when God was pleased to let him see a crucified Saviour.' Very well; and what is this brought to prove? Why, (1), that I am an enthusiast; (2), that I 'encourage the
25 notion of the real, corporal presence in the sacrifice of the Mass'. How so? 'Why, this is as good an argument for transubstantiation as several produced by Bellarmin.'[c] Very likely it may; and as good as several produced by you for the enthusiasm of the Methodists.

24. In that 'seraphic rhapsody of divine love',[d] as you term it,

---

[a] [*Enthusiasm*,] p. 45. [Lavington opened: 'No marvel, then, if the presumption riseth still higher into a fancy of *perfection*, an *unsinning* state and *unspotted*; while other wretched mortals lie grovelling in the mire of vice, or at least in an *imperfect* way. To such a high-flown pitch may a frantic imagination be carried.']

[b] [Ibid.,] p. 49.　　　　　　　　　　　　　　　　　[c] [Ibid.,] p. 53.

[d] [Ibid.,] p. 57 [i.e. a part of an unsigned letter inserted in Wesley's *Journal* under the date Dec. 5, 1738].

---

[1] Lavington, *Enthusiasm*, p. 49.

[2] See Thomas Church, *Remarks on the Rev. Mr. John Wesley's Last Journal*, p. 60; Wesley, *An Answer to the Rev. Mr. Church's Remarks on the Rev. Mr. John Wesley's Last Journal*, III. 5, and *The Principles of a Methodist Farther Explained*, IV. 2, in Vol. 9 of this edition.

which you condemn in the lump as rant and madness, there are several scriptural expressions, both from the Old and New Testament. At first I imagined you did not know them; those being books which you do not seem to be much acquainted with. But upon laying circumstances together, I rather suppose you was glad of so 5 handsome an opportunity to make as if you aimed at *me*, that you might have a home stroke at some of those old enthusiasts.

25. The next words which you cite from me as a proof of my enthusiasm are: 'The power of God was in an unusual manner present.'[a] I mean, many found an unusual degree of that peace, joy, 10 and love, which St. Paul terms, 'the fruit of the Spirit'.[1] And all these, in conformity to his doctrine, I ascribe to 'the power of God'. I know you, in conformity to your principles, ascribe them to the power of nature. But I still believe, according to the old scriptural hypothesis, that whenever in hearing the Word of God men are 15 filled with peace and love, 'God confirms that Word by the Holy Ghost given unto those that hear it.'[2]

26. As a farther proof of my enthusiasm you mention 'special directions, missions, and calls by immediate revelation'.[b] For an instance of which you cite those words: 'I know, and am assured, 20 that God sent forth his light and his truth.'[3] I did know this. But do I say, by immediate revelation? Not a tittle about it. This is your own ingenious improvement upon my words.

'However, it was by a "special direction", for your own words in the same paragraph are: "From the direction I received from God 25 this day, touching an affair of the greatest importance."'[c]

What, are these words in the same paragraph with those, 'I know, and am assured, God sent forth his light and his truth'? Why then do you tear the paragraph in two, and put part in your sixty-seventh, part in your sixty-eighth, and sixty-ninth pages? O, for a plain 30 reason: to make it look like two instances of enthusiasm—otherwise it could have made but one at the most.

But you cannot make out one till you have proved that these directions were by 'immediate revelation'. I never affirmed they were. I now affirm they were not. Now, sir, make your best of them. 35

---

[a] [Ibid.,] p. 61. [b] [Ibid.,] p. 67. [c] [Ibid.,] pp. 68–9.

[1] Cf. Gal. 5: 22; Eph. 5: 9.
[2] Lavington, *Enthusiasm*, p. 61, citing Wesley's *Journal*, though the citation is inaccurate. [3] Lavington cites Wesley's *Journal* for Mar. 4, 1737.

You add, 'Let me mention a few directions coming by way of command. . . . Mr. Wesley "came to Mr. Delamotte's, where I expected a cool reception. But God had prepared the way before me." '[a] What! By a command to Mr. Delamotte? Who told you
5 so? Not I. Nor anyone else: only your own fruitful imagination.

27. Your next discovery is more curious still: that 'Itinerants . . . order what they want at a public house, and then tell the landlord that he will be damned if he takes anything of them.'[b]

I was beating my brain to find out what Itinerant this should be,
10 as I could not but imagine some silly man or other, probably styling himself a Methodist, must somewhere or other have given some ground for a story so punctually delivered. In the midst of this, a letter from Cornwall informed me it was I—I myself was the very man—and acquainted me with the place and the person to whom
15 I said it. But as there are some particulars in that letter (sent without a name) which I did not well understand, I transcribe a few words of it in hopes that the author will give me fuller information: 'As to the bishop's declaring what the landlord of Mitchell says in respect of your behaviour, I don't at all wonder at the story.' 'The
20 bishop's declaring'! Whom can he mean? Surely not the Right Reverend Dr. George Lavington, Lord Bishop of Exeter! When, or to whom, did he declare it? At Truro, in Cornwall? Or in Plymouth, at his Visitation? To all the clergy who were assembled before God to receive his pastoral instructions? His lordship of
25 Exeter must certainly have more regard to the dignity of the episcopal office!

28. But to proceed. I was not 'offended with the Moravians' for warning men 'against mixing nature with grace',[c] but for their doing it in such a manner as tended to destroy all the work of grace
30 in their souls. I did not blame the thing itself, but their *manner* of doing it. And this you know perfectly well. But with you truth must always give way to wit. At all events you must have your jest.

29. Had you had any regard to truth, or any desire to represent things as they really are, when you repeated Mr. Church's objection
35 concerning *lots* you would have acknowledged that I have answered it at large. When you have replied to that answer, I may add a word more.[1]

---

[a] [*Enthusiasm*,] p. 69.   [b] [Ibid.,] pp. 69–70.   [c] [Ibid.,] p. 71.

---

[1] Lavington, *Enthusiasm*, § 27, pp. 71–6, ridicules Wesley's use of bibliomancy and

30. You are sadly at a loss under the article of 'ecstasies and raptures' to glean up anything that will serve your purpose. At last, from ten or twelve tracts, you pick out two lines, and those the same you had mentioned before: 'My soul was got up into the holy mount. I had no thought of coming down again into the body.'[1] And truly you might as well have let these alone. For if by ecstasy you mean trance, here is no account of any such; but only of one 'rejoicing in God with joy unspeakable and full of glory'.[2]

With the 'girl of seven years old'[a] I have nothing to do; though you honestly tack that relation to the other in order to make me accountable for both. But all is fair toward a Methodist.

31. What I assert concerning Peter Wright[b] is this: (1), that he gave me that relation (whether I believed it or no, I did not say); (2), that he died within a month after. Now, sir, give us a cast of your office. From these two propositions extract a proof of my being an enthusiast.

You may full as easily prove it from these, as from the words you quote next: 'God does now give remission of sins, and the gifts of the Holy Ghost; and often in dreams and visions of God.'[c] But afterwards (you say) I 'speak more distrustfully'. Indeed I do not; but I guard against enthusiasm in those words, part of which you have recited. The whole paragraph runs thus:

From those words, 'Beloved, believe not every spirit, but try the spirits whether they be of God',[3] I told them they were not to judge of the spirit whereby anyone spoke either by appearances, or by common report, or by their own inward feelings; no, nor by any dreams, visions, or revelations, supposed to be made to their souls, any more than by their tears or any involuntary effects wrought upon their bodies. I warned them all these were in themselves of a doubtful, disputable nature; they *might be* from God, and they *might not*; and were therefore

---

[a] [Ibid.,] p. 77 [citing an instance from Gibson's *Observations*, p. 19, culled from John Lewis's *An Account of the Most Remarkable Particulars relating to the Present Progress of the Gospel*].

[b] [Ibid.,] p. 79 [For this incident, cf. *Journal*, Mar. 28, 1736].

[c] [Ibid.,] p. 79.

---

lots. Wesley refers him to his second letter to the Revd. Thomas Church, *The Principles of a Methodist Farther Explained*, IV. 3–4, which deals with this matter. On pp. 74–5 Lavington has quoted Church's *Farther Remarks*, which Wesley was answering.

[1] Lavington, *Enthusiasm*, p. 77, quoting once more the unsigned letter noted in § 24 above.

[2] Cf. 1 Pet. 1: 8.   [3] 1 John 4: 1.

not simply to be relied on (any more than simply to be condemned) but to be tried by a farther rule—to be brought to the only certain test, the law and the testimony.[1]

Sir, can you show them a better way?

5   32. The last proof that you produce of my enthusiasm is my 'talking of the great work which God is now beginning to work upon earth'.[a] I own the fact. I do talk of such a work. But I deny the consequence. For if God has begun a great work, then the saying he has is no enthusiasm.

10   To bring sinners to repentance, to save them from their sins, is allowed by all to be the work of God. Yea, and to save one sinner is a great work of God; much more to save many.

But many sinners are saved from their sins at this day, in London, in Bristol, in Kingswood, in Cornwall; in Newcastle upon Tyne,
15   in Whitehaven, in many other parts of England; in Wales, in Ireland, in Scotland; upon the continent of Europe; in Asia and in America. This I term *a great work of God*; so great as I have not read of for several ages.

You ask 'how I know' so great a work is wrought now? 'By
20   inspiration?' No; but by common sense. I know it by the evidence of my own eyes and ears. I have seen a considerable part of it; and I have abundant testimony, such as excludes all possible doubt, for what I have not seen.

33. But you are so far from acknowledging anything of this as to
25   conclude, in full triumph, 'that this new dispensation is a composition of enthusiasm, superstition, and imposture'.[b] It is not clear what you mean by a new 'dispensation'. But the clear and undeniable fact stands thus: A few years ago Great Britain and Ireland were covered with vice from sea to sea. Very little of even the form of
30   religion was left; and still less of the power of it. Out of this darkness God commanded light to shine. In a short space he called thousands of sinners to repentance. They were not only reformed from their outward vices, but likewise changed in their dispositions and tempers; filled with 'a serious, sober sense of true religion',[2]
35   with love to God and all mankind, with an holy faith producing good works of every kind, works both of piety and mercy.

---

[a] [*Enthusiasm*,] p. 80.   [b] [Ibid.,] p. 81.

---

[1] *Journal*, June 22, 1739.   [2] Lavington, *Enthusiasm*, p. 82.

What could the god of this world do in such a case to prevent the spreading of this 'serious, sober religion'? The same that he has done from the beginning of the world. To hinder the light of those whom God had thus changed from shining before men he gave them all in general a nickname—he called them 'Methodists'. And this name, as insignificant as it was in itself, effectually answered his intention. For by this means that light was soon obscured by prejudice, which could not be withstood by Scripture or reason. By the odious and ridiculous ideas affixed to that name they were condemned in the gross, without ever being heard. So that now any scribbler with a middling share of low wit, not encumbered with good nature or modesty, may raise a laugh on those whom he cannot confute, and run them down whom he dares not look in the face. By this means even a comparer of Methodists and Papists may blaspheme the great work of God, not only without blame, but with applause; at least from readers of his own stamp. But it is high time, sir, you should leave your skulking place. Come out, and let us look each other in the face. I have little leisure and less inclination for controversy. Yet I promise, if you will set your name to your Third Part, I will answer all that shall concern me, in that as well as the preceding.[1] Till then I remain,

Sir,
Your friend and well-wisher,
John Wesley

Canterbury,
   Feb. 1, 1749/50

POSTSCRIPT

When you come to relate those 'horrid and shocking things'[2] there may be a danger you are not aware of. Even you yourself may fall (as little as you intend or suspect it) into seriousness. And I am afraid if once you put off your fool's coat, if you stand naked

---

[1] Throughout the greater part of Wesley's exchanges with Lavington, he was consistently trying to drive his opponent from the covert of anonymity. He disliked dealing with critics who refused to accept responsibility for the accusations they levelled against his movement. Cf. the letter of Nov. 27, 1750, addressed to Lavington, in which he assumed that the bishop could not possibly approve of the scurrilous methods employed by the 'Comparer'.

[2] Lavington, *Enthusiasm*, p. 81.

before cool and sober reason, you yourself may appear as inconsiderable a creature—to use your own phrase—'as if your name was Perronet'.[1]

FINIS

[1] Lavington, *Enthusiasm*, Pt. II, Preface, p. iv: 'Nor could you have been more light and insignificant, unless your name had been Perronet.' The Revd. Vincent Perronet, vicar of Shoreham, had been one of the first to reply to *The Enthusiasm of Methodists, etc.* It was for Perronet that Wesley had written *A Plain Account of the People called Methodists* (see Vol. 9 of this edition).

A SECOND
LETTER

To the AUTHOR of the

ENTHUSIASM

OF

METHODISTS

AND

PAPISTS

COMPAR'D.

Ecce•iterum Chrispinus! Juv.

LONDON:

Printed by H. Cock, in *Bloomsbury-Market*, and sold at the *Foundery*, near *Upper-Moorfields*; by *J. Robinson*, in *Ludgate-Street*; by *T. Trye*, near *Gray's-Inn-Gate*, *Holborn*; by *T. James*, under the *Royal-Exchange*; and G. *Englefield*, in *West-street*, near the *Seven Dials*.
M.DCC.LI.

[N.B. The motto is from Juvenal, *Satires*, iv. 1 — 'Crispinus once again!' (Loeb).]

TO THE
Right Reverend the LORD
BISHOP of EXETER.[1]

My Lord,

1. I was grieved when I read the following words in the Third Part of *The Enthusiasm of Methodists and Papists compared*: '"A sensible, honest woman[2] told the Bishop of Exeter, in presence of several witnesses, that Mr. John Wesley came to her house, and questioned her whether she had 'an assurance of her salvation'? Her 5 answer was that she *hoped* she should be saved, but had no absolute *assurance* of it. 'Why then', replied he, 'You are in hell; you are damned already.' This so terrified the poor woman, who was then with child, that she was grievously afraid of miscarrying, and could not in a long time recover her right mind. For this, and the Metho- 10 dists asking her to live upon free cost,[3] she determined to admit no more of them into her house." So much is *her own account* to his lordship, on whose authority it is here published.'[4]

2. This renewed the concern I felt some time since, when I was informed (in letters which I have still by me) of your lordship's 15 publishing this account both at Plymouth in Devonshire and at Truro in Cornwall, before the clergy assembled from all parts of those counties at the solemn season of your lordship's visiting your diocese. But I was not informed that your lordship showed a deep

---

[1] For details of the editions published during Wesley's lifetime and of the variant readings from the edited text (based on the first edition, London, Cock, 1751), see the appendix to this volume, pp. 556–7. For full bibliographical details see *Bibliography*, No. 193.

As noted above, the first part of Wesley's *Second Letter* to his anonymous critic comprises an open letter specifically addressed to Bishop Lavington.

[2] Mrs. Morgan, wife of the keeper of the Plume of Feathers inn at Mitchell, or St. Michael, a village in the parish of Newlyn and St. Enoder, about seven miles NNE. of Truro, Cornwall.

[3] i.e. to lodge and eat at the inn free—Methodist itinerants frequently depended upon such generous hospitality during their travels.

[4] [George Lavington,] *The Enthusiasm of Methodists and Papists Compared: Part III*, London, Knapton, 1751, p. 5. Wesley had probably passed through Mitchell during the week beginning July 19, 1747, and Lavington received the account from Mrs. Morgan the following summer.

concern for the honour of God, which you supposed to be so dreadfully violated, or a tender compassion for a presbyter whom you believed to be rushing into everlasting destruction.

3. In order to be more fully informed, on Saturday August 25,
5 1750, Mr. Trembath[1] of St. Gennys, Mr. Haime[2] of Shaftesbury, and I, called at Mr. Morgan's at Mitchell. The servant telling me her master was not at home, I desired to speak with her mistress, the 'honest, sensible woman'.[3] I immediately asked, 'Did I ever tell you or your husband that you would be damned if you took any
10 money of me?' (So the story ran in the First Part of the Comparison; it has now undergone a very considerable alteration).[4] 'Or did you or he ever affirm' (another circumstance related at Truro) 'that I was rude with your maid?' She replied vehemently, 'Sir, I never said you was, or that you said any such thing. And I don't suppose
15 my husband did. But we have been belied as well as our neighbours.' She added, 'When the bishop came down last, he sent us word that he would dine at our house; but he did not, being invited to a neighbouring gentleman's. He sent for me thither, and said, "Good woman, do you know these people that go up and down? Do you
20 know Mr. Wesley? Did not he tell you, you would be damned if you took any money of him? And did not he offer rudeness to your maid?" I told him, "No, my lord; he never said any such thing to me, nor to my husband that I know of. He never offered any rudeness to any maid of mine. I never saw or knew any harm of him. But
25 a man told me once (who, I was told, was a Methodist Preacher) that I should be damned if I did not know my sins were forgiven."'

4. This is *her own account* given to me. And an account it is irreconcilably different (notwithstanding some small resemblance in the last circumstance) from that she is affirmed to have given
30 your lordship. Whether she did give that account to your lordship or no, your lordship knows best. That the Comparer affirms it is no proof at all, since he will affirm anything that suits his purpose.

5. Yet I was sorry to see your lordship's authority cited on such an occasion, inasmuch as many of his readers, not considering the
35 man, may think your lordship did really countenance such a writer: one that turns the most serious, the most awful, the most venerable

---

[1] John Trembath, one of Wesley's senior itinerants, a native of St. Gennys, who had served Wesley in Cornwall.

[2] John Haime (1710–84), a native of Shaftesbury, and a soldier–preacher whom Wesley had recently enlisted into his itinerancy.   [3] See § 1 above.

[4] Cf. *A Letter to the Author of* The Enthusiasm of Methodists, etc., § 27.

things into mere farce; that makes the most essential parts of real, experimental religion, matter of low buffoonery; that beginning at the very rise of it in the soul, namely 'repentance toward God',[1] 'a broken and a contrite heart',[2] goes on to 'faith in our Lord Jesus Christ',[3] whereby 'he that believeth is born of God',[4] to 'the love of God shed abroad in the heart',[5] attended with 'peace and joy in the Holy Ghost';[6] to our subsequent 'wrestling not only with flesh and blood, but with principalities and powers, and wicked spirits in high places',[7] and thence to 'perfect love',[8] the loving the Lord our God with 'all our heart, mind, soul, and strength';[9] and treats every one of these sacred topics with the spirit and air of a merry-andrew. What advantage the common enemies of Christianity may reap from this your lordship cannot be insensible.

6. Your lordship cannot but discern how the whole tenor of his book tends to destroy the Holy Scriptures, to render them vile in the eyes of the people, to make them stink in the nostrils of infidels. For instance: after reading his laboured ridicule of the sorrow and fear which usually attend the first repentance (called by St. Chryso-stom, as well as a thousand other writers, 'the pangs or throes of the new birth') what can an infidel think of those and the like ex-pressions in Scripture—'I have roared for the very disquietness of my heart';[10] 'Fearfulness and trembling are come upon me, and an horrible dread hath overwhelmed me'?[11] After his flood of satire on all kind of conflicts with Satan, what judgment can a deist form of what St. Paul speaks concerning the various wrestlings of a Christian with the wicked one?[12] Above all, how will his bringing the lewd heathen poets to expose the pure and spiritual love of God naturally cause them to look with the same eyes on the most elevated passages of the inspired writings? What can be more diverting to them than to apply his γλυκύπικρος ἔρωτος (bitter-sweet of love)[13] to many ex-pressions in the Canticles? (On which undoubtedly he supposes *The Fair Circassian*[14] to be a very just paraphrase!) 'Ay', say they, 'the very case: "Stay me with apples; for I am sick of love".'[15]

[1] Acts 20: 21.   [2] Ps. 51: 17.   [3] Acts 20: 21.   [4] Cf. 1 John 5: 1.   [5] Cf. Rom. 5: 5.
[6] Rom. 14: 17.   [7] Cf. Eph. 6: 12.   [8] 1 John 4: 18.   [9] Cf. Luke 10: 27, etc.
[10] Ps. 38: 8 (B.C.P.).   [11] Ps. 55: 5 (B.C.P.).   [12] See Eph. 6: 12.   [13] Cf. Sappho, 40.
[14] *The Fair Circassian, a Dramatic Performance*. Done from the original by a Gentle-man-Commoner of Oxford [by R.D., i.e., Samuel Croxall]. It appeared in 1720—the year in which Wesley went up to Christ Church, Oxford. The work was very popular. By 1721 it had passed through four editions; by 1756 it had reached the twelfth edition. The 'original' to which the sub-title refers is, of course, the Song of Solomon.
[15] Cf. S. of S. 2: 5.

7. Probably the Comparer will reply, 'No: I do not ridicule the things themselves; repentance, the new birth, the fight of faith, or the love of God—all which I know are essential to religion—but only the folly and the enthusiasm which are blended with these by the Methodists.' But how poor a pretence is this! Had this really been the case, how carefully would he have drawn the line under each of these heads between the sober religion of a Christian and the enthusiasms of a Methodist? But has he done this? Does he take particular care to show under each what is true, as well as what is false, religion? Where the former ends and the latter begins? What are the proper boundaries of each? Your lordship knows he does not so much as endeavour it, or take any pains about it; but indiscriminately pours the flood out of his unclean mouth upon all repentance, faith, love, and holiness.

8. Your lordship will please to observe that I do not here touch in the least on the merits of the cause. Be the Methodists what they may—fools, madmen, enthusiasts, knaves, impostors, Papists, or anything—yet your lordship perceives this does not in any degree affect the point in question. Still it behoves every Christian, nay every reasonable heathen, to consider the subject he is upon, and to take care not to bring this into contempt (especially if it be of the last importance), however inexcusable or contemptible his opponents may be.

9. This consideration, my lord, dwelt much upon my mind when I read the former parts of the Comparison. I immediately saw there was no encountering a buffoon by serious reason and argument. This would naturally have furnished both him and his admirers with fresh matter of ridicule. On the other hand, if I should let myself down to a level with him, and by a less serious manner of writing than I was accustomed to, I was afraid of debasing the dignity of the subject. Nay, and I knew not but I might catch something of his spirit. I remembered the advice: 'Answer not a fool according to his folly, lest thou also be like unto him.' And yet I saw there must be an exception in some cases, as the words immediately following show: 'Answer a fool according to his folly, lest he be wise in his own conceit.'[a] I conceive, as if he had said, 'yet it is needful in some cases to "answer a fool according to his folly". Otherwise he will be "wiser in his own conceit than seven men that can render

---

[a] Prov. 26: 4, 5.

a reason".'¹ I therefore constrained myself to approach as near as I dared to his own manner of writing. And I trust the occasion will plead my excuse with your lordship and all reasonable men.

10. One good effect of my thus meeting him on his own ground is visible already. Instead of endeavouring to defend, he entirely gives up the First Part of his Comparison. Indeed I did not expect this when I observed that the Third Part was addressed to me. I took it for granted that he had therein aimed at something like a reply to my answer. But going on I found myself quite mistaken. He never once attempts a reply to one page, any otherwise than by screaming out, 'Pertness, scurrility, effrontery', and in subjoining that deep remark, 'Paper and time would be wasted on such stuff.'ᵃ

11. I cannot but account it another good effect that he is something less confident than he was before. He is likewise (not more angry or more bitter, for that cannot be but) a few degrees more serious. So that I plainly perceive this is the way I am to take if I should have leisure to answer the Third Part. Although it is far from my desire to write in this manner—it is as contrary to my inclination as to my custom.

12. But is it possible that a person of your lordship's character should countenance such a performance as this? It cannot be your lordship's desire to pour contempt on all that is truly venerable among men! To stab Christianity to the heart under the colour of opposing enthusiasm! And to increase and give a sanction to the profaneness which already overspreads our land as a flood.

13. Were the Methodists ever so bad, yet are they not too despicable and inconsiderable for your lordship's notice? 'Against whom is the King of Israel come out? Against a flea? Against a partridge upon the mountains?'² Such they undoubtedly are, if that representation of them be just which the Comparer has given. Against whom (if your lordship espouses his cause) are you stirring up the supreme power of the nation? Against whom does your lordship arm the ministers of all denominations, particularly our brethren of the Established Church; inciting them to point us out to their several congregations as not fit to live upon the earth? The effects of this have already appeared in many parts both of Devonshire and Cornwall. Nor have I known any considerable riot in any part of England for which such preaching did not pave the way.

ᵃ [Lavington, *Enthusiasm*,] Third Part, Preface, p. xv.

¹ Prov. 26: 16.   ² Cf. 1 Sam. 26: 20.

14. I beg leave to ask, would it be a satisfaction to your lordship if national persecution were to return? Does your lordship desire to revive the old laws, *de haeretico comburendo*?[1] Would your lordship rejoice to see the Methodists themselves tied to so many stakes in
5　Smithfield? Or would you applaud the execution, though not so legally or decently performed by the mob of Exeter, Plymouth Dock, or Launceston? My lord, what profit would there be in our blood? Would it be an addition to your lordship's happiness? Or any advantage to the Protestant cause? Or any honour either to our
10　Church or nation?

15. The Comparer doubtless would answer, 'Yes: for it would prevent the horrid consequences of your preaching.' My lord, give me leave to say once more:

　　I willingly put the whole cause upon this issue. What are the general
15　consequences of our preaching? Are there more *tares* or *wheat*? More *good men destroyed* (as Mr. Church once supposed) or *wicked men saved*? The last places in your lordship's diocese where we began constant preaching are near Liskeard in Cornwall, and at Tiverton in Devonshire. Now let any man inquire here, (1). What kind of people
20　were those a year ago, who now constantly hear this preaching? (2). What are the *main doctrines* the Methodists have been teaching this twelve-month? (3). What *effect* have these doctrines had upon their hearers? And if you do not find, (1), that the greater part of these were a year or two ago notoriously wicked men; (2), yet the
25　main doctrines they have heard since were, 'Love God and your neighbour, and carefully keep his commandments'; and (3), that they have since exercised themselves herein, and continue so to do—I say, if any reasonable man, who will be at the pains to inquire, does not find this to be an unquestionable fact, I will openly acknowledge
30　myself an enthusiast, or whatever else he shall please to style me.[a]

16. I beg leave to conclude this address to your lordship with a few more words transcribed from the same letter.

'Allow Mr. Wesley (says Mr. Church) but these few points, and he

---

[a] *Second Letter to Mr. Church*, p. 74 [i.e. *The Principles of a Methodist Farther Explained*, VI. 8. Wesley modifies his original text to suit Lavington's circumstances.]

[1] *De haeretico comburendo* (2 Henry IV, c. 15), an Act passed in 1401 to assist in the suppression of Lollardry. By its provisions, a person suspected of heresy was tried in the ecclesiastical courts by canon law. If the bishop pronounced him guilty, he was to be handed over to the secular authorities to be burnt alive—to deter others. The statute was repealed in the reign of Elizabeth I.

will defend his conduct beyond expectation.'[1] That is most true. If I '*have* indeed *been advancing* nothing but the true knowledge and love of God'; if God has made me an *instrument* in *reforming* many sinners, and bringing them to *inward and pure religion*; and if many of these continue holy to this day, and free from all wilful sin: then may I, even   5 I, use those awful words, 'He that despiseth me, despiseth him that sent me.' But I never expect the world to allow me one of these points. However, I must go on, as God shall enable me. I must lay out whatsoever talents He entrusts me with (whether others will believe I do it or no) in advancing the true Christian knowledge of God, and the love   10 and fear of God among men; in reforming (if so be it please him to use me still) those who are yet without God in the world; and in propagating inward and pure religion, righteousness, peace, and joy in the Holy Ghost.[2]

Sincerely wishing your lordship all happiness in time and in   15 eternity,

I remain,
Your lordship's most
Obedient servant,
John Wesley   20

Nov. 27, 1750

---

[1] Wesley, *The Principles of a Methodist Farther Explained*, p. 75, and Church, *Some Farther Remarks on the Rev. Mr. John Wesley's Last Journal*, p. v, read 'beyond exception'.

[2] Wesley, *The Principles of a Methodist Farther Explained*, VI. 9; the closing reference is to Rom. 14: 17.

A SECOND
LETTER

To the AUTHOR of the
ENTHUSIASM
OF
METHODISTS, &c.

Sir,

1. You have undertaken to prove (as I observed in my former *Letter*, a few sentences of which I beg leave to repeat)[1] that the 'whole conduct of the Methodists is but a counterpart of the most wild 5 fanaticisms of popery'.[a]

You endeavour to support this charge by quotations from our own writings, compared with quotations from popish authors.

It lies upon me to answer for one. But in order to spare both you and myself, I shall at present consider only your Second Part, and 10 that as briefly as possible. Accordingly I shall not meddle with your other quotations, but leaving them to whom they may concern shall examine whether those you have made from my writings prove the charge for which they were made or not.

If they do, I submit. But if they do not, if they are 'the words of 15 truth and soberness',[2] it is an objection of no real weight against any sentiment just in itself, though it should also be found in the writings of Papists; yea, of Mahometans or pagans.

2. In your first section, in order to prove the 'vain boastings of the Methodists',[3] you quote a part of the following sentence: 'When 20 hath religion, I will not say since the Reformation, but since the

---

[a] Preface to the First Part [of *The Enthusiasm of Methodists, etc.*], p. 3.

---

[1] The whole of this first section is an adaptation of §§ 1 and 2 of Wesley's *A Letter to the Author of The Enthusiasm of Methodists, etc.*, largely word for word, this letter promising to consider Lavington's Second Part, while the former one dealt with the first.

[2] Acts 26: 25.   [3] Cf. *Enthusiasm*, Pt. II, Sect. I, § 3, pp. 12–27.

time of Constantine the Great, made so large a progress in any nation within so short a space?'¹ (I beg any impartial person to read the whole passage, from the eighty-fourth to the ninetieth page of the third *Appeal*.)² I repeat the question, giving the glory to God. And, I trust, without either boasting or enthusiasm.　　　　　　　5

In your second, you cite (and murder) four or five lines from one of my *Journals* as instances of 'the persuasive eloquence' of the Methodist Preachers.ª But it unfortunately happens that neither of the sentences you quote were spoke by any preacher at all. You know full well the one was used only in a private letter, the other by 10 a woman on a bed of sickness.

3. You next undertake to prove 'the most insufferable *pride* and *vanity* of the Methodists'.ᵇ For this end you quote five passages from my *Journals* and one from the third *Appeal*.

The first was wrote in the anguish of my heart, to which I gave 15 vent (between God and my own soul) by breaking out, not into 'confidence of boasting',³ as you term it, but into those expressions of bitter sorrow: 'I went to America to convert the Indians. But O! who shall convert me!'ᶜ Some of the words which follow you have picked out, and very honestly laid before your reader without 20 either the beginning or end, or one word of the occasion or manner wherein they were spoken.

Your next question is equally fair and generous. 'Are they read in philosophy? So was I, etc.'ᵈ This whole 'string of self-commendation', as you call it, being there brought, *ex professo*,⁴ to prove that 25 notwithstanding all this, which I once piqued myself upon, I was at that hour in a state of damnation!

The third is a plain narrative of the manner wherein many of Bristol expressed their joy on my coming unexpectedly into the room, after I had been some time at London. And this, I conceive, 30

ª [*Enthusiasm*, Pt. II, Sect. II,] pp. 1, 9. [There is some error in Wesley's citation, for Sect. II comprises pp. 5–12, and the actual phrase quoted by Wesley occurs on p. 5. It is difficult to identify any specific quotations from Wesley, and Lavington gives no citations.]

ᵇ [Ibid.,] Sect. 3, p. 12, etc.

ᶜ 1st *Journal*, p. 67, etc. [Jan. 24, 1738, quoted in *Enthusiasm*, Pt. II, p. 21.]

ᵈ Ibid., p. 68, etc. [Feb. 1, 1738, quoted ibid.]

---

¹ Wesley, *A Farther Appeal*, Pt. III, I. 7. The quotation in Lavington's *Enthusiasm* (Pt. II, p. 4) reads: 'No work has been wrought so swiftly, so extensively, since Constantine the Great.'   ² Ibid., I. 4–14.

³ 2 Cor. 11: 17.   ⁴ 'Professedly, by open acknowledgment.'

will prove the charge of high treason, as well as that of 'insufferable *pride* and *vanity*'.[a]

You say, fourthly, a dying woman, who had earnestly desired to see me, cried out as I entered the room, 'Art thou come, thou
5 blessed of the Lord?'[b] She did so. And what does this prove?

The fifth passage is this: 'In applying which my soul was so enlarged that methought I could have cried out (in another sense than poor, vain Archimedes) "Give me where to stand, and I will shake the earth."'[1] My meaning is, I found such freedom of thought
10 and speech (jargon, stuff, enthusiasm to you) that methought could I have then spoken to all the world, they would all have shared in the blessing.

[4.] The passage which you quote from the third *Appeal*[2] I am obliged to relate more at large:
15 'There is one more excuse for denying this work of God, taken from the instruments employed therein; that is, that they are wicked men. And a thousand stories have been handed about to prove it....'

'Yet I cannot but remind considerate men in how remarkable a manner the wisdom of God has for many years guarded against
20 this pretence with regard to my brother and me in particular.' This pretence, i.e. 'of not employing fit instruments'. These words are yours, though you insert them as mine. The pretence I mentioned was, 'That they were wicked men.' And how God guarded against this is shown in what follows: 'From that time both my brother and
25 I (utterly against our will) came to be more and more observed and known, till we were more spoken of than perhaps two so inconsiderable persons ever were before in the nation. To make us more public still, as *honest* madmen at least, by a strange concurrence of providences overturning all our preceding resolutions we were hurried
30 away to America.'

Afterward it follows: 'What persons could in the nature of things have been (antecedently) less liable to exception, with regard to their moral character at least, than those the all-wise God hath now employed? Indeed I cannot devise what manner of men could have

---

[a] 4th *Journal*, p. 85 [May 18, 1741, quoted ibid., pp. 21-2].
[b] Ibid., p. 96 [July 31, 1741, quoted ibid., p. 22. Lavington implies that this took place in 'a religious meeting'. The biblical quotation is from Gen. 24: 31].

---

[1] *Journal*, May 20, 1739, quoted *Enthusiasm*, Pt. II, p. 22. For the reference to Archimedes, cf. *A Letter to the Bishop of London*, § 20, p. 350 above.
[2] *A Farther Appeal*, Pt. III, III. 18, quoted *Enthusiasm*, Pt. II, p. 22.

been more unexceptionable on all accounts. Had God endued us with greater natural or acquired abilities, this very thing might have been turned into an objection. Had we been remarkably defective, it would have been matter of objection on the other hand. Had we been *Dissenters* of any kind, or even Low-Churchmen (so called), it would have been a great stumbling-block in the way of those who are "zealous for the church".[1] And yet had we continued in the impetuosity of our High Church zeal, neither should we have been willing to converse with Dissenters, nor they to receive any good at our hands.'[2] Sir, why did you break off your quotation in the middle of this paragraph, just at 'more unexceptionable on all accounts'? Was it not on purpose to give a wrong turn to the whole? To conceal the real and obvious meaning of my words, and put one upon them that never entered into my thoughts?

5. You have reserved your strong reason for the last, namely, my own confession. 'Mr. Wesley says himself, "By the most infallible of proofs, *inward feeling*, I am convinced of pride, etc."'[3] Sir, be pleased to decipher that 'etc.' Or I will spare you the pains, and do it myself by reciting the whole sentence:

By the most infallible of proofs, inward feeling, I am convinced:
(1). Of unbelief, having no such faith in Christ as will prevent my heart from being troubled, which it could not be if I believed in God, and rightly believed also in him.
(2). Of pride throughout my life past, inasmuch as I thought I had what I find I have not.[a]

Now, sir, you have my whole confession. I entreat you to make the best of it.

'But I myself acknowledge three Methodists to have fallen into pride.' Sir, I can tell you of three more. And yet it will not follow that the doctrines I teach 'lead men into *horrid pride and blasphemy*'.[4]

6. In the close of your fourth section you charge me with 'shuffling and prevaricating' with regard to 'extraordinary gifts and miraculous powers'.[5] Of these I shall have occasion to speak by and by. At

---

[a] 1st *Journal*, p. 64 [Jan. 8, 1738].

[1] Cf. Acts 21: 20.
[2] *Farther Appeal*, Pt. III, III. 19, quoted *Enthusiasm*, Pt. II, p. 22.
[3] Lavington, *Enthusiasm*, Pt. II, p. 24.
[4] Ibid., p. 26. On pp. 25–6 Lavington had given 'several instances' of such a 'tendency to pride', including three from Wesley's *Journal* for Sept. 3, 1740, which apparently led to his condensed summary of Lavington's charges.   [5] Ibid., p. 36.

present I need only return the compliment, by charging you with gross, wilful prevarication from the beginning of your book to the end. Some instances of this have appeared already. Many more will appear in due time.

5   7. Your fifth charges me with an 'affectation of prophesying'.[1] Your first proof of it is this:

'It was about this time that the soldier was executed. For some time I had visited him every day. But when the love of God was shed abroad in his heart,[2] I told him, "do not expect to see me any 10 more. . . . I believe Satan will separate us for a season." Accordingly, the next day I was informed the commanding officer had given strict orders that neither Mr. Wesley nor any of his people should be admitted.'[a] I did believe so, having seen many such things before; yet without affecting a spirit of prophecy.

15   But that I do claim it you will prove, secondly, from my mentioning 'the great work which God *intends*, and is now *beginning* to work over all the earth'.[3] By what art you extract such a conclusion out of such premises, I know not. That God *intends* this, none who believe the Scripture doubt. And that he has *begun* it, both in Europe and 20 America, any who will make use of their eyes and ears may know without any 'miraculous gift of prophesying'.

8. In your sixth section you assert that I lay claim to other *miraculous gifts*.[b] As you borrow this objection from Mr. Church, I need only give the same answer I gave before.

25   'I shall give' (says Mr. Church) 'but one account more, and that is what you give of yourself.' The sum whereof is 'At two several times, being ill and in violent pain, I prayed to God, and found immediate ease.' I did so. I assert the fact still. 'But if these' (you say) 'are not miraculous cures, all this is rank enthusiasm.'

30   I will put your argument in form:

He that believes those are miraculous cures which are not, is a rank enthusiast.
But you believe those to be miraculous cures which are not:
Therefore you are a rank enthusiast.

---

[a] 4th *Journal*, p. 30 [Mar. 29, 1740, quoted less fully in *Enthusiasm*, p. 40].
[b] [*Enthusiasm*, Pt. II,] pp. 45, etc.

---

[1] Lavington, *Enthusiasm*, Pt. II, p. 36.   [2] See Rom. 5: 5.
[3] *Enthusiasm*, Pt. II, p. 40, citing 2nd *Journal*, pp. 19 and 35, the first quotation apparently in justification of 'intends' (*Journal*, May 4–10, 1738), and the latter one a quotation from the *Journal* for June 17, 1738.

Before I answer, I must know what you mean by 'miraculous'. If you term everything so which is 'not strictly accountable for by the ordinary course of natural causes', then I deny the latter part of the second proposition. And unless you can make this good, unless you can prove the effects in question are strictly accountable for by the ordinary course 5 of natural causes, your argument is nothing worth.[a]

Having largely answered your next objection relating to what I still term, 'a signal instance of God's particular providence', I need only refer you to those answers, not having leisure to say the same thing ten times over.[b]   10

Whether I sometimes claim, and sometimes disclaim miracles, will be considered by and by.

[9.] In your seventh section you say, 'I shall . . . now give some account . . . of their grievous *conflicts* and *combats* with Satan.'[c] O, sir, spare yourself, if not the Methodists! Do not go so far out of 15 your depth. This is a subject you are as utterly unacquainted with as with justification or the new birth.

But I attend your motions. 'Mr. Wesley', you say, 'was advised . . . to [observe] a very high degree of silence. . . . And he spoke to none at all for two days, and travelling fourscore miles together.'   20

'The same whim (you go on) has run through several of the religious orders. . . . Hence St. Bonaventura says that silence in all religious is necessary to perfection. . . . St. Agatho held a stone in his mouth for three years, till he had learned taciturnity. . . . St. Alcantara carried several pebbles in his mouth for three years like- 25 wise, and for the same reason.—Theon observed a continual silence for thirty years.—St. Francis observed it himself, and enjoined it upon his brethren. The rule of silence was religiously observed by St. Dominic.'[1]

I have repeated more of your words than I otherwise should, in 30 order to show to a demonstration that a man of a lively imagina- tion may run a parallel to any length without any foundation in nature.

---

[a] *First Letter to Mr. Church*, p. 45 [*An Answer to the Rev. Mr. Church's Remarks*, III. 12, quoting Thomas Church, *Remarks on the Rev. Mr. John Wesley's Last Journal*, pp. 72–3].
   [b] Ibid., p. 42 [III. 8, and] *Second Letter*, p. 46 [*The Principles of a Methodist Farther Explained*, IV. 5. The 'signal instance' is from Wesley's *Journal* for Feb. 17, 1741].
   [c] [*Enthusiasm*, Pt. II,] p. 51, etc.

---

[1] *Enthusiasm*, Pt. II, pp. 61–2.

You begin: 'The same whim' which led Mr. Wesley to observe an absolute silence for two days—and so run on to St. Bonaventura, St. Agatho, and I know not whom. But did Mr. Wesley observe an 'absolute silence' for two days? No; not for one hour. My words, 'I spoke to none at all for fourscore miles together', imply neither more nor less than that I spoke to none 'concerning the things of God', as it is in the words immediately preceding.ᵃ And you know this as well as I. But 'tis all one for that. Wit, not truth, is the point you aim at.

My supposed inconsistency with regard to the Moravians, which you likewise drag in (as they say) by head and shoulders, I have shown again and again to be no inconsistency at all; particularly in both the letters to Mr. Church.

10. Well, but as to *conflicts* with Satan: 'Nor can Mr. Wesley (you say) escape the attacks of this infernal spirit', namely, suggesting distrustful thoughts, and buffeting him with inward temptations.[1] Sir, did you never hear of anyone so attacked, unless among the Papists or Methodists? How deeply then are you experienced both in the ways of God, and the devices of Satan?

You add, with regard to a case mentioned in the fourth *Journal*,ᵇ 'Though I am not convinced that these *fits of laughing* are to be ascribed to Satan, yet I entirely agree that they are *involuntary* and *unavoidable*.'[2] I am glad we agree so far. But I must still go farther. I cannot but ascribe them to a preternatural agent, having observed so many circumstances attending them which cannot be accounted for by any natural causes.

Under the head of conflicts with Satan you observe farther: 'Mr. Wesley says, while he was preaching the devil knew his kingdom shook, and therefore stirred up his servants to . . . make a noise';[3] that September 18 'The prince of the air made another attempt in defence of his tottering kingdom';[4] and that another time 'the devil's children fought valiantly for their master'.[5] I own the whole charge. I did say all this. Nay, and if need were I should say it again.

ᵃ 4th *Journal*, p. 86 [June 8, 1741. The phrase 'absolute silence' is used by Lavington of the mystics and religious orders].
ᵇ [Ibid.,] p. 37 [May 9, 1740].

---

[1] *Enthusiasm*, Pt. II, p. 70.   [2] Ibid., p. 72.
[3] Ibid., p. 73, citing *Journal* for May 13, 1740.
[4] Ibid., citing *Journal* for Sept. 18, 1740.
[5] Ibid., citing *Journal* for May 3, 1741.

You cite one more instance from my fourth *Journal*: 'The *many-headed beast* began to roar again.'[1] So your head is so full of the subject that you construe even poor Horace's *bellua multorum capitum*[2] into the devil!

These are all the combats and conflicts with Satan which you can 5 prove I ever had. O, sir, without more and greater conflicts than these none shall see the Kingdom of God.

11. In the following sections you are equally out of your element. The first of them relates to 'spiritual desertions';[a] all which you make the subject of dull ridicule, and place to the account of enthu- 10 siasm. And the case of all you give in the following words: 'We may look upon enthusiasm as a kind of drunkenness, filling and intoxicating the brain with the heated fumes of spirituous particles. Now no sooner does the inebriation go off, but a coldness and dullness takes place.'[3]   15

12. As wildly do you talk of the doubts and fears incident to those who are 'weak in faith',[b] I cannot prevail upon myself to prostitute this awful subject by entering into any debate concerning it with one who is innocent of the whole affair. Only I must observe that a great part of what you advance concerning me is entirely wide of 20 the question. Such is all you quote from the first, and a considerable part of what you quote from my second *Journal*. This you know in your own conscience; for you know I speak of myself during the whole time as having no faith at all. Consequently, the 'risings and fallings' I experienced then have nothing to do with those 'doubts 25 and fears which many go through *after* they have by faith received remission of sins'.[4]

The next words which you cite, 'thrown into great perplexities', I cannot find in the page you refer to.[5] Neither those that follow. The sum of them is, that at that time I did not feel the love of God, 30 but found deadness and wanderings in public prayer, and coldness even at the Holy Communion. Well, sir, and have you never found in yourself any such coldness, deadness, and wanderings? I am

---

[a] [*Enthusiasm*, Pt. II,] § 8, p. 75, etc.   [b] [Ibid.,] § 9, p. 79, etc.

[1] Ibid., citing *Journal* for Oct. 26, 1740.
[2] 'Many-headed monster', Horace, *Epistles*, I. i. 76. *Belua* is the more usual spelling.
[3] *Enthusiasm*, Pt. II, p. 79.   [4] Ibid., p. 80.
[5] Ibid., p. 81. Lavington apparently summarizes thus the questionings in Wesley's *Journal* entry for Feb. 1, 1738, but inserts this summary without distinction among his quotations from Wesley.

persuaded you have. And yet surely your brain is always cool and temperate! Never 'intoxicated with the heated fumes of spirituous particles'!

13. If you quote, not incoherent scraps (by which you may make anything out of anything), but entire connected sentences, it will appear that the rest of your quotations make no more for your purpose than the foregoing. Thus, although I allow that on May 24 [1738] 'I was much buffeted with temptations, but I cried to God and they fled away; that they returned again and again; I as often lifted up my eyes, and he sent me help from his holy place'; it will only prove the very observation I make myself: 'I was fighting both "under the law" and "under grace". But then I was sometimes, if not often, conquered; now I was always conqueror.'[a]

That sometime after I 'was strongly assaulted again, and after recovering peace and joy, was thrown into perplexity afresh by a letter asserting that no doubt or fear could consist with true faith; that my weak mind could not then bear to be thus sawn asunder', will not appear strange to any who are not utter novices in experimental religion.[1] No more than that one night the next year 'I had no life or spirit in me, and was much in doubt whether God would not lay me aside and send other labourers into his harvest.'[2]

14. You add, 'He owns his frequent relapses into sin for near twice ten years. Such is the case of a person who tells us that he carefully considered every step he took; . . . one of intimate communication with the deity.'[3] Sir, I did not tell you that; though according to custom you mark the words as mine. 'Tis well for you that *forging quotations* is not felony.

My words are: 'O what an hypocrite have I been (if this be so) for near twice ten years! But I know it is not so. I know every one "under the law" is even as I was'; namely from the time I was twelve years old till considerably above thirty.

---

[a] 3rd *Journal*, pp. 30, 31 [actually 2nd *Journal*, § 16 of Wesley's 'conversion' narrative, May 24, 1738. Lavington, *Enthusiasm*, Pt. II, p. 82, had quoted (without citing the source) fragments only from §§ 14–16: 'At length, my heart was strangely warmed,—had an *assurance of forgiveness.*—The *enemy* suggested, this cannot be faith,—was much *buffeted with temptations*: but cried out, and they fled away. They returned again, and again, etc.'].

---

[1] Lavington, *Enthusiasm*, Pt. II, p. 83, incorrectly citing '2 Journ. pag. 27'. The phrases come from *Journal*, June 3–7, 1738.

[2] Ibid., correctly cited from *Journal*, June 22, 1739.

[3] Ibid., citing *Journal*, Aug. 31, 1739.

'And is it not strange (you say) that such a one should be destitute of means to resolve his scruples? Should be ever at variance with himself, and find no place to fix his foot?'

Good sir, not too fast. You quite outrun the truth again. Blessed be God, this is not my case. I am not destitute of means to resolve 5 my scruples. I have some friends, and a little reason left. I am not ever at variance with myself; and have found a place to fix my foot:

> Now I have found the ground wherein
> Firm my soul's anchor may remain;
> The wounds of Jesus, for my sin   10
> Before the world's foundation slain.[1]

And yet one of your assertions I cannot deny: namely, that you 'could run the parallel' between me and 'numbers of fanatical Papists'. And that not only with regard to my temper, but my stature, complexion, yea (if need were) the very colour of my hair.   15

15. In your next section you are to give an account of the 'spiritual succours and advantages received either during these trials or very soon after'.[a] 'Tis no wonder you make as lame work with these as with the conflicts which preceded them. 'As the heart knoweth its own bitterness, so a stranger doth not intermeddle with his 20 joy.'[2] But 'tis no business of mine, as you have not done me the honour to cite any of my words in this Section.

16. 'The unsteadiness of the Methodists both in sentiments and practice' is what you next undertake to prove.[b] Your loose declamation with which you open the cause I pass over, as it rests on your 25 own bare word; and haste to your main reason, drawn from my sentiments and practice with regard to the Moravians.

'He represents them' (you say) 'in the blackest colours; . . . yet declares, "in the main they are some of the best people in the world". . . . His love and esteem for them increases more and more. 30 . . . His own disciples among the Methodists go over to them in crowds. But still Methodism is the strongest barrier against the Moravian doctrines and principles.'[3]

---

[a] [*Enthusiasm*, Pt. II,] § 10, p. 92 etc.   [b] [Ibid.,] § 11, p. 95 etc.

---

[1] John and Charles Wesley, 'Redemption Found', *Hymns and Sacred Poems*, 1740, p. 91 (*Poet. Wks.*, I. 279), the first four lines of the opening stanza of John Wesley's translation of a hymn by Johann Andreas Rothe (1688–1758).

[2] Cf. Prov. 14: 10.

[3] *Enthusiasm*, Pt. II, p. 97; Lavington's one citation in this passage is incorrect.

Sir, I bear you witness you have learnt one principle at least from those with whom you have lately conversed; namely, that no faith is to be kept with heretics—of which you have given us abundant proof. For you know I have fully answered every article of this
5 charge, which you repeat as if I had not opened my lips about it. You know that there is not one grain of truth in several things which you here positively assert. For instance, 'His love and esteem of them increases more and more.' Not so, no more than my love and esteem for *you*. I love you both; but I do not much esteem either.
10 Again, 'His own disciples among the Methodists go over to them in crowds.' When? Where? I know not that ten of my disciples, as you call them, have gone over to them for twice ten months. O sir, consider! How do you know but some of your disciples may tell your name?

15 17. With the same veracity you go on. 'In *The Character of a Methodist* those of the sect are described as having all the virtues that can adorn the Christian profession. But in their *journals* you find them waspish, condemning all the world except themselves; and among themselves perpetual broils and confusions, with various
20 other irregularities and vices.'[1]

I answer, (1). The tract you refer to (as is expressly declared in the preface) does not describe what the Methodists are already, but what they desire to be, and what they will be then when they fully practise the doctrine they hear. (2). Be pleased to point the pages in my
25 *Journals* which mention those 'various irregularities and vices'. Of their 'perpetual broils and confusions' I shall speak under their proper head.[2]

You add, 'Sometimes they are so far from fearing death that they wish it. But the keenness of the edge is soon blunted. . . . They
30 are full of dreadful apprehensions . . . that the clergy *intend to murder* them.'[3] Do you mean me, sir? I plead not guilty. I never had any such apprehension. Yet I suppose you designed the compliment for me, by your dragging in two or three broken sentences from my first *Journal*. But how little to the purpose, seeing at the time that
35 was written I had never pretended to be above the fear of death. So that this is no proof of the point in view, of the 'unsteadiness of my sentiments or practice'.

[1] *Enthusiasm*, Pt. II, p. 98. For *The Character of a Methodist* see Volume 9 of this edition, *The Methodist Societies: History, Nature and Design*; see also *Bibliography*, No. 57.   [2] See §§ 32–5 below.   [3] *Enthusiasm*, Pt. II, p. 99.

18. You proceed, 'One day they fancy it their duty to preach; the next, they "preach with great reluctance".'¹ Very true! But they fancy it their duty still; else they would not preach at all. This therefore does not prove any 'inequality either of sentiment or practice'.   5

'Mr. Wesley is sometimes "quite averse from speaking", and then perplexed with the doubt, "Is it a prohibition from the good Spirit? Or a temptation from nature and the evil one?"'²

Just of a piece with the rest. The sentence runs thus: 'I went several times with a design to speak to the sailors, but could not. 10 I mean, I was quite averse from speaking. . . . Is not this what men commonly mean by, "I could not speak"? And is this a sufficient cause of silence, or no? Is it a prohibition from the good Spirit? Or a temptation from nature or the evil one?'ᵃ Sir, I was in no doubt at all on the occasion. Nor did I intend to express any in these 15 words; but to appeal to men's conscience whether what they call a prohibition from the good Spirit be not a mere temptation from nature or the evil one.

19. In the next Section you are to show the 'art, *cunning*, and *sophistry*' of the Methodists, who 'when hard pressed by argument 20 run themselves into inconsistency and *self-contradiction*: and occasionally either defend or give up some of their favourite notions and principal points'.ᵇ

I dare say, sir, you will not put them to the trial. *Argument* lies out of the way of one,   25

Solutos
*Qui captat risus hominum famamque dicacis.*³

But to the proof. 'Mr. Wesley (you say) at one time declares for a disinterested love of God'; at another declares, 'There is no one caution in all the Bible against the selfish love of God.'⁴   30

Nay, sir, I will tell you what is stranger still. Mr. Wesley holds *at one time* both sides of this contradiction. I now declare, both that

---

ᵃ 1st *Journal*, p. 63 [Jan. 2, 1738].
ᵇ [*Enthusiasm*, Pt. II,] § 12, p. 102.

---

¹ Ibid., p. 100.   ² Ibid., p. 101.
³ Horace, *Satires*, I. iv. 82–3. Wesley's translation: 'one that affects the droll, and loves to raise a horse-laugh' (*Works*, Vol. 32 (1774), Appendix).
⁴ *Enthusiasm*, Pt. II, pp. 102–3, citing Wesley's *Journal*, Aug. 8, 1740, § 12

'all true love is disinterested, "seeketh not her own" ;[1] and that there is no one caution in all the Bible against the selfish love of God.'

What, have I the *art* to slip out of your hands again? 'Pardon me (as your old friend says) for being jocular.'[2]

5   20. You add (*altius insurgens*),[3] 'but it is a considerable offence to charge another wrongfully and contradict himself about the doctrine of assurances'.[4] To prove this upon me you bring my own words. 'The assurance we preach is of quite another kind from that Mr. Bedford writes against. We speak of an assurance of our present
10 pardon; not, as he does, of our final perseverance.'[a]

'Mr. Wesley might have considered (you say) that when they talk of "assurance of pardon and salvation", the world will extend the meaning of the words to our eternal state.' I do consider it, sir. And therefore I never use that phrase, either in preaching or writing.
15 'Assurance of pardon and salvation' is an expression that never comes out of my lips. And if Mr. Whitefield does use it, yet he does not *preach* such an assurance as the privilege of all Christians.

'But Mr. Wesley himself says that though a "full assurance of faith does not necessarily imply a full assurance of our future
20 perseverance", yet "some have both the one and the other". And now what becomes of his charge against Mr. Bedford? And is it not mere evasion to say afterwards, "This is not *properly* an assurance of what is future"?'[5]

Sir, this 'argument' *presses* me very *hard*! May I not be allowed
25 a little *evasion* now? Come, for once I will try to do without it, and to answer flat and plain.

And I answer, (1), that faith is one thing, the 'full assurance of faith'[6] another; (2), that even the *'full assurance of faith'* does not imply the *'full assurance of perseverance'*. This bears another name,
30 being styled by St. Paul 'the full assurance of hope'.[7] (3). Some Christians have only the first of these. They have faith, but mixed with doubts and fears. Some have also the full assurance of faith,

---

[a] 3rd *Journal*, p. 9 [Oct. 6, 1738. See above, *A Letter to the Author of the Enthusiasm of the Methodists*, § 21].

---

[1] 1 Cor. 13: 5.

[2] J. Addison, *The Drummer, or the Haunted House* (1716), Act II, Sc. i. Addison and Lavington were fellow Whigs.

[3] 'Mounting higher.' Cf. Virgil, *Aeneid*, xii. 902.   [4] *Enthusiasm*, Pt. II, p. 103.

[5] Ibid., pp. 103-4, citing Wesley's sermon *Free Grace*, § 14.

[6] Heb. 10: 22.   [7] Heb. 6: 11.

a full conviction of *present pardon*: and yet not the *full assurance of hope*—not a full conviction of their *future perseverance*. (4). The faith which we preach as necessary to all Christians is the first of these, and no other; Therefore, (5), it is no evasion at all to say, 'This (the faith which we preach as necessary to all Christians) is not *properly* an assurance of what is future.' And consequently my charge against Mr. Bedford stands good: 'That his sermon on assurance is an *ignoratio elenchi* (an ignorance of the point in question) from beginning to end.' Therefore neither do I 'charge another *wrongfully*, nor *contradict myself*, about the doctrine of assurances'.

21. To prove my *art*, *cunning*, and *evasion*, you instance next in the case of *impulses* and *impressions*. You begin: 'With what pertinacious confidence have impulses, impressions, feelings, etc., been advanced into *certain rules* of conduct? Their followers have been taught to depend upon them, as sure guides and *infallible proofs*.'[1]

To support this weighty charge you bring one single scrap, about a line and a quarter from one of my *Journals*. The words are these: 'By the most *infallible of proofs*, *inward feeling*, I am convinced.' Convinced of what? It immediately follows: 'Of unbelief, having no such faith as will prevent my heart from being troubled.'[2]

I here assert that *inward feeling*, or consciousness, is the *most infallible of proofs* of unbelief, of the want of such a faith as will prevent the heart's being troubled. But do I here 'advance impressions, impulses, feelings, etc., into "certain rules" of conduct'? Or anywhere else? You may just as well say I advance them into certain proofs of transubstantiation.

Neither in writing, in preaching, nor in private conversation, have I ever 'taught any of my followers to depend upon them as sure guides or infallible proofs' of anything.

Nay, you yourself own I have taught quite the reverse—and that at my very first setting out. Then, as well as ever since, I have told the societies they were not to judge 'by their own *inward feelings*'. 'I warned them all these were in themselves of a doubtful, disputable nature. They *might* be from God, or they *might not*, and were therefore . . . to be tried by a farther rule, to be brought to the only certain test, the law and the testimony.'[a]

---

[a] 3rd *Journal*, pp. 60, 61 [June 22, 1739].

[1] *Enthusiasm*, Pt. II, pp. 104-5.
[2] The reference is apparently to Lavington's *Enthusiasm*, Pt. II, p. 116, citing Wesley's *Journal*, Jan. 8, 1738, though at much greater length than stated.

This is what I have taught from first to last. And now, sir, what becomes of your heavy charge? On which side lies the 'pertinacious confidence' now? How clearly have you made out my 'inconsistency and self-contradiction'? And that I 'occasionally either defend or
5 give up my favourite notions and principal points'?

22. 'Inspiration, and the extraordinary calls and guidances of the Holy Ghost', are what you next affirm to be *given up*.[a] Not by me. I do not *give up* one tittle on this head which I ever maintained. But observe. Before you attempt to prove my 'giving them up',
10 you are to prove that I laid claim to them—that I laid claim to some *extraordinary* inspiration, call, or guidance of the Holy Ghost.

You say my *concessions* on this head (to Mr. Church) are *ambiguous* and *evasive*.[1] Sir, you mistake the fact. I make no concessions at all, either to him or you. I give up nothing that ever I advance on this
15 head. But when Mr. Church charged me with what I did not advance I replied, 'I claim no other direction of God's [Spirit] but what is common to all believers. . . . I pretend to be no otherwise *inspired* than you are, if you love God.' Where is the *ambiguity* or *evasion* in this? I meant it for a flat denial of the charge.

20 23. Your next section *spirat tragicum satis*,[2] charges the Methodists 'with *scepticism and infidelity*, with doubts and denials of the truth of revelation, and atheism itself'.[b] The passages brought from my *Journals* to prove this charge, which you have prudently transposed, I beg leave to consider in the same order as they stand
25 there.

The first you preface thus: 'Upon the people's *ill usage* (or *supposed* ill usage) of Mr. Wesley in Georgia, and their speaking of all manner of evil, *falsely* (as he says), against him; and trampling under foot the word, after having been very attentive to it, what an emotion
30 in him is hereby raised! "I do hereby bear witness against myself that . . . *I could scarce refrain from giving the lie to experience, reason, and Scripture all together.*" '[3]

---

[a] [*Enthusiasm*, Pt. II,] § 13, p. 106, etc.
[b] [Ibid.,] § 14, p. 110, etc; 1st *Journal*, p. 14 [i.e. Mar. 7, 1736, though apparently this is a misprint for Lavington's opening citation, i.e. 3rd *Journal*, p. 11, Wesley's confession of his own spiritual state, Oct. 14, 1738].

---

[1] *Enthusiasm*, Pt. II, p. 108, citing Wesley's *Answer to the Rev. Mr. Church's Remarks*, III. 5.
[2] Horace, *Epistles*, I. i. 166: 'he has some tragic inspiration'.
[3] *Enthusiasm*, Pt. II, p. 111, citing *Journal* for Mar. 7, 1736.

The passage as I wrote it stands thus:

> Sunday, March 7. I entered upon my ministry at Savannah. . . . In the Second Lesson (Luke 18) was our Lord's prediction of the treatment which he himself (and consequently his followers) were to meet with from the world. . . .
>
> Yet notwithstanding these plain declarations of our Lord, notwithstanding my own repeated experience, notwithstanding the experience of all the sincere followers of Christ whom I ever talked with, read or heard of; nay, and the reason of the thing, evincing to a demonstration that all who love not the light must hate him who is continually labouring to pour it in upon them; I do here bear witness against myself that when I saw the number of people crowding into the church, the deep attention with which they received the word, and the seriousness that afterwards sat on all their faces, I could scarce refrain from giving the lie to experience, and reason, and Scripture all together. I could hardly believe that the greater, the far greater part of this attentive, serious people, would hereafter trample under foot that word, and say all manner of evil falsely of him that spoke it.

Sir, does this prove me guilty of '*scepticism* or *infidelity*'? Of 'doubting or denying the truth of revelation'? Did I speak this 'upon the people's using me ill, and saying all manner of evil against me'? Or am I here describing any 'emotion raised in me hereby'? Blush, blush, sir, if you *can* blush. You had here no possible room for mistake. You grossly and wilfully falsify the whole passage to support a groundless, shameless accusation.

24. The second passage (written January 24, 1737/8) is this. 'In a storm I think, "What if the gospel be not true? Then thou art of all men most foolish. For what hast thou given thy goods, thy ease, thy friends, thy reputation, thy country, thy life? For what art thou wandering over the face of the earth? A dream? A cunningly devised fable?"'[a]

I am here describing the thoughts which passed through my mind when I was confessedly an unbeliever. But even this implies no scepticism, much less atheism: no 'denial of the truth of revelation'; but barely such transient doubts as I presume may assault any thinking man that knows not God.

The third passage (which you tack to the former as if they were one and the same) runs thus: 'I have not such a peace as excludes the possibility either of doubt or fear. When holy men have told me

[a] 1st *Journal*, p. 67 [quoting at the end 2 Pet. 1: 16].

I had no faith, I have often doubted whether I had or no. And those doubts have made me very uneasy, till I was relieved by prayer and the Holy Scriptures.'ᵃ

Speak frankly, sir, does this prove me guilty of 'scepticism,
5 infidelity, or atheism'? What else does it prove? Just nothing at all but the 'pertinacious confidence' of him that cites it.

25. You recite more at large one passage more. The whole paragraph stands thus:

St. Paul tells us, 'the fruit of the Spirit is love, joy, peace, long-
10 suffering, gentleness, meekness, temperance'.¹ Now although, by the grace of God in Christ, I find a measure of some of these in myself, viz., of peace, long-suffering, gentleness, meekness, temperance; yet others I find not. I cannot find in myself the love of God or of Christ. Hence my deadness and wanderings in public prayer. Hence it is that
15 even in the Holy Communion I have rarely any more than a cold attention. Hence when I hear of the highest instance of God's love my heart is still senseless and unaffected. Yea, at this moment (October 14, 1738) I feel no more love to him than one I had never heard of.ᵇ

To any who knew something of inward religion I should have
20 observed that this is what serious divines mean by 'desertion'. But all expressions of this kind are jargon to you. So allowing it to be whatever you please, I ask only, 'Do you know how long I continued in this state? How many years, months, weeks, or days? If not, how can you infer what my state of mind is now from what it was above
25 eleven years ago?'

Sir, I do not tell you, or any man else, that 'I cannot *now* find the love of God in myself'; or that *now*, in the year 1751, 'I rarely feel more than a cold attention in the Holy Communion.' So that your whole argument, built on this supposition, falls to the ground
30 at once.

26. Sensible, I presume, of the weakness of this *reason*, you immediately apply to the *passions*, by that artful remark: 'Observe, reader, this is the man who charges our religion as no better than "the *Turkish pilgrimages to Mecca or the popish worship of our Lady*
35 *of Loretto*"!'² 'Our religion'! How naturally will the reader suppose

---

ᵃ 3rd *Journal*, p. 12 [Oct. 14, 1738].
ᵇ Ibid., p. 11 [quoted in *Enthusiasm*, Pt. II, p. 110].

---

¹ Gal. 5: 22–3.
² *Enthusiasm*, Pt. II, p. 110, citing *A Farther Appeal*, Pt. III, I. 2, q.v.

that I fix the charge either on the *Protestant* religion in general, or on that of the *Church of England* in particular! But how far is this from the truth!

My words concerning those who are commonly called religious are:

> Wherein does their religion consist? 'In righteousness and true holiness'?[1] In love stronger than death? Fervent gratitude to God, and tender affection to all his creatures? Is their religion the religion of the heart? A renewal of the soul in the image of God? Do they resemble him they worship? Are they free from pride, from vanity, from malice, from envy? From ambition and avarice, from passion and lust, from every uneasy and unlovely temper? Alas! I fear neither they (the greater part at least) nor you have any more notion of this religion than the peasant that holds the plough of the religion of a gymnosophist.
>
> 'Tis well if the *genuine religion* of Christ has any more alliance with what you call 'religion' than with the Turkish pilgrimages to Mecca, or the popish worship of our Lady of Loretto. Have not *you* substituted in the place of the religion of the heart something (I do not say, equally *sinful*, but) equally vain and foreign to the 'worshipping of God in spirit and in truth'?[2] What else can be said even of prayer, public or private, in the manner wherein you generally perform it? As a thing of *course*, running round and round in the same dull track, without either the knowledge or the love of God? Without one heavenly *temper* either attained or improved?[a]

Now, sir, what room is there for your 'own exclamations': What sort of heavenly temper is his? How can he possibly, consistently with charity, call this our '*general* performance'?[3] Sir, I do not. I only appeal to the conscience of *you* (and each particular reader) whether this is, or is not, the manner wherein *you* (in the singular number) *generally* perform public or private prayer. 'How possibly, without being omniscient, can he affirm that *we* (I presume you mean, all the members of our Church) pray without one heavenly *temper*? Or know anything at all of our *private devotions*? How monstrous is all this!' Recollect yourself, sir. If your terror is real, you are more afraid than hurt. I do not affirm any such thing. I do not take upon me to *know* anything at all of your private devotions.

---

[a] *Farther Appeal*, Third Part, p. 82 [I. 2].

[1] Eph. 4: 24.　　　　　　　　　　　　　　　　[2] Cf. John 4: 23, 24.

[3] After a series of exclamations on p. 111 (of which Wesley quotes the first two) Lavington closed his paragraph: 'Let his own exclamation be the answer, "O! what mockery of God is this!"'—the closing exclamation of the passage from *A Farther Appeal* quoted above.

But I suppose I may *inquire* without offence, and beg you seriously to examine yourself before God.

So you have brought no one proof that *scepticism, infidelity,* and *atheism* are either *constituent parts* or *genuine consequences* of Methodism. Therefore your florid declamation in the following pages is entirely out of its place. And you might have spared yourself the trouble of accounting for what has no being but in your own imagination.

27. You charge the Methodists next with an *'uncharitable spirit'.*[a] All you advance in proof of this, as if it were from my writings, but without naming either page or book, I have nothing to do with. But whatever you tell me where to find I shall carefully consider.

I observe but one single passage of this sort. And that you have worn threadbare already: 'By the most infallible of proofs, inward feeling, I am convinced . . . of levity and luxuriancy of spirit . . . by speaking words not tending to edify; but most by my *manner of speaking of my enemies.'*[1] Sir, you may print this, not only in *italics,* but in CAPITALS, and yet it would do you no service. For what I was convinced of then was not uncharitableness but, as I expressly mentioned, 'levity of spirit'.

28. 'Of the same *uncharitable nature* (you say) is their *application of divine judgments* to their opposers.'[b] You borrow two instances from Mr. Church. But you omit the answers, which I shall therefore subjoin.

His words are: 'You describe heaven as executing judgments, immediate punishments, on those who oppose you. You say, "Mr. Molther was taken ill this day. I believe it was the hand of God that was upon him." I do. But I do not say as a judgment for opposing *me.* That *you* say for me.'

'Again, you mention', says Mr. Church, 'as an "awful providence", the case of a poor wretch who was last week cursing and blaspheming, and had boasted to many that he would come on Sunday, and no man should stop his mouth. "But on Friday God laid his hand upon him, and on Sunday he was buried." I do look on this as a manifest judgment of God on a hardened sinner for his complicated wickedness.'[c]

---

[a] [*Enthusiasm,* Pt. II,] § 15, p. 115, etc.   [b] [Ibid.,] § 16, p. 119, etc.
[c] *First Letter to Mr. Church,* p. 42 [i.e. *An Answer to the Rev. Mr. Church's Remarks,* III. 9. Cf. Wesley, *Journal,* Oct. 23, 1740].

---

[1] *Enthusiasm,* Pt. II, pp. 116–17.

To repeat these objections without taking the least notice of the answers is one of the usual proofs of your *charitable spirit*.

29. You pass on 'to the Methodists' *uncharitable* custom of summoning their opponents *to the bar of judgment*'.ᵃ

You bring two passages from my writings to prove this. The first is: 'Calling at Newgate (in Bristol) I was informed that the poor wretches under sentence of death were earnestly desirous to speak with me; but that Alderman Beacher¹ had sent an express order that they should not. I cite Alderman Beacher to answer *for these souls* at the judgment seat of Christ.'²

Why do you leave out those words, 'for these souls'? Because they show the sentence means neither more nor less than 'if *these souls* perish he, not I, must answer for them at the great day'.

The second passage is still more wide from the point. The whole of it is as follows:

> I have often inquired who were the authors of this report (that I was a Papist) and have generally found they were either bigoted Dissenters or (I speak it without fear or favour) ministers of our own Church. I have also frequently considered what possible ground or motive they could have thus to speak: seeing few men in the world have had occasion so clearly and openly to declare their principles as I have done both by preaching, printing, and conversation, for several years last past. And I can no otherwise think than that either they spoke thus (to put the most favourable construction upon it) from gross ignorance; they knew not what popery was; they knew not what doctrines these are which the Papists teach; or they wilfully spoke what they knew to be false, probably thinking thereby to do God service. Now take this to yourselves, whoever ye are, high or low, Dissenters or Churchmen, clergy or laity, who have advanced this shameless charge, and digest it how you can.
>
> But how have ye not been afraid, if ye believe there is a God, and that he knoweth the secrets of your hearts (I speak now to you preachers, more especially, of whatever denomination) to declare so gross, palpable

---

ᵃ [*Enthusiasm*, Pt. II,] § 17, p. 123, etc.

---

¹ Alderman Michael Beacher, one of the sheriffs of Bristol, and brother of the Revd. Henry Beacher of Temple Church, who in July 1740 repulsed Charles Wesley and a group of colliers from the Lord's Table. In the eighteenth century gaolers were answerable to the aldermen for the administration of the prisons, and so were very susceptible to pressure from that quarter. Although the spellings 'Becher' and 'Beecher' are found, both John and Charles Wesley spelt the name 'Beacher', as did Lavington.

² Wesley, *Journal*, Apr. 2, 1740; cf. *Enthusiasm*, Pt. II, p. 124.

a lie, in the name of the God of truth? I cite you all before 'the Judge of all the earth'[1] either publicly to prove your charge, or by publicly retracting it to make the best amends you can, to God, to me, and to the world.[a]

5 Sir, do I here 'summon my opponents *to the bar of judgment*'? So you would make me do, by quoting only that scrap, 'I cite you all before "the Judge of all the earth"!' You then add, with equal charity and sincerity, 'Here you have the *true spirit of an enthusiast*, flushed with a *modest* assurance of his *own salvation*, and the *charit-*
10 *able* prospect of the *damnation* of others.' O Sir, never name modesty more!

Here end your laboured attempts to show the *uncharitable spirit* of the Methodists, who, for anything you have shown to the contrary, may be the most charitable people under the sun.

15 30. You charge the Methodists next 'with violation and contempt of *order and authority*', namely the authority of the governors of the Church.[b] I have answered every article of this charge in the Second and Third Parts of the *Farther Appeal*, and the Letter to Mr. Church. When you have been so good as to reply to what is there
20 advanced, I may possibly say something more.

What you offer of *your own* upon this head I shall consider without delay.

'*Women and boys* are actually employed in this ministry of *public preaching*.'[2] Please to tell me where? I know them not, nor ever
25 heard of them before.

You add what is more marvellous still: 'I speak from *personal knowledge* . . . that sometimes, a little before the delivering of the elements (at the Communion), three or four Methodists together will take it into their heads to go away; that sometimes while the
30 sentences of the *Offertory* were reading they have *called out* to the minister who carried the basin, . . . *reproaching* him for asking *alms* of *them*; that sometimes when the minister has delivered the bread into their hands, instead of *eating* it, they would slip it into their pockets.'[3] Sir, you must show your face before these stories will find
35 credit on your bare asseveration.

'Yet they are surprised (you say) that every man in his senses don't without the least hesitation *join* them.'[4]

---

[a] *Journal*, pp. 75, 76 [Aug. 27, 1739].   [b] [*Enthusiasm*, Pt. II,] § 18, p. 124.

[1] Gen. 18: 25.   [2] *Enthusiasm*, Pt. II, p. 126.
[3] Ibid., pp. 127–8.   [4] Ibid., p. 128.

Sir, I am surprised (unless you are not in your senses) at your advancing such a barefaced falsehood.

31. You go on. 'Under this head may not improperly be considered their undutiful behaviour to the *civil powers*.'¹ What proof have you of this? Why, a single sentence, on which I laid so little stress myself that it is only inserted by way of parenthesis in the body of another sentence: 'Ye learned in the law, what becomes of Magna Charta, and of English liberty and property? Are not these mere sounds, while on any pretence there is such a thing as a *press-gang* suffered in the land?'²

Upon this you descant: 'The legislature . . . has at several times made Acts for pressing men. . . . But no matter for this; touch but a Methodist, . . . and all may perish, rather than a soldier be pressed. . . . He who had before bound himself not to speak a tittle of worldly things is now bawling for liberty and property.'

Very lively this. But I hope, sir, you do not offer it by way of *argument*. You are not so unlearned in the law as not to know that the legislature is out of the question. The legislature six years ago did not appoint *press-gangs*, but legal officers, to press men. Consequently this is no proof (and find another if you can) of our *undutiful* behaviour to the *civil powers*.

32. 'Another natural consequence (you say) of Methodism, is their mutual *jealousies* and *envyings*, their manifold *divisions*, fierce and rancorous *quarrels* and *accusations* of one another.'ᵃ

I shall carefully attend whatever you produce on this head. And if you prove this, I will grant you all the rest.

You first cite those words: 'Musing on the things that were past, and reflecting how many that came after me were preferred before me, I opened my Testament on those words . . . : 'The Gentiles, which followed not after righteousness, have attained to righteousness; but Israel, which followed after the law of righteousness, hath not attained to the law of righteousness.'''ᵇ

And how does this prove the 'manifold divisions' and 'rancorous quarrels' of the Methodists?

Your second argument is: 'Mr. Whitefield told me he and I preached two different gospels (his meaning was that he preached

---

ᵃ [*Enthusiasm*, Pt. II,] § 19, p. 134.

ᵇ 4th *Journal*, pp. 14–15 [Dec. 6, 1739, cited in *Enthusiasm*, Pt. II, p. 135. Both in the *Journal* and this *Second Letter* Wesley's quotation from Rom. 9: 30–1, reads 'but Israel . . . have not'].

¹ Ibid., p. 133.   ² Wesley, *Journal*, July 21, 1739.

particular, and I universal redemption) and therefore he would not join with me, but publicly preach against me.'ᵃ

Well, sir, here was doubtless a 'division' for a time; but no 'fierce and rancorous quarrel' yet.

5 You say, thirdly: 'They write and publish against each other.'¹ True; but without any degree either of *fierceness* or *rancour*.

You assert, fourthly: 'Mr. Wesley in his sermon on *Free Grace* opposes the other for the horrible blasphemies of his horrible doctrine.'²

10 Sir, away with your flourishes and write plain English. I opposed the doctrine of predestination which he held. But without any degree either of *rancour* or *fierceness*. Still therefore you miss the mark.

You quote, fifthly, these words: 'I spent an hour with Mr. Stonehouse. O what πι θανολογία (persuasiveness of speech) is here!
15 Surely all the deceivableness of unrighteousness.'ᵇ But there was no *fierceness* or *rancour* on either side.

The passage, a fragment of which you produce as a sixth argument, stands thus: 'A few of us had a long conference together. Mr. C[ennick] now told me plainly he could not agree with me,
20 because I did not preach the truth, particularly with regard to election.'ᶜ He did so; but without any *rancour*. We had a long conference; but not a *fierce* one.

You seventhly observe, 'What scurrility of language the Moravians throw out against Mr. Wesley!'³ Perhaps so. But this will not
25 prove that 'the Methodists quarrel with each other'.

'And how does he turn their own artillery upon them!'⁴ This is your eighth argument. But if I do, this no more proves the '*mutual quarrels* of the Methodists' than my turning your own artillery upon *you*.

30 33. Having by these eight irrefragable arguments clearly carried the day, you raise your crest and cry out, 'Is this Methodism?

And reign such mortal feuds in heavenly minds?'⁵

ᵃ 4th *Journal*, p. 77 [Mar. 28, 1741, cited in *Enthusiasm*, Pt. II, p. 135].
ᵇ Ibid., p. 59 [Oct. 22, 1740. For the Revd. George Stonehouse see above, p. 184].
ᶜ Ibid., p. 63 [Dec. 20, 1740; cited in *Enthusiasm*, Pt. II, p. 136. John Cennick (1718–55), evangelist and hymn-writer, assisted both Whitefield and Wesley as teacher and preacher in the Bristol area, but broke with Wesley in 1741, Whitefield in 1745, when he joined the Moravians. Cf. §§ 35, 48 below].

---

¹ *Enthusiasm*, Pt. II, p. 135.   ² Ibid., p. 136.   ³ Ibid., p. 136.   ⁴ Ibid., p. 137.
⁵ Ibid., p. 138, quoting both the Latin 'Tantaene animis coelestibus irae?' from Virgil, *Aeneid*, i. 11, and its translation as reproduced by Wesley.

Truly, sir, you have not yet brought one single proof (and yet, I dare say, you have brought the very best you have) of any such feuds among the Methodists as may not be found among the most heavenly minded men on earth.

But you are resolved to pursue your victory, and so go on. 'What are we to think of these charges, of Whitefield, and Wesley, and the Moravians, one against another?'[1] The Moravians, sir, are out of the question; for they are no Methodists. And as to the rest, Mr. White-field charges Mr. Wesley with holding universal redemption, and I charge him with holding particular redemption. This is the stand-ing charge on either side. And now, sir, what are we to think! Why, that you have not proved one point of this charge against the Methodists.

However, you stumble on. 'Are these things so? Are they true, or are they not true? If not true, they are grievous *calumniators*; if true, they are detestable *sectarists*. Whether true or false, the allega-tion stands good, of their fierce and rancorous *quarrels*, and mutual heinous *accusations*.'[2]

Sir, has your passion quite extinguished your reason? Have *fierceness* and *rancour* left you no understanding? Otherwise how is it possible you should run on at this senseless, shameless rate? These things are *true* which Mr. Whitefield and Wesley object to each other. He holds the decrees; I do not. Yet this does not prove us 'detestable sectarists'. And whether these things are true or false, your allegation of 'our fierce and rancorous *quarrels*, and mutual heinous *accusations*' cannot stand good without better proof than you have yet produced.

34. Yet with the utmost confidence, *quasi re bene gesta*,[3] you pro-ceed, 'And how stands the matter among their disciples? . . . They are *all* together by the ears, embroiled and broken with *unchristian quarrels and confusions*.'[4]

How do you prove this? Why thus: 'Mr. Wesley's fourth *Journal* is mostly taken up in enumerating their *wrath, dissensions*, and *apostasies*.'[5] No, sir, not a tenth part of it; although it gives a full and explicit account of the greatest dissensions which ever were among them.

---

[1] Ibid.   [2] Ibid.
[3] Cf. Plautus, *Amphitruo*, line 784; Ennius, *Annales*, line 547. Wesley's translation, 'as if you had carried your point' (*Works*, Vol. 32 (1774), Appendix).
[4] *Enthusiasm*, Pt. II, pp. 138-9.   [5] Ibid., p. 139.

But to come to particulars. You first cite these words: 'At Oxford but a few who *had not forsaken them*'.[1]

My words are: 'Monday, October 1, 1738, I rode to Oxford, and found a few who *had not yet forsaken the assembling themselves* together.'[a] This is your first proof 'that the Methodists are *all* together by the ears'. Your second is its very twin brother. 'Tuesday, 2. I went to many who once heard the word with joy; but "when the sun arose, they withered away".'[b]

Your third is this: 'Many were induced (by the Moravians) to deny the gift of God, and affirm they never had any faith at all.'[c] You are at liberty to enjoy this argument also; and let it prove what it can prove.

You fourthly cite these words: 'Many of our sisters are shaken, ... grievously torn by reasonings. . . . But few come to Fetter Lane, and then after their names are called over they presently depart. Our brethren here' (those who were proselytes to the Moravians) 'have neither wisdom enough to guide, nor prudence enough to let it alone. . . . They (the Moravians) have much confounded some of our sisters, and many of our brothers are much grieved.'[d]

This proves thus much, that *one* society was *at that time* divided; but not 'that the Methodists' in general were even then '*all* together by the ears'.

The passage you quote in the fifth place is: 'I believe [Hutton, etc.] are determined to go on according to Mr. Molther's direction, and I suppose (says the writer of the letter) above half our brethren are on their side. But they are so very confused, they don't know how to go on, and yet are unwilling to be taught except by the Moravians.'[e]

Add to this (I recite the whole passages in order, not as you had mangled and then jumbled them together): 'Wednesday, December 19. I came to London, though with a heavy heart. Here I found every day the dreadful effects of our brethren's reasoning and disputing with each other. Scarce one in ten retained his first love; and most of the rest were in the utmost confusion' (they were so, more or less, for several months) 'biting and devouring one another.'

---

[a] 3rd *Journal*, p. 84.   [b] Ibid., p. 85 [Oct. 2, 1738, quoting Matt. 13: 6, etc.].
[c] 4th *Journal*, p. 8 [Nov. 7, 1739].   [d] Ibid., p. 17 [Dec. 13, 1740].
[e] Ibid., p. 18 [Dec. 14, 1739].

---

[1] *Enthusiasm*, Pt. II, pp. 139–40.

This also proves so much, neither more nor less [than] that *some* of the Methodists were then in confusion. And just so much is proved by your sixth quotation. 'Many were wholly unsettled' (by the Moravians, taking advantage of my absence) 'and lost in vain reasonings and doubtful disputations . . . not likely to come to any true foundation.'[a]

Your seventh quotation (I recite the whole sentence) runs thus: 'April 19. I received a letter . . . informing me that our poor brethren at Fetter Lane were again in great confusion.'[b] This quotation proves just as much as the preceding; or as the following. 'The plague (of false stillness) was now spread to them also'; namely, to the 'little society at Islington'.[c]

Your ninth is this: 'I went to the society, but I found their hearts were quite estranged. Friday 4. I met a little handful of them who still stand in the old paths.'[d]

Thus far you have been speaking of the Methodists in London. And what have you proved concerning them? Only that the Moravians mixing with them *twelve years* ago, while they were young and unexperienced, set them a-disputing with each other, and thereby occasioned much confusion for *several months*. But you have not proved that 'the Methodists' in general were even then '*all* together by the ears': and much less that they have been so ever *since*, and that they are so *now*.

35. I now attend you to Kingswood. Not to 'Bristol and Kingswood', which you artfully join together. The society at Bristol was no more concerned with the disputes in Kingswood than with those in London.

Here the first quotation, though containing but two lines, is extracted from three different paragraphs; in one of which I say, 'I had many unpleasing accounts (in December, 1740) concerning our little society in Kingswood'; in the second, 'I went to Kingswood, if haply I might repair the breaches which had been made' (by the predestinarian preachers); in the third, 'I laboured to heal the jealousies and misunderstandings which had arisen.'[e]

The second passage, part of which you quote, is this: 'I returned early in the morning to Kingswood. But my congregation was gone

[a] Ibid., pp. 21, 22 [Dec. 31, 1739].
[b] Ibid., p. 34 [Apr. 19, 1740].
[c] Ibid., p. 36 [Apr. 25, 1740].
[d] Ibid., p. 47 [July 2, 1740].
[e] Ibid., p. 62 [Dec. 12, 14, 15, 1740, quoted in *Enthusiasm*, Pt. II, p. 141].

to hear Mr. C[ennick], so that I had not above two or three men and as many women.'ᵃ

The third is: 'January 1. I explained, "If any man be in Christ he is a new creature."¹ But many of our brethren had no ears to hear,
5 having disputed away both their faith and love.'ᵇ

The fourth: 'February 21. I inquired concerning the divisions and offences which began afresh to break out in Kingswood. In the afternoon I met a few of the bands; but it was a cold uncomfortable meeting.'ᶜ

10 You have picked out here and there a word from several pages in order to furnish out a fifth quotation. The most material part of it is this: 'Saturday 28. I read the following paper at Kingswood: "For their scoffing at the Word and ministers of God, for their backbiting and evil-speaking, I . . . declare the persons above-mentioned to be
15 no longer members of this society." 'ᵈ

'And we had great reason to bless God, that after fifty-two were withdrawn we had still upwards of ninety left.'ᵉ

Who those other forty were that (you say) left them I know not.² Perhaps you may inform me.

20 Upon the whole, all these quotations prove only this: that about eleven years ago Mr. C[ennick], falling into predestination, set the society in Kingswood a-disputing with each other, and occasioned much confusion for some months. But still you have not gone one step toward proving (which is the one point in question) 'that the
25 Methodists in general were even then *all* together by the ears'; and much less, 'that they have been so ever since, and that they *are* so *now*'.

However you fail not to triumph (like Louis le Grand after his victory at Blenheim):³ 'What shall we say now? Are these the fruits
30 of Methodism?'⁴ No, sir. They are the fruits of opposing it. They are the tares sown among the wheat.⁵ You may hear of instances of the same kind both in earlier and later ages.

ᵃ [4th *Journal*,] p. 64 [Dec. 26, 1740. For Cennick see § 32 above].   ᵇ Ibid., p. 65.
ᶜ Ibid., p. 70.   ᵈ Ibid., pp. 72–3.   ᵉ Ibid., p. 74 [Mar. 8, 1741].

¹ 2 Cor. 5: 17.
² Lavington, *Enthusiasm*, p. 141, has: 'Fifty-two leave them, and again about forty.'
³ Blenheim, the village on the Danube which was the scene in 1704 of the great victory of the army of the Grand Alliance, led by the Duke of Marlborough and Prince Eugene, over the forces of the French and the Bavarians. For the reaction of Louis XIV, cf. P. Sagnac et A. de Saint-Léger, *Louis XIV*, p. 472.
⁴ *Enthusiasm*, Pt. II, p. 141.   ⁵ See Matt. 13: 25.

You add, 'This is bad enough; but it is not the worst. For consider what becomes of those that leave them.'[1] Why, sir, what if 'their last end be worse than their first'?[2] Will you charge this upon *me*? By the same rule you must have charged upon the apostles themselves whatever befell those who having 'known the way of righteousness', afterwards 'turned back from the holy commandment once delivered to them'.[3]

36. You conclude this section: 'Mr. Wesley will probably say, "Must I be answerable for the Moravians, against whom I have preached and written?" True, since he and the Moravians quarrelled. But who gives them a box on the ear with the one hand, and embraces them with the other? Who first brought over this wicked generation? Who made a Moravian his spiritual guide? . . . Who *fanaticized* his own followers, . . . and deprived them of their senses? Whose societies (by his own confession) run over in shoals to Moravianism, forty or fifty at a time? Would they have split upon this rock, if they had not been first Methodists? . . . Lastly, where is the spawn of Moravianism so strongly working as in the children of Methodism?'[4]

Sir, you run very fast. And yet I hope to overtake you by and by. Mr. Wesley, you say, has preached against the Moravians since he quarrelled with them. Sir, I never quarrelled with their persons yet. I did with some of their tenets long ago. He 'gives them a box on the ear with the one hand, and embraces them with the other'. That is, I embrace what is good among them, and at the same time reprove what is evil. 'Who *first* brought over this wicked generation?' Not I, whether they be wicked or not. I once thought I did; but have since then seen and acknowledged my mistake. 'Who made a Moravian his spiritual guide?' Not I; though I have occasionally consulted several. 'Who *fanaticized* his own followers, . . . and deprived them of their senses?' Not I. Prove it upon me if you can. 'Whose societies (by his own confession) run over in shoals to Moravianism, forty or fifty at a time?' Truly not mine. Two and fifty of Kingswood society ran over to Calvinism, and a year before part of Fetter Lane society gradually went over to the Moravians. But I know none of ours that went over 'in shoals'. They never, that I remember, gained five at a time; nor fifty in all (to the best of my knowledge) for these last ten years. 'Would they (of Fetter Lane) have split on

---

[1] *Enthusiasm*, Pt. II, p. 142.
[2] Cf. Matt. 12: 45.
[3] Cf. 2 Pet. 2: 21.
[4] *Enthusiasm*, Pt. II, p. 145.

this rock, if they had not first been Methodists?' Undoubtedly they would; for several of them had not first been Methodists; Mr. Viney,[1] for instance (as well as several others) was with the Germans before ever he saw me. 'Lastly, where is the spawn of Moravianism working so strongly as in the children of Methodism?' If you mean the errors of Moravianism, they are not working at all in the generality of the children of Methodism; the Methodists in general being thoroughly apprised of, and fully guarded against them.

So much for your modest assertion that 'the Methodists *in general* are *all* together by the ears'—the very reverse of which is true. They are, *in general*, in perfect peace. They enjoy in themselves the peace of God, which passeth all understanding.[2] They are at peace with each other. And as much as lieth in them, they live peaceably with all men.[3]

37. Your next charge is that Methodism has a 'tendency to undermine morality and good works'.[a] To prove this you assert, (1), 'that the Methodists are trained up to wait *in quietness* for sudden conversion; whence they are naturally led to neglect the *means of salvation*'. This is a mistake all over. For neither are they taught to wait in *quietness* (if you mean any more than patience by that term) for either sudden or gradual conversion; neither do they in fact neglect *the means*. So far from it, they are eminently exact in the use of them.

You assert, (2), 'The doctrine of *assurance of pardon and salvation, present and future*, . . . causes a false security, to the neglect of future endeavours.' Blunder upon blunder again. That all Christians have an assurance of *future* salvation is no Methodist doctrine: and an assurance of *present pardon* is so far from causing negligence that it is of all others the strongest motive to vigorous endeavours after universal holiness.

You assert, (3), '*Impulses* and *impressions*, being made the *rule of duty*, will . . . lead into dangerous errors.' Very true. But the Methodists do not make 'impulses and impressions' the 'rule of duty'. They totally disclaim any other rule of duty than the written Word.

---

[a] [*Enthusiasm*, Pt. II,] § 20, p. 146 etc.

---

[1] Richard Viney, a tailor, and a leading member of the Fetter Lane religious society which Wesley helped to form. In 1738 Viney acted as interpreter for Peter Böhler, the German Moravian who powerfully influenced Wesley. Viney travelled to Holland with Wesley in June 1738, and later became an avowed Moravian.

[2] Phil. 4: 7.   [3] Rom. 12: 18.

You assert, (4), 'A claim of unsinning perfection' (I mean by perfection, the loving God with all our heart) 'drives some into frenzies, others into despair.' Sir, I doubt the fact.

You assert, (5), 'The Moravian Methodists trample down morality, and multitudes of the Wesleyans have been infected.' The 'Moravian Methodists'! You may as well say the Presbyterian Papists. The Moravians have no connexion with the Methodists. Therefore whatever they do (though you slander them, too) they and not we are to answer for. The Methodists at present, blessed be God, are as little infected with this plague (of condemning or neglecting good works) as any body of people in England or Ireland.

38. From these loose assertions you proceed to quotations from my writings, every one of which I shall consider, to show that not in one or two, but in every one you are a wilful prevaricator and false accuser of your neighbour.

You say, first, 'The Moravians'—Hold, good sir! You are out of the way already. You well know the Moravians are to answer for themselves. Our present question concerns the Methodists only .

You say, secondly, 'A general temptation prevails among *the societies* of Methodists of leaving off good works.'[a] Sir, you are wrong again. 'The societies of Methodists' are not there spoken of; but the *single society* of Fetter Lane. Among these only that temptation *then* prevailed.

You quote, thirdly, as my words, 'The poor, confused, shattered society *had erred from the Faith*.' My own words are, 'I told the poor, confused, shattered society, *wherein* they had erred from the faith';[b] namely with regard to the ordinances; not in general, as your way of expressing it naturally imports. Nor had *all* the society erred even in this point. Many of them were still unshaken.

You quote, fourthly, 'A woman of Deptford spoke great words and true. She ordered Mr. Humphreys to leave off doing good.'[1]

Must not every reader suppose, as you have placed these words, that they were all spoke at one time? And that 'the great words and true' were those whereby she 'ordered Mr. Humphreys to leave off doing good'?

What then must every honest man think of you, when he observes

---

[a] 4th *Journal*, p. 39 [June 5, 1740, cited in *Enthusiasm*, Pt. II, p. 148].
[b] Ibid. [June 11, 1740, quoted ibid.]

---

[1] *Enthusiasm*, Pt. II, p. 148, quoting Wesley's *Journal* for June 9 and 19, 1740.

that one half of the sentence (which you thus artfully put together) stands in another page, and at a considerable distance from the other? And that I immediately subjoin to the latter clause, 'We talked largely with her, and she was humbled to the dust under a
5 deep sense of the advantage Satan had gained over her.'

You quote, fifthly, a part of the following sentence to prove that I 'undermine morality and good works':

'His judgment concerning holiness is new. He no longer judges it to be an outward thing, to consist either in doing no harm, in doing
10 good, or in using the ordinances of God.' (And yet how strongly do I insist upon all these! Sir, do not you know this?) 'He sees it is the life of God in the soul, the image of God fresh stamped on the heart.'[1] It is so. Sir, can you deny it? What then will you prove by this?

15 You quote, sixthly, part of these words:

'They speak of holiness as if it consisted chiefly, if not wholly, in these two points: first, the doing no harm; secondly, the doing good (as it is called), i.e. the using the means of grace, and helping our neighbour.'[a]

20 And this you term 'disparaging good works'! Sir, these things, considered barely as to the *opus operatum*,[2] are not good works. There must be something good in the heart before any of our works are good. Insomuch that 'though I give all my goods to feed the poor, and have not *this*, it profiteth me nothing'.[3]

25 You 'observe by the way, the *mystic divinity* was once the *Methodists' doctrine*'.[4] Sir, you have stepped out of the way, only to get another fall. The mystic divinity was never the Methodists' doctrine. They could never swallow either John Tauler[5] or Jacob Behmen;[6] although they often advised with one that did.

---

[a] 3rd *Journal*, p. 82 [Sept. 13, 1739; Wesley is discussing points in which he differs from some clergy of the Church of England].

---

[1] *Journal*, Oct. 9, 1738. Lavington's *Enthusiasm*, Pt. II, p. 149, quotes almost the whole of the second sentence, but not the first or the third.

[2] 'The act done': see note on p. 122 above.

[3] Cf. 1 Cor. 13: 3.

[4] *Enthusiasm*, Pt. II, p. 150: Lavington refers to §§ 7–8 of the *Journal* for May 24, 1738.

[5] Johann Tauler (1300–61), German Dominican mystic, famous as a preacher and director of souls, and eminently practical in his presentation of the Mystic Way.

[6] Jakob Boehme (1575–1624), German theosophical author. Wesley's spelling of the name vacillated between 'Behme' and 'Behmen', though the latter is used throughout this edition. Cf. Introduction, p. 10.

39. You say, seventhly, 'I don't find that Mr. Wesley has ever cited those express passages of St. James.'[1] Sir, what if I had not? (I mean, in print). I do not cite every text from Genesis to the Revelation. But it happens I have. Look again, sir; and by and by you may find where.

You say, eighthly, Mr. Wesley affirms that the condition of our justification is 'faith alone and not good works'.[2] Most certainly I do. And I learnt it from the eleventh and twelfth Articles and from the Homilies of our Church. If you can confute them, do. But I subscribe to them, both with my hand and heart.

You say, ninthly: 'Give me leave to make a remark. "The Methodists wandered many years in the new path of salvation by faith and works", . . . which was the time, too, of their highest *glory and popularity*. During this time they were *seducing their disciples into* the most destructive errors.'[3] Excuse me, sir. While they preached salvation by faith and works they had no *disciples* at all (unless you term a few pupils such); nor had they any *popularity* at all. They then enjoyed (what they always desired) a quiet, retired life. But whatever disciples we had, they were not *seduced by us* into the error of justification by works. For they were in it before ever they saw our face, or knew there were such men in the world.

You say, tenthly, 'Mr. Wesley only contends that it is *possible* to *use* them without *trusting* in them.' Not in that page; because the proposition I am confuting is: ''Tis *not possible* to *use* them without *trusting* in them.'[a]

You added, 'And now, are not such disparaging expressions' (a *mere possibility* of using them without trusting in them) 'a great discouragement to practice?'

O sir, when will you deviate into truth? Dare you affirm, without any regard to God or man, 'Mr. Wesley only contends for a *mere possibility* of using the means without trusting in them'?

To go no farther than the very first page you refer to. My express words are these:

'I believe the way to attain faith is to wait for Christ, . . . in using all the means of grace.'

---

[a] 4th *Journal*, p. 20 [part of a summary of a conference with Molther on Dec. 31, 1739; in fact Wesley does use the disowned phrase on the following page, referring to the means of grace. Lavington's *Enthusiasm*, Part II, p. 152, had cited both pages 20 and 21, as well as page 105 of this *Journal*].

---

[1] *Enthusiasm*, Pt. II, p. 150.   [2] Ibid.   [3] Ibid., p. 151.

'Because I believe these . . . do ordinarily convey God's grace (even) to unbelievers.'ª Is this 'contending only for a *mere possibility* of using them without trusting in them'?

Not only in this, and many other parts of the *Journals*, but in
5 a sermon wrote professedly on the subject,¹ I contend that all the ordinances of God are the stated channels of his grace to man; and that it is our bounden duty to use them all, at all possible opportunities. So that to charge the Methodists in general, or me in particular, with undervaluing or disparaging them, shows just as
10 much regard for justice and truth as if you was to charge us with Mahometanism.

40. Tedious as it is to wade through so many dirty pages, I will follow you, step by step, a little farther. Your eleventh proof that we 'undermine morality and good works' is drawn from the follow-
15 ing passage:

I know everyone 'under the law'² is even as I was for near twice ten years. Everyone, when he begins to see his fallen state and to feel the wrath of God abiding on him, relapses into the sin that most easily besets him, *soon after* repenting of it. Sometimes he avoids, and at many
20 other times he cannot persuade himself to *avoid* the occasions of it. Hence his relapses are *frequent*, and of consequence his 'heart is hardened'³ more and more. . . . Nor can he, with all his *sincerity*, avoid any one of these four marks of *hypocrisy*, till 'being justified by faith' he 'hath peace with God through our Lord Jesus Christ.'ᵇ

25 You, sir, are no competent judge in the cause. But to any who has experienced what St. Paul speaks in his seventh chapter to the Romans I willingly submit this whole question. *You* know by experience that if anger was the sin that did so easily beset you, you relapsed into it (for days, or months, or years) *soon after* repenting
30 of it. Sometimes you *avoided* the *occasions* of it; at other times you did not. Hence your relapses were *frequent*, and your heart was *hardened* more and more. And yet all this time you was *sincerely* striving against sin. You could say, without *hypocrisy*, 'the thing which I do, I allow not; the evil which I would not, that I do. . . .

ª [4th *Journal*], p. 20.
ᵇ 3rd *Journal*, pp. 78, 79 [Aug. 31, 1739; the closing quotation is from Rom. 5: 1].

---

¹ 'The Means of Grace', first published in *Sermons on Several Occasions* (1746), and reprinted separately the following year.
² Rom. 6: 14.   ³ Cf. Mark 6: 52.

To will is even now present with me; but how to perform that which is good, I find not.'[1]

But the Jesuits, you think, 'could scarce have granted salvation upon easier terms. Have no fear, ye Methodists.'[2] Sir, I do not grant salvation (as you call it) upon so easy terms. I believe a man in this state is in a state of damnation. 'Have no fear!' say you? Yea, but those who are thus 'under the law' are in fear all the day long. 'Was there ever so pleasing a scheme?' Pleasing with a vengeance! As pleasing as to be in the belly of hell.[3] So totally do you mistake the whole matter, 'not knowing what you speak nor whereof you affirm'.[4]

You are indeed somewhat pitiable in speaking wrong on this head because you do it in ignorance. But this plea cannot be allowed when you gravely advance that trite, threadbare objection concerning the Lord's Supper, without taking any notice that I have answered it again and again, both to Mr. Church and to the late Lord Bishop of London.[5]

41. Your thirteenth proof is this: 'Mr. Wesley has taught us that *infirmities are no sins.*'[6] Sir, you have taught me to wonder at nothing you assert; else I should wonder at this. The words I suppose you refer to stand in the *Sermon on Salvation by Faith* (though you do not choose, for a plain reason, to show your reader where they may be found): 'He that is by faith born of God, sinneth not, (1), by any habitual sin; nor (2), by any wilful sin; nor (3), by any sinful desire; for he continually desireth the holy and perfect will of God; nor (4), doth he sin by infirmities, whether in act, word, or thought. For his infirmities have no concurrence of his will, and without this they are not properly sins.'[7] And this you seriously declare 'is a loop-hole to creep out of every moral and religious obligation'![8]

In the same paragraph you say I have strongly affirmed that 'all our works and tempers are evil continually;[a] that our whole heart is altogether corrupt and abominable, and consequently our whole

<hr />

[a] 3rd *Journal*, pp. 10, 70 [Oct. 14, 1738; July 31, 1739].

[1] Cf. Rom. 7: 15, 18.   [2] *Enthusiasm*, Pt. II, pp. 156–7.
[3] Jonah 2: 2.   [4] Cf. 1 Tim. 1: 7.
[5] *Enthusiasm*, Pt. II, pp. 157–8, citing Wesley's *Journal* for June 28, 1740, claiming that for Holy Communion 'no previous fitness is required . . . but a sense of our state, of our utter sinfulness and helplessness'. Cf. *An Answer to the Rev. Mr. Church's Remarks*, III. 3 (see Vol. 9 of this edition), and *A Letter to the Bishop of London*, § 10, above.
[6] *Enthusiasm*, Pt. II, p. 159.
[7] *A Sermon on Salvation by Faith*, II. 6; cf. II. 5.   [8] *Enthusiasm*, Pt. II, p. 159.

life;[a] all our works, the most specious of them, our righteousness, our prayers, needing an atonement themselves'.[b]

I do strongly affirm this. But of whom? In all these places but the last *of myself only*. In every one but this I speak in the singular number, and of myself, when confessedly *an unbeliever*. And of whom do I speak in that last place? Of *unbelievers*, and them only. The words are, 'All our tempers and works *in our natural state* are only evil continually.'[c]

Now, sir, where is *your* loop-hole to creep out? If you have none, I fear every impartial man will pass sentence upon you, that you have no regard either to *moral* or *religious obligations*

I have now weighed every argument you have brought to prove that the Methodists 'undermine morality and good works'.[1] A grievous charge indeed! But the more inexcusable is he who advances it, but is not able to make it good in any one single instance. Pardon my pertness, sir, in not barely *affirming* (that is *your* manner) but *proving* this; nay, and in telling you that you cannot make amends to God, to me, or to the world, without a retractation as public as your calumny.

42. You add, 'How the case stands in fact as to the number of converts among the Methodists, and *real reformation of life* to the certain and known duties of the gospel, is matter of difficult determination.'[2] Not at all. What is easier to be determined, than (1), that A. B. of Exeter or Tiverton was for many years a notorious drunkard, common swearer, or sabbath-breaker; (2), that he is not so now; that he is *really reformed* from drunkeness, swearing, sabbath-breaking, to sobriety and the other 'certain and known duties of the gospel'!

'But from what inquiry you can make there is no reason to think them, for the generality, better than their neighbours.'[3] Better than their neighbours? Why, are they no worse than their neighbours? Then what have you been doing all this time? But whether they are better or worse than their neighbours, they are undeniably better

---

[a] 1st *Journal*, p. 69 [Feb. 1, 1738].

[b] 2nd *Journal*, p. 23 [May 24, 1738; cf. Feb. 1, 1738].

[c] *Journal*, p. 70 [July 31, 1739. Wesley's footnotes here are in confusion, but in fact this is the last citation appended to the previous paragraph, even though the quotation there does not correspond to it, while an earlier citation (to 2nd *Journal*, p. 9) does partly match this].

---

[1] See § 37 above.   [2] *Enthusiasm*, Pt. II, p. 161.   [3] Ibid., pp. 161-2.

than themselves; I mean, better than they were before they heard this preaching, in the 'certain and known duties of the gospel'.

But you desire us to 'consider their black art of calumny; their uncharitableness; their excessive pride and vanity; their scepticism, doubts, and disbelief of God and Christ; their disorderly practices and contempt of authority; their bitter envying and inveterate broils among themselves; their coolness for good works'.[1] Sir, we will consider all these, when you have proved them. Till then, this is mere *brutum fulmen*.[2]

43. You proceed: 'If we take Mr. Wesley's own account, it falls very short of any *considerable reformation*.'[3] You mean; if we take *that part* of his account which you are pleased to transcribe. *Atticam elegantiam!*[4] But let any impartial man read my whole account, and then judge.

However, hence you infer that 'the new reformers have made but a slow and slight progress in the reformation of manners'.[5]

As a full answer to this I need only transcribe a page or two from the last *Appeal*:

God begins a glorious work in our land. You set yourself against it with your might; to prevent its beginning where it does not yet appear, and to destroy it wherever it does. In part you prevail. You keep many from hearing the Word that is able to save their souls. Others who have heard it, you induce to turn back from God, and to list under the devil's banner again. Then you make the success of your own wickedness an excuse for not acknowledging the work of God! You urge that not *many* sinners were reformed; and that *some* of those are now as bad as ever!

Whose fault is this? Is it ours? Or your own? Why have not thousands more been reformed? Yea, for every one who is now turned to God, why are there not ten thousand? Because you and your associates laboured so heartily in the cause of hell; because you and they spared no pains either to prevent or to destroy the work of God! By using all the power and wisdom you had you hindered thousands from hearing the gospel, which they might have found to be the power of God unto salvation.[6] Their blood is upon *your* heads. By inventing, or countenancing, or retailing lies, some refined, some gross and palpable, you

---

[1] Ibid., p. 162.

[2] 'A harmless thunderbolt'. Pliny, *Natural History*, II. xliii.

[3] *Enthusiasm*, Pt. II, p. 162.

[4] 'Attic refinement'. Cf. Cicero, *De Finibus bonorum et malorum* (*On the Purpose of Good and Evil*), iii. 2.

[5] *Enthusiasm*, Pt. II, p. 163.   [6] Rom. 1: 16.

hindered others from profiting by what they did hear. *You* are answerable to God for these souls also. Many who began to taste the good word, and run the way of God's commandments, by various methods you prevailed on to hear it no more. So they soon drew back to perdition. 5 But know that for every one of these also, God will require an account of *you* in the day of judgment![1]

And yet, in spite of all the malice, and wisdom, and strength, not only of men, but of 'principalities and powers', of 'the rulers of the darkness of this world', of the 'wicked spirits in high places',[2] there are 10 thousands found who are 'turned from dumb idols to serve the living and true God'.[3] What a harvest then might we have seen before now, if all who say they are 'on the Lord's side'[4] had come, as in all reason they ought, 'to the help of the Lord against the mighty'.[5] Yea, had they only *not opposed* the work of God, had they only *refrained from* 15 his messengers, might not the trumpet of God have been heard long since in every corner of our land? And thousands of sinners in every county been brought to 'fear God and honour the king'?[a]

44. Without any regard to this, your next assertion is that the Methodists are 'carrying on the work of popery'.[b] This also being 20 a charge of a very high nature, I shall particularly consider whatever you advance in defence of it.

Your first argument is: 'They have a strain of Jesuitical sophistry, artifice and craft, evasion, reserve, equivocation, and prevarication.' So you *say*. But you do not so much as aim at any proof.

25 Your second argument is: 'Mr. Wesley says, when a Methodist was receiving the Sacrament, God was pleased to let him see a crucified Saviour.'[6] Sir, Mr. Wesley does not say this. It is one that occasionally wrote to him. But if he had, what would you infer? That he is a Papist? Where is the consequence? Why, you say, 'Was 30 not this as good an argument for transubstantiation as several produced by the Papists?' Yes, exactly as good as either their arguments or yours. That is, just good for nothing.

Your third argument runs thus: 'We may see in Mr. Wesley's writings that he was once a *strict Churchman*, but gradually put on

---

[a] [*A Farther Appeal*, Pt. III,] p. 127, etc. [III. 33-4; the closing quotation is from 1 Pet. 2: 17].
[b] [*Enthusiasm*, Pt. II,] Sect. 21, p. 164 etc.

[1] See Matt. 12: 36.   [2] Cf. Eph. 6: 12.   [3] Cf. 1 Thess. 1: 9.
[4] Exod. 32: 26.   [5] Judg. 5: 23.
[6] *Enthusiasm*, Pt. II, pp. 164-5, citing *Journal*, Dec. 5, 1738—a letter from an unknown correspondent.

a more *catholic spirit*, tending at length to Roman Catholic. . . . He rejects any design to convert others *from any communion*; and consequently *not from popery*.'[1]

This is half true (which is something uncommon with you) and only half false. It is true that for thirty years last past I have 'gradually put on a more catholic spirit', finding more and more tenderness for those who differed from me either in *opinions* or *modes of worship*. But it is not true that I 'reject any design of converting others from any communion'. I have, by the blessing of God, converted several from popery, who are now alive and ready to testify it.

Your fourth argument is that in *A Collection of Prayers* I cite the words of an ancient liturgy 'for the faithful departed'.[2] Sir, whenever I use those words in the Burial Service I pray to the same effect: 'That we, with all those who are departed in thy faith and fear, may have our perfect consummation of bliss, both in body and soul.'[3] Yea, and whenever I say 'Thy Kingdom come'; for I mean both the kingdom of grace and glory. In this kind of general prayer therefore, for the faithful departed, I conceive myself to be clearly justified both by the earliest antiquity, by the Church of England, and by the Lord's Prayer; although the Papists have corrupted this scriptural practice into praying for those who die in their sins.

45. Your fifth argument is: That they use '*private confession*', in which 'every one is to speak the state of his heart, with his several temptations and deliverances', and 'answer as many searching questions as may be'.[4] 'And what a scene (say you) is hereby disclosed! What a filthy jakes opened, when the most searching questions are answered without reserve!' Hold, sir, unless you are answering for yourself. This undoubtedly you have a right to do. You can tell best what is in your own heart. And I cannot deny what you say. It may be a very filthy jakes, for ought I know. But pray do not

[1] Ibid., p. 166.

[2] Ibid., pp. 166–7. *A Collection of Forms of Prayer for Every Day of the Week* was first published in 1733. The section for Saturday evening of the greatly revised fifth edition of 1740 (and other editions stemming from it) contains a prayer for the dead from St. Mark's Liturgy, the traditional eucharistic liturgy of the Alexandrian Church. See *Bibliography*, No. 1, and Vol. 8 of this edition, *Prayers Private and Public*.

[3] As usual Wesley quotes the Book of Common Prayer from memory, varying from the original, which reads '. . . that are departed in the true faith of thy holy name, may have our perfect consummation and bliss, . . .'

[4] *Enthusiasm*, Pt. II, p. 167, citing *A Plain Account of the People called Methodists*, VI. 3 (see Vol. 9 of this edition, *The Methodist Societies: History, Nature and Design.*)

measure others by yourself. The hearts of believers 'are purified through faith'.¹ When these open their hearts one to another there is no such scene disclosed. Yet temptations to pride in various kinds, to self-will, to unbelief in many instances, they often feel in them-
5 selves (whether they give any place to them or no) and occasionally disclose to their brethren.

But this has no resemblance to *popish confession*—of which you are very sensible. For you cite my own words: 'The popish confession is the confession made by a single person to a priest; whereas
10 this is the confession of several persons conjointly, not to a priest, but to each other.'² You add, 'Will Mr. Wesley abide by this, and freely answer a question?' I will. For I desire only 'by manifestation of the truth to commend myself to every man's conscience in the sight of God'.³

15 Your question is: 'After private confessions taken in their bands, are not *reports* made to Mr. Wesley?' I answer, no; no reports are made to me of the particulars mentioned in private bands. 'Are no delinquents, male and female, *brought before him separately and confessed* by him?' No; none at all. You ask, 'How then do I know
20 the outward and inward states of those under my care?'⁴ I answer, by examining them once a quarter, more or less, not separately, but ten or fifteen together.

Therefore every unprejudiced person must see that there is no analogy between the popish confession to a priest, and our 'confess-
25 ing our faults one to another, and praying one for another', as St. James directs.⁵ Consequently neither does this argument, though urged with all your art and force, amount to any shadow of proof that 'the Methodists are carrying on the work of popery'.

46. Your sixth argument, such as it is, stands thus: 'Another
30 tendency to popery appears, by the notion of a *single drop of Christ's blood being a sufficient atonement for the sins of the whole world*. For however pious this may appear, it is absolutely false and papistical.'⁶ Sir, this argument is perfectly new and entirely your own. It were great pity to disturb you in the enjoyment of it.

---

¹ Cf. Acts 15: 9.   ² *Enthusiasm*, Pt. II, p. 168.   ³ Cf. 2 Cor. 4: 2.
⁴ Lavington cites Wesley's claim to this effect in *A Farther Appeal*, Pt. III, III. 17.
⁵ Jas. 5: 16.
⁶ *Enthusiasm*, Pt. II, p. 170. This idea also Lavington derived from the anonymous letter quoted by Wesley in his *Journal*, Dec. 5, 1738, which he cites. The writer says: 'And so strong was my faith, that if I had had all the sins of the whole world laid upon me, I knew and was sure one drop of his blood was sufficient to atone for all.'

A seventh argument you ground on those words in the *Plain Account of the People called Methodists*: '"'Tis a point we chiefly insist upon, that *orthodoxy*, or right opinions, is *a very slender part* of religion, if *any part of it at all*." The plain consequence whereof is (so you affirm) that teaching and believing the fundamental errors of popery, . . . with the whole train of their abominations and idolatries, are of very little moment, if any.'[1] Strain again, sir; pull hard, or you will never be able to drag this conclusion out of these premisses.

I assert, (1), that in a truly religious man, 'right opinions *are a very slender part* of religion'; (2), that in an irreligious, a profane man, they are not *any part of religion at all*; such a man not being one jot more religious because he is *orthodox*. Sir, it does not follow from either of these propositions that *wrong opinions* are not an hindrance to religion; and much less, that 'teaching and believing the fundamental errors of popery, *with the whole train of their abominations and idolatries*' (practised, I presume you mean, as well as taught and believed) 'are of very little moment, if any'.

I am so far from saying or thinking this that in my printed letter to a priest of that communion (did you never read it, or hear of it before?) are these express words: 'I pity you much, having the same assurance that Jesus is the Christ, and that no Romanist can expect to be saved according to the terms of his covenant.'[a] Do you term this 'an extenuation of their abominations? A reducing them to almost a mere nothing.'[2]

47. You argue, eighthly, thus: 'The Methodist doctrine of impressions and assurances holds equally for popish *enthusiasts*.'[3] This needs no answer. I have already shown that the Methodist doctrine in these respects is both scriptural and rational.

Your ninth argument is: 'Their sudden . . . conversions stand upon the same footing with the popish.' You should say, 'are a proof that they are promoting popery.' I leave you to enjoy this argument also.

But the dreadful one you reserve for the last, namely, our 'recommending popish books. . . . One is the life of Mr. de Renty, of which

---

[a] 3rd *Journal*, p. 77 [27 Aug., 1739].

[1] Ibid., p. 171, citing *A Plain Account of the People called Methodists*, I. 2.
[2] Ibid., pp. 171–2.
[3] Ibid., p. 172. For Wesley's answer see above, §§ 20–1.

Mr. Wesley has published *An extract.*[1] To prove your inimitable fairness here, you scrape up again all the trash wherein the weak writer of that life abounds, and which I had pared off and thrown away. Sir, could you find nothing to your purpose in the *Extract* itself? I fancy you might; for I have purposely left in two or three particulars to show of what communion he was, which I did not think it right to conceal.

You go on: 'Francis of Sales is another Papist much commended by Mr. Wesley, and who he doubts not is in Abraham's bosom . . . . He is the Methodist's bosom friend.'[2]

I believe he is in Abraham's bosom. But he is no 'bosom friend of the Methodists'. I question whether one in five hundred of them has so much as heard his name. And as for me, neither do I 'commend him much, nor recommend' him at all. His life I never saw, nor any of his works but his *Introduction to a Holy Life*. This the late Dr. Nicholls translated into English, published and strongly *recommended*. Therefore if this be a proof of promoting popery, that censure falls not on me but him.[3]

I have now considered all the arguments you have brought to prove that the Methodists are 'carrying on the work of popery', And I am persuaded every candid man who rightly weighs what has been said with any degree of attention, will clearly see, not only that no one of those arguments is of any real force at all, but that you do not believe yourself; you do not believe the conclusion which you *make as if* you would prove. Only you keep close to your laudable resolution of throwing as much dirt as possible.

48. It remains only to gather up some of your fragments, as still farther proofs of your integrity.

You graciously say, 'I don't lay much stress upon the charge of some of the angry Moravians against Mr. Wesley and brother for preaching popery.'[4] Sir, if you had, you would only have hurt yourself. For (1), the Moravians never, that I know of, brought this charge at all; (2), when Mr. C[ennick] and two other predestinarians (these were the persons) affirmed 'they had heard both my brother

---

[1] *Enthusiasm*, Pt. II, pp. 172–3. For Wesley, *An Extract of the Life of Monsieur de Renty* (1741), see *Bibliography*, No. 43. For another tribute to de Renty see above, *A Farther Appeal*, Pt. II, III. 12 and note.

[2] Ibid., p. 176.

[3] William Nicholls (1664–1712), *An Introduction to a Devout Life, by Francis Sales. . . . Translated and reformed from the errors of the popish edition* (1701).

[4] *Enthusiasm*, Pt. II, p. 179.

and me preach popery', they meant neither more nor less thereby
than the doctrine of a universal redemption.[1]

'Some connection between the doctrines of the Methodists and
Papists hath been shown through this whole Comparison.'[2] Shown!
But how? By the same art of wire-drawing and deciphering which 5
would prove an equal connexion between the Methodists and
Mahometans.

'Jesuits have often mingled, and been the ringleaders among our
enthusiastic sectaries.'[3] Sir, I am greatly obliged to you for your
compliment, as well as for your parallel of Mr. Faithful Commin.[4] 10

And pray, sir, at what time do you think it was that I first
'mingled with those enthusiastic sectaries'? When I came back from
Germany? Or when I returned from Georgia? Or while I was at
Lincoln College? Although the plot itself might be laid before, when
I was at Christ Church, or at the Charterhouse School. 15

But 'a Jesuit's or enthusiast's declaring against popery is no test
of their sincerity'.[5] Most sure; nor is a nameless person's declaring
against Methodism any proof that he is not a Jesuit. I remember well
when a well-dressed man, taking his stand not far from Moorfields,
had gathered a large company, and was vehemently asserting that 20
'those rogues the Methodists were all Papists'; till a gentleman
coming by fixed his eye on him and cried, 'Stop that man; I know
him personally; he is a Romish priest.'

I know not that anything remains on this head which bears so
much as the face of an argument. So that of all the charges you have 25
brought (and truly you have not been sparing) there is not one
wherein your proof falls more miserably short than in this, that 'the
Methodists are advancing popery'.

49. I have at length gone through your whole performance,
weighed whatever you cite from my writings, and shown at large 30
how far those passages are from proving all or any part of your
charge. So that all you attempt to build on them, of the pride and
vanity of the Methodists;[a] of their shuffling and prevaricating;[b] of

---

[a] § 3.   [b] § 4.

[1] See *Journal*, Feb. 28, 1741. For Cennick see § 32 above.
[2] *Enthusiasm*, Pt. II, p. 179.   [3] Ibid.
[4] Ibid., pp. 180–4. Father Faithful Commin was a Dominican friar, sent to England
as a Roman Catholic missionary in the reign of Queen Elizabeth. He was examined
before the queen and Archbishop Parker. He escaped to Rome, and the pope gave him
2,000 ducats in recognition of his services.   [5] Ibid., p. 184.

their affectation of prophesying;[a] laying claim to the miraculous favours of heaven;[b] unsteadiness of temper;[c] unsteadiness in sentiment and practice;[d] art and cunning;[e] giving up inspiration and extraordinary calls;[f] scepticism, infidelity, atheism;[g] un-
5 charitableness to their opponents;[h] contempt of order and authority;[i] and fierce, rancorous quarrels with each other;[j] of the tendency of Methodism to undermine morality and good works;[k] and to carry on the good work of popery[l]—all this fabric falls to the ground at once, unless you can find some better foundation to support it.

10   50. These things being so, what must all unprejudiced men think of you and your whole performance? You have advanced a charge, not against one or two persons only, but indiscriminately against a whole *body of people*, of His Majesty's subjects, Englishmen, Protestant, members, I suppose, of your own Church; a charge
15 containing abundance of articles, and most of them of the highest and blackest nature. You have prosecuted this with unparalleled bitterness of spirit and acrimony of language; using sometimes the most coarse, rude, scurrilous terms; sometimes the keenest sarcasms you could devise. The point you have steadily pursued in *thus*
20 prosecuting *this* charge is, first, to expose the whole people to the hatred and scorn of all mankind, and next, to stir up the *civil powers* against them. And when this charge comes to be fairly weighed, there is not a single article of it true! The passages you cite to make it good are one and all such as prove nothing less than the points
25 in question; most of them such as you have palpably maimed, corrupted, and strained to a sense never thought of by the writer; many of them such as are flat against you, and overthrow the very point they are brought to support. What can they think but that this is the most shocking violation of the Christian rule: 'Thou shalt
30 love thy neighbour as thyself';[1] the most open affront to all justice, and even common humanity; the most glaring insult upon the common sense and reason of mankind which has lately appeared in the world.

     If you say, 'But I have proved the charge upon Mr. Whitefield.'
35 Admit you have (which I do not allow) Mr. Whitefield is not 'the Methodists'. No, nor the societies under his care; they are not

---

a § 5.   b § 6.   c § 9.   d § 11.   e § 12.   f § 13.
g § 14.   h § 15, etc.   i § 18.   j § 19, etc.   k § 20.   l § 21.

---

[1] Matt. 19: 19, etc.

a third, perhaps not a tenth part of the Methodists. What then can excuse your ascribing *their* faults (were they proved) to the *whole body*? You indict ten men. Suppose you prove the indictment upon one, will you *therefore* condemn the other nine? Nay, let every man bear his own burden, since every man must give an account of himself to God.

I had occasion once before to say to an opponent, 'You know not to show mercy.'[1] Yet that gentlemen did regard truth and justice. But you regard neither mercy, justice, nor truth. To vilify, to blacken, is your one point. I pray God it may not be laid to your charge! May he show you mercy, though you show none!

I am, sir,

Your friend and well-wisher,

John Wesley

---

[1] Cf. *The Principles of a Methodist Farther Explained*, IV. 2: 'O sir, you put me in mind of him who said, "I know not to show mercy"!'

A

SECOND LETTER

TO THE

Lord Bishop of *Exeter,*

In Answer to

His Lordship's late Letter.

By *JOHN WESLEY,* M.A.

The Second Edition.

LONDON:

Printed by H. Cock, in *Bloomsbury-Market*; and sold at the *Foundery,* near *Upper-Moorfields*; by *J. Robinson,* in *Ludgate-Street*; by *T. Trye,* near *Gray's-Inn-Gate, Holborn*; by *T. James,* under the *Royal-Exchange*; and G. *Englefield,* in *Weft-street,* near the *Seven Dials.* M.DCC.LII.

A
SECOND LETTER, &c.[1]

My Lord,

In my late letter to your lordship I used no ceremony: I suppose it was not expected from one who was so deeply injured. And I trust I used no rudeness; if I did, I am ready to ask your lordship's pardon. 5

That letter 'related to a matter of fact published on your lordship's authority, which I endeavoured to falsify', and your lordship now again endeavours to support.[a]

The facts alleged are: First, That I told Mrs. Morgan at Mitchell, 'You are in hell; you are damned already'; Secondly, That I asked 10 her to 'live upon free cost'; Thirdly, That she determined to admit no more Methodists into her house.

At first I thought so silly and improbable a story neither deserved nor required a confutation; but when my friends thought otherwise I called on Mrs. Morgan, who denied she ever said any such thing. 15 I wrote down her words, part of which I transcribed in my letter to your lordship, as follows:

> On Saturday, August 25, 1750, Mr. Trembath of St. Gennys, Mr. Haime of Shaftesbury, and I, called at Mr. Morgan's at Mitchell. The servant telling me her master was not at home, I desired to speak 20 with her mistress, the 'honest, sensible woman'. I immediately asked, 'Did I ever tell you or your husband that you would be damned if you took any money of me?' (So the story ran in the first part of the Comparison: it has now undergone a very considerable alteration.) 'Or did you or he ever affirm' (another circumstance related at Truro) 'that 25

[a] *The Bishop of Exeter's Letter*, pp. 2–3 [i.e. *The Bishop of Exeter's Answer to Mr. J. Wesley's late Letter to his Lordship*, London, Knapton, 1752, pp. 1–2. For the original charge in its full detail see Lavington, *Enthusiasm*, Pt. III, p. 51, and for Wesley's rebuttal the opening sections of his *Second Letter to the Author of the Enthusiasm of Methodists and Papists Compared*].

---

[1] No copy is known of the presumptive first edition of 1752. For variant readings from the edited text (based on the second edition, London, Cock, 1752) and the version in the *Works*, Vol. 17 (1773) see the Appendix to this volume, p. 557. For further details, see *Bibliography*, No. 195.

I was rude with your maid?' She replied vehemently, 'Sir, I never said you was, or that you said any such thing. And I don't suppose my husband did. But we have been belied as well as our neighbours.' She added, 'When the bishop came down last, he sent us word he would

5 dine at our house; but he did not, being invited to a neighbouring gentleman's. He sent for me thither, and said, "Good woman, do you know these people that go up and down? Do you know Mr. Wesley? Did not he tell you, you would be damned if you took any money of him? And did not he offer rudeness to your maid?" I told him, "No,

10 my lord; he never said any such thing to me, nor to my husband that I know of. He never offered any rudeness to any maid of mine. I never saw, or knew any harm by him. But a man told me once (who, I was told, was a Methodist Preacher) that I should be damned, if I did not know my sins were forgiven."'[1]

15 Your lordship replies, 'I neither sent word that I would dine at their house, nor did I send for Mrs. Morgan. . . . Every word that passed between us was at her own house at Mitchell.'[a] I believe it; and consequently, that the want of exactness in this point rests on Mrs. Morgan, not on your lordship.

20 Your lordship adds, 'The following attestations will sufficiently clear me from any imputation, or even suspicion, of having published a falsehood.' I apprehend otherwise. To waive what is past, if the facts now published by your lordship, or any part of them, be not true, then certainly your lordship will lie under more than a

25 'suspicion of having published a falsehood'.

The attestations your lordship produces are: First, those of your lordship's chancellor[2] and archdeacon:[3] Secondly, those of Mr. Bennet.[4]

The former attest that in June or July, 1748, Mrs. Morgan did

30 say those things to your lordship.[b] I believe she did, and therefore acquit your lordship of being the *inventor* of those falsehoods.

Mr. Bennet avers that in January last Mrs. Morgan repeated to him what she had before said to your lordship.[c] Probably she might;

---

[a] [*The Bishop of Exeter's Answer*,] p. 7.   [b] [Ibid.,] pp. 8–10.
[c] [Ibid.,] pp. 11–12.

[1] Wesley, *Second Letter to the Author of The Enthusiasm of the Methodists and Papists Compared*, § 3, reprinted in *The Bishop of Exeter's Answer*, pp. 5–7.
[2] Revd. John Fursman, Chancellor of Exeter Cathedral.
[3] Revd. William Hole, Archdeacon of Barnstaple.
[4] Revd. Thomas Bennet, Vicar of St. Enoder, who served the village of Mtichell.

having said those things once, I do not wonder if she said them again.

Nevertheless, before Mr. Trembath and Mr. Haime she denied every word of it.

To get over this difficulty, your lordship publishes a second letter from Mr. Bennet, wherein he says: 'On March 4th last Mrs. Morgan said, "I was told by my servant that I was wanted above stairs; where, when I came, the chamber door being open, I found them (Mr. Wesley and others) round the table on their knees."' He adds, 'That Mrs. Morgan owned one circumstance[1] in it was true; but as to the other parts of Mr. Wesley's letter to the bishop, she declares 'tis all false.'

I believe Mrs. Morgan did say this to Mr. Bennet, and that therefore neither is he 'the maker of a lie'.[2] But he is the relater of a whole train of falsehoods, and those told merely for telling sake. I was never yet in any chamber at Mrs. Morgan's. I was never *above stairs* there in my life. On August 25, 1750, I was *below stairs* all the time I was in the house. When Mrs. Morgan came in I was *standing* in the large parlour; nor did any of us *kneel* while we were under the roof. This both Mr. Trembath and Mr. Haime can attest upon oath, whatsoever Mrs. Morgan may declare to the contrary.

But she declared farther (so Mr. Bennet writes), 'That Mr. John Wesley some time ago said to a maid of hers such things as were not fit to be spoken . . .'[a] And Mr. Morgan declared that he 'did or said such indecent things to the above-named maid' (the same fact, I presume, only a little embellished) 'in his chamber, in the night, that she immediately ran downstairs, and protested she would not go near him or any of the Methodists more'.[b]

To save trouble to your lordship as well as to myself I will put this cause upon a very short issue. If your lordship will only prove that ever I lay one night in Mr. Morgan's house; nay, that ever I was in the town of Mitchell after sunset, I will confess the whole charge.

What your lordship mentions 'by the way' I will now consider: 'Some of your western correspondents imposed upon the *leaders of*

---

[a] [*Answer*,] p. 11. [b] [Ibid.,] p. 12.

---

[1] i.e. Wesley's statement that she denied making the charge that he 'attempted to debauch a maid'. [2] Cf. Rev. 21: 27.

Methodism, by transmitting to London a notoriously false account of my Charge to the clergy. . . . Afterwards the Methodists confessed themselves to have been deceived; yet some time after the Method- ists at Cork in Ireland, your own brother at the head of them,
5 reprinted the same lying pamphlet, as my performance.'ᵃ

My lord, I know not who are your lordship's Irish correspondents; but here are almost as many mistakes as lines. For, (1). They were none of *my* correspondents who sent that account to London; (2). It was sent not to the 'leaders of Methodism', but to one who was
10 no Methodist at all; (3). That it was a false account, I do not know. But your lordship may easily put it out of dispute. And many have wondered that your lordship did not do so long ago, by printing the Charge in question; (4). I did never confess it was a 'false account', nor any person by my consent, or with my knowledge; (5). That
15 account was never reprinted at Cork at all; (6). When it was re- printed at Dublin your lordship had not disowned it; (7). My brother was not in Dublin when it was done; nor did either he or I know of it till long after.

Therefore, when my brother was asked how he could reprint
20 such an account after your lordship had publicly disowned it I do not at all wonder that 'he did not offer a single word in answer'.¹

Whether this, as well as my former letter, be 'mere rant and declamation',² or plain and sober reason, I must refer to the world and your lordship's own conscience.
25   I am, my lord,
                       Your lordship's most obedient servant,
                                  John Wesley
Newcastle upon Tyne,
    May 8, 1752

ᵃ [Ibid.,] pp. 4–5.

---

¹ *Answer*, p. 5.   ² Ibid., p. 15.

A Letter to The Rev. Mr. Horne

Introduction

On Sunday, June 7, 1761, the Revd. George Horne (1730–92), fellow of Magdalen College, preached before the University of Oxford. His text was James 2:24, and his aim was to demonstrate that justification is not by faith alone, but by faith and works together. The doctrine taught by St. Paul, he argued, coincides exactly with that taught by St. James, and this balanced emphasis represents the teaching of the Church of England. This by itself would not necessarily have demanded an answer from Wesley, but early in the sermon he introduced a comment which could hardly be ignored. Horne had referred to the threat of antinomianism. 'And what wonder', he continued,

> that this or any other heresy should be introduced and propagated if men, instead of having recourse to the Catholic doctors of the ancient church, and to such of our divines as have trodden in their steps, will extract their theology from the latest and lowest of modern sectaries, thus beginning where they should end? if instead of drawing living water for the use of the sanctuary from the fresh springs of primitive antiquity, they take up with such as comes to them at second or third hand from the Lake of Geneva? if the spirit of a Cyprian exerted in the maintenance of the *vigor episcopatus* and the institution of the church be accounted for bigotry and narrowness, and Clement and Ignatius pass for but very moderate divines, when compared with the new lights of the Tabernacle and the Foundery? Should this method of studying divinity prevail, to the exclusion of the other, there will soon be neither order left in the church, nor certainty in the faith.[1]

The personal innuendo demanded a reply: Horne explicitly attributed antinomianism to the Methodists, in spite of the fact that Wesley had been struggling for years to dissociate his movement from the taint of this heresy. But there was a further consideration: implicit in Horne's sermon was a theology which Wesley regarded

---

[1] George Horne, *Works wrought through Faith a Condition of our Justification*, p. 6. (In *The Works of the late Right Reverend George Horne, D.D.* (4 vols., London, 1831) this sermon appears as Discourse LXII in Vol. 3). The Tabernacle and the Foundery were respectively the headquarters in London of Whitefield and of Wesley.

as dangerous, and which directly challenged his own teaching on justification. Early in his discourse the preacher provided a summary of the theme he proposed to develop.

> That faith is such a necessary condition [of salvation], all Christians are agreed. That works are so likewise I shall prove—from Scripture testimonies; from Scripture examples; from the nature of faith; from the nature of justification; and from the process at the day of Judgment: after which I shall show from St. Paul's own words that he preaches the very same doctrine with St. James; and close the whole with the state of that doctrine given by Bishop Bull in the noble confession of his faith in this particular made by him when on his deathbed.[1]

Wesley believed that this was theologically pernicious. In his reply he undertook to prove that justification by faith alone is both scriptural and Anglican, proclaimed by St. Paul and expounded in the Homilies and in the Thirty-nine Articles. Repentance, justification, faith, good works, and the relation between all of these demand and receive careful examination. Wesley's letter provides a condensed exposition of many of the central elements in his system of theology.

Wesley replied to Horne with a degree of respect that contrasts sharply with his attitude to Bishops Lavington and Warburton. This was natural. The tone of Horne's sermon is serious and reasonable. It is a worthy discussion of an important subject. It is wholly free from the scurrility which marked much contemporary polemics.

But Horne was guilty of an offence which Wesley always found it hard to overlook: he had attacked a theological position without bothering to read what its upholders had already advanced in its support. The *Appeals*—particularly *A Farther Appeal*—would have prevented many misconceptions at the outset. Since Horne was apparently not familiar with the work, Wesley included in his letter copious extracts from the earlier tract. When Wesley prepared a collected edition of his *Works* he omitted most of these quotations, but in doing so he considerably altered the impact of this letter. In this edition they have been restored.

Of all the men with whom he engaged in controversy, few held a higher place in his esteem than George Horne. When Wesley

---

[1] Ibid., pp. 8–9. The passage to which Horne refers is in Robert Nelson, *The Life of Dr. George Bull* (1713), p. 463. On Bishop George Bull, cf. below, p. 453 n. 5.

decided that he must reply to Horne's sermon, he did so with a combination of reluctance and relief. 'O that I might dispute with no man! but if I must dispute, let it be with men of sense.'[1] He regarded Horne's Commentary on the Psalms (1771) as 'the best that ever was wrote',[2] and he used it as a criterion by which to judge florid and pretentious writers. 'Give me', he exclaimed, 'plain, strong Dr. Horne.'[3]

Horne's career was marked by steady though not spectacular promotion. When he preached before the University he was thirty years old and had been a fellow of Magdalen for ten years. In 1768 he became president of the college. In 1776 he was vice-chancellor of the University of Oxford. He was chaplain-in-ordinary to King George III from 1771 to 1781; in the latter year he was appointed Dean of Canterbury. In 1790 he was consecrated Bishop of Norwich, but his health had already broken, and he died within two years.

George Horne was a man of intelligence and integrity. When Dr. Johnson and Boswell had tea with him at Oxford in 1776 they were obviously impressed with his qualities.[4] He was a High Churchman of the eighteenth-century type; so was Wesley. Ironically, in his attack on heretical tendencies, he advocated reliance on precisely the theological sources from which Wesley himself chiefly drew. Horne was an earnest man; consequently, though he criticized the leading Methodists, he was regarded as sympathetic to Methodism itself. In 1761, a year before he preached his sermon on justification, six undergraduates, accused of Methodist views, were expelled from St. Edmund Hall, Oxford. Horne strongly disapproved of the action taken by the academic authorities.

Wesley's respect for Horne remained undiminished to the end. Shortly after Horne became Bishop of Norwich, he was asked if he had any objection to Wesley preaching in the parish church of Diss, Norfolk. 'None at all', he replied; Wesley was 'an ordained minister of the Church of England', and he had no intention of allowing him to be harassed in his diocese.[5]

---

[1] *Journal*, Mar. 8, 1762.

[2] *Journal*, Mar. 27, 1783.

[3] Letter to Miss Thornton, Feb. 4, 1787. Wesley's respect for Horne is clearly reflected in § 10 of the present work.

[4] James Boswell, *Life of Samuel Johnson*, Chapter XXXI.

[5] *Journal*, Oct. 20, 1790. Cf. also *Memoirs of the Life of Dr. Horne*, by William Jones, in *The Works of Horne*, Vol. I. Jones was a close friend of Horne; as 'Jones of Nayland' he was a well-known High-Churchman.

The text reproduced is basically that of the only separate edition, printed by William Strahan for Flexney, London, no date (1761). For the variants in the version published in *Works*, Vol. 17 (1772), see the appendix to this volume, p. 557. For further bibliographical details see *Bibliography*, No. 246.

A

LETTER

TO THE

Rev. Mr. HORNE:

OCCASIONED

By his late SERMON

Preached before the

UNIVERSITY of OXFORD.

LONDON,

Printed: and fold by W. FLEXNEY, near Gray's-Inn-
Gate, Holbourn; by G. KEITH, in Gracechurch-
ftreet; by T. JAMES, under the Royal-Exchange.

A
LETTER

TO THE

Rev. Mr. HORNE

Reverend Sir,

When you spoke of '*heresies* making their periodical revolutions', of '*antinomianism* rampant among us', and immediately after of 'the *new lights* at the Tabernacle and Foundery',[1] must not your hearers naturally think that Mr. Whitefield and I were reviving those heresies? But do you know the persons of whom you speak? Have you ever conversed with them? Have you read their writings? If not, is it kind, is it just, to pass so severe a censure upon them? Had you only taken the trouble of reading one tract, the *Appeal to Men of Reason and Religion*, you would have seen that a great part of what you affirm is what I never denied. To put this beyond dispute I beg leave to transcribe some passages from that treatise, which will show not only what I teach now, but what I have taught for many years. I will afterward simply and plainly declare wherein I as yet differ from you. And the rather, that if I err therein you may, by God's assistance, convince me of it.

I. 1. *Justification* sometimes means our acquittal at the last day.[2] But this is altogether out of the present question—that justification whereof our Articles and Homilies speak, meaning present forgiveness and acceptance with God, who therein 'declares his righteousness', or mercy, by or 'for the remission of the sins that are past'.[a]

---

[a] *Farther Appeal*, Part I, pp. 1–2 [I. 2]; Rom. 3: 25.

---

[1] George Horne, *Works wrought through faith a condition of our justification. A Sermon preached before the University of Oxford, at St. Mary's, on Sunday, June 7, 1761*, Oxford, The Clarendon Press, n.d. (cited below in accordance with Wesley's practice as *Sermon*), pp. 5–6. For the Tabernacle and the Foundery, see above, p. 437 n.

[2] When reprinting the *Letter* in his *Works* Wesley omitted all of Part I except the opening and closing sentences, clearly because this exposition of Methodist teaching on justification was little more than a slightly abridged extract from *A Farther Appeal*, Part I, §§ I. 2–II. 11, which was reproduced elsewhere in the *Works*.

2. I believe the *condition* of this is faith: I mean, not only that without faith we cannot be justified, but also that as soon as anyone has true faith, in that moment he is justified.[a]

5   Good works follow this faith, but cannot go before it:[b] much less can sanctification, that is a continued course of good works, springing from holiness of heart. But it is allowed that entire sanctification goes before our justification at the last day.

It is allowed also that repentance[c] and 'fruits meet for repentance'[d] go before faith. Repentance *absolutely must* go before faith; fruits meet

10   for it, if there be opportunity. By repentance I mean conviction of sin producing real desires and sincere resolutions of amendment; and by 'fruits meet for repentance', forgiving our brother,[e] ceasing from evil, doing good,[f] using the ordinances of God,[g] and in general obeying him according to the measure of grace we have received.[h] But these I

15   cannot as yet term 'good works', because they do not spring from faith and the love of God.

3. Faith, in general, is a divine, supernatural ἔλεγχος of things not seen;[i] not discoverable by our bodily senses, as being either past, future, or spiritual. Justifying faith implies, not only a divine ἔλεγχος

20   that 'God was in Christ, reconciling the world to himself'[1] but a sure trust and confidence that Christ died for *my* sins, that he 'loved *me*, and gave himself for *me*'.[j] And the moment a penitent sinner believes this, God pardons and absolves him.

And as soon as his pardon or justification is witnessed to him by the

25   Holy Ghost, he is saved. He loves God and all mankind. He has 'the mind that was in Christ',[2] and power to 'walk as he also walked'.[3] From that time—unless he 'makes shipwreck of his faith'[4]—salvation gradually increases in his soul. For 'so is the kingdom of God, as if a man should cast seed into the ground, . . . and it springeth up, first the

30   blade, then the ear, after that the full corn in the ear'.[k]

4. Many persons seem to be very confused as to the nature of justification, and speak as if they had never heard of any justification antecedent to that of the last day. To clear up this, there needs only a close inspection of our Articles and Homilies, wherein justification is

35   always taken for the present remission of our sins.

But many are the objections which have been warmly urged against the condition of justification, faith alone. A late writer, in particular,

---

[a] [*Farther Appeal*, Pt. I,] p. 2.   [b] Luke 6: 43.   [c] Mark 1: 15.   [d] Matt. 3: 8.
[e] Matt. 6: 14, 15.   [f] Luke 3: 4, 9, etc. [cf. Isa. 1: 16, 17.]   [g] Matt. 7: 7.
[h] Matt. 25: 29.   [i] Heb. 11: 1.   [j] Gal. 2: 20.
[k] Mark 4: 26–8 [*A Farther Appeal*, Pt. I, I. 4].

[1] 2 Cor. 5: 19.   [2] Cf. Phil. 2: 5.   [3] Cf. 1 John 2: 6.
[4] Cf. 1 Tim. 1: 19 (*Notes*).

affirms this doctrine is both unscriptural and contrary to the doctrine of the Church of England.[1]

5. To prove it is unscriptural he alleges that 'sanctification, according to Scripture, must go before it', to evince which he cites the following texts: 'Preach repentance and remission of sins';[a] 'Repent and be baptized every one of you . . . for the remission of sins';[b] 'Repent and be converted, that your sins may be blotted out.'[c]

I conceive these, and all the Scriptures which can be quoted to prove sanctification antecedent to justification (if they do not relate to our final justification), prove only (what I never denied) that repentance or conviction of sin, and 'fruits meet for repentance', precede that faith whereby we are justified; but by no means that the love of God, or any branch of true holiness, must or can precede faith.[2]

6. It is objected, secondly, that justification by faith alone is not the doctrine of the Church of England.

In order to be clearly and fully satisfied what the doctrine of the Church of England is (as it stands opposite to the doctrine of the *antinomians* on the one hand, and to that of *justification by works* on the other) I will simply set down what occurs on this head either in her liturgy, Articles, or Homilies:

Spare thou them, O God, which *confess their faults*. Restore thou them that are *penitent*; according to thy promises declared unto mankind in Christ Jesus our Lord.[3]

He pardoneth and absolveth all them that *truly repent* and *unfeignedly believe* his holy gospel.[4]

Almighty God, who dost forgive the sins of them that are *penitent*, create and make in us new and contrite hearts; that we, *worthily lamenting our sins* and *acknowledging our wretchedness*, may obtain of thee perfect remission and forgiveness, through Jesus Christ our Lord.[d]

---

[a] Luke 24: 47.   [b] Acts 2: 38.   [c] Acts 3: 19.
[d] [B.C.P.] Collect for Ash Wednesday.

---

[1] See *A Farther Appeal*, Pt. I, II. 1. In the passage to which he refers, Wesley has been defining the crucial theological terms which he used (justification, sanctification, new birth, faith); he now turns to consider objections to his position. In this quotation from his own work he has condensed what he had previously written. He had referred specifically to two works published anonymously, *The Notions of the Methodists fully disproved by setting the doctrine of the Church of England concerning justification and regeneration in a true light* (1743) and *The Notions of the Methodists farther disproved . . .* (1743). These were attacks on *An Earnest Appeal*, and aimed to show that Wesley's doctrine was not scriptural, nor was it the teaching of the Church of England.

[2] Ibid., II. 2.

[3] B.C.P., Morning Prayer, General Confession.   [4] Ibid., Absolution.

Almighty God . . . hath promised forgiveness of sins to all them that with *hearty repentance* and *true faith* turn unto him.ᵃ

Our Lord Jesus Christ . . . hath left power . . . to absolve all sinners who *truly repent* and *believe* in him.ᵇ

5 Give him unfeigned *repentance* and steadfast *faith*, that his sins may be blotted out.ᶜ

He is a merciful receiver of all true, *penitent* sinners, and is ready to pardon us if we come unto him with *faithful repentance*.ᵈ

Infants indeed our Church supposes to be justified in baptism, 10 although they cannot then either *believe* or *repent*. But she expressly requires both *repentance* and *faith* in those who come to be baptized when they are of riper years.

As earnestly therefore as our Church inculcates justification by faith alone, she nevertheless supposes repentance to be previous to faith, and 15 'fruits meet for repentance'; yea, and universal holiness to be previous to final justification, as evidently appears from the following words:

Let us beseech him . . . that the rest of our lives may be pure and holy, so that at the last we may come to his eternal joy.ᵉ

May we seriously apply our hearts to that holy and heavenly 20 wisdom . . . here, which may in the end bring us to life everlasting.ᶠ

Raise us from the death of sin unto the life of righteousness, . . . that at the last day we may be found acceptable in thy sight.ᵍ

If we from henceforth walk in his ways, . . . seeking always his 25 glory, . . . Christ . . . will set us on his right hand.ʰ

[7.]¹ We come next to the Articles of our Church. The former part of the ninth runs thus:

Of Original or Birth Sin

Original sin is the fault and corruption of the nature of every 30 man, . . . whereby man is very far gone from original righteousness, and is of his own nature inclined to evil, so that the flesh lusteth always contrary to the spirit: and therefore in every person born into the world it deserveth God's wrath and damnation.

ᵃ [B.C.P.,] Communion Office.   ᵇ [Ibid.,] Visitation of the Sick.
ᶜ Ibid.   ᵈ [Ibid.,] Commination office.
ᵉ [Ibid., Morning and Evening Prayer,] Absolution.
ᶠ [Ibid.,] Visitation of the Sick.   ᵍ [Ibid.,] Burial Office.
ʰ [Ibid.,] Commination Office.

¹ From here to the end of Part I Wesley did not number his sections, contrary to his usual practice and the example of *A Farther Appeal*. Section numbers have been supplied at the same places as in *A Farther Appeal*.

Art. X. Of Free Will

The condition of man after the fall of Adam is such that he cannot turn and prepare himself by his own natural strength and good works to faith and calling upon God. Wherefore we have no power to do good works pleasant and acceptable to God, without the grace of 5 God by Christ preventing us that we may have a good will, and working with us when we have that good will.

Art. XI. Of the Justification of Man

We are accounted righteous before God only for the merit of our Lord and Saviour Jesus Christ, by faith, and not for our own works 10 or deservings. Wherefore that we are justified by faith only is a most wholesome doctrine, and very full of comfort, as is more largely expressed in the Homily of Justification.

I believe this Article relates to the *meritorious cause* of justification, rather than to the *condition* of it. On this therefore I do not build any- 15 thing concerning it, but on those that follow.

Art. XII. Of Good Works

Albeit that good works, which are the fruits of faith and follow after justification, cannot put away our sins; yet are they pleasing and acceptable to God in Christ, and do spring out necessarily of a true 20 and lively faith; insomuch that by them a lively faith may be as evidently known as a tree may be known by the fruit.

We are taught here, (1), that good works, in general, follow after justification; (2), that they spring out of a true and lively faith (that faith whereby we are justified); (3), that true, justifying faith may be 25 as evidently known by them as a tree is discerned by the fruit.

Does it not follow that the supposing any good works to go *before* justification is full as absurd as the supposing an apple or any other fruit to grow before the tree?

But let us hear the Church speaking yet more plainly.   30

Art. XIII. Of Works done before Justification

Works done before the grace of Christ and the inspiration of his Spirit (i.e. before justification, as the title expresses it), are not pleasant to God, forasmuch as they spring not of faith in Jesu Christ . . .: yea rather, for that they are not done as God hath willed 35 and commanded them to be done, we doubt not but they have the nature of sin.

[8.] It remains to consider what occurs in the Homilies, first with regard to the *meritorious cause* of our justification, agreeable to the eleventh, and then with regard to the *condition* of it, agreeable to the twelfth and thirteenth Articles.

These things must go together in our justification: upon God's part, his great mercy and grace; upon Christ's part, the satisfaction of God's justice; and upon our part, true and lively faith in the merits of Jesus Christ.[a]

So that the grace of God doth not shut out the justice (or righteousness) of God in our justification; but only shutteth out the righteousness of man . . . as to *deserving* our justification.

And therefore St. Paul declareth nothing on the behalf of man concerning his justification, but only a true faith.

And yet that faith doth not shut out repentance, hope, love, to be joined with faith (that is, *afterwards*—see below) in every man that is justified. . . . Neither doth faith shut out the righteousness of our good works, necessarily to be done afterwards; but it excludeth them, so that we may not do them to the intent to be made just (or to be justified) by doing them.

That we are justified by *faith alone* is spoken to take away clearly all *merit* of our works, and wholly to ascribe the merit and deserving of our justification unto Christ only.[b]

The true meaning of the saying, 'we be justified by faith only', is this: we be justified by the merits of Christ only, and not of our own works.[c]

[9.] Thus far touching the *meritorious cause* of our justification, referred to in the eleventh Article. The twelfth and thirteenth are a summary of what now follows with regard to the *condition* of it.

Of (justifying) true faith three things are specially to be noted: (1), that it bringeth forth good works; (2), that without it can no good works be done; (3), what good works it doth bring forth.[d]

Without faith can no good work be done, accepted, and pleasant unto God. For 'as a branch cannot bear fruit of itself (saith our Saviour Christ) except it abide in the vine, so cannot you, except you abide in me'.[1] Faith giveth life to the soul; and they be as much dead to God that lack faith, as they be to the world whose bodies lack souls. Without faith all that is done of us is but dead before God. Even as a picture is but a dead representation of the thing itself, so be the works of all unfaithful (unbelieving) persons before God. They be but shadows of lively and good things, and not good things indeed.

---

[a] Homily on Salvation, Part 1. [b] Ibid., Part II.
[c] Ibid., Part III. [d] Sermon on Faith, Part I.

[1] Cf. John 15: 4.

For true faith doth give life to the works, and without faith no work is good before God.ᵃ

We must set no good works before faith, nor think that before faith a man may do any good works; for such works are as the course of an horse that runneth out of the way, which taketh great labour, 5 but to no purpose.ᵇ

Without faith we have no virtues, but only the shadows of them. All the life of them that lack true faith¹ is sin.ᶜ

As men first have life, and after be nourished, so must our faith go before, and after be nourished with good works. And life may be 10 without nourishment, but nourishment cannot be without life. . . .

I can show a man that by faith without works lived and came to heaven. But without faith never man had life. The thief on the cross only believed, and the most merciful God justified him. . . . Truth it is, if he had lived and not regarded faith and the works thereof, he 15 should have lost his salvation again. But this I say, faith by itself saved him. But works by themselves never justified any man.ᵈ

Good works go not before in him which should afterward be justified. But good works do follow after, when a man is first justified.ᵉ   20

[10.] From the whole tenor then of her liturgy, Articles, and Homilies, the doctrine of the Church of England appears to be this:

(1). That no good work, properly so called, can go *before* justification;

(2). That *no degree* of true sanctification can be previous to it;

(3). That as the *meritorious cause* of justification is the life and death 25 of Christ, so the *condition of it is faith, faith alone*; and

(4). That both inward and outward holiness are consequent on this faith, and are the ordinary, stated condition of final justification.

[11.] And what more can you desire, who have hitherto opposed justification by faith alone, merely upon a principle of conscience, 30 because you was zealous for holiness and good works? Do I not effectually secure these from contempt, at the same time that I defend the doctrines of the Church? I not only allow, but vehemently contend, that none shall ever enter into glory who is not holy on earth, as well in heart as 'in all manner of conversation'.² I cry aloud, 'Let all 35

ᵃ Homily, 'Of Works annexed to Faith', Part I. [Wesley's original incorrectly reads 'ibid. Part III' here, but gives the correct citation three paragraphs later.]
ᵇ Ibid.   ᶜ Ibid.   ᵈ [Ibid.]
ᵉ Homily on Fasting, Part I [quoting Augustine, *De Fide et Operibus*, cap. 4.].

---

¹ The original, correctly quoted in *A Farther Appeal*, has 'the true faith'.
² 1 Pet. 1: 15.

that have believed be careful to maintain good works;'[1] and, 'Let everyone that nameth the name of Christ depart from all iniquity.'[2] I exhort even those who are conscious they do not believe, 'Cease to do evil, learn to do well;'[3] 'The kingdom of heaven is at hand;' therefore
5   repent, and 'bring forth fruits meet for repentance'.[4] Are not these directions the very same in substance which you yourself would give to persons so circumstanced? What means then the endless 'strife of words'?[5] Or 'what doth your arguing reprove?'[6]

[12.] Many of those who are perhaps as 'zealous of good works'[7] as
10   you, think I have allowed you too much. Nay, my brethren, but how can we help allowing it, if we allow the Scriptures to be from God?

For is it not written, and do not you yourselves believe: 'Without holiness no man shall see the Lord'?[8] And how, then, without fighting about words, can we deny that holiness is a condition of final
15   acceptance? And, as to the first acceptance or pardon, does not all experience as well as Scripture prove that no man ever yet truly 'believed the gospel'[9] who did not first repent? That none was ever yet truly 'convinced of righteousness' who was not first 'convinced of sin'?[10] Repentance therefore in this sense we cannot deny to be necessarily
20   previous to faith. Is it not equally undeniable that the running back into known wilful sin (suppose it were drunkenness or uncleanness) stifles that repentance or conviction? And can that repentance come to any good issue in his soul, who resolves not to forgive his brother? Or who obstinately refrains from what God convinces him is right,
25   whether it be prayer or hearing his Word? Would you scruple yourself to tell one of these, 'Why, if you *will* thus drink away all conviction, how should you ever truly know your want of Christ? Or consequently, believe in him? If you *will* not forgive your brother his trespasses, neither will your heavenly Father forgive you *your* trespasses.[11] If you
30   will not ask, how can you expect to receive?[12] If you will not hear, how can "faith come by hearing"?[13] It is plain, "You grieve the Spirit of God.'[14] You *will not* have him to reign over you. Take care that he do not utterly depart from you. For "unto him that hath shall be given; but from him that hath not (i.e. uses it not) shall be taken away even
35   that which he hath."'[15] Would you scruple on a proper occasion to say this? You could not scruple it if you believe the Bible. But in saying this you allow all which I have said, viz., that previous to justifying faith there *must* be repentance, and if opportunity permits, 'fruits meet for repentance'.[16]

[1] Cf. Titus 3: 8.   [2] 2 Tim. 2: 19.   [3] Isa. 1: 16, 17.   [4] Matt. 3: 2, 8.
[5] Cf. 1 Tim. 6: 4.   [6] Job 6: 25.   [7] Titus 2: 14.   [8] Cf. Heb. 12: 14.
[9] Cf. Mark 1:15.   [10] Cf. John 16: 8 (*Notes*).   [11] See Matt. 6: 15.
[12] See Matt. 7: 8.   [13] Rom. 10: 17.   [14] Cf. Eph. 4: 30.
[15] Cf. Matt. 25: 29.   [16] Matt. 3: 8.

[13.] And yet I allow you this, that although both repentance and the fruits thereof are in *some sense* necessary before justification, yet neither the one nor the other is necessary in the *same sense* or in the *same degree* with faith. Not in the *same degree*: for in whatever moment a man believes (in the Christian sense of the word) he is justified, his sins are blotted out, 'his faith is counted to him for righteousness'.[1] But it is not so at whatever moment he repents, or brings forth any or all the fruits of repentance. Faith alone therefore justifies, which repentance alone does not, much less any outward work. And consequently none of these are necessary to justification in the *same degree* with faith.

Nor in the *same sense*: for none of these has so direct, immediate a relation to justification as faith. This is *proximately* necessary thereto; repentance, *remotely*, as it is necessary to the increase or continuance of faith.[2] And even in this sense these are only necessary on supposition —if there be time and opportunity for them; for in many instances there is not, but God cuts short his work and faith prevents the fruits of repentance. So that the general proposition is not overthrown, but clearly established by these concessions; and we conclude still, both on the authority of Scripture and the Church, that faith alone is the proximate condition of justification.[3]

II. 1. I have now[4] shown at large what is the doctrine I teach with regard to justification, and have taught ever since I was convinced of it myself by carefully reading the New Testament and the Homilies. In many points, I apprehend, it agrees with yours; in some, it does not. These I come now to consider. May God enable me to do it in love and meekness of wisdom!

You say, page seven: 'Happy times, when "faith" and "a good life" were synonymous terms.' I conceive, they never were. Is not faith the root, a good life the tree springing therefrom?

Page nine: 'That good works are a necessary condition of our justification may be proved, (1), from express testimonies of Scripture. So Isaiah 1: 16: "Cease from evil, learn to do well." Then

---

[1] Cf. Rom. 4: 5.

[2] Wesley here follows the hastily revised text of the later editions of *A Farther Appeal*, rather than the erratum which restored the line erroneously omitted from the first edition, so that the passage read: 'repentance, *remotely*, as it is necessary to the increase or continuance of faith: and the fruits of repentance still more remotely, as they are necessary to repentance'.

[3] *A Farther Appeal*, Pt. I, I. 1–II. 11, i.e. pp. 1–15 of the original. In the *Works* reprint of this *Letter* Wesley numbered this closing proposition '2, the first being the opening sentence of I. 1.

[4] *Works*, 'I have here shown', apparently referring to *A Farther Appeal*, the lengthy quotations from which he had omitted.

"your sins that were as scarlet shall be white as snow". Here "ceasing from evil", and "learning to do well", are the conditions of pardon.' I answer: without them there is no pardon, yet the immediate condition of it is faith. He that believeth, and he alone,
5 is justified before God. 'So Ezekiel 33: 14: If the sinner "turn from his evil ways" and "walk in the statutes of life", then "all his sins shall not be once mentioned to him".' Most sure: that is, if he believe; else, whatever his outward walking be, he cannot be justified.

10 The next Scripture you cite,[a] Matthew 11: 28, proves no more than this, that none find 'rest to their souls' unless they first 'come to' Christ (namely, by faith) and then obey him.

But 'he says, "Ye are my friends, if ye do whatsoever I command you."'[1] He does so; but how does it appear that this relates to
15 justification at all?

'St. Peter also declares: "In every nation he that feareth God and worketh righteousness is accepted of him."'[b] He is; but none can either fear God or work righteousness till he believes, according to the dispensation he is under. 'And St. John, "He that doth righteous-
20 ness is righteous."'[2] I do not see that this proves anything. 'And again, "If we walk in the light, as God is in the light, then have we communion with him, and the blood of Jesus Christ his Son cleanseth us from all sin."'[c] This would prove something if it could be proved that 'cleansing us from all sin' meant only justification.

25 'The Scriptures insist upon the necessity of repentance in particular for that purpose. . . . But repentance comprehends compunction, humiliation, hatred of sin, confession of it, prayer for mercy, ceasing from evil, a firm purpose to do well, restitution of ill-got goods, forgiveness of all who have done us wrong, and works of
30 beneficence.'[d] I believe it does comprehend all these, either as parts or as fruits of it. And it comprehends 'the fear', but not 'the love of God'—that flows from a higher principle. And he who loves God is not barely in the right way to justification; he is actually justified. The rest of the paragraph asserts just the same thing which
35 was asserted in those words, 'previous to justifying faith must be repentance, and if opportunity permits, "fruits meet for

---

[a] *Sermon*, p. 10. [b] Acts 10: 35. [c] 1 John 1: 7.
[d] [*Sermon*,] pp. [10], 11, 12.

---

[1] John 15: 14. [2] 1 John 3: 7.

repentance".'[1] But still I must observe that 'neither one nor the other is necessary, either in the *same sense* or in the *same degree* with faith'.[2] No Scripture testimony can be produced which any way contradicts this.

2. 'That works are a necessary condition of our justification may be proved, secondly, from Scripture examples, particularly those recited in the eleventh chapter of the Epistle to the Hebrews. These all "through faith wrought righteousness"; without working righteousness they had never "obtained the promises".'[a] I say the same thing: none are finally saved but those whose 'faith worketh by love'.[3]

'Even in the thief upon the cross, faith was attended by repentance, piety, and charity.' It was: repentance went before his faith; piety and charity accompanied it. 'Therefore he was not justified by faith alone.' Our Church, adopting the words of St. Chrysostom,[4] expressly affirms in the passage above cited, he was justified by faith alone. And her authority ought to weigh more than even that of Bishop Bull,[5] or that of any single man whatever. Authority, be pleased to observe, I plead against authority, reason against reason.

It is no objection that the faith whereby he was justified immediately *produced* good works.

3. How we are justified by *faith alone*, and yet by such a faith as is *not alone*, it may be proper to explain. And this also I choose to do, not in my own words, but in those of our Church:

'Faith doth not shut out repentance, hope, love, and the fear of God, to be joined with faith in every man that is justified; but it

---

[a] [Ibid.,] p. 13 [cf. Heb. 11: 33.]

---

[1] Matt. 3: 8; see above, §§ I. 2, 12.   [2] See above, § I. 13.

[3] Cf. Gal. 5: 6.

[4] St. John Chrysostom (*c.* 347–407), one of the greatest of patristic preachers and expositors, was a theological authority whom Wesley held in the highest esteem and whom he frequently quoted. It was therefore reassuring to him that the *Homilies* appealed to Chrysostom so often; quotations from him are second in number only to those from St. Augustine. For Chrysostom's reference to the faith of the penitent thief, see *Two Homilies on Eutropius*, Homily II, 17.

[5] George Bull (1634–1710), Bishop of St. David's, was a leading High-Churchman of the later Stuart period. His *Harmonia Apostolica* (concerning which Horne quoted the verdict that it was 'the triumph of the Church of England') was regarded as an authoritative attack on the more Protestant interpretations of justification. Bull claimed that Pauline views on the question had to be interpreted in the light of the Epistle of St. James. In the course of his sermon, Horne referred several times to Bishop Bull.

shutteth them out from the office of justifying. So that although they be all present together in him that is justified, yet they justify not all together.' Neither doth faith shut out 'good works, necessarily to be done *afterwards*, of duty towards God'.[a]

5 'That we are justified only by this faith in Christ, speak all the ancient authors: specially Origen, St. Cyprian, St. Chrysostom, Hilary, Basil, St. Ambrose, and St. Augustine.'[1]

4. You go on: 'Thirdly, if we consider the nature of faith, it will appear impossible that a man should be justified by that alone.
10 Faith is either an *assent* to the gospel truths, or a *reliance* on the gospel promises. I know of no other notion of faith.'[b] I do: an 'ἔλεγχος of things not seen';[2] which is far more than a bare assent, and yet *toto genere* different from a reliance. Therefore if you prove that neither an assent nor a reliance justifies, nor both of them
15 together, still you do not prove that we are not justified by faith, even by faith alone. But how do you prove that we cannot be justified by faith as a reliance on the promises? Thus: 'Such a reliance must be founded on a consciousness of having performed the conditions; and a reliance so founded is the result of works wrought *through*
20 *faith*.' No. Of works wrought *without* faith; else the argument implies a contradiction. For it runs thus (on the supposition that 'faith' and 'reliance' were synonymous terms): such a reliance is the result of works wrought through such a reliance.

5. Your fourth argument against justification by faith alone is
25 drawn from the *nature* of justification. This, you observe, 'implies a prisoner at the bar, and a law by which he is to be tried; and this is not the law of Moses, but that of Christ, requiring repentance and faith, with their proper fruits, . . . which now through the blood of Christ are accepted and "counted for righteousness".'[c] St. Paul
30 affirms this concerning faith in the fourth chapter of his Epistle to the Romans.[3] But where does he say that either repentance or its fruits are 'counted for righteousness'? Nevertheless I allow that the law of Christ requires such repentance and faith before justification as, if there be opportunity, will bring forth 'the fruits of righteous-
35 ness'.[4] But if there be not, he that repents and believes is justified

---

[a] Homily on the Salvation of Man [Pt. I.]   [b] [*Sermon*,] p. 15.
[c] [Ibid.,] p. 16.

---

[1] *Homilies*, Of Salvation, Pt. II.
[2] Heb. 11: 1.   [3] Rom. 4: 3, 5.   [4] Phil. 1: 11.

notwithstanding. Consequently these alone are necessary, *indispens-ably necessary* conditions of our justification.

6. Your last argument against justification by faith alone 'is drawn from the method of God's proceeding at the last day'. He will then 'judge every man according to his *works*'.[1] 'If therefore works wrought through faith are the ground of the sentence passed upon us in that day, then are they a necessary condition of our justification.'[a] In other words, 'If they are a condition of our *final*, they are a condition of our *present* justification.' I cannot allow the consequence. All holiness must precede our entering into glory. But no holiness can exist till, 'being justified by faith, we have peace with God through our Lord Jesus Christ'.[2]

7. You next attempt to reconcile the writings of St. Paul with justification by works. In order to this you say: 'In the three first chapters of his Epistle to the Romans he proves that both Jews and Gentiles must have recourse to the gospel of Christ. To this end he convicts the whole world of sin. And having "stopped every mouth",[3] he makes his inference, "Therefore by the deeds of the law there shall no flesh be justified."[4] "We conclude then (says he) a man is justified by faith, without the deeds of the law."[5] But here arise two questions. First, what are the works excluded from justifying? Secondly, what is the faith which justifies?'[b]

'The works excluded are heathen and Jewish works, set up as meritorious. This is evident from hence, that heathens and carnal Jews are the persons against whom he is arguing." Not so. He is arguing against all mankind: he is 'convicting the whole world of sin'.[6] His concern is to 'stop every mouth' by proving that 'no flesh', none born of a woman, no child of man, can 'be justified by his own works'.[7] Consequently he speaks of *all* the works of *all* mankind antecedent to justification, whether Jewish or any other, whether supposed *meritorious* or not, of which the text says not one word. Therefore *all* works antecedent to justification are excluded, and faith is set in *flat opposition* to them. 'Unto him that worketh not, but believeth, his faith is counted to him for righteousness.'[8]

'But what is the faith to which he attributes justification? That

[a] [Ibid.,] pp. [17,] 19.   [b] [Ibid.,] pp. [19], 20, 21, 22.

---

[1] Cf. 2 Cor. 5: 10, which Horne later quoted by way of proof.   [2] Rom. 5: 1.
[3] Cf. Rom. 3: 19.   [4] Rom. 3: 20.   [5] Rom. 3: 28.
[6] Cf. Rom. 3: 19.   [7] Cf. Rom. 3: 20.   [8] Cf. Rom. 4: 5.

"which worketh by love", which is the same with the "new creature", and implies in it the "keeping the commandments of God".[1]

It is undoubtedly true that nothing avails for our final salvation
5 without καινὴ κτίσις, 'a new creation', and consequent thereon a sincere, uniform keeping of the commandments of God. This St. Paul constantly declares. But where does he say this is the condition of our justification? In the Epistles to the Romans and Galatians particularly, he vehemently asserts the contrary; earnestly
10 maintaining that nothing is *absolutely necessary* to this but 'believing in him that justifieth the ungodly'[2]—not the godly, not him that is already 'a new creature',[3] that previously keeps all the commandments of God. He does this *afterward*. When he is justified by faith —then his 'faith worketh by love'.

15 'Therefore there is no condemnation to them that are in Christ Jesus',[4] justified by faith in him, provided that they 'walk in him whom they have received',[5] 'not after the flesh but after the spirit'.[6] But should they turn back and walk again after the flesh, they would again be under condemnation. But this no way proves that 'walking
20 after the spirit' was the condition of their justification.[a]

Neither will anything like this follow from the Apostle's saying to the Corinthians, 'Though I had all faith, so as to remove mountains, and have not charity, I am nothing.'[7] This only proves that miracle-working faith may be where saving faith is not.

25 8. To the argument, 'St. Paul says "Abraham was justified by faith"' you answer, 'St. James says "Abraham was justified by works."'[b] True. But he neither speaks of the same justification, nor the same faith, nor the same works. Not of the same justification: for St. Paul speaks of that justification which was five and twenty
30 years before Isaac was born,[c] St. James of that wherewith he was justified when 'he offered up Isaac on the altar'.[8] It is *living* faith whereby St. Paul affirms we are justified; it is *dead* faith whereby St. James affirms we are not justified. St. Paul speaks of works antecedent to justification; St. James of works consequent upon it.
35 This is the plain, easy, natural way of reconciling the two apostles.

---

[a] [*Sermon,*] p. 23.　　　　[b] [Ibid.,] p. 24.　　　　[c] Gen.

[1] *Sermon*, pp. 22, 23. Cf. Gal. 5: 6; 6: 15; 1 Cor. 7: 19; all of which Horne cited.
[2] Rom. 4: 5.　　　[3] 2 Cor. 5: 17; Gal. 6: 15.　　　[4] Rom. 8: 1.
[5] Cf. Col. 2: 6.　　[6] Rom. 8: 15.　　[7] Cf. 1 Cor. 13: 2.　　[8] Cf. Jas. 2: 21.

The fact was manifestly this: (1). When Abraham dwelt in Haran, being then seventy-five years old, God called him thence. He 'believed God, and he counted it to him for righteousness'.[1] That is, he was 'justified by faith', as St. Paul strenuously asserts. (2). Many years after Isaac was born (some of the ancients thought, three and thirty), 'Abraham showing his faith by his works'[2] offered him up upon the altar. (3). Here the faith by which, in St. Paul's sense, he was justified long before, 'wrought together with his works',[3] and he was justified in St. James's sense; that is (as the Apostle explains his own meaning) 'by works his faith was made perfect'. God confirmed, increased, and perfected the principle from which those works sprang.

9. Drawing to a conclusion you say: 'What pity so many volumes should have been written upon the question whether a man be justified by faith OR works, seeing they are two essential parts of the same thing.'[a] If by works you understand 'inward and outward holiness', both faith and works are essential parts of Christianity. And yet they are essentially different, and by God himself contradistinguished from each other—and that in the very question before us, 'him that worketh not, but believeth'.[4] Therefore whether a man be justified by faith *or* works is a point of the last importance: otherwise our reformers could not have answered to God their spending so much time upon it. Indeed they were both too wise and too good men to have 'wrote so many volumes' on a trifling or needless question.[5]

10. If in speaking on this important point (such at least it appears to *me*), I have said anything offensive, any that implies the least degree of anger or disrespect, it was entirely foreign to my intention; nor indeed have I any provocation. I have no room to be angry at

---

[a] [*Sermon,*] p. 25.

[1] Gen. 15: 6; cf. Rom. 4: 3.   [2] Cf. Jas. 2: 18.   [3] Jas. 2: 22 (*Notes*).
[4] Rom. 4: 5.
[5] See the Minutes of the first Conference, June 25, 1744:

Q[uestion] 14. St. Paul says, Abraham was not justified by works; St. James, he was justified by works. Do not they then contradict each other?

A[nswer]. No. (1). Because they do not speak of the same justification. St. Paul speaks of that justification which was when Abraham was 75 years old, above 20 years before Isaac was born; St. James of that justification which was when he offered up Isaac on the altar. (2). Because they do not speak of the same works. St. Paul speaks of works that precede faith, St. James of works that spring from faith.

your maintaining what you believe to be the truth of the gospel, even though I might wish you had omitted a few expressions,[1]

Quas aut incuria fudit
Aut humana parum cavit natura.[2]

5 In the general, from all I have heard concerning you I cannot but very highly esteem you in love. And that God may give you both 'a right judgment in all things, and evermore to rejoice in his holy comfort',[3] is the prayer of,

Reverend Sir,

10   Your affectionate brother and servant,

John Wesley

---

[1] See *Sermon*, p. 25: 'What pity is it then that so many volumes should have been written to the infinite vexation and disturbance of the church, upon the question—whether a man be justified by *faith*, OR *works*; seeing they are two essential parts of the same thing?'

[2] Horace, *Art of Poetry*, 352–3; in the appendix to Vol. 32 of his *Works* (1774) Wesley translates: 'Such as escaped my notice; or such as may be placed to the account of human infirmity'.

[3] B.C.P., Collects, Whit Sunday.

A Letter to the Bishop of Gloucester

Introduction

William Warburton was the most perverse and abusive of all Wesley's opponents. He was also the most eminent, and Wesley could hardly afford to ignore his attack. Warburton's distinction was due not to his position in the church—after all, Gibson and Lavington were also bishops—but to his standing in the world of letters. Without benefit of university education, Warburton had settled in a country parish and by voracious reading had laid the foundation of a reputation for omniscience. Richard Bentley, the greatest of English classical scholars, remarked that Warburton was a man with a monstrous appetite for knowledge but a very bad digestion.[1] His earliest major work (and probably his best) was *The Alliance between Church and State* (1736). Two years later he published the first part of his most celebrated work, *The Divine Legation of Moses*. This was one of the strangest literary phenomena of the age—a vast unwieldy work, crammed with ill-digested erudition and marked by dogmatic arrogance and an undisciplined love of paradox. 'It includes in itself', said Lowth, 'all history, chronology, criticism, law, politics, from the law of Moses to the late Jew-bill, and from Egyptian hieroglyphics to modern rebus-writing; and to it we are to have recourse, as to an infallible oracle, for the resolution of every question in literature.'[2] The book was never finished; it is a colossal fragment, marred by slipshod scholarship allied with the affectation of infallibility. But it made an immense impression at the time, and established its author's reputation. Warburton, now a famous man, began savagely to attack his fellow authors. Initially he slaughtered the dim figures in the underworld of 'Grub-street', but he stepped into a wider sphere when he became the friend of Alexander Pope, the authorized interpreter of his poetry, and finally his literary legatee. As a result of this alliance, Warburton arrogated to himself the position of chief arbiter of literary taste. He felt entitled to assault some of the best-known figures of the age;

[1] Cf. J. H. Monk, *Life of Richard Bentley*, (2nd ed., 1833), II. 410.
[2] Robert Lowth, *A Letter to the Right Reverend Author of the Divine Legation of Moses* (1765), p. 18.

they have rewarded his abuse by preserving him from the oblivion into which he would otherwise have fallen. He attacked David Hume, who complained that he suffered from 'all the illiberal petulance, arrogance, and scurrility which distinguish the Warburtonian school'.[1] He attacked Gibbon, and the historian distilled his resentment in a characteristically polished piece of invective.

> The learning and abilities of the author had raised him to a just eminence; but he reigned the dictator and tyrant of the world of literature. The real merit of Warburton was degraded by the pride and presumption with which he pronounced his infallible decrees; in his polemic writings he lashed his antagonists without mercy or moderation, and his servile flatterers, . . . exalting the master critic far above Aristotle and Longinus, assaulted every modest dissenter who refused to consult the oracle and adore the idol.[2]

It is difficult for modern readers, tamed by the law of libel as well as by more humane standards of literary civility, to comprehend the level to which Warburton had debased the exchange of views on literary subjects. A crass arrogance, a vindictive spite, a coarse and noisy contradiction, an avowed aim to humiliate and destroy every antagonist—these were the hallmarks of Warburton's reign as dictator of taste. A victim need have failed only in some minor point of deference, he need only have questioned some preposterous paradox to bring down upon himself the tyrant's wrath. His behaviour corresponded to his avowed intent. 'I shall hang him and his fellows', he wrote, 'as they do vermin in a warren, and leave them to posterity to stink and blacken in the wind.'[3]

Warburton's career is a long sequence of discreditable brawls. In most of them he silenced his opponents, even if he did not overthrow them. But finally, in one of the most celebrated controversies of the century, Warburton met an antagonist who was more than his match. Warburton had felt that Robert Lowth, then professor of poetry at Oxford and subsequently Bishop of London, had indirectly reflected on him in his published lectures on Hebrew poetry. Lowth's interpretation of the book of Job differed from Warburton's, and this was regarded as a piece of unpardonable presumption. So Warburton chastised him. Lowth did not submit in silence. In 1765

[1] David Hume, *My Own Life*, *Philosophical Works* (Edinburgh, 1854), Vol. I, p. xcviii.
[2] Edward Gibbon, *The Autobiographies of Edward Gibbon*, ed. by J. Murray (London, 1896), p. 281.
[3] Warburton to Birch, in John Nichols, *Literary Anecdotes*, V. 548.

he published his *Letter to the Right Reverend Author of the Divine Legation of Moses*. The eighteenth century produced no more polished example of the controversialist's art. With suave irony Lowth stripped away Warburton's defences, and exposed the hollow shabbiness of his pretensions. Warburton did not even attempt a reply. His authority was badly shaken; as time passed it became increasingly clear that his prestige had received a wound from which it would never recover.[1]

In 1762, however, the decline and fall of Warburton's authority still lay in the future. In that year he picked a quarrel with the free-thinkers and religious enthusiasts of his day, and published a two-volume work entitled *The Doctrine of Grace: or, the Office and Operations of the Holy Spirit vindicated from the insults of infidelity and the abuse of fanaticism*.[2] Warburton was not primarily a theologian, but he was a prominent religious leader with a clearly defined theological position. He stood in the Latitudinarian and rationalist tradition. His critics regarded him as an undisguised Pelagian. He could hardly be expected to agree with Wesley. Wesley found himself the main target of Warburton's attacks, and decided that the work demanded a reply. Warburton's eminence in the literary world guaranteed a respectful hearing for his aspersions. His book might easily prejudice people who otherwise would judge Wesley's mission on its own merits. Warburton's reputation as an author who annihilated his critics made Wesley's decision to refute him one that presupposed some courage. Wesley, of course, feared the face of no man, and in any case Warburton epitomized many of the qualities which he found most offensive in an opponent. Warburton had ignored most of Wesley's explanations of his methods and all his defences of his work. He had, it is true, read certain instalments of the *Journal*, and on these he based his diatribe against the Methodists. But he had treated his source with a contemptuous carelessness which made little effort to penetrate to Wesley's real meaning. His misquotations were so many and so flagrant that Wesley concluded that he was dealing with an author devoid of intellectual integrity. This explains the severe tone which Wesley often adopts in his reply.

---

[1] Wesley's comment, on reading Lowth's *Letter*, is interesting: 'If anything human could be a cure for pride, surely such a medicine as this would!' *Journal*, Jan. 9, 1766.

[2] The first edition is dated 1763, though Wesley answered it in November 1762. The explanation is that works published in the later months of one year were often given the date of the following year. Warburton's correspondence shows that as early as 1738 he was repeating unfriendly gossip about the Wesleys.

Warburton devoted the early chapters of *The Doctrine of Grace* to an attack on the views of that sceptical, semi-deist divine, Conyers Middleton.[1] In Part II he turned to deal with Wesley. Fanaticism, he argued, had replaced superstition as the major threat to an intelligent faith, and all 'the features of modern fanaticism' could be 'seen in the famed leader of the Methodists, Mr. John Wesley'.[2] Because of 'a change in economy', the 'dispensations of the Holy Spirit'[3] are now very different from what they were in the primitive days of Christianity. The church is now firmly established; it no longer needs the gifts appropriate to earlier times, and yet 'this extraordinary man [Wesley] hath in fact laid claim to almost every apostolic gift and grace'.[4] Warburton then set forth at large the absurd pretensions which he detected in Wesley—his struggles with the Devil, the signs and wonders associated with his mission, his claim to the New Birth, the assumption that he spoke by the Spirit, his gifts of healing and exorcism, and the divine judgements which overtook his adversaries. Warburton paused for a moment to expose the dangerous antecedents of Wesley's doctrines—Boehme, Law, Zinzendorf, and the Moravians—and then returned to more direct assaults. Wesley claimed to be promoting the interests of faith; actually he was merely trampling on the rights of reason. Methodist teaching was incompatible with that of the Church of England. An examination of Wesley's career suggested that it was absurd for him to claim the gifts of the Spirit, since he was not peaceable, gentle, meek, or easy to be entreated. Indeed, he was clearly guilty of fraud and fanaticism. He was a hypocrite, an 'enthusiast' with an unbalanced hankering after persecution. As Warburton triumphantly concluded, Wesley was 'ready to exhibit to us every feature of fanaticism in its turn'.[5] The tone of Warburton's attack is arrogant and self-assured. Wesley's letter seems, by contrast, reasonable and self-possessed. He never forgets the measure of respect to which a bishop is entitled, but he feels free to expose with great candour the faults of mind and temper which he detects in *The Doctrine of Grace*.[6]

---

[1] Conyers Middleton (1683-1750) was a fellow of Trinity College, Cambridge, and University Librarian.

[2] Warburton, *The Doctrine of Grace*, in *Works* (1811 ed.), VIII. 322.

[3] Ibid., p. 318. [4] Ibid., p. 322. [5] Ibid., p. 426.

[6] There is a tradition that Warburton submitted his manuscript to Wesley before publication, in order to give Wesley a chance to correct any errors (cf. James Everett, *Adam Clarke Portrayed* (1843), I; 244; cf. also Thomas Jackson, *Recollections of my own*

Wesley took some pains with his reply. Though he wrote it in the space of five days, he weighed the issues with care, and submitted his work to the criticism of others.[1] He believed that a compressed style would be most effective. 'I think the danger in writing to Bishop Warburton is rather that of saying too much than too little. The least said is the soonest amended, and leaves an ill-natured critic the least to take hold of.'[2] Wesley conceded the ability of his opponent, but was surprised to discover the extent of his deficiencies as a scholar. 'He is a man of sense,' he remarked, 'but I verily think that he does not understand Greek.'[3] He also concluded that the bishop did not understand the New Testament. Wesley believed that he had offered a restrained refutation; should Warburton reply, he would feel free to be a good deal more outspoken.[4] But Warburton maintained a discreet silence.

For a summary of the four editions published during Wesley's lifetime, a stemma illustrating the transmission of the text, and a list of the substantive variant readings from the edited text (based on the first edition, London, no printer named, 1763), see the Appendix to this volume, pp. 557–8. For full bibliographical details see *Bibliography*, No. 256. For the numbering of the divisions see note 1, p. 477.

Life and Times, p. 245). But there is little in either Warburton's work or Wesley's to lend credence to the tradition. The tone of both works makes it unlikely, and Warburton's book does not correspond with the description Wesley was supposed to have given of it: 'The MS. abounded with quotations from poets, philosophers, etc., both in Greek and Latin.'

[1] *Journal*, Nov. 22 to 26, 1762.   [2] Letter to Samuel Furly, Dec. 20, 1762.
[3] Letter to Charles Wesley, Dec. 11, 1762; cf. to the same, Jan. 5, 1763.
[4] Letter to Samuel Furly, Mar. 10, 1763.

A

LETTER

TO THE

RIGHT REVEREND

The Lord Bifhop of GLOUCESTER.

Occafioned by his T R A C T,

ON THE

OFFICE AND OPERATIONS

OF THE

HOLY SPIRIT.

By J O H N W E S L E Y, M. A.
Late Fellow of LINCOLN COLLEGE, OXFORD.

LONDON printed:
And fold at the FOUNDERY, near Moorfields.
MDCCLXIII

A

LETTER

TO THE

RIGHT REVEREND

The Lord Bishop of GLOUCESTER

[1.] My Lord

Your lordship well observes: 'To employ *buffoonery* in the service of religion is to violate the majesty of truth, and to deprive it of a fair hearing. To examine, men must be *serious*.'ᵃ I will endeavour to be so in all the following pages. And the rather, not only because 5 I am writing to a person who is so far and in so many respects my superior, but also because of the importance of the subject. For is the question only what I am, a madman, or a man in his senses; a knave, or an honest man? No; this is only brought in by way of illustration. The question is of the office and operation of the Holy 10 Spirit: with which the doctrine of the new birth, and indeed the whole of real religion, is connected. On a subject of so deep concern I desire to be serious as death. But at the same time your lordship will permit me to use great plainness. And this I am the more emboldened to do because by naming my name your lordship, as 15 it were, condescends to meet me on even ground.

I shall consider, first, what your lordship advances concerning *me*; and then what is advanced concerning the operations of the Holy Spirit.

I. [1.] First, concerning *me*. It is true I am here dealing in *crambe* 20 *repetita*¹—reciting objections which have been urged and answered an hundred times. But as your lordship is pleased to repeat them again, I am obliged to repeat the answers.

ᵃ [William Warburton, Bishop of Gloucester, *The Doctrine of Grace; or, the Office and Operations of the Holy Spirit vindicated from the insults of infidelity, and the abuses of fanaticism . . .*, in two volumes, paginated continuously, London, for A. Millar, 1763,] Preface, p. xi. [Here, as usual, Wesley abridges what he quotes.]

¹ 'Cabbage twice cooked, the same old story'. Juvenal, *Satires*, vii. 154. Cf. *A Farther Appeal*, Pt. II, III. 15.

Your lordship begins: 'If the *false prophet* pretend to some *extraordinary* measure of the Spirit, we are directed to try that spirit by James 3: 17.'ᵃ I answer, (1), (as I have done many times before) I do not pretend to any *extraordinary* measure of the Spirit.
5 I pretend to no other measure of it than may be claimed by every Christian minister. (2). Where are we directed to 'try prophets' by this text? How does it appear that it was given for any such purpose? It is certain we may try *Christians* hereby, whether they are real or pretended ones. But I know not that either St. James, or any other
10 inspired writer, gives us the least hint of trying *prophets* thereby.

Your lordship adds: 'In this rule or direction for the *trial of spirits* the marks are to be applied only *negatively*. . . . The man in whom they are not found hath not . . . "the wisdom from above".¹ But we are not to conclude that he has it in whom any or all of them
15 are found.'ᵇ We are not to conclude that he is a prophet; for the Apostle says nothing about prophets. But may we **not** conclude the man in whom all these are found has 'the wisdom from above'? Surely we may; for these are the essential parts of that wisdom. And can he have *all the parts* and not have *the whole*?

20 Is not this enough to show that the Apostle is here giving 'a set of marks', not 'to detect impostor-*prophets*'² but impostor-*Christians*? Those that impose either upon themselves or others, as if they were Christians, when they are not?

[2.] In what follows I shall simply consider the argument, without
25 directly addressing your lordship.

'Apply these marks to the features of modern *fanatics*, especially Mr. John Wesley. . . . He has laid claim to almost *every apostolic gift*, in *as full and ample* a manner as they were possessed of old.'ᶜ

The *miraculous gifts* bestowed upon the apostles are enumerated
30 in two places. (1). 'In my name they shall cast out devils; they shall speak with new tongues; they shall take up serpents; if they drink any deadly thing, it shall not hurt them; they shall lay hands on the sick and they shall recover.'ᵈ (2). 'To one is given the word of

---

ᵃ [Warburton, *Doctrine of Grace*,] p. 117. [In fact Warburton gives the passage from James in the body of his text—'The wisdom that is from above is first pure, then peaceable, gentle and easy to be entreated, full of mercy and good fruits, without partiality, and without hypocrisy'—and the citation in a footnote.]

ᵇ [Warburton, *Doctrine of Grace*,] pp. 117–18.

ᶜ [Ibid.,] p. 119.   ᵈ Mark 16: 17, 18.

---

¹ Cf. Jas. 3: 17.   ² Warburton, *Doctrine of Grace*, p. 118.

wisdom, to another the word of knowledge, to another faith, to another the gifts of healing, to another the working of miracles, to another prophecy, to another the discernment of spirits, to another tongues, to another the interpretation of tongues.'ᵃ

Do I lay claim to *almost every one* of these, 'in as *full and ample* 5 a manner as they were possessed of old'?

Five of them are enumerated in the former catalogue; to three of which—'speaking with new tongues, taking up serpents, drinking deadly things'—it is not even pretended I lay any claim at all. In the latter, nine are enumerated. And as to seven of these, none has 10 yet seen good to call me in question—'miraculous wisdom, or knowledge, or faith, prophecy, discernment of spirits, strange tongues, and the interpretation of tongues'. What becomes then of the assertion that I lay claim to 'almost every one of' them, in the most 'full' and 'ample' manner? 15

[3.] Do I lay claim to *any one* of them? To prove that I do my own words are produced: extracted from an account of the occurrences of about sixteen years.

I shall set them down naked and unadorned. (1). May 13, 1740: 'The devil stirred up his servants to make all the noise they could.' 20 (2). May 3, 1741: 'I explained to a vast multitude of people, "What doth the Lord require of thee, but to do justly, to love mercy, and to walk humbly with thy God."¹ The devil's children fought valiantly for their master, that his kingdom should not be destroyed. And many stones fell on my right hand and on my left.' (3). April 1, 25 1740: 'Some or other of the children of Belial had laboured to disturb us several nights before. Now all the street was filled with people shouting, cursing, and swearing, and ready to swallow the ground with rage.'ᵇ (4). June 27, 1747: 'I found only one person among them who knew the love of God before my brother came. No 30 wonder the devil was so still; for "his goods were in peace".'² (5). April 29, 1752: 'I preached at Durham to a quiet, stupid congregation.'ᶜ (6). May 9, 1740: 'I was a little surprised at some who were buffeted of Satan in an unusual manner, by such a spirit of laughter as they could in no wise resist. I could scarce have believed the 35

ᵃ 1 Cor. 12: 8–10.
ᵇ [Warburton, op. cit.,] p. 120 [Warburton's citations are all from Wesley's 4th *Journal* extract.]
ᶜ [Ibid.,] p. 121 [quoting Wesley's 7th and 9th *Journal* extracts].

¹ Mic. 6: 8.   ² Cf. Luke 11: 21.

account they gave me, had I not known the same thing ten or eleven years ago'—when both my brother and I were seized in the same manner. (If any man calls this *hysterics*, I am not concerned; I think and let think.) (7). May 21, 1740: 'In the evening such a spirit of
5 laughter was among us that many were much offended. But the attention of all was soon fixed on poor L[ucreti]a S[mith], whom we all knew to be no dissembler. One so violently and variously torn of the evil one did I never see before. Sometimes she laughed till almost strangled; then broke out into cursing and blaspheming. At last she
10 faintly called on Christ to help her. And the violence of her pangs ceased.' (Let any who please impute this likewise to hysterics. Only permit *me* to think otherwise.) (8). May 17, 1740: 'I found more and more undeniable proofs that we have need to watch and pray every moment. Outward trials indeed were now removed. But so
15 much the more did inward trials abound; and "if one member suffered, all the members suffered with it".¹ So strange a sympathy did I never observe before; whatever considerable temptation fell on any one unaccountably spreading itself to the rest, so that exceeding few were able to escape it.'ᵃ
20   [4.] I know not what these eight quotations prove, but that I believe the devil still variously tempts and troubles good men, while he 'works with energy in the children of disobedience'.² Certainly they do not prove that I lay claim to any of the preceding gifts. Let us see whether any more is proved by the ten next quota-
25 tions. (1). 'So many living witnesses hath God given that his hand is still stretched out to heal' (namely, the souls of sinners, as the whole paragraph fixes the sense) 'and that signs and wonders are even now wrought'ᵇ (namely in the conversion of the greatest sinners). (2). 'Among the poor colliers of Placey,³ John Lane, then
30 nine or ten years old, was one of the first that found peace with God.'ᶜ (3). 'Mrs. Nowers said her little son appeared to have a continual fear of God, and an awful sense of his presence. . . . A few days since (she said) he broke out into prayers aloud, and said, "I shall go to heaven soon." This child (when he began to have the

---

ᵃ [Warburton, op. cit.], pp. 122–3 [citing Wesley's 4th *Journal* extract.]
ᵇ [Ibid.,] p. 124 [citing 3rd *Journal*, but no specific reference].
ᶜ Ibid. [citing 9th *Journal*, May 16, 1752].

---

¹ Cf. 1 Cor. 12: 26.   ² Cf. Eph. 2: 2.
³ i.e. Plessey, a hamlet 6 miles SSE. of Morpeth, Northumberland.

fear of God) was (as his parents said) just three years old.'¹ (4). I did receive that 'account of the young woman of Manchester from her own mouth'.² But I pass no judgment on it, good or bad; nor (5). On 'the *trance*' (as her mother called it) of S. T., neither denying nor affirming the truth of it.ᵃ (6). 'You deny that God does work these effects; at least, that he works them in this manner. I affirm both. I have seen very many persons changed in a moment, from the spirit of fear, horror, despair, to the spirit of love, joy, and peace. . . . In several of them this change was wrought in a dream, or during a strong representation to their mind of Christ, either on the cross, or in glory.'ᵇ

'But here the symptoms of grace and of perdition are interwoven and confounded with one another.'ᶜ No. Though light followed darkness, yet they were not interwoven, much less confounded with each other. (7). 'But some imputed the work to the force of imagination, or even to the delusion of the devil.'ᵈ They did so; which made me say, (8), 'I fear we have grieved the spirit of the jealous God by questioning his work.'ᵉ (9). Yet he says himself, 'These symptoms I can no more impute to any natural cause than to the Spirit of God. I make no doubt it was Satan tearing them as they were coming to Christ.'ᶠ But 'these symptoms', and 'the work' mentioned before, are wholly different things. The *work* spoken of is the conversion of sinners to God; these *symptoms* are cries, and bodily pain. The very next instance makes this plain: (10), 'I visited a poor old woman. Her trials had been uncommon—inexpressible agonies of mind, joined with all sorts of bodily pain; not, it seemed, from any natural cause, but the direct operation of Satan.'ᵍ

Neither do any of these quotations prove that I lay claim to any *miraculous* gift.

'Such was the evangelic state of things when Mr. Wesley first entered on this ministry; who, seeing himself surrounded with

---

ᵃ [Ibid.,] p. 126 [citing 6th *Journal*, Aug. 29, 1746].
ᵇ [Ibid.,] p. 127 [where Warburton cites defence of visions and dreams in 3rd *Journal*, May 20, 1739].
ᶜ [Ibid.,] pp. 127–8.
ᵈ [Ibid.,] p. 128 [citing 3rd *Journal*, June 16, 1739].
ᵉ Ibid. [citing 3rd *Journal*, July 23, 1739].
ᶠ [Ibid.,] p. 129 [citing 5th *Journal*, Mar. 13, 1743].
ᵍ [Ibid.,] pp. 129–30 [citing 8th *Journal*, Aug. 9, 1750].

---

¹ Warburton cites 6th *Journal*, June 28, 1746.
² This account of a vision Warburton cites from 7th *Journal*, Aug. 29, 1748.

subjects so harmoniously disposed, thus triumphantly exults. . . .'¹
To illustrate this, let us add the date. 'Such was the evangelic state
of things, August 9, 1750 (on that day I preached that sermon)
when Mr. *Wesley first entered on this* ministry.' Nay, that was in the
5 year 1738.² So I triumphed, because I saw what would be twelve
years after!

[5.] Let us see what the ten next quotations prove. (1). 'In
applying these words, "I came not to call the righteous, but sinners
to repentance",³ my soul was so enlarged that methought I could
10 have cried out—in another sense than poor, vain, Archimedes⁴—
"Give me where to stand, and I will shake the earth." 'ᵃ I meant
neither more nor less (though I will not justify the use of so strong
an expression) than that I was so deeply penetrated with a sense of
the love of God to sinners that it seemed if I could have declared it
15 to all the world they could not but be moved thereby.

'Here then was a scene well prepared for a good actor, and excel-
lently *fitted up* for *the part* he was to play.'ᵇ But how came so good
an actor to begin playing the part twelve years before the scene was
fitted up?

20 'He sets out with declaring his mission. . . . (2). "I cried aloud,
'All things are ready; come ye to the marriage.'⁵ I then delivered
my message." 'ᶜ And does not every minister do the same whenever
he preaches?

But how is this? 'He *sets out* with declaring his mission'? Nay,
25 but this was ten years after my setting out!

(3). 'My heart was not wholly resigned. Yet I know he heard my
voice.'ᶜ (4). 'The longer I spoke the more strength I had, till at
twelve I was as one refreshed with wine.'ᵈ (5). 'I explained the

---

ᵃ [Warburton, op. cit.,] p. 130 [quoting 3rd *Journal*, May 20, 1739].
ᵇ [Ibid.,] p. 131.
ᶜ [Ibid.,] p. 132 [1st *Journal*, Mar. 4, 1737, incorrectly cited by Warburton].
ᵈ [Ibid.,] pp. 132–3 [citing 7th *Journal*, Oct. 9, 1747].

---

¹ Warburton, op. cit., p. 130, moving from the *Journal* for Aug. 9, 1750, without
any intermediate step, to speak of a sermon preached from a text discovered by opening
the Bible at random on May 20, 1739.
² Wesley's error in the year apparently arose because Warburton furnished only the
reference, 'Journ. from August 12, 1738, to November 1, 1739'.
³ Mark 2: 17; Luke 5: 32.
⁴ For other references to Archimedes, see *A Letter to the Bishop of London*, § 20;
A Second Letter to the Author of the Enthusiasm of Methodists, etc., § 3.
⁵ Cf. Matt. 22: 4.
⁶ Warburton, op. cit., pp. 131–2, citing 7th *Journal*, Aug. 23, 1747.

nature of inward religion, words flowing upon me faster than I could speak.'ᵃ (6). 'I intended to have given an exhortation to the society. But as soon as we met the spirit of supplication fell upon us (on the congregation as well as me) so that I could hardly do anything but pray and give thanks.'ᵇ I believe every true Christian may experience all that is contained in these three instances. (7). 'The spirit of prayer was so poured upon us all that we could only speak to God.'ᶜ (8). 'Many were seated on a wall, which in the middle of the sermon fell down; but not one was hurt at all. Nor was there any interruption, either of my speaking, or of the attention of the hearers.'ᵈ (9). 'The mob had just broke open the doors, and while they burst in at one door, we walked out at the other. Nor did one man take any notice of us, though we were within five yards of each other.'ᵉ The fact was just so. I do not attempt to account for it; because I cannot. (10). 'The next miracle was on his friends.' They were no friends of mine. I had seen few of them before in my life. Neither do I say or think it was any miracle at all that they were all 'silent while I spake'; or that 'the moment I had done, the chain fell off, and they all began talking at once'.¹

Do any or all of these quotations prove that I 'lay claim to *almost every* miraculous gift'?

[6.] Will the eight following quotations prove any more? (1). 'Some heard perfectly well on the side of the opposite hill, which was seven score yards from the place where I stood.'ᶠ I believe they did, as it was a calm day, and the hill rose gradually like a theatre. (2). What I here aver is the naked fact. Let everyone account for it as he sees good. 'My horse was exceeding lame. And my head ached much. I thought, 'Cannot God heal man or beast, by means, or without?' Immediately my weariness and headache ceased, and my horse's lameness in the same instant.'ᵍ It was so; and I believe thousands of serious Christians have found as plain answers to prayer as this. (3). William Kirkman's case proves only that God

---

ᵃ [Ibid.,] p. 133 [citing 5th *Journal*, Jan. 24, 1743].
ᵇ Ibid. [citing 7th *Journal*, Aug. 2, 1748].
ᶜ Ibid. [citing 5th *Journal*, Aug. 23, 1743].
ᵈ [Ibid.,] p. 134 [citing 7th *Journal*, May 5, 1747].
ᵉ [Ibid.,] pp. 134–5 [citing 7th *Journal*, Feb. 12, 1748].
ᶠ [Ibid.,] p. 136 [citing 9th *Journal*, Apr. 5, 1752].
ᵍ [Ibid.,] pp. 136–7 [citing 6th *Journal*, Mar. 17, 1746].

---

¹ Warburton, op. cit., p. 135, citing 7th *Journal*, Sept. 18, 1748.

does what pleases him; not that I make myself either 'a great saint or a great physician'.ᵃ (4). 'R. A. was freed at once, without any human means, from a distemper naturally incurable.'ᵇ He was; but it was before I knew him. So what is that to me? (5). 'I found
5 Mr. Lunell in a violent fever. He revived the moment he saw me, and began to recover from that time. Perhaps for this also was I sent.'ᶜ I mean, perhaps this was one end for which the providence of God brought me thither at that time. (6). 'In the evening I called upon Ann Calcut. She had been speechless for some time. But
10 almost as soon as we began to pray God restored her speech. . . . And from that hour the fever left her.'¹ (7). 'I visited several ill of the spotted fever, which had been extremely mortal. But God had said, "Hitherto shalt thou come."² I believe there was not one with whom we were but he recovered.'ᵈ (8). 'Mr. Meyrick . . . had been
15 speechless and senseless for some time. A few of us joined in prayer. Before we had done his sense and his speech returned. Others may account for this by natural causes. I believe this is the power of God.'ᵉ

But what does all this prove? Not that I claim any gift above other
20 men; but only that I believe God now hears and answers prayer, even beyond the ordinary course of nature. Otherwise the clerk was in the right, who (in order to prevent the *fanaticism* of his rector) told him, 'Sir, you should not pray for fair weather yet, for the moon does not change till Saturday.'
25 [7.] While the two accountsᶠ which are next recited lay before me, a venerable old clergyman calling upon me, I asked him, 'Sir, would you advise me to publish these strange relations, or not?' He answered, 'Are you sure of the facts?' I replied, 'As sure as that I am alive.' 'Then', said he, 'publish them in God's name, and be
30 not careful about the event.'

ᵃ [Warburton, op. cit.], p. 137 [citing 7th *Journal*, May 27, 1749: cf. *A Plain Account of the People called Methodists*, XII. 4 (Vol. 9 of this edition)].

ᵇ [Ibid.,] p. 138 [incorrectly citing 8th *Journal*, Apr. 8, 1750, for which see following note. The incident here referred to occurs in the *Journal* under Oct. 12, 1754].

ᶜ Ibid. [citing 5th *Journal*, p. 34, but actually 8th *Journal*, Apr. 8, 1750].

ᵈ [Ibid.] p. 139 [citing 4th *Journal*, Nov. 16, 1740].

ᵉ Ibid. [citing 5th *Journal*, Dec. 20, 1742].

ᶠ [Ibid.,] pp. 143-4 [citing 3rd *Journal*, Oct. 23-9, 1739; the young women were Sally Jones and Lucy Clear of Kingswood].

¹ Warburton, op. cit., pp. 138-9, citing 5th *Journal*, Mar. 31, 1742.
² Job 38: 11.

The short of the case is this. Two young women were tormented of the devil in an uncommon manner. Several serious persons desired my brother and me to pray with them. We (with many others) did, and they were delivered. But where meantime were 'the exorcisms in form, according to the Roman fashion'? I never used them. I never saw them. I know nothing about them.

[8.] 'Such were the blessings which Mr. Wesley *distributed* among his friends. For his enemies he had in store the *judgments* of heaven.'[a] Did I then ever *distribute* or profess to distribute these? Do I *claim* any such power? This is the present question. Let us calmly consider the eight quotations brought to prove it.

(1). 'I preached at Darlaston, late a den of lions. But the fiercest of them God has called away, by a train of surprising strokes.'[b] But not by me. I was not there. (2). 'I preached at R., late a place of furious riot and persecution; but quiet and calm since the bitter rector is gone to give an account of himself to God.'[c] (3). 'Hence we rode to T[odmorde]n, where the minister was slowly recovering from a violent fit of the palsy, with which he was struck immediately after he had been preaching a virulent sermon against the Methodists.'[d] (4). The case of Mr. W[esto]n was dreadful indeed, and too notorious to be denied.[e] (5). 'One of the chief of those who came to make the disturbance on the first instant, hanged himself.'[f] (6). 'I was quite surprised when I heard Mr. R[omley] preach. That soft, smooth, tuneful voice, which he so often employed to blaspheme the work of God, was lost without hope of recovery.'[g] (7). 'Mr C[owley] spoke so much in favour of the rioters that they were all discharged. A few days after, walking over the same field, he dropped down and spoke no more.'[h]

And what is the utmost that can be inferred from all these passages? That I *believe* these things to have been judgments. What if I did? To *believe* things are judgments is one thing; to *claim* a power of inflicting judgments is another. If indeed I *believe* things

---

[a] [Ibid.,] p. 144.

[b] Ibid. [citing 8th *Journal*, Apr. 2, 1751].

[c] [Ibid.,] p. 145 [citing 9th *Journal*, Apr. 11, 1752].

[d] Ibid. [citing 9th *Journal*, June 9, 1752].

[e] Ibid. [citing 5th *Journal*, Aug. 23, 1743, relating the incident of a Bristol clergyman who suffered a fatal fit while preaching against the Methodists].

[f] [Ibid.,] p. 146 [citing 4th *Journal*, Apr. 12, 1740].

[g] Ibid. [citing 7th *Journal*, July 3, 1748, describing a visit to Epworth, where Romley, the rector, had opposed the Methodists].

[h] [Ibid.,] pp. 146–7 [citing 7th *Journal*, Nov. 14, 1748].

to be judgments which are not, I am to blame. But still this is not 'claiming any miraculous gift'.

But 'you cite one who forbade your speaking to some dying criminals to answer for their souls at the judgment seat of Christ'.ᵃ

5 I do; but be this right or wrong, it is not claiming a power to *inflict judgments*.

Yes, it is: for 'these judgments are fulminated with the air of one who had the divine vengeance at his disposal'.ᵇ I think not; and I believe all impartial men will be of the same mind.

10 [9.] 'These are some of the *extraordinary gifts* which Mr. Wesley claims.'ᶜ I claim no 'extraordinary gift' at all. Nor has anything to the contrary been proved yet, so much as in a single instance.

[10.] 'We come now to the application of this sovereign test'— James 3: 17.¹ But let us see that we understand it first. I beg leave

15 to consider the whole. 'Who is a wise and knowing man among you? Let him show his wisdom', as well as his faith, by *his works*, not by words only. 'But if ye have bitter zeal and strife in your heart, do not glory and lie against the truth'; as if any such zeal, anything contrary to love, could consist with true wisdom. 'This wisdom

20 descendeth not from above, but is earthly, sensual, devilish. For where *bitter* zeal and strife are, there is confusion and every evil work. But the wisdom which is from above' (which every one that hath is a real Christian, and he only) 'is first pure' (free from all that is 'earthly, sensual, devilish'), 'then peaceable' (bringing,

25 loving, making peace), 'gentle' (soft, mild, yielding, not morose or sour), 'easy to be entreated' (to be persuaded or convinced, not stubborn, self-willed, or self-conceited), 'full of mercy' (of tenderness and compassion), 'and good fruits' both in the heart and life. Two of these are immediately specified: 'without partiality' (loving

30 and doing good to all, without respect of persons), 'and without hypocrisy' (sincere, frank, open).²

I desire to be tried by this test. I try myself by it continually; not indeed whether I am a *prophet* (for it has nothing to do with this) but whether I am a *Christian*.

ᵃ [Warburton, op. cit.], p. 147 [quoting 4th *Journal*, Apr. 2, 1740, though Warburton's citation is incorrect].
ᵇ Ibid.   ᶜ [Ibid.,] p. 149.

---

¹ Warburton, op. cit., p. 149 (i.e. the second page so numbered, beginning the text of Vol. II).
² Jas. 3: 13–17 (cf. Wesley's *Notes*).

[11.]¹ The present question then is—not what is Mr. Law, or what are the Moravians,² but—what is John Wesley? And,

(I). Is he *pure* or not? 'Not pure; for he separates reason from grace.'ᵃ A wonderful proof! But I deny the fact. I never did separate reason from grace. 'Yes, you do. For your own words are: "The 5 points we chiefly insisted on were four. (1). That *orthodoxy* or *right opinion* is at best but a very slender part of religion, if it can be allowed to be any part of it at all." '''ᵇ

After premising that it is our bounden duty to labour after a *right judgment* in all things, as a *wrong judgment* naturally leads to 10 wrong *practice*, I say again, *right opinion* is at best but a very *slender part* of religion (which properly and directly consists in right tempers, words, and actions) and frequently it is *no part* of religion. For it may be where there is no religion at all: in men of the most abandoned lives; yea, in the devil himself. 15

And yet this does not prove that I 'separate reason from grace', that I 'discard reason from the service of religion'. I do continually 'employ it to distinguish between right and wrong opinions'. I never affirmed 'this distinction to be of little consequence', or denied 'the gospel to be *a reasonable service*'.ᶜ 20

[12.] But 'the apostle Paul considered *right opinion* as a full third part at least of religion. For he says, "The fruit of the Spirit is in all goodness, and righteousness, and truth." By "goodness" is meant

---

ᵃ [Warburton, op. cit.,] p. 156.
ᵇ [Ibid.,] p. 157 [citing *A Plain Account of the People called Methodists*, I. 2].
ᶜ [Ibid.,] pp. 157–8.

---

¹ The numbering of the divisions in this work presents one of the worst problems in Wesley's writings. In the original a new division here is headed 'I.'—ignoring the fact that this occurs within the first of two parts numbered 'I.' and 'II.' Nor is this second 'I.' succeeded by 'II.' or 'III.' The following sentence begins the first of five major subsections numbered '1.' to '5.', dealing with Warburton's application of James 3: 15 to Wesley, and comprising the remainder of Pt. I. In this edition these have been noted as '(I).' to '(V).' Within these five sub-sections occur other divisions, subdivisions, and sub-subdivisions, always indicated (when noted at all) by various series of Arabic numerals whose relationships become very confusing. (In part Wesley's numbering follows that of Warburton.) We have made an attempt at denoting these relationships by using differentiated Arabic numerals together with differentiated Roman numerals, in the following sequence: I; (I).; 1.; (1). or (i). In order to maintain continuity within each of the two parts we have supplied a series of Arabic section numbers (enclosed within square brackets) in Wesley's manner; these sometimes correspond with divisions or sub-divisions numbered by Wesley, which have thus been merged into a unified system. For the comfort of the reader the headlines omit the brackets.

² With which pp. 150–7 n. of *The Doctrine of Grace* dealt.

the conduct of particulars to the whole; and consists in habits and social virtue; and this refers to *Christian practice*. By "righteousness" is meant the conduct of the whole to particulars; and consists in the gentle use of church authority; and this refers to *Christian discipline*.
5 By "truth" is meant the conduct of the whole, and of particulars to one another, and consists in *orthodoxy* or *right opinion*; and this refers to *Christian doctrine*.'ᵃ

My objections to this account are, (1), it contradicts St. Paul; (2), it contradicts itself.

10 First: it contradicts St. Paul. It fixes a meaning upon his words foreign both to the text and context. The plain sense of the text taken in connexion with the context is no other than this: 'The fruit of the Spirit'ᵇ (rather, 'of the light', which Bengelius¹ proves to be the true reading, opposite to 'the unfruitful works of darkness',
15 mentioned verse eleven) 'is (consists in) all goodness, kindness, tender-heartedness',ᶜ opposite to 'bitterness, wrath, anger, clamour, evil-speaking';ᵈ 'in all righteousness', rendering unto all their dues, opposite to 'stealing';ᵉ 'and in all truth', veracity, sincerity, opposite to 'lying'.ᶠ

20 [13.] Secondly, that interpretation contradicts itself—and that in every article. For (i), if by 'goodness' be meant the conduct of 'particulars to the whole', then it does not consist in 'habits of social virtue'. For *social virtue* regulates the conduct of particulars, not so properly to the whole as to each other. (ii). If by 'righteousness'
25 be meant the conduct of 'the whole to particulars', then it cannot consist in the 'gentleness of church authority'; unless church governors are the whole church, or the parliament the whole nation. (iii). If by 'truth' be meant 'the conduct of the whole, and of particulars to one another', then it cannot possibly consist 'in
30 *orthodoxy* or *right opinion*'. For *opinion*, right or wrong, is not conduct. They differ *toto genere*. If then it be *orthodoxy*, it is not 'the *conduct* of the governors and governed toward each other'. If it be their *conduct* toward each other, it is not *orthodoxy*.

ᵃ [Warburton, op. cit.], pp. 158-9. ᵇ Eph. 5: 9. ᶜ Eph. 4: 32.
ᵈ Ver. 31. ᵉ Ver. 28. ᶠ Ver. 25.

---

¹ J. A. Bengel, a famous Lutheran biblical scholar, whose edition of the Greek New Testament, with critical notes, was an important landmark in the scientific study of the text. In 1742 he published his *Gnomon Novi Testamenti*, an exegetical commentary which combined great insight with epigrammatical brevity. Wesley used it extensively in his *Explanatory Notes upon the New Testament*, for which see Vols. 5-6 of this edition.

Although therefore it be allowed that right opinions are a great
help, and wrong opinions a great hindrance, to religion, yet till
stronger proof be brought against it that proposition remains
unshaken—'Right opinions are a slender part of religion, if any
part of it at all.'[a]   5

(As to the affair of Abbé Paris, whoever will read over with calmness and impartiality but one volume of Monsieur Montgéron will
then be a competent judge. Meantime I would just observe that if
these miracles were real, they strike at the root of the whole papal
authority, as having been wrought in direct opposition to the famous   10
Bull *Unigenitus*.[b])

Yet I do not say, 'Errors in faith have little to do with religion';
or that they 'are no let or impediment to the Holy Spirit'.[c] But
still it is true that 'God (generally speaking) begins his work at the
heart.'[d] Men usually feel *desires* to please God before they *know*   15
how to please him. Their *heart* says, 'What must I do to be saved?'[1]
before they *understand* the way of salvation.

[14.] But see 'the character he gives his own saints! "The more
I converse with this people, the more I am amazed. That God hath
wrought a great work is manifest (by saving many sinners from their   20
sins). And yet the main of them are not able to give a rational

---

[a] [Warburton, op. cit.,] p. 160; [see also p. 157 and § 11 above.]

[b] [Ibid.,] p. 161 [citing 8th *Journal*, Jan. 11, 1750. In the *Journal* Wesley recorded his
reaction to Montgéron's work: 'I read, to my no small amazement, the account given
by Monsieur Montgéron, both of his own conversion and of the other miracles wrought
at the tomb of Abbé Paris. I had always looked upon the whole affair as a mere legend,
as I suppose most Protestants do: but I see no possible way to deny these facts without
invalidating all human testimony. I may full as reasonably deny there is such a person
as M. Montgéron, or such a city as Paris in the world. Indeed in many of these instances
I see great superstition, as well as strong faith. But the "times of ignorance" God does
"wink at" still; and bless the faith, notwithstanding the superstition.'

The Abbé François de Paris (1690–1727), a deacon in the Roman Catholic Church,
joined the Jansenist party during the bitter conflict that raged in France during the
latter part of the seventeenth century and (more intermittently) throughout much of the
eighteenth. He was buried in the churchyard of St. Médard, and the miracles performed
at his grave caused such great excitement that the churchyard was closed by royal
command. Carré de Montgéron, a radical sceptic, was converted as a result of his pilgrimages to St. Médard. In *La Vérité des Miracles opérés par l'intercession de M. de Paris*
he described his experiences and defended his belief in the miracles. The Bull *Unigenitus*
(Sept. 8, 1713), specifically directed against Quesnel's annotated translation of the New
Testament, was one of the most controversial documents elicited by the Jansenist
controversy].

[c] [Ibid.,] pp. 161–2.   [d] [Ibid.,] p. 162 [citing 7th *Journal*, May 22, 1749].

---

[1] Acts 16: 30.

account of the plainest principles of religion."'¹ They were not able then, as there had not been time to instruct them. But the case is far different *now*.

Again, did I 'give this character', even then, of the people called
5 Methodists in *general*? No, but of the people of a *particular* town in Ireland, where nine in ten of the inhabitants are Romanists.

'Nor is the observation confined to the people. He had made a proselyte of Mr. D[rake] vicar of B[eighton]. And to show he was no discredit to his master, he gives him this character: "He seemed
10 to stagger at nothing, though as yet his understanding is not opened."'ᵃ

Mr. D[rake] was never a proselyte of mine; nor did I ever see him before or since. I endeavoured to show him that we 'are justified by faith'. And he did not object; though neither did he *understand*.

15 [15.] 'But in the first propagation of religion God began with the *understanding*, and rational conviction won the *heart*.'ᵇ Frequently, but not always. The jailor's *heart* was touched first; then he *understood* what he 'must do to be saved'.² In this respect, then, there is nothing *new* in the present work of God. So the lively story from
20 Molière is just nothing to the purpose.³

In drawing the parallel between the work God has wrought in England and in America I do not so much as *insinuate* 'that the understanding has nothing to do in the work'.ᶜ Whoever is engaged therein will find full employment for all the understanding which
25 God has given him.

'On the whole, therefore, we conclude that [that] wisdom which divests the Christian faith of its *truth* and the test of it—*reason* —and resolves all religion into spiritual *mysticism* and *ecstatic*

ᵃ [Warburton, op. cit.], p. 162, [citing 9th *Journal*, Apr. 14,1752. The Revd. John Drake was vicar of Beighton, Derbyshire, 1733–63].
ᵇ [Ibid.,] p. 163.   ᶜ [Ibid.,] p. 165.

---

¹ Warburton, op. cit., p. 162, quoting 7th *Journal*, May 22, 1749.
² Cf. Acts 16: 30.
³ Wesley's remark is intelligible only in the light of Warburton's comment (op. cit., pp. 163–4): 'But, for this discordancy between *his* mission and St. Paul's he has a salvo: he observes occasionally, in several places in his *Journal*, that God *now* not only does a *new work*, but by *new ways*. This solution of our spiritual empiric will perhaps put the reader in mind of the quack in Molière who, having placed the *liver* on the left side and the *heart* on the right, and being told that the structure of the parts was certainly otherwise, replied: "Oui, cela étoit autre fois ainsi; mais nous avons changé tout cela, et nous faisons maintenant la médecine d'une méthode toute nouvelle." ' Cf. Molière, *Le Médecin malgré lui*, Acte II, Scène vi.

raptures, . . . cannot be the wisdom from above, whose characteristic is *purity.*'ª

Perhaps so, but *I* do not 'divest faith, either of truth or reason'; much less do I 'resolve all into *spiritual mysticism* and *ecstatic raptures*'. Therefore suppose *purity* here meant *sound doctrine* 5 (which it no more means than it does a sound constitution) still it touches not *me*, who, for anything that has yet been said, may teach the *soundest doctrine* in the world.

(II). [16.] 'Our next business is to apply the other marks to these *pretending sectaries*. The first of these, *purity*, respects the nature of 10 "the wisdom from above",¹ or in other words the *doctrine* taught.'ᵇ Not in the least. It has no more to do with *doctrine* than the whole text has with *prophets*. 'All the rest concern the *manner* of teaching.' Neither can this be allowed. They no farther concern either teaching or teachers than they concern all mankind. 15

But to proceed. 'Methodism signifies only the *manner of preaching*; not either an *old* or a *new* religion; it is the *manner* in which Mr. Wesley and his followers attempt to propagate the "plain, old religion".'ᶜ And is not this 'sound doctrine'? Is this '*spiritual mysticism*' and '*ecstatic raptures*'? 20

'Of all men Mr. Wesley should best know the meaning of the term, since it was not a *nickname* imposed on the sect by its enemies, but an appellation of honour bestowed upon it by themselves.'² In answer to this I need only transcribe what was published twenty years ago: 25

> Since the name first came abroad into the world many have been at a loss to know what a Methodist is; what are the *principles* and the *practice* of those who are commonly called by that name; and what are the *distinguishing marks* of the sect 'which is everwhere spoken against'.³

And it being generally believed that I was able to give the clearest 30 account of these things (as having been one of the first to whom the name was given, and the person by whom the rest were supposed to be directed) I have been called upon, in all manner of ways and with the utmost earnestness, so to do. I yield at last to the continued importunity both of friends and enemies; and do now give the clearest account 35 I can, in the presence of the Lord, the judge of heaven and earth, of the *principles* and *practice* whereby those who are called Methodists are distinguished from other men.

ª [Ibid.,] pp. 165–6.   ᵇ [Ibid.,] pp. 166–7.   ᶜ [Ibid.,] pp. 167–8.

¹ Cf. Jas. 3: 17.   ² [Warburton, op. cit.,] p. 167.   ³ Acts 28: 22.

I say 'those who are called Methodists', for let it be well observed
that this is *not a name which they take upon themselves*, but one *fixed on
them* by way of reproach, without their approbation or consent. It was
first given to three or four young men at Oxford by a student of
5   Christ Church, either in allusion to the ancient sect of physicians so
called (from their teaching that almost all diseases might be cured by
a specific *method* of diet and exercise) or from their observing a more
regular method of study and behaviour than was usual with those of
their age and station.ᵃ

10   I need only add that this nickname was imposed upon us before
this 'manner of preaching' had a being. Yea, at a time when I
thought it was as lawful to cut a throat as to *preach out of a church*.
[17.] 'Why then will Mr. Wesley so grossly misrepresent his
adversaries as to say that when they speak against Methodism they
15   speak against the *plain, old doctrine* of the Church of England?'ᵇ
This is no misrepresentation. Many of our adversaries, all over the
kingdom, speak against us *eo nomine*¹ for preaching *these doctrines—
justification by faith* in particular.

However, 'a *fanatic manner* of preaching, though it were the
20   doctrine of an apostle, may do more harm, to society at least, than
reviving *old* heresies or inventing *new*. It tends to bewilder the
imaginations of some, to inflame the passions of others, and to
spread disorder and confusion through the whole community.'ᶜ
I would gladly have the term defined. What is 'a *fanatic manner
25   of preaching*'? Is it *field preaching*? But this has no such effect, even
among the wildest of men. This has not 'bewildered the imaginations' even of the Kingswood colliers, or 'inflamed their passions'.
It has not spread disorder or confusion among them, but just the
contrary. From the time it was heard in that chaos,

30   Confusion heard the voice, and wild uproar
            Stood ruled, and order from disorder sprung.²

ᵃ Preface to *The Character of a Methodist*. [A 'student' at Christ Church is equivalent
to a 'fellow' at other Oxford colleges.]
ᵇ [Warburton, op. cit.,] p. 168.   ᶜ [Ibid.,] p. 169.

---

¹ 'On this account, for this cause.'
² Cf. Milton, *Paradise Lost*, iii. 710–13:

            Confusion heard his voice, and wild Uproar
            Stood ruled, stood vast Infinitude confined;
            Till, at his second bidding, Darkness fled,
            Light shone, and order from disorder sprung.

'But St. James, who delivers the test for the trial of these men's pretensions,' (the same mistake still) 'unquestionably thought a fanatic spirit did more mischief in the *mode* of teaching than in the *matter* taught; since of six marks *one* only concerns *doctrine*, all the rest the *manners* of the teacher.'ᵃ Nay, all six concern *doctrine* as much as one. The truth is they have nothing to do either with *doctrine* or *manner*.

'From St. Paul's words, "Be instant, in season, out of season",¹ he infers more than they will bear; and misapplies them into the bargain.'ᵇ When and where? I do not remember applying them at all.

'When *seasonable* times are appointed for holy offices, to fly to *unseasonable* is factious.'ᶜ But it is not clear that five in the morning and seven in the evening (our usual times) are *unseasonable*.

[18.] We come now directly to the second article. '"The wisdom from above is peaceable.". . . But the propagation of Methodism has occasioned many and great violations of peace. In order to know where the blame hereof lies let us inquire into the temper which *makes for peace*. For we may be assured the fault lies not there where such a temper is found.'ᵈ Thus far we are quite agreed. 'Now the temper which makes for peace is *prudence*.' This is *one* of the tempers which make for peace; others are kindness, meekness, patience. 'This our Lord recommended by his own example.ᵉ. . . But this Mr. Wesley calls "the mystery of iniquity" and "the offspring of hell".'ᶠ No, not this; not the prudence which our Lord recommends. I call that so, and that only, which *the world*, the men who know not God, style 'Christian prudence'. By this I mean subtlety, craft, dissimulation; study to please man rather than God; the art of trimming between God and the world, of serving God and mammon. Will any serious man defend this? And *this* only do I condemn.

[19.] But you say '*good sort of men*, as they are called, are *the bane of all religion*'.ᵍ And I think so. By this 'good sort of men' I mean 'persons who have a liking to but no *sense* of religion'; no real fear or love of God; no truly Christian tempers. 'These steal away the

ᵃ [Ibid.,] p. 170.   ᵇ [Ibid.,] p. 171.   ᶜ [Ibid.,] pp. 171–2.
ᵈ [Ibid.,] pp. 172–3.   ᵉ [Ibid.,] pp. 174–7.
ᶠ [Ibid.,] pp. 178–9 [citing 2nd *Journal* (1st ed.), Feb. 26, 1738, and 3rd *Journal*, June 11, 1739].
ᵍ [Ibid.,] pp. 179–80 [citing 3rd *Journal*, Mar. 28, 1739, § 8 of the letter to his father].

¹ 2 Tim. 4: 2.

little *zeal* he has, that is, persuade him to be peaceable.'[1] No; persuade me to be like themselves—without love either to God or man.

'Again, speaking of one he says, "Indulging himself in *harmless*
5 *company*" (vulgarly so called) "he first made shipwreck of his *zeal*, then of his *faith*."[2] In this I think he is right. The *zeal* and *faith* of a *fanatic* are such exact tallies that neither can exist alone. They came into the world together to disturb society and dishonour religion.'

10 By *zeal* I mean the flame of love, or fervent love to God and man; by *faith*, the substance or confidence of things hoped for, the evidence of things not seen.[3] Is this the *zeal* and *faith* of a *fanatic*? Then St. Paul was the greatest fanatic on earth. Did these come into the world to *disturb society* and *dishonour religion*?

15 'On the whole we find Mr. Wesley, by *his own confession*, entirely destitute of . . . prudence. Therefore it must be ascribed to the want of this if his preaching be attended with tumult and disorder.'[a] By 'his own confession'? Surely no. This I confess, and this only: What is falsely called prudence I abhor; but *true* prudence I love and
20 admire.

[20.] However, 'you set at nought the discipline of the Church by invading the province of the parochial minister'.[b] Nay, if ever I preach at all, it must be in the province of some parochial minister. 'By assembling in undue places and at unfit times.' I know of no
25 times unfit for those who assemble. And I believe Hanham Mount and Rose Green were the most proper places under heaven for preaching to the colliers in Kingswood.[4] 'By *scurrilous invectives* against the governors and pastors of the national Church.' This is an entire mistake. I dare not make any 'scurrilous invective' against

---

[a] [Warburton, op. cit.], pp. 180–1.   [b] [Ibid.,] p. 182.

[1] Wesley here conflates the quotation from his *Journal* and Warburton's interpretation of it.

[2] Warburton, op. cit., p. 180, citing 1st *Journal* (1st ed.), May 18, 1737.

[3] See Heb. 11: 1.

[4] Kingswood, a colliery village about four miles east of Bristol, was the scene of some of the more remarkable of Wesley's early successes. Here he started a school which has had a distinguished history. Two open-air preaching places in the area were especially important, Hanham Mount and Rose Green. For Hanham Mount see *A Letter to the Author of the Enthusiasm of Methodists*, etc., § 4 and note. Rose Green was 'a plain upon the top of a high hill', ringed with spoil-heaps from old coal-pits (cf. *Letters*, Apr. 9, 1739 to James Hutton).

any man. '*Insolencies* of this nature provoke warm men to tumult.'
But these 'insolencies' do not exist; so that whatever tumult either
warm or cool men raise, I am not chargeable therewith.

'To know the *true character* of Methodism.' The present point is
to know the *true character* of *John Wesley*. Now in order to know this
we need not inquire what others were before he was born. All
therefore that follows of old *Precisians*, *Puritans*, and *Independents*
may stand just as it is.ᵃ

[21.] But 'Mr. Wesley *wanted* to be persecuted.'ᵇ As this is
averred over and over I will explain myself upon it, once for all.
I never desired or *wanted* to be persecuted.

> Lives there who loves his pain?¹

I love and desire to 'live peaceably with all men'.² 'But persecution would not come at his call.'³ However, it came uncalled; and
more than once or twice it was not 'mock persecution'. It was not
only the 'huzzas' of the mob—showers of stones are something
more than 'huzzas'. And whoever saw the mob either at Walsall
or Cork (to instance in no more) saw that they were not 'in jest' but
in great earnest, eagerly athirst, not for *sport* (as you suppose), but
for *blood*.

But though I do not *desire* persecution, I *expect* it. I must, if I
believe St. Paul: 'All that will live godly in Christ Jesus shall suffer
persecution';ᶜ either sooner or later, more or less, according to the
wise providence of God. But I believe 'all *these* things work together
for good to them that love God'.⁴ And from a conviction of this they
may even *rejoice* when they are 'persecuted for righteousness' sake'.⁵

Yet as I seldom 'complain of ill treatment', so I am never '*dissatisfied* with good'.ᵈ But I often wonder at it. And I once expressed
my wonder, nearly in the words of the old Athenian: 'What have
we done that the world should be so civil to us?'⁶

You conclude the head, 'As he who persecutes is but the tool of
him that *invites* persecution' (I know not who does) 'the crime
finally comes home to him who set the rioter at work.'ᵉ And is

---

ᵃ [Ibid.,] pp. 184–6.   ᵇ [Ibid.,] p. 187.   ᶜ 2 Tim. 3: 12.
ᵈ [Warburton, op. cit.,] p. 188.   ᵉ [Ibid.,] pp. 190–1.

¹ Milton, *Paradise Lost*, iv. 888.   ² Rom. 12: 18.
³ Warburton, op. cit., p. 187.   ⁴ Rom. 8: 28.   ⁵ Matt. 5: 10.
⁶ Cf. *Journal*, June 30, 1747, where Wesley uses these words but does not identify
them as a quotation.

this all the proof that I am not *peaceable*? Then let all men judge if the charge is made good.

(III). [22.] 'The next mark of the celestial wisdom is, it is "gentle, and easy to be entreated";[1] . . . compliant and even obsequious to all men'. And how does it appear that I am wanting in this? Why, he is 'a severe condemner of his fellow citizens, and a severe exactor of conformity to his own observances'. Now the proof: (1). 'He tells us this in the very appellation he assumes.'[a] Nay, I never *assumed* it at all. (2). But 'You say, "Useless conversation is 'an abomination to the Lord'." And what is this but to withstand St. Paul to the face?'[2] Why, did St. Paul join in or commend 'useless conversation'? I rather think he reproves it. He condemns as σαπρὸς λόγος, *putrid*, *stinking* conversation, all that is not good, all that is not 'to the use of edifying', and meet to 'minister grace to the hearers'.[b] (3). Mr. Wesley 'resolved never to laugh, . . . nor to speak a tittle of worldly things'[c]—'though others may, nay must'.[3] Pray add that, with the reason of my so resolving, namely, that I expected to die in a few days. If I expected it now, probably I should resume the resolution. But be it as it may, this proves nothing against my being both 'gentle' and 'easy to be entreated'. (4). 'He says Mr. Gr[iffith] was a clumsy, overgrown, hard-faced man.'[d] So he was. And this was the best of him. I spare him much in saying no more. But he is gone. Let his ashes rest. (5). 'I heard a most miserable sermon full of dull, senseless, improbable lies.'[4] It was so, from the beginning to the end. I have seldom heard the like. (6). '"The persecution of St. Ives" (which ended before I came; what I saw, I do not term 'persecution') "was owing to the indefatigable labours of Mr. H[oblyn] and Mr. S[ymonds]—gentlemen

---

[a] [Warburton, op. cit.], pp. 191-2.   [b] Eph. 4: 29.

[c] [Warburton, op. cit.,] p. 193 [cf. *Journal*, Feb. 28, 1738. On that date Wesley 'renewed and wrote down my former resolutions'. Warburton quotes a couple of clauses —neither accurately nor in proper sequence].

[d] [Ibid.,] p. 194 [citing 8th *Journal*, Mar. 28, 1750. Griffith twice broke in upon Wesley—once on board ship, during an abortive crossing from Anglesey to Ireland, and again the following night when, with a mob at his heels, he beset the house in Holyhead where Wesley was staying].

---

[1] Jas. 3: 17.

[2] Warburton, op. cit., pp. 192-3, citing 4th *Journal*, Sept. 3, 1741 (Wesley's letter to the church at Herrnhut, note to § 2).

[3] Cf. note 'c' above. This clause is part of Wesley's 'resolutions', but Warburton omitted it when quoting the passage.

[4] Warburton, op. cit., citing 5th *Journal*, Jan. 30, 1743.

worthy to be had in everlasting remembrance." Here he tells us it is his purpose to gibbet up the names of his two great persecutors to everlasting infamy.'a These gentlemen had occasioned several innocent people to be turned out of their livelihood; and others to be outraged in the most shocking manner, and beat only not to death. My purpose is by setting down their names to make others afraid so to offend. Yet I say still, 'God forbid that I should *rail* either at a Turk, infidel, or heretic.' But I will bring to light the actions of *such* Christians to be a warning to others. And all this I judge to be perfectly consistent with 'the spirit of *meekness*'.b

(IV). [23.] The fourth mark is 'full of mercy and good fruits'.1 'Let us inquire into the "mercy and good fruits" of Mr. Wesley.'c

(1). And first: 'He has no mercy on his opposers. They pass with him under no other title than that of the "devil's servants" and the "devil's children".d This is far from true. Many have opposed, and do oppose me still, whom I believe to be the children and servants of God. 'We have seen him dispatching the principal of these children of the devil, without mercy, to their father.'e No, not one. This has been *affirmed* over and over, but never proved yet. I 'fling about no exterminating judgments of God'; I 'call down no fire from heaven'. 'But it would be for the credit of these *new saints* to distinguish between *rage* and *zeal*.' That is easily done: *rage* is furious fire from hell; *zeal* is loving fire from heaven. (2). 'If what has been said above does not suffice, turn again to Mr. Wesley's *Journals*. "Mr. S., while he was speaking to the society against my brother and me, was struck raving mad."'f He was so, before an hundred witnesses; though I was *the last* to believe it. 'But, it seems, God is at length entreated for him, and has restored him to a sound mind.' And is my *relating* this *fact* an instance of '*dooming* men to *perdition*'? (3). 'John Haydon . . . cried aloud, "Let the world see the judgment of God."'g He did. But let John Haydon look to that. It was he said

a [Ibid.,] p. 195 [citing 6th *Journal*, Apr. 6, 1744: the *Journal*, followed by Warburton, prints the names of both men].

b [Ibid.,] pp. 195–6 [citing 4th *Journal*, Sept. 3, 1741, unfinished letter of 1738 to the Moravian Church].

c [Ibid.,] p. 198.   d Ibid.   e [Ibid.,] p. 199.

f [Ibid.,] p. 200 [citing 6th *Journal*, July 15, 1744].

g [Ibid.,] p. 201 [citing 3rd *Journal*, May 2, 1739. Haydon, a weaver of Bristol, though normally a man of sedate habits, had temporarily been swept into irrationality].

1 Jas. 3: 17.

so, not I. (4). 'I was informed of an *awful providence*. A poor
wretch, who was here the last week cursing and blaspheming, and
labouring with all his might to hinder the word of God, had afterwards boasted he would come again on Sunday, and no man should
5 stop his mouth then. But on Friday God laid his hand upon him,
and on Sunday he was buried.'ᵃ And was not this an 'awful providence'? But yet I do not 'doom even him to perdition'. (5). 'I saw
a poor man, once joined with us, who wanted nothing in this world.
A day or two before he hanged himself, but was cut down before he
10 was dead. He has been crying out ever since, God had left him
because he had left the children of God.'¹ This was *his* assertion,
not *mine*. I neither affirm nor deny it. (6). The true account of Lucy
Godshall is this:

I buried the body of Lucy Godshall. . . . After pressing toward the
15   mark for more than two years, since she had known the pardoning love
of God, she was for some time weary and faint in her mind, till I put
her out of the bands. God blessed this greatly to her soul, so that in
a short time she was admitted again. Soon after, being at home, she
felt the love of God in an unusual manner poured into her heart. She
20   fell down upon her knees, and delivered up her soul and body into the
hands of God. In the instant the use of all her limbs was taken away, and
she was in a burning fever. For three days she mightily praised God,
and rejoiced in him all the day long. She then cried out, 'Now Satan
hath desired to have me, that he may sift me as wheat.' Immediately
25   darkness and heaviness fell upon her, which continued till Saturday
the fourth instant. On Sunday the light shone again upon her heart.
About ten in the evening one said to her, 'Jesus is ready to receive your
soul.' She said, 'Amen! Amen!', closed her eyes, and died.ᵇ

Is this brought as a proof of my *inexorableness*! Or of my 'dooming
30 men to perdition'?
  (7). 'I found Nicholas Palmer in great weakness of body and
heaviness of spirit. We wrestled with God in his behalf; and our
labour was not in vain. His soul was comforted; and a few hours
after he quietly fell asleep.'² A strange proof this, likewise, either of

---

ᵃ [Warburton, op. cit.,] pp. 201–2 [citing 4th *Journal*, Oct. 23, 1740].
  ᵇ 4th [i.e. 5th] *Journal*, p. 71 [Sept. 9, 1742, quoted more briefly by Warburton,
op. cit., pp. 202–3].

---

¹ Warburton, op. cit., p. 202, citing 6th *Journal*, Aug. 25, 1745.
  ² Wesley, 5th *Journal*, Sept. 29, 1741, quoted more briefly by Warburton, op. cit.,
p. 203.

inexorableness or of 'dooming men to perdition'! Therefore this charge, too, stands totally unsupported. Here is no proof of my *unmercifulness* yet.

[24.] '*Good fruits* come next to be considered, which Mr. Wesley's idea of true religion does not promise. He saith (I will repeat the words a little at large, that their true sense may more clearly appear): "In explaining those words, 'The kingdom of God (or true religion) is not meat and drink',¹ I was led to show that religion does not *properly consist* in harmlessness, using the means of grace, and doing good—that is, helping our neighbours, chiefly by giving alms; but that a man might both be harmless, use the means of grace, and do much good, and yet have no true religion at all."'ᵃ He may so. Yet whoever has true religion must be 'zealous of good works'.² And zeal for all good works is, according to *my* idea, an essential ingredient of true religion.

'Spiritual cures are all the *good fruits* he pretends to.'ᵇ 'Not quite all', says William Kirkman, with some others.³ 'A few of his spiritual cures we will set in a fair light. . . . "The first time I preached at Swalwell" (chiefly to colliers and workers in the ironwork[s]) 'none seemed to be much convinced, only *stunned*." '⁴ I mean *amazed* at what they heard, though they were the first principles of religion. 'But he brings them to their senses with a vengeance.' No, not *them*. These were different persons. Are they lumped together in order to set things in a 'fair light'? The whole paragraph runs thus:

I carefully examined those who had lately cried out in the congregation. Some of these, I found, could give no account at all how or wherefore they had done so; only that of a sudden they dropped down, they knew not how; and what they afterward said or did they knew not. Others could just remember they were in fear, but could not tell what they were in fear of. Several said they were afraid of the devil; and this was all they knew. But a few gave a more intelligible account of the piercing sense they then had of their sins, both inward and outward, which were set in array against them, round about; of the dread they were in of the wrath of God, and the punishment they had deserved, into which they seemed to be just falling, without any way to escape.

ᵃ [Warburton, op. cit.,] p. 203 [citing 4th *Journal*, Nov. 24, 1739: Wesley conflates two passages from the entry under that date].
ᵇ [Ibid.,] pp. 204-5.

---

¹ Rom. 14: 17. ² Titus 2: 14. ³ See above, § 6 (3).
⁴ Warburton, op. cit., p. 205, citing 5th *Journal*, Dec. 28, 1742.

One of them told me: 'I was as if I was just falling down, from the highest place I had ever seen. I thought the devil was pushing me off, and that God had forsaken me.' Another said: 'I felt the very fire of hell already kindled in my breast; and all my body was in as much pain
5   as if I had been in a burning fiery furnace.' What wisdom is this which 'rebuketh these, that they should hold their peace'? Nay, let such an one cry after Jesus of Nazareth, till he saith, 'Thy faith hath made thee whole'!ᵃ

[25.] Now follow the proofs of my driving men mad. (1). 'Another
10 of Dr. Munro'sᴵ patients came to ask my advice. I found no reason to believe she had been any otherwise mad than everyone is that is *deeply convinced of sin*.'ᵇ Let this prove all that it can prove. (2). 'A middle-aged woman was *really distracted*.'² Yes, before I ever saw her, or she me. (3). 'I could not but be under some concern
15 with regard to one or two persons who were tormented in an unaccountable manner, and seemed to be indeed "*lunatic* as well as *sore vexed*".'³ True; for a time. But the deliverance of one of them is related in the very next paragraph. (4). 'Two or three are *gone quite distracted*; that is, they "mourn and refuse to be com-
20 forted" till they have redemption.'ᶜ (5). 'I desired one to visit Mrs. G. in Bedlam, put in by her husband as a madwoman.'⁴ But she never was mad in any degree, as he himself afterwards acknowledged. (6). 'One was so deeply convinced of her ungodliness that she cried out day and night, "Lord, save, or I perish!" All the
25 neighbours agreed she was stark mad.'⁵ But I did not make her so. For this was before she ever saw my face. Now let everyone judge whether here is yet a single proof that I drive men mad.

[26.] 'The time when this spiritual madness was at its height he calls a *glorious time*.'ᵈ I call that a 'glorious time' when many
30 notorious sinners are converted to God (whether with any outward

---

ᵃ 4th [i.e. 5th] *Journal*, p. 82 [Dec. 30, 1742].
ᵇ [Warburton, op. cit.,] p. 208 [citing 3rd *Journal*, Sept. 21, 1739].
ᶜ [Ibid.,] p. 209 [citing 3rd *Journal*, Oct. 17, 1739].
ᵈ [Ibid.,] p. 210 [citing 5th *Journal*, Feb. 20, 1742].

ᴵ Dr. James Munro, authority on mental illness, and chief physician at the Bethlehem Hospital. Here and in the *Journal* Wesley spells the name 'Monro'.
² Warburton, op. cit., p. 208, citing 3rd *Journal*, Sept. 28, 1739.
³ Ibid., citing 3rd *Journal*, Oct. 12, 1739; cf. Matt. 17: 15.
⁴ Ibid., p. 209, citing 4th *Journal*, Aug. 28, 1740.
⁵ Ibid., p. 209, citing 5th *Journal*, June 17, 1742.

symptoms or none; for those are no way essential) and when many are in the 'triumph of faith',¹ greatly 'rejoicing in God *their* Saviour'.²

'But though Mr. Wesley does so well in turning fools into madmen, yet his craftsmaster is certainly one Mr. Wheatley,³ of whom he gives this extraordinary account: "A poor woman (on Wednesday, 5 17th September, 1740) said it was four years (namely, in September, 1736, above a year before I left Georgia) since her son, by hearing a sermon of Mr. Wheatley's, fell into great uneasiness. She thought he was ill and would have sent for a physician. But he said, 'No, no; send for Mr. Wheatley.' He was sent for, and came; and after asking 10 a few questions, told her: 'The boy is mad. Get a coach, and carry him to Dr. Munro. Use my name. I have sent several such to him.'" Who this Mr. Wheatley is I know not.'ᵃ He was lecturer at Spitalfields Church. The event was, after the apothecary had half murdered him, he was discharged, and the lad soon recovered his 15 strength. His senses he never had lost. The supposing this was a blunder from the beginning.

'These are the exploits which Mr. Wesley calls *blessings from God.*'ᵇ (Certainly I do; both *repentance* and *faith*). 'And which therefore we may call the *good fruits* of his ministry.' (May God 20 increase them an hundredfold!) 'What the Apostle calls *good fruits*, namely, *doing much good*, Mr. Wesley tells us belongs not to *true religion.*' I never told any man so yet. I tell all men just the contrary.

I may then safely leave all mankind to judge whether a single article of the charge against me has yet been made good. So much 25 for the first charge that I am a *madman*. Now for the second, that I am a *knave*.

(V). [27.] The proof is short: 'Every enthusiast is a knave; but he is an enthusiast; therefore he is a knave.' I deny both the first and second proposition. 'Nay, the first is proved thus: "Enthusiasm 30 must always be accompanied with craft and knavery."'ᶜ It *often* is so, but not *always*; for there may be *honest enthusiasts*. Therefore the whole account of that *odd combination* which follows is ingenious but proves nothing.ᵈ

ᵃ [Ibid.,] p. 211 [citing 4th *Journal*, Sept. 17, 1740].
ᵇ [Ibid.,] p. 212 [Warburton incorrectly cites for this the previous passage].
ᶜ [Ibid.,] p. 213.   ᵈ [Ibid.,] pp. 214–18.

¹ Cf. *Journal*, June 22, 1740.   ² Cf. Luke 1: 47.
³ The Revd. Mr. Wheatley is not to be confused with James Wheatley, Wesley's preacher, whose name frequently appears in later instalments of the *Journal*.

Yet I must touch upon one or two parts of it. 'An enthusiast thinks he is dispensed with in breaking—nay, that he is authorized to break—the common laws of morality.'[1] Does every enthusiast? Then I am none; for I never thought any such thing. I believe no
5 man living is authorized to break, or dispensed with in breaking, any law of morality. I know whoever (habitually) 'breaks one of the least of these shall be called least in the kingdom of heaven'.[2]

'Can any but an enthusiast believe that he may use guile to promote the glory of God?'[3] Yes, ten thousand that are no enthusiasts
10 firmly believe this. How few do we find that do not believe it? That do not plead for 'officious lies'? How few will subscribe to St. Augustine's declaration (to which I assent with my whole heart): 'I would not tell a wilful lie to save the souls of the whole world.'[4]

But to return. '"The wisdom from above is without partiality
15 and without hypocrisy."[5] "Partiality" consists in dispensing an unequal measure in our transactions with others; "hypocrisy", in attempting to cover that unequal measure by prevarication and false pretences.'[6]

The former of these definitions is not clear; the latter neither
20 clear nor adequate to the defined.

[28.] But let this pass. My partiality is now the point. What are the proofs of it? (1). 'His followers are always the "children of God"; his opposers, the "children of the devil".'[a] Neither so, nor so. I never affirmed either one or the other universally. That *some* of the former
25 are children of God, and *some* of the latter children of the devil, I believe. But what will this prove?

'His followers are directed by *inward feelings*, the *impulses* of an inflamed fancy' (no more than they are directed by the Alcoran), 'his opposers by the Scripture.' What, while they are cursing,
30 swearing, blaspheming; beating and maiming men that have done them no wrong; and treating women in a manner too shocking to be repeated?

(2). The next proof is very extraordinary. My words are: 'I was with two persons who, I doubt, are properly enthusiasts; for, first,

---

[a] [Warburton, op. cit.,] p. 220.

---

[1] Warburton, op. cit., p. 216.   [2] Cf. Matt. 5: 19.
[3] Warburton, op. cit., p. 218.
[4] Augustine, *Contra Mendacium* (*Against Lying*), cap. 15 (Migne, *Patrologia Latina*, XL. 540). Wesley also quoted this sentence in *A Farther Appeal*, Pt. II, II. 24.
[5] Cf. Jas. 3: 17.   [6] Warburton, op. cit., p. 219.

they think to attain the end without the means, which is enthusiasm properly so called. Again, they think themselves inspired of God and are not. But false, imaginary inspiration is enthusiasm. That theirs is only imaginary inspiration appears hence—it contradicts "the law and the testimony".'ᵃ

Now, by what art of man can this be made a proof of my *partiality*? Why, thus: 'These are wise words. But what do they amount to? Only to this; that these two persons would not take out their patents of inspiration from his office.' But what proof is there of this round assertion? Truly, none at all.

[29.] Full as extraordinary is the third proof of my *partiality*. 'Miss Gr. told Mrs. Sp. Mr. Wesley was a Papist. Upon this Miss Gr. is anathematized. And we are told that, *in consequence*, she had lately been *raving mad*, and as such was *tied down* in her bed. Yet *all these* circumstances of madness have befallen his favourite saints, whom he has vindicated from the opprobrium.'ᵇ

The passage in my *Journal* stands thus: 'Mrs. Spa——¹ told me, two or three nights since, "Miss Gr. met me, and said, 'I assure you, Mr. Wesley is a Papist.'" . . . Perhaps I need observe no more upon this than that Miss Gr. had lately been raving mad, in consequence of a *fever* (not of an *anathema* which never had any being); that as such she was tied down in her bed; and as soon as she was suffered to go abroad went to Mr. Whitefield to inquire of him whether *he* was not a Papist. But he quickly perceived she was only a lunatic, the nature of her disorder soon betraying itself.' Certainly then my allowing *her* to be mad is no proof of my *partiality*. I will allow everyone to be so who is attended with '*all these* circumstances of madness'.

(4). 'He pronounces sentence of enthusiasm upon another, and tells wherefore without any disguise: "Here I took leave of a poor *mad*, *original* enthusiast, who had been scattering lies in every quarter."'² It was the famous John Adams, since confined at Box, whose capital lie, the source of the rest, was that he was a prophet greater than Moses or any of the apostles. And is the pronouncing *him* a madman a proof of my *partiality*?

ᵃ [Ibid.,] p. 221 [citing 3rd *Journal*, Jan. 17, 1739; cf. Isa. 8: 20].
ᵇ [Ibid.,] pp. 221–2 [citing 5th *Journal*, Sept. 24, 1742].

---

¹ The additional 'a' here given beyond the 'Sp.' of the *Journal* tends to confirm the conjecture that this was Mrs. Sparrow, a Bristol Methodist. Miss Gr—— was possibly Miss Gregory (cf. Wesley's diary, Feb. 27, 1741).
² Warburton, op. cit., p. 222, citing 6th *Journal*, June 19, 1745.

[30.] (5). 'I had much conversation with Mr. Simpson, an *original enthusiast*. I desired him in the evening to give an exhortation. He did so, and spoke many good things in a manner peculiar to himself' (without order or connexion, head or tail; and in a language
5 very near as mystical as that of Jacob Behmen.) 'When he had done I summed up what he had said, methodizing and explaining it. O what pity it is this well-meaning man should ever speak without an interpreter!'ᵃ

Let this passage likewise stand as it is, and who can guess how it
10 is to prove my *partiality*? But by a sleight of hand the thing is done. 'How differently does Mr. Wesley treat these two enthusiasts? The first is accused of spreading lies "of his master"'; (No, he never was any disciple of mine:) 'on which Mr. Wesley "*took his leave of him*"—a gentle expression to signify the thrusting him out
15 head and shoulders from the society of saints.' It signifies neither more nor less than that I went out of the room and left him. 'The other's enthusiasm is made to consist only in "*want of method*".' No. His enthusiasm did not *consist in this*. It was the cause of it. But he was quite another man than John Adams; and I believe,
20 a right *honest man*.

[31.] (6). 'I was both surprised and grieved at a genuine instance of enthusiasm. J[ohn] B[rown], who had received a sense of the love of God a few days before, came riding through the town, hollowing and shouting, and driving all the people before him, telling them
25 God had told him he should be a king, and should tread all his enemies under his feet. I sent him home immediately to his work, and advised him to cry day and night to God that he might be lowly in heart, "lest Satan should again get an advantage over him".'ᵇ

What this proves, or is intended to prove, I cannot tell. Certainly
30 neither this nor any of the preceding passages prove the point now in question, my *partiality*. So this likewise is wholly unproved still.

[32.] 'We shall end, where every fanatic leader ends, with his *hypocrisy*.'ᶜ Five arguments are brought in proof of this. I shall take them in their order. (1). 'After having heaped up miracles one upon
35 another he sneaks away under the protection of a puny wonder: "About five I began near the Keelmen's Hospital, many thousands

---

ᵃ [Warburton, op. cit.,] p. 223 [citing 6th *Journal*, Aug. 17, 1745. Wesley invited Simpson to give an exhortation, 'that I might understand him the more thoroughly'. Warburton wrote a tract giving an account of Simpson's enthusiasm].

ᵇ [Ibid.,] pp. 224–5 [citing 5th *Journal*, Nov. 28, 1742, the account of this same John Brown's conversion; cf. p. 226, citing ibid., Dec. 4, 1742].   ᶜ [Ibid.,] p. 227.

standing round. The wind was high just before, but scarce a breath
was felt all the time we assembled before God. I praise God for
this also. Is it enthusiasm *to see God in every benefit we receive?*"
It is not; the enthusiasm consists in believing those benefits to be
conferred through a change in the established course of nature. . . .   5
But here he *insinuates* that he meant no more by his *miracles* than
the seeing God in every benefit we receive.'ᵃ That sudden and total
ceasing of the wind I impute to the *particular providence of God.*
This I mean by *seeing God* therein. But *this* I knew many would
count *enthusiasm.* In guarding against it I had an eye to that single   10
incident and no other. Nor did I *insinuate* anything more than
I expressed, in as plain a manner as I could.

   [33.] A little digression follows: 'A friend of his advises not to
establish the power of working miracles as the great criterion of
a divine mission; seeing the agreement of doctrines with Scripture   15
is the only infallible rule.'ᵇ 'But Christ himself establishes the power
of working miracles as the great criterion of a divine mission.'ᶜ
True, of a mission to be the Saviour of the world; to put a period
to the Jewish and introduce the Christian dispensation. And whoever pretends to *such a mission* will stand in need of *such credentials.*   20

   [34.] (2). 'He shifts and doubles no less' (neither less, nor more)
'as to the *ecstasies* of his saints. Sometimes they are of God, sometimes of the devil. But he is constant in this, that *natural causes* have
no hand in them.'¹ This is not true. In what are here termed 'ecstasies'—strong joy or grief, attended with various bodily symptoms—   25
I have openly affirmed again and again that *natural causes* have a part.
Nor did I ever shift or double on the head. I have steadily and uniformly maintained that if the mind be affected to such a degree, the
body must be affected, by the laws of the vital union. The mind,

   ᵃ [Ibid.,] pp. 228–9 [citing 9th *Journal,* May 17, 1752: the italics are Warburton's].
   ᵇ [Ibid.,] pp. 229–30 [citing 3rd *Journal,* July 31, 1739, quoting 'a little discourse
concerning enthusiasm . . . published about this time'. The title by which its author
referred to this item was 'Rules and Considerations'; it appeared as No. 25 in a series
published in the *Gloucester Journal,* and was signed 'Country Common Sense'. The
author was the Revd. Josiah Tucker, vicar of All Saints, Bristol, and subsequently
incumbent of St. Stephen's, Bristol, and Dean of Gloucester. Wesley's *The Principles of
a Methodist* (1740) was a reply to Tucker. Wesley praised him as a courteous critic, with
a high regard both for his own integrity and for the truth. (Cf. *A Letter to the Rev. Mr.
Baily of Cork* (1750), I. 1; both this and the *Principles* will be found in Vol. 9 of this
edition)].   ᶜ [Ibid.,] pp. 230–1.

   ¹ Warburton, op. cit., pp. 231–2.

I believe, was in many of those cases affected by the spirit of God; in others by the devil; and in some, by both; and in consequence of this, the body was affected also. (3). 'Mr. Wesley says, "I fear we have grieved the spirit of the jealous God by questioning his work",
5 and "by blaspheming it, by imputing it to nature or even to the devil".'ᵃ True; by imputing the conviction and conversion of sinners, which is the work of God alone (because of these unusual circumstances attending it) either to nature or to the devil. This is flat and plain. No *prevarication* yet. Let us attend to the next proof
10 of it: 'Innumerable cautions were given me not to regard visions or dreams, or to fancy people had remission of sins because of their cries, or tears, or outward professions. The sum of my answer was: You deny that God does now work these effects; at least, that he works them in this manner. I affirm both. I have seen very many
15 persons changed in a moment from a spirit of fear, horror, despair, to a spirit of love, joy, peace. What I have to say touching visions and dreams is this: I know several persons in whom this great change was wrought in a dream, or during a strong representation to the eye of their mind of Christ, either on the cross, or in glory.
20 This is the fact.' Let any judge of it as they please. And that such a change was then wrought appears (not from their shedding tears only, or falling into fits, or crying out; these are not the fruits, as you seem to suppose, whereby I judge, but) from the whole tenor of their life, till then many ways wicked, from that time holy and just
25 and good. 'Nay, he is so convinced of its being the *work of God* that the *horrid blasphemies* which ensued he ascribes to the abundance of joy which God had given to a poor madwoman.'ᵇ Do I ascribe those *blasphemies* to her 'joy in God'? No; but to her *pride*. My words are: 'I met with one who, having been lifted up with the
30 abundance of joy which God had given her, had fallen into such blasphemies and vain imaginations as are not common to men. In the afternoon I found another instance, nearly, I fear, of the same kind; one who set her *private revelations*, so called, on the selfsame foot with the written word.'
35 [35.] But how is this to prove *prevarication*? 'Why, on a sudden, he *directly revokes* all he had advanced. He says, "I told them they were not to judge of the spirit whereby anyone spoke, either by *ap-*

ᵃ [Warburton, op. ⸢cit.,] pp. 232–3 [citing 3rd *Journal*, an incorrect reference, and June 16, 1739.]
  ᵇ [Ibid.,] pp. 233–4 [citing 3rd *Journal*, May 20, 1739, and 4th *Journal*, Sept. 3, 1740].

pearances, or by *common report*, or by their own *inward feelings*. No, nor by any 'dreams, visions or revelations'[1] supposed to be made to the soul, any more than by their tears, or any *involuntary effects* wrought upon their bodies. I warned them that all these things were in themselves of a *doubtful, disputable* nature. They *might* be from 5 God, or they *might not*; and were therefore not simply to be relied on, any more than simply to be condemned, but to be tried by a farther rule, to be brought to the only certain test, 'the law and the testimony'."[2] Now is not this a *formal recantation* of what he had said just above?'[a] Nothing less, as I will show in two minutes to every 10 calm impartial man. What I say now I have said any time this thirty years; I have never varied therefrom for an hour. 'Every thing *disputable* is to be brought to the *only certain test*, "the law and the testimony".' 'But did not you talk just now of *visions* and *dreams*?' Yes, but not as of a *test* of anything; only as a *channel* 15 through which God is sometimes pleased to convey 'love, joy, peace; long-suffering, gentleness, goodness; fidelity, meekness, temperance' —the indisputable 'fruit of his Spirit'.[3] And these, we may observe, wherever they exist must be *inwardly felt*. Now where is the *pre-varication*? Where the *formal recantation*? They are vanished into 20 air.

[36.] But here is more proof: 'At length he gives up all these *divine agitations* to the devil. "I inquired", says he, "into the case of those who had lately cried out aloud during the preaching. . . . I found this had come upon every one of them in a moment, without any pre- 25 vious notice. . . . In that moment they dropped down, lost all their strength, and were seized with violent pain. . . . Some said they felt as if a sword were running through them; . . . others, as if their whole body was tearing in pieces. *These symptoms* I can no more impute to any *natural cause* than to the Spirit of God. I make no 30 doubt but it was *Satan tearing them* as they were coming to Christ." '[b]

'Now these were the *very symptoms* which he had before ascribed to the Spirit of God.'[c] Never in my life. Indeed some of them I never met with before. Those outward symptoms which I had met with before, bodily agitations in particular, I did not ascribe to the 35 Spirit of God, but to the *natural union* of the soul and body. And those symptoms which I now ascribe to the devil, I never ascribed

---

[a] [Ibid.,] pp. 234–5 [citing 3rd *Journal*, June 22, 1739].
[b] [Ibid.,] pp. 236–7 [citing 5th *Journal*, Mar. 12, 1743].   [c] [Ibid.,] p. 237.

[1] Cf. Dan. 1: 17; 2 Cor. 12: 1.   [2] Cf. Isa. 8: 20.   [3] Cf. Gal. 5: 22–3 (cf. *Notes*)·

to any other cause. The second proof of my *prevarication* or *hypocrisy* is therefore just as conclusive as the first.

[37.] (3). Now for the third: 'Mr. Wesley before spoke contemptuously of *orthodoxy*, to take in the sectaries. But when he
5 would take off churchmen, then orthodoxy is the *unum necessarium*.'[1]
Did I ever say so? No more than (in the other extreme) 'speak contemptuously' of it. 'Yes', you say, 'I described the *plain*, *old* religion of the Church of England which is now almost everywhere spoken against, under the *new* name of Methodism.'[2] Very well;
10 and what shadow of *prevarication* is here? May I not still declare the 'plain, old religion of the Church of England', and yet very consistently aver that *right opinion* is a very slender part of it?

[38.] (4). The next passage, I am sorry to say, is neither related with seriousness nor truth. 'We have seen him *inviting* persecution.'[3]
15 Never; though I '*rejoiced*' in the instance alleged, at having an opportunity of calling a multitude of the most abandoned sinners to repentance.

What is peculiarly unfair is, the lame, false account is palmed upon *me* by 'so he himself tells the story'.[4] I must therefore tell the
20 story once more, in as few words as I can.

Sunday, August 7, 1737. I repelled Mrs. W[illiamson] from the communion. Tuesday 9, I was required by Mr. Bailiff Parker to appear at the next court. Thursday 11, Mr. Causton, her uncle, said to me, 'Give your reasons for repelling her before the whole con-
25 gregation.' I answered, 'Sir, if you insist upon it, I will.' But I heard no more of it. Afterward he said (but not to *me*) 'Mr. Wesley had repelled Sophy out of revenge, because he had made proposals of marriage to her which she rejected.' Tuesday 16, Mrs. Wi[lliamson] made affidavit of it. Thursday, September 1, a grand jury, *prepared*
30 by Mr. Causton, found that 'John Wesley had broken the laws of the realm, by speaking and writing to Mrs. Wi[lliamson] against her husband's consent, and by repelling her from the communion.'

---

[1] Warburton, op. cit., pp. 238–9.

[2] Ibid., p. 239, citing 3rd *Journal*, Oct. 15, 1739.

[3] Ibid., pp. 239–40, citing 4th *Journal*, Sept. 14, 1740.

[4] Ibid., pp. 240–4, citing 1st *Journal*, pp. 44–56. The first instalment of Wesley's *Journal* devotes a great deal of space to his perplexed relations with Sophia Hopkey, who finally married Mr. Williamson, and whom Wesley repelled from the Lord's Table. Charity is needed if the retelling of the story is not to prove damaging to Wesley's reputation for wisdom or even common sense. Warburton treats the episode with an understandable lack of sympathy, but presses it into service to attack Wesley on other and more serious grounds.

Friday, [September] 2, was the third court day at which I appeared since my being required so to do by Mr. Parker. I moved for an immediate hearing; but was put off till the next court day. On the next court day I appeared again, as also at the two courts following; but could not be heard. Thursday, November 3, I appeared in court again; and yet again on Tuesday, November 22, on which day Mr. C[auston] desired to speak with me, and read me an affidavit in which it was affirmed that I 'abused Mr. C[auston] in his own house, calling him liar, villain, and so on'. It was likewise repeated that I had been reprimanded at the last court by Mr. C[auston] as an enemy to and hinderer of the public peace.

My friends agreed with me that the time we looked for was now come. And the next morning, calling on Mr. C[auston] I told him I designed to set out for England immediately.

Friday, December 2, I proposed to set out for Carolina about noon. But about ten the magistrates sent for me, and told me I must not go out of the province; for I had not answered the allegations laid against me. I replied, 'I have appeared at six or seven courts in order to answer them. But I was not suffered so to do.' After a few more words I said, 'You use me very ill. And so you do the trustees. You know your business, and I know mine.'

In the afternoon they published an order forbidding any to assist me in going out of the province. But I knew I had no more business there. So as soon as evening prayer was over, the tide then serving, I took boat at the Bluff for Carolina.

This is the plain account of the matter. I need only add a remark or two on the pleasantry of my censurer. 'He had recourse, as usual, to his *revelations*: "I consulted my friends whether God *did not call* me to England."'[a] Not by *revelations*—these were out of the question —but by clear, strong reasons. 'The magistrate soon quickened his pace, by declaring him an enemy to the public peace.'[1] No; that senseless assertion of Mr. C[auston] made me go neither sooner nor later. 'The reader has seen him long *languish* for persecution.'[1] What, before November, 1737? I never *languished* for it either before or since. But I *submit* to what pleases God. 'To hide his *poltroonery* in a bravado he gave public notice of his apostolical intention.'[b] Kind and civil! I may be excused from taking notice of what follows. It is equally serious and genteel.

[a] [Warburton, op. cit.,] p. 242 [quoting 1st *Journal*, Nov. 22, 1737].   [b] [Ibid.,] p. 243.

[1] Warburton, op. cit., p. 242.

[39.] 'Had his *longings* for persecution been without *hypocrisy*. . . .'
The same mistake throughout! I never longed or *professed* to long
for it at all. But if I had *professed* it ever *since* I returned from
Georgia, what was done *before* I returned could not prove *that*
5 *profession* to be *hypocrisy*. So all this ribaldry serves no end; only
to throw *much dirt*, if haply some may stick.

Meantime, how many untruths are here in one page?ª (i) 'He
made the path doubly perplexed for his followers.' (ii). 'He *left
them to answer* for his crimes.' (iii). 'He *longed* for persecution.'
10 (iv). 'He went as far as Georgia *for it*.' (v). 'The truth of his mission
was *questioned by the magistrate*; and (vi), *decried by the people*',
(vii), 'for his *false morals*'. (viii). 'The *gospel was wounded* through
the sides of its *pretended missionary*.' (ix). 'The first Christian
preachers offered up themselves'; (so did I.) 'Instead of this, our
15 *paltry mimic*. . . .' *Bona verba*! Surely a writer should *reverence himself*, how much soever he *despises* his opponent. So upon the whole
this proof of my *hypocrisy* is as lame as the three former.

[40.] (5). 'We have seen above how he sets all *prudence* at defiance.'[1]
None but *false* prudence. 'But he uses a different language when his
20 rivals are to be restrained.' No; always the same, both with regard
to *false* prudence and *true*.

'But take the affair from the beginning. He began to suspect
rivals in the year thirty-nine. For he says, "Remembering how many
that came after me were preferred before me." '[2] The very next
25 words show in what sense. They 'had attained unto the law of
righteousness';[3] I had not. But what has this to do with *rivals*?

However, go on. 'At *this time* (December 8, 1739) his opening the
Bible afforded him but small relief. He sunk so far in his despon-
dency as to doubt if God would not lay him aside and send other
30 labourers into his harvest.'[4] But this was *another time*. It was June 22.
And the occasion of the doubt is expressly mentioned: 'I preached,
but had no life or spirit in me, and was much in doubt' on *that
account*. Not on account of Mr. Whitefield. He did not '*now* begin
to set up for himself'.[4] We were in full union; nor was there the
35 least shadow of *rivalry* or contention between us. I still sincerely
'praise God for his wisdom in giving different talents to different

---

ª [Warburton, op. cit.,] p. 244.

[1] Warburton, op. cit., p. 248.
[2] Ibid., citing 4th *Journal*, Dec. 8, 1739; cf. John 1: 15.   [3] Cf. Rom. 9: 31.
[4] Warburton, op. cit., p. 249, citing 3rd *Journal*, June 22, 1739.

preachers';[a] and particularly for his giving Mr. Whitefield the talents which I have not.

[41.] (6). What farther proof of *hypocrisy*? Why, 'he had given innumerable flirts of contempt in his *Journals against human learning*'.[b] Where? I do not know. Let the passages be cited. Else let me 5 speak *for it* ever so much, it will prove nothing. 'At last he was forced to have recourse to what he had so much scorned, I mean *prudence*.'[c] All a mistake. I hope never to have recourse to *false prudence*. And *true prudence* I never scorned.

'He might have met Mr. Whitefield half-way; but he was too 10 formidable a *rival*. With a less formidable one he pursues this way. "I laboured", says he, "to convince Mr. Gr[een]"[1] (my assistant, not *rival*) "that he had not done well in confuting, as he termed it, the sermon I preached the Sunday before. . . . I asked, 'Will you meet me half-way?' (The words following put my meaning beyond 15 all dispute.) 'I will never publicly *preach against you*. Will not you, against *me*?'" Here we see a fair invitation to Mr. Gr[een] to play the hypocrite with him.'[d] Not in the least. Each might simply deliver his own sentiments without *preaching against* the other. 'We conclude that Mr. Wesley, amidst his warmest exclamations against 20 *all prudence*, had still a succedaneum which *he* indeed *calls prudence*. But its true name is craft.'[e]

Craft is an essential part of *worldly prudence*. This I detest and abhor. And let him prove it upon me that can. But it must be by

[a] [Ibid.,] p. 250, [citing 8th *Journal*, Jan. 28, 1750.]   [b] [Ibid.,] p. 251.
[c] [Ibid.,] p. 254.
[d] [Ibid.,] pp. 255–6 [citing 9th *Journal*, May 12, 1754].   [e] [Ibid.,] p. 257.

---

[1] Probably the Revd. John Green, whom Wesley had brought from his curacy in Thurnscoe, Yorkshire, to assist in the oversight of the London Methodists. He became antinomian in his views, in 1746 published a pamphlet attacking the doctrine propounded in Wesley's 1744 Conference, and continued to prove unreliable, though in 1749 he was again helping the Wesleys. From the title-pages of his publications in 1746 and 1752 he lived in Great St. Andrew's Street, Seven Dials, and in the former year (after his first break with Wesley) taught school in his home. Wesley's West Street Chapel was in Seven Dials, and it was probably here that he preached on May 5, 1754 by Wesley's invitation, with the results noted. In later years he threw in his lot with the Countess of Huntingdon. (See Charles Wesley, *Journal*, I. 428, 429, 452; II. 179; [Seymour], *Countess of Huntingdon*, I. 217, 358, 388; II. 350.)

The concluding sentences of Wesley's account of his confrontation with Green should be added: 'But he disclaimed any such agreement; and walked away, as one who did not design to come any more. He told all he met, I had put him away. Indeed, not I: but I adore the providence of God. He has put himself away; nor shall I desire him to come again till he has a more sound judgment, or a more teachable spirit.'

better arguments than the foregoing. *Truly Christian prudence*, such as was recommended by our Lord, and practised by him and his apostles, I reverence and desire to learn, being convinced of its abundant usefulness.

5   [42.] I know nothing material in the argument which I have left untouched. And I must now refer it to all the world whether, for all that has been brought to the contrary, I may not still have a measure of the 'wisdom from above, which is first pure, then peaceable; gentle, easy to be entreated; full of mercy, and good fruits; without
10   partiality and without hypocrisy'.[1]

[43.] I have spoke abundantly more concerning myself than I intended or expected. Yet I must beg leave to add a few words more. How far I am from being an enemy to *prudence* I hope appears already. It remains to inquire whether I am an enemy to
15   *reason* or *natural religion*.

'As to the first, he frankly tells us the father of *lies* was the father of *reasonings* also. For he says, "I observed more and more the advantage Satan had gained over us. Many were thrown into *idle reasonings*."'[a] Yes, and they were hurt thereby. But *reason* is good,
20   though *idle reasonings* are evil. Nor does it follow that I am an enemy to the one because I condemn the other.

[44.] 'However, you are an enemy to *natural religion*. For you say, a Frenchman gave us a full account of the Chicasaws. "They do nothing but eat and drink and smoke from morning till night, and
25   almost from night till morning. For they rise at any hour of the night when they awake, and after eating and drinking as much as they can, go to sleep again."' 'Hence we could not but remark what is "the religion of nature", properly so called, or that religion which flows from *natural reason* unassisted by *revelation*.'[b] I believe this
30   dispute may be cut short by only defining the term. What does your lordship mean by 'natural religion'? A *system of principles*? But I mean by it, in this place, *men's natural manners*. These certainly 'flow from their *natural passions and appetites*', with that degree of *reason* which they have. And this, in other instances, is not contemp-
35   tible; though it is not sufficient to teach them true religion.

---

[a] [Warburton, op. cit.,] p. 289 [citing 4th *Journal*, Nov. 7, 1739].
[b] [Ibid.,] pp. 289–90 [citing 2nd *Journal*, July 9, 1737, in which Wesley alludes unobtrusively to William Wollaston's work *The Religion of Nature Delineated*].

---

[1] Cf. Jas. 3: 17, and § [10] above.

II. I proceed to consider, in the second place, what is advanced concerning the operations of the Holy Spirit.

[1]. 'Our blessed Redeemer promised to send among his followers the Holy Ghost, called "the Spirit of truth and the Comforter",[1] which should co-operate with man in *establishing his faith* and in *perfecting his obedience*; or in other words, should *sanctify him to redemption*.'[a]

Accordingly 'the *sanctification* and *redemption* of the world man cannot frustrate nor render ineffectual. For it is not in his power to make that to be undone which is *once done and perfected*.'[b]

I do not comprehend. Is *all* the world *sanctified*? Is not to be sanctified the same as to be *made holy*? Is *all* the world *holy*? And 'can no man frustrate' his own sanctification?

[2.] 'The Holy Ghost establishes our faith and perfects our obedience by *enlightening the understanding* and *rectifying the will*.'[c]

'In the former respect, (1) he gave the *gift of tongues* at the day of Pentecost.'[2]

'Indeed *enthusiasts* in their ecstasies have *talked very fluently* in languages they had a very imperfect knowledge of in their sober intervals.'[3] I can no more believe this on the credit of Lord Shaftesbury and a popish exorcist than I can believe the tale of 'an hundred people *talking without tongues*' on the credit of Dr. Middleton.[4]

'The other gifts of the Spirit St. Paul reckons up thus: "To one is given the word of wisdom, to another the word of knowledge, to another the gifts of healing, to another working of miracles, to another prophecy, to another the discerning of spirits."'[d] But why are the other three left out—'faith', 'divers kinds of tongues', and 'the interpretation of tongues'?

[3.] I believe 'the word of wisdom' means light to explain the manifold wisdom of God in the grand scheme of gospel salvation; 'the word of knowledge', a power of explaining the Old Testament types and prophecies. 'Faith' may mean an extraordinary trust in God under the most difficult and dangerous circumstances; 'the

---

[a] [Ibid.,] p. 2.   [b] [Ibid.,] p. 337.   [c] [Ibid.,] p. 3.
[d] [Ibid.,] p. 23 [cf. 1 Cor. 12: 8–10].

---

[1] Cf. John 15: 26.   [2] Warburton, op. cit., p. 4.   [3] Ibid., p. 16.
[4] Shaftesbury, *Letter concerning Enthusiasm*, § 6; Conyers Middleton, *A Free Inquiry into the Miraculous Powers which are supposed to have subsisted in the Christian Church*, etc. (1749), p. 182. Cf. Wesley, *A Letter to Conyers Middleton* (1749), VI. 12, in Vol. 13 of this edition.

gifts of healing', a miraculous power of curing diseases; 'the discerning of spirits', a supernatural discernment whether men were upright or not, whether they were qualified for offices in the church, and whether they who professed to speak by inspiration really did
5 so or not.

[4.] But 'the richest of the fruits of the Spirit is the *inspiration of Scripture*'.[a] 'Herein the promise that "the Comforter should abide with us for ever"[1] is eminently fulfilled. For though his ordinary influence *occasionally* assists the faithful of all ages, yet his *constant*
10 abode and *supreme illumination* is in the Scriptures of the New Testament.'[b] 'I mean, he is there only as the *illuminator of the understanding.*'[2]

But does this agree with the following words? 'Nature is not able to keep a mean. But *grace* is able; for "the spirit helpeth our in-
15 firmities". We must apply to "the Guide of truth", to prevent our being "carried about with divers and strange doctrines".'[c] Is he not then *everywhere*, to *illuminate the understanding* as well as to *rectify the will*? And indeed, do we not need the one as continually as the other?

20 [5.] 'But how did he inspire the Scripture? He so directed the writers that *no considerable error* should fall from them.'[d] Nay, will not the allowing there is *any error* in Scripture shake the authority of the whole?

Again, what is the difference between the *immediate* and the
25 *virtual* influence of the Holy Spirit? I know Milton speaks of '*virtual* or *immediate* touch'.[3] But most incline to think *virtual touch* is no touch at all.

'Were the style of the New Testament *utterly rude and barbarous*, and *abounding with every fault* that can possibly deform a language,
30 this is so far from proving such language not divinely inspired that it is one certain mark of this original.'[e]

A vehement paradox this. But it is not proved yet, and probably never will.

'The labours of those who have attempted to defend the purity of
35 Scripture Greek have been very idly employed.'[f]

---

[a] [Warburton, op. cit.,] p. 30. [b] [Ibid.,], p. 39. [c] [Ibid.,] pp. 339-40.
[d] [Ibid.,] p. 45. [e] [Ibid.,] p. 55. [f] [Ibid.,] p. 66.

---

[1] Cf. John 14: 16. [2] Warburton, op. cit., p. 41 n.
[3] Ibid., pp. 48 ff.; Milton, *Paradise Lost*, viii. 617.

Others think they have been very wisely employed, and that they have abundantly proved their point.

[6.] Having now 'considered the operations of the Holy Spirit as "the Guide of truth", who clears and enlightens the understanding, . . . I proceed to consider him as "the Comforter", who purifies 5 and supports the will.'[a]

Sacred antiquity is full in its accounts of the *sudden* and *entire* change made by the Holy Spirit in the dispositions and manners of those whom it had enlightened; instantaneously effacing their evil habits, and familiarizing them to the performance of every good action.[b] 10

No natural cause could effect this. Neither *fanaticism* nor *superstition*, nor both of them, will account for so *sudden* and *lasting* a conversion.

Superstition never effects any considerable change in the *manners*. Its utmost force is just enough to make us exact in the ceremonious offices of religion, or to cause some acts of penitence as death 15 approaches.[c]

Fanaticism, indeed, acts with greater violence, and by influencing the will frequently forces the manners from their bent, and sometimes effaces the strongest impressions of custom and nature. But this fervour, though violent, is rarely *lasting*; never so long as to establish the *new* 20 *system* into an *habit*. So that when its rage subsides, as it very soon does, but where it drives into downright madness, the bias on the will keeps abating, till all the former habitudes recover their relaxed tone.[d]

Never were reflections more just than these. And whoever applies them to the matters of fact which daily occur all over England, and 25 particularly in London, will easily discern that the changes *now* wrought cannot be accounted for by *natural causes*: not by *superstition*, for the *manners* are changed, the whole life and conversation; not by *fanaticism*, for these changes are so '*lasting* as to establish the *new system* into a *habit*'; not by mere *reason*, for they are *sudden*; 30 therefore they can only be wrought by the Holy Spirit.

As to Savonarola's being a fanatic, or assuming the person of a prophet, I cannot take a popish historian's word.[1] And what a man says on the rack proves nothing; no more than his dying silent. Probably this might arise from shame and consciousness of having 35 accused himself falsely under the torture.

---

[a] [Ibid.,] p. 89.   [b] [Ibid.,] pp. 89–90.   [c] [Ibid.,] p. 91.   [d] [Ibid.,] p. 92.

[1] See Warburton, op. cit., pp. 93–4. The historian cited by Warburton was Guicciardini.

[7.] 'But how does the Spirit, as comforter, "abide with us for
ever"? He "abides with the church for ever", as well *personally*, in
his office as *comforter*, as *virtually*, in his office of *enlightener*.'ᵃ

Does he not then abide with the church *personally* in both these
5 respects? What is meant by 'abiding virtually'? And what is the
difference between 'abiding virtually' and 'abiding personally'?

'The only question will be, "Does he still exercise his office *in
the same extraordinary manner* as in the apostles' days?"'ᵇ

I know none that affirms it. 'St. Paul has determined this question.
10 "Charity (says he) never faileth. But whether there be prophecies,
they shall fail; whether there be tongues, they shall cease; whether
there be knowledge, it shall vanish away."'ᶜ

The common opinion is that this respects another life, as he enforces
his argument by this observation, 'Now we see through a glass darkly;
15 but then face to face. Now we know in part; but then shall we know,
even as also we are known.'ᵈ

But the Apostle means charity is to accompany the church in *all its
stages*; whereas *prophecy* and all the rest are only bestowed *during its
infant state*, to support it against the delusions and powers of darkness.ᵉ
20 The Corinthians abounded in these *gifts*, but were wanting in
charity. And this the Apostle here exposes, by proving charity to be
superior to them all, both in its *qualities* and *duration*. The three first
verses declare that the other gifts are useless without charity. The next
four specify the qualities of charity; the remaining six declare its con-
25 tinuance. 'Charity never faileth; but whether there be prophecies,
they shall fail; whether there be tongues, they shall cease; whether
there be knowledge, it shall vanish away.' I.e., when that *Christian life*,
the lines of which are marked out by the gospel, shall arrive to its *full
vigour and maturity*, then the temporary aids given to subdue prejudice
30 and to support the weak shall, like scaffolding, be removed.ᶠ

In other words, when that *Christian life*, wherein the apostles and
first Christians were but *infants*, shall arrive to its *full vigour* and
maturity in their successors, then miracles shall cease. But I fear
that time is not yet come. I doubt none that are now alive enjoy
35 more of the vigour and maturity of the Christian life than the very
first Christians did.

'To show that the loss of these will not be regretted when the

---

ᵃ [Warburton, op. cit.,] p. 96.   ᵇ [Ibid.,] p. 97.
ᶜ [Ibid., pp. 98–9, citing] 1 Cor. 13: 8, etc.   ᵈ [Warburton, op. cit.,] p. 99.
ᵉ [Ibid.,] p. 100.   ᶠ [Ibid.,] p. 102.

church has advanced from a state of *infancy* to *manhood*' (Alas the
day! Were the *apostles* but *infants* to *us*?) 'he illustrates the case by
an elegant similitude. "When I was a child I spake as a child, ... but
when I became a man, I put away childish things." . . . His next
remark, concerning the defects of human knowledge, is only an 5
occasional answer to an objection. And the last verse shows that the
superior duration of charity refers to the present life only. "Now
abideth faith, hope, charity, these three; but the greatest of these
is charity." That is, you may perhaps object, faith and hope will
likewise remain in the church when prophecy, tongues, and know- 10
ledge are ceased. They will so; but still charity is the greatest,
because of its excellent qualities.'[a]

[8.] 'The last verse shows'! Is not this begging the question?
How *forced* is all this! The plain natural meaning of the passage is,
'Love' (the absolute necessity and the nature of which is shown in 15
the foregoing verses) has another commendation—'it never faileth';
it accompanies and adorns us to eternity. 'But whether there be
prophecies, they shall fail'—when all things are fulfilled, and God
is all in all. 'Whether there be tongues, they shall cease.' One
language shall prevail among all the inhabitants of heaven, while the 20
low, imperfect languages of earth are forgotten. The knowledge
likewise we now so eagerly pursue 'shall then vanish away'. As
starlight is lost in that of the midday sun, so our present knowledge
in the light of eternity. 'For we know in part, and we prophesy in
part.' We have here but short, narrow, imperfect conceptions, even 25
of the things round about us, and much more of the deep things of
God. And even the prophecies which men deliver from God are far
from taking in the whole of future events. 'But when that which is
perfect is come', at death, and in the last day, 'that which is in part
shall be done away'. Both that low, imperfect, glimmering light 30
which is all the knowledge we can now attain to; and these slow and
unsatisfactory methods of attaining as well as of imparting it to
others. 'When I was a child, I talked as a child, I understood as
a child, I reasoned as a child.' As if he had said, 'In our present state
we are mere infants compared to what we shall be hereafter.' 'But 35
when I became a man, I put away childish things'; and a proportion-
able change shall we all find when we launch into eternity. 'Now we
see' even the things which surround us 'by means of a glass' or
mirror, in a dim, faint, obscure manner, so that everything is a kind

[a] [Ibid.,] pp. 103, 105.

of *riddle* to us; but then we shall see, not a faint reflection, but the objects themselves, 'face to face', directly and distinctly. 'Now I know but in part.' Even when God reveals things to me, great part of them is still kept under the veil. 'But then shall I know, even as
5 I also am known'—in a clear, full, comprehensive manner, in some measure like God, who penetrates the centre of every object, and sees at one glance through my soul, and all things. 'And now', during the present life, 'abide these three, faith, hope, love; but the greatest of these'—in its duration, as well as the excellence of its
10 nature—'is love.' Faith, hope, love, are the sum of perfection on earth; love alone is the sum of perfection in heaven.

[9.] 'It appears then that the miraculous powers of the church *were to cease upon its perfect establishment.*'ᵃ Nothing like it appears from this Scripture. But supposing it did, is Christianity *perfectly*
15 *established* yet? Even nominal Christianity? Mr. Brerewood¹ took large pains to be fully informed. And according to his account five parts in six of the known world are Mahometans or pagans to this day. If so, Christianity it yet far from being *perfectly established*, either in Europe, Asia, Africa, or America.
20 [10.] 'Having now established the *fact* (wonderfully established!), we may inquire into the *fitness* of it. There were two causes of the extraordinary operations of the Holy Spirit, one to manifest his mission (and this was done once for all), the other to comfort and instruct the church.'ᵇ
25 'At his first descent on the apostles he found their minds rude and uninformed; strangers to all heavenly knowledge, and utterly averse to the gospel. He illuminated their minds with all necessary truth. For a *rule of faith* not being yet composed' (No? Had they not 'the law and the prophets'?)² 'some *extraordinary infusion* of his virtue
30 was still necessary. . . . But when this rule was perfected, *part of this office* was *transferred upon the sacred canon*; and his enlightening

---

ᵃ [Warburton, op. cit.,] p. 107.   ᵇ [Ibid.,] p. 110.

¹ Edward Brerewood (1565?–1613) was educated at Brasenose College, Oxford, and became the first professor of astronomy at Gresham College, London. He wrote *Enquiries touching the Diversities of Languages and Religions through the chief parts of the world.* The book was published posthumously in 1614, and passed through several editions in English and French. Wesley refers to Brerewood's evaluation of the religious situation in his sermons on 'The General Spread of the Gospel', § 1, and 'Causes of the Inefficacy of Christianity', § 3, and in *The Doctrine of Original Sin*, II. 1.

² Matt. 22: 40.

grace was not to be expected in such abundant measure as to make the recipients *infallible guides*.'[a]

Certainly it was not. If this is all that is intended, no one will gainsay.

'Yet modern *fanatics* pretend to *as high a degree* of divine com- 5 munications, as if no such rule were in being' (I do not); 'or at least as if that rule needed the *farther assistance* of the Holy Spirit to explain his own meaning.'[1] This is quite another thing. I do firmly believe (and what serious man does not)—*omnis scriptura legi debet eo spiritu quo scripta est*: we need the same Spirit to *understand* the 10 Scripture which enabled the holy men of old to *write* it.[2]

'Again, the whole strength of human *prejudices* was then set in opposition to the gospel, to overcome the obstinacy and violence of which nothing less than the power of the Holy One was sufficient. . . . At present, whatever *prejudice* may remain, it *draws the other* 15 *way*.'[b] What, toward holiness? Toward temperance and chastity? Toward justice, mercy, and truth? Quite the reverse. And to overcome the obstinacy and violence of the heart-prejudices which still lie against these, the power of the Holy One is as necessary now as ever it was from the beginning of the world. 20

[11.] 'A farther reason for the ceasing of miracles is the peace and security of the church. . . . The *profession* of the Christian faith is now attended with *ease* and *honour*.'[3] 'The profession', true; but not the *thing* itself, as 'all that will live godly in Christ Jesus' experience.[4] 25

'But if miracles are not ceased, why do you not prove your mission thereby?'[5] As your lordship has frequently spoke to this effect, I will now give a clear answer. And I purposely do it in the same words which I published many years since.

---

[a] [Ibid.,], pp. 111–12.   [b] [Ibid.,] p. 113.

---

[1] Warburton, op. cit., p. 112.

[2] Cf. *Imitatio Christi*, I. v, *Omnis scriptura sacra eo spiritu debet legi, quo facta est*, with its translation in Wesley, *The Christian's Pattern* (*Bibliography*, No. 4, 1735, p. 11), 'All Scripture is to be read with the same Spirit wherewith it was written.' Wesley uses variants of the same translation in the preface to his *Explanatory Notes upon the Old Testament* (*Bibliography*, No. 294, 1765), and in a later undated letter to Dean William Digby, in which he cites his source as Kempis.

[3] Warburton, op. cit., p. 114.

[4] 2 Tim. 3: 12.

[5] Cf. Warburton, op. cit., pp. 114–15, 119–50, 230–1, whose general theme Wesley summarizes in this question; cf. Wesley's letter to 'John Smith', Mar. 22, 1748, § 11.

[12.]¹

I have in some measure explained myself on the head of miracles in the Third Part of the *Farther Appeal*.² But since you repeat the demand (though without taking any notice of the arguments there advanced)
5 I will endeavour once more to give you a distinct, full, and determinate answer. And first, I acknowledge that I have seen with my eyes, and heard with my ears, several things which, to the best of my judgment, cannot be accounted for by the *ordinary* course of *natural causes*, and which, I therefore believe, ought to be 'ascribed to the extraordinary
10 interposition of God'.³ If any man choose to style these *miracles*, I reclaim not. I have diligently inquired into the facts. I have weighed the preceding and following circumstances. I have strove to account for them in a *natural* way; but could not without doing violence to my reason. Not to go far back, I am clearly persuaded that the sudden
15 deliverance of John Haydon was one instance of this kind, and my own recovery on May the tenth another.⁴ I cannot account for either of these in a *natural* way. Therefore I believe they were both *supernatural*.

I must, secondly, observe that the truth of these facts is supported
20 by the same kind of proof as that of all other facts is wont to be, namely, the testimony of competent witnesses. And that the testimony here is in as high a degree as any reasonable man can desire. Those witnesses were many in number. They could not be deceived themselves; for the fact in question they saw with their own eyes, and
25 heard with their own ears. Nor is it credible that so many of them would combine together with a view of deceiving others; the greater part being men who feared God, as appeared by the general tenor of their lives. Thus, in the case of John Haydon, this thing was not contrived and executed in a corner, and in the presence of his own family only,
30 or three or four persons prepared for the purpose. No; it was in an open street in the city of Bristol, at one or two in the afternoon. And the doors being open from the beginning, not only many of the neighbours from every side, but several others (indeed whosoever desired it) went in, till the house could contain no more. Nor yet does the account
35 of my own illness and recovery depend, as you suppose, on *my bare*

¹ For this lengthy quotation from *The Principles of a Methodist Farther Explained*, V. 1–8, Wesley gives each of the original section numbers, which have here been altered to 12–19.
² See *A Farther Appeal*, Pt. III, III. 28–9.
³ Thomas Church, *Some Farther Remarks on the Rev. Mr. John Wesley's last Journal* (1746), p. 142.
⁴ For the case of John Haydon, a weaver of Bristol, see *Journal*, May 2, 1739 (cf. above, I. 23 (3)). In IV. 11 of *The Principles of a Methodist Farther Explained* (from which he is now quoting) Wesley had just described his own recovery.

word. There were many witnesses, both of my disorder on Friday and
Saturday, and my lying down most part of Sunday (a thing they were
well satisfied could not be the effect of a slight indisposition), and all
who saw me that evening plainly discerned (what I could not wholly
conceal) that I was in pain; about two hundred of whom were present 5
when I was seized with the cough, which cut me short so that I could
speak no more, till I cried aloud, 'Lord, increase my faith. Lord,
confirm the word of thy grace.' The same persons saw and heard that
at that instant I changed my posture, and broke out into thanksgiving;
that quickly after I stood upright (which I could not before) and showed 10
no sign either of sickness or pain.

Yet I must desire you well to observe, thirdly, that my will, or
choice, or desire, had no place either in this, or any case of this kind
that has ever fallen under my notice. Five minutes before, I had no
thought of this. I expected nothing less. I was willing to wait for a 15
gradual recovery, in the ordinary use of outward means. I did not look
for any other cure till the moment before I found it. And it is my belief
that the case was always the same with regard to the most 'real and
undoubted miracles'. I believe God never interposed his miraculous
power but according to his own sovereign will; not according to the 20
will of man, neither of him by whom he wrought, nor of any other man
whatsoever. The wisdom, as well as the power, are his; nor can I find
that ever, from the beginning of the world, he lodged this power in
any mere man, to be used whenever that man saw good. Suppose therefore there was a man now upon earth who did work 'real and undoubted 25
miracles'; I would ask, by whose power doth he work these? And at
whose pleasure? His own, or God's? Not his own; but God's. But
if so, then your demand is made not on man, but on God. I cannot
say it is modest thus to challenge God; or well suiting the relation of
a creature to his Creator.   30

[13.] However, I cannot but think there have been already so many
interpositions of divine power, as will shortly leave you without excuse
if you either deny or despise them. We desire no favour; but the justice
that diligent inquiry may be made concerning them. We are ready to
name the persons on whom the power was shown, which belongeth to 35
none but God (not one or two, or ten or twelve only); to point out their
places of abode. And we engage they shall answer every pertinent
question fairly and directly; and if required shall give all these answers
upon oath, before any who are empowered to receive them. It is our
particular request that the circumstances which went before, which 40
accompanied, and which followed after the facts under consideration,
may be thoroughly examined, and punctually noted down. Let but this
be done (and is it not highly needful it should? at least by those who

would form an exact judgment?) and we have no fear that any reasonable man should scruple to say, 'This hath God wrought.'¹

As there have been already so many instances of this kind, far beyond what we dared to ask or think, I cannot take upon me to say
5 whether or no it will please God to add to their number. I have not herein 'known the mind of the Lord', neither am I 'his counsellor'.² He may, or he may not; I cannot affirm or deny. I have no light, and I have no desire either way. 'It is the Lord; let him do what seemeth him good.'³ I desire only to be as clay in his hand.

10 [14.] But what if there were now to be wrought ever so many 'real and undoubted miracles'? (I suppose you mean by 'undoubted' such as being sufficiently attested, *ought not* to be doubted of.) Why, this, you say, 'would put the controversy on a short foot, and be an effectual proof of the truth of your pretences'. By no means. As common as this
15 assertion is, there is none upon earth more false. Suppose a teacher was now, on this very day, to work 'real and undoubted miracles', this would extremely little 'shorten the controversy' between him and the greater part of his opposers. For all this would not force them to believe; but many would still stand just where they did before; seeing men may
20 'harden their hearts'⁴ against miracles, as well as against arguments.

So men have done from the beginning of the world; even against such signal, glorious miracles, against such interpositions of the power of God, as may not be again till the consummation of all things. Permit me to remind you only of a few instances; and to observe that the argu-
25 ment holds *a fortiori*—for who will ever be empowered of God again to work *such* miracles as these were? Did Pharaoh look on all that Moses and Aaron wrought as an 'effectual proof of the truth of their pretences'? Even when 'the Lord made the sea to be dry land, and the waters were divided'; when 'the children of Israel went into the midst
30 of the sea, and the waters were a wall on the right and on the left'ᵃ Nay:

> The wounded dragon raged in vain;
> And fierce the utmost plagues to brave,
> Madly he dared the parted main,
> And sunk beneath th' o'erwhelming wave.⁵

35 Was all this an 'effectual proof of the truth of their pretences' to the Israelites themselves? It was not; they 'were still disobedient at the

ᵃ Exod. 14: 21-2.

¹ Cf. Num. 23: 23.   ² 1 Cor. 2: 16; cf. Isa. 40: 13.
³ 1 Sam 3: 18.   ⁴ Josh. 11: 20.
⁵ Charles Wesley, 'The Fifty-first Chapter of Isaiah', Pt. II, st. 4, in *Hymns and Sacred Poems* (1749), I. 21 (*Poet. Wks.*, IV. 303). The original reads: 'While bold thine utmost plague to brave'.

sea, even at the Red Sea'![1] Was the giving them day by day 'bread from heaven'[2] an effectual proof to those 'two hundred and fifty of the princes of the assembly, famous in the congregation; men of renown', who said with Dathan and Abiram, 'Wilt thou put out the eyes of these men? We will not come up.'[a] Nay, when 'the ground clave asunder that was 5 under them, and the earth opened her mouth and swallowed them up'![b] Neither was this an *effectual proof* to those who saw it with their eyes, and heard the cries of those who went down into the pit. But the very next day they 'murmured against Moses and against Aaron, saying: Ye have killed the people of the Lord.'[c] Was not the case generally 10 the same with regard to the prophets that followed? Several of whom 'stopped the mouths of lions, quenched the violence of fire', and did many other mighty works; yet their own people received them not. Yet 'they were stoned, they were sawn asunder; they were slain with the sword; they were destitute, afflicted, tormented!'[3]—utterly contrary to 15 the commonly received supposition that the working 'real, undoubted miracles' must bring all controversy to an end and convince every gainsayer.

Let us come nearer yet. How stood the case between our Lord himself and his opposers? Did he not work 'real and undoubted miracles'? 20 And what was the effect? Still when 'he came to his own, his own received him not'.[4] Still 'he was despised and rejected of men'.[5] Still it was a challenge not to be answered, 'Have any of the rulers or of the Pharisees believed on him?'[6] After this, how can you imagine that whoever works miracles must convince 'all men of the truth of his pre- 25 tences'?

I would just remind you of only one instance more. 'There sat a certain man at Lystra, impotent in his feet, being a cripple from his mother's womb, who never had walked. The same heard Paul speak; who steadfastly beholding him, and perceiving he had faith to be 30 healed, said with a loud voice, Stand upright on thy feet. And he leaped and walked.' Here was so 'undoubted a miracle' that the people 'lifted up their voices, saying, The Gods are come down in the likeness of men'. But how long were even these convinced of 'the truth of his pretences'? Only till 'there came thither certain Jews from Antioch 35 and Iconium'; and then they stoned him (as they supposed) to death![d] So certain it is that no miracles whatever that were ever yet wrought in the world were 'effectual to prove' the most glaring truth to those who hardened their hearts against it.

[a] Num. 16: 12, 14.　　　　　　　　　　　[b] Num. 16: 31–2.
[c] Num. 16: 41.　　　　　　　　　　　　　[d] Acts 14: 8–19, etc.

[1] Ps. 106: 7 (B.C.P.).　　[2] Neh. 9: 15; Ps. 105: 40.　　[3] Cf. Heb. 11: 33, 34, 37.
[4] John 1: 11.　　　　　　[5] Cf. Isa. 53: 3.　　　　　　　[6] John 7: 48

[15.] And it will equally hold in every age and nation. 'If they hear not Moses and the prophets, neither will they be convinced (of what they desire not to believe) though one rose from the dead.'¹ Without a miracle, without one rising from the dead, ἐὰν τις θέλῃ ποιεῖν, 'if any man be willing to do his will, he shall know of the doctrine, whether it be of God'.² But if he is not 'willing to do his will' he will never want an excuse, a plausible reason for rejecting it. Yea, though ever so many miracles were wrought to confirm it. For let ever so much 'light come into the world', it will have no effect (such is the wise and just will of God) on those who 'love darkness rather than light'.³ It will not convince those who do not simply desire to 'do the will of their Father which is in heaven'.⁴ Those 'who mind earthly things',⁵ who (if they do not continue in any gross outward sin, yet) love pleasure and ease, yet seek profit or power, preferment or reputation. Nothing will ever be an effectual proof to these of the holy and acceptable will of God, unless first their proud hearts be humbled, their stubborn wills bowed down, and their desires brought, at least in some degree, into obedience to the law of Christ.

Hence, although it should please God to work anew all the wonders that ever were wrought on earth, still these men, however *wise* and *prudent* they may be in things relating to the present world, would fight against God and all his messengers, and that in spite of all these miracles. Meanwhile God will reveal his truth *unto babes*,⁶ unto those who are meek and lowly, whose desires are in heaven, who want to 'know nothing save Jesus Christ and him crucified'.⁷ These need no outward miracles to show them his will; they have a plain rule—the written Word. And 'the anointing which they have received of him abideth in them, and teacheth them of all things'.ᵃ Through this they are enabled to bring all doctrines 'to the law and the testimony'.⁸ And whatsoever is agreeable to this they receive, without waiting to see it attested by miracles. As, on the other hand, whatsoever is contrary to this they reject; nor can any miracles move them to receive it.

[16.] Yet I do not know that God hath anywhere precluded himself from thus exerting his sovereign power, from working miracles in any kind or degree, in any age to the end of the world. I do not recollect any Scripture wherein we are taught that miracles were to be confined within the limits either of the apostolic or the Cyprianic age, or of any period of time, longer or shorter, even till the restitution of all things.

ᵃ 1 John 2: 27.

---

¹ Cf. Luke 16: 31. ² John 7: 17 (Cf. *Notes*). ³ Cf. John 3: 19.
⁴ Cf. Matt. 12: 50. ⁵ Phil. 3: 19. ⁶ Matt. 11: 25.
⁷ Cf. 1 Cor. 2: 2. ⁸ Cf. Isa. 8: 20.

I have not observed, either in the Old Testament or the New, any intimation at all of this kind. St. Paul indeed says once, concerning two of the miraculous gifts of the Spirit (so I think that text is usually understood), 'whether there be prophecies, they shall fail; whether there be tongues, they shall cease';[1] but he does not say either that these or any other miracles shall cease, till faith and hope shall cease also; till they shall all be swallowed up in the vision of God, and love be all in all.

I presume you will allow there is one kind of miracles (loosely speaking) which are not ceased; namely, τέρατα ψεύδους, 'lying wonders',[2] diabolical miracles, wrought by the power of evil spirits. Nor can you easily conceive that these will cease as long as the 'father of lies'[3] is the 'prince of this world'.[4] And why should you think that the God of truth is less active than him, or that he will not have his miracles also? Only not as man wills, neither when he wills; but according to his own excellent wisdom and goodness.

[17.] But even if it were supposed that God does now work beyond the operation of merely natural causes, yet what impression would this make upon *you*, in the disposition of mind you are now in? Suppose the trial was repeated, and made again tomorrow. One informs you the next day, 'While a clergyman was preaching yesterday where I was, a man came who had been long ill of an incurable distemper. Prayer was made for him, and he was restored to perfect health.'

Suppose now that this was a real fact. Perhaps you would scarce have patience to hear the account of it; but would cut it short in the midst with, 'Do you tell this as something *supernatural*? Then miracles are not ceased.' But if you should venture to ask, 'Where was this? And who was the person who prayed?' And it was answered, 'At the Foundery, near Moorfields; the person who prayed was Mr. Wesley': what a damp comes at once! What a weight falls on your mind, at the first setting out! 'Tis well if you have any heart or desire to move one step farther. Or if you should, what a strong additional propensity do you now feel to deny the fact! And is there not a ready excuse for so doing? 'O! They who tell the story are *his own people*; most of whom, we may be sure, will *say* anything for him, and the rest will *believe* anything.' But if you at length allowed the fact, might you not find means to account for it by *natural* causes? 'Great crowds, violent heats', with 'obstructions and irregularities of the blood and spirits',[5] will do wonders. If you could not but allow it was more than *natural*, might not some plausible reason be found for ranking it among the

---

[1] 1 Cor. 13: 8. [2] 2 Thess. 2: 9. [3] Cf. John 8: 44. [4] John 12: 31, etc.
[5] See Thomas Church, *Remarks on the Reverend Mr. John Wesley's last Journal* (1745), p. 69, quoted in Wesley, *The Principles of a Methodist Farther Explained*, IV. 8.

'lying wonders', for ascribing it to the devil rather than God? And if, after all, you was convinced it was the finger of God, must you not still bring every doctrine advanced 'to the law, and to the testimony'¹—the only sure and infallible test of all? What then is the use of this con-
5   tinual demand, 'Show us a sign and we will believe'?² What will you believe? I hope no more than is written in the Book of God. And thus far you might venture to believe, even without a miracle.

[18.] Let us consider this point a little farther. 'What is it you would have us prove by miracles? The doctrines we preach?' We prove these
10 by Scripture and reason; and if need be, by antiquity. What else is it then we are to prove by miracles? At length we have a distinct reply. 'Wise and sober men will not otherwise be convinced' (i.e. unless you prove it by miracles) 'that God is, by the means of such teachers and such doctrines, working a great and extraordinary work in the earth.'³
15 So then the determinate point which you, in their name, call upon us to prove by miracles is this: 'that God is, by these teachers, working a great and extraordinary work in the earth'.

What I mean by 'a great and extraordinary work' is the bringing *multitudes* of *gross, notorious sinners*, in a *short space*, to the *fear* and
20 *love* and *service* of God, to an *entire change of heart and life*.

Now, then, let us take a nearer view of the proposition, and see which part of it we are to prove by miracles.

Is it, (1), that A. B. was for many years without God in the world,⁴ a common swearer, a drunkard, a sabbath-breaker?
25 Or, (2), that he is not so now?

Or, (3), that he continued so till he heard this man preach, and from that time was another man?

Not so. The proper way to prove these facts is by the testimony of competent witnesses. And these witnesses are ready, whenever required,
30 to give full evidence of them.

Or, would you have us prove by miracles, (4), that this was not done by our own power or holiness? That God only is able to raise the dead, to quicken those who are dead in trespasses and sins?⁵

Surely no. Whosoever believes the Scriptures will want no new proof
35 of this.

Where then is the *wisdom* of those men who demand miracles in proof of such a proposition? One branch of which—'that such sinners are reformed by means of these teachers'—being a plain fact, can only be proved by testimony, as all other facts are; and the other—'that

---

¹ Isa. 8: 20.   ² Cf. John 6: 30.
³ Thomas Church, *Some Farther Remarks on the Rev. Mr. John Wesley's Last Journal* (1746), preface, p. vi.
⁴ Eph. 2: 12.   ⁵ See Eph. 2: 1.

this is a "work of God", and a "great and more than ordinary work"'—needs no proof, as carrying its own evidence to every thinking man.

[19.] To sum up this. No truly *wise* or *sober* man can possibly desire or expect miracles to prove either, (1), that these *doctrines* are true—this must be decided by Scripture and reason; or, (2), that these *facts* 5 are true—this can only be proved by testimony; or, (3), that to *change* sinners from darkness to light is the 'work of God' alone, only using what instruments he pleases—this is glaringly self-evident; or, (4) that *such a change* wrought in *so many notorious sinners* within so *short* a time is a great and *extraordinary* work of God. What then is it remains 10 to be proved by miracles? Perhaps you will say, it is this, 'That God has *called* or *sent* you to do this.' Nay, this is implied in the third of the foregoing propositions. If God has actually *used* us therein, if *his work* hath in fact prospered in our hands, then he hath *called* or *sent* us to do this. I entreat reasonable men to weigh this thoroughly, whether the 15 fact does not plainly prove the *call?* Whether he who thus *enables* us to save souls alive does not *commission* us so to do? Whether, by giving us the *power* to pluck these brands out of the burning,[1] he does not authorize us to exert it? O that it were possible for you to consider calmly whether the *success* of the gospel of Jesus Christ, even as it is 20 preached by us, the least of his servants, be not itself a *miracle* never to be forgotten! One which cannot be denied, as being visible at this day, not in one but an hundred places; one which cannot be accounted for by the *ordinary* course of any *natural causes* whatsoever; one which cannot be ascribed, with any colour of reason, to diabolical agency; and 25 lastly, one which will bear the infallible test, the trial of the written Word.[a]

[20.] But [you may say,] 'Why do you talk of the *success* of the gospel in England, which was a Christian country before you was born?' Was it indeed? Is it so at this day? I would explain myself a little on this 30 head also.

And (1), none can deny that the people of England, in general, are *called* Christians. They are *called* so, a few only excepted, by others as well as by themselves. But I presume no man will say the *name* makes the *thing*; that men *are* Christians barely because they are *called* so. 35 It must be allowed, (2), that the people of England, generally speaking, have been *christened* or baptized. But neither can we infer, 'These were *once* baptized; therefore they are Christians now.' It is allowed, (3), that many of those who were once *baptized*, and are *called* Christians to this

---

[a] Second Letter to Dr. Church, p. 55 & seq. [i.e. *The Principles of a Methodist Farther Explained*, V. 1-8, for which see Vol. 9 of this edition.]

---

[1] See Zech. 3: 2.

day, *hear* the word of God, attend *public prayers*, and partake of the *Lord's Supper*. But neither does this prove that they *are* Christians. For notwithstanding this, some of them live in open sin; and others (though not conscious to themselves of *hypocrisy*, yet) are utter strangers
5   to the *religion of the heart*; are full of pride, vanity, covetousness, ambition; of hatred, anger, malice, or envy; and consequently, are no more *spiritual* Christians than the open drunkard or common swearer.

Now these being removed, where are the Christians from whom we may properly term England 'a Christian country'? The men who have
10   'the mind which was in Christ',[1] and who 'walk as he also walked';[2] whose inmost soul is renewed after the image of God; and who are outwardly holy, as he who hath called them is holy?[3] There are doubtless a few such to be found. To deny this would be 'want of candour'.[4] But how few? How thinly scattered up and down? And as for a Christian
15   *visible church*, or a body of Christians visibly united together, where is this to be seen?

> Ye different sects, who all declare
> 'Lo! Here is Christ!', or 'Christ is there!'
> Your stronger proofs *divinely* give,
20   > And *show* me where the Christians live![5]

And what use is it of, what good end does it serve, to term England 'a Christian country'? Although 'tis true most of the natives are *called* Christians, have been *baptized*, frequent the *ordinances*; and although here and there a real Christian is to be found, 'as a light shining in
25   a dark place',[6] does it do any honour to our great Master among those who are not *called* by his name? Does it recommend Christianity to the Jews, the Mahometans, or the avowed heathens? Surely no one can conceive it does. It only makes Christianity stink in their nostrils. Does it answer any *good end* with regard to those who are called by this
30   worthy name? I fear not; but rather, an exceeding bad one. For does it not keep multitudes easy in their *heathen practice*? Does it not make or keep still greater numbers satisfied with their *heathen tempers*? Does it not directly tend to make both the one and the other imagine that they *are* what indeed they *are not*? That they *are* Christians, while
35   they are utterly without Christ, and without God in the world?[7] To close this point. If men are not Christians till they are renewed after the image of Christ, and if the people of England, in general, are not

---

[1] Cf. Phil. 2: 5.   [2] Cf. 1 John 2: 6.   [3] See 1 Pet. 1: 15.

[4] See Church, *Some Farther Remarks*, Preface, p. v.

[5] Charles Wesley, 'Primitive Christianity', st. 9; this poem was appended to *An Earnest Appeal*, for which see above, p. 91.

[6] Cf. 2 Pet. 1: 19.   [7] Eph. 2: 12.

thus renewed, why do we term them so? 'The god of this world hath' long 'blinded their hearts.'[1] Let us do nothing to increase that blindness; but rather to recover them from that 'strong delusion', that they may no longer 'believe a lie'.[2]

Let us labour to convince all mankind that to be a *real* Christian is 5 'to love the Lord our God with all our heart, and to serve him with all our strength';[3] 'to love our neighbour as ourselves',[4] and therefore to do unto every man as we would he should do unto us.[a]

[21.] To change one of these heathens into a real Christian, and to continue him such, all the *ordinary operations* of the Holy Spirit 10 are absolutely necessary.

'But what are they?' I sum them up (as I did in the *Farther Appeal to Men of Reason and Religion*[5]) in the words of as learned and orthodox a divine as ever England bred.

> Sanctification being opposed to our corruption, and answering fully 15 to the latitude thereof, whatsoever holiness and perfection is wanting in our nature must be supplied by the Spirit of God. Wherefore, we being by nature totally void of all saving truth, and under an impossibility of knowing the will of God; . . . this 'Spirit searcheth all things, yea, even the deep things of God',[6] and revealeth them unto the sons 20 of men; so that thereby the darkness of their understanding is expelled, and they are enlightened with the knowledge of God. . . . The same Spirit which revealeth the object of faith generally to the universal church, . . . doth also illuminate the understanding of such as believe, that they may receive the truth. For 'faith is the gift of God',[7] not only 25 in the object, but also in the act . . . And this gift is a gift of the Holy Ghost working within us. . . . And as the increase [and] perfection,[8] so the original of faith is from the Spirit of God . . . by an internal illumination of the soul.
>
> The second part of the office of the Holy Ghost is the renewing of 30 man in all the parts and faculties of his soul. For our natural corruption consisting in an aversation of our wills, and a depravation of our

---

[a] Second Letter to Dr. Church, p. 67 & seq. [i.e. *The Principles of a Methodist Farther Explained*, VI. 3–4, for which see Vol. 9 of this edition. For the closing clause see Matt. 7: 12.]

---

[1] 2 Cor. 4:4.   [2] 2 Thess. 2: 11.
[3] Cf. Matt. 22: 37, etc.   [4] Cf. Matt. 22: 39, etc.
[5] Pt. I, V. 23, which Wesley copies (with some minor variants) rather than making a new extract from Pearson's *Exposition of the Creed*.
[6] 1 Cor. 2: 10.   [7] Eph. 2: 8.
[8] Wesley's text reads 'increase of perfection'. See note 3, p. 164 above.

affections, an inclination of them to the will of God is wrought within us by the Spirit of God. . . .

The third part of his office is to lead, direct, and govern us in our actions and conversations . . . 'If we live in the Spirit', quickened by his
5 renovation, we must also 'walk in the Spirit',[1] following his direction, led by his manuduction. We are also animated and acted by the Spirit of God who giveth 'both to will and to do';[2] And 'as many as are *thus* led by the Spirit of God, are the sons of God'.[a] Moreover, that this direction may prove more effectual, we are guided in our prayers by the
10 same Spirit, according to the promise, 'I will pour upon the house of David, and upon the inhabitants of Jerusalem, the spirit of grace and supplication.'[b] Whereas then 'this is the confidence we have in him, that if we ask anything according to his will, he heareth us';[3] and whereas 'we know not what we should pray for as we ought, the Spirit
15 itself maketh intercession for us with groaning that cannot be uttered; and he that searcheth the heart knoweth what is the mind of the Spirit, because he maketh intercession for the saints according to the will of God'.[c] From which intercession (made for all true Christians) he hath the name of the 'Paraclete' given him by Christ, who said, 'I will pray
20 the Father, and he will give you another Paraclete.'[d] For 'if any man sin, we have a Paraclete with the Father, Jesus Christ the righteous', saith St. John;[4] 'who maketh intercession for us', saith St. Paul.[e] And we have 'another Paraclete',[f] saith our Saviour; 'which also maketh intercession for us',[g] saith St. Paul. A Paraclete then, in the notion of
25 the Scriptures, is an intercessor.

It is also the office of the Holy Ghost to 'assure us of the adoption of sons',[5] to create in us a sense of the paternal love of God toward us, to give us an earnest of our everlasting inheritance. 'The love of God is shed abroad in our hearts by the Holy Ghost which is given unto us.'[6]
30 'For as many as are led by the Spirit of God, they are the sons of God.'[7] 'And because we are sons, God hath sent forth the Spirit of his Son into our hearts, crying, Abba, Father.'[8] 'For we have not received the spirit of bondage again to fear, but we have received the Spirit of adoption, whereby we cry, Abba, Father: the Spirit itself bearing wit-
35 ness with our spirit, that we are the children of God.'[h]

As therefore we are born again by the Spirit, and receive from him our regeneration, so we are also by the same Spirit 'assured of our adoption'.[9] Because being sons, 'we are also heirs, heirs of God, and

---

[a] Rom. 8: 14. [b] Zech. 12: 10. [c] Rom. 8: 26–7. [d] John 14: 16.
[e] Rom. 8: 34. [f] John 14: 16. [g] Rom. 8: 27. [h] Rom. 8: 15–16.

---

[1] Gal. 5: 25. [2] Phil. 2: 13. [3] 1 John 5: 14. [4] Cf. 1 John 2: 1.
[5] Cf. Gal. 4: 5. [6] Rom. 5: 5. [7] Rom. 8: 14. [8] Cf. Gal. 4: 6.
[9] Cf. Gal. 4: 5.

joint heirs with Christ',[1] by the same Spirit we have the pledge or
rather the 'earnest of our inheritance'.[2] For 'he which establisheth us in
Christ, and hath anointed us, is God; who hath also sealed us, and hath
given us the earnest of his Spirit in our hearts';[3] so that we are 'sealed
with that Holy Spirit of promise, which is the earnest of our inheri-   5
tance'.[4] The Spirit of God, as given to us in this life, . . . is to be looked
upon as an earnest, being part of that reward which is promised, and
upon performance of the covenant which God hath made with us,
certainly to be received. . . .[5]

It now rests with your lordship to take your choice; either to con-   10
demn or to acquit both. Either your lordship must condemn Bishop
Pearson for an enthusiast . . . or you must acquit me: for I have his
express authority on my side concerning every text which I affirm to
belong to all Christians.

[22.] But I have greater authority than his, and such as I reverence   15
only less than the oracles of God. I mean that of our own Church. I
shall close this head by setting down what occurs in her authentic
records concerning either our 'receiving the Holy Ghost', or his
ordinary operations in all true Christians.

In her daily service she teacheth us all to beseech God 'to grant us . . .   20
his Holy Spirit, that those things may please him which we do at this
present, and that the rest of our life may be pure and holy';[6] to pray
for our sovereign lord the king, that God would 'replenish him with the
grace of his Holy Spirit';[7] for all the royal family, that 'they may be
endued with his Holy Spirit and enriched with his heavenly grace';[8]   25
for all the clergy and people, that he would 'send down upon them the
healthful Spirit of his grace';[9] for the catholic Church, that 'it may be
guided and governed by his good Spirit';[10] and for all therein who at any
time 'make their common supplications unto him',[11] that 'the fellowship or communication of the Holy Ghost may be with them all ever-   30
more'.[12]

Her collects are full of petitions to the same effect: 'Grant that we . . .
may daily be renewed by thy Holy Spirit.'[a] 'Grant that in all our

---

[a] [B.C.P., Collects,] Collect for Christmas Day.

[1] Rom. 8: 17.   [2] Eph. 1: 14.   [3] Cf. 2 Cor. 1: 21-2.   [4] Eph. 1: 13, 14.
[5] Here ends Wesley's quotation from Pearson's *Exposition of the Creed*. After adding
the closing comment from *A Farther Appeal*, Pt. I, V. 23, he continues to quote, again
with only minor variants, the succeeding sections of the work, V. 24-7.
[6] B.C.P., Morning Prayer, Absolution.   [7] Ibid., Prayer for the King's Majesty.
[8] B.C.P., Morning Prayer, Prayer for the Royal Family.
[9] Ibid., Prayer for the Clergy and People.
[10] Ibid., Prayers, For all Conditions of Men.
[11] Ibid., Morning Prayer, etc., A Prayer of St. Chrysostom.
[12] Ibid., Benediction (2 Cor. 13: 14).

sufferings here for the testimony of thy truth, we may . . . by faith behold the glory that shall be revealed, and being filled with the Holy Ghost may love and bless our persecutors.'a 'Send thy Holy Ghost, and pour into our hearts that most excellent gift of charity.'b 'O Lord,

5 from whom all good things do come, grant to us thy humble servants, that by thy holy inspiration we may think those things that are good, and by thy merciful guidance may perform the same.'c 'We beseech thee, leave us not comfortless, but send to us the Holy Ghost to comfort us.'d 'Grant us by the same Spirit to have a right judgment in all

10 things, and evermore to rejoice in his holy comfort.'e 'Grant us, Lord, we beseech thee, the Spirit, to think and do always such things as be rightful.'f 'O God, forasmuch as without thee we are not able to please thee, mercifully grant that thy Holy Spirit may in all things direct and rule our hearts.'g 'Cleanse the thoughts of our hearts by the inspiration

15 of thy Holy Spirit, that we may perfectly love thee, and worthily magnify thy holy name.'h

'Give thy Holy Spirit to this infant (or this person) that he may be born again.' 'Give thy Holy Spirit to these persons (N.B. already baptized) that they may continue thy servants.'i

20 'Almighty God, who hast vouchsafed to regenerate these persons by water and the Holy Ghost, . . . strengthen them with the Holy Ghost, the Comforter, and daily increase in them the manifold gifts of thy grace.'i

From these passages it may sufficiently appear for what purposes

25 every Christian, according to the doctrine of the Church of England, does now 'receive the Holy Ghost'.2 But this will be still more clear from those that follow; wherein we may likewise observe a plain, rational sense of God's *revealing* himself to us, of the *inspiration* of the the Holy Ghost, and of a believer's *feeling* in himself the mighty work-

30 ing of the Spirit of Christ.

[23.] 'God gave them of old grace to be his children, as he doth us now. But now, by the coming of our Saviour Christ, we have received more abundantly the Spirit of God in our hearts.'j

'He died to destroy the rule of the devil in us, and he rose again to

35 send down his Holy Spirit to rule in our hearts.'k

---

a [B.C.P., Collects,] Saint Stephen's Day. b [Ibid.,] Quinquagesima Sunday.
c [Ibid.,] Fifth Sunday after Easter. d [Ibid.,] Sunday after Ascension Day.
e [Ibid.,] Whitsunday. f [Ibid.,] Ninth Sunday after Trinity.
g [Ibid.,] Nineteenth Sunday after Trinity. h [B.C.P.,] Communion Office.
i [Ibid.,] Office of Confirmation. j Homily on Faith, Part II.
k Homily on the Resurrection.

1 B.C.P., Baptism, Baptism of Adults. 2 Acts 8: 15, 19.

'We have the Holy Spirit in our hearts as a seal and pledge of our everlasting inheritance.'[a]

'The Holy Ghost sat upon each of them like as it had been cloven tongues of fire, . . . to teach . . . that it is he that giveth eloquence and utterance in preaching the gospel, which engendereth a burning zeal 5 towards God's Word, and giveth all men a tongue, yea, a fiery tongue.' (N.B. Whatever occurs in any of the *Journals* of God's 'giving me utterance' or 'enabling me to speak with power' cannot therefore be quoted as enthusiasm, without wounding the Church through my side.) 'So that if any man be a dumb Christian, not professing his faith 10 openly, . . . he giveth men occasion to doubt . . . lest he have not the grace of the Holy Ghost within him.'[b]

'It is the office of the Holy Ghost to sanctify; which, the more it is hid from our understanding' (i.e. the particular manner of his working), 'the more it ought to move all men to wonder at the secret and mighty 15 workings of God's Holy Spirit which is within us. For it is the Holy Ghost that doth *quicken* the minds of men, *stirring up* godly motions in their hearts. Neither does he think it sufficient inwardly to work the new birth of men, unless he does also dwell and abide in them. "Know ye not", saith St. Paul, "that ye are the temples of God, and that his 20 Spirit dwelleth in you?"[1] "Know ye not that your bodies are the temples of the Holy Ghost which is within you?"[2] Again he saith, "Ye are not in the flesh, but in the spirit."[3] For why? "The Spirit of God dwelleth in you."[4] To this agreeth St. John: "The anointing which ye have received (he meaneth the Holy Ghost) abideth in you."[c] And St. 25 Peter saith the same: "The Spirit of glory and of God resteth upon you."[5] O what comfort is this to the heart of a true Christian, to think that the Holy Ghost dwelleth in him! "If God be with us", as the Apostle saith, "who can be against us?" . . .[6] He giveth patience and joyfulness of heart in temptation and affliction, and is therefore worthily 30 called "the Comforter".[d] He doth instruct the hearts of the simple in the knowledge of God, and his Word; therefore he is justly termed "the Spirit of truth".[e] And, N.B., "where the Holy Ghost doth instruct and teach there is no delay at all in learning." '[f]

From this passage I learn, (1), that ever true Christian now receives 35 the Holy Ghost, as the Paraclete, or Comforter promised by our Lord;[g] (2), that every Christian receives him as 'the Spirit of truth' (promised

---

[a] Ibid.   [b] Homily on Whitsunday, Part I.
[c] 1 John 2: 27.   [d] John 14: 16.   [e] John 16: 13.
[f] Ibid. [i.e. Homily on Whit Sunday, Pt. I, citing Bede, Hom. 9. sup. Lucam.]
[g] John 14: [16; 16:] 13.

[1] Cf. 1 Cor. 3: 16.   [2] Cf. 1 Cor. 6: 19.   [3] Rom. 8: 9.
[4] 1 Cor. 3: 16.   [5] 1 Pet. 4: 14.   [6] Cf. Rom. 8: 31.

John sixteen) 'to teach him all things';[1] and, (3), that the anointing mentioned in the first Epistle of St. John 'abides in every Christian'.[2]

[24.] 'In reading of God's word, he profiteth most . . . who is most inspired with the Holy Ghost.'[a]

5 'Human and worldly wisdom is not needful to the understanding the Scripture, but the revelation of the Holy Ghost, who inspireth the true meaning unto them who with humility and diligence search for it.'[b]

'Make him know and *feel* that there is no other name given under heaven unto men whereby we can be saved.'[3]

10 'If we *feel* our conscience at peace with God through remission of our sins, . . . all is of God.'[c]

'If you *feel* such a faith in you, rejoice in it, . . . and let it be daily increasing by well working.'[d]

'The faithful may *feel* wrought tranquillity of conscience, the increase 15 of faith and hope, with many other graces of God.'[e]

Godly men *feel* inwardly God's Holy Spirit inflaming their hearts with love.'[f]

'God give us grace to know these things, and *feel* them in our hearts! This knowledge and *feeling* is not of ourselves. . . . Let us therefore 20 meekly call upon the bountiful Spirit, the Holy Ghost, . . . to *inspire* us with his presence, that we may be able to hear the goodness of God to our salvation. For without his lively *inspiration* we cannot so much as speak the name of the Mediator: 'No man can say Jesus is the Lord, but by the Holy Ghost.'[4] Much less should we be able to believe and 25 know these great mysteries that be opened to us by Christ. . . . But "we have received" (saith St. Paul) "not the spirit of the world, but the Spirit which is of God"; for this purpose, "that we may know the things which are freely given to us of God".[5] In the power of the Holy Ghost resteth all ability to *know* God and to *please* him. . . . It is he 30 that *purifieth* the mind by his secret working. He *enlighteneth* the heart to conceive worthy thoughts of Almighty God. He sitteth on the *tongue* of man to stir him to speak his honour. He only ministereth spiritual *strength* to the powers of the *soul* and *body*. . . . And if we have any gift whereby we may profit our neighbour, all is wrought by this 35 one and selfsame spirit.'[g]

[a] Homily on reading the Scripture, Part I.
[b] Ibid., Part II, quoting Chrysostom. [c] Homily on Rogation week, Part III.
[d] Homily on Faith, Part III. [e] Homily on the Sacrament, Part I.
[f] Homily on certain places of Scripture, Part I.
[g] Homily for Rogation week, Part III.

[1] Actually John 14: 26. [2] Cf. 1 John 2: 27.
[3] Cf. Acts 4: 12; *Homilies*, Of the Passion. [4] Cf. 1 Cor. 12: 13.
[5] Cf. 1 Cor. 2: 12.

[25.] Every proposition which I have anywhere advanced concerning those operations of the Holy Ghost which I believe are common to all Christians in all ages is here clearly maintained by our own church.

Being fully convinced of this, I could not well understand for many years how it was that on the mentioning any of these great truths, even among men of education, the cry immediately arose, 'An enthusiast, an enthusiast!' But I now plainly perceive this is only an old fallacy in a new shape. To object 'enthusiasm' to any person or doctrine is but a decent method of begging the question. It generally spares the objector the trouble of reasoning, and is a shorter and easier way of carrying his cause.

For instance, I assert that 'till a man "receives the Holy Ghost",[1] he is without God in the world; that he cannot know the things of God unless God *reveal* them unto him by his Spirit; no, nor have even one holy or heavenly temper without the inspiration of the Holy One.'[2] Now should one who is conscious to himself that he has experienced none of these things attempt to confute these propositions either from Scripture or antiquity it might prove a difficult task. What then shall he do? Why, cry out, 'Enthusiasm! Fanaticism!' and the work is done.[3]

[26.] 'But is it not mere *enthusiasm* or *fanaticism* to talk of the *new birth*?' So one might imagine from the *manner* in which your lordship talks of it. 'The Spirit did not stop till it had manifested itself in the last effort of its power, the *new birth*.'[a] 'The *new birth* began in storms and tempests, in cries and ecstasies, in tumults and confusions.'[b] 'Persons who had no sense of religion, that is, no ecstatic feelings or pains of the *new birth*.'[c] 'What can be the issue of the *new birth*, attended with those infernal throes?'[d] 'Why would he elicit sense from these Gentiles, when they were finally to be deprived of it in ecstasies and *new births*?'[e] All these circumstances Mr. Wesley has 'declared to be *constant symptoms* of the *new birth*.'[f]

So the *new birth* is, throughout the whole tract, the standing topic of *ridicule*!

[27.] 'No, not the new birth itself, but your enthusiastic, ridiculous *account* of it.' What is then *my* account of the new birth? I gave it some years ago in these words:

It is that great change which God works in the soul when he brings

---

[a] [Warburton, op. cit.,] p. 124.   [b] [Ibid.,] p. 126.   [c] [Ibid.,] p. 180.
[d] [Ibid.,] pp. 169-70.   [e] [Ibid.,] p. 225.   [f] [Ibid.,] p. 222.

[1] Cf. John 20: 22; Acts 8: 15.   [2] See note to *A Farther Appeal*, Pt. I, V. 27.
[3] *A Farther Appeal*, Pt. I, V. 24-7.

it into life; when he raises it from the death of sin to the life of righteousness. It is the change wrought in the whole soul by the almighty Spirit of God when it is 'created anew in Christ Jesus';[1] when it is 'renewed after the image of God'[2] 'in righteousness and true holiness';[3] when the love of the world is changed into the love of God, pride into humility, passion into meekness, hatred, envy, malice into a sincere, tender, disinterested love to all mankind. In a word, it is that change whereby the 'earthly, sensual, devilish'[4] mind is turned into 'the mind which was in Christ Jesus'.[a]

This is *my account* of the new birth. What is there *ridiculous* or *enthusiastic* in it?

[28.] 'But what do you mean by those *tempests*, and *cries*, and *pains*, and infernal *throes* attending the new birth?' I will tell you as plainly as I can, in the very same words I used to Dr. Church— after premising that some experience much, some very little of these *pains* and *throes*:

'When men feel in themselves the heavy burden of sin, see damnation to be the reward of it, behold with the eye of their mind the horror of hell; they tremble, they quake, and are inwardly touched with sorrowfulness of heart, and cannot but accuse themselves, and open their grief unto Almighty God, and call unto him for mercy. This being done seriously, their mind is so occupied, partly with sorrow and heaviness, partly with an earnest desire to be delivered from this danger of hell and damnation, that all desire of meat and drink is laid apart, and loathing of all worldly things and pleasures comes in place; so that nothing then liketh them more than to weep, to lament, to mourn, and both with words and behaviour to body to show themselves weary of life.'[5]

Now permit me to ask, 'What if, before you had observed that these were the very words of our own Church, one of your acquaintance or parishioners had come and told you that ever since he heard a sermon at the Foundery he "saw damnation" before him, and "beheld with the eye of his mind the horror of hell"? What if he had "trembled" and "quaked", and been so taken up, "partly with sorrow and heaviness, partly with an earnest desire to be delivered from the danger of hell and damnation", as "to weep, to lament, to mourn, and both with words and behaviour to show himself weary of life?" Would you have scrupled

---

[a] Vol. 4 of *Sermons* [i.e. 'The New Birth', II. 5. The closing quotation is from Phil. 2: 5.]

---

[1] Cf. Eph. 2: 10. [2] Cf. Col. 3: 10. [3] Cf. Eph. 4: 24. [4] Jas. 3: 15.
[5] *Homilies*, Of Fasting, Pt. I, quoted also in *A Farther Appeal*, Pt. I, VII. 12.

to say, "Here is another deplorable instance of the Methodists driving men to distraction"'?[a]

[III.] To show whether I represent religion as a *reasonable service*, I cannot but add one extract more from a letter I sent to Dr. Middleton a considerable time before his death:[1]   5

We have been long disputing about Christians, about Christianity, and the *evidence* whereby it is supported. But what do these terms mean? Who is a Christian indeed? What is real, genuine Christianity? And what is the surest and most accessible evidence (if I may so speak) whereby I may know that it is of God? May the God of the Christians 10 enable me to speak on these heads in a manner suitable to the importance of them!

Section (I). 1. I would consider, first, Who is a Christian indeed? What does that term properly imply? It has been so long abused, I fear, not only to mean nothing at all, but, what was far worse than nothing, 15 to be a cloak for the vilest hypocrisy, for the grossest abominations and immoralities of every kind, that it is high time to rescue it out of the hands of wretches that are a reproach to human nature; to show determinately what manner of man he is to whom this name of right belongs.   20

2. A Christian cannot think of the Author of his being without abasing himself before him; without a deep sense of the distance between a worm of earth and him that sitteth on the circle of the heavens.[2] In his presence he sinks into the dust, knowing himself to be less than nothing in his eye; and being conscious, in a manner words 25 cannot express, of his own littleness, ignorance, foolishness. So that he can only cry out from the fullness of his heart, 'O God! What is man![3] What am I!'

3. He has a continual sense of his dependence on the Parent of good for his being, and all the blessings that attend it. To him he refers 30 every natural and every moral endowment, with all that is commonly ascribed either to fortune or to the wisdom, courage, or merit of the possessor. And hence he acquiesces in whatsoever appears to be his will, not only with patience, but with thankfulness. He willingly resigns

---

[a] Second Letter to Dr. *Church* [i.e. *The Principles of a Methodist Farther Explained*, VI. 4].

---

[1] *A Letter to the Reverend Dr. Conyers Middleton, occasioned by his late Free Enquiry* (1749). Wesley published Pt. VI of this work separately as *A Plain Account of Genuine Christianity*, and the text here is based on the 1761 edition of that extract. (See *Bibliography*, No. 160, and Vol. 13 of this edition.)

[2] See Isa. 40: 22.   [3] Ps. 8: 4, etc.

all he is, all he has, to his wise and gracious disposal. The ruling temper of his heart is the most absolute submission and the tenderest gratitude to his sovereign benefactor. And this grateful love creates filial fear: an awful reverence toward him, and an earnest care not to give place to
5 any disposition, nor to admit an action, word, or thought, which might in any degree displease that indulgent power to whom he owes his life, breath, and all things.

4. And as he has the strongest affection for the fountain of all good, so he has the firmest confidence in him; a confidence which neither
10 pleasure nor pain, neither life nor death can shake. But yet this, far from creating sloth or indolence, pushes him on to the most vigorous industry. It causes him to put forth all his strength in obeying him in whom he confides. So that he is never faint in his mind, never weary of doing whatever he believes to be his will. And as he knows the most
15 acceptable worship of God is to imitate him he worships, so he is continually labouring to transcribe into himself all his imitable perfections: in particular his justice, mercy, and truth, so eminently displayed in all his creatures.

5. Above all, remembering that God is love, he is conformed to the
20 same likeness. He is full of love to his neighbours: of universal love, not confined to one sect or party, not restrained to those who agree with him in opinions, or in outward modes of worship, or to those who are allied to him by blood, or recommended by nearness of place. Neither does he love those only that love him, or that are endeared to him by
25 intimacy of acquaintance. But his love resembles that of him whose mercy is over all his works. It soars above all these scanty bounds, embracing neighbours and strangers, friends and enemies; yea, not only the good and gentle, but also the froward, the evil and unthankful. For he loves every soul that God has made; every child of man, of
30 whatever place or nation. And yet this universal benevolence does in no wise interfere with a peculiar regard for his relations, friends, and benefactors; a fervent love for his country; and the most endeared affection to all men of integrity, of clear and generous virtue.

6. His love, as to these, so to all mankind, is itself generous and dis-
35 interested; springing from no view of advantage to himself, from no regard to profit or praise; no, nor even the pleasure of loving. This is the daughter, not the parent of his affection. By experience he knows that *social love* (if it mean the love of our neighbour) is absolutely, essentially different from *self-love*, even of the most allowable kind.
40 And yet it is sure, that, if they are under true regulations, each will give additional force to the other, till they mix together never to be divided.

7. And this universal, disinterested love is productive of all right

affections. It is fruitful of gentleness, tenderness, sweetness; of humanity, courtesy, and affability. It makes a Christian rejoice in the virtues of all, and bear a part in their happiness, at the same time that he sympathizes with their pains and compassionates their infirmities. It creates modesty, condescension, prudence, together with calmness and evenness of temper. It is the parent of generosity, openness, and frankness, void of jealousy and suspicion. It begets candour, and willingness to believe and hope whatever is kindly and friendly of every man; and invincible patience, never overcome of evil, but overcoming evil with good.[1]

8. The same love constrains him to converse, not only with a strict regard to truth, but with artless sincerity and genuine simplicity, as one in whom there is no guile.[2] And not content with abstaining from all such expressions as are contrary to justice or truth, he endeavours to refrain from every unloving word, either to a present or of an absent person; in all his conversation aiming at this, either to improve himself in knowledge or virtue, or to make those with whom he converses some way wiser, or better, or happier than they were before.

9. The same love is productive of all right actions. It leads him into an earnest and steady discharge of all social offices, of whatever is due to relations of every kind; to his friends, to his country, and to any particular community whereof he is a member. It prevents his willingly hurting or grieving any man. It guides him into an uniform practice of justice and mercy, equally extensive with the principle whence it flows. It constrains him to do all possible good, of every possible kind, to all men; and makes him invariably resolved in every circumstance of life to do that, and that only, to others, which, supposing he were himself in the same situation, he would desire they should do to him.[3]

10. And as he is easy to others, so he is easy in himself. He is free from the painful swellings of pride, from the flames of anger, from the impetuous gusts of irregular self-will. He is no longer tortured with envy or malice, or with unreasonable and hurtful desire. He is no more enslaved to the pleasures of sense, but has the full power both over his mind and body, in a continued cheerful course of sobriety, of temperance, and chastity. He knows how to use all things in their place, and yet is superior to them all. He stands above those low pleasures of imagination which captivate vulgar minds, whether arising from what mortals term greatness, or novelty, or beauty. All these too he can taste, and still look upward; still aspire to nobler enjoyments. Neither is he a slave to fame; popular breath affects not him; he stands steady, and collected in himself.

[1] See Rom. 12: 21.   [2] John 1: 47.   [3] See Matt. 7: 12.

11. And he who seeks no praise cannot fear dispraise. Censure gives him no uneasiness, being conscious to himself that he would not willingly offend, and that he has the approbation of the Lord of all. He cannot fear want, knowing in whose hand is the earth and the fullness thereof,[1] and that it is impossible for him to withhold from one that fears him any manner of thing that is good. He cannot fear pain, knowing it will never be sent unless it be for his real advantage, and that then his strength will be proportioned to it, as it has always been in times past. He cannot fear death, being able to trust him he loves with his soul as well as his body; yea, glad to leave the corruptible body in the dust till it is raised incorruptible and immortal. So that in honour or shame, in abundance or want, in ease or pain, in life or death, always and in all things he has learned to be content,[2] to be easy, thankful, joyful, happy.

12. He is happy in knowing there is a God, an intelligent cause and Lord of all, and that he is not the produce either of blind chance or inexorable necessity. He is happy in the full assurance he has that this Creator and end of all things is a being of boundless wisdom, of infinite power to execute all the designs of his wisdom, and of no less infinite goodness to direct all his power to the advantage of all his creatures. Nay, even the consideration of his immutable justice, rendering to all their due, of his unspotted holiness, of his all-sufficiency in himself, and of that immense ocean of all perfections which centre in God from eternity to eternity, is a continual addition to the happiness of a Christian.

13. A farther addition is made thereto while in contemplating even the things that surround him that thought strikes warmly upon his heart:

These are thy glorious works, Parent of good;[3]

while he takes knowledge of the invisible things of God, even his eternal power and wisdom, in the things that are seen,[4] the heavens, the earth, the fowls of the air, the lilies of the field.[5] How much more while, rejoicing in the constant care which he still takes of the work of his own hand, he breaks out in a transport of love and praise: 'O Lord, our governor! How excellent is thy name in all the earth! Thou that hast set thy glory above the heavens!'[6] While he, as it were, sees the Lord sitting upon his throne, and ruling all things well; while he observes the general providence of God so extended with his whole creation, and surveys all the effects of it in the heavens and earth, as a well pleased spectator; while he sees the wisdom and goodness of his general government descending to every particular, so presiding over the whole uni-

---

[1] See Ps. 24: 1. [2] See Phil. 4: 11. [3] Milton, *Paradise Lost*, v. 153.
[4] See Rom. 1: 20. [5] See Matt. 6: 26–8. [6] Cf. Ps. 8: 1 (B.C.P.).

verse as over a single person, so watching over every single person as if he were the whole universe; how does he exult when he reviews the various traces of the almighty goodness in what has befallen himself in the several circumstances and changes of his own life! All which, he now sees, have been allotted to him and dealt out in number, weight, 5 and measure. With what triumph of soul, in surveying either the general or particular providence of God, does he observe every line pointing out an hereafter, every scene opening into eternity!

14. He is peculiarly and inexpressibly happy in the clearest and fullest conviction, 'This all-powerful, all-wise, all-gracious being, this 10 governor of all, loves *me*. This lover of my soul is always with me, is never absent, no, not for a moment. And I love him; there is none in heaven but thee, none on earth that I desire beside thee.[1] And he has given me to resemble himself; he has stamped his image on my heart. And I live unto him; I do only his will; I glorify him with my body 15 and my spirit. And it will not be long before I shall die unto him; I shall die into the arms of God. And then farewell sin and pain; then it only remains that I should live with him for ever.'

15. This is the plain, naked portraiture of a Christian; be not prejudiced against him for his name. Forgive his particularities of opinion 20 and (what you think) superstitious modes of worship. These are circumstances but of small concern, and do not enter into the essence of his character. Cover them with a veil of love, and look at the substance—his tempers, his holiness, his happiness.

Can calm reason conceive either a more amiable or a more desirable 25 character?

Is it your own? Away with names! Away with opinions! I care not what you are called. I ask not—it does not deserve a thought—what opinion you are of, so you are conscious to yourself that you are the man whom I have been (however faintly) describing. 30

Do not you know, you ought to be such? Is the governor of the world well pleased that you are not?

Do you (at least) desire it? I would to God that desire may penetrate your inmost soul, and that you may have no rest in your spirit till you are not only almost, but altogether a Christian![2] 35

Section (II). 1. The second point to be considered is, What is real, genuine Christianity, whether we speak of it as a principle in the soul, or as a scheme or system of doctrine?

Christianity, taken in the latter sense, is that system of doctrine which describes the character above recited, which promises it shall be 40 mine (provided I will not rest till I attain) and which tells me how I may attain it.

---

[1] See Ps. 73: 25.   [2] See Acts 26: 28, and Wesley's sermon thereon.

2. First, it *describes* this character in all its parts, and that in the most lively and affecting manner. The main lines of this picture are beautifully drawn in many passages of the Old Testament. These are filled up in the New, retouched and finished with all the art of God.

5   The same we have in miniature more than once; particularly in the thirteenth chapter of the former Epistle to the Corinthians, and in that discourse which St. Matthew records as delivered by our Lord at his entrance upon his public ministry.

3. Secondly, Christianity *promises* this character shall be mine if
10 I will not rest till I attain it. This is promised both in the Old Testament and the New. Indeed the New is, in effect, all a promise, seeing every description of the servants of God mentioned therein has the nature of a command, in consequence of those general injunctions: 'Be ye followers of me, as I am of Christ';[a] be ye 'followers of them who
15 through faith and patience inherit the promises'.[b] And every command has the force of a promise, in virtue of those general promises: 'A new heart will I give you, and I will put my spirit within you; and cause you to walk in my statutes, and ye shall keep my judgments and do them';[c] 'This is the covenant that I will make . . . after those days, saith the
20 Lord; I will put my laws into their minds, and write them in their hearts.'[d] Accordingly, when it is said, 'Thou shalt love the Lord thy God with all thy heart, and with all thy soul, and with all thy mind';[e] it is not only a direction what I shall do, but a promise of what God will do in me; exactly equivalent with what is written elsewhere, 'The
25 Lord thy God will circumcise thy heart and the heart of thy seed' (alluding to the custom then in use) 'to love the Lord thy God with all thine heart and with all thy soul.'[f]

4. This being observed, it will readily appear to every serious person who reads the New Testament with that care which the importance of
30 the subject demands, that every particular branch of the preceding character is manifestly promised therein; either explicitly, under the very form of a promise, or virtually, under that of a description or command.

5. Christianity tells me, in the third place, how I may attain the
35 promise; namely, by faith.

But what is faith? Not an opinion, no more than it is a form of words; not any number of opinions put together, be they ever so true. A string of opinions is no more Christian faith than a string of beads is Christian holiness.

40   It is not an assent to any opinion, or any number of opinions. A man may assent to three, or three and twenty creeds; he may assent to

---

[a] 1 Cor. 11: 1.   [b] Heb. 12.   [c] Ezek. 36: 26–7.
[d] Heb. 8: 10.   [e] Matt. 22: 37.   [f] Deut. 30: 6.

all the Old and New Testament (at least as far as he understands them) and yet have no Christian faith at all.

6. The faith by which the promise is attained is represented by Christianity as a power wrought by the Almighty in an immortal spirit inhabiting an house of clay, to see through that veil into the world of spirits, into things invisible and eternal; a power to discern those things which with eyes of flesh and blood no man hath seen or can see: either by reason of their nature, which (though they surround us on every side) is not perceivable by these gross senses, or by reason of their distance, as being yet afar off, in the bosom of eternity.

7. This is Christian faith in the general notion of it. In its more particular notion it is a divine evidence or conviction wrought in my heart that God is reconciled to *me* through his Son; inseparably joined with a confidence in him as a gracious, reconciled Father, as for all things, so especially for all those good things which are invisible and eternal.

To believe (in the Christian sense) is, then, to walk in the light of eternity; and to have a clear sight of, and confidence in, the Most High, reconciled to me through the Son of his love.

8. Now how highly desirable is such a faith, were it only on its own account! For how little does the wisest of men know of anything more than he can see with his eyes! What clouds and darkness cover the whole scene of things invisible and eternal! What does he know even of himself, as to his invisible part? What of his future manner of existence? How melancholy an account does the prying, learned philosopher (perhaps the wisest and best of all heathens), the great, the venerable Marcus Antoninus give of these things! What was the result of all his serious researches? Of his high and deep contemplation? 'Either dissipation' (of the soul as well as the body into the common, unthinking mass); 'or reabsorption into the universal fire, the unintelligent source of all things; or, some unknown manner of conscious existence after the body sinks to rise no more.'[1] One of these three, he supposed, must succeed death: but which he had no light to determine. Poor Antoninus! With all his wealth, his honour, his power, with all his wisdom and philosophy!

> What points of knowledge did he gain?
> That life is sacred all—and vain!
> Sacred how high? And vain how low?
> He could not tell—but died to know.[2]

---

[1] Marcus Aurelius Antoninus, *Meditations*, iv. 21.
[2] John Gambold, the closing quatrain of 'Epitaph', published by Wesley in his *Collection of Moral and Sacred Poems* (1744), III. 195. The original reads: 'He knew not here, but died to know.'

9. He 'died to know'! And so must you, unless you are now a partaker of Christian faith. O consider this. Nay, and consider, not only how little you know of the immensity of the things that are beyond sense and time, but how uncertainly do you know even that little? How
5 faintly glimmering a light is that you have! Can you properly be said to *know* any of these things? Is that knowledge any more than bare conjecture? And the reason is plain. You have no senses suited to invisible or eternal objects. What desiderata then, especially to the rational, the reflecting part of mankind, are these: a more extensive
10 knowledge of things invisible and eternal; a greater certainty in whatever knowledge of them we have; and, in order to both, faculties capable of discerning things invisible.

10. Is it not so? Let impartial reason speak. Does not every thinking man want a window, not so much in his neighbour's, as in his own
15 breast? He wants an opening there, of whatever kind, that might let in light from eternity. He is pained to be thus feeling after God so darkly, so uncertainly; to know so little of God, and indeed so little of any beside material objects. He is concerned that he must see even that little not directly, but in the dim, sullied glass of sense; and conse-
20 quently so imperfectly and obscurely that it is all a mere enigma still.

11. Now these very desiderata faith supplies. It gives a more extensive knowledge of things invisible, showing what eye had not seen, nor ear heard, neither could it before enter into our heart to conceive.[1] And all these it shows in the clearest light, with the fullest certainty and
25 evidence. For it does not leave us to receive our notice of them by mere reflection from the dull glass of sense; but resolves a thousand enigmas of the highest concern by giving faculties suited to things invisible. O who would not wish for such a faith, were it only on these accounts! How much more, if by this I may receive the promise, I may
30 attain all the holiness and happiness implied therein!

12. So Christianity tells me; 'And so I find it', may every real Christian say: 'I now am assured that these things are so: I experience them in my own breast. What Christianity (considered as a doctrine) promised, is accomplished in my soul.' And Christianity, considered
35 as an inward principle, is the completion of all those promises. It is holiness and happiness, the image of God impressed on a created spirit; 'a fountain of peace and love springing up into everlasting life'.[2]

Section (III). 1. And this I conceive to be the strongest evidence of the truth of Christianity. I do not undervalue traditional evidence. Let
40 it have its place and its due honour. It is highly serviceable in its kind, and in its degree. And yet I cannot set it on a level with this.

It is generally supposed that traditional evidence is weakened by

[1] See 1 Cor. 2: 9.   [2] Cf. John 4: 14.

length of time, as it must necessarily pass through so many hands in a continual succession of ages. But no length of time can possibly affect the strength of this internal evidence. It is equally strong, equally new, through the course of seventeen hundred years. It passes now, even as it has done from the beginning, directly from God into the 5 believing soul. Do you suppose time will ever dry up this stream? O no; it will never be cut off:

> *Labitur et labetur in omne volubilis aevum.*[1]

2. Traditional evidence is of an extremely complicated nature, necessarily including so many and so various considerations that only 10 men of strong and clear understanding can be sensible of its full force. On the contrary, how plain and simple is this! And how level to the lowest capacity! Is not this the sum? 'One thing I know: I was blind, but now I see.'[2] An argument so plain that a peasant, a woman, a child may feel its force. 15

3. The traditional evidence of Christianity stands as it were a great way off; and therefore although it speaks loud and clear, yet makes a less lively impression. It gives us an account of what was transacted long ago, in far distant times as well as places. Whereas the inward evidence is intimately present to all persons, at all times, and in all 20 places. It is nigh thee, in thy mouth, and in thy heart, if thou believest in the Lord Jesus Christ. 'This (then) is the record', this is the evidence emphatically so called, 'that God hath given unto us eternal life, and this life is in his Son'.[3]

4. If then it were possible (which I conceive it is not) to shake the 25 traditional evidence of Christianity, still he that has the internal evidence (and every true believer hath the witness or evidence in himself) would stand firm and unshaken. Still he could say to those who were striking at the external evidence, 'Beat on the sack of Anaxagoras.'[4] But you can no more hurt *my* evidence of Christianity than the tyrant 30 could hurt the spirit of that wise man.

5. I have sometimes been almost inclined to believe that the wisdom of God has, in latter ages, permitted the external evidence of Christianity to be more or less clogged and encumbered for this very end, that men (of reflection especially) might not altogether rest there, but 35

---

[1] 'On it glides, and on it will glide, rolling its flood forever.' Horace, *Epistles*, I. ii. 43. Wesley's translation ('Latin Sentences Translated', *Works* (1774), Vol. 32, Appendix): 'It flows on, and will for ever flow.'

[2] Cf. John 9: 25.   [3] 1 John 5: 11.

[4] Anaxagoras (*c.* 500–428 B.C.) was a Greek philosopher from Asia Minor who, by settling in Athens, made the city the chief centre of philosophic speculation. The 'sack of Anaxagoras' is a reference to his experiment, mentioned by Aristotle, of 'straining wineskins and showing the resistance of the air' (Aristotle, *Physics*, 4. 213 a 22).

be constrained to look into themselves also, and attend to the light shining in their hearts.

Nay, it seems (if it be allowed for us to pry so far into the reasons of the divine dispensations) that particularly in this age God suffers all
5 kinds of objections to be raised against the traditional evidence of Christianity, that men of understanding, though unwilling to give it up, yet at the same time they defend this evidence may not rest the whole strength of their cause thereon, but seek a deeper and firmer support for it.

10 6. Without this I cannot but doubt whether they can long maintain their cause; whether, if they do not obey the loud call of God, and lay more stress than they have hitherto done on this internal evidence of Christianity, they will not, one after another, give up the external, and (in heart at least) go over to those whom they are now contending with:
15 so that in a century or two the people of England will be fairly divided into real deists and real Christians.

And I apprehend this would be no loss at all, but rather an advantage to the Christian cause; nay, perhaps it would be the speediest, yea, the only effectual way of bringing all reasonable deists to be Christians.

20 7. May I be permitted to speak freely? May I, without offence, ask of you that are called Christians, what real loss would you sustain in giving up your present opinion that the Christian system is of God? Though you bear the name, you are not Christians now: you have neither Christian faith nor love; you have no divine evidence of things
25 unseen;[1] you have not entered into the holiest by the blood of Jesus;[2] you do not love God with all your heart; neither do you love your neighbour as yourself.[3] You are neither happy nor holy, you have not learned in every state therewith to be content:[4] to rejoice evermore, even in want, pain, death; and in everything to give thanks.[5] You are
30 not holy in heart: superior to pride, to anger, to foolish desires. Neither are you holy in life: you do not walk as Christ also walked.[6] Does not the main of *your* Christianity lie in your opinion, decked with a few outward observances? For as to morality, even honest heathen morality (O let me utter a melancholy truth), many of those whom you style
35 deists, there is reason to fear, have far more of it than you.

8. Go on, gentlemen, and prosper. Shame these nominal Christians out of that poor superstitition which they call Christianity. Reason, rally, laugh them out of their dead, empty forms, void of spirit, of faith, of love. Convince them that such unmeaning pageantry (for such
40 it manifestly is if there is nothing in the heart correspondent with the outward show) is absolutely unworthy, you need not say of God, but

---

[1] See Heb. 11: 1. [2] See Heb. 10: 19. [3] Luke 10: 27, etc.
[4] See Phil. 4: 11. [5] 1 Thess. 5: 18. [6] See 1 John 2: 6.

even of any man that is endued with common understanding. Show them that while they are endeavouring to please God thus they are only beating the air.[1] Know your time; press on; push your victories, till you have conquered all that know not God. And then he whom neither they nor you know now shall arise and gird himself with 5 strength,[2] and go forth in his almighty love, and sweetly conquer you altogether.

9. O that the time was come! How do I long for you to be partakers of the exceeding great and precious promises![3] How am I pained when I hear any of *you* using those silly terms which the men of form have 10 taught you, calling the mention of the holy thing you want, 'cant'!, the deepest wisdom, the highest happiness, 'enthusiasm'! What ignorance is this! How extremely despicable would it make you in the eyes of any but a Christian! But he cannot despise you, who loves you as his own soul, who is ready to lay down his life for your sake. 15

10. Perhaps you will say, 'But this internal evidence of Christianity affects only those in whom the promise is fulfilled. It is no evidence to *me*.' There is truth in this objection. It does affect them chiefly: but it does not affect them only. It cannot in the nature of things be so strong an evidence to others as it is to them. And yet it may bring a 20 degree of evidence, it may reflect some light on you also.

For, first, you see the beauty and loveliness of Christianity, when it is rightly understood. And you are sure there is nothing to be desired in comparison of it.

Secondly, you know the Scripture promises this, and says it is 25 attained by faith, and by no other way.

Thirdly, you see clearly how desirable Christian faith is, even on account of its own intrinsic value.

Fourthly, you are a witness that the holiness and happiness above described can be attained no other way. The more you have laboured 30 after virtue and happiness, the more convinced you are of this. Thus far, then, you need not lean upon other men; thus far you have personal experience.

Fifthly, what reasonable assurance can you have of things whereof you have not personal experience? Suppose the question was, 'Can the 35 blind be restored to sight?' This you have not yourself experienced. How then will you know that such a thing ever was? Can there be an easier or surer way than to talk with one or some number of men who were blind, but are now restored to sight? They cannot be deceived as to the fact in question; the nature of the thing leaves no room for 40 this. And if they are honest men (which you may learn from other circumstances) they will not deceive you.

[1] See 1 Cor. 9: 26.   [2] See 2 Sam. 22: 40; Ps. 18: 39.   [3] See 2 Pet. 1: 4.

Now transfer this to the case before us; and those who were blind but now see, those who were sick many years but now are healed, those who were miserable but now are happy, will afford *you* also a very strong evidence of the truth of Christianity; as strong as can be in the nature of things till you experience it in your own soul. And this, though it be allowed they are but plain men, and in general of weak understanding; nay, though some of them should be mistaken in other points, and hold opinions which cannot be defended.[1]

I have now finished, as my time permits, what I had to say either concerning myself or on the operations of the Holy Spirit. In doing this I have used great plainness of speech, and yet, I hope, without rudeness. If anything of that kind has slipped from me I am ready to retract it. I desire on the one hand to 'accept no man's person';[2] and yet on the other to give 'honour to whom honour is due'.[3]

If your lordship should think it worth your while to spend any more words upon me, may I presume to request one thing of your lordship—to be more *serious*? It cannot injure your lordship's *character*, or your *cause*. Truth is great, and will prevail.[4]

Wishing your lordship all temporal and spiritual blessings, I am,

My lord,

Your lordship's dutiful son
and servant,
John Wesley

November 26,
1762

---

[1] Wesley, *A Plain Account of Genuine Christianity*, 1761 edition, from *A Letter to the Rev. Dr. Conyers Middleton*, Pt. VI.

[2] Cf. Gal. 2: 6.   [3] Cf. Rom. 13: 7.

[4] See 1 Esd. 4: 41—in Vulgate, 'Magna est veritas et praevalet.'

APPENDIX

Wesley's Text: Editions, Transmission, Variant Readings

Two major problems face the editor of the works of a long-deceased author, first the securing of the best text, and second its presentation to the reader. In the case of a prolific and busy author such as John Wesley the first presents serious difficulties. In spite of a search through hundreds of libraries in the western world many early editions of his writings remain undiscovered, and of a few ephemera which he certainly published no copies appear to have survived. Nevertheless of about 450 publications issued by John and Charles Wesley either jointly or separately some two thousand editions appearing during their lifetimes have been discovered, many in unique copies. Where several editions of any work are extant it is usually possible (though sometimes only by following up minute clues) to determine their order and their relationship to each other, and thus to trace the history of the transmission of the text.

To ascertain which text best reflects the most fully deliberate expression of Wesley's thought three main alternatives offer themselves. (1) Obviously attractive is the last edition known to have received his personal revision, but his practice of preparing a new edition from the one most readily available (usually the most recent) frequently combines with careless printing and hasty proof-reading to undermine its value. As a result of accumulated and compounded errors, Wesley was sometimes faced with nonsense in later editions, and his makeshift corrections are usually poorer than the original text, which he seems never to have consulted because of the many other demands upon his time. (2) His effort during the years 1771–4 to prepare an authorized collected edition of his *Works* in thirty-two volumes suffers similarly from haste. Some passages were omitted deliberately, but others by accident, for the volumes were more poorly printed than usual. Wesley recognized that this venture had not fulfilled his original purpose of standardization, and seems never to have followed this abridged text in later editions of his publications. A few years earlier he had asked his brother Charles to prepare a definitive edition of the *Appeals*, which he regarded highly, and textual evidence demonstrates that for the 1765 printing of *An Earnest Appeal* at least two editions were consulted, but here again the attempt was only partly successful. (3) For our 'copy-text', therefore, we turn to the first edition, the only one printed directly from the author's manuscript, and therefore the one likely to reproduce most faithfully his original intentions.

Incorporated in the text of the first edition are all revisions which certainly or almost certainly derive from the author, but not those which more probably originated with a compositor or proof-reader, such as the many 'indifferent readings' (minor stylistic changes not affecting the sense) introduced during Wesley's later years. Excluded also are such things as the changing statistics of Methodist membership, and abridgements made only in the collected *Works*. Every plausible variant from the resulting edited text found in any known British edition published during Wesley's lifetime has been noted in the appendix. Manifest errors and 'accidentals'—differences in typography, spelling, or punctuation—have been excluded. When the true reading for an error arising during the printing processes is obvious the correction is made silently, but if any doubt exists the conjecture is substituted within square brackets, and the actual reading or readings shown in a footnote. For most of Wesley's publications we have furnished a stemma—a diagram tracing the descent of the text from the first through later editions, which occasionally separate into several families of text. By means of this apparatus it is possible to reconstruct the substantive text of any known edition published during Wesley's lifetime.

In securing and preserving the text, with its variants, therefore, the specialist scholar has been kept firmly in mind. In order that this apparatus should not intimidate the general reader, however, it has been placed in an appendix, and only a few variant readings have been selected for incorporation in the footnotes to the body of the text. Nor does this particular volume exhibit many of the textual complexities to be found in some others. The largest number of editions noted for any work included here is the ten for *An Earnest Appeal*, and these separate into only two lines of descent, though they exhibit some cross-influence such as is unusual in Wesley's publications.

In reproducing this text the antiquarian approach has deliberately been avoided, although we have neither eliminated nor added nor changed a word without informing the reader, nor felt justified in bringing Wesley's grammar up to date by altering 'you was', 'this was wrote', 'he had forgot', etc., to their modern equivalents. We have felt no compunction, however, about clothing his words in a different typographical dress —the style of printing familiar to him only during his later years, after the typographical revolution which took place in the middle years of the century.

Wesley's later *spelling* is almost uniformly modern, and we are attempting to make it consistent throughout this edition, even where he himself (or his printers) used different forms—except in a few instances. Thus we find in his original text both 'throughly' and 'thoroughly', 'toward' and 'towards', words which overlapped in meaning, were similar in spelling, but differed in pronunciation. Some differences in form clearly held for him grammatical significance, such as his use of 'counsel' and 'practise' as verbs and 'council' and 'practice' as nouns. In these instances we follow the orthography which he seems to have preferred, as also in his use of contractions such as ''tis' and 'don't', and special Methodist usages such as 'connexion' and 'Foundery'. Common abbreviations, however, which unlike contractions did not represent Wesley's spoken word—he *said* 'don't'; he did not say 'wch', i.e. 'which'—have been silently extended, except when concealment was apparently intended, or where some doubt remains; in these instances the extension is enclosed within square brackets.

The prolific *capitals* and *italics* of Wesley's earlier years have been reduced to a minimum. We have retained capitals, however, for some common nouns used by him in a technical sense, such as 'Assistant', 'Leaders', and 'Circuit'. He regularly italicized quotations from the Bible, even when those quotations were inexact in adding or omitting unimportant words or in changing the tense of verbs or the person of pronouns. These passages we have placed within quotation marks to indicate Wesley's intention, and where the quotation is more than minimally inexact we have prefixed 'cf.' when citing the source if he displayed it as a quotation, and 'see' where he did not.

To indicate the more important *ellipses* we have sometimes supplied '. . .'. Occasionally Wesley himself did mark the omission of a whole clause or more by a dash or a double dash (although these indications were frequently lost from later editions, perhaps because their significance was misunderstood), but never did this for a word or phrase whose absence did not disturb the general sense of the passage reproduced; in this we have followed his own practice rather than compel the reader to wander through a jungle of ellipses. Nor have we attempted to distinguish between those ellipses indicated by Wesley himself and those supplied by the editors, in this one instance breaking our rule that editorial interventions should be enclosed within square brackets or footnoted.

Wesley's style varied enormously, and with it his *punctuation*, from a series of staccato sentences (or even phrases masquerading as sentences) to a complete paragraph consisting of one complex (and occasionally confusing) sentence. Much of his punctuation was rhetorical rather than syntactical—indicating places where he would pause for effect rather than logical divisions of thought. In general we have followed the safer course of omission rather than of alteration, aiming at 'open' or minimal punctuation when the language is flowing and the meaning clear. Wherever there is any doubt about the original meaning, however, and wherever it seems possible that some significant nuance might be lost by any alteration, the punctuation of the copy-text is retained. Thus we have followed Wesley in treating many subordinate clauses as if they were complete sentences, and have retained the comma which he frequently used instead of 'that' in introducing other subordinate clauses. Wesley employed parentheses somewhat lavishly, and in this we have usually followed his text, as also in his device of interjecting a brief parenthetic comment into a quotation without closing and reopening the quotation with additional quotation marks. We have also followed his practice of inserting direct speech into a quotation (especially a scriptural quotation, where this is normal in the Authorized Version) without adding internal quotation marks. We have omitted the quotation marks frequently added by Wesley when he was clearly recording indirect speech.

Citations and other reference material furnished by Wesley himself, whether enclosed within parentheses, added at the ends of paragraphs, or placed in footnotes, have in this edition been gathered together in a series of footnotes lettered a, b, c, etc. Editorial additions to these notes are enclosed within square brackets. Footnotes originating with the editors are given in a numbered series below Wesley's notes. The largest proportion of these trace those passages indicated by Wesley's italicization as scriptural quotations. We have also footnoted the more lengthy and striking quotations from the Bible which Wesley did not italicize, but because he apparently regarded these phrases as parts of the normal scriptural texture of his language rather than self-conscious quotations we have not enclosed them within quotation marks.

Wesley's *paragraph structure* has been retained intact. The numbering of his sections and sub-sections has occasionally been varied in order to clarify the organization of his material, especially by distinguishing between different numerical sequences, which are often confusingly interwoven; he seems never to have used letters to enable his readers to distinguish between different sequences, and we have felt it right in this to follow his own practice.

In many of his publications Wesley furnished *headlines*, occasionally with the addition of section numbers. For the convenience of the reader we have used these aids uniformly, as well as adding line numbers.

In order to achieve as great a measure of uniformity as possible both in securing and in styling Wesley's text, the present writer was appointed textual editor for the whole Wesley corpus, and the responsibility for any errors in collation or inconsistencies in the presentation of the text—and such there will inevitably be!—must be accepted by him.

In the following pages we list all editions of the works in this volume known to have been published during Wesley's lifetime. Only the briefest details are given; for fuller accounts the *Bibliography* should be consulted. Because the numbering of the editions (when present) is sometimes chaotic, the editions are arranged in chronological order and designated A, B, C, etc. (For the purpose of tracing the history of the text a resetting in a collected volume is counted a new 'edition' equally with an independent publication.) Normally a new edition was printed from a copy of one of its predecessors which had been corrected or revised in manuscript by Wesley or one of his proof-readers. Occasionally two or even more families of text thus arose, and these are here shown in the stemma by the descending lines which connect the letters denoting the various editions— a solid line if the relationship is undoubted, a dotted line if it is hypothetical. Usually only one earlier edition was thus employed for the preparation of another, but on rare occasions there is evidence of the blending of chosen readings from two different progenitors. In these instances two lines of descent converge on the later edition, as is the case with *An Earnest Appeal*. All plausible variant readings noted which involve the omission, addition, or alteration of any word (but not differences in typography, spelling, or punctuation, nor manifest errors) are here recorded, with the editions in which they occur. A variant reading described as 'D→' is to be found in edition 'D' and in all those which stemmed from it, but in those only, i.e. not in others belonging to a different family of text, even though later in date.

F. B.

An Earnest Appeal

- A. Newcastle, Gooding, 1743
- B. 2nd, Bristol, Farley, 1743
- C. 3rd, Bristol, Farley, 1744
- D. 4th, Dublin, Powell, 1747
- E. 3rd Bristol, Farley, 1749
- F. 5th, Dublin, Powell, 1750
- G. 6th, Bristol, Pine, 1765
- H. 6th, Bristol, Pine, 1771
- I. *Works*, 14. 104–77, Bristol, Pine, 1772
    [I*e*, errata sheet to *Works*, Vol. 14]
    [I*m*, copy of *Works*, Vol. 14, containing Wesley's manuscript alterations]
- J. 7th, London, Paramore, 1786

The MS. for 'A' clearly received John Wesley's fullest attention. For 'B' he added his brother's poem, 'Primitive Christianity', and introduced a handful of small changes. In 'C' he corrected an error about the Council of Trent, and probably made one other minor alteration. The correction of proofs, at least from this stage onwards, was apparently left to one or other of his colleagues, who may well have been responsible for introducing some minor changes not affecting the sense, though other alterations were brought about by the printing errors which occurred in almost every edition, and sometimes led to *ad hoc* changes by either Wesley or his proof-readers. For 'G' Wesley asked his brother Charles to undertake a careful revision, from which three small changes have been retained in the edited text, as possibly securing John's approval. Certainly John himself revised the work for 'I', but unfortunately some of his changes were necessitated by previous errors, others the result of a hasty reading during which the context was insufficiently considered, still others a simple reversing of the order of words with no change in meaning. In 'J' there seems to be no evidence of Wesley's active interposition, though many minor changes were introduced by his proof-reader.

Page	Line	
46	7	B → omit 'is the'.
	8	I omits 'in the heart'.
	11	B → omit 'in'.
	21–2	A, 'Now faith . . . is *[Pragmaton elenchos ou blepomenon]*' in text, with footnote: '* The Reader is desired to excuse our want of Greek Types.'
47	7	'saying' inserted in J only.
	33	J, 'not they'.
50	3	J omits 'own'.
	18	H → omit 'so'.
52	2	I omits 'which you have', restored by I*m*, but not by I*e*.
	5	J, 'your hearts'.
	12–14	I omits 'of our love . . . that golden rule'; I*e* alters the resulting defective text to 'more equitable rule than this (the only adequate'; from this I*m* retains 'than this', and restores all the original passage except the introductory 'of our love, than'.
	21	J, 'may not one'.
54	29	J omits 'if'.
55	11	A, 'We join then with you'.
56	6	B → 'ancient and modern'.
59	17	J, 'you truly believe the Scripture?'
61	1–2	D, F, 'And this is all?'
	32	Original 'find' corrected to 'afford' in I*e*, I*m*.
62	4	H, I, J, 'he that hath much'.
63	21	H, I, J, omit 'You cannot love God: for you love praise.'
64	15	B → omit 'yet'.
	18	J, 'go to church'.
65	2	H omits 'we' from 'would we'; I, 'I would'; J, 'we would'.

Page	Line	
	20	D → (except G), 'cannot commit sin'.
	27	A–H, 'wished what'.
	29	J omits 'it'.
	31	J omits 'strong'.
66	15–16	A–F, 'come down the mount'; G, I, 'come down from the mount' J, 'come down out of the mount'.
	22	G, 'Have not you'.
67	5	J, 'anyone who believes'.
	9–10	A–F, H, I, 'wished by all'.
	15	A–C, E, G, I, 'no word is impossible'.
68	16–18	A, B, E, G, '59. If we consider the time when this decree was passed, namely just after the publication of our Homilies, it will appear more than probable that the very design of the Council was to anathematize the Church of England, as being now convict by her own confession of "that damnable and heretical doctrine". For the very words in the Homily on Salvation are:'
	17	H, I, J, 'convicted'.
69	6–7	J, to believe the Scriptures, and that the articles'.
	13–14	D →, G →, 'let him be an *anathema maranatha*'.
	18	A, 'Or if not'.
70	8–9	E, 'one who loves God'.
	17	J, 'He who is offended'.
	34	Only I*e*, I*m* cite Acts 2: 41.
71	8–9	A–F, 'by the same spirit'.
	17–18	J, 'when God speaketh there is none'.
	19–20	E, 'good works'.
	32	I, 'that they would be better'; J, 'they would be better'.
	33	A–C, 'it would do them good'.
72	3	I omits 'very'.
	5	H, I, J, 'You seek rest'.
	29–30	J, 'It may be so; or it may not.'
74	4	I, 'on the Lord's side against us?'; I*m* deletes 'against us'.
	14	I, 'could believe it.'
	33	I omits 'any of'.
75	5	E, 'a river's side'.
	5–6	J, 'a sufficient precedent'.
	16	H, I, J, 'to church, to the Lord's Table'.
	24	H, I, J, 'my brethren the clergy'.
76	3	A has no footnote.
	10	I, 'Have ye not'.
	14	E, G, 'and to be spent'.
	21	J omits 'even the Church'.
77	11	In A the parenthetic clause is a footnote.
	11–13	I, 'among whom the pure word of God is preached, and the sacraments duly administered'.
	28–9	D →, 'Church of England, France, or any other'.
78	4	H, J, 'else the faith'.

Page	Line	
78	13	J, 'I am reconciled'.
	19	I omits 'and hearing'; restored by I*m*, but not by I*e*.
79	21	B →, 'All Fridays'.
	34	J, 'In cathedral or collegiate.'
80	5	A–F, H, I, 'curates'.
	12	A, 'give knowledge'.
81	28	In A the footnote began: 'The Author of a Tract just printed here'.
82	24	J, 'cannot conceive it yourself'.
	33 to	A, 'They were before "joined to all their brethren" of the Church
83	1	of England by "assembling themselves together" . . .'
	6–7	B → omit 'that'; H, J, 'i.e. *he doth not*'; I, 'i.e. *do not*'.
	17	J, 'our desolated Church'.
	27	J, 'puts me upon'.
84	4	J, 'do ye know'.
	13	B →, 'silver or gold'.
	18–19	B → 'bishop of London'.
	21–2	G, '. . . and Kingswood, and at all other places where any collection at all is made'; from this I omits the first 'at' and the second 'at all'.
	25	B →, 'any who desire it'.
85	7	J, 'and so to the last'.
	9	I omits 'chiefly'.
	16–17	A, 'for the men and women'.
	19	B →, 'has been hitherto'.
	23	I, 'school'.
86	9	J, 'independent of anyone'.
	13	I, 'nature, temper', restored to 'natural temper' by I*m*, but not by I*e*.
	17	I, 'But suppose the balance'.
87	25	All except A, I*m* read 'but by the grace of God'.
88	1	G appends within parenthesis, 'and my books'; to this I adds, 'or what may happen to be due on account of them', but omits 'and the little arrears of my fellowship'.
	2	E, 'I have lived'.
	16–17	H, J, 'those who are called'.
	19–20	I, 'want even of'.
	25	A, 'an eye and ear witness'.
	31	D → (inc. G, I), 'If you had been then'.
89	7–8	I only adds 'of time'.
	9	J omits 'did or'.
	10	I, 'have vehemently'.
	17	I omits 'vile or'; restored by I*m*, but not I*e*.
	21–2	J omits 'by being careful to maintain good works'.
90	20	I adds, 'Written in the year 1744.'
	90–4	A, F, G omit the poem.
91	31	E, '"Lo! here is Christ!" and, "Christ is there!"'

Page	Line	
92	22	J, 'the sanctifying word'.
94	6	H, I, 'the saints'.
	7	H, J, 'Enjoy his grace'.

A Farther Appeal, Part I

A. London, Strahan, 1745

B. 4th, Bristol, Grabham, 1758

C. *Works*, 14. 178–331 (1772)

D. 5th, London, Hawes, 1778

E. 5th, London, Paramore, 1786

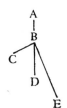

It is just possible that there were editions intervening between 'A' and 'B', and possibly one revised by Charles Wesley in 1765, corresponding to the revised editions of *An Earnest Appeal* and *A Farther Appeal*, Parts II and III, though none has been discovered. The only certain editorial interposition by John Wesley is in 'C', though it also seems probable that he personally made a few corrections in 'B'.

Page	Line	
106	2	D, 'continual'.
108	17	A, ראה.
114	37	E, 'a horse'.
116	3	E, 'the endless'.
	29–30	E omits 'Take care . . . from you.'
	30	B–D, 'that he does not'.
117	15–16	A omits 'faith: and the . . . necessary to', which is reinserted by an erratum slip found only in some copies. B → (obviously using uncorrected copy) continue the omission, but alter the resultant nonsense from 'continuance of repentance' to 'continuance of faith'.
	29	C adds footnote, 'The (then) Archbishop of York.'
118	7	C, 'are they the words'.
120	37	A → have 'enemy of Christianity', apparently an inadvertent misquotation of Gibson's original 'enemy of mankind'. A → also omit the original's 'their'.
121	14	C, 'sincere and careful'.
	24	C omits 'better', replaced by C*m*.
	26–7	C, 'roarings, screamings'.
	27	A, B, D, E, 'roarings and madnesses'.
124	2	D, 'indeed to be'.
	21–2	A, B, D, E, 'my express words are that immediately follow, specifying'.

Page	Line	
125	9	E, 'appeared'.
	19	A, ‏חוח, ארקסך‎.
		C*m* adds translation of the Latin in a footnote: 'I will love thee from my inmost bowels.'
126	14	C, 'going in any way'.
127	5	C, 'is not so easily'.
129	37	B, D, 'recreation'.
132	34	D, 'As direct a one'.
133	27–8	E 'Now, though we have . . ., this cannot bind us.'
134	30–1	E, 'forgiveness of sin'.
135	4	E omits 'next'.
136	14	C, 'may be surely?'
137	16	E, 'which is the sense'.
142	20	C, 'I deny this "original . . .".'
149	9	B → omit 'an'.
	15–16	C omits '(or with regard to)'.
	36	E, 'law and to'.
150	18	'chapter of the Romans.'
152	17	C, 'in the demonstration'.
	20	C, 'Spirit and power'.
	22	A → read 'Yes', apparently a printing error for 'Yet'.
155	18	E omits 'ancient'.
156	18	C, 'passages that'.
158	31–2	E, 'Spirit bearing witness'.
160	7	E, 'making intercession'.
162	1	D, 'men's wisdom'.
	2	D, 'wisdom of man'.
	9	E, 'does not cite it'.
	34–5	A, B, D, E, 'his Anointing (his Spirit), he teacheth'.
163	30	D, 'Wherefore, seeing by'; E omits 'being'.
	31	E omits 'of all saving truth, and . . . impossibility'.
164	14	C, 'aversion'.
	15	C, 'and inclination'.
	20	D, 'and actuated'.
167	2–3	C omits 'We beseech thee, . . . comfort us.'
	5	C omits citation 'c'.
168	22	A, B, D, E, 'which is within you'.
169	2	E, 'teach all things'.
	13–14	E, 'our sins'.
170	18	C, 'by the Spirit'.
172	7	E, 'such receiving'.
	25	E, 'of the doctrine'.
173	24	E, '*Whole Duty.*'
174	16	D, E, 'narrow the way'.
175	21	E omits 'this'.
176	20–1	D, 'I do not so much as remember'.
177	15	A, B, D, E, 'such doctrine'.

Page	Line	
178	10	C only adds '(except that the people crowded so)'.
	11	A, B, D, E, 'till long after'.
	35	A, B, D, E, 'Roman laws'.
		C, 'the devil gods'.
182	8	D, 'designs'.
	19	C, 'and places'.
183	16	A, B, D, E, 'congregation'.
184	1–2	E, 'or administer the sacrament'.
186	15	E, 'I have been considering'.
187	17	D omits 'all'.
	34	D, 'preaching of the gospel'.
188	16	D omits 'plain'.
189	10	A, B, D, E, 'direction'.
190	14	E omits 'have'.
	24	C, '*you like?*'
	25	E, 'loaded'.
191	29	E, 'will not you'.
	34	A, B, D, E, 'as who would say'.
193	25	B–E, 'revilings'.
199	32	E, 'had never'.
201	20	C adds 'Dec. 22, 1744.'
	22	C, 'thy guiding eye'.
202	13–22	C omits letter.

A Farther Appeal, Parts II, III

A. London, Strahan, 1745

B. 3rd, Bristol, Farley, 1746

C. 4th, London, Strahan, 1746

D. 4th, Bristol, Pine, 1765

E. *Works*, 15. 3–193 (1772) [E*e*, E*m*, as I*e*, I*m*, p. 543]

F. 5th, London, Paramore, 1781

G. 6th, London, Paramore, 1786

It is possible that there did exist a second edition, but none has been discovered, only variant issues of the first. The textual evidence implies that Wesley himself introduced a few revisions into both 'B' and 'C'. 'D' was apparently revised by Charles Wesley. 'E' was certainly revised by John Wesley, sometimes over-hastily, and with large omissions from the account of the Wednesbury riots. It seems unlikely that he was closely concerned in seeing 'F' and 'G' through the press.

Page	Line	
203		*Title.* The title page is almost a replica of that for Pt. I (see p. 103 above), but B → change the motto to Isa. 58: 1. The first issue of 'A' retains 'Price Bound One Shilling', but this is amended in the second issue (along with minor typographical variants in the first gathering) to 'Price Unbound One Shilling'.
204	25	B, D → omit 'very'.
	30	B, D →, 'their spot was not'.
205	12	F →, 'said God'.
206	7	F →, 'said the prophet'.
	16	F →, 'are gone out'.
	22	F →, 'inflames'.
	27	B, D →, 'their calves'.
207	4	F →, 'harlots' house'.
209	6	F →, 'hearts'.
	12	F →, 'regarded'.
	25	E omits 'it'.
211	5	F →, 'said God'.
	26–7	F →, 'said the prophet'.
	29	B, D →, 'hearts'.
212	6	F →, 'he said'.
	8–9	D → omit 'Yea, they are'.
	23–4	B, D →, 'There is whoredom in Ephraim'; C, 'There is whoredom at Ephraim';
	25	F, 'said God'.
213	17	D, E, 'The Lord had said'.
	24–5	D →, 'shall not return'.
	33	F →, 'pitied'.
214	23	G, 'our salvation'.
215	12	F →, 'their sight'.
	17	A, C, 'or nobleman's'.
	21	A, C, F →, 'into confusion'.
	30–1	F →, 'at best only an'.
216	9	B, D →, 'is an institution'.
	35	A, 'hath brought'.
217	2	F → omit 'yet'.
	18	D → omit 'may'.
	19	E, 'but the old'.
219	29–30	G, 'a public house'.
	30–1	A →, 'of vice', but E*e*, E*m*, 'on vice'.
220	26	F →, 'juries'.
	32	C, 'leaves you to no'.
221	4	G omits second 'the'.
	37	G, 'statutes'.
222	15–19	E, '(2) Such as he shall find at sports and pastimes on that day. (3) Such as he shall find tippling in public houses; (4) Shopkeepers selling or exposing goods on the Lord's day; and lastly, Such as . . .'.

Page	Line	
222	22–3	E, 'duly, according to your knowledge'.
	32	D →, 'this realm'.
223	18	G, 'to prevent'.
	22	E, 'to the next'.
225	12–13	A–D, F →, 'once in seven years (if not oftener)'; E, '(if requested)'. Ee, Em, '(if required)'.
	14	F → omit 'by'.
	25	F →, 'a hundred'.
	28	E, F → omit 'a'.
226	7	D →, 'to venture'.
	19	F →, 'He hath left'.
227	27	D →, 'not finding'.
	28	F →, 'man-servants and maid-servants'.
228	1	E, 'one branch or other'.
	2	E, 'mouths'.
	4	A →, 'And when'; Ee, Em, 'Even when'.
	18	F →, 'run upon'.
	23	G, 'rebellings'.
	34	E omits footnote.
229	23	A–D, F →, 'work'.
	28	A–D, F →, 'disencumbering themselves from'.
230	18	A →, 'eat'; Ee, Em, 'ate'.
232	25–6	G, 'men of note'.
233	4	D →, 'What will he do?'
	35	F → omit 'more'.
234	8	A–D, F →, 'those twenty'.
	30	G, 'expenses'.
235	2	G, 'shameful mockery'.
237	10	D →, 'are we not'.
	21	G, '*honest* price'.
238	2	A–D, F →, 'Who of those that'.
	5	D →, 'rank'.
	15	G, 'opinionated'.
	20	D →, 'For are not'.
	27–8	G, 'not only foreigners only'.
	32	F →, 'go on foot'.
239	5	F →, 'near to me'.
	21–2	A–D, F →, 'Whatsoever you sow'.
	29	E omits Wesley's footnote.
	34	F →, 'an empty'.
240	12–14	E omits 'We had had plenty . . . borders'.
	14	D →, 'say not'.
241	3	G, 'evident that'.
	4	G omits 'then'.
242	3	D, F →, 'Are your countrymen'.
	20	A, C, 'Either the form or the power'.
243	5	D →, 'not to be silent'.

Page	Line	
243	12–13	F →, 'a horrible'.
244	6	E, 'holy and profane'.
245	8	B, D →, 'these words'.
	13	C, 'not of those'.
	18	D →, 'hath not'.
246	12	A–D, F →, 'and the women-servants'.
	22	A–D, F →, 'do it not'.
	22–3	D →, 'give any account'.
	29	F →, 'is of the stoutest heart'.
	32	G, 'to seek and to save'.
248	5	B, D, F →, 'One of those who'.
	9	A, C, 'healed the heart'.
	19	G, 'upon a wall'.
250	17	C, 'toward men'.
	32	F →, 'if not in all'.
		G, 'no small'.
251	18	G, 'God hath sent forth'.
	30	A–D, F →, 'provided they'.
252	8	B, D →, '*conviction?*'
	31	A–D, F →, 'either of'.
	36	F →, 'he who hath'.
253	21–2	F →, 'And you may all your life have' (omitting phrase later).
	31	F → omit 'own'.
254	5–6	D →, 'enter within'.
255	3	A, C, 'my friends'.
	12	E, 'may always be'.
	32	A–D, F →, 'such trifles'.
256	14–15	A, C, lack 'the expense'.
	33	A, C, 'who are *Speakers*'.
	34–5	A, C, 'bear it or no'.
257	3	Wesley's parenthetic explanation appears in C only, which had no textual descendants.
	4	B →, C, add footnote
	n. 'a'. *l.* 1	F →, 'You say, "We do . . ."'.
	ll. 10–11	B, D →, 'But you did not bestow all that you had to spare from them on the poor belonging to other societies.' (Wesley seems to have handed different versions of this note to Farley and Strahan for incorporation in their respective editions, B and C.)
	7	A, C, 'Speaker'.
	7–8	F →, 'Preacher, in particular upon those who'.
258	5	D →, 'Are not you'.
	15	D →, 'Yea, all that which'.
259	29	A, C, 'My friends'.
	33	E, 'whatever you once were'.
259	39	F →, 'leaving you unto'.
260	30	D → omit 'own'.

Page	Line	
261	12	F →, 'a holy nation'.
	16	E, 'the seed of Abraham'.
	19	A, C, 'thus far'.
	25	E omits 'and (3).' '(3).' replaced by E*e*, E*m*.
262	12	G, 'of the earth'.
	18	B, D →, 'you in this no more hear'. [? a compositor's error for an intended revision, 'in this you no more hear'.]
	29	D, 'baring' [probably a misprint for the original, but possibly an error for 'barring']; F →, 'except'.
263	12	E, F →, 'that are called'.
264	22	D, F →, 'You are only'.
265	34	G omits 'you do not . . . together: although'.
266	3	D →, 'what would you do'.
	15	G omits 'flux of'.
267	20	B, D → omit 'all'.
	28	D, F →, 'men who profess'.
268	20	D →, 'his creator'.
	28	D →, 'I might discern'.
269	9	A–D, F →, 'more easily intelligible'.
	15	D, F →, 'worketh in all'.
270	3–4	A–D, F →, 'comfort'.
	8	C omits 'it'.
	22–3	A, C, 'giveth to all liberally'.
	31	A, C, 'that love'.
271	11	D–F, 'was such'.

A Farther Appeal, Part III

Page	Line	
273	1	A–E, 'renewal of soul'.
274	16	A, C, 'same alarm'.
275	2	G, 'and to swear'.
277	18	F →, 'had appeared'.
278	24	F → omit 'indifferent . . . nothing'.
279	20	G omits 'lately'.
280	6–7	D, F →, 'it is spread'.
	21	D →, 'inference'.
	33	G, 'still hangs'.
281	23	G, 'the inferences'.
282	15 to	
283	14	E omits § 6.
282	21	G, 'Joshua Yardly'.
283	23	G, 'his house'.
	26	A, C, 'stones and bricks'; G, 'the bricks and stones'.
284	11–14	E omits paragraph.
	17	D →, 'rose'.
	23	E omits 'broke it open'.
	26–31	E omits paragraph.

Page	Line	
285	17	F →, omit 'necessary'.
	18	F → omit 'of'.
	25–6	G, 'into the frost'.
	33	A–C, 'John and wife'.
286	20	F →, 'counters'.
	28	A–D, F →, 'these parsons'.
287	4–5	F →, 'those people'.
	8	F →, 'take that'.
287	23 to 289 31	E omits this passage.
292	11	F → omit 'own'.
293	9	A–D, F →, 'shall have'.
294	5–6	E, 'by many or few'.
	19–20	A–D, F →, 'another grievous offence'.
296	17–18	B, D →, 'locked up every passage'.
297	16	B, D →, 'not better'.
299	17	B, D, F →, 'I did not'.
301	18	E omits 'that'.
	20	F → omit 'little'.
	35–6	E, 'thirty thousand'.
302	8	B, D →, omit 'an'.
	17	B, D →, 'Scriptures'.
303	22	F →, 'God had employed'.
304	25	B, D →, 'special care'.
306	7–8	A, C, 'in the wilderness'.
307	32	D, F →, 'of our souls'; E, 'of poor souls'.
	39	A, C, 'place'.
310	25	C, 'ye believe'.
311	6	C, 'yet there is'.
	11	C, 'and Pharisees'.
	24	F →, 'this doctrine'.
312	3	A–D, F →, 'into the no less damnable sin of schism'; E, 'into no less damnable sin than that of schism', altered to edited text by E*e*, E*m*.
	16	F →, 'adulterers and murderers'.
	20	E omits 'in'; *Ee, Em* supply 'by'.
	29	F → omit 'all who die . . . that is'.
313	13	A, C, 'than ever'.
	29	A–D, F →, 'his own soul'.
	39	A–D, F →, 'this drunkard's'.
315	27	F →, 'a hundred'.
	37	A, C, 'but the meanest'.
316	12	A–D, F →, 'God hath'.
317	8	B, D →, 'neither rewarded'.
318	32	D →, 'stumbling-block'.
		A–D, F →, 'That never was yet'.
323	16	E, 'see and regard'.
324	7	G, 'hear the rod'.

A Letter to the Bishop of London

A. London, Strahan, 1747

B. Dublin, Powell, 1748

C. 2nd, Bristol, Farley, 1749

D. *Works*, 16. 222–46 (1772) [D*e* = errata]

Minor revisions may have been made in each edition by John Wesley, though Charles Wesley was possibly more active than his brother in preparing 'B' and 'C'. Some of the alterations in 'D' result from the altered text of 'C'.

Page	Line	
335	11	A, B, 'what is in'.
338	10–11	'Nay, whether ... should?' is inked through in some copies of A, omitted from B, but present in C, D.
	16	D omits 'an'.
		C → omit 'the'.
	18	D*e*, 'believe it'.
339	7	C, 'ignorant of'.
340	2	C → 'as it is done in heaven'.
	3	D, 'This is to be'.
	18	D omits 'but'.
	22	A–C, 'those loose'.
342	28	D, 'to do'.
343	7	C →, 'before God'.
	8	A, B, 'more sacred things'.
	11	A adds, 'or of a boy in the third class of Westminster School', struck through in ink in all known copies, and omitted from B →.
	27	C →, 'as we can to our'.
344	22	C omits 'in'.
345	2	B, 'When I could have'.
	4–5	A, B, 'use of both'.
	8	A, B, 'frequently advised'.
	15	C → omit 'an'.
	31	C →, 'God and man'.
346	14, 20	A → read 'station' in first instance, A–C 'stations' in second, altered to 'station'. Gibson's original reads 'stations'.
	34	C →, 'now come'.
347	26	B omits 'no Papists'.
	27	C → omit 'left'.
348	4	A, B, '"arm", "fortify"'.
	23	C →, 'of the poor'.
349	13	A, 'How any can now advance'; B, 'how they can now advance'.
350	24	A, B, 'gospel I preach'.
	31	A, B, 'their several places'.

Page Line
351   6   A–C, 'given to man'.
       11–12 C, 'hearing it all'; D, 'hearing at all'.

A Letter to the Author, etc.

A. London, Cock, [1750]

B. Dublin, Powell, 1750

C. *Works*, 16. 254–76 (1772)

It is uncertain whether 'C' derives from 'A' or 'B', though the former is more likely. Wesley clearly attempts some revision in 'C'.

371   11   A, B, 'fruits of the Spirit'.
372   2   C, 'Mr. Wesley says, "I came . . ." '——a grammatical improvement, but an alteration of Lavington's original text.
       18–19 C, 'in respect to your'.
373   18–19 C, 'gift of the Holy Ghost'.

A Second Letter to the Author, etc.

A. London, Cock, 1751

B. *Works*, 16. 277–354 (1772)

380   11   A, 'Or you'.
       24   A, 'by him'.
381   10–11 A, 'treats on every'.
       26   A, 'how far will'.
384   18   A, 'and Tiverton'.
387   24–5   A, 'self-condemnation'.
388   11   A, 'spoke'.
       33   A, 'had'.
393   11   A, 'cause of all'.
       23–4   A, 'that whole time'.
395   1   B omits 'not'.
398   7   B, 'assurance'.
       21   A, 'And it is not'.
399   12   A, *'impulses, impressions'*.
       22   A, *'infallible proof'*.
       27   B omits 'in preaching'.
400   20   A, 'charging'.
       32   A, *'altogether'*.
401   35   A, 'doubt'.
402   34–5   A, 'Lady at Loretto'—which is Lavington's incorrect quotation from Wesley.

Page Line
403　9　A, 'renewal of soul'.
405　16　B, 'such report'.
406　27　B omits the first 'the'.
426　12–13　A, 'them have'.

A Second Letter to the Lord Bishop of Exeter

A. London, Cock, 1752 [no copy known]

B. 2nd, London, Cock, 1752

C. *Works*, 17. 3–9 (1773)

434　19　C, 'your worship'.
435　32　C, 'Mrs. Morgan's house'.

A Letter to the Rev. Mr. Horne

A. London, [Strahan] for Flexney, n.d. [1761]

B. *Works*, 17. 55–66 (1773)

443　17 to
451　20　B omits all except opening and closing phrases.
451　21　B, 'I have here shown'.
453　26　B, 'Faith does not'.

A Letter to the Lord Bishop of Gloucester

A. London, n.p., 1763

B. 2nd, Bristol, Pine, 1763

C. Dublin, n.p., 1763

D. *Works*, 18. 276–372 (1773)

Wesley seems to have made some revisions in 'C', as also for 'D', though this latter is worse printed than is usual for the *Works*, and its variant readings therefore the more suspect. The minor alterations in 'B' are probably the work of Charles Wesley or some other proof-reader.

471　5–6　D, 'those effects'.
　　28　D, 'those quotations'.
472　13　A, B, D, 'than I was'.
476　24　D, '*peaceable*, benign'.
478　15　D, 'it consists in'.
481　27–8　D, '*principles* and *practice*'.

Page	Line	
482	22	D, 'imagination'.
487	16	A–C, 'be children'.
488	31	A–C, 'Nich. Palmer'.
491	22	A–C, 'belong not'.
493	23–4	A, B, D, '*she* was not'.
495	20	D, 'in such need'.
497	15	D, 'unless only'.
506	7	D omits 'only'.
509	15	A, B, D, 'prejudices'.
510	11	D omits 'I have . . . facts'.
511	9	D, 'at the instant'.
513	29	D, 'had never'.
514	22–3	D, 'of these miracles'.
515	16	A–C, 'wisdom and greatness'.
	24	A–C, 'was real fact'.
516	3	D, 'and the testimony'.
	13	A–C, 'prove this by'.
	34–5	D omits 'Whosoever believes . . . of this'.
517	1	D omits 'great and'.
521	11	D, 'or acquit both'.
	26–7	B, D, 'the helpful spirit'.
525	34	A, C, 'that my account'.
526	3	D, 'when he is'.
527	3 to	
538	8	D omits.
532	27	B, 'all thy heart'.
533	9	B, 'are not perceivable'.

INDEX OF SCRIPTURAL REFERENCES

This index covers all cited references to Scripture (*a*) by Wesley himself and (*b*) by the authors whom he quotes. The latter—comparatively few, because it is not editorial policy to footnote quotations within quotations—are differentiated by enclosing the page numbers within parentheses. More than one citation of a text on the same page is indicated by a figure within brackets immediately after the page number.

OLD TESTAMENT

GENERAL INDEX

The alphabetical arrangement of entries is on a word-by-word basis. Foreign words and phrases are listed under the appropriate language, and in the case of Greek and Hebrew they are preceded by a transliteration and arranged accordingly. References in footnotes are indicated by the addition of '*n*' after the page number.

The abbreviation 'W' is used throughout for the surname 'Wesley', either alone when the reference is to John Wesley, or following the Christian name of other members of the family. The entry under 'Wesley, John' is confined to personal characteristics and major periods and events in his life. For his sermons and other publications (of which lists are given), see under the titles, although works by other authors are given under the author's name.　　　　J. A. V.